How to Think and Write

How to THINK & WRITE

H. Edward Richardson

University of Louisville

Scott, Foresman and Company

Library of Congress Catalog Card No. 70–121068

Copyright © 1971 by Scott, Foresman and Company,
Glenview, Illinois 60025.
Philippines Copyright 1971 by Scott, Foresman and
Company.
All Rights Reserved.

Printed in the United States of America.
Regional offices of Scott, Foresman and Company are
located in Atlanta, Dallas, Glenview, Palo Alto, Oak-
land, N. J., and London, England.

*This book is for
my mother
Mary Marcella Osborne Richardson
and my father
Samuel A. Richardson*

In the first century A.D. the Roman rhetorician Quintilian observed that good writing is clear thinking made visible. Whatever methods language teachers have employed since, I believe most of them have worked toward Quintilian's vision. The major purpose of *How to Think and Write* is to help the student think clearly and transmit his thoughts into lucid composition.

The Introduction contains an explanation of how to use the text. In addition to the Introduction, Part I of this text consists of eight chapters, each followed by a set of questions keyed to readings in Part II. Ideally, the teacher will assign in sequential order these eight chapters and selected questions, because they provide a basis for discussing, implementing, and emphasizing the major points of Part I of *How to Think and Write*. The readings in Part II, though of considerable independent value, have been selected and keyed to the chapters of Part I in an attempt further to emphasize those chapters.

The organization of this book is flexible. Although many teachers may wish to move directly from Chapter 1 through Chapter 8, assigning all or some of the questions, others may wish to use the text for an intensive six- or eight-week unit on thinking and writing. It is also possible to use Part I or portions of it for demonstrating and emphasizing such widely divergent aspects of the English language as its origins and changing nature; its symbolical functions; its effects upon human behavior; the recognition of generalizations and how to deal with them; common problems in abstraction and logic; ambiguities, the essence of good and poor analogies, propaganda, up-labeling and down-labeling; the language of literature; the importance of context, meaning, and relativity in thinking and writing; humor through change of context, and ways to deal with linguistic problems of increasing complexity which often defy ordinarily useful but limited methods of verbal analysis.

In addition, *How to Think and Write* emphasizes the correctness of basic English and thus provides both teacher and student with a mechanism for integrating any good handbook of English with the text. The composition symbol chart (pp. 8–9), is a means by which the student may readily check his progress and may have it checked in classes and conferences with his teacher. But as important as basic

English skills are, the emphasis placed upon them makes up the rationale only for the introductory portion of this text. The eight chapters which follow are its raison d'être: they provide a means for the student to become aware of, to define, and to achieve those qualities of thinking which are necessary for good writing.

In this Preface and in the Introduction I have suggested only some of the ways in which this text may be used. An author may anticipate an instructor's approaches; he may offer departures from them; and he may suggest new approaches of his own devising. He cannot hope, however, to treat all possible approaches. Nor should he. The authorial voice must inevitably give way to the instructor's design and performance. Anyone who has taught realizes that the ultimate success of any text lies with the instructor and what he and his students bring to it and do with it.

Teaching is an art, requiring more than we can achieve, demanding more than we can give. It is my hope that *How to Think and Write* will serve as an incentive for instructors to use in different ways their present methods of instruction, and to meld them with even some of the new ways offered for confronting the seemingly overwhelming task of imparting basic skills and the higher proficiencies of thinking and writing to students of English. For a teacher's best endures, bound in time through the written word of his students.

And that is enough.

H.E.R.

Louisville, Kentucky

TABLE OF CONTENTS

Traditional Fallacies

The Special Child

Affirmation of Life

PART
1

INTRODUCTION

Most teachers of English realize that the achievement of passable skills in composition, though worthwhile, is only a minor achievement. Teachers expect a solid "C" student in freshman English to possess an ability to apply with consistency the rules of punctuation, spelling, capitalization, and construction, and to have an awareness of paragraph and theme organization. Students who have only begun to develop these skills in high school soon learn that their full achievement is a requisite of success in college, and that composition skills receive continued and repeated emphasis in most freshman English programs. Yet even as English teachers pencil red marks on themes, and students then wincingly read them, both probably sense that mastery of such skills alone is a second-rate achievement. Such an awareness in no way denigrates the value of the skills, but it does serve to help the student to adjust his perspective and to recognize the basics for what they are: good tools with which to express what he is thinking—but only tools.

But even consummate mastery of the skills will never transform careless thinking or trite expression or vague generalization into good composition. What we write on paper is a mirror image of our minds. Good writing does not proceed from superficial thinking, and far too often students fail to pull the stuff of originality from their minds; it is easier to rely on what they have heard or read, and to take those words and phrases and parrot them. When a teacher asks for original expression, the student who has developed a parroting habit will often simply dip into his trough of received word and thought patterns; and as such a habit becomes deeply ingrained, a student's thought processes become imprisoned by the word symbols with which he "thinks." His mind no longer governs the words he uses; rather, his words tend to dominate— to choose—his thoughts. Indeed, by building up a store of second-hand word patterns, he is stifling his potential for original thinking and writing. For such a student, mastery of composition skills can at best provide only an artificial solace.

The purpose of this book is to take the student from the basic skills into the higher competencies of thinking and writing, a process not so complex as it may at first seem. Before the student can begin to break through the word barriers that stifle his originality, he must first become aware of the degree to which his thinking is limited by his reliance on generalizations that mean little or nothing. He must be taught to recognize the triteness of his word patterns and to become aware of the tedium of their content. He should learn that just as the world about him is not static, neither should his language be rigid, unchanging, frozen by conventional usage.

The words we use too often determine, to a large extent, the world we see, or *perceive*. In learning how to handle generalizations, the student should apprise himself of the problems of abstraction in language, of how he often becomes entangled in words and then fruitlessly endeavors to solve the riddle of what he really wants to say by using still more words in a kind of revolving verbal magic—abstract word-juggling, which only leads him farther from his ever diminishing purpose, or, worse, into the delusion that he has said something meaningful. One purpose of this text is to alert the student to that illusion.

Another major purpose of this text is to enable the student of English to identify some problems in logic. Among them are the common fallacies which the unknowing student fails to pierce; the confusion of words with objects (the frequent result of which is to preclude further thinking); and the bewildering masses of "up-labeling" and "down-labeling" which confront him on every side, not only from other people (in and out of the college community), but in books, newspapers, and magazines, and on radio and television. The illogical language of advertising illustrates the point, of course—from the fantastic merits of the latest filter cigarette, Circean perfume, or hypnotic shaving lotion to the pejorative treatment of some political opponent's abilities, ethics, patriotism, and private life.

By applying concepts derived from *How to Think and Write,* students may eventually learn to deal with more complex problems in language which challenge them to implement the higher competencies of expression while, at the same time, increasing their opportunities to apply the basic tools of composition—or, in a broad sense, of literacy itself.

Each of the chapters in this book dealing with *competency* contains at its conclusion, under the heading "Questions on Readings," questions relevant to the material treated in that particular chapter. (Readings are also organized thematically beginning with Part II; see p. 153.) The selections are organizationally interrelated with the textual material of Part I. They deal with such topics as science and the humanities; language and reality; war and dehumanization; the campus today, rebellion and conformity; the search for identity; love, sex, and censorship; individual responsibility; God, man, and moral consciousness; literature and good writing; and our "Age of Controversy." The final section is purposely emotive in tone; therefore it includes articles and excerpts related to controversial topics and selected to generate strong (affective) responses from students, who, consistent with the thesis of this text, will at the same time be linking their thoughts to written expression in new ways. Topics covered in "The Age of Controversy" include racial prejudice; traditional fallacies; existentialism (non-meaning, frustration, and resolution); the special child; and affirmation of life.

Although the readings have a thematic organization of their own, their central purpose lies in the illumination they provide of points sequentially developed in Part I. The logical placement of "Questions on Readings" is, therefore, at the conclusion of each of the chapters in Part I. For example, one of the "Questions on Readings" in Chapter 2: "Symbols, not Things," relates to the close examination of generalizations in that chapter. The student is expected to read C. P. Snow's essay "The Two Cultures" in Part II and to apply what he has learned in Chapter 2 to the question:

> *1. What* generalizations *are evident in C. P. Snow's statement in "The Two Cultures": "The traditional culture, which is, of course, mainly literary, is behaving like a state whose power is rapidly declining—standing on its precarious dignity, spending far too much energy on Alexandrian intricacies, occasionally letting fly in fits of aggressive pique quite beyond its means, too much on the defensive to show any generous imagination to the forces which must inevitably reshape it" (p. 156)?*

The student should see that Snow's statement asserts a generalization that lumps all the past under the fiction "traditional culture," a fallacious assumption which, the student has learned, can be termed the "*is* of identity," in which the symbol is taken for the reality through the mode of assertion itself, as if a "traditional culture" really existed as an indisputable, classifiable entity. The student will, doubtless, also point up other inherent weaknesses in the statement, such as the author's endowing "traditional culture" (should such a classification be tentatively granted) with organic qualities neatly pigeonholed as "defensive," lacking in "generous imagination," and doomed to inevitable reshaping. Through the treatment of such patterns of thought and expression in Chapter 2, the student learns that such assertions as these of Snow's would, generally, preclude any further dialogue between a scientist and a humanist, for Snow's terms would be unacceptable, especially to the humanist, who would probably suggest another definition of terms. The readings thus serve the major function of furnishing the student with carefully selected examples of interesting topics which permit him to apply in an organized fashion various points of *competency.*

The major distinction of *How to Think and Write,* then, is that it provides college students of English a means by which they may become aware of, define, and move toward those qualities of thinking which form the framework of good writing; they move toward competence.

How to Think and Write may be used either as a major or as a supplementary text to prepare English students not merely to be aware of, but to be functionally aware of "subverbal" levels of reality as they write, so that the words they use develop naturally from their thought processes in such a way that their words serve their ideas, and so that they communicate without loss or giving in to secondary desires and accompanying tangential verbiage—the vague generalization and the easy *cliché*. Neither will the student mistake words for realities, for he will have learned that words themselves can only partially convey the essence of his thinking. Since the emphasis in this text is placed on thinking as it relates to written expression, it seems axiomatic that, with the skillful guidance of the instructor, the students should begin to move away from a blind adherence to preconceptions, a condition which often characterizes limited experience. Similarly, students should tend to become more open-minded and critically thoughtful. They will no longer be content to take as their own what they have gleaned from the latest editorial or slanted piece of news coverage. Nor will they be content to parrot what they have absorbed from others, who may have predigested the "facts," but who, in their statements, tell more about the way they feel than about the things themselves. Without solid evidence, thinking students will defer making up their minds; and without the facts, they will certainly withhold judgment. In short, they will become less prejudiced and more original. Finally, as they develop the ability to think clearly and to transmute their thoughts cleanly into written expression, they will have gone beyond the minimal competencies of the English language which are expected of them as college students.

HOW TO USE THE COMPOSITION SYMBOL CHART

The "Composition Symbol Chart" on pp. 8–9 is designed to help students in their continuing efforts to achieve literacy, including such fundamentals as the elimination of major errors, the mastery of expected refinements of punctuation, the improvement of mechanics, diction, paragraph development, and paragraph and theme organization. The symbols of correction employed are in common use; the designations of errors are treated in most handbooks of English. Using his particular handbook, the student first reviews the most common errors in literacy listed, along with any others which may be emphasized in his English class. For ease of future reference and continuity of study, he should then write the page numbers from his handbook, treating these errors within the spaces provided in the column "Page References Keyed to Handbook." The final column, "Special Problem Areas," provides spaces to be checked for individual areas of difficulty which the student may encounter; these of course become evident through repetition of the same errors from theme to theme.

With a conscientious use of this chart, any student who is serious about mastering the basic elements of composition will begin to assume a greater degree of personal responsibility than he may yet have experienced in striving toward that goal. Moreover, as each student accepts the responsibility of carefully studying his handbook, and keeping a record of and reviewing special problem areas, his instructor will have more time in which to help him move toward the higher competencies of English expression which truly successful students are expected to achieve.

COMPOSITION SYMBOL CHART

	CORRECTION SYMBOL	DESIGNATION OF ERRORS	PAGE REFERENCES KEYED TO HANDBOOK	SPECIAL PROBLEM AREAS

TWELVE MAJOR ERRORS

1.	*Ad*	Adjective or adverb error
2.	*Ca*	Case error
3.	*CF*	Comma fault or splice
4.	*Con*	Construction error
5.	*Dangl*	Dangling modifier
6.	*Frag*	Fragmentary sentence
7.	*FS*	Fused sentence or run-on sentence
8.	*Pn Ag*	Pronoun agreement error
9.	*Ref*	Reference error of pronouns
10.	*S-V ag*	Subject-verb agreement error
11.	*//*	Parallelism error
12.	*T*	Tense error

OTHER ERRORS

13.	*Abbr*	Abbreviation
14.	*Ab*	Abstract
15.	*Amb*	Ambiguous
16.	*Apostr*	Apostrophe
17.	*Awk*	Awkward
18.	*Cap*	Capitalization error
19.	*Cl*	Clarity
20.	*C*	Comma error
21.	*Clic*	Cliché
22.	*Coh*	Coherence
23.	*Comp*	Comparison of adjectives and adverbs
24.	*D*	Diction error
25.	*Div*	Division of words
26.	*Fact*	Factual accuracy questionable
27.	*Fr*	Form of manuscript faulty
28.	*Fig*	Figurative language faulty
29.	*Gen*	Generalization inaccurate
30.	*Hy*	Hyphen
31.	*Inf*	Informal language inappropriate
32.	*Ital*	Italics
33.	*Log*	Logic faulty
34.	*Mod*	Modification error

	CORRECTION SYMBOL	DESIGNATION OF ERRORS	PAGE REFERENCES KEYED TO HANDBOOK	SPECIAL PROBLEM AREAS
32.	*Ital*	Italics		
33.	*Log*	Logic faulty		
34.	*Mod*	Modification error		
35.	*No*	Number error		
36.	*Org*	Organization faulty		
37.	¶	Paragraph		
38.	¶ *dev*	Paragraph development weak		
39.	*Pass*	Passive voice weak		
40.	*Per*	Person error		
41.	*Pl*	Plural		
42.	*P*	Punctuation error		
	:	Colon		
	⌃	Comma		
	—	Dash		
	!	Exclamation mark		
	( )	Parenthesis		
	⊙	Period		
	?	Question mark		
	⌄⌄ or ⌄	Quotation marks		
	⊙	Semicolon		
43.	*Rec*	Recast sentence		
44.	*Red*	Redundant		
45.	*Rel*	Relation not clear		
46.	*Rep*	Repetitious		
47.	*Restr*	Restrictive element— no commas		
	Nonrestr	Nonrestrictive element— commas needed		
48.	*sp*	Spelling error		
49.	*Stat*	Static sentence patterns —variety needed		
50.	*Sub*	Subordination		
51.	*Trans*	Transition weak		
52.	*Tr*	Transpose order		
53.	V	Verb form wrong		
54.	VP	Viewpoint (shift of, wrong or questionable)		
55.	W	Word wrong or omitted		
56.		Remove the circled item		

OTHER DESIGNATED ERRORS (to be added by instructor)

57.				
58.				
59.				
60.				
61.				

OUR CHANGING LANGUAGE

THE DEFINITIONS OF LANGUAGE

Language has been defined in many ways, none of them quite adequate. Language can be conceived of as a system of noises and marks, arbitrary in nature, to convey meaning—the noises and marks being symbolical in that they stand for objects, ideas, places, and other things. (Speech is, doubtless, the essence of any language.) But a moment's reflection will demonstrate the inadequacy of this "definition," for it does not cover any of the "sign languages" used by certain primitive tribes, or by the deaf and dumb. Among some peoples, for instance, speech must be accompanied by gestures—to such an extent that communication is nearly impossible in the dark. (Even in English, it is difficult to define such a term as "spiral staircase" without gestures.) In addition, there are other forms of symbolic expression such as music and mathematics. Dictionaries vary in their definitions of *language,* but most emphasize such aspects of meaning as *expression, communication, thoughts, feelings, vocal sounds,* other *conventionalized signs or symbols to which meaning is attributed, written symbols,* and, last but foremost, *speech.*

Thinking usually accompanies either spoken or written expression, and we usually think in words, no matter what our language. Language functions to *communicate ideas,* from the simplest to the most complex. Language serves to impart effective expression of emphatic thoughts and conscious feelings, too, which are closely related to reality. For example, *"Oh!"* may indicate sudden pain, surprise, fear, or even mystery. Although not every language is accompanied by a written expression of it in a form which endures, one function of many languages at present is the preservation of ideas developed in it, resulting in collections of writings, in books, and in libraries. In this way, ideas are pooled over whole eras of time, generations remote from each other can symbolically "work together," and cultures are preserved for posterity.

THE ORIGINS OF ENGLISH

We shall probably never know precisely how language originated, but we do know that language *evolved* over a long period of time, and that it is still evolving and changing. Scholars have attempted to place as many languages as possible into groups which bear some resemblance to each other. (For example, there are about thirty groups of languages on the American continent—but knowledge of all of them is incomplete.) English derives from the Indo-European, which itself had at least eight branches embracing languages as widely separated as Sanskrit, Persian, Armenian, Greek, Albanian, Latin and the Romance languages (such as French, Spanish, Italian), Celtic (ancient Gauls, Welsh, Scotch, Irish), the Balto-Slavic branch (including Russian and Polish), and the Germanic or Teutonic. Within this last branch, Germanic or Teutonic, were three subbranches: (1) Gothic or East German, now extinct; (2) North German, from which the Scandinavian languages developed; and (3) West German, out of which sprang High German, Low German, Frisian—and English. According to the Venerable Bede (673–735), author of the *Ecclesiastical History of the English Nation,* there were three groups who settled England: the Angles (from central Denmark); the Saxons (who lived just south of the Angles in Holstein); and the Jutes (from Jutland, in the extreme northern peninsula of Denmark). The word *English* itself can be traced back through the Middle English *Englysch* to the Anglo-Saxon *englisc* or *aenglish,* called *lingua Anglorum* (language of the Angles) by Bede in Latin, and designated as *englisc* by King Alfred the Great of Wessex (871–899).

The three historical periods of the development of English (although there has been no break in the language's steady evolution, as the dates might seem to indicate) are generally given:

    I. Old English, 450 to 1066
    II. Middle English, 1066 to 1500
    III. Modern English, 1500 to the present.

The changes in English during this period of approximately fifteen hundred years have been profound in all aspects: vocabulary, grammar, spelling, and, of course, pronunciation. Compare, for example, some lines from the famous Old English poem "The Wanderer" with a statement of the same lines in modern English:

> 'Hwǣr cwōm mearg? hwǣr cwōm mago? hwǣr cwōm māþþum-
>   gyfa?
> hwǣr cwōm symbla gesetu? hwǣr sindon seledrēamas?
> Ēalā beorht bune! ēalā byrnwiga!
> ēalā þēodnes þrym! hū sēo þrāg gewāt,
> genāp under nihthelm, swā hēo nō wǣre!

> "Where is the war-steed? Where is the warrior? Where his gen-
>   erous lord?
> Where now the feasting-places? Where now the mead-hall
>   pleasures?

Alas, bright cup! Alas, armed warrior!
Alas, glorious kings! How the time has slipped away
Darkened into night, as if it never were!"

Many of the Old English words have not changed as much as this excerpt from "The Wanderer" would indicate, however. The nouns *cyning* (king), *scip* (ship), *land* (land), *talu* (account), *golf* (glove), and the adjective *gōd* (good) are not remote from modern English. Thus, in Old English "that good king" would have been written, "*sē gōd cyning.*" Similarly, consider the principal parts of the following verbs:

drīfan (drive), *drāf* (drove), *gedrifen* (driven)
helpan (help), *healp* (helped), *geholpen* (helped)
feohtan (fight), *feaht* (fought), *gefohten* (fought)
beran (bear), *bāer* (bore), *geboren* (borne)
gifan (give), *gēaf* (gave), *gegifen* (given)
fēallan (fall), *fēoll* (fell), *gefeallen* (fallen).

The English language was changed from its Old English form, structure, and vocabulary largely because of the strong Norman French influence that developed after the Battle of Hastings in 1066. However, Old English remained the language of the people—the vernacular—even though French was spoken in the courts. The English language was so deeply rooted in the people that by about 1387 Chaucer's famous "Prologue" to his *Canterbury Tales* was written not in French, but in Middle English—a kind of Anglo-Norman English:

Whan that Aprill with his shoures soote
[*When April with his showers sweet*]

The droghte of March hath perced to the roote,
[*The drought of March has pierced to the root,*]

And bathed every veyne in swich licour
[*And bathed every vein in such liquor*]

Of which vertu engendred is the flour;
[*Of which virtue is engendered the flower;*]

English has continued to change throughout its modern period, as a glance at the King James version of the Bible or the plays of Shakespeare will reveal, and it continues to change today. In the late nineteenth century, William Skeat's *Etymological English Dictionary* indicated that only about 20 percent of English was native, over 30 percent was derived from French, about 15 percent from Latin, about 13 percent from Greek, and the rest from several other languages. The creation and borrowing of new words continues, of course, and has never been as pronounced as it is in the twentieth century in Anglo-American English.

THE CHANGE OF MEANING

Meaning changes as thought processes change. Since the circumstances with which man deals change about him, should his language not change, man would be a rigid, static, and—eventually—an extinct creature. The ways in which meaning changes are innumerable, but three should be mentioned here:

1. The meaning of a word can be restricted or narrowed.
2. The meaning can be transferred or changed until original concepts may be altogether lost.
3. The meaning may be extended, and the word may gain a variety of meaning.

An example of the first kind of change is the Old English *deor,* and the Middle English *dere* or *deer,* which meant until Shakespeare's time any small, wild animal, but has since been narrowed to mean a specific kind of animal.

Gossip is a good example of the transfer of meaning which continues until the original concept is lost. From the Old English, the original form was *godsibbe,* which literally meant "related to God," or more precisely, "a baptismal sponsor." In Middle English, the form was "gossib," and the meaning had transferred to the more general "companion," "close friend," or "one who talks a lot." Now the meaning has degenerated into "one who indulges in rumors or idle talk about others," and the tone of the word is derogatory.

A good example of the extension of meaning is the Old and Middle English *bord,* which originally meant a "flat piece of wood." Later the word was applied to a table for meals made up of several wooden "boards"; then *board* referred to the meals themselves served on the table, then to meals provided regularly for pay, as in the expression "room and board." Since people sat around a table and talked, in addition to eating, the word *board* was eventually applied to any deliberating body or organization, such as a board of education.

The transfer of meaning continues also in the form of *metaphor* (an indirect comparison of two unlike objects), as when we apply *sharp* to a person who dresses fashionably, or *dull* to a color, or *heavy* to an emotional attitude (a *heavy* heart). Extensions of meaning are also evident in such words as *grate, pen, sole,* and *swallow.* There is nothing permanent or sacred about words; it is normal that men continue their process of adjusting language to fit the demands of reality which must be faced in different ways with the passage of time.

WORD CHANGES

It is both instructive and amusing to observe how words originate, and how they "turn around on themselves," so to speak, and come to mean something entirely different, sometimes the opposite of their original meanings. *Budget,* for example, came originally from the Latin *bulga* through the French and Middle English *bougette,* meaning initially "a bag or pouch of leather." The contents of the bag became the substance of the word, particularly the plan or schedule for arranging expenses during a certain time over against the income for that time. The word has been extended to more complex aspects of modern finance and also applies to plans involving those other than money; for example, one may *budget* time.

Calm was borrowed from the Greek *kauma*, meaning "burning heat," through the Latin *cauma*, "heat of the sun." Because people in Italy and other southern regions avoided the noonday sun with a period of midday rest, the word came to mean "still, quiet, and tranquil."

Cheat is derived from the Middle English *chete* or *escheat*, originally from the Old French *escheoir*; it once meant "to look after lands that had gone back to the state through forfeiture, *e.g.*, through a lack of legal heirs." *Escheators*, doubtless, were notoriously fraudulent, for the word shifted in meaning to the practice of deception; in verb form, "to swindle, trick, and defraud."

Easel today means the stand for an artist's painting and connotes the creative atmosphere of a studio. But the original word is less romantic; borrowed from the Dutch *ezel*, which meant "ass," the term was derived from the association with an animal used for support, as we today use a carpenter's "horse," or "sawhorse," a brace for sawing boards. The word was not borrowed until the seventeenth and eighteenth centuries, when the Dutch became famous for their oil painting.

Neighbor in Old English was a combination of two words: *néah* (nigh or near) and *gebūr* (freeholder, farmer, or peasant). Originally, then, in an agrarian age, the word *néahgebūr* meant literally "the near farmer." In Middle English the form was *neighbour* or *nyebour,* and soon meant a person who lives close to another. In Modern English the nearness of the meaning is generally retained, although one meaning is "fellow man," as in Christian usage, "Love thy neighbor."

Rehearse derives from the Old French *hercier* and Middle English *rehercen,* meaning "to harrow," as a farmer "harrows" a plowed field, breaking up the large clods into finer pieces, thus going over and over the same earth until it is fit for planting. In Modern English the word is now applied to speakers and actors rather than to farmers.

Silly, the Old English form for which was *saelig,* meant "happy, prosperous, blessed" (akin to *selig,* blessed). The Middle English form had changed to *seli* or *sili,* but the meaning was largely retained as "good, blessed, innocent." Gradually, it degenerated to mean "unworldly" and "foolish." Now it denotes "feeble-minded," "foolish, stupid, ludicrous"; and in colloquial usage "dazed" and "senseless." *Silly* now implies "irrational behavior."

Stickler, from the Old English *stihtan* and Middle English *stightlen,* was used by Shakespeare to mean a sportsman who parts combatants, somewhat as a referee does in a present-day boxing match, thus connoting fair play. Technically, it also meant "to rule, order, or dispose of," although in Modern English a *stickler* denotes one who is fussy about small matters.

Tawdry is a verbal composite of *St.* (Saint) and *Audrey,* which was the name of an annual October fair held in Norwich, England. At this fair cheap, gaudy articles were sold. The shortened merging of the syllables of *St. Audrey* into *tawdry* developed directly out of the designation of these cheap and tasteless items bought or won at St. Audrey's Fair.

Yuletide in Old English had the forms of *géol, giul, jul,* and *geohol,* and designated a heathen festival in midwinter. The Middle English form was *yul,* which is related to the Icelandic *jol,* a possible antecedent form of "jolly." Related to the Christmas season, then, *Yuletide* became literally "the happy time," and so it remains.

QUESTIONS ON READINGS

SCIENCE AND THE HUMANITIES IN CONFLICT.

In *An Essay on Man: An Introduction to the Philosophy of Human Culture,* Ernst Cassirer wrote, "No longer in a merely physical universe, man lives in a symbolic universe. Language, myth, art, and religion are parts of this universe. They are the varied threads which weave the symbolic net, the tangled web of human experience. . . . No longer can man confront reality immediately; he cannot see it, as it were, face to face. Physical reality seems to recede in proportion as man's symbolic activity advances. Instead of dealing with the things themselves man is in a sense constantly conversing with himself. He has so enveloped himself in linguistic forms, in artistic images, in mythical symbols or religious rites that he cannot see or know anything except by the interposition of this artificial medium. His situation is the same in the theoretical as in the practical sphere. Even here man does not live in a world of hard facts, or according to his immediate needs and desires. He lives rather in the midst of imaginary emotions, in hopes and fears, in illusions and disillusions, in his fantasies and dreams. 'What disturbs and alarms man,' said Epictetus, 'are not the things, but his opinions and fancies about the things.' " After reading this statement, do you feel that man's language may be a handicap rather than an advantage? Explain. If this is so in art and religion, as Cassirer indicates, is it also true in the sciences? Explain.

LANGUAGE AND REALITY

The expression "A rolling stone gathers no moss" (p. 183) is attributed to Publilius Syrus in the first century B.C. Would you say that the entire context of the adage has changed in any way from its classical meaning? Discuss. Is the expression ambiguous? How?

Read John Kenneth Galbraith's "The Age of the Wordfact" (p. 208). Discuss the meaning of "wordfact." Can language really "improve" the "reality"? If your answer is "Yes," then explain it. If it is "No," also explain your rationale. After studying the entire article, would you conclude that language is indeed "changeable"? If so, how? What are *nuances* of meaning? How can nuances be emphasized in such a way as to "improve" impressions through language? Discuss. Do you think that "wordfact" will be incorporated into the English language as a new word? Why or why not?

Read the abridgment from H. L. Mencken's chapter "American Slang." What part does slang play in our changing language? Discuss in detail. Is "Yesterday's slang is tomorrow's language" a maxim which you can support with illustrations from Chapter 1? Discuss.

Susanne K. Langer, in the excerpt from *Philosophy in a New Key* (p. 212), gives us new light on the origin of language, in addition to the treatment of the subject in Chapter 1. Discuss the meaning of *symbol* and *symbolizing* in relation to Langer's views. How do her insights serve to clarify the evolution or changing nature of language?

In "The Psychology of Semantics" (p. 216), Edward L. Thorndike states, "Meanings are in persons' minds, not in words. . . ." What have you learned in Chapter 1 which tends to support Thorndike's view? Discuss. Give examples to strengthen your own contention. How does Thorndike's statement support the idea that the thought is father to the word? Discuss.

WAR AND DEHUMANIZATION

Peruse Joseph Wood Krutch's article, "Man's Ancient, Powerful Link to Nature: A Source of Fear and Joy" (p. 253). Later, you will have opportunity to go into the article in more detail, but for the present, do you think that language as such is part of man's nature? Krutch indicates that the modern world tends to separate man from what is natural. Do you agree? If so, do you see any ways in which some language is "more natural," so to speak, than other language? Discuss. What aspects of modern civilization tend to make man's language more "artificial" and less "natural"? Assuming the relevance of the question, discuss its implications.

THE CAMPUS TODAY: REBELLION AND CONFORMITY

Examine H. Lynn Sheller's address, "What the Students Are Saying to Us" (p. 274). What does the author indicate about student reaction to such terms as "economic imperialism," "bureaucratic," "machine-like society," "the system," "abstract values," "conformity," "role playing," "free speech," and especially *"in loco parentis"*? In what ways does Sheller demonstrate that language is, indeed, fluid rather than rigid, changing rather than stagnant? Discuss. What insights does he offer for the so-called "generation gap" in relationship to language, both from the standpoints of speaking *and* listening? In what ways does he suggest a dialogue of understanding between students on the one hand, and faculty and administrators (and even parents) on the other? Discuss. What does Sheller mean by "barriers that inhibit communication between students and teachers" (p. 278)? Can you give examples from your own experience, either direct or indirect, to illustrate Sheller's meaning? Is language really language *if it fails to communicate*? Discuss. Can you think of examples of the use of language which do, indeed, fail to communicate? Specify. Finally, describe in your own words your "ideal" of what the author terms "a climate favorable to the intellectual development of students."

THE SEARCH FOR IDENTITY

T. S. Eliot wrote in his drama *The Elder Statesman,* "What do you call a failure? The worst kind of failure, in my opinion, is the man who has to keep on pretending to himself that he's a success—the man who in the morning has to make up his face before he looks in the mirror" (p. 295). Look up the meanings of the words *failure* and *success* in a dictionary. How do people misinterpret the meanings of these words in their daily lives? In Chapter 1 we received an impression in miniature of how our English words have changed in form and meaning, as well as in pronunciation and grammar, over a period of about fifteen hundred years. Do you detect any change in meaning in present-day concepts of *failure* and *success*? Discuss.

LOVE, SEX, AND CENSORSHIP

Read and carefully interpret the two poems by Robert Browning, "Meeting at Night" and "Parting at Morning" (p. 309). Define the word *love,* checking its derivation and denotations in a dictionary. Are these "love poems" according to your definition? Definitions? How do Browning's poems illustrate the different meanings of *love*? Discuss.

INDIVIDUAL RESPONSIBILITY

Read the poem "The Love Song of J. Alfred Prufrock," by T. S. Eliot. Relate portions of the poem to the quotation from *The Elder Statesman* (p. 295) above. After a close checking of the derivation and meanings of the word *love,* what new light does Eliot shed on the meaning of "Love Song"? Are his meanings *ironic* (unexpected)? Discuss. How does the poem demonstrate the changing aspects of language? Discuss.

GOD, MAN, AND MORAL CONSCIOUSNESS

Study Shakespeare's excerpt from *The Merchant of Venice,* Act II, Scene I (p. 418), beginning with Salarino's question, which may be paraphrased, "Why, I feel certain, if he doesn't pay in time, you won't really take from him a pound of flesh, for what advantage would it be to you?" Check the word *paraphrase* in your dictionary. What do the stems *para* and *phrazein* mean literally? Read carefully Shylock's answer. Then put it into your own words, never repeating more than three of Shakespeare's original words in sequence. Does this exercise convince you that Shakespeare wrote Modern English, albeit early Modern English (1500 to the present)? Aside from expressions clarified in the footnotes, do you have any difficulty with the passage? What words bespeak most concretely Shylock's feeling of equality with other human beings, especially Christians? Pick out at least three words and check their derivation or etymology; for example, Shakespeare's *laugh'd* is derived from Middle English forms *laughen, lahen;* earlier Anglo-Saxon *hleahhan;* Greek *lachen;* Old High German *hlahhan;* and ultimately the Indo-European *gleg,* which meant "to cry out" "to sound," related to *clangor* or a loud sound. What do your findings in etymology indicate about how language changes? To bring your points full-circle, what are the various meanings of *laugh* at present? In what different ways may the word be used? How does Shylock use the word within the context of his statement? Is his usage a broad or limited meaning of *laugh?*

LITERATURE AND GOOD WRITING

After reading Walt Whitman's "O Captain! My Captain!" (p. 403), examine the denotations of the words *rack, port, keel, vessel, father,* and *Captain.* In none of the ways in which Whitman used these words do they mean literally what their denotations (dictionary meanings) indicate, do they? Why then has Whitman used such words? Do you agree that some language is used in order to convey *feeling* and *emotion* rather than information? How does Whitman appeal to the five senses with the use of certain words in the poem? Specify. What is *imagination?* Has Whitman achieved the dimension of language which we call *imagination* with this poem? Discuss. Relate aspects of *symbolism* to your discussion.

AGE OF CONTROVERSY

Look up the word *existentialism* in a dictionary, noting that its present meaning includes an interpretation by Jean-Paul Sartre which is quite different from its original meaning (from Middle English and Latin *existentia,* or "fact of being or existence"). One aspect of Sartre's concept of *existentialism,* although it is here somewhat oversimplified, is that man exists in a universe without purpose, and that he must strive against an inimical environment through the use of his own lonely powers of reason and free will. Now read carefully the excerpt from the Venerable Bede's *Ecclesiastical (Church) History of the English Nation* (p. 440). Do you see any relationship between the Sartre concept of *existentialism* and that of Old English royalty and followers before their conversion to Christianity? Describe. The anecdote of the sparrow and its flight through the bright room is a vivid Old English story. What is its purpose? Do you see points of identity between King Edwin and his men's reaction to the "purposelessness of existence" and that of men today? Discuss. In what ways, then, does this excerpt indicate that our language retained its meanings? Changed in its meanings? Discuss.

SYMBOLS, NOT THINGS

THE WORD IS NOT THE THING, BUT MERELY STANDS FOR THE THING

A symbol requires a thought. A word is a symbol, and for it to have any meaning it must cause a thought—nearly always a thought which is, to some extent, shared by other human beings. Some words are obviously symbolical; that is, a letter or group of letters written or spoken expressing talk—talk or speech which, in turn, stands for something: objects, qualities, processes, quantities, concepts both concrete and abstract. Obvious symbols in the culture of the United States are the cross, which represents Christianity; the dove, which stands for peace; the plowshare, which is emblematical of agriculture. A flag is symbolical of a nation; a crown, of the king; the altar, of religion; the pen, of arts and sciences; and the sword, of war. But in this sense *all* words are representations, symbols—not just the obvious ones. Yet in the modern world, we often talk and behave as if words possessed some kind of magic, powerful substance inhering in them. Moreover, people generally tend to think of a word as having only one function, when in actuality it may have several functions.

When we are very young we conceive the miracle of language. We begin to use it, and ultimately the usage becomes automatic. We take the splendor of our language for granted. Perhaps for this reason we may tend to confuse words for things, symbols for objects or ideas. Yet, just as we know that the diagram is not the machine, the musical score is not the sound, or the map is not the territory, we surely realize (especially if we habitually remind ourselves of the fact) that *the word is not the thing, but merely stands for the thing.* Such a realization is fortunate, for it aids us immeasurably in conceiving accurately of reality, and people who live their lives close to reality are usually better adjusted than those who tend to be unrealistic—hence, they are happier, more efficient, healthier human beings. Being aware of the world as it is, they are bothered less by changes in a dynamic society; they are aware that language is simply a flexible tool which must be used with limitations, and kept in focus within the ever-changing dimensions of human existence.

An illustration of the flexibility of language may help us to perceive more accurately than we may at present the importance of distinguishing words from things, and to see how human misfortune can result when we fail to do so. We need a word for our illustration. Let us consider *cat*. The word *cat* may mean many things, and it may be used in a number of ways. *Cat* may refer to a domesticated mammal, lithe and soft-furred, often kept as a pet. Depending upon its gender, it may be called "Tom" or "Pussy." *Cat* may also mean any of Tom's or Pussy's bigger and wilder relatives in the *feline* family—a cougar, leopard, lion, tiger, or wildcat. However, the *referent* of the word *cat* (that is, the thing to which the word *refers*) may not be a feline animal at all, but instead a human being with feline traits—for example, a supple girl with a triangular face and large green eyes, or a spiteful woman. *Cat* may also mean a kind of tripod, a fish, a whip, a caterpillar tractor, a bat used in a game of tipcat or the game itself, a movable military shelter, a part of a ship to which an anchor may be hoisted, or a tackle for hoisting the anchor itself. *Cat* in all these situations, being the name of something, is used as a noun; but it may also be used as a verb, designating action, movement, and, hence, a more immediate involvement than a parallel noun form is usually capable of connoting. In nautical language, *to cat* may mean to hoist an anchor of a ship up to the cathead, or it may mean to flog or whip with a cat-o'-nine-tails. Similarly, *catting* or *catted* may refer to these processes in the present tense or past tense respectively. But in none of these situations is *cat* or any of its forms the thing itself. It is merely the label, the *symbol* of the thing. The reality exists *under the level of language,* subverbally, without the word.

Because language changes to reflect the reality of a world in flux, *cat* may spring over its boundaries of standard usage and in some circles refer to a musician, an especially animalic personality, or simply a lively person. Used in this way, *cat* is more nearly always a slang term, and the slang versions vary in specificity. Among some university students, for example, *cool cat* may designate anything from the latest "mod" attire to an attractive quality such as *savoir-faire* (a ready knowledge of the what, when, and how of saying, doing, acting). A *fat cat* may designate wealth, or a "big spender." Traditionally, the word *cat* has been used by poets and writers for its richly varied connotations. An early example is the nursery tale dating back to the sixteenth century, "Puss 'n Boots," in which the astonishingly resourceful cat suggests the qualities of individuality, cleverness, pride, earnest friendship, and loyalty. In William Blake's poem "The Tiger," the most famous lines connote not only the power, grandeur, and majesty of the jungle creature, but also suggest, even within the intimations of terror, the awesome beauty and inscrutable mystery of God's universe:

Tiger! Tiger! burning bright
In the forests of the night,
What immortal hand or eye
Could frame thy fearful symmetry?

.   .   .   .

When the stars threw down their spears,
And water'd heaven with their tears,
Did he smile his work to see?
Did he who made the Lamb make thee?

The word *cat* has commended itself to generations of literary artists, English-speaking and otherwise, as a term of endearment. Tolstoy in 1877 employed the form as a Russian diminutive in treating as the center of a delicate romance the Princess "Kitty" Shcherbatskaya in *Anna Karenina*. Ernest Hemingway had the hero of his famous novel *A Farewell to Arms* (1929) apply it to the heroine, Catherine, in one of the tenderest of Hemingway's love scenes. Ten years later, William Faulkner used the term in a more animalic sense to describe his heroine Charlotte in *The Wild Palms*. Today we sometimes hear the word as the special language of a trade or profession, nor is all such language (or *argot*) slang. For example, jazz musicians in a jam session may refer to an outstanding performer as a "real cat," implying a definite technical and artistic skill. But we also hear the word used as general slang. To illustrate, the word *cat* may be used as a verb, directed toward the intensification of the personal traits of human types already mentioned, although such usages are not yet considered to be standard English.

Even so, the usage hangs on. Thus, say a girl—we'll call her Barbara—meets a boy—Jim—on the campus and asks him where his roommate Clyde is, and Jim responds "Oh, he's out *cattin'* around somewhere." Barbara knows that Clyde, depending upon the nature of his lively activities, is "around somewhere" engaged in them.

"What do you mean, *catting*?" she inquires, and—Jim's response may depend upon his attitude toward Barbara, the context of her question, the circumstances of their conversational exchange, the tone of her voice. Is she really curious? Does she want information? Is her tone casual, concerned, flippant, flirtatious? The point is that the meaning of *cat* or *catting*, as a general slang term, has a whole range of possibilities, and the communication of Barbara and Jim, as well as their mutual concepts of Clyde, depends upon a highly complex contextual setting. For the word is not a thing at all, but only a *symbol* of the thoughts of each—as particular or as general as each intends. It is up to Barbara and Jim (and, less directly, Clyde) to establish precisely what they mean in the use of their remarks *if communication of accurate information is their purpose*. Confusion, doubt, misunderstanding, and even irrational responses, may result if communication breaks down— that is, if their *references*, or mutual thought processes, do not in this instance at least generally coincide. Here, the word "cat" or "catting"—

if it is not properly understood in its precise context by people who, we can assume, are concerned about what they really mean—may become a bugaboo that disorders their human affairs. And yet, why should it? Words by themselves—without human thought processes—are meaningless.

But people, even intelligent students at universities, may confuse the word for the thing, or the expression for the reality. Let us assume, for example, that Barbara's feelings toward Clyde are deeply personal; they have, in fact, discussed marriage. Thus, while Jim's use of the general slang term *"cattin'"* meant precisely in his mind that Clyde, having just tuned up the engine of his convertible Camaro, was out on the highway giving the car a trial run, Barbara's response to his expression was entirely different from what he intended. Her whole attitude toward Clyde is personal and romantic; she feels possessive toward him, although she does not like to let her feelings show, except in what she considers to be properly secluded moments, and even then she does not feel completely free to express her emotions. Although she is aware of the general nature of the slang term *cat,* her attitudes are colored by her knowledge of the nocturnal habits of mature domestic cats, and for her the term is slanted toward an elemental or sexual connotation; the images which come to her mind are not of Clyde's Camaro but rather a vague montage of Clyde's dancing with other girls, one after the other. Before she can reflect further or delay her responses or ask any more questions for information, she hears herself crying out, *"Oh, he is, is he?"* and to Jim's bewilderment, she bursts into tears and rushes away.

The possible endings to this little melodrama are as numerous as human responses to such a combination of circumstances can be. Clyde, too "proud" to discuss with his roommate the debacle which ensues (as we imagine it does), mopes and does not speak to Barbara for weeks, and then one of them has a date with another person. There is a rapid exchange of "I'll show you" situations, and ultimately, the possible engagement is impossible. Or perhaps from Barbara's **actions** Clyde assumes that she despises him for some reason that he cannot fathom, but he is too "proud" to discuss the matter with her. They never date each other again. Or perhaps Clyde more sensibly discusses his problem with his roommate, hears Jim's account of his meeting with Barbara, and begins to see the whole matter in an understandable perspective.

THE CHILD AND THE ADULT

When the little two-year-old boy hugs the German shepherd dog and says, "Hello, Pussycat," we smile at his innocent mistake; the child has confused the name with the object. Similarly, children may define "punctuation" as "being on time" or "blood vessels" as "little red sailboats that carry blood through people." The adult response to such confusions of words with what they stand for (the *symbol* with the *referent*) is one of tolerant amusement. After all, children are children.

But what of the woman in a shoe shop during a sale who eventually refuses to purchase a "bargain" because, as the shoes are being boxed and wrapped, she notices that the size labeled on the box is not "her size" despite the fact that she has previously tried on dozens of pairs and, after long consideration, has "made up her mind" and told the exhausted salesman that these are "just what I wanted" and that they "fit perfectly"? She feels that her refusal to purchase a "7-B" when she has worn a "6½-B" for years is entirely reasonable and rational. But she has ignored the fact that the shoes "fit perfectly." Perhaps the shoes were manufactured on a comparatively smaller last than those she previously purchased, or these shoes may have been made with a thicker inner leather lining, or the woman may have gained weight; but none of these possibilities occurs to her. For her, the *reality* is less meaningful than the *label*. She will pay more money for a pair of 6½-B, nonbargain shoes because she cannot distinguish between the *symbol* ("7-B") and the *referent* (a pair of shoes described as "just what I wanted" and which "fit perfectly").

THE LEVELS OF MEANING

There may be numerous levels of meaning, sense, import, purport, and signification of a word. Let us consider at least four which will help us to understand better the nature of language and reality:

1. *The meaning without the word.*
2. The dictionary meaning of the word (*denotation*).
3. The associated meanings of the word (*connotations*).
4. The *private meaning* of the word (remote from reality).

We have seen that the word *cat* has many dictionary meanings. Yet the *reality* which the word represents is always *subverbal:* the *reality* exists without the word. Can one "define" such a word subverbally—*cat*, itself, for example? The answer is Yes, but without using words; by pointing, by studying the object directly from various angles, by applying the various human senses to it—but *not* by using words. Once a person's findings are reported in words, he is at least one level removed from the reality itself. Thus, a chemist may observe and study the properties of a substance that he later discovers to be an element: let us say it is a gaseous element with a pungent, suffocating odor, yellowish-green in color, two and one-half times heavier than atmospheric air, and soluble in water; it is found in numerous compounds, one of the most prevalent being common salt, a compound with sodium; it is found to be usable in the arts as an ingredient of paints; in the process of vulcanizing; and as a bleaching and disinfecting agent. The element is named "chlorine." When the chemist studies the element directly, as did Sir Humphry Davy, he may work *subverbally,* directly with the substance, and *see it clearly with all his senses,* as it were, *rather than through the blurred lenses of words.* In doing so, he is working in an area closer to reality than any verbal level can be. The original discoverer, the inventor, the poet, the student who sees things "freshly," the individual "genius" often deals with reality subverbally. Hence, he often brings new knowledge and new insights to mankind—as Davy brought the knowledge of chlorine and its benefits to us. We understand what the thinking men have done through the medium of words, of course, preferably through a careful "*denoting*" of experiences; that is, a rendering of observations through direct, explicit words—"dictionary words" which report the barest physical descriptions and characteristics of such discoveries and insights.

This is often true even when an eloquent writer, for example, touches us deeply through his use of words. Because he has consciously communicated something he has experienced or felt in an *original* way, and because he has communicated in words which have been carefully chosen to convey in a fresh way the vividness of his feeling, he moves us to new insights and depths of feeling which we may never have experienced through the use of language. Consider, for example, Shakespeare's treatment of the death of the tragic hero Prince Hamlet. Hamlet wants his best friend, Horatio, to clear his name, a duty which only Horatio can perform. It is a classic noble farewell and expression of the last wish of a dying man:

> *"If thou didst ever hold me in thy heart,*
> *Absent thee from felicity awhile,*
> *And in this harsh world draw thy breath in pain,*
> *To tell my story."*

And then, with these lines, consider Horatio's assuaging words to his dying friend,

> *"Good night, sweet prince;*
> *And flights of angels sing thee to thy rest!"*

Notice how Shakespeare's choice and arrangement of words force us to feel and to understand in a singular way the emotional impact of the whole scene. For a dying man to state a conditional "If thou didst ever" is extraordinary enough, but the direct metaphor "hold me in thy heart" states *concretely* much that is usually abstract. *Hold* itself is a kinesthetic image, indicating muscular movement, and *heart* gives concrete substance to what might otherwise be stated as a more abstract condition of profound friendship and devotion. The metaphor is thus intense, pressuring into its unique poetic form more emotion than the ordinary language of information is capable of. "Absent thee from felicity awhile" is an especially original condensation of broadly ramified ideas; it makes what is general more nearly exact, and the compression of the statement, coming from the lips of a dying man, emerges with eloquent lucidity, simplicity, and euphony. The gentle tone of this line, pointing out an all too human frailty—the personal selfishness of humanity set over against the death of one's best friend—is juxtaposed with "And in this harsh world draw thy breath in pain," with the initial emphasis on "harsh world," a direct contrast to the gentle tone of Hamlet's personal request to Horatio. *Harsh* denotes the crude, uneven, rough aspects of human existence—the sharp, grating, and discordant experiences common to all mature, sensitive people. But notice that the word which Shakespeare chose *sounds* discordant and grating—onomatopoeic. Hence, the word *harsh*, in addition to its explicit or *denoted* meaning, becomes richly *connotative*, suggesting and conveying associations and overtones, even in the dimension of sound. The portion of Hamlet's statement "draw thy breath in pain" is also an intense and highly compressed image, associating breathing (life itself) with that which hurts, an odd (paradoxical) contrast on the literal level; but the *connotation* of the words is understandable in the context of Hamlet's meaning. His tragic life is certainly more than a literal "story" to be "told" also, for the drama of *Hamlet, Prince of Denmark,* as told by Shakespeare, has gripped the hearts, minds, and imaginations of thinking people for nearly four centuries. The concrete power and rich connotations of its language, the rhythmical arrangement of words, its style and substance have made it, as Matthew Arnold noted, one of the "touchstones" of great poetry.

The fourth category of meaning may be a *private level,* one which is remote from reality. Just as the denotation of a word is one level removed from reality, and connotations (or associated meanings) are two levels removed from reality, the private meaning—not being either a legitimate denotation or connotation—is often farther removed from reality than three levels. More often than not, one may maintain that the private meaning is cut off, separated from reality. An extreme example of this can be seen in the response of some people to the personage of Napoleon Bonaparte. He was, of course, a real person, who occupied time and space from the year 1769 to 1821. This personage may be said to denote an emperor of France from 1804 to 1815, an enlightened despot, a reformer of French law, a leader of popular revolutions, and an overthrower of monarchies. Acceptable connotations would be a "military genius," "a man of slight stature who became a giant among men," perhaps even the famous French medal "the Legion of Honor" itself, which Napoleon established. But a highly private response to the symbol *Napoleon* would be for an individual in the present to walk around in a cocked hat, wearing an early nineteenth-century French military tunic with brass buttons, his hand thrust between the buttons in a typical "Napoleonic" pose. Unless the individual were an actor in a play, a person on his way to a masquerade ball, or a *poseur* for some other rational purpose (such as a photographer's model or a college student being initiated into a fraternity by such hazing), he would most certainly be acting in an irrational manner. (If human beings respond on a "private level" to very many aspects of their lives, they may, depending upon the extent and frequency with which they respond privately, be "unsane," although we should remember that all individuals at some time and under various conditions of extreme stress are capable of responding "privately" and irrationally.)

SUBVERBAL REALITY AND PROBLEMS OF GENERALIZATIONS

Rather than responding to various aspects of life with his own private meanings remote from reality, the user of language needs to conceive of and understand as fully as possible words as they relate to the world outside of himself. People who are aware of the subverbal levels of reality are more flexible in their attitudes than those who are not; generally, they are more objective (hence, less prejudiced), and are more intelligent and useful citizens. If people can recognize *generalizations* for what they are—vague words or patterns of words which often leave out important details and concrete terms, often broadly emphasizing more than what is meant and employing abstract terms to hazy ends—they have taken the first important step toward becoming oriented to the reality of humanity and the world about themselves. If we would be properly oriented with things as they are, then we should train ourselves to be aware of the reality without the word.

CLEAR THINKING IS THE MAJOR PREREQUISITE OF GOOD WRITING

Such a goal is easier to state in words than to practice. Since language naturally tends to be about language and therefore strays farther from —rather than moves closer to—reality, then obviously most language tends toward abstraction. Most speaking and most writing is poor speaking and writing. If a person cannot recognize generalizations to begin with, then he will speak and write in generalizations. Also, he will think in generalizations, for speaking and writing are merely reflections of our thought processes. Most students write somewhat as water runs off a rock, seeking the worn grooves of downward progress. They may write naturally, but they often write without power or purpose, without force or grace; and just as, through the years, draining water wears troughs of the lowest, easiest ways, so does an original human thought often lose its singularity by its route of expression, either in speech or writing, emerging as a *cliché* or some other kind of dull, inaccurate expression. Too often we avoid the responsibility of thinking altogether by permitting our minds to fall back on familiar and comfortable generalizations; or we "parrot" other people's thoughts by using their words rather than our own; or we sometimes sacrifice the truth of what we really mean to a mode of expression which sounds clever to us, but which says something other than what we actually mean. In seeking *to think* and *to write* in lucid and original ways, we must begin with *clear thinking*. There is no point in expressing well what is essentially lazy, sloppy, generalized thinking.

Language is an expression of human thought processes and, as such, it becomes an aspect of human behavior. Just as one can study language from the standpoints of grammar, derivation, morphology, and orthography, he can also study language in relation to the human responses to it. As we have seen, problems in human behavior often

arise because of the misunderstanding of language. Study and correction of human responses to *symbols* (usually words) seem, therefore, to
be necessary and valid pursuits.

Another problem in human behavior stems from man's failure to
interpret properly not only *symbols*, but also *signs*. Although there are
many kinds of signs, for our purposes signs differ essentially from
symbols in that symbols involve conscious thought processes (*references*), while a sign is a thing which refers directly to another thing. No
"symbolizing" takes place if a sign functions as a sign. *A sign "points
to" the existence, either past, present, or future, of something else.* A
sign *indicates;* it does not *represent.* For example, wet streets may be a
sign of rain. (Animals other than man use signs. A rabbit thumps at
danger; birds cry out. Bees "dance" to give the distance and direction of
nectar.)

Words, too, may be used as signs: a word can be a sign for an
animal, while it is symbol for a man. To illustrate, assume that Jack
calls on his friend Morton at Morton's house. Morton has left the door
open, for he will return soon, and his dog is there. Jack enters, and
since he has been there before, Morton's dog Sport is friendly and does
not bark. Jack calls, "Morton!" and as he calls certain thought processes
are occurring in his mind. He can think of Morton, even though Morton
is not present. But while Jack is thinking, the dog has run to the
doorway to look for his master. For to the dog, the shouted word
"Morton!" is a sign, pointing directly to his master.

This concept of signs explains how horses supposedly "count," or
parrots "talk." They are often trained simply to respond to the signs of
their masters. So far as is known, man is the only symbol-making
creature; only he can make symbols which *represent* something, and
only he can write them down. He is the only creature who can hold onto
ideas. In this sense, man is the only "time-binding" creature.

But man can, and sometimes does fail to interpret signs correctly.
Involuntary gestures or manners of talking can be misinterpreted, even
in habitual conversation. For example, in the United States most people
when engaged in close conversation tend to stand about two feet apart;
in England, the comparable separation is closer to three feet. Thus, if
an American talks closely with an Englishman whom he has recently
met, the two may come away with mistaken impressions about each
other. The American, in attempting to be friendly, has been misunderstood as being "forward." The Englishman, by custom standing a bit
farther away from the social talker, is conceived of by the American as
being somewhat "aloof." One may well imagine the reaction of either to
the Arab, who in a close conversation likes to feel the other speaker's
breath on his face; or the Arab himself to either "foreigner," who, in
backing away all the time, is certainly deemed "unfriendly," or perhaps
one who "thinks himself superior to Arabs"!

Similarly, a sudden gesture, such as the tendency of Americans to
throw up their arms and wave with visible energy—especially when
accompanied by a loud shout, such as "Oh, Joe!" or "Hi, Jane!" or
simply a vociferous "How are you, Buddy!"—may be perfectly accept-

able in Yuma, Arizona, Dalton, Georgia, Rumford, New Hampshire, or a thousand other American cities and towns. But the same sudden gestures and loud shout (even if of well-meant greeting) would be construed in most of China as an insult. . . . We shall have more to say about words and human behavior in the next chapter.

QUESTIONS ON READINGS

SCIENCE AND THE HUMANITIES IN CONFLICT

What *generalizations* are evident in C. P. Snow's statement in "The Two Cultures": "The traditional culture, which is, of course, mainly literary, is behaving like a state whose power is rapidly declining—standing on its precarious dignity, spending far too much energy on Alexandrian intricacies, occasionally letting fly in fits of aggressive pique quite beyond its means, too much on the defensive to show any generous imagination to the forces which must inevitably reshape it" (p. 156)? As a beginning, do you see in his use of the term "traditional culture" any vagueness? Considering the term as a *symbol,* to what does it *refer?*

Examine Snow's central statement: "It is the traditional culture, to an extent remarkably little diminished by the emergence of the scientific one, which manages the western world." What, in your view, does *traditional* mean to Snow (p. 156)? Do you think that Snow has in any way confused the word *traditional* for what it may stand? In determining your answer, examine the word from the four levels of language treated in Chapter 2.

Read the excerpts from Charles Dickens' *Hard Times.* Notice especially the description of the schoolroom, the character and philosophy of Thomas Gradgrind, and the girl Sissy Jupe and her innocent views of life. Thomas Gradgrind describes himself as "A man of realities . . . of facts. . . . A man who proceeds upon the principle that two and two are four, and nothing over" (p. 167). The students to whom the "facts" are to be presented are described as "little pitchers before him, who were to be filled so full of facts" (p. 167). In these and other portions of *Hard Times,* do you see any examples of the confusion of *symbols* with the *realities* for which they stand? Do you find any evidence of *private meanings* for symbols, and possibly sad, if not tragic, consequences resulting from them? Discuss.

In his address "On Education," Albert Einstein discusses the use of "fear" and "force" as motivations in education (p. 174). What do these terms mean to him? Do you agree? In his view what is the "most important method of education" (p. 174)? Does his reasoning for this view strike you as being logical and close to reality? What is his opinion of the "most important motive for work in the school" (p. 175)? Do you agree? Why or why not? In connection with the viewpoints of C. P. Snow and F. R. Leavis, how does Einstein illuminate the relative importance of the "general ability of independent thinking and judgment" as opposed to "special knowledge" (p. 176)? In regard to the whole question of science and the humanities in conflict, which one of the three thinkers strikes you as using words which are closest to reality? Give examples to support and qualify your views.

LANGUAGE AND REALITY

In what ways does Helene and Charlton Laird's "How Did Language Begin?" (p. 178) reflect the point that words ideally should be related closely with reality? Assuming that language began on such a primitive level, then what conditions in the civilization of man have changed, resulting in a more abstract and less concrete language? Are such abstractions necessary? Are some abstractions necessary and some not?

Give examples to support your views.
Consider the following famous statements:
1. The best is yet to be. (p. 180)
2. With a grain of salt. (p. 185)
3. A new broom sweeps clean. (p. 182)
Before reading Magill's analysis of the original contexts of these statements, discuss the possible meanings. Then read the analyses. What do the discrepancies indicate about the nature of language? Do all statements—even famous ones—mean the same thing to all people?

Emerson wrote in "Language" (p. 214), "A man's power to connect his thought with its proper symbol, and so to utter it, depends upon the simplicity of his character, that is, upon his love of truth and his desire to communicate it without loss. The corruption of man is followed by the corruption of language." How do we lose meaning through a failure to be "simple," or through our lack of a "love of truth," or a "desire to communicate without loss"? Discuss.

WAR AND DEHUMANIZATION

Read Wilfred Owen's poem "Dulce et Decorum Est" (p. 222). In what ways do the words (*symbols*) which Owen chooses give us a more realistic picture of war than would, say, a sentence from a typical Fourth of July speech made by a windy orator? Discuss especially the *denotations* and *connotations* of "old beggars," "Knock-kneed," "coughing like hags," "trudge," "limped," "blood-shod," "lame," and "blind." Similarly, choose words in the remaining three stanzas which, in your opinion, are closer to the *realities* of wars than *abstractions* would be. Are there any *abstractions* in the final stanza of the poem? If so, are they *functional;* that is, do they serve a definite purpose? What?

In Dylan Thomas' statement, "War Can't Produce Poetry" (p. 224), he writes, "Poets can stop bullets, but bullets can't stop poets." Is this statement close to reality? In what way or ways? Is Thomas precisely clear about what he means when he says that war cannot produce poetry? Explain.

In "Man's Ancient, Powerful Link to Nature: A Source of Fear and Joy," Joseph Wood Krutch writes that "man is, of course, himself a part of Nature" (p. 253). What specifically do Krutch's words *denote;* that is, how is man a part of nature in a literal sense? Explain what he means when he writes of man, "Nature is what he tries to get away from and then something he wishes to keep" (p. 253). What does the word *paradox* mean? In Krutch's opinion, what is the major paradox of man in his relationship with nature (p. 254)?

THE CAMPUS TODAY: REBELLION AND CONFORMITY.

In what ways does Mario Savio's essay "An End to History" apply to his concept of college administrators and bureaucracies" (p. 262)? What are the denotations of *administrator* and *bureaucracy*? Denotatively, do you think that Savio's views are absolutely right, partly right and partly wrong, or completely wrong? Give specific reasons for your views. Do you think he is justified in maintaining that "bureaucracies" tend to "begin as tools" and as "means to certain legitimate goals," but "end up feeding their own existence" (p. 262)? Discuss. Following this statement, Savio contends, "The conception that bureaucrats have is that history has in fact come to an end. . . . We proceed by standard procedures as we are" (p. 262). Is this statement a *generalization*? What specific illustrations exist to prove his point; which to disprove it? After reading the entire essay, do you see possible "private meanings" which may have caused Savio to slant his argument? What are they? Be specific.

Included in the subsection which deals with the poetry from *Tomorrow's People,* is a poem by K. D. Petrey entitled "Of This Town" (p. 262). Read the poem carefully. The only stanza which mentions a "sheriff" is the third: "Moonshine rolls from the blood-stained hills./ Drunken officers delight in finding parked kids-/ while *the county sheriff* has a son by a local woman" (italics added). Now read the article in the same subsection, "Poems Stir Dispute," especially the reference to a poem "by sophomore K. D. Petrey," which "refers to a sheriff of an unnamed county" (p. 271). According to the article, "The Harlan County Sheriff, Jason Howard, telephoned Pennington demanding an explanation of Petrey's poem. Pennington explained that the poem was literary and not political, but he feels that the Sheriff was unsatisfied by the explanation. According to Pennington, Howard told him, 'You either clear this up or I'll be in to see you'" (p. 271). Assuming all these statements to be sound, how has the sheriff possibly confused a symbol in the poem ("*the county sheriff*") with his "*private meaning*" of the poem? Discuss the various possibilities. Discuss other ways in which the symbols of the poem have been confused with realities. Give other examples of highly "private meanings," including human responses which are remote from reality. Finally, what are the differences between *art* and *reality*, the *painting* and the *landscape*, the *statue* and the *man*? What are the similarities?

Read the poem "Variety's the Spice of Life" (p. 286), an excerpt from William Cowper's longer work *The Task*. Paraphrase the *denotative* significance of the words. Do you see any significance between your paraphrase of the lines and the world about us? Distinguish between a situation in which "change" would be practicable, and one in which it would not be. Why are men and women so "studious of mutation" that they will "discard a real elegance" for a "monstrous novelty and strange disguise"? Is the poem still timely? Do individuals to which these lines apply tend to confuse, in any way, the *symbol* for the *referent*? How? Discuss.

THE SEARCH FOR IDENTITY

Sherwood Anderson's old writer with the white mustache, in "The Book of the Grotesque," "like all of the people in the world, had got, during his long life, a great many notions in his head" (p. 296). First, "there were a great many thoughts [in the world] but no such thing as a truth. Man made the truths himself. . . ." Man also gave them names. What are the ones which Anderson mentions? Then it was the writer's "notion" that the people came along and "snatched up the truths," one or more; and "It was the truths that made the people grotesques . . . the moment one of the people took one of the truths to himself, called it his truth, and tried to live his life by it, he became a grotesque and the truth he embraced became a falsehood" (p. 297). Is Anderson saying that people give names to thoughts—words to ideas—and then exalt these ideas beyond their realistic import? If so, are such people fanatics? Give illustrations to support your answers. Do such people tend to mistake the *symbol* for the *reality*? Are their responses in regard to such symbols (or "truths") sometimes *remote from reality*? Explain.

Russell Baker's comical treatment of the subject in "Identity Crisis (Thing That Counts: Knowing Who You Aren't)" (p. 300) involves a basic confusion common to children, adolescents, and adults, who unconsciously picture themselves in roles of varying degrees of heroism, from Tom Mix and Tarzan to Clark Gable, Lincoln, Hemingway, and Einstein. Do you know of any such people who consciously or unconsciously mimic such a hero or heroine? Despite Baker's paradoxical treatment of the subject, do you think that people who live a significant portion of their lives under such illusions are truly happy or well-adjusted? Why or why not? In confusing their own personal lives with those of famous personages—even unconsciously—in what ways are their lives beset with continuing patterns of frustration and demoralization? Discuss. On the other hand, how would a more balanced view of one's life—that is, one's operating closer to reality than his daydreaming thoughts are indicative of—truly contribute to a personal self-discovery which could be solidly satisfying, happy, and productive? Discuss.

LOVE, SEX, AND CENSORSHIP

Read carefully and paraphrase Shakespeare's "Sonnet 116." Contrast the concept of love treated in this poem with various aspects of Barbara and Clyde's relationship narrated in Chapter 2. Discuss the differences. Which "love" do you think is closer to reality, more mature and enduring? Give specific details to support your views. Finally, what *concrete* terms give distinctive weight and integrity to Shakespeare's concept of a love which is closer to reality? If you find the poem convincing, try to explain why you feel as you do.

Vance Packard in "The Built-in Sexual Overtone" relates *symbols* and *referents* in advertising. "Ad men at conventions," he relates, "tell the story of the wistful girl who surveyed all the passionate labels on a perfume counter and asked bashfully if the store perhaps had something for beginners" (p. 328). One of the most remarkable merchandising feats, revealing the unconscious sexual yearnings of men, is the "Mistress-versus-Wife" concept of the automobile purchaser (p. 329). If the man sees in a flashy convertible a "symbolic mistress," which "sets him daydreaming of youth, romance," and "adventure," and if he sees in the four-door sedan the married "plain girl," then the symbolic union between the wife and mistress becomes nothing less than *the hardtop!* How do you explain the fact that the hardtop became "the most successful new auto style introduced in the American market for several years"? How does Packard explain it? In both the example of the wistful girl and the daydreaming purchaser of the automobile, what *symbols* have been confused with what *realities*? How close to reality are the thinkers who purchase these products, primarily on the basis of the "built-in sexual overtone"?

How did the manufacturers of Marlboro cigarettes use the "built-in sexual overtone" (p. 330)? What intentional confusion of the *symbol* with the *referent* was created by the Color Research Institute? What is the symbolical confusion created by the "virile-looking men deep in work," the sailors, cowboys, and the tattoos? What is the symbolical relationship between a tattoo on the one hand, and "delinquents in reformatories" or an "interesting past" on the other? Ethics aside, discuss how deliberate confusions of symbols with objects can step up the sales of a product.

INDIVIDUAL RESPONSIBILITY

Philip H. Phenix in the excerpt from *Realms of Meaning* gives credit to Martin Buber, the famous theologian, in stating, "*I-Thou* is a 'primary word,' not in the sense of a spoken utterance, but as a creative event [italics added]. I-Thou rises out of the 'reality of combination.' . . . In the I-Thou relation the attitude of manipulation is absent. One does not try to *use* the other with whom he stands in relation, but rather affirms and respects the other's being" (p. 353). Can you think of human relationships in which one person attempts to *use* the other for a selfish purpose rather than to respect him as a fellow human being? Do people, then, sometimes confuse another human being for a kind of "it"? Explain. Phenix states, "Another concept in personal relations is *love*. Love is also an ambiguous term. In the present connection it does not refer to a subjective experience, state of feeling or passion. It means simply the reality of the active, caring, responsible relation of an 'I' to a 'Thou.' The antithesis of love is not hate, which still manifests a kind of relation, but indifference, the cold exclusion of others by behaving as if they did not exist" (p. 354). Is *love* a generalization? Referring to the Barbara-Clyde incident in Chapter 2, relate the "I-Thou" concept of love to the possible solutions of the couple's problem. Does the "I-Thou" concept of love tend to make the abstract concrete? How? Is it possible, on the other hand, to have an "I-It" relationship and "call" it *love*, really believe that it is *love*? Explain. Give examples.

GOD, MAN, AND MORAL CONSCIOUSNESS

In Mark Twain's chapter "You Can't Pray a Lie" (p. 368), from *The Adventures of Huckleberry Finn*, the scenes of which are laid in the frontier slave society of the Mississippi River valley in the 1850's, the Negro slave Jim is adjudged to be "property" by the legal slaveocracy of the period. Discuss the basic discrepancies between the "human being Jim" and the concept of "Jim as property." The Egyptians also considered the Israelites to be "property" according to Biblical accounts (see *Exodus*, II, 1–10; IV, 1–9, 20; and XIV, 8–9). The Romans also treated captured Greeks as slaves, some of them serving as teachers of Roman children. The Mohammedans imported slaves, both Negro and white. Slavery began gradually to be replaced by another institution, serfdom, following the fall of the Roman empire. But Huck's society approved of slavery as a legal institution, and under its provisions the "stealing" of a slave was a crime. Huck is consciously convinced that he has done the wrong thing in helping Jim to "be free" (a crime in his society), so he "kneeled down" to pray, but, as he puts it, "the words wouldn't come. Why wouldn't they?" Answer Huck's question. What was Huck's lie that he was attempting to pray? Explain. He then writes Miss Watson, Jim's "legal owner," giving her the information on Jim's whereabouts and then "felt good and all washed clean of sin for the first time. . . ." Explain Huck's sudden elation. Is his "good feeling" related in any way to the approval of his society rather than to the satisfaction of his personal conscience? Discuss. At length, Huck begins once again to think of the basic humanity of Jim in concrete ways. How is the abstract of "Jim's humanity" made concrete and convincing, even in summary? Point out the details which indicate Jim's basic humanity and selflessness. Huck then tears up the letter to Miss Watson and states, "All right, then, I'll *go* to hell." Discuss the complexity of the situation for a thirteen- or fourteen-year-old boy such as Huck. How does the incident, especially as it is revealed through the mind of an innocent boy, cast an unfavorable light on the true nature of the institution of slavery? Does the institution crumble before the reader's eyes? Why? Even though Huck feels that he will "*go* to hell," is the reader convinced? Why or why not? Finally, what confusions between *symbol* and *referent* are indicated in this memorable scene, involving the development of moral consciousness?

Consider the following statements from the political advertisement "Help Build the Spiritual Strength of Our Nation," urging the candidacy of Congressman James B. Utt: (1) "I have been concerned with the decay of the moral fiber of our nation"; (2) ". . . . For this reason, I introduced a resolution in the Congress . . . to insert the words 'Under God' in our Pledge of Allegiance"; and "For the same reason, I . . . introduced a resolution seeking to affirm the basic belief in God and to have it become part of our Constitution." In these statements are some obvious *generalizations*. Pick them out; as a beginning, give the *denotation* of "the decay of the moral fiber of our nation." What is meant specifically? Give indications of a possible confusion of *words* with *realities* in the remaining statements. Discuss. Could you think of a more concrete indication of a "basic belief in God" than the placing of the phrase into the Constitution? Discuss "abstractness" and "concreteness" in connection with Mr. Utt's arguments. Read the entire advertisement. Can you think of any truly concrete issues which are treated in the piece which would, in your judgment, tend to support his candidacy as a member of the House of Representatives? Discuss.

LITERATURE AND GOOD WRITING

"How to Write and Be Read" is for college English students one of the most informative essays in this section. Jacques Barzun, its author, states that "as soon as you put pen to paper, somebody may be puzzled, angry, bored, or ecstatic . . ." (p. 406). Have you ever thought of your own writing as producing such effects? Barzun also notes that most students "know that they have to write and . . . most of them want to be well thought of" (p. 408). If writing is a reflection of the mind of its producer, and if no good piece of writing will ever proceed from a superficial mind, then in what ways can one's writing make its producer be "well thought of"? Is one's writing as important as one's clothes? One's looks? Just how important is writing well? Barzun even goes so far as to state that "the proper aim of writing should be to make it a pleasure" (p. 408). Do you agree? Why or why not? "Just what are you trying to tell me?" is a question, Barzun notes, which the teacher should have the student keep foremost in his mind when writing. "It is in that spirit that student writing must be read, corrected, and if need be,

rewritten" (p. 408). What indications do you see in the essay that let
you know that Barzun is interested primarily in the thought processes
of the student; that is, thought processes that say something well?
What does he mean by "spineless, vague, and incoherent prose" (p.
409)? He gives several examples from what he terms by allusion "the
softer pedagogy." Later, he notes, "the softness goes to the very roots of
the mind and turns it into mush" in the victims of "the softer pedagogy"
(p. 412). Then he gives several examples of poor writing. Discuss these
examples, noting as precisely as you can the weaknesses in the surplus
of abstractions, and the lack of concrete terms which communicate
directly and with exactitude. From these examples, would you agree
that the so-called Educator's patois is "easily the worst English now
spoken" (p. 413)? Why? Paraphrase Barzun's statement, "a tolerable
paragraph must have gone through six or seven versions, and be ready
to follow athletically on the trail of articulate thoughts, rather than look
for the soapy incline to muddled meaning" (p. 414). What is Barzun
hoping to make explicit in this colorful statement as it relates to
thinking and writing? Give examples. Do you agree with the great
English poet Lord Byron that "easy writing makes damned hard reading"? Why? From Barzun's essay, would it be accurate to maintain that
good writing is always characterized by clear thinking and forceful
expression on the part of the writer, and that it tends to generate
thinking as well as enjoyment on the part of the reader? Does the good
writer, then, have something *real* to communicate? Does the poor writer
often simply write words, thus saying very little, if anything?

AGE OF CONTROVERSY

Read the first paragraph of the excerpt from Thoreau's *Walden* (p. 454).
Demonstrate by choosing portions of the paragraph that Thoreau was
attempting to live close to reality, subverbally, genuinely. Pick out
several words or phrases which indicate concretely his purposes in
going to the woods to live. What did *live* mean for Thoreau? Later
Thoreau raises the question, "Why should we live with such hurry and
waste of life" (p. 456)? How does he make this question meaningful
through concrete illustrations? What is Thoreau's view of "shams and
delusions" as opposed to his view of "reality" (p. 457)? Consider the
portion beginning, "If you stand right fronting and face to face to a
fact, you will see the sun glimmer on both its surfaces. . . ." (p. 458).
Discuss the forceful qualities of Thoreau's prose. In spite of the fact
that Thoreau has been sometimes considered an eccentric individualist,
both in his own time and ours, do these concluding statements strike
you as being close to reality, and therefore especially sane? Discuss.

3

WORDS AND HUMAN BEHAVIOR

Born 384 years before Jesus of Nazareth, Aristotle took all knowledge as his province and made lasting achievements in the sciences, arts, in metaphysics, ethics, politics, and logic. His influence has continued for over two thousand years, and the weight of it is difficult to estimate, but in logic it would not be an overstatement to say that his concepts have profoundly influenced our whole view of life. His logic was concerned with the forms of knowing, and the ways in which we perceive reality symbolically are traceable to certain aspects of his methodology which have, through the ages, virtually become laws. Among them are three *generalizations* based on his logic:

1. *Law of identity.* A thing is what it is. A is A.
2. *Law of the excluded middle.* A thing is either one thing or not that thing. It is either A or not A.
3. *Law of contradiction.* A thing cannot be both a thing and not a thing. It cannot be both A and *non-A*.

On the surface, these laws seem logical enough. Indeed, they may seem only common sense. And they probably work in most situations to which they have application. But they are not entirely accurate, and they can and frequently do lead to errors, especially in situations in which they are only partially applicable, or in which they are not applicable at all.

Let us apply Aristotle's laws to three situations to which they may appear to be related. First, let us apply the *law of identity* to a convict. A thing is what it is. Thus, "a convict is a convict." But suppose an individual committed a crime in 1950—let us say that he embezzled funds—and was apprehended, convicted, and then served two years in the penitentiary. Technically he had paid his debt to society by 1952, and in doing so realized his mistake, regretted his crime. After completing his prison sentence, he tries to get a job, but because of his record as a "convict," he is refused employment. Despite the admission of his crime, and the fact that he has paid his debt to society, he is still looked upon as a "convict." In his efforts to find a job, the man effaces his own pride and explains carefully to all prospective employers that he can be trusted and will be loyal, not only because he fears prison, but also because he wants to atone for his crime. "Give me a chance," he asks, but every prospective employer turns a deaf ear to his plea. To them, he is a "convict." Assuming that the man *is* a "changed person" and has truly reformed, then such prospective employers are turning away a man who feels a profound obligation to be trustworthy and loyal. They are unreasonably bound by Aristotle's *law of identity:* "A convict is a convict." What they have ignored are the other facts in the situation, the man's attitudes and the condition of time; it is true that the man *was* a convict for two years, but after 1952 he ceased, technically, to be a convict.

One weakness of the *law of identity,* then, is that people tend to overapply it as a tool; hence, it may often lose its usefulness and lead to erroneous thought processes.

Second, let us apply the *law of the excluded middle* to a concept or a quality. Let us consider the qualities of "hotness" and "coldness." According to Aristotle's law, a thing is either hot or it is not hot; it is either cold or it is not cold. The law also applies to an individual. He is either "hot" or he is not "hot." He is either "cold" or he is not "cold." Imagine a bucket of very hot water on a table, not boiling water, but so hot that you cannot keep your hands in it more than two or three seconds without scalding them. Next, imagine that on the same table is a bucket of ice water so cold that it is on the verge of freezing. Now assume that you place both of your hands into the hot water. You feel immediately the sensation of "hotness," and have to jerk your hands out of the water to keep from scalding them. Aristotle's *law of the excluded middle* works. The water is either hot, or it is not hot. Clearly, the water is hot, and you have felt the sensation of "hotness." Do the same with the cold water and you feel the sensation of "coldness." But now let us assume that, using the same two buckets, you plunge one hand into the hot water and one hand into the cold water *at the same time.* You sense both "hotness" and "coldness" at the same time. Relative to your sensations, Aristotle's *law of the excluded middle* does not work; *for you are "hot" and "cold" at the same time.*

One weakness of the *law of the excluded middle,* then, is that it does not take into consideration such variables.

Third, let us consider the *law of contradiction.* A thing cannot be both a thing and not that thing. Newtonian physics may provide some examples which will permit us to see some of the weaknesses of this law. Imagine yourself in a completely enclosed elevator. Affixed to the center of the top of the elevator is a very long cable. If you are standing on the center of the floor of the elevator and if the elevator is drawn straight up at a definite speed, you will feel the force of your mass being drawn to the spot on which you are standing, the center of the floor of the elevator. You may call this force "gravity," which, according to Newtonian physics, is that force which tends to draw all bodies in the earth's sphere toward the center of the earth. But now assume that the far end of the long cable—the same long cable affixed to the center of the top of the elevator—is attached to a central point or axis outside the earth's gravitational field. The elevator is then whirled in a huge arc around this point in such a manner and at such a speed that inside the elevator you exert the same force of mass against the center of the bottom of the elevator on which you are standing as in the first illustration. (Whirling a bucket of water around in a circle about your shoulder would be roughly analogous. The water stays in the bucket; dependent upon the speed of your "whirling," you can feel the force of the mass of the water pulling against your shoulder.) Assuming that mass and velocity (speed) are equal in both illustrations (relative to you inside the elevator), there is no difference between the force called "gravity," and the one called "centrifugal force." Here, then, a thing certainly can be both *gravity* and *centrifugal force;* or to put it another way, there is no essential difference between the two supposedly different kinds of forces *relative to you enclosed in the elevator.* The *law of contradiction* in this instance, then, is inaccurate. Newtonian physics was basically Aristotelian in its orientation. Scientists such as Einstein and Lorentz have since emphasized the theory of the relative (rather than absolute) character of motion, velocity, mass, and other factors of import, such as the interdependence of matter, time, and space in dealing more accurately than did Newton with the realities of man's universe.

MODERN CONCEPTS OF LANGUAGE AND REALITY

No doubt the bad reasoning in our examples results from an over-extension of Aristotle's principles. But over against the helpful, yet comparatively rigid, laws of Aristotle are a number of concepts drawn from studies in "language logic," or the relationships between the language we use and the actualities of the external world. These studies began over two thousand years ago with Plato, who held in his *Dialogues* that the knowledge of things is not to be derived from names, but that things must be studied and investigated in themselves. The Englishman John Locke, in *An Essay Concerning Human Understanding* (1660), observed that words were merely "sensible marks of ideas," and that words alone stand for nothing except as they signify "the ideas in the mind of him that uses them, how imperfectly soever or carelessly those ideas are collected from the things which they are supposed to represent." Locke also noted that speakers are prone to "suppose their words to be marks of the ideas in the minds also of other men with whom they communicate," and to assume that they are speaking "of things as they really are." Therefore, "they often suppose *their words* to stand . . . for the reality of things." Such observations have continued sporadically, but it was not until the latter nineteenth and early twentieth centuries that inquiries into the relationships between language, thought processes, and reality became intensified. Many of these more recent inquiries have shown that there are serious discrepancies between the language we use and the actualities of the external world. Many modern thinkers believe that our words too often reflect distorted images of reality which lead to misconceptions that, in turn, give rise to unrest, distrust, suspicions, fears, hatreds, and wars.

In the first half of the twentieth century, one group of modern thinkers—men who broke through the rigid shells of Aristotelian thought processes which tend to isolate man from reality—in discussing new ways of approaching problems in mathematics and physics, initiated new systems of symbolic logic which led to such developments as atomic fission and cybernetics (comparative studies of the human nervous system and calculating machines complicated enough to reflect it). Another group concentrated upon efforts to make language more consistent with a constructive behavior of mankind. They believed that language—as a tool for man's thinking, his communication with others, and his behavior both individually and collectively—was faulty. Foremost among this latter group was a Polish emigrant, Alfred Korzybski, who came to the United States during the Hitler regime in Germany. Korzybski was an engineer and mathematician who believed in a new focus for language, one in which scientific thinking would be based upon three premises which were virtual obverse reflections of Aristotle's laws:

1. *Nonidentity.* Using an analogy of a word to a map, the map is not the territory, but *represents* the territory.

2. *Non-allness.* Continuing the analogy of a word to a map, no map can represent *all the territory;* something *is always* left out.

3. *Self-reflexiveness.* Just as one can have a map, *language can be about language* in an ever-diminishing reflexiveness. An example of this concept would be two mirrors placed opposite each other, each reflecting the other's reflection, and the reflections reflecting each other's reflection, *ad infinitum;* or the old label on a Quaker oat box, which contains the picture of a Quaker holding a Quaker oat box, which contains the picture of a Quaker holding a Quaker oat box, *ad infinitum.*

Let us briefly apply Korzybski's premises to the same sets of circumstances to which we applied Aristotle's laws. First, applying the premise of nonidentity to the example of the convict, the word "convict" is not confused with the thing as it was in the *law of identity,* for the premise of nonidentity holds that the word merely *represents* the object to which it applies. It is not the *same thing* as that object in reality. If we say that the man *is* a "convict," then we have linked the two nouns "man" and "convict," and in doing so we may mistakenly assume that the characteristics *exist* in the man without reference to the individual, his attitudes, the time, conditions, or dates. With the premise of *nonidentity,* on the other hand, we automatically assume that the word "convict" merely represents the "man." Consequently, there is no inherent existence of "convict-ness," so to speak, *inside* the "man." Thus, we do not tend to oversimplify or to "overdefine" the word *convict.* What we are really thinking when we are aware of the premise of *nonidentity* in such a sentence as "The man is a convict," is more nearly: "The man may be classified as a convict under certain conditions; however, the word *convict* is *not* the man; it merely *represents* the man."

Second, the premise of *non-allness,* holding as it does that no word can represent all that there is to a given concept and that *something is always left out,* would never lead us to a two-valued attitude toward the qualities of "hotness" and "coldness." Instead of the two-valued response to reality often generated by Aristotle's *law of the excluded middle,* the premise of *non-allness* guides us to "multiordinal" or "infinite-valued" responses. In short, we realize that there may be many possibilities instead of merely two implied by the "is" or "is not" of the *law of the excluded middle.* Thus, under similar laboratory conditions of buckets of hot and cold water, we can readily see how in one situation plunging both hands into the hot water would cause the sensation of heat; into the cold water, the sensation of cold. But we are ready for other possibilities, for we know that we may be "hot" or "cold" under other circumstances. Some possibilities for "hot" are heat waves, hot range burners, sitting too close to a hot radiator, being overdressed in a close space; or for "cold," one may be caught without a coat in a blizzard, work in a frozen food locker, be seated in an unheated room in mid-January in Amherst, Massachusetts, etc. We are also aware that at certain times of the year, a Californian may be able to ski in the morning on mountain slopes and on the same day go surfing in the Pacific. And if we plunge one of our hands into a bucket of hot water, the other into a bucket of cold water, we can feel the sensations of heat and cold simultaneously. The concept of *non-allness* makes us aware of such variables in reality.

Third, the premise of self-reflexiveness alerts us to a probability: once we begin with a "system" of reasoning or understanding, we tend to stay with it, to elaborate upon it, and to embellish it. Concepts once stated in language are somewhat like conditions created by a pebble thrown into the center of a pool of still water: concentric rings begin to form about it, then more rings. The circles continue to move out one after the other, each retracing the pattern of the former, circle after circle. . . . Thus Newton's classic Law of Gravitation, in order to be consistent with other phenomena about which he had made "laws," such as his Law of Inertia—the tendency of a body to stay at rest or, if moving, to continue to do so in a straight line unless acted upon by some other force: *the amount of force necessary to move a body depends on the mass or weight of that body*—had to account for certain conflicts. For example, consistent with Galileo's discovery, an iron safe and a marble-sized ball bearing, if dropped simultaneously from the top of the Eiffel Tower, would hit the ground at the same time, for they fall at the same speed, assuming that the air resistance is constant. The conflict between the Law of Inertia and the Law of Gravitation is obvious. If, in dealing with inertia, mass is a factor—if indeed four mules hitched to the iron safe are required to pull it over the earth, while the smallest toddler can roll the ball bearing across the ground— then how is it that the iron safe and the ball bearing fall from the Eiffel

Tower at the same speed? Isn't mass a factor *vertically* as well as *horizontally*? Consistent with the tendency of language to become ever more *self-reflexive*, Newton made up an explanation in words: gravity in some strange way exerts its force just enough to attract the body to itself by overpowering the inertia of the body, *no matter what its size*. The explanation was weak, but convenient enough to go virtually unchallenged until the twentieth century. The example of the elevator previously given demonstrates basically that, under certain conditions, one cannot distinguish so-called "gravity" from "centrifugal force." Yet, Newton had begun with sound and workable ideas. He liked the idea of different kinds of absolute "forces," like "gravity" and "inertia." However, when he carried them too far, they became illusory and inaccurate. The language with which he attempted to expand his ideas became increasingly *self-reflexive*, and he constructed his own trap with words which continued to move away from the very reality he sought. Now Einstein's "Principle of Equivalence of Gravitation and Inertia" supersedes Newton's separate categories of "forces," and in so doing gives us a more accurate picture of nature and our universe.

We have seen that the "levels of language" vary from *the meaning without the word* (subverbal level) to private meanings which are remote from reality. Korzybski and others of similar mind wanted man to keep his thoughts and verbal symbols as close to the actual world as possible. They believed that if man could habitually conceive of things without words, could reorient himself to the external world and the natural function of his own nervous system, he could begin to overcome his linguistic limitations. His individual and social maladjustments could be brought into clear focus. Seeing them without blurred verbal concepts, he could then deal with them less emotionally, more objectively, and more intelligently.

The theory is an interesting one, for if man could even partially achieve such goals—if he could even begin to reduce his misunderstandings and confusions—then the world would be a sounder and better place in which to live than it is at present. Perhaps we have already begun to make some progress; certainly, new scientific developments traceable to new forms of symbolic mathematics are obvious. But what of the everyday problems and conflicts with which man is confronted? Let us consider a hypothetical case, a history of an accident, which may challenge us to respond in numerous ways—ways which reflect Aristotle's concepts as well as those which are more indicative of modern concepts of language and reality.

THE STORY OF AN ACCIDENT

An accident occurs. Twelve people, excluding the driver, see it or a portion of it. Briefly, here is what happens: a 1941 "open-top" Ford sedan—the convertible effect having been achieved by the removal of the original hard top, leaving the car looking as if it has been cut off from the body at windowsill level with a can opener—is moving east on

Water Street. At the sound of a siren, the driver suddenly accelerates. He swerves into a left turn, going north on Second Street, despite the fact that Second Street is clearly marked with a red sign at the corner indicating that the driver is entering a "One Way" street, and he is going the wrong way. Also, several cars are parked aslant on the driver's right, against his direction, as he proceeds northward on Second Street; and no lanes are marked which would indicate a two-way street. The driver comes to a screeching halt at the corner of Main and Second Streets, where he attracts much attention. First, he is going the wrong way on a one-way street. His car is unusual, and the noise of his brakes causes at least a dozen people to turn toward him. They see hunched over the steering wheel a figure who has long hair and wears sun glasses, has on what looks like a checked tablecloth with a slit in the top, and wears it in the style of the ponchos of Spanish America. Around his neck are several loose strands of glass-like beads. As the cars begin to move with the green light east and west on Main Street, this driver suddenly gives his car full throttle and beats them to the center of the intersection, apparently trying to turn left. But he is going so fast that he loses control. Two cars on Main Street stop to give him room, but he skids diagonally into the northwest telephone pole on the corner of the intersection, hitting it so hard and at such an angle that his car rebounds from the pole and backs eastwardly across Second Street with such force that it bounces against a telephone booth. The two objects appear to "shake" each other. Both are visibly vibrating as the car rolls to a stop in the middle of Second Street. A little girl who was leaving the telephone booth has been knocked down by the concussion and is lying on the sidewalk—close by are a startled bypasser and a policeman. Just as the car comes to a stop, the door on the driver's side comes open, and the driver falls out onto the pavement of Main Street, apparently unconscious. The rest of his garb then becomes visible. His trousers are of a faded blue denim, and he is wearing Socrates sandals, his big toes sticking through leather thongs in each. A clinking sound is heard as a bottle labeled Old Factory Whistle rolls out behind him on the pavement. On the windshield of the car are the initials "UCLA."

Of the twelve people who have witnessed the accident, the immediate reactions of each is given as follows (for the location of each observer, see the diagram of the accident):

1. The first man says to his companion, "Look at that! He almost hit us. Tore the creosote out of that telephone pole! Drunk as a skunk!"

2. His companion is angry. "The damn fool almost hit us! I must have caught a splinter from that pole—something's hurtin' my arm. All these young kids are alike nowadays!"

3. The middle-aged lady cries out, "Oh my Lord! He's a hippie! Look at him lying there. Probably on LSD, and there's a bottle, too! There goes a policeman now. Why don't they enforce the law and put drunks like him behind bars!"

4. The little girl making the phone call had seen the car ricocheting off the telephone pole across the street and in her direction, had hung up the phone, and had tried to get out of the booth, but all she will

remember is a loud noise and herself screaming. Now she is unconscious and lying on the sidewalk.

5. The first policeman—a sturdy man—steps off the curb twirling his billy. "Kid's either drunk or on dope. I'll get him for drunken driving, going the wrong way on a one-way street, disorderly conduct maybe. Damn radical trouble-making Communists! Probably on his way to some civil rights march! He'll never get there if I've got anything to do with it. I want to see him in the cooler, and any other hophead I can." He notices the other policeman, a younger man, hesitating on the sidewalk. He thinks, "Young Mike's standin' there like an idiot. Aeh, he's got no guts. He'll never make Captain. . . ."

6. The second policeman, Mike, hesitates. "This happened suddenly," he thinks. "A lot will have to be investigated here." In a moment he takes in the main incidents, but withholds any opinions because two events are of major concern to him. First, he begins to move toward the little girl who is lying on the sidewalk, wondering if she is seriously hurt. He is also concerned about the condition of the peculiar looking driver, and surmises that he, too, may need medical attention. Just before he reaches the little girl, he realizes that he should also call a squad car to the scene to restore order, thus reducing the gathering congestion and the possibility of any further accidents. But, he thinks, "First the girl, then the ambulance, then the driver, and then the squad car."

7. The man standing by himself on the corner has never seen anything like this. He is stunned. "Something awful has happened!" he shouts. But no one hears him. He is terrified, paralyzed into immobility. The blood is racing through his head, and he remembers when he was a little boy he was hurt in an accident. He feels faint and leans against the corner of the building.

8. The driver of the car going east on Main Street is sweating profusely. He has just thrown on his brakes, been missed by the cutting car now wrecked a few feet away from him, is cursing the driver. "You almost killed me, you ———! All these college kids are alike! Look at that bum!" He nods toward the prone driver and for the first time notices the bottle. He begins to curse again, this time shaking his fist.

9. The driver going west on Main Street is astonished by what he has seen and is trying to take it all in. He sees the old car wrecked a few feet to his right and in front of him and wonders what has happened. The behavior of the driver, he thinks, was most peculiar. He is more curious, though, about the men at the corner near the telephone pole who were almost hit by the old car, and the little girl, over whom he sees the second policeman leaning. He backs his car out of the mainstream of traffic, gets out, and goes to help the policeman.

10. The driver of the car going south on one-way South Second Street slows down, his heart thumping heavily under his ribs. "That hippie almost hit my tail!" he thinks. He is a drug salesman with an appointment with a medical doctor in the next block, and he is already late. "Better not to get involved anyway," he thinks. He is planning to take the doctor to lunch and he thinks he will have to drive the doctor

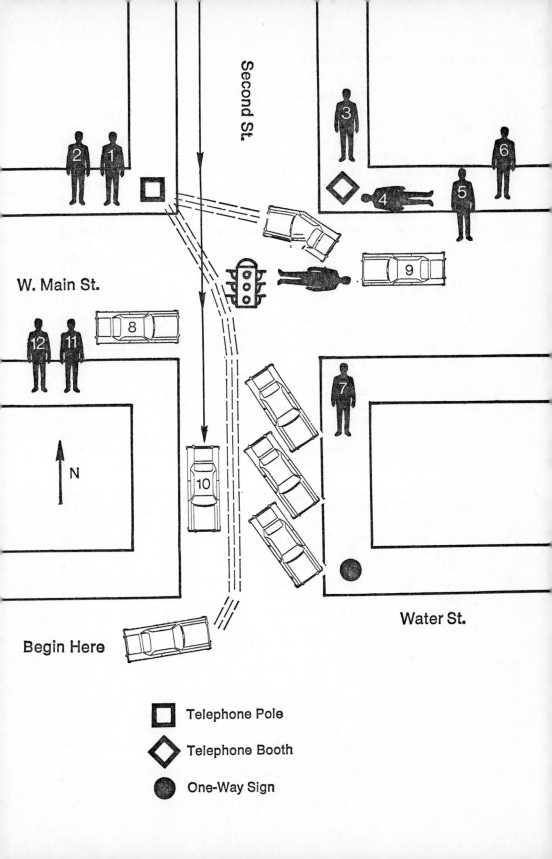

Second St.

W. Main St.

N

Begin Here

Water St.

Telephone Pole

Telephone Booth

One-Way Sign

around the scene of the accident to avoid losing time on the way to the restaurant. "Bad luck for me," he thinks. The thought of stopping does not enter his mind.

11. Holding hands with his girlfriend, a college sophomore looks back over his shoulder and says to her, "Look at that nut from UCLA. He's mashed his wheels." The two walk away.

12. His girlfriend hardly notices the accident, except for the decal on the windshield. "Oh, well, what can you expect from a Uclan?" She feels a twinge of conscience when they do not at least consider approaching the accident, but the two smile at each other and go on up the street.

ANALYSIS

Before we can see how accurate the initial responses of the twelve witnesses to the hypothetical accident are, we need to understand the remaining "facts" of the incident. Further investigation reveals the following information: Three hours before the accident, a student from the University of Southern California had parked his "remodeled" car on Hoover Boulevard in Los Angeles. As he got out of the car he reminded himself that he would need to replace the decal with a "USC" sticker—the one with "Tommy Trojan" on it—but he had not yet had time, having just acquired the car from a neighbor's son, whose hobby was reconstructing automotive oddities. He had been so occupied with his thoughts, and the fact that he was dangerously late to class, that he left his key in the car. Less than ten minutes later, a drunk wandered by looking for a place to rest, and got into the car, cuddling his only possession, a bottle of Old Factory Whistle. Just as he was getting comfortable, he looked up, saw two policemen approaching in a cruiser, and left the back seat, forgetting his only possession in his hurry to get away. About thirty minutes later, a juvenile delinquent—fifteen-year-old Cletus Tussy came along—an escapee from a reformatory in South Carolina who had somehow made his way cross-country to Los Angeles in time to attend a "love-in" the night before at Griffith Park, where he was given his strange attire. Cletus had never driven a car before, but seeing the key and savoring the familiar condition of the old car (like the ones in his uncle's junkyard) were motivation enough. If it was a good old car, maybe he could learn to drive well enough to get all the way back home. For an hour after starting the car and getting it into the street, he "practiced driving," then drove out of the heavy traffic until he reached the suburban community in which he had his unfortunate accident. He was just getting the car under control when he reached Water Street. The sudden sound of a siren scared him into thinking the police were after him, so without thinking or looking, he turned left and entered a one-way street. . . .

In analyzing these twelve immediate responses to the hypothetical accident, we can see how readily Aristotelian concepts function in people's thought processes and speech, and how rarely the more desirable premises of modern concepts of language and reality are brought into play:

1. The response of the first man is emotional; his remarks are personal. From the many events in front of him, he has abstracted only three: he and his companion were almost hit; the telephone pole was damaged; and the driver was drunk. The last observation is an overdefinition of Aristotle's *law of identity;* for from the actions of the driver and the presence of the bottle with the whiskey label on it, he assumes the driver was drunk.

2. The companion of the first man responds with an even more obvious "private meaning." His response, too, is emotional and personal. He thinks he may have been hurt by flying splinters when what he really feels is a nervous twinge in his arm. He fails to see much of what has happened, and likewise fails to apply the premise of *non-allness.* Assuming that the driver is a "young kid," he is not *all* "young kids."

3. The middle-aged lady's response is highly "private" and remote from reality. She finds solace in calling the prone driver a "hippie," which he may or may not be; to this extent, she has confused the *symbol* with the *reality.* By the driver's actions, she overdefines Aristotle's *law of identity,* for she equates "hippie" with "LSD." Her desire for vengeance is remote from reality; for, under the circumstances, if she were responding close to subverbal reality, she would be trying to do something constructive rather than to retreat into the abstraction of words. But seeing the policeman has started her train of thought away from reality; her thoughts are becoming more *self-reflexive.*

4. The little girl, in pausing to hang up the telephone even in the face of imminent danger, when a split-second may have allowed her to escape the accident unscathed, evinces a *conditioned response* taught to her by her environment; the pattern of action is so deeply engrained that even in dire circumstances she fails to "symbolize" with originality, which would have protected her. For her the ritual of hanging up the telephone is a behavior pattern which even *subverbal* instinct cannot overcome. If she had been trained to respond to reality, below the level of words (say, by perceptual training in elementary school rather than drill work in good manners), she might have saved herself a concussion.

5. The hefty policeman applies Aristotle's *law of the excluded middle* to the prone driver, although he first uses the *law of identity,* equating behavior with drunkenness or drug use, and in doing so *overdefines* both laws. His other responses are highly private and remote from reality. He confuses symbols with realities, and eventually becomes *self-reflexive* as his thoughts run off tangentially on his fellow policeman. This policeman's thought processes are already deeply imprisoned by rigidities and assumptions.

6. The second policeman, Mike, applies the concept of *non-allness* in pausing to take in the whole scene. He is naturally curious about the accident, but he is rational in the course of action he follows. He quickly abstracts what to him are the most urgent matters concerning the incident, and begins to move as soon as he can to protect human life

and to restore order. He is also remarkably restrained in deferring judgments, for he knows he has at hand only the "facts" he has seen. Much remains to be investigated. He responds close to reality, and his actions as they are commenced seem "subverbally" close.

7. The man who is stunned into a fainting condition by seeing the accident has a *unilateral* rather than *multiordinal* response. In addition, his interpretation is related to himself irrationally; his response is highly "private." It is so remote from reality that he goes into a *self-reflexive* trance, recalling his own childhood accident. He *overdefines* the accident in relation to himself. He fails to separate the part from the whole (*nonidentity*), and he fails to see other aspects of the accident (*non-allness*). His behavior, perhaps more than all the others, is *unsane*.

8. The driver of the car going east on Main Street is also *unsane*, although the circumstances of his own near accident make his emotional response more understandable than that of the fainting man on the southeastern corner. In cursing the driver, he is expressing his *feeling* rather than communicating information. He fails to apply the premise of *nonidentity* in confusing the prone driver's actions with his intentions and in assuming that the prone driver has been drinking. His anger is *emotive* rather than *rational;* to that extent, his behavior is *unsane*.

9. The driver going west on Main Street is in his responses closer to reality than all others except Mike, the young trained policeman, for he withholds most of his reactions, feeling that the circumstances are "peculiar" or lacking in a firm, factual basis. He also abstracts the important events, and soon begins to take constructive action, first by getting his car out of what could rapidly become a traffic jam. He has applied the modern concepts of thought inherent in *nonidentity* and *non-allness,* and has refused to let his thoughts become so remote from the reality at hand that they are *self-reflexive*. His behavior is quite *sane*.

10. The salesman is "private" in his responses to reality; he is also selfish and irresponsible. Perhaps justifying his own inaction, he calls the prone driver "hippie," thus overapplying Aristotle's *law of identity,* confusing *symbols* with *realities*. Further, he confuses the supposition, even if it is true, with the justification of his own irresponsibility, as if to say, "Since he is a hippie, he is not a human being deserving of any help I might be able to give him!" The irrationality of this kind of *self-reflexive* thinking gets him conveniently out of the situation—or so his verbal illusion convinces him. Ironically, of all those who could rush a doctor to the scene most quickly, this man is in the position to do so. But he turns away from reality and human responsibility. His behavior is not only selfish, it is irrational. His behavior is so remote from the demands of reality, especially the interdependence of human society, that it is not merely negligent; it is *unsane*.

11. The college sophomore assumes that the prone driver is a "nut"; that is, he equates the driver's erratic actions with a mental condition. He also fails to apply *nonidentity* to the decal "UCLA," but

extends Aristotle's *law of identity* to encompass the driver. The fact that the accident has occurred is noticed, but his indifferent response indicates that he considers human beings objects rather than fellowmen; no *feeling* is necessary. Hence, he walks away with his girl friend, self-centered and socially remote from the demands of reality in an interdependent human relationship.

12. The girl's reaction is similar to the boy's, except that she reiterates the *law of identity* with emphasis, equating the decal with the driver. In addition, she is guilty of a failure to apply *non-allness*. To her, apparently, all students at UCLA, or "Uclans," are like this one. Here she also mistakes the *symbol* for the *reality*. In not going to the aid of those who need it, her response is also highly *private* and remote from reality.

QUESTIONS ON READINGS

SCIENCE AND THE HUMANITIES IN CONFLICT

Notice Miguel de Unamuno's "definition" under the heading Some Definitions of "Science" and the "Humanities": "True science teaches, above all, to *doubt* and to be *ignorant*" (p. 156, italics added). Ordinarily we think of science as an exact and classified body of knowledge, connoting confidence and a specialized precision of details within the area of knowledge concerned. What are the *denotations* of "doubt" and "ignorant"; how, then, could science teach one "to doubt" and "to be ignorant"? How does Unamuno's concept fly in the face of Aristotelian "laws"; how does such a definition reveal an awareness of *nonidentity* and *non-allness*? Discuss.

Do you see any connection between Aristotle's *law of the excluded middle* and the entire Snow-Leavis Controversy (p. 156)? If so, what? Give specific page references.

In "On Education," Albert Einstein applies concepts of *non-allness* to the idea of the importance of education: "The school has always been the most important means of transferring the wealth of tradition from one generation to the next" (p. 173). How does Einstein demonstrate that new reasons exist which add to the meaning of his statement, thus bringing into consideration more aspects of "allness"? Give specific examples.

LANGUAGE AND REALITY

How does H. L. Mencken's excerpt "American Slang" (p. 196), taken from *The American Language,* reveal the inadequacy of Aristotle's *law of identity* in the treatment of language—specifically words themselves? How would *non-allness* give a more accurate understanding of the nature of language, especially how it grows, changes, and takes on new meanings and new forms of usage? *Nonidentity?* Can you think of any illustrations from your own experience of strong "rigidity" in the use of language, which in turn tend to make the viewer see the world as a restricted vision, so to speak?

WAR AND DEHUMANIZATION

In his statement entitled "War, Poetry, the Individual" (p. 224), John Manifold suggests that one can do only three things about war. What are they? Does Manifold indicate, in making such a statement, a lack of application of *non-allness*? If you think so, then what are some other possibilities besides the three he suggests? We tend to think of war as being all bad, on the one hand, or good on the other—which is, of course, an overdefinition of the *law of the excluded middle*. What good things does Manifold think can come out of war? Bad things? Things that go on unchanged? Why does he like certain words to which he has been exposed, "precise words" as he calls them? What do the words mean? Discuss them. Do any of his observations disturb you? Discuss.

Marx and Engels in *The Communist Manifesto* (p. 226) draw a strong line of demarcation between *bourgeoise* and *proletarians*. The two are referred to as "two great hostile camps" (p. 227). What aspects of Aristotle's *law of identity* and the *law of the excluded middle* do you see in the categorization? The writers also maintain that "today the proletariat alone is a really revolutionary class" (p. 229). How would an application of the premise of *nonidentity* bring the writers closer to reality? Do you see evidence of overdefinition in the statement? Discuss. In relating "proletarians and Communists," Marx and Engels state that the Communists "have no interests separate and apart from those of the proletariat as a whole. They do not set up any sectarian principles of their own, by which to shape and mould the proletarian movement." In your study of Communists, do you see any need to apply *non-allness* and *self-reflexiveness* to this statement, thus bringing the contention into a more accurate focus with the reality? Discuss.

Read thoroughly Harry M. Caudill's excerpts from *Night Comes to the Cumberlands: A Biography of a Depressed Area*. Note the "highland slaveholder" (p. 239) and his method of recruiting mountaineers for the Confederacy. How do his threats demonstrate the tendency of language to become *self-reflexive*? Continue reading. Notice that Caudill gives as reasons for the mountaineers' enlisting boredom and loneliness. Discuss *non-allness* in connection with Civil War enlistments, including what might be termed the natural training of the mountaineer in walking long distances, shooting, and leading a hard life in a harsh land. Do you see an overapplication of the *law of identity* in the behavior of some of the highlanders in taking their vengeance out on neighbors of the opposite side, or a lack of awareness of *nonidentity*? Discuss the "ever-deepening hatred, outbreaks of *violence* in connection with widows and orphans in the southern mountains." Is there a *self-reflexiveness* operating in human responses leading to violence, long-lasting hatreds, bitternesses—what might be termed "harvests of blood"? Discuss. Discuss the applications of the *law of identity*, the *law of the excluded middle*, and the *law of contradiction* in connection with the ninety-year-old mountaineer's anecdote of the Civil War (p. 241). Discuss the *law of identity* and premise of *nonidentity* as they relate to the tragic commentary of Frank Wilkeson of New York (p. 243). Caudill goes on to state, "Perhaps in no other region of the United States except the Southern mountains were the lives and property of a great number of pro-Union civilians lost in the war" (p. 244). How does such a state-

ment apply to the *non-allness* of the phrase "victory in war"? Discuss.
Using *nonidentity* as an approach, try to give concrete examples of the
Civil War as it affected this region. Discuss. Discuss also the aftermath
of the Civil War as it related to the Kentucky mountain feuds (p. 244).
Specifically, how did the famous "Hatfield-McCoy War" begin (p. 245)?
Notice Randall McCoy's cannibalistic vow of vengeance (p. 246). His
response to reality is, of course, highly private and remote from reality
—even *unsane*—but how has he overapplied the *law of identity* in
relation to his desire for vengeance? Note the incidents which "trig-
gered" several of the feuds. Try to see them through erroneous applications of Aristotelian views, or a failure to be aware of modern concepts
of language and reality. Discuss. Do you see any connection between
the initial responses of the twelve witnesses to "The Story of an Accident" in Chapter 3, and the responses of the participants in the mountain feuds?

THE CAMPUS TODAY: REBELLION AND CONFORMITY

Read instructor Lee Pennington's "Introduction" to the student magazine *Tomorrow's People* (p. 265). The piece deals with a poet, what he
is, and what he tries to be. Look over these statements. How does
Pennington apply concepts of *non-allness* to his writing? *Nonidentity?*
Discuss.

In contrast, read Kyle Vance's "Students' Poems Whip Up Furor at
Cumberland" (p. 272). How do various portions of this article demonstrate erroneous applications of the *law of identity* and the *law of the
excluded middle?* The *law of contradiction?* What do you think Pennington and his students were trying to do in writing and publishing
their work?

Applying similar critical approaches, read and discuss Angie M. Skidmore's poem "Fool's Intersanctum" (p. 267) and James D. Asher's "By
Love Possessed" (p. 268).

At the opposite extreme from rebellion is conformity. Read "What
Factors Contribute to Compliance?" (p. 280). Note especially the Milgram electrical shock experiment which demonstrates the tendency of
people to "overconform," so to speak. In effect they are failing to be
aware of *nonidentity* in certain situations where *nonidentity* is essential. Admittedly, certain kinds of conformity are highly desirable if we
desire a civilized society, but rigidity of conformity may lead the person
to a very serious error in which he fails "to distinguish between
situations in which compliance is appropriate and those in which it is
not" (p. 286). Discuss the entire experiment and all of its details. How
do you explain "overconformity"? How do you explain that the more
aware a person is of the victim's presence, "the lower the mean maxi-

mum shock level, and the more subjects defied the experimenter" (p. 285)? What are the dangers of excessive conformity?

THE SEARCH FOR IDENTITY

Read Ernest Hemingway's "Une Génération Perdue" ("the lost generation"), an excerpt from *A Moveable Feast*. Have you ever heard the phrase, "the lost generation"? What did you think it meant? After reading Hemingway's chapter, have you altered your ideas in any way? How? Discuss the *law of identity* and the premise of *nonidentity* in connection with your views. Notice closely the scene in which Gertrude Stein first applied the term to Hemingway's generation (Hemingway was then in his mid-twenties): "All of you young people who served in the war. You are a lost generation" (p. 294). Discuss *nonidentity* and *non-allness* in relation to this statement. How did Hemingway eventually interpret her statement? Did he reject the statement? He later thought, as he wrote, "But the hell with her lost-generation talk and all the dirty, *easy labels*" (italics added). What did Hemingway mean by "easy labels"? Was he himself applying *non-allness* and *nonidentity* to Gertrude Stein's generalization? If so, how? Discuss.

LOVE, SEX, AND CENSORSHIP

Read the poems "Upon Julia's Clothes" (p. 306), by Robert Herrick, and Shelley's "Love's Philosophy" (p. 306). Would you call both of these "love poems"? Why do you identify them as you do? In Herrick's poem, he writes more of Julia's clothes than of Julia; yet, the reader "knows" what Herrick means. What does he mean? Has Herrick purposely confused Julia's clothes with the girl herself? If so, why? Purposeful indirection is sometimes called *irony*. Is Herrick's poem *ironic*, and therefore original and penetrating? Apply the concept of *non-allness* to the poet's intention. For example, how does the sound of the poem add to its meaning? Shelley applies the *law of identity* to fountains, rivers, oceans, winds, and Heaven in the first stanza. The comparison (indirect) of two objects is a *metaphor;* how do the comparisons help the poet to make his point in a new way? Is this a legitimate use of the *law of identity*, even though it involves a temporary suspension of literal rationality in order to understand and enjoy the poem? Discuss. The *metaphor* gives way to *personification* in the second stanza, and Shelley intentionally identifies unlike objects. Why does he do so? Concerning his intention, apply *non-allness* to such aspects of the poem as sound. How does the sound relate to the total impression of the poem?

Read the excerpt from the then-controversial *Maggie: A Girl of the Streets* (1893). Is the relationship between Pete and Maggie one of love? Discuss their relationship as an "I-It" rather than an "I-Thou" arrangement. In this connection discuss the morning meeting between

Pete and Maggie (p. 315), especially their conversation. How does Pete erroneously identify "respectability" with a rejection of responsibility on his part? Discuss. Is Maggie bright? Pete? How are both Pete and Maggie subjected to group pressures, which ultimately lead to Maggie's suicide? What effect do the characters produce in the excerpt? Consider the following: the woman who ridicules Pete (p. 315), the laughing man who hears her say "Who?" (p. 316), and the stout gentleman who "saved his respectability by a vigorous side-step" (p. 317). In Chapter XVII, Maggie's descent from man to man, place to place, light to darkness, and river to silence is treated symbolically; that is, each character, place, and incident seem to *represent* whole attitudes compressed into a short space. Discuss the chapter as symbolic, relating concepts of the *law of identity,* the *law of the excluded middle, non-identity,* and *non-allness* to your interpretation of the episodes.

INDIVIDUAL RESPONSIBILITY

John Donne in portions of "Meditations 16 and 17" gives us the legend of the bell and proceeds to use the device to speak of life, death, human concern, and immortality. Concerning death, note the conclusion of "Meditation 16." Death is ordinarily associated with lifelessness, fear, and panic; but Donne gives us new insights. Apply *non-allness* to the concept of death. He continues in "Meditation 17" to write of the universality of mankind as well as the church in which his convictions lay. How does he transcend the *law of identity,* as well as other Aristotelian approaches, with his contention that "No man is an Island. . . . It tolls for thee" (p. 335)? Read over the famous concluding analogy of man and island carefully. Apply *non-allness* to his concept of individuality; human responsibility; brotherly love. Discuss.

Read carefully the two articles by Loudon Wainwright, "The Dying Girl That No One Helped" (p. 355) and "A Very Special Murderer" (p. 357). Summarize the circumstances of Kitty Genovese's death. Having done so, explain in both Aristotelian terms and modern concepts of language and reality the behavior of the "38 heedless witnesses to the murder" of the girl. Compare and contrast the reactions of these witnesses with those of the twelve witnesses of the hypothetical accident in Chapter 3. How do people tend to overapply the *law of identity* with *self?* How do they ignore the concept of *non-allness* in relation to *self* and *others?* Relate to the idea of human responsibility for individuals.

GOD, MAN, AND MORAL CONSCIOUSNESS

Read the "Epigraph" from Albert Einstein's "I Believe" (p. 361). In our culture there are many approaches to the concept of God and the nature of God. What is Einstein's? Is it *unidimensional* or *multidimensional?* How does his expression of his own feeling of "religiousness" connote humility, mystery, and challenge? In approaching the nature of God, how does he employ modern concepts of language and reality, including *nonidentity, non-allness,* and, to some extent, an awareness that language tends to become *self-reflexive?*

Analyze thoroughly the excerpt from the controversial novel based on the life of Jesus of Nazareth, Nikos Kazantzakis' *The Last Temptation of Christ* (p. 374). The setting is the home of old Zebedee, father of James and John; thus, the action is set close to the shores of the Sea of Galilee. Zebedee is concerned about these men in his home, living in it, using his sleeping mats, drinking his wine, and eating his food. Notice the anecdote Jesus relates concerning the rich man. How can you apply the concept of *non-allness* to richness in this parable? Young Nathanael is concerned about his lack of knowledge concerning religious matters —especially "the Law," or the *Old Testament.* Again, Jesus in answering him about the "Two paths lead to God's bosom" (p. 376) instructs Nathanael, applying the breadth of the mystery of a superior being by suggesting that "mind" (intellect) and "heart" (feeling) are two ways, and that one is not superior to the other. In addition, Jesus gives the anecdotes of the poor man Hillel, the rich man Eleazar, and the rake Joseph. Here, Jesus makes the *abstract concrete,* but in doing so he brings the reader closer to reality. He also suggests the *non-allness* of what religious authorities have to say about men and God. One of the most astonishing applications of *non-allness* made by the author is that applied to Matthew, who records Jesus' actions and words, and Peter's dream, which he relates to Matthew. Is the miracle of walking on water a dream or reality? Apply Aristotle's *law of the excluded middle;* apply *non-allness.* Discuss. Apply also the erroneous *law of identity* to the legend that the "son of the Carpenter of Nazareth" is a reincarnated John the Baptist (p. 380). Obviously such legends stem from the overapplication of such thought processes. Do you agree? Discuss the character of Jonah, who enters and almost throws his boots at Jesus after being ignored so completely. How does Jesus apply *non-allness* to certain of the old commandments, such as killing, adultery, honoring one's parents? Discuss the figure, "Man is a frontier, the place where earth stops and heaven begins" (p. 382). Interpret the meaning. How does the concept inherent in the statement, "Man is of earth as well as of Heaven" again apply *non-allness* to certain Aristotelian approaches —Man is either of Heaven or not of Heaven, for example? Discuss the soul-body argument of Judas Iscariot and Jesus. In what ways are the apostles, as treated with the vision of the novelist, revolutionaries? Do you see evidence of a "generation gap" between their ideas and those of their parents, Zebedee and Jonah? Discuss. How does Matthew apply *non-allness* in his recordings of the events of his time? Discuss.

Having examined the "Epigraph" of Einstein and the excerpt from Kazantzakis' controversial novel on Christ, now read the brief portion from C. H. Dodd's *The Authority of the Bible* (p. 382). According to Dodd, what is the *denotation* of the phrase "Word of God"? He maintains that it is not clear ("equivocation"). Can you think of situations in which people, even well-meaning people, use the phrase consistent with Aristotle's concepts associated with the *law of identity*? Give examples. Dodd then explains that "Word of God" is metaphorical, or a kind of *personification* (i.e., making God human as if he could speak and write in words). However, we all know, as Dodd points out, that words are merely means for the conveyance of thought. Thus, the Word "is not the utterance of God *in the same sense*" in which it is the utterance of men." Read the application of the idea of Paul's Epistle to the Romans. How does Dodd apply here the premise of *nonidentity*? *Non-allness*? Does Dodd imply that those who use such simple expressions as "Word of God" leave the more important aspects of religious belief unanswered in doing so? How? What does he mean when he says, "The mystery of revelation is not to be so lightly disposed of"? Discuss.

LITERATURE AND GOOD WRITING

Consider Horace's statement, used as the "Epigraph" to this section, "Literature and Good Writing": "Knowledge is the foundation and source of good writing" (p. 387). If words are simply "marks" which *represent* something, then how accurate is this statement? How is Horace's statement consistent with the modern concept of language and reality associated with the premise of *nonidentity*? *Self-reflexiveness*? What is the relationship of this statement and the importance of good grammar? Is good grammar enough in good writing? Assuming that good grammar is important, then beyond that basic skill, what is the point of writing well about little? About what has already been said better? About old ideas?

Henry David Thoreau in the excerpt from *A Week on the Concord and Merrimack Rivers* (p. 393) applies the concept of *non-allness* to the idea of antiquity. What is it that America possesses that is as old as that which Greece possesses? Discuss. Concerning good writing, Thoreau states, "If you can speak what you will never hear,—if you can write what you will never read, you have done rare things" (p. 394). Associate this statement with Horace's, treated above. What has *originality* to do with good writing? What are the two classes of "men called poets"? What is the difference between the poet of genius (inspiration) and the one of intellect (taste)? Discuss. Which is like Bristol spar? Like granite? Which is the more enduring? The greater? Discuss. Is there really a kind of immortality in good writing? Give a denotation of "immortality"; then apply Aristotle's *law of contradiction,* then the premise of *non-allness* in giving your answer.

AGE OF CONTROVERSY

Read carefully the excerpts from Barrows Dunham's "That There Are Superior and Inferior Races" (p. 418). The opening passage tells a story. The surprised man, who denigrates Jews, overapplies Aristotle's *law of identity*. Explain why he may think as he does. In Dunham's comments upon the Fair Employment Practices Bill, he quotes several United States Congressmen of the 1940's. What is the significance of the general laughter at the sound of the name "Dombrowski" in the Senate of the United States? Apply the *law of identity* (overidentification and oversimplification) to the incident. Apply *non-allness* for a more accurate analysis. What caused the laughter? What other responses would have been closer to reality? Discuss the tragedy of Maidanek, Poland, in and about 1944 as treated by Dunham. How can one overidentify from fear? Discuss. Treat the unsane actions of the Nazis from the standpoint of *self-reflexiveness*. How can a theory be so remote from reality? Is it possible that a whole society can be unsane? Why is *unsane* a more accurate word than *insane*? Relate Aristotle's *law of the excluded middle* to your discussion, and answer the question, "May a person be definitely *sane* at one time and definitely *insane* at another; or do one's actions tend toward *sanity* or *unsanity* (a lack of saneness)?" Why does Dunham relate the incident at the dinner table with the "death factory at Maidanek" (p. 420)? Relate *self-reflexiveness* to his intentions. What are the connections between racial prejudice and *self-reflexiveness*? Read the rest of Dunham's excerpt, noting closely the four propositions of racism (p. 421). After observing Dunham's arguments, apply to these tenets of racism the *law of the excluded middle, non-allness,* and the tendency to respond in symbols which are remote from reality. What are the advantages of rational approaches to such problems as racism? Note Dunham's statement, "A believing Nazi was fully persuaded that his victims were scarcely distinguishable from animals" (p. 422). Apply overidentity, rigidity, and the deadening of individual *thought references* to this idea. Also consider the confusion of symbol with referent, as in the "I-It" concept of human relationships. In the subsection "The Critique of Racism," Dunham makes the statement, "The largest brain thus far found is that of an imbecile, whilst several men of great intelligence have had rather small brains. The size of the human brain and the shape of the human head have nothing whatever to do with intelligence" (p. 425). Apply the modern concept of language *nonidentity* to this statement. Discuss other kinds of false associations of ideas such as this one. How is skin color determined, according to Dunham? Discuss. Apply *non-allness* and *nonidentity* to the colors generally associated with races, "white," "black," and "yellow." What does Dunham mean when he contends, "We are all brothers *in* the skin, as well as under it" (p. 425), italics added)? Discuss *blood* as a *symbol* (p. 426). How do "racial blood ties" provide nations "an excuse for foreign conquest" and enable them "to divide their own populations at home"? Why would nations wish to do so? Discuss the *law of identity* as it relates to accompanying manipulations of human passions and irrationalities, and to what we may term "social unsaneness." Is blood a bearer of heredity? Discuss. Dunham makes the statement that "human behavior is determined by environmental influences" (p. 428). Do you agree? Apply *non-allness* to this statement, and in this connection give "social reasons" that racial minorities are often the last to be hired. Is this situation as true today as it was in 1948, at the time of the publication of *Man Against Myth*? Discuss. Finally, discuss the *law of identity* in relation to the concept of prejudice, racial and other kinds. Respond to Dunham's idea that so-called "Aryan races" are, if we go by the record of the murder of other peoples, *morally inferior* to all other groups of people. Discuss Jonathan Swift's statement concerning "Aryans" as "the most pernicious race of little odious vermin, that Nature ever suffered to crawl upon the surface of the earth" (p. 429). However, relate *non-allness* to the statement. Do you think that Dunham successfully proves racism to be a "myth"? What is his hope for humanity? Do you think that "democratic peoples of the world" can prevail against the "violence and hate" which we associate with racism—racism of all kinds? Discuss. Include alternatives.

4
GENERALIZATIONS

The word is not the thing, but merely stands for the thing. We have seen that words are marks on something—paper or stone, for example —or are noises people make which become language when the noises are understood by another person to stand for things. Only men can use words as language. Language is like fire; it can be extremely useful and extremely dangerous, although most of the time it is neither one nor the other, but rather a human comfort. It is preeminently a human characteristic. It is best used when it is most efficiently controlled for the purpose at hand. We have seen how language can lead to misunderstandings, broken relationships, human misery. We hear children misuse words, and we smile with understanding. We understand less how adults abuse language, and we seldom smile about such situations, especially if they are personal.

Language has several levels of meaning, as we have seen. At one extreme is the *meaning without the word;* at the other, the *private meaning of the word,* remote from reality. Between these extremes are two other levels which we have examined in Chapter 2: the *denotations* of the word (dictionary meanings), and the *connotations* (associated meanings of the word generally shared by others). Many problems arise in the use of language because people speak or write without an awareness of the *meaning without the word,* or what we may term the *subverbal* reality which one attempts to transmute into words which communicate. As we have seen, many people use language without an awareness of the necessity for a close relationship to *subverbal* realities. Thus, they frequently speak and write in *generalizations.* Generalizations are characterized by vague words or patterns of words which often lack concrete terms, leave out important details, and employ abstract terms to hazy ends. Often, generalizations broadly emphasize more, or less, or even something other than what is intended. None of us is immune to the tendency to use lazy patterns of expression, but in using old words we lose the opportunities for fresh thought processes, as well as the expression of such desirable thought processes to others. Worse, we tend to stunt our potential abilities to think; for since we think in words (*symbols*), if we develop rigid habits of expression, an inevitable recoil takes place. Our hackneyed word patterns tend to "trap" our thoughts, as it were, and we find our thoughts bound by the very words with which we think.

Whether we like it or not, we have also seen that there is a close relationship between words and human behavior. If a man uses the same word in the same way long enough, he may stop "thinking." Then the word becomes a *sign* pointing directly to the object. Living thought dies. Although some signs are useful, if man "overuses" words as signs, he tends to behave as animals behave—with conditioned responses, rigid behavior patterns, thoughtless actions, and actions which may, indeed, be easily controlled by others who *do* think when they use words. Hence, students give "standardized answers," "ride a pony in Latin class," "give the teacher what he wants," "echo quotations," and talk and write "in their sleep," their mental feet padding along well-worn verbal paths from which their thoughts seldom wander. Even when man "thinks," he can easily misuse language, for man tends to *pattern* thinking. His patterns become the "easiest way" for expression; in turn, his thoughts are bound by the very symbols he verbalizes. Significantly, he is limited by the oral and written expression he uses, sees, hears, and exchanges with others, for his thought patterns are often shaped by these influences. Moreover, man is a creature of his culture, and he tends to reflect well-established cultural patterns. In the Western world, man consciously and unconsciously applies Aristotelian concepts to reality—the *law of identity, the law of the excluded middle,* and the *law of contradiction.* As we have seen, these generalizations are often helpful and workable, but they are at best merely tools with which to approach the complexities of reality. Like a good crescent wrench, adjustable within limits, these generalizations do not *always* fit the job one encounters. Moreover, the so-called laws of Aristotle can be used so habitually that the individual who applies them may repeatedly run into conflicts, frustrations, and inaccurate oversimplifications. However, when he adds modern concepts of language and reality to the traditional ones of Aristotle, he often finds that problems diminish. He may begin to operate closer to *subverbal* levels of reality. Implementation of the premises of *nonidentity, non-allness,* and *self-reflexiveness* often clarify apparent inconsistencies, contradictions, and various misunderstandings. Perhaps most importantly, when conscientiously applied even to complex human problems, these approaches tend to aid the individual in moving away from thought processes which may be remote from reality (*private meanings*), and toward *subverbal* levels of reality (*meanings without words*).

Socrates said, "The unexamined life is not worth living." If man can avail himself of the proper tools with which to examine his thought processes, he may be able to break out of his illusory verbal prisons and become, to a greater extent than he has ever known, an open-minded, freer thinking human being. He may even expose his own self-defeating "limitations" for the nonsubstantive illusions they are, whether or not they may have been previously rationalized by laziness, cynicism, environmental vapidness, or any other of a hundred and one excuses. He may discover that his potential for thinking and learning are measurably broadened, his knowledge deepened, and his hope for constructive human endeavor restored with vigor and determination.

HOW TO DEAL WITH GENERALIZATIONS

Here are some common generalizations:
1. America is the greatest country on earth.
2. Women drivers are dangerous.
3. Liberals are Communists.
4. Conservatives are Fascists.
5. That was the greatest game I ever saw.
6. The foremost goal of American education is democracy in the classroom.
7. The modern generation has gone to the dogs.
8. People over thirty cannot be trusted.
9. In a democracy all people are equal.
10. Happiness is the best goal in life.

Generalizations give us the main or overall features of something; they are not specific and detailed, but instead are vague, imprecise. They are convenient as elements of language, and indeed often necessary, since we often speak in a kind of verbal shorthand:

"Hi, George," Doris says, on her way to class. "Beautiful day!"

"Great day!" George replies in passing.

These statements contain obvious generalizations, but the purpose of the speakers is not so much to convey information as it is to greet each other socially, and perhaps to express something of how each feels, not only literally toward the day but also toward each other. It would be silly for George to think, "Now I wonder what Doris means by *beautiful day*? The leaves are falling, wind's up, winter's coming on." It would be even sillier for him to stop her and to inquire about her meaning of *beautiful*. Such generalizations are understandable without more than a flash of conscious effort.

However, if a student, after reading a long assignment on geopolitics, is asked to write a detailed essay on the subject "Distinctive Aspects of the United States of America," and he begins his essay with the generalization, "America is the greatest country on earth," and proceeds in the same generalized vein, without giving specific information to make his generalizations meaningful, then he will probably get an "F" on his paper. He may object: "Look, there's not a grammatical error in it," but the instructor will reply, "Your paper is an assemblage of generalizations."

Those interested in modern language concepts—a person such as Korzybsky—not only were convinced that people could use language more intelligently and effectively if they attempted to get closer to meanings which lie under the level of language itself (*subverbal* realities), but also believed that this desirable goal could be approached more successfully by the definite processes of (1) *indexing,* and (2) *dating* generalizations. These men were deeply concerned by the tendency of speakers and writers to generalize concerning groups of people. For example, speakers and writers often apply the characteristics of a unique individual to a whole group, or the qualities of the particular to the class; or they may reverse the process and apply generalized group concepts to a singular individual. Thus, if one wishes to think close to reality, he must *index* misleading generalizations, such as, "Englishmen are aloof." After recognizing the generalization, one must *index* it: "Englishman[1] is different from Englishman[2]; and Englishman[3] is distinctively unlike Englishman[4]." The specifics could be elaborated upon. The basic idea of indexing, of course, is to help people to avoid illogical groupings and sweeping generalizations—and, hence, to avoid thought processes which are remote from reality.

Similarly, those who implement modern language concepts are aware that the world constantly changes. People change, too. Altogether, the world is in flux. Yet, the behavior responses of most people are, comparatively, more fixed than the fluctuating circumstances would seem to justify. The symbol system with which they think, the language they use, and the interrelationships between the two are rigid. We are often imprisoned by a *jargon* (specialized vocabularies of those in the same work). Thus, if one wishes to think close to reality, he must *date* a fact or event in order to place it in time, in order to place it accurately relative to change, to place, and to circumstances. In Chapter 1, several examples were given of words that have undergone changes in meaning as well as in form. Human attitudes, which words symbolize, also change.

Now let us examine with the processes of *indexing* and *dating* the common generalization which began the paper on which our unfortunate student received a grade of "F": *America is the greatest country on earth.* It is the kind of generalization we hear frequently. The student was simply "parroting" what he had heard—and in so doing was avoiding the responsibility of thinking. If the student wishes to bring his thought processes closer to reality, he should first recognize the entire statement as a sweeping generalization. First, *America* is itself a generalization, for there are several Americas. To *index,* let us consider North America, Central America, and South America. Our student should have used the more precise *United States of America* to distinguish it from other Americas of the Western Hemisphere. The superlative *greatest* denotes, among other qualities, the highest degree of superiority of others of the same kind. In this context, however, *greatest* is so broad as to be nearly meaningless. Some of the ways in which the student could have indexed *greatest* are *area, population, antiquity* (or *history*), *industrial production, natural resources, shipping, education, churches, arts, judicial system, medical research* and *health standards, space research, military power,* and *gross national product.* But let us consider three countries—the United States of America, Great Britain (or the United Kingdom of Great Britain and Northern Ireland), and Russia (the Union of Soviet Socialist Republics).

As of 1950, the United States had an *area* of about 3,022,387 square miles; Great Britain, 99,667 square miles; and Russia, 8,358,567 square miles. From the standpoint of *population,* the United States was in 1950 inhabited by about 150,000,000 people; Great Britain by about 50,368,455 people; and Russia by about 193,000,000 people. Of the three countries, historical records indicate that Great Britain is the *oldest* country. The Celts, related to the Gauls of France, had settled in what is now England and Wales by 600 B.C., and the Iberians (from what is now the Spanish peninsula) had been there long before. Although one estimate of the number of American Indians is 8,400,000 for the entire New World in 1492, and evidences of the "mound builders" in areas of what is now the United States are even more ancient, for purposes of present national identity we usually use the early seventeenth century, when Jamestown and Plymouth were settled, as the time of our national origin. Politically, the English list as their first ruler King Egbert, whose reign began A.D. 829. The citizens of the United States generally consider 1776, when the Declaration of Independence was signed, as the date of their political origin. Russia's federation was not created until 1917, but the national descent can be traced historically from Slavic tribes from the Carpathian Mountains of the ninth and tenth centuries A.D. who eventually spread out and united with groups in the huge area between the Baltic and Black seas. Christianization came somewhat later than in England, the Russians accepting the doctrine in the late tenth century at Constantinople. Russia's political unity began much later than England's, however, in the fourteenth century under the reign of Grand Prince Ivan I.

From the process of *indexing* the student's statement, "America is the greatest country on earth"—at least from the statistics and records available as of 1950 dealing with *area, population,* and *antiquity*—we can see that the student was inaccurate, for literally the United States is far from the "greatest" in any of these three specific areas. Probably the student meant to write about his feeling for his country, his sense of patriotism, unaware that he had chosen one of the most difficult subjects even for great poets to put into fresh and convincing words. Or he may have meant to write, "As of 1960 the United States had the highest gross national product of any country in the world," a statement which he could have substantiated with some research. But this is clear: he did not say what he intended to say, probably because his thought processes did not direct, choose, and control the words he used. As a result his communication was faulty through generalization.

The process of *dating* could be applied to the same statement, but since the applications are so obvious, let us instead illustrate the process with the symbol *economics*. For example, *economics* of 1700 in the Western world were essentially commercial and agrarian. Thus, *economics* dealt with the production, transportation or distribution, and consumption of basically agrarian wealth, and with the related problems of labor, finance, and taxation (although in the 1700's taxes were minimal compared to those of today). Most of the Western world followed the teachings of Adam Smith's *The Wealth of Nations* (1776), which both directly and indirectly did much to make *laissez-faire* (literally, "leave alone," but applied to economics so as to mean, "let each individual pursue his own interests without governmental interference") the dominant economic theory. The *laissez-faire* theory worked with some success in a time when most people lived on farms and produced their goods with hand tools. Theirs was a domestic production, labor having been systematized for ages, and a minimal interchange of items of trade kept life simple.

But by the 1760's the so-called Industrial Revolution was introduced into England by a series of inventions which, at first, appeared to promise man a bright future. After all, James Hargreaves' spinning jenny (1767) could operate eight spindles instead of one, and was soon to operate eighty! Dr. Edward Cartwright's power loom (1784) made domestic or home production of cloth obsolete, and in America, Eli Whitney's cotton gin (1792) cleaned 300 pounds of cotton of its seeds in a single day, whereas only one pound could be cleaned by hand. But new production raised new problems in distribution: new roads had to give way to new ways of haulage; by 1769 James Watt improved the steam engine, making it a modern machine; and since speed was needed, the power of Watt's new engine was harnessed first to vessels, then to carriages on rails in the early 1800's. Thus, the *economics of 1700* were no longer applicable to the *economics of 1850;* for the whole means of production, distribution, and consumption of wealth were vastly different.

Nor was all as rosy as had been predicted, for with the new realities created by the Industrial Revolution, new problems were created for people everywhere. First of all, the benefits of the increased output of goods were unequally distributed. Owners and industrialists, now called capitalists, seemed to get the lion's share, while the great numbers of people, now called laborers, who had moved from their farms into cities and factories, gained little from the new technology. Indeed, they encountered much suffering. Industrial injustices prevailed. The domestic craftsman could no longer compete with the manufacturer of mass-produced goods. While cities and factories expanded, the family unit on the farm was depleted. Eventually a sharp conflict developed between the workers and the owners—so sharp that a two-class society tended to develop, giving rise to new questions of labor and capital. In turn, new governmental regulations were needed to combat what a growing number of people considered economic atrocities. The spirit of their outrage can be felt in the sardonic lines of a poem by Sarah N. Cleghorn, as she turned the wrath of her pen upon child-labor exploiters:

> The golf links lie so near the mill
> That almost every day

The laboring children can look out
And see the men at play.

In fairness to Adam Smith, however, one should point out that his book was taken up by selfish economic individualists of the eighteenth and nineteenth centuries in order to justify their own preconceived notions of freedom. They had confused, perhaps purposely in many cases, political freedom with economic freedom. Even though the Industrial Revolution was not fully under way when he wrote, Smith recognized that some forms of governmental provisions would be needful: public health, support of education, safeguards against injustices, and various undertakings for the welfare of mankind which possibly could not be developed by private enterprise. By and large, these aspects of Smith's economic theory were overlooked or conveniently ignored. In the United States, the Industrial Revolution—with its accompanying benefits and problems—did not gain a significant momentum until the first half of the nineteenth century.

By 1950, *economics* had changed even more, for we had begun to enter an industrial-cybernetic-atomic age. Just as machines had replaced human hands in spinning thread by the 1770's in England, complex electronic calculating machines have in our era been adapted to numerous industries, replacing thousands of workers. Government regulations and controls now seem to be the rule rather than the exception. In the United States, for example, governmental regulation of public utilities and industries involved in interstate commerce has long been established. In England, the railroads and medical facilities have been regulated by the government. Policies of taxation, social security, improved roads, public school systems, workmen's compensation, and welfare are common to us all. Other governmental measures to stave off recessions and depressions, as well as legislation to diminish gold drains and to reduce inflation, are well known. Although private enterprise exists today in the United States, it does so within certain legal regulations and restrictions. There is no longer any such thing as *free* enterprise in the sense that the merchants and property owners of Adam Smith's age understood and used the term.

Yet people continue to use the term *economics*—as well as the related words *free enterprise, private enterprise,* and *laissez-faire*—as if such terms had *one meaning* throughout *all time.* Such generalizations are self-deluding and serve only to lead the individual's thoughts farther from, rather than closer to, the real meanings which underlie the level of language. A person who examines the complex problems of economics today can solve little if he generalizes in ways which are remote from reality. If he brings fresh thoughts to these problems, as did Sir Alfred Ewing, the President of the British Association for the Advancement of Science in 1932, he may well question the whole premise of technological progress and even become critical of it; he may point to the continual perplexity and frustration which have begun to concern man. *The Times* (September 1, 1932) reported some of Ewing's refreshing observations and questions on the subject. They are still timely enough to quote:

> *To go back is impossible; how shall industrialized Man proceed? Where will he find himself if he follows this path or that? An old exponent of applied mechanics may be forgiven if he expresses something of the disillusion with which, now standing aside, he watches the sweeping pageant of discovery and invention in which he used to take unbounded delight. It is impossible not to ask: Whither does this tremendous procession tend? What, after all, is its goal? What is its probable influence upon the future of the human race?*

In *indexing* the problems of economics of the twentieth century, Sir Alfred Ewing also demonstrated a *dating* of the problems. He was, in effect, raising some fundamental questions of moral responsibility in economics (our production, distribution, and consumption of goods, and related problems of labor, finance, and taxation). In avoiding generalized observations, he thereby opened up new areas for investigation. By choosing his words as he did, he challenged mankind to reexamine itself in regard to the whole question of economics, and added the dimension of morals to the dimension of ever-changing techniques.

THE CLICHÉ AS GENERALIZATION

Cliché, originally a French term meaning a stereotype plate, also means figuratively in French, a stereotyped phrase. A stereotype plate is a block for making prints, a kind of stamp reproducing its own image over and over again; applied to the words, phrases, and sentences people use, the meaning of cliché is immediately vivid, for one receives the impression of a person not thinking at all, but rather stamping words, phrases, and sentences in print with a printing block or a rubber stamp. Once the general procedure is learned, the person does not even need to think. He does his task mechanically with a kind of figurative *stamp, stamp, stamp,* and then one sees in print or hears spoken the old, hackneyed, outmoded phrases. A cliché means, then, an expression that has become trite. It may once have been unique and striking, but its original luster has become dulled and abused through overuse. Here are some clichés:

Mother Nature	Sweet as candy
Beautiful as a sunset	Skinny as a rail
Not a cloud in the sky	Fat as a butterball
Pretty as a picture	Drab as Monday's wash
The deep purple night	Smooth as silk

Black as midnight	Awkward as a bull in a china
Light as day	shop
Bigger and better	Tall, dark, and handsome
Down in the dumps	Green as grass
Sadder but wiser	Great
A good boy	Cool (as a cucumber)
A nice girl	Uptight
A person of high character	Magnificent
Pure as the driven snow	Very (good)
Lovely as a rose	Real(ly) good
Cute as a button	Still as a mouse
Blue as the sky	A deep dark mystery
Dark as pitch	Loomed on the horizon
A glorious time	In terms of (as a loose con-
A fetching dress	nective)
Lovely as a dream	A great deal of

Like a *generalization,* the *cliché* helps us to avoid thinking. The cliché allows us to continue to "talk in our sleep," or to "live in our *word world* of dreams," quite remote from reality. When we use clichés, however, the very reality which we want to convey is often lost. Certainly it is reduced in value from the priority of what we really intend to relay to anyone with whom we wish to communicate. We can avoid clichés—which are really extreme, compressed forms of generalizations—in the same way that we avoid generalizations: first, we recognize the expression as a cliché; then we *index* it; then we *date* it. For example, we tell a brief story or anecdote about "a good boy," and thus demonstrate his goodness with a specific point in time. One remembers how effectively this was done to indicate the honesty of Abraham Lincoln—his walking miles through bad weather to return the change a customer had left at Offutt's store in New Salem, Illinois. Thus, we break through the cliché into substantive thought with concrete and vivid details. If possible, we place the event in time, relative to change and circumstances, and in so doing date the time-space event. Our thinking, in turn, becomes less rigid, more original, and more incisive.

MORE ON GENERALIZATIONS

Economy of thought leads us to generalize. Some generalizations, as has been pointed out, are necessary. In conversations between members of a family, fellow workers, or associates, or those at social gatherings, people are not so much interested in the weather or politics as they are in how each person affects the other—what we sometimes call social rapport. Each person deeply treasures a self-image which he wishes to project successfully to other people. As words of greeting and enthusiastic salutation, generalizations are easy and useful. But generalizations are misleading when they are mistakenly accepted for thought processes; sometimes they can be charged with peril. It is temptingly easy to proceed from "this person" to "all of these people"—and then we have a generalization of what is essentially group or racial prejudice. Or consider, "Exercise is good for people," instead of "Exercise of certain kinds under certain circumstances is usually beneficial." Or again, "Men are stronger than women," instead of "Selected men under specific conditions and for specific tasks are stronger than selected women under specific conditions for the same tasks."

A generalization holds that different things are alike. If a medical doctor generalizes excessively, he may begin to prescribe the same medicine for all illnesses, or he may tend to become a faddist and to use one method to treat various ailments. One generalizes his way into spiritual, political, social, and physical oversimplifications, just as a student who likes to read may become a bookworm, blind to the real world of action and change about him. One generalizes because it is convenient—but inaccuracies inevitably result. One may understand such terms as generation gap when he realizes that generalizations cover, as so many layers, the possibilities of understanding between parent and offspring. Many older people have formed their generalizations and, unfortunately, have become rigidly comfortable with them. Younger people see differences. They see that their parents have overdefined similarities; but ironically younger people, too, tend to repeat the faults of new generalizations paralleling those of the older people. The young are great imitators. In time, and perhaps unconsciously, they adhere to their visions of reality as rigidly as their parents ever did, even though their visions may be different ones. Thus, we conceive of a new generation emerging with somewhat different generalizations.

Our language is like a pair of spectacles through which we perceive, and once we become accustomed to the lenses, we act as if they are not there. To be aware of generalizations and to be alert to them is one way in which we can begin to check our distortions.

QUESTIONS ON READINGS

SCIENCE AND THE HUMANITIES IN CONFLICT

Read the definition of "technocracy" by William H. Smyth: "Scientific reorganization of national energy and resources, coordinating industrial democracy to effect the will of the people" (p. 156). The statement contains several generalizations; the most glaring is, perhaps, "the will of the people," which supposes the organic fiction of something that has no meaning on the subverbal level of reality. Pick out other *generalizations* in his statement. First recognize them; then demonstrate how he could have dealt more effectively with them. The large number of *generalizations* in the statement makes its validity suspect, does it not? Discuss.

Read *Gulliver's Travels* (p. 161). Early in the chapter, Swift mentions the "blown bladder," a device by which the Laputans get each other's attention for communication, for they are "so taken up with intense speculations" that they cannot speak or listen to others "without being roused by some external taction upon the organs of speech and hearing." Thus, the Laputans keep a domestic servant called "a flapper" with them whenever they "walk abroad or make visits." *Satire* is a literary device with which a writer, with humor and wit, tries to expose human frailties and the weaknesses of humanity and its institutions. His hope is not only to entertain, but also to promote improved conditions. Here Swift has *generalized* about a certain profession or area of knowledge in human affairs. What is it? Read the chapter and give examples of how Swift *indexes* his satire. In doing so, does he stimulate you to think in new ways, perhaps with original thoughts? How? In your discussion treat the ways in which food is carved; the tailoring of Gulliver's clothes; the nature of the music for court entertainment; the views of the inhabitants of the floating island toward the people on earth below them (Lagado) and their "petitions," sent up to the King like so many kites of school boys; their descriptions of the "beauty of a woman"; the architecture of their houses; the superior attitude of the scientists in their mathematical approach to news, politics, and public affairs (In this connection, can you relate the present-day conflict between the forces of Snow and Leavis in any new ways?); their fears of "impending dangers" and consequent loss of sleep; the attitudes of the vivacious women of the island and their familiarities with their lovers before the "husband . . . so rapt in speculation"; and the desire for the reality of the earth of Lagado below the floating island of Laputa.

Now, relate the substance of Swift's satire in Chapter II to the "Epigraph" of Oliver Wendell Holmes, "Science is a first-rate piece of furniture for a man's upper-chamber, if he has common-sense on the ground floor." *Index* and *date* your observations of the relationships. Try to avoid *generalizations* in your statements.

LANGUAGE AND REALITY

The denotation of war is "open armed conflict between countries or within a country," but it can refer also to any active hostility, strife, or conflict. Actually, the statement attributed to General of the Union army, William Tecumseh Sherman, "War is hell" (p. 184) is a *generalization*. *Index* and *date* the context of the statement as it is recorded historically. Why did Sherman add, ". . . but if it has to come I am here"? Does he suggest by so doing that war may be justified under certain circumstances? What circumstances? Discuss. *Index* and *date* your remarks.

Read Susanne K. Langer's excerpt from *Philosophy in a New Key* (p. 212). When people say that animals can *understand* or *talk*, are they generalizing? In answering the question, refer to Langer's example of Kohler's apes: they could use a stick to reach a banana outside of their cage only so long as the stick and the banana could be seen in one glance; in other words, they could not retain the *thought process* (or *symbol*) of the two acting together without the actual physical presence of the stick and the banana simultaneously within their vision. But how does the child differ from the ape in this respect? Then, can apes "talk" or even "think" as human beings "conceptualize"? Is this example of Kohler's apes an *indexing* of a generalization? Discuss. How does Langer *index* and *date* the generalization of the origin of language which she makes? Discuss.

Read the first section of Eleazer Lecky's "Words and Things" (p. 217). Note that the article begins with two proverbs that have become virtual *clichés:* "Look before you leap," and "He who hesitates is lost." How does he demonstrate that they are *generalizations*? How does he move conceptualizing concerning these proverbs closer to *subverbal* reality? Discuss. Other adages? How has the word *logos* been treated as a *generalization*, especially by the Greeks and in Christian theology? Lecky states, "That words are not things is not a modern discovery." How does he *index* and *date* this important concept? Give examples of Wordsworth, Coleridge, and Feidelson's contrary contentions; that is, that words can be things. Why does Lecky *index* these views? How does he make the generalization of *symbol* more concrete through *indexing*? How does he show the flexibility of *symbols*? Discuss his definitions of *words*. How does he *index meaning*? *Context*? Discuss.

WAR AND DEHUMANIZATION

Examine the two introductory quotations of Mao Tse-Tung. Is each a *generalization*? Can you give the meaning of each clearly? What are some problems in understanding the author? Discuss. Now read "The War Objective," from *Mao Tse-Tung: Selected Works* (p. 231). Quoting himself, Mao Tse-Tung states, "The objective of war is nothing but 'to preserve oneself and to annihilate the enemy.'" Explore the *generalizations* of this statement. How does the author *index* and *date* "annihilate"? Do the processes give added validity to his statement? Discuss. Mao Tse-Tung writes of "heroic sacrifice in war," which is, of course, a *generalization*. By what means does he make the *generalization* meaningful? Discuss. Does the author index the term "tactics" in a convincing way? How?

THE CAMPUS TODAY: REBELLION AND CONFORMITY

Examine the section which concerns itself with *Tomorrow's People* (p. 265). After reading the "Introduction" and the poems, what do you think the authors were attempting to accomplish by publishing their work in the magazine? Choose one poem which you consider to be controversial; then choose another which, in your judgment, is uncontroversial. Do you find generalizations in both? Discuss. Consider Jesse Stuart's statement about the poems in *Tomorrow's People* as "maybe not good poetry, but mighty powerful writing." Do you consider this statement a generalization? Discuss. In relation to the two poems which you have considered, *index* and *date* the applicability of Stuart's statement. Glance over the two newspaper articles, "Poems Stir Dispute" (p. 270) and "Students' Poems Whip Up Furor at Cumberland" (p. 272). Pick out several generalizations which strike you as especially glaring. Demonstrate how the "dispute" and "furor" could have been reduced or eliminated through *indexing* and *dating* on the part of certain individuals whose responses were so sweepingly generalized that their behavior appeared, as reported, to be remote from reality. Discuss. Finally, what is the basic generalization made here—and made with marked inaccuracy—in connection with art on the one hand, and reality on the other? Discuss.

THE SEARCH FOR IDENTITY

Read the excerpt from Ralph Waldo Emerson's "The American Scholar" (p. 298). He commences by stating that the books of an older period will not fit that of the succeeding generation. Do you agree? Is Emerson's statement an unjustifiable generalization? Discuss. He goes on to state the dangers of reading. One is that the "love of the hero corrupts into worship of his statue," another that man can cease to think inspired thoughts and instead succumb to uninspired reading and "we have the bookworm." Again, "Books are the best of things, well used; abused, among the worst." He mentions the individual who "over-responds" to a book, so to speak, or one who is "warped" by its attraction "clean out of . . . orbit." His statement echoes the old adage, "God deliver me from the man who has read but one book!" In what ways are his observations *indexes* of a generalization? Discuss.

Speaking of scholars especially, and American scholars in particular, Emerson observes, "Whatever talents may be, if the man create not, the pure efflux of the Deity is not his . . . ." Is he suggesting here that all American scholars have the obligation to do fresh work, i.e., to create? Discuss and index *create*. What does Emerson mean when he states, "Books are for the scholar's idle times. When he can read God directly, the hour is too precious to be wasted in other men's transcripts of their readings"? Especially, is "read God directly" clear to you? Is it a generalization? A metaphor? Does an American scholar have an obligation toward the external, real world? Discuss.

Emerson wrote, "One must be an inventor to read well." Does he *index* his meaning? How? Discuss his technique of *indexing*. Is the maxim, "One is capable of getting out of a book what he can bring to it" as effective as the similar one Emerson employs? Why or why not? He indexes different kinds of reading. For example, we read "history and exact science" for information; hence, Emerson labels such reading "laborious." Is this view a generalization? Discuss. When he speaks of colleges teaching us "elements" and aiming "to drill," whereas they should be teaching us "to create," is he *generalizing*? Is his observation a fair one? Why or why not? What justification does he give for our institutions of higher learning teaching youth to create? Does he *index* the results? In designating gowns and pecuniary foundations does he expose any generalizations concerning knowledge—real knowledge? Discuss and *index*. According to Emerson, what are the real aspects of "wealth" in our colleges and universities? Is his generalization justified? Discuss. How do Emerson's observations relate to the general theme of one's search for identity? Must one generalize to see the relationships? Explain.

LOVE, SEX, AND CENSORSHIP

The literary comedian Charles Farrar Browne (Artemus Ward) wrote "Artemus Ward: Among the Free Lovers" (p. 313) in 1862. One student in a college class recently made the statement that Artemus Ward was "not funny and his ideas are dated." What is your reaction to the student's observations? Do they contain generalizations? If so, *index* them. *Date* them. For the sake of discussion, take an opposing view. Likening the "Free Lovers" to the "Hippies" of the mid-1960's, could you *index* any similarities? Discuss.

INDIVIDUAL RESPONSIBILITY

In the excerpt from "The American Democrat" (p. 336), James Fenimore Cooper differentiated between the *aristocrat* and the *democrat*, while at the same time *indexing* similarities between them. He wrote "To call a man who has the habits and opinions of a gentleman, an aristocrat from that fact alone, is an abuse of terms. . . ." The observation contains, of course, a generalization. Here the part ("habits") is confused for the whole. Similarly, "Some men fancy," Cooper wrote, "that a democrat can only be one who seeks the level, social, mental and moral, of the majority, a rule that would at once exclude all men of refinement, education, and taste from the class." How does Cooper in this statement pierce the inaccuracy of the basic generalization that one who believes politically in democracy is common in every way? Discuss his methods of *indexing*.

What is Cooper's opinion of "indiscriminate association"? In answering this question, note that the meaning of "indiscriminate" can be *"lacking in ability to distinguish things"* or *"failure to make distinctions in treatment."* Is it a generalization to assume that *discrimination* should always be associated with *prejudice,* which means "making up one's mind without facts"? Discuss.

Note Cooper's definition of democracy and what it means. In this connection, do people sometimes erroneously generalize about such terms as social democracy, religious democracy, intellectual democracy, when they perhaps should be limiting their observations more precisely to political democracy? To clarify this question, attempt to *index* social democracy, religious democracy, and intellectual democracy. What does the cliché "democracy in the classroom" really mean? *Index* and *date* your answer.

GOD, MAN, AND MORAL CONSCIOUSNESS

Read the two poems "God Lay Dead in Heaven," by Stephen Crane, and "God's Funeral," by Thomas Hardy (p. 365). Note that both poems were written two generations before the present-day "God is dead" controversy. Crane's poem has been interpreted to mean that without a belief in God, man would be destroyed by the monsters of desire, selfishness, and greed. Is this a generalization? If so, *index* it.

Hardy's poem depicts a funeral cortege. Although we understand it to be an imaginative projection of "God's Funeral" in a sense, Hardy *indexes* what are, in effect, man's ever-changing concepts of God. How? Discuss his observations, and, if possible, date them. It has been pointed out that the poem ends on a note of religious doubt. Do you agree? If it is "a note of doubt," is it "thoughtful doubt"? *Index.*

LITERATURE AND GOOD WRITING

Examine again the excerpt from Thoreau's "Nature and Antiquity: The Poet of Genius and the Poet of Taste" (p. 393). We often generalize about age, oldness, or antiquity. We may equate such divergent ideas as age-wisdom, years-experience, antiquity-value (or -tradition), centuries-culture; and yet Emerson wrote, "We do not count a man's years, until he has nothing else to count." What did Emerson mean? Concerning cultural antiquity, what does Thoreau have to say about its quality relative to the antiquity of nature? How does he *index* the idea of antiquity and thus broaden our concept of it?

Specifically, how does Thoreau avoid *generalizing* about genius and talent as prerequisites of good writing? How does he *index* the "writer of genius"? The "writer of talent"? Does he *date* by implication the two kinds of writers? According to Thoreau, which is the greater writer? Can you supply reasons for your answer by pointing to Thoreau's text? Can you implement Thoreau's concepts of genius and talent *in re* writers whom you have read? Illustrate and discuss.

AGE OF CONTROVERSY

In this chapter, you read, ". . . speakers and writers often apply the characteristics of a unique individual to a whole group, or the qualities of the particular to the class; or they may reverse the process and apply generalized group concepts to a singular individual." Examine this statement within the context of illogical groupings and sweeping generalizations which keep one's thought processes from operating close to reality and encourage those which tend to be remote from reality. Within the context of *prejudice* (an opinion or judgment made before facts are known), look over carefully Shylock's speech from *The Merchant of Venice* (p. 418) and read, along with it, the excerpt from James Gould Cozzens' novel *By Love Possessed* (p. 430). What *generalizations* do you note in both excerpts? Do you observe any *sweeping generalizations*? Discuss them if you find any. Now, compare and contrast the two excerpts from the standpoints of *indexing* and *dating*. As a result of your analysis, which statement seems closer to reality, more remote from reality? That of Shylock or that of Julius Penrose? Distinguish between characters and authors. What do you suppose were Shakespeare's intentions in presenting such a character? Cozzens' purposes? Discuss.

5

COMMON PROBLEMS IN ABSTRACTION AND LOGIC

SOME COMMON PROBLEMS IN ABSTRACTION

We have seen that one of the modern concepts of language and reality is the *self-reflexiveness* of language itself. We talk about something, and when we do we tend to move away from that thing. Our conversational exchanges become as so many widening, concentric circles in water around the thing—the place where the stone was dropped. To put the matter another way, the words we first choose and use are only symbols of reality. The more we talk about that reality, the farther we move from it. It happens in our conversations nearly every day. Consider the verbal interchange of these five students:

1st Student (physics major, a "folk-rock" fan): "Heard a great guitar last night."

2nd Student (a music major): "Who?"

1st Student: "Magic Sam. Ash Grove. Electrific—sparks flying!"

2nd Student: "Ever hear Andrés Segovia?"

1st Student: "Andy who?"

3rd Student (P.E. major, an amateur drummer): "Take your strings. Give me skins."

4th Student (an art major): "You ever seen Picasso's *Antique Head?*"

1st Student: "What's with Picasso?"

4th Student: "Well, it's got a guitar in it. I think it's a guitar. Could be a mandolin. . . ."

5th Student (an English major): "Speaking of guitars, I just read Wallace Stevens' 'Man with a Blue Guitar.' "

1st Student: "I give up."

5th Student: "You don't dig poetry, huh?"

3rd Student: "Got somethin' against skins, too."

4th Student: "Say, Picasso's *my bag!*"
2nd Student: "Magic Sam! You don't know psychedelia from academe."
1st Student (leaving): "Zilch. I give up . . ."

Not only do people tend to stray from the subjects about which they think or the point they begin to discuss, but in so doing they tend to misunderstand others. Sometimes such misunderstandings develop into arguments. More frequently, communication simply breaks down. Even under these circumstances, people may continue to assert their feelings through language, even aggressively; but such actions do not result in communication. Rather, they result in frustration. "I didn't really mean that," we may say. But the damage is done. Genuine interchanges of thought processes are too often cut off in the bloom of our very human yearnings to express ourselves and to understand how others think about subjects of interest to us. We want to expand our minds, to learn about new ideas, to satisfy our curiosities and to keep them growing. We have discovered that the more we know, the more aware we become of how very much remains unknown. Just as an explorer discovers new lands and brings an awareness of them into the known world, he also glimpses vast reaches of other new, unexplored regions. So is it with us all—so many voyagers in a mysterious universe. Together with others we can learn more than we know, and we can all benefit.

Too often, however, our motivations are high but our performances are low. Whatever these motivations may be, the specific of language frequently gives way to the general, and the general to the abstract. In Chapter 2 we examined the subverbal level of reality in relation to language, and especially in relation to specific problems of generalizations (p. 28). There we saw that clear thinking, involving a more or less constant reference to a subverbal level of reality, is the major prerequisite of lucid expression.

In writing, as in speech, however, a consciousness of the subverbal level of reality is quickly forgotten. Unfortunately, most people tend to use words "about words" in such a way that whatever is under discussion becomes ever more remote from those basic realities which underlie the verbal level. To illustrate, here is a list of words. See if you can determine which terms are more concrete than others, or less abstract than others:

List for Discussion, Categorizing, Qualifying

1. Guide, rule, Taft-Hartley Law, legislation, regulation.
2. Probity, morality, candor, clean hands, singleness of heart, Abraham Lincoln (example of honesty), honesty.
3. Mendacity, disrepute, faithlessness, Benedict Arnold (example of betrayal), laxity, knavery, graft, treachery, a "false heart," "forked-tongue," Machiavellian.
4. Darkness, opacity, mysterious night, gloaming, nighttime, nightfall.

5. Pain, headache, migraine, smart, twinge, indigestion, heartburn, grippe, seizure, fever, intestinal disorder, an acute and contagious disease, virus, inflammation of the respiratory tract, muscular discomfort, intestinal disorder, influenza.
6. Radical, one wanting change, insurgent, a Tory, a Continental, flower child, hippie, a beatnik, a yippie, Red, anarchist, Henry David Thoreau (example of action treated in "Civil Disobedience"), Henry Clay, George Washington, rioter, Zola.
7. Bird, blackbird, thrush, red-winged blackbird, martin, starling, crow, raven.
8. Fish, bass, fresh-water fish, salt-water fish.

In Item 1 above, *guide* represents more abstract concepts than *rule* or *regulation*. Relative to the other words in the list, *regulation* seems to be more concrete than either *rule* or *guide*, since it suggests a precedent of rule, hence *law*. Since *legislation* may involve the development of any number of laws, then obviously *Taft-Hartley Law* is the more concrete term in Item 1 relative to, or within the context of, rules of man which are enforced by the particular controlling authority. Still, we can see at a moment's glance that relative to other contexts, certain of the other words may be more or less concrete than the remaining words within the group. For example, from the context of discovery, *guide* is the most concrete; from measurement, *rule*; from creation of laws, *legislation*; and from either the executive branch of government or a watchmaker's shop, *regulation*.

All this is to say that there is a kind of scale of context related to the usage of a word, that no single view of a word is necessarily superior to another, especially outside a specific context; and that it is important to keep in mind, if we are to remain close to the subverbal levels of reality, that contexts vary in abstractness or concreteness depending upon our point of reference—what we are looking for, so to speak, which in turn depends on many other considerations.

THE RELATIVITY OF CONCRETENESS AND ABSTRACTNESS

Years ago you might have read a story something like this: Once upon a time there was a little boy named Joey. He very much wanted a pet. His father was a farmer, known by the neighbors as "Farmer Calvin." Farmer Calvin raised all kinds of livestock on his farm, as well as many kinds of grain and some tobacco. He also had large stands of timber which he sold to the lumber companies. Joey Calvin could have had a dog or a cat for a pet. He could have raised a calf or a lamb of his own, or he could have had a pony or a duck. But he had once heard his father say that the pig was the brightest of all farm animals, and the most valuable, too, and that for every person in the country, there was at least half a pig. Joey liked the sounds pigs made when they ate corn and special feeds. They lived with the joy of life. They relished good food enough to "grunt" their joy. He even could have had a pet squirrel or fox, for Farmer Calvin had caught them in cunning traps; but more than anything else, Joey wanted a pig for a pet. One day, big Mathilda, who had won the blue-ribbon sow prize at the state fair more than once, gave birth to a litter of pigs. After much persuasion by Joey, Farmer Calvin gave an astonished shake of his head and agreed that Joey could have his choice of the farrow for a pet of his own, but only until the pig was old enough for marketing. "After all," his father said, "farming is a business here."

Joey nodded in agreement. "I'll feed him myself," he said. "I'll take care of him and maybe someday show him at the state fair."

Joey chose the prettiest Poland China pig he had ever seen. Farmer Calvin remarked, "You've got a good eye for stock, son. That one may develop into a good boar pig."

"I'll name him Blue-boar," Joey said proudly. And that night he went to sleep with happy dreams, for he had a pet all his own—a pet pig that he had wanted, it seemed, as long as he could remember.

As time passed, Blue-boar grew up and so did Joey, whose demonstrated abilities and absorbing interest in rural education made him a natural leader in the Four-H Club. Since Blue-boar was his special project, Joey carefully fed and cared for the porker, charting his diet, checking the increase in poundage, firmness, skin condition, and other aspects of health against his feeding, shelter, exercise, and vitamin input. In time, Blue-boar became the State Champion, and with the honor and traditional blue ribbon went the prize of a future college scholarship, just as soon as Joey Calvin would be eligible to receive it.

So, then, relative to the boy Joey Calvin, the pig Blue-boar has a fairly definite context: to Joey, Blue-boar is a pet and an emblem of a way of life that is beginning to fascinate him and motivate him in new directions. But let us also examine the following contexts.

To Farmer Calvin, the pig represents a farm asset and source of professional pride, as well as a source of pride in his son.

To Farmer Calvin's financial advisor, accountant, and tax specialist, Blue-boar represents a simple economic asset, translatable to dollars and cents.

To the Director of the State Department of Agricultural Statistics, part of whose job is to project growth in the state's hog production, Blue-boar presents not only impressive individual statistics, but also an optimistic hope for the future growth of hog production.

To the Bureau of Internal Revenue, Blue-boar emerges in the form of a taxable source for national income—hence, part of the nation's wealth, bearing a less direct relationship to the wealth of the world.

To most of the people at the state fair, including many who witnessed the judging or saw Blue-boar's picture with Joey standing at his side receiving the blue ribbon, the pig represents another championship hog—an especially neat pig with black and white markings.

To Dr. Oswald Steward, Director of Research in Animal Husbandry at the state university, who helped judge the contest, Blue-boar is a superb specimen of the large swine (family *Suidae,* genus *Sus*), Poland China.

To Dr. Steward's colleague, Dr. Winthrop Hamm, a geneticist, Blue-boar is an experimental object which he hopes to obtain through the university for a special research project in the development of improved strains and breeds of domesticated swine.

To Professor Hyman Levin, a histologist of national renown, and consultant to Drs. Hamm and Steward, the pig represents so much specific tissue: cellular, connective, epithelial, muscular, nerve, fatty, bone, and cartilage or gristle. He and his research assistant scientifically examine the tissue and prepare a detailed report of the quality of the minute structures of the animal's tissues.

The diagram should help us understand the relativity of concreteness and abstraction.

The simple story of Blue-boar may give us the impression that his "basic reality" is that of a pet, his relationship with Joey. Relative to Joey, the impression is basically accurate. Blue-boar has also come to represent other ideas to Joey: he is a symbol of his interest in agriculture, perhaps his future leadership in the agrarian community, and unconsciously, perhaps, a means of earning his father's respect. But a glance at the "Cycle of Relativity" indicates that there are at least *eight other* legitimately "real" views of Blue-boar, too—beginning with what may appear to be the most concrete at the top-left of the cycle (histologist) and moving counterclockwise around the cycle to the geneticist, somewhat less detailed and concrete, and so forth on to what may appear to be the most abstract of all levels, the concept of Blue-boar as an extremely small part of the national income and a country's wealth, which may be considered as part of the world's wealth, *ad infinitum*.

However, one could make out a good case that No. 4 on the "Cycle of Relativity" is the most concrete, assuming that most people would see Blue-boar as a pig with recognizable physical characteristics, hence different from other animals—simply a pig, albeit an outstanding one. Again, assuming that farming is a business to be judged ultimately in terms of dollars and cents, one could contend that the accountant's view of Blue-boar is the most "objective," and, hence, the most "concrete" meaning or significance of the pig. Similarly, from other points of view, Blue-boar is understood as more than livestock to be raised for profit, or a pet to be loved; he becomes an object of scientific research leading to new knowledge in the breeding of swine. As a source for study, the possibilities are endless, not only in the realms of husbandry but, perhaps less directly, in medical science.

As helpful as the terms *concrete* and *abstract* may be; that is, as usable as they are in keeping us close to subverbal levels, they are not always enough. The "Cycle of Relativity" helps us to see that the *context of meaning* often governs the significance and accuracy of individual views. Blue-boar may be considered as a *time-space event*. Linked to time and space, he contains an infinitude of characteristics which may extend from human concepts of the smallest microscopic details to the most inferential macrocosmic details. Just as all forms of life move, change, do not remain static, neither should our views of life be rigid and unilateral (one-valued) or dualistic (two-valued). Hence, the

microcosmic

1. Histologist's concept of porcine tissues, endless in details of cellular structure, *ad infinitum*

2. Geneticist's view of the pig as a research object to improve strains of breeding, retaining highly selective characteristics of the specific pig but leaving out many of the barest physical traits

3. Livestock Judge's concept of the prize-winning specimen of domesticated swine (family *Suidae*, genus *Sus*), Poland China—selective criteria highly subjective, and theoretical, but including many details subject to abstraction by the human nervous system

4. People's view of the Pig as pig with recognizable physical characteristics intact, but conceived of generally as a model swine representative of the animal group, rather than as the individualized "Blueboar," distinct from the group

5. Joey Calvin's concept of Blueboar as a pet, but with widening connotations—a symbol of agricultural interest, a new role of leadership, personal and family pride, a college scholarship

macrocosmic

6. Farmer Calvin's concept of the pig as a farm asset, but with widening connotations—a symbol of his son's interest in his own work, a source of family and professional pride, a means of his son's future education

7. Accountant's concept of the pig as a financial asset only—increasingly inferential level of conception retains few characteristics indentifiable as "pig"

8. Statistician's view—even more highly inferential, only vaguely related to a descriptive level of pig as a recognizable time-space event, understood basically as impressive individual statistics related to quantitative and qualitative growth of an economic product, "hog production"

9. Bureau of Internal Revenue's concept of income, wealth, endless in inference, related to gross national production, national economic welfare, related to a medium of exchange in relation to the wealth of the world —constant movement *ad infinitum*

INFINITY OF DETAILS

TIME
SPACE
EVENT
of the PIG
[Life Force of]
[Existence of Pig]

CONCRETENESS
And
ABSTRACTION:
The Cycle of Relativity

"Cycle of Relativity" should be conceived of as a fluid cycle. There are samenesses running through the differences, even though many similarities, as so much sediment, drop out of the flow as we move from one concept to another. As long as we conceive of what the human mind and nervous system abstract from the time-space event of Blue-boar, there are at least a few details carried through the entire counterclockwise current—all the way from the infinity of details on the microcosmic level of conception, counterclockwise around the cycle to the infinity of details on the macroscopic level.

The ability to examine a time-space event, whether it is a pig or something else, with the multiplicity of views implied by the "Cycle of Relativity" is extremely important in keeping ourselves close to subverbal levels of reality—in knowing where we are, so to speak, so that we can move more logically to where we may wish to go. Thus we are not "cut off" into stagnant, water-locked areas; we can cross the boundaries of narrower concepts, voyage through related areas of meaning, and encompass new ideas with many approaches. We need not give merely one or two answers to a problem when there may be dozens. Specialists in modern concepts of language often term this kind of knowledge and implementation of ideas a *multivalued* or *multiordinal* orientation.

SOME COMMON PROBLEMS IN LOGIC

The word *logic* is derived through the Middle English from the Greek *logikós,* which meant "of speech or reason." Logic is still closely related to *words and thinking.* As an area of knowledge, it concerns us with the principles by which we deal as correctly as possible with inferences, or the ways in which we think based on evidence, circumstances, statements, or "facts." Logic may involve various methods of reasoning or argumentation, but whatever those methods may be, the goal usually involves a movement toward judgments, utterances, and actions which are as sound as possible.

In spite of our efforts to achieve increasingly sounder judgments in our daily lives, old habits of thought tend to mislead and deceive us. False and mistaken ideas, opinions, illogical modes of argument—in short, not only abuses of logic, but failures to apply logic—lead us into repeated misconceptions. Because of the compression of social relationships today, nearly instantaneous communication systems, closer political and economic interdependence between groups as well as nations, and what may be termed the cultural explosions taking place all over the world, it is more important than ever that citizens in general, and educated people in particular, be able to see through *fallacies* which are so ruinous in their pervasive results, appealing as they do to lower emotions, clouded understanding, and at best the bare rudiments of thinking. Following is a list of some of the most destructive fallacies which men permit to disrupt and topple their most constructive efforts:

1. *The broad generalization (Secundum quid).* If one reasons from the particular instance to the general conclusion, he is guilty of this kind of generalization, sometimes termed a sweeping generaliza-

tion, also related to the hasty generalization. Such unjustified concepts as those symbolized by the words *always, never, all, none,* and such superlatives as *the best* or *greatest* or *the worst I've ever seen,* and *everybody knows* frequently introduce these generalizations. The fallacy of such statements as those introduced by the words *always* or *none* can be indicated by pointing out the exceptions which make them false. Such fallacies are especially dangerous, often leading to fractured human relationships, prejudice, and continuing ignorance. *Examples:* "To move three times is as bad as having a burn out." (Actually, the moving of a family may result in improvement of opportunities.) "Teague O'Reagan and Paddy Flannagan, Irish immigrants, are fast-talking, unscrupulous opportunists. They may have kissed the Blarney stone, but they're dishonest and undependable fellows who wouldn't hesitate to make off with your daughters and then leave them in the lurch. Irishmen are all alike." (Two examples, even if they are accurately represented, do not make up the characteristics of all people of any nation.)

2. *The generalized prediction (extrapolation).* One extrapolates when he makes predictions on the basis of variables within the known range, thus inferring the unknown. Although extrapolations may be done with some accuracy statistically, assuming that a sufficient number of the variables within the known range are solid enough—as in samplings for political opinion polls, or actuarial calculations of premium-risk ratios for life insurance companies—they lose accuracy rapidly when the variables increase or lack solidity.

Example: "Nifty Sal has closed first in her last four races, so she's going to win the Goldenrod Stakes at Churchill Downs." (It is true that Nifty Sal has won her last four races, but the purses were all $3000 or under, and she has never faced the competition she must meet in the Goldenrod Stakes where the purse may be as high as $50,000 to $60,000. Another of many variables omitted in the generalized prediction is that the race is seven furlongs, two furlongs longer than any in which she has competed; and she tends to "wind" quickly after five furlongs.

3. *The argument against the man (Ad hominem).* The proponents of this fallacy evade the issue by abusing the person both directly and indirectly.

Example: "Hemingway could not have been very intelligent or much of a writer because he had four wives." (The question of the quality of Hemingway's writing is evaded by a personal attack, specifically on the man's marital problems.) When the attack is directed to the person himself, as if to say, "Consider the source" (*tu quoque*), the issue is also evaded illogically, as in the question, "*You* a doctor, and advocating socialized medicine?" Again, if a young husband criticizes his wife for wearing miniskirts, and she replies, "Look at who's talking, old piano legs in his surfing trunks!" she evades the issue. Direct, mutual fault-finding, frequent among people everywhere, usually solves little and leads to spiraling irrelevancies.

4. *The cause-effect fallacy (Post hoc ergo propter hoc).* A noted

dean of women once gave a university president's wife a peck of mushrooms she had picked for a special dinner for notable guests. Being somewhat dubious about the dean's ability to distinguish mushrooms from poisonous toadstools, the president's wife had her cook, Rachel, feed some of them to her aging dog, Byron, early the day of the dinner. By afternoon, Byron seemed as peppy as ever, so she assumed the mushrooms were mushrooms after all and ordered them prepared for dinner. During the dinner, Rachel entered and told the president's wife, "Old Byron is dead," and went back to the kitchen. Recovering momentarily from horror, the president's wife informed the group of her fears. University officials moved quickly, physicians came to the presidential mansion with stomach pumps, necessary functions were performed. After the last guest had shakily departed and the president's wife could manage it, she went into the kitchen to mourn the remains of the dog. "Rachel, where is . . . poor old Byron?" Rachel paused with moist and shining eyes. "Why, he's outside, M'am, on the sidewalk. And the driver that hit him didn't even stop!" (This kind of fallacy involves an erroneous assumption of a causal connection simply because one situation follows another situation. Many superstitions are based on the cause-effect fallacy, such as "Crossing the path of a black cat brings bad luck." Similarly, people will often make such fallacious statements as, "There was a hundred percent chance of rain today, but just because I carried my umbrella, it didn't rain.")

5. *The false analogy.* The analogy is frequently a treacherous basis of reasoning since few objects or ideas which are *different* are even basically *alike* except in the most obvious ways and to the most shallow of minds.

Example: "Don't walk on the grass. How would you like to be walked on?" (a crude but revealing example). "A governor of a state should be a good businessman because running a government is like running a business." (Running a government and running a corporation really do not have much in common, except for obvious ancillary skills. To illustrate, the primary motivations respectively of government and business are service and profit; often these motivations are mutually exclusive of each other.) Good and poor analogies are treated in more detail in the next chapter.

6. *Appeal to authority* (*Ad verecundiam*). Employment of this fallacy requires that such devices as the names of great or influential people, impressive quotations of personages, and weighty statistics be linked to the points at issue, often when the linkage has little if any relevance to the issue. Advertisers rely upon this fallacy, attracting people to their clients' products by linking such irrelevant items as "beverage-distinction," "car-sexy girl," "cosmetics-romance," "soda-pop-youth," "cereal-younger generation," "fuel-tiger," "cigarette-nature," "deodorant-marriage," "patent medications-financial raises." Closely related to abuse of logic is the "He himself says so" (*ipse dixit*) fallacy, which is based on traditional views engendered through long periods of time and thus treasured by people. For example, "Benjamin Franklin said, 'A small leak will sink a great ship,' so don't let the smallest

mistake get by you, or we'll be ruined." (Obviously Benjamin Franklin was generally a reliable person and, in many areas of knowledge, an expert of his age, but he is sometimes quoted out of context or for purposes which may not be related to the issue. If the statement above were made by a landowner to a farm worker who was preparing to shuck corn, it would not make much sense because obviously some ears would be missed in any case. If a banker made the statement to a new teller, it would have more relevance, but tellers often make mistakes and banks are not ruined as a result. If a demolition expert made the statement to an apprentice about to defuse a "block-buster," it would be more obviously relevant.)

7. *Appeal to the public* (*Ad populum*). Those who use this fallacy link whatever issue is involved to unrelated "emotion-rousers" to gain support. The aim is invariably to arouse popular passions for personal interests; it is the bandwagon technique, unfortunately and all too often producing results which involve destructive or wasteful action without much thought. Those who cannot address themselves to standards of quality often point to big numbers, overwhelming size, and growth instead, thus appealing to the most superficial of public responses in efforts to justify actions or, let us say, an educational program on the primary basis of quantity.

A classic example in English literature of appeal to the public is Mark Antony's speech to the Roman citizens over the slain body of Julius Caesar (Act III, Sc. ii), beginning,

> *Friends, Romans, countrymen, lend me your ears;*
> *I come to bury Caesar, not to praise him. . . .*

and proceeding to play upon the heartstrings of the populace. Antony comes "to bury Caesar, not to praise him" (appeal to common decency, expected ritual, the impressive antithesis which dramatically balances "bury" against the opposite "praise" for emotional effect); Antony says, "The evil that men do lives after them;/ The good is often interred with their bones" (The aphorism was commonly known and, identified with Caesar, the mass appeal to forget his faults and remember his goodness is pronounced with memorable irony.). Antony continues to move the masses with statements of Caesar's friendship, faithfulness, sense of justice, generosity, self-sacrifice, humility:

> *I thrice presented him a kingly crown,*
> *Which he did thrice refuse: was this ambition?*
> *Yet Brutus says he was ambitious;*
> *And, sure, he is an honorable man.*

By his use of the phrase "honorable man," Antony is, of course, being intensely ironic and satiric (*antiphrasis*). He means just the opposite. The subtle, yet forceful, repetition wins over his audience by a gradual revelation of the truth to them through the popular device of wearing the heart up the sleeve, so to speak, rather than on it. Antony goes on to

add the quality of love and to cry out with an emotion that is shared by
the citizenry:

> . . . *Bear with me;*
> *My heart is in the coffin there with Caesar,*
> *And I must pause till it come back to me.*

As the citizens are moved to the "great wrong" done Caesar, Antony
raises their very self-images by stating,

> *But yesterday the word of Caesar might*
> *Have stood against the world: now lies he there,*
> *And none so poor to do him reverence. . . .*

contending in the final line above that Caesar was such a simple man of
the people that the lowest, humblest citizen would find the great man
somehow more humble than he—that is, noble Caesar was (again,
ironically) beneath their regard, indeed *too low for their reverence.*
Such a statement would tend to create added depths of generosity in the
listeners, and to move them indeed to sympathy for the "underdog."
Antony goes on to assert his intentions while pretending to deny them
(*apophasis*), moving the emotions and imaginations, while simultaneously exalting his audience's self-conception:

> *O masters, if I were disposed to stir*
> *Your hearts and minds to mutiny and rage,*
> *I should do Brutus wrong, and Cassius wrong,*
> *Who, you all know, are honorable men:*
> *I will not do them wrong; I rather choose*
> *To wrong the dead, to wrong myself and you,*
> *Than I will wrong such honorable men.*

Within these last words, of course, the popular opinion becomes identified with Caesar and Mark Antony himself, and the thin, entering
wedge splits the conspirators (Brutus, Cassius, and the other killers of
Caesar) from the sympathy of the masses. Antony now sees that he has
the people completely with him, and proceeds to drive his points home
with a variety of *ad populum* devices: first, the scrolled will of Caesar
itself; then the view of Caesar's bloody body around which Antony has
arranged the citizens; and ultimately the *apostrophe*, often used in
patriotic oratory, invoking aid beyond the present tangibles from transcendental and god-like power:

> *Judge, O you gods, how dearly Caesar loved him!*

At the very point that Antony has turned the citizenry into a mob, he
restrains them and appeals to them through the very self-abnegation
that fills them further with their own sense of power and superiority:

I come not, friends, to steal away your hearts:
I am no orator, as Brutus is;
But, as you know me all, a plain blunt man,
That love my friend; and that they know full well
That gave me public leave to speak of him:
For I have neither wit, nor words, nor worth,
Action, nor utterance, nor the power of speech,
To stir men's blood: I only speak right on;
I tell you that which you yourselves do know;
Show you sweet Caesar's wounds, poor poor dumb mouths,
And bid them speak for me: but were I Brutus,
And Brutus Antony, there were an Antony
Would ruffle up your spirits and put a tongue
In every wound of Caesar that should move
The stones of Rome to rise and mutiny.

The roundabout and indirect method of the last five lines above is a skillfully handled device (*periphrasis*) for informing the masses that Brutus would hold himself above them; that he, as leader of the conspirators, is the one deserving of whatever hostility they may feel. In effect, he concludes with a metaphor that says, when stated directly, "In consideration of Brutus and the crime of his co-conspirators in taking great Caesar's life, one would have to be veritable 'stone' not to be moved 'to rise and mutiny.'"

Yet, in this incomparable oration, Antony does not conclude until he drives home the concrete illustrations of Caesar's will. Antony states that Caesar leaves seventy-five drachmas to each Roman citizen, and his walks, arbors, and orchards on the side of the Tiber River nearest the Roman Forum and Capitol as public parks. The *ad rem* "vested interest" is the capstone of Mark Antony's funeral oration, a triumph in the art of *ad populum* appeal; for Mark Antony knows that as close to their hearts as the fickle memories of Caesar may be at the moment, money in the pocket is closer still. Within the *ad populum* scope of appeal, of course, is the *ad hominem* argument against Brutus and the other conspirators, who serve as a purposeful source for the hostilities radiating from the white-hot passions to which Mark Antony has adroitly inflamed the mob.

8. *Begging the question* or *arguing in a circle* (circulus in probando —sometimes known as "restating the premise"). Such a fallacy assumes what it states. For example, "Joan is a happy girl because she is always full of fun," or "John is a poor student because he makes low grades." The effect of *begging the question* often appears to be simply a statement of illusory value, which adds little if any information and wastes time in speech, space in writing. The machine-age aphorism "Engage mind before throwing mouth into gear" seems to be an excellent motto for those who tend to beg the question.

9. *Overidentity* or *the fallacy of false identity*. One would do well to remember that the *"is of identity"* itself, stated in words, becomes merely a *representation* of reality. When one commits the fallacy of

overidentity or false identity, he confuses different things for the same thing. The abstract example "A is A" possesses, as an underlying basis, the assumption of the similarity of individual characteristics—such as physical association, kinship, and verbal association. By the same illogical reasoning, innocence as well as guilt may be identified by association.

Example: "Martin Luther King was a Communist because he was always stirring things up and causing riots." (Martin Luther King, who was a Nobel laureate of peace, represented minority and poverty groups. His eloquent arguments transcended the narrow confines of racial boundaries. He was a highly educated Baptist minister who believed in the "egalitarian dream" of man, much as it is stated in the Declaration of Independence and guaranteed in the Constitution of the United States. Aside from the *ad hominem* and *ad populum* undercurrents of the statement above, it is obviously a false identity of "Communist," disorder and "riots," on the one hand, with the *esse* of Martin Luther King, on the other. This procedure is an oversimplification of issues; it stems, perhaps, from grasping too quickly at the straws of causation. Consequently, one evades the need to face up to the real issues of difference which he may have had with the views espoused by Martin Luther King.)

10. *The excluded middle fallacy.* This fallacy involves the assumption that a thing is either "A or not A." Thus, a thing is either true or false, right or wrong, practical or foolish. Such a fallacy is extremely dangerous because it oversimplifies thinking, sometimes into absurdly inaccurate extremes. Its implications have been treated in greater detail in Chapter 3.

    Example: "Is Dustin very bright?"
        "I don't know."
        "Well, he's either bright or he isn't."
(Actually, a huge middle range of possibilities is excluded in this kind of conversation. Dustin may be bright in some ways and, to varying degrees, more or less bright in others. He may be good in mathematics but poor in history, or bright in art but average in French. Sometimes aspects of the truth may appear to involve extremes, but the center of gravity of "the whole truth," were it subject to the measurement of weight, would most often be found somewhere between the extremes.)

QUESTIONS ON READINGS

SCIENCE AND THE HUMANITIES IN CONFLICT

In the essay "On Education," Einstein deals with the abstraction of *education* as "means" and "methods," thus making what tends to be abstract more concrete (p. 173). Discuss his treatment of education as "means" and as "methods." Specifically, how does he make the abstract more concrete?

LANGUAGE AND REALITY

Think about the well-known expression, "Carry a message to Garcia," and its various forms, such as, "He really carried the message to Garcia, didn't he?" Think of all the meanings (contexts) possible for this old saying, then read the precise context of the quotation from Elbert Hubbard's essay, treated in Magill's *Quotations in Context* (p. 181). Does the example illustrate how words about words (*self-reflexiveness*) and the accompanying movement away from precise use of even famous old sayings can break down communication? Discuss.

WAR AND DEHUMANIZATION

Examine again in this chapter the chart, "Concreteness and Abstraction: The Cycle of Relativity" (p. 82). In place of Blue-boar, the pig, consider instead the "I" (or *persona*) of T. S. Eliot's poem, "The Love Song of J. Alfred Prufrock" (p. 346). Noting that there are ten approaches to the time-space event of Blue-boar indicated by the chart, including the pig itself as life force, develop a similar illustration demonstrating various views of Eliot's poem—especially the "I" of the poem.

Among possible approaches which could be developed are (1) the "I" literally as the poet, T. S. Eliot himself (although Eliot first wrote the poem in 1910 when he was twenty-two years old, hardly the age of Prufrock); (2) the "I" in a general relationship to the "you," representing the poet and the reader respectively; (3) "you and I" as woman and her lover (After all, "Love Song" is part of the title.); (4) the "you and I" as two modern twentieth-century men in a dialogue; (5) a lonely "I" talking to himself (hence, "you"); (6) the inner self ("you") juxtaposed with the outer self ("I"); (7) the "you" as an individual's real but submerged nature in the modern world and the "I" who wears a mask, so to speak, with which he faces the society of which he is a part; (8) psychologically, the "you" as the *id* (source of the libido and instinctive energy dominated by the pleasure principle) and the "I" as *ego* (conscious controller of the id and its pleasure-energized impulses); (9) the natural "I" accompanied by a Romantic "you," both struggling against a modern world which tends to dehumanize people—or an undiscovered "I" seeking its identity with a "soul-mate" ("you") in the form of heroic tradition (e.g., St. John, Hamlet, Ulysses) representative of exaltation of the individual, but discovering only a mechanized world in which man and nature alike have been thwarted by artificial and unnatural forces, leaving the individual to be drowned in a sea of anonymity; and (10) the "you and I" not as human beings at all, but rather as Dantesque spirits (Note the epigraph) moving into an earthly Hell of modern man's own making.

Give examples of how Eliot makes any one of these or selected approaches to "The Love Song of J. Alfred Prufrock" *concrete*. Discuss. Is Eliot at times purposely *abstract*? If so, why? Discuss also the relativity of the poem as a whole to selected ones of the ten possible views of "you and I" presented above. Is any one view the most concrete, the most abstract, the most *relative*—hence, the most accurate? Discuss. Referring closely to the analysis of the chart in Chapter 5 (p. 82), as well as to the poem itself, evolve the relationships carefully. Such a procedure will help you to keep remarks and discussion as close as possible to *subverbal levels* of reality.

Can you find elements of accuracy in all ten approaches to the "you and I" of the poem offered above? Discuss. More elements of accuracy in some approaches may prevail than in others. Discuss. Do such approaches lead naturally to various interpretations of the poem about which you may not have otherwise thought? Discuss. Is it possible that the poem may have many levels of meaning, all of them relevant to some extent, and, hence, to some extent accurate? By using *multiordinality* in analyzing Eliot's work, is it possible to understand and enjoy the poem more fully? Does increasing one's understanding of the poem decrease one's appreciation of it? Increase it? Discuss.

THE CAMPUS TODAY: REBELLION AND CONFORMITY

Although you may have read the material in relation to the question in Chapter 4, examine again the entire section which concerns itself with *Tomorrow's People* beginning on page 265. Referring to the chart, "Concreteness and Abstraction: The Cycle of Relativity" (p. 82), its analysis, and especially "An application of multiordinality" (p. 83), draft another list of possible approaches to the time-space event of the publication of the controversial student magazine. Distinguish between *unilateral* and *multiordinal* approaches. How does an awareness of many views of the magazine help us to conceive more accurately than may occur otherwise, a better balanced sense of reality concerning the publication and all its parts? With such an awareness of the publication of the magazine and the circumstances surrounding it, could improved communication between various contending individuals and groups be developed? Between the students and the college? The students, college, and community? The magazine sponsors and the college administration? The magazine sponsors and allegedly threatening persons in the community? After attempting to understand the relativity of various points of view, discuss the elements of accuracy of the views as you see them. Are some more accurate than others when balanced against the wholistic concept of *multiordinal* approaches? Is any particular view most or least accurate? Support your views by a careful application of *concrete* and *abstract* points, but do not forget to include *relativity* in expressing your views.

THE SEARCH FOR IDENTITY

Read over Russell Baker's "Identity Crisis (Thing That Counts: Knowing Who You Aren't)" (p. 300). After doing so, apply *concrete* terms to counter the following *generalizations:*

1. "The psychiatric fad these days is 'identity.' "
2. Some people enjoy "slashing other persons' egos" by telling them, "The trouble with you is that you don't know who you really are."
3. People solve an "identity crisis" by *discovering* "who they really are."
4. Making allowances for Baker's humorous tone, is there nevertheless some truth in his contention that "sudden" self-discovery would "depress most people"? Answer with specific examples or anecdotes.
5. Is it normal for most people to live with "illusions"? Specifically, how may doing so result in happiness? Unhappiness? Destruction and tragedy?
6. Baker notes, "Happy progress through life requires a gradual shucking off of . . . identity illusions." Being as concrete as possible, indicate just how one may achieve this kind of progress.
7. Is it true that adolescents evince a confusion of identities? Give examples from recollections of your own adolescence or childhood.
8. How closely should one "identify with" his heroes—for example, Lincoln, Einstein, Eisenhower, Hemingway, John F. Kennedy, Martin Luther King, your own hero of the 1970's? Concretely treat advantages, disadvantages. If possible, give specific illustrations of your views.

On a more serious side of the matter than Baker's article would indicate, Stanley H. King, in his article "Emotional Problems of College Students: Facts and Priorities," published in the *AAUP Bulletin,* vol. 50 (December 1964), pp. 327–332, addresses himself to a deep concern with psychological conditions occurring more frequently among college students than among those in other periods of life. Specific conditions include "apathy," "acute confusional and agitated states," "the prolongation of the dependence of adolescence into adulthood," and "the now familiar syndrome known as the 'identity crisis.'" King further notes that indications of the identity crisis include "unconscious rebellion, vacillation, indecision, psychosis," and that the identity crisis may result in college dropouts—the rate of which varies from a low of about 15 percent in some colleges to a high of 50 percent in others. Do students within your acquaintance ever evince any of these syndromes, indicating an approaching identity crisis? How would you recognize such traits, aside from those involving clearly aberrant behavior? Be as specific as possible.

From the comments and illustrations given in Baker's article, and observations of King's reported findings, could you compose a definition of "identity crisis"? Compare your own effort with those of other students. Then consider such patterns of crisis in biographical treatments of famous people as you may find them available. For example, you could select crucial periods in the lives of Martin Luther, King Henry V of England, Abraham Lincoln, Karl Marx, Charles Darwin, Sigmund Freud, Albert Schweitzer, George Bernard Shaw, Thomas Wolfe, William Faulkner, and Dwight Eisenhower. Can you think of others? Be as specific as possible in defining the "identity crisis."

LOVE, SEX, AND CENSORSHIP

In Chapter 5, review the final section, "Some common problems in logic" (p. 83). Of the ten fallacies treated, how many can you apply to Plato's statement dealing with censorship from *The Republic* (p. 318)? In particular consider the following ideas:
1. Establishing a censorship of the writers.
2. The censors' receiving any tale of fiction which is good and rejecting the bad.
3. Letting mothers and nurses tell their children authorized stories only.
4. Most tales now in use must be discarded.
5. Expulsion of artists who fail "to express the image of the good in their works."
6. The prohibition of "forms of vice and intemperance and meanness and indecency in sculpture," the prohibition of artists who do not conform, "lest the taste of our citizens be corrupted."
7. Allowing people to grow up "amid images of moral deformity."
8. Insisting that only artists "gifted to discern the true nature of the beautiful and graceful" be permitted to practice their art.
9. With such ideas of art, and laws to enforce them, the youth will "dwell in a land of health," and "receive the good in everything; and beauty."

10. The purpose of art is to "draw the soul from earliest years into likeness and sympathy with the beauty of reason."

Now, in contrast with Plato's stated concept of art, read closely the excerpt from Stephen Crane's once-controversial novel, *Maggie: A Girl of the Streets* (p. 314). Is there any logic in the old aphorism that the ugly truth is better for a young person than the pretty lie? Discuss. In principle, do you think Plato would have allowed Crane to produce such fiction in his ideal Republic? Why or why not?

Contrast Henry James' statements from "The Art of Fiction" with those of Plato's views of art:

1. Fiction "must take itself seriously for the public to take it so" (p. 319).
2. " 'Art,' in our Protestant communities, where so many things have got so strangely twisted about, is supposed in certain circles to have some vaguely injurious effect upon those who make it an important consideration, who let it weigh in the balance" (p. 321).
3. "A novel is in its broadest definition a personal, a direct impression of life: that, to begin with, constitutes its value, which is greater or less according to the intensity of the impression" (p. 322).
4. "We must grant the artist his subject, his idea, his *donnée;* our criticism is applied only to what he makes of it" (p. 323).
5. "I have no right to tamper with your flute and then criticize your music" (p. 324).
6. "One perceives . . . that the province of art is all life, all feeling, all observation, all vision. . . . it is all experience" (p. 325).
7. "The moral consciousness of a child is as much a part of life as the islands of the Spanish Main . . ." (p. 325).
8. "Will you not define your terms and explain how (a novel being a picture) a picture can be either moral or immoral? You wish to paint a moral picture or carve a moral statue: will you not tell us how you would set about it" (p. 326)? ". . . the deepest quality of a work of art will always be the quality of the mind of the producer . . ." (p. 326).
9. "No good novel will ever proceed from a superficial mind . . ." (p. 326).
10. James' final statement of advice for the writer was this: "Remember that your first duty is to be as complete as possible— to make as perfect a work. Be generous and delicate, and then, in the vulgar phrase, go in" (p. 327).

INDIVIDUAL RESPONSIBILITY

In our time much is made of the concept of "civil disobedience," or passive resistance. Read carefully the excerpts from Henry David Thoreau's essay "Civil Disobedience," and relate the following to the common fallacies indicated:

1. "That government is best which governs least . . . . That government is best which governs not at all" (p. 338). (the broad generalization, *secundum quid*)
2. "Others—as most legislators, politicians, lawyers, ministers, and office-holders—serve the state chiefly with their heads; and, as they rarely make any moral distinctions, they are as likely to serve the devil, without *intending* it, as God" (p. 338). (the *excluded middle fallacy*)
3. "All men recognize the right of revolution . . . when its tyranny or its inefficiency are great and unendurable" (p. 338). (the *broad generalization; overidentity* or *false identity*)
4. "I should like to have them order me . . . to march to Mexico; —see if I would go," and yet these very men have each, directly by their allegiance, and so indirectly, at least, by their money [taxes], furnished a substitute" (p. 339). (the *cause-effect fallacy, post hoc ergo propter hoc;* i.e., Thoreau equates conscientious objection with "allegiance," and taxes with the furnishing of a substitute soldier for the Mexican War; of course, he equates the Mexican War with the extension of slaveocracy only.)
5. "Action from principle, the perception and the performance of right, changes things and relations; it is essentially revolutionary . . . . It not only divides States and churches, it divides families; ay, it divides the *individual,* separating the diabolical in him from the divine" (p. 340). (*the broad generalization; the excluded middle fallacy*)
6. "Why does [government] not cherish its wise minority? Why does it cry and resist before it is hurt? Why does it not encourage its citizens to be on the alert to point out its faults, and *do* better than it would have them? Why does it always crucify Christ, and excommunicate Copernicus and Luther, and pronounce Washington and Franklin rebels" (p. 340)? (the *broad generalization; appeal to authority, ad verecundiam*)
7. Notice how carefully Thoreau avoids the *broad generalization* throughout the paragraph beginning, "If the injustice is part of the necessary friction of the machine of government, let it go: perchance it will wear smooth . . ." (p. 340). However, when he gets to the word "injustice" in the same paragraph, and adjures the reader to "break the law. Let your life be a counter friction to stop the machine," does he engage in the fallacy of *overidentity*? Discuss. In the concluding sentence of the paragraph, however, he warns such a person: "What I

have to do is to see, at any rate, that I do not lend myself to the wrong which I condemn" (p. 340). What does Thoreau mean here? Can you relate revolutionary action to the activist's lending himself "to the wrong which [he] condemn[s]"? Discuss. What is Thoreau's implication concerning such a person's "civil disobedience" becoming a clear example of *begging the question (arguing in a circle, circulus in probando)*? Of the responsibility of "break[ing] the law," which a pacific resister must accept as Thoreau accepted his jailing? Discuss.

8. In the paragraph beginning, "I do not hesitate to say, that those who call themselves Abolitionists should at once effectually withdraw their support . . ." (p. 341), does Thoreau employ any fallacies? Especially consider the *appeal to the public (ad populum)*. Similarly toward the close of the next paragraph, in which he uses the expression "honest men," then "honest man" (p. 341). Discuss.

9. Relate *false analogy* to Thoreau's figure beginning, "But even suppose blood should flow. Is there not a sort of blood shed when the conscience is wounded" (p. 342)?

10. Compare the quality of the analogy beginning, "It was like traveling into a far country . . ." (p. 344). Analyze closely. Is this a comparatively better analogy than the preceding one? Discuss the reasons for your opinion as concretely as possible.

GOD, MAN, AND MORAL CONSCIOUSNESS

Read and reflect upon Robert Frost's poem "Stopping by Woods on a Snowy Evening" (p. 362). On the surface, the poem seems to be about nature. Specifically, the person in the poem (*persona*)—not necessarily the poet himself—thinks he knows who owns the woods. It is a man who lives in the village. So, he thinks, the owner will not see him stopping to "watch his woods fill up with snow." The *persona* muses about his horse's reaction in stopping there in the cold winter night and assumes, when the horse shakes his harness bells, that the animal must think it strange not to be moving along, as usual, toward whatever destination the *persona* has. But the *persona* remains in the snowy night, listening to the wind, watching the downy flakes of snow move easily in it. Then he comments directly on the beauty of the woods, giving specific details, but remembers that he has a long way to go before he sleeps. He repeats the idea.

Recalling how people tend to be *self-reflexive* in responding to reality, what else beyond nature may readers see in Frost's poem? In your discussion consider these possible themes:

1. Man as a creature of nature, yet isolated from it.
2. Man as a creature with obligations beyond what he may wish to do—with duties.
3. Man as a moral creature who must forego his natural and

pleasurable desires to achieve what he deems to be higher purposes in life.

4. Man as a natural creature in conflict with his artificial role in an industrialized society.

5. A parable of the life and death of man.

Now read Dr. Tom Dooley's letter from the book *Promises to Keep* (p. 363). Notice the parallels between the letter and Frost's poem—specifically the title. Also observe the parallels of nature: the late night, the miles of distance from home, the wind, and the obviously more violent aspects of nature (the monsoons and floods of northern Laos). Considering the title of *Promises to Keep,* how do you think the author of the book interpreted Frost's poem, especially in terms of human obligations, duties, and responsibilities? Whereas Frost's poem may be looked upon as both specific and universal, the letter of Tom Dooley is directly to the point, is it not? Or is it? Discuss. How close to *subverbal* levels is Tom Dooley's language? Give examples. Is Dooley's presentation *multiordinal*? Logical? Giving specific illustrations, is the letter free from logical fallacies? Discuss. Finally, what aspects of logic can you apply to Tom Dooley's arguments urging the young doctor to come to Laos? Be specific.

LITERATURE AND GOOD WRITING

Professor Kelly Thurman's article "Teaching Literature by a Synaptic Method" might well be called "The Confessions of a Teacher of Literature" in that he points out the weaknesses of what he terms *"synoptic"* ways of teaching, and the strengths of the more advanced learning of a *"synaptic"* process of learning—a full, richer, more meaningful and enduring experience for students.

In examining the ten common fallacies in your text, apply as many as possible to Professor Thurman's article, noting in particular the positive relationships between logic and statements in the article. For example, how does Thurman avoid abstractions in stating the "nature of literature" in the first paragraph, and thus avoid the *broad generalization*? In the second paragraph, he lists four specific kinds of students of literature and implies several other kinds. Why is he so specific? Notice in the following two paragraphs he discusses numerous methods of learning literature and proceeds to give a thorough description of *"synoptic results"* (p. 404).

He contends, however, that even old approaches to learning about literature can be made "freshly and imaginatively and creatively" through "the *synaptic* approach" (p. 405). How does he then make the term "*synaptic* approach" *concrete* rather than *abstract*? Discuss. Notice how Thurman avoids stating the "synaptic method" as one particular thing. How does he deal with the term *concretely,* and at the same time avoid the *fallacy of false identity* or the *"is of identity"*? Discuss.

Thurman states that "few teachers would quarrel with the worth" of *synoptic* "enterprises" (i.e., many of the established ways of teaching and learning literature), but goes on to say, "I do question the methodology employed" (p. 405). In stating the matters which concern him in such a way, how does he thereby avoid the *excluded middle fallacy?* Discuss. Note especially how the author uses analogies in treating his example of *Romeo and Juliet.* Holding himself guilty of lecturing with *synoptic* methods, he writes, ". . . to my chagrin, I discover that the 'inoculation' lasts only through the final examination" (p. 405). In relation to a *synaptic* approach, on the other hand, he emphasizes creative and highly meaningful learning in linking it to an age-old event, common to most people: "To every man falling in love is original, creative, committing, containing. Likewise are one's responses to works of art . . ." (p. 405). Within the context are these analogies *logical?* Discuss. How does Thurman avoid *broad generalizations* by suggesting characterization and language as two approaches to learning literature which will help the student past "the pre-packing stage" (p. 406), help him to think and express himself in more imaginative, creative, and memorable ways—in short, help him to participate in the *synaptic* experience of learning literature and to enjoy "journeys on the road to fuller self-containment"? Referring to the article, discuss.

AGE OF CONTROVERSY

Traditional fallacies still prevail in modern society. Read the selected portions of Remy de Gourmont's essay "The Disassociation of Ideas" (p. 432). Applying examples from "Some common problems in logic" in your text, examine the author's emphasis on "disassociation" of commonly jointed ideas. You might begin with *overidentity* (the *fallacy of false identity* or the *"is of identity"*), treat the *excluded middle fallacy,* and then work back to the more subtle implications of such fallacies as *appeal to the public, cause-effect,* and the *generalized prediction.* Among your observations of the author's work, relate the tendency of the creative intelligence to associate ideas, then to relate them habitually until they become "so durable that they seem everlasting" (p. 432). In the applications of logic to the article, discuss Gourmont's concepts of "commonplaces" or "*clichés*" (p. 432) and his questions concerning the military idea (p. 435), liberty-nature-man-privilege (p. 437); art-beauty (p. 437); beauty-sexual illusion-carnal pleasure (p. 438); beauty-femininity-art (p. 438); art-ideas-self-realization (p. 438); woman-feminine education (p. 439); and the numerous false associations listed and commented on in the last three paragraphs of the essay (p. 439). Treat also the *logic* of Gourmont's concept of what may be termed the nature of and necessity for "disassociation" (e.g., see p. 433).
Read Ben Jonson's brief poem "It Is Not Growing like a Tree" (p. 432). Applying what you have learned from Gourmont's essay in relation to the common fallacies treated in Chapter 5, comment meaningfully upon the aspects of this work.

6

VERBAL CONFUSIONS: THE USE AND ABUSE OF LANGUAGE

CONFUSION OF WORDS WITH OBJECTS

There is the story of the woman at a party in Philadelphia who was introduced to another guest, a Dr. Longabaugh. The woman maneuvered Dr. Longabaugh into a corner and, pursuing her advantage, began to relate to him her life history of physical problems, in some instances going into graphic details concerning a periodically low blood count, labor pains, the possible deleterious effects of birth control pills, and other such intimate matters. As many doctors will on such occasions, Dr. Longabaugh nodded understandingly and intoned a professional "Hmmmm," actions which the woman took to be sure signs of his astuteness and interest. She was encouraged to continue, and was working her way back through her childhood diseases and some traumatic sexual experiences in Peoria, Illinois, where she had grown up, when Dr. Longabaugh interrupted her: "Peoria!" he exclaimed with a broad grin—"That's where I had my first congregation!"

For the woman, *doctor* was equated with *medical doctor*, a confusion of the word with the reality, the symbol with the referent. This most obvious kind of verbal confusion was treated in some detail in Chapter 2: the incident of Barbara's confusion of the verb form *catting*; how a child may confuse a German shepherd dog with a "pussy-cat"; or how a grown woman looking for a bargain at a shoe sale may mistake a specified shoe size for an actual fit. We have seen also how a great artist like Shakespeare chooses the right word and arrangements of words, as in Hamlet's farewell speech to Horatio, and, in effect, forces the reader to perceive the experience sensuously, emotionally, and imaginatively.

The confusion of words with objects, ideas with expressions, and thoughts with composition all seem to derive from certain basic problems which may be summarized as follows:

1. *Overidentity*—the overapplication of Aristotle's law of identity (see Chapter 3).
2. *Private meanings of words*—an "intensional response," usually remote from reality, frequently unilateral or two-valued in application; in relation to the latter condition, Aristotle's law of the excluded middle and law of contradiction may be involved in producing the limited thought responses of private meanings (see Chapter 2).
3. *Unrecognized generalization*—failure to think, "glossing" habits of thought, imprisonment by jargons, failure to handle the generalization effectively (for example, by indexing and dating), often resulting in verbal haziness and virtual meaninglessness as higher levels of communication are sought (see Chapter 4).
4. *Self-reflexiveness of language*—the failure to be aware of the tendency of words to become increasingly abstract, or an inability to be aware of the level of reference or the specific context, which itself may simply be one of many such levels of context, even in relationship to what may appear to be a simple referent (Blue-boar, the pig) or ideas (appreciation of a folk-rock guitarist).
5. *Lack of multiordinality*—to this extent the modern concept of language known as *non-allness* (see Chapter 3) may be ignored, or the application of a many-valued orientation toward symbols (words) may be overlooked (see item 4 above).

AMBIGUITIES

Closely related to the confusion of words with objects are ambiguities —words, remarks, expressions which may have two or more possible meanings. Often they are uncertain and vague, even within the context of familiar conversations. At one extreme is the kind of ambiguity known as a *double entendre;* at the other is the word, phrase, or statement which is so vague as to be nearly meaningless. The double entendre often connotes a risqué or indecorous mistake in word choice, as, for example, the college student who wrote of Hemingway's hero and heroine in *A Farewell to Arms,* "The lieutenant loved her so much he could not leave her behind[,] alone in Milano." Unfortunately, the student left out the comma.

Among other causes of ambiguities are (1) vague pronoun references, (2) unclear or misplaced modifiers, (3) overzealous compression of statements, (4) faulty poetical inversions and other figurative expressions, and (5) incomplete comparisons.

The vague pronoun reference either altogether lacks an antecedent for the pronoun, or else the antecedent appears to possess two or more meanings instead of the desired single, clear meaning:

1. *Error:* "*They* produce good roads in New York." (To whom does the vague pronoun "they" refer—the people of New York? those who work on the roads? the road engineers? the state highway

commissioner and his staff? the members of the state legislature?)

Sample correction: "The state highway commissioner and his staff produce good roads in New York."

2. *Error:* "The sophomore talked a lot about the technical aspects of planning a series of downs, kicking, passing, and running; but the fact remains that he could not do *it*." (Could not do what—talk about these things? plan a series of downs? kick? pass? run? perform the technical aspects? or do all of these things?)

    Sample correction: "The sophomore talked a lot about the technical aspects of planning a series of downs, the logic of kicking, passing, and running, but the fact remains that he lacked the size, speed, and skill to become a good quarterback."

3. *Error:* "When Brutus rose to address Caesar in the Senate-House, *he* did not know that *he* would be murdered within the minute." (*He* grammatically, if not historically, could refer either to Brutus or to Caesar.)

    Sample correction: "When Brutus rose to address the Senate-House, Caesar did not realize that he would be murdered within the minute by Brutus and the other conspirators."

Unclear or misplaced modifiers vary from the most obvious kinds of dangling elements and unrelated phrases to the more subtle misplacing of single words such as *only*, perhaps the worst offender:

1. *Error:* "*After swimming the Hellespont,* anyone could see that Byron was a brave man." (Did *anyone* swim the Hellespont? Does *anyone* need to swim the Hellespont in order to see that Byron was a brave man?)

    Sample correction: "In swimming the Hellespont, Byron demonstrated his bravery to everyone." (The phrase now clearly modifies Byron.)

2. *Error:* "*After baking in the oven at 325 degrees for two hours,* my aunt made quite an impression on her guests with a most unusual dessert." (*What* or *who* baked for two hours?)

    Sample correction: "My aunt's unusual dessert, after baking in the oven at 325 degrees for two hours, made quite an impression on her guests." (The dangling phrase is eliminated.)

3. *Error:* "The flowers on the altar are given in honor of Mrs. Helen F. Pearson *recently hospitalized by the Women's Society of Christian Service*." ("Recently hospitalized" and "by the Woman's Society of Christian Service," are misplaced modifiers.)

    Sample correction: "The flowers on the altar are given by the Women's Society of Christian Service in honor of Mrs. Helen F. Pearson, who recently has been hospitalized."

4. Here are two simple examples of misplaced prepositional phrases:

    Error: "I saw a man going down the street on a horse *with a wooden leg*." (A horse with a wooden leg?)

Error: "Did you see the chick on the beach carrying a radio *with a pink bikini?*" (A radio with a pink bikini?)

5. Consider the placement of the frequent offender *only* as it modifies and alters the meaning of the basic sentence below:

Only ten people showed up for the class picnic. (Only ten and no more.)

Ten people *only* showed up for the class picnic. (They only showed up but did not stay for or participate in the festivities.)

Ten people showed up *only* for the class picnic. (They showed up only for the class picnic, not for the class photograph which was taken later.)

Ten people showed up for the *only* class picnic. (There was never another class picnic.)

Ten people showed up for the class picnic *only*. (They did not show up for any other scheduled event.)

The compression of statements can sometimes be dramatically effective, as it is in Julius Caesar's classic "*Veni, vidi, vinci*" (I came, I saw, I conquered), or the laconicism attributed to General William Tecumseh Sherman, "War is hell." Both are expressive short statements, eloquent in meaning and implication. Compare with these, however, the ambiguous sign recently seen along the New Jersey coast:

Had the figure "$50.00" preceded *FINE*, then there would be no ambiguity, for *FINE* would then clearly refer to a monetary punishment. Without the qualification of the sum, however, *FINE* may denote, especially to one not familiar with American English usage, that this particular beach area is the appropriate place for dumping trash.

Similarly, captions or headlines for newspapers sometimes indicate a sacrifice of clarity to brevity. All these ambiguities, for example, contain names of counties in Kentucky:

Wolfe Man Arrested
Concealed Automatic Found on Hancock Man
Defeat Goes to Laurel Team
Bourbon Schools Ready for Holiday
Snake-handlers Congregate in Pike
Graves Robbers Nabbed

Murder Charge Filed in Bath
Oil Struck in Clay
Divorce in Union
Letcher Man Indicted for Pollution

The following quotation from a freshman paper demonstrates many faults. Aside from those of grammar, construction, and a general lack of originality, an overall ambiguity pervades the excerpt:

> Not just dancing and living it up, knowing the hard life they have lived, my parents sacrificing to get me into college, my obligation to them and myself along with self-respect just to stay there, the hope of making them and the girl back home (and maybe here, too, who knows?) happy, using my talents although I know that "all work and no play makes Jack a dull boy," I've still got to do it —must make a success in college, so much depends on it.

During a conference with his English instructor which followed, the freshman saw that his major problem was, as he put it, "trying to say too much in too little space," or overzealous compression. His revision demonstrates more care in working out precisely what he intended to say, and is written in a much less ambiguous way:

> People have different reasons for getting a college education. In my own opinion, the main reason for going to college is to develop whatever natural talents I may possess. I realize that I must work hard in order to learn as much as I can, but I have the motivation to do so. My mother and father have worked hard to pay my college expenses, and I feel a profound sense of obligation to them. I want them to be proud of me, not ashamed. If a person does not have much respect for himself, then few others will respect him. My own self-respect, then, is another motivation for my succeeding in college.
>
> There are many temptations to take a student away from his work. The old adage, "All work and no play makes Jack a dull boy" is as true as ever; certainly social life—the parties, dances, and friendships—is an important part of a college education. However, for me, at least, academic work must take precedence over "the happy time" and "the golden memories." Thomas Carlyle once advised a student to "do the nearest duty," and "the next will become clearer." If I work hard and learn all that I can in college, maybe the future will take care of itself, whether I share it with the girl back home or that girl I've yet to meet.

Although the revision still lacks originality and has other weaknesses, what was once a jumbled run-on sentence forming a kind of amorphous paragraph now has become two paragraphs, the first with seven sentences and the second with five. The first coherently relates the student's major motivations for procuring a college education, and the second subsumes under his major goal various temptations which tend to lure him away from his studies. The excerpt no longer suffers from

ambiguity caused by the over-compression of ideas into a weak structure which simply will not bear the weight.

Faulty poetical inversions and other figurative expressions may
result in ambiguities. When an element is taken out of its normal place
in a sentence, it is called an "inversion." Inversion is practiced for both
emphasis and poetic effect. If the inversion is achieved smoothly and
with skill, the results are usually good. For example, consider the
natural order of the sentence "We shall leave the room at ten o'clock."
The inverted "At ten o'clock, we shall leave the room" emphasizes the
time at which the leaving will take place. In the sentence, "From the
direction of the end of the long aisle of canned juices, fruits, and
vegetables, terminating with the refrigerated dairy products, came the
resonating sounds of the manager's footsteps," the inversion distorts the
natural order of the sentence and creates an artificial effect; worse yet,
the delayed information which would naturally come first in the normal
sentence may create a puzzling, if momentary, ambiguity. In addition,
the poetic tone is out of place in such informational writing. The
inversion is faulty.

One of the most grotesque examples of a garbled figurative expression is Castlereagh's, "I must *embark* into the feature on which this
question chiefly *hinges.*" Here is a mixed metaphor, nearly as blatant as
"*sailing* down the long *road* of life." The problem occurs when different
kinds of figures (nautical-mechanical or sea-land in these cases) are
juxtaposed within an already compressed verbal form, especially in a
context which cannot withstand the strain. An exception is the so-called
mixed metaphor of Hamlet's famous soliloquy in which he appears to
question the wisdom of quiet submission to his woes or a dramatic
suicide in the lines: "to suffer / The slings and arrows of outrageous
fortune / Or to *take arms* against *a sea* of troubles. . . ." Shakespeare
was probably not making a direct comparison of two unlike objects
here, but rather alluding to the custom of the old Celtic warriors who in
ceremonious desperation went down to the sea and met the waves,
sword in hand, fighting until the ocean closed over them, thus ending
their troubles in a symbolic battle. Even so, the lines are often misread
metaphorically as a mixing of a military image with an oceanic image.
The results of such metaphors may be construed as comical. Mark
Twain deliberately mixed several Shakespearian metaphors in the outrageous speech of the rapscallion King in *Huckleberry Finn,* the nonsense of it aside:

> *To be, or not to be; that is the bare bodkin*
> *That makes calamity of so long life;*
> *For who would fardels bear, till Birnam Wood do come to Dunsi-*
> *   nane,*
> *But that the fear of something after death*
> *Murders the innocent sleep,*
> *Great nature's second course,*
> *And makes us rather sling the arrows of outrageous fortune*
> *Than fly to others that we know not of.*

There's the respect that must give us pause:
Wake Duncan with thy knocking! I would thou couldst; . .
For who would bear the whips and scorns of time,
The oppressor's wrong, the proud man's contumely,
The law's delay, and the quietus which his pangs might take, .
In the dead waste and middle of the night, when churchyards
    yawn
In customary suits of solemn black,
But that the undiscovered country from whose bourne no traveler
    returns,
Breathes forth contagion on the world,
And thus the native hue of resolution, like the poor cat i' the adage,
Is sicklied o'er with care,
And all the clouds that lowered o'er our housetops,
With this regard their currents turn awry,
And lose the name of action.
'Tis a consummation devoutly to be wished. But soft you, the fair
    Ophelia:
Ope not thy ponderous and marble jaws,
But get thee to a nunnery—go!

Other ambiguities emerge through incomplete comparisons, of which there are various forms. Comparisons usually should be filled out completely, shortened only in loose, informal speech, or in situations when the unfinished comparison is understood through custom, as in "His reasoning is *clearer*"; "It is always *wiser* to plan for the future"; and "Everyone considered it *better* to laugh." Similarly, superlative rather than comparative forms of adjectives may be used in speech and informal expressions: "Charles Laughton was a *most remarkable* actor"; "Socrates was a *most unselfish* teacher"; and "Jonathan Winters is *the funniest* man." Here the superlative forms logically serve the function of emphasis (intensive forms), as well as that of comparison.

But consider these shortened ambiguous forms:

Error: "He is obligated to Hershel more *than you*." (He is obligated to Hershel more than *you are*? He is obligated to Hershel more than *to you*?)

Error: "I enjoy John Gary more than other ballad singers." (I enjoy John Gary more *than other ballad singers do*? I enjoy John Gary more *than I do other ballad singers*?)

In order to be clear, the comparison should be completed consistent with the writer's intention.

Another kind of ambiguity is created in "double comparisons" involving the use of sentence elements introduced by *as* and *if*, respectively. If the double comparison follows the "*as . . . as, if . . . than*" structure, the comparison is at least logical, if not stylistically graceful, as in "The cut-glass punch bowl was *as* beautiful *as, if* not more beautiful *than*, the antique silver monteith." But consider:

(about 200 words) From page 190, *The Adventures of Huckleberry Finn* by Samuel L. Clemens. By permission of Harper & Row, Publishers, Inc.

Error: "Dark hair is *as* beautiful, *if* not more beautiful *than* blonde hair." (The second comparative *as* is lacking, so the ambiguity arises, *as beautiful than blonde hair?*).

However, many English stylists object to the awkwardness of the comparative structure—"*as . . . as, if . . . than*" sometimes termed a "suspended construction"; that is, the logic of the comparison is suspended, or delayed, creating a momentary gap in logic. The whole structure may be handled more smoothly and logically by recasting the suspended construction, eliminating the "*as . . . as, if . . . than*" formula altogether, and instead moving a brief conditional comparison to the end of the sentence:

Unambiguous, natural: "The cut-glass punch bowl was as beautiful as the antique silver monteith, if not more so."

Or: "Dark hair is as beautiful as blonde hair, if not more beautiful."

Finally, in order to avoid ambiguities through incomplete comparisons, one should remember to include *other* after *than* or *as* in comparing things of the same class, of which the compared thing is a part:

Ambiguous: "Lew Alcindor was taller than any man on the UCLA basketball team." (Since Alcindor was a member of the team, he could not be taller than himself. If Alcindor had not been on the team, then the comparison would be clear for two classes would be involved, not one.)

Clear: "Lew Alcindor was taller than any other man on the UCLA basketball team."

GOOD AND POOR ANALOGIES

An *analogy* may be looked upon as a kind of elaborated comparison, not unlike an extended metaphor, in which one object or conception is explained in terms of another. Any two analogous items are on the surface unlike, but to the extent that they share numerous similarities, the analogy may be stronger. To the extent that the similarities are limited, the analogy may be more ineffective and weaker. Thus, the sign which declaims,

Don't walk on the grass.
How would you like to be walked on?

is a poor analogy, for grass and human beings really do not have much in common except to the most superficial minds.

In much the same way, advertisements are often based on weakly associated concepts; at best, shaky analogies result. Thus, a perfume ad depicts a bottle of the fragrant liquid superimposed over a lovely woman in filmy chiffon; on the bottle is the caption: "*Interlude* like love . . . must be experienced." Or consider, "*Intimate*—the fragrance that won't let go." In both advertisements, the analogies are poor because so few characteristics are shared in common between human beings and their affairs, including intimate relationships between men and women, and liquid extracts of the scent of flowers, either naturally prepared or synthesized. Nor does a "distinguished man" have any relationship with a decanter of bourbon; or malt liquor with a bull; and certainly cigarettes bear little relationship to the Elysian mise en scène of an eternal spring.

In addition to the number of similarities which strengthen an analogical figure, a second requirement may be the number of ways in which the two unlike items may resemble each other. A wide class, for example, with many parallel subclasses, forms a matrix in which two unlike items can be developed analogically in a greater number of ways. Eugene O'Neill's character Yank in the naturalistic drama *The Hairy Ape* is compared to the primate mammal physically, mentally, economically, and socially—even to the point of his being isolated and, in a very real sense, captured, used, and "caged" by society—so that the artistic analogy emerges with a many-faceted power. Stephen Crane achieves some startling effects when he analogically places Maggie Johnson's mother next to a ferocious red fire engine, but the two classes (human being-machine) form a much more restricted matrix; hence, the ways in which the two base cases can potentially resemble each other are considerably narrowed.

A third quality of a rich analogy is the obverse of the first: just as the two unlike cases brought together for treatment should have many points in common, they should also be characterized by as few dissimilarities as possible.

Perhaps the most important aspect of a strong analogy is its pertinence, the immediacy with which it bears upon, explains, and illuminates the purpose of the speaker or writer. All other criteria—the number of similarities, the potential ways in which the base cases may be compared, and the fewest possible dissimilarities—may give way to this overriding standard which ultimately determines the effectiveness of the analogy. Thus, William Makepeace Thackeray concluded his masterpiece *Vanity Fair* with this analogy:

> *Ah!* Vanitas Vanitatum! *which of us is happy in this world? Which of us has his desire? or, having it, is satisfied?*—Come, children, let us shut up the box and the puppets, for our play is played out [*second emphasis added*].

The basic comparison here, although the readers are likened to children, is that of a *box, puppets,* and *play* to the book itself, *Vanity Fair*.

A box, of course, may contain puppets just as a novel may figuratively be considered to contain characters, and the action of a novel may be logically compared to that of a play. Other similarities emerge. Thus, on the surface, the analogy holds consistently; still, there are some weaknesses in it. A critic such as Henry James may well have argued with Thackeray over the basic comparison of both the novel and its characters to a box and puppets to be hauled out of a closet and played with, then put up again, somewhat as a toy is dispensed with, because James believed that a novel should deal with reality rather than sheer imagination. He wrote in *The Art of Fiction* that good writing must capture "the colour of life." Yet, in the context of all that precedes the conclusion of *Vanity Fair,* its conclusion remains so strikingly relevant with its intonation of wisdom, human insight, imaginative exaltation, and a calm and reflective affirmation of the human condition, in spite of its transitory vanities, that the analogy triumphs over its imperfections.

Here is a list of analogies for examination and discussion:

1. "All the world's a stage,
   And all the men and women merely players:
   They have their exits and their entrances;
   And one man in his time plays many parts. . . ."
                                           —Shakespeare, *As You Like It,* II, vii.

2. ". . . a tactful, tolerant, complex, loving man, who goes at his days as if they were lions and he had to slay seven by nightfall."
           —Stewart Stern, "Paul Newman," "Double Exposure,"
                                   McCalls, XCIV (October 1966), 106.

3. Every forest is a floodgate.

4. ". . . Nay there is no Stond [obstacle] or Impediment in the Wit, but may be wrought out by Fit *Studies:* Like as Diseases of the Body, may have Appropriate Exercises. Bowling is good for the Stone and Reines [inner organs]; Shooting for the Lungs and Breast; Gentle Walking for the Stomacke; Riding for the Head; And the like. So if a Mans Wit be Wandring, let him *Study* the *Mathematicks;* For in Demonstrations, if his Wit be called away never so little, he must begin again: If his Wit be not Apt to distinguish or find differences, let him *Study* the *Schoolemen;* For they are *Cymini sectores* [patient, exacting]. If he be not Apt to beat over Matters, and to call up one Thing, to Prove and Illustrate another, let him *Study* the *Lawyers Cases:* So every Defect of the Minde, may have a Speciall Receit [recipe or antidote]."
                           —Sir Francis Bacon, "Of Studies," 1625 ed.

5. "We are more popular than Jesus Christ now."
                     —John Lennon of the Beatles, as reported
                               in *Time,* November 4, 1966, p. 50.

6. "There is a moment in the history of every nation, when, proceeding out of this brute youth, the perceptive powers reach their ripeness and have not yet become microscopic: so that man, at that instant, extends across the entire scale, and, with

his feet still planted on the immense forces of night, converses by his eyes and brain with solar and stellar creation. That is the moment of adult health, the culmination of power."
—Ralph Waldo Emerson, Representative Men.

7. No bourbon, no time, is as good as *Old Factory Whistle:* one blast—and you're through for the day!

8. In the Einstein universe there are no straight lines, there are only great circles. Space, though finite, is unbounded; a mathematician would describe its geometrical character as the four-dimensional analogue of the surface of a sphere. In the less abstract words of the late British physicist, Sir James Jeans:

"A soap-bubble with corrugations on its surface is perhaps the best representation, in terms of simple and familiar materials, of the new universe revealed to us by the Theory of Relativity. The universe is not the interior of the soap-bubble but its surface, and we must always remember that while the surface of the soap-bubble has only two dimensions, the universe bubble has four—three dimensions of space and one of time. And the substance out of which this bubble is blown, the soap-film, is empty space welded onto empty time."
—Lincoln Barnett, The Universe and Dr. Einstein.
New York: William Sloane Associates, 1957, pp. 93–94.

THE USE AND ABUSE OF LANGUAGE: WORD MAGIC

Talleyrand, the French statesman and diplomat who participated in the Congress of Vienna (1815), once said, "Speech was given to man *to disguise* his thoughts" (italics added). The English philosopher and mathematician Bertrand Russell, pointing to the cleverness of Talleyrand's quip, qualified its accuracy for men of less intelligence than that of Talleyrand, contending that "Speech was given to man *to prevent* thought" (italics added).

Among the more obvious uses of language are these:

1. *General communication*—to greet, to converse with others, and to convey ideas verbally; to exchange verbal and written messages; to write, to use the telephone, to telegraph, and to signal in established ways.

2. *Specific information*—to tell, enlighten; to impart knowledge, facts, and to give intelligence.

3. *Hortative use*—to advise, incite by words or advice; to exhort another by words.

4. *Persuasion*—to argue an opinion or to influence thoughts by arguments and reasons; to induce one to accept an opinion or belief; sometimes to plead or to urge; the persuasive use of language may connote more subtle, less direct, and less personal motivations in the use of language than the hortatory.

THE LANGUAGE OF LITERATURE

Of course, language is used in many more ways than these. For example, literary artists such as the Beowulf poet, Chaucer, Spenser, Milton, Pope, Wordsworth, Byron, Keats, Browning, Whitman, Yeats, and Eliot used the language of literature which, although it may partake of all those uses indicated above, is quite different from any one of them. To illustrate, John Keats, at once the youngest of the Romantic poets and first to die, began his poem "The Eve of St. Agnes" with these lines:

> St. Agnes' Eve—Ah, bitter chill it was!
> The owl, for all his feathers, was a-cold;
> The hare limp'd trembling through the frozen grass,
> And silent was the flock in woolly fold:
> Numb were the Beadsman's fingers, while he told
> His rosary, and while his frosted breath,
> Like pious incense from a censor old,
> Seem'd taking flight for heaven, without a death. . . .

Certainly there is an informational level of language here; indeed, the poet both communicates with and informs the reader. But he also appeals to the reader's senses, especially the tactile, visual, auditory, and olfactory. There are also images of motion, contrast, and faint suggestions of time and suspense. These lines have been called the coldest ever written in the English language; but whatever our concept of them may be, they do create a sensuous dimension of language, which, in turn, gives rise to a more or less emotional dimension. And it is the emotional dimension which renders the upper current of the imaginative dimension—the essential ingredient of the language of literature.

THE LANGUAGE OF PROPAGANDA

As language may be used for thrilling, noble, and inspirational purposes, it may also be used as means to predatory ends. The end may be highly personal in nature, selfish, and ulterior. Thus, advertisers may employ language for economic reasons through mass media, and in so doing "use" people. The motivations of advertisers and their clients, although not necessarily lacking in benefits for mankind, are usually and primarily based on profit, often to the sacrifice of the quality of the product, as well as increased cost to the consumer.

Similarly, politicians, and even more frequently dictators, through organized and concerted group efforts, set forth certain policies, doctrines, information (often distorted or exaggerated), and facts (frequently slanted favorably or unfavorably, incomplete, taken out of context, and over- or underidentified), thus spreading their "system of principles," when, in actuality, their purposes may not be to improve the social, political, economic, moral, or spiritual problems of human beings, but rather to gain personal power, and to perpetuate it by any means. Thus, they may treat others who may have different ideas as objects rather than as human beings, even to the point of disposing or purging (murdering). These are *pathogenic* uses of language; they emerge from minds which are, to varying degrees, diseased, but not necessarily unintelligent. Consider this statement:

> *All propaganda must be popular and its intellectual level must be adjusted to the most limited intelligence among those it is addressed to. . . .*
>
> *The more modest its intellectual ballast, the more exclusively it takes into consideration the emotions of the masses, the more effective it will be. And this is the best proof of the soundness or unsoundness of a propaganda campaign, and not success in pleasing a few scholars or young aesthetes. . . .*
>
> *The function of propaganda is . . . not to weigh and ponder the rights of different people, but exclusively to emphasize the one right which it has set out to argue for. Its task is not to make an objective study of the truth, in so far as it favors the enemy, and then set it before the masses with academic fairness; its task is to serve our own right, always and unflinchingly. . . .*
>
> *The people in their overwhelming majority are so feminine by nature and attitude that sober reasoning determines their thoughts and actions far less than emotion and feeling. . . .*
>
> *English propagandists understood all this most brilliantly— and acted accordingly. They made no half statements that might have given rise to doubts.*
>
> *Their brilliant knowledge of the primitive sentiments of the broad masses is shown by their atrocity propaganda, which was adapted to this condition. As ruthless as it was brilliant, it created the preconditions for moral steadfastness at the front, even in the face of the greatest actual defeats, and just as strikingly it pilloried the German enemy as the sole guilty party for the outbreak of the War: the rabid, impudent bias and persistence with which this lie was expressed took into account the emotional, always extreme, attitude of the great masses and for this reason was believed. . . .*
>
> *The purpose of propaganda is . . . to convince, and what I mean is to convince the masses. But the masses are slow-moving, and they always require a certain time before they are ready even to notice a thing, and only after the simplest ideas are repeated thousands of times will the masses finally remember them. . . . a slogan must be presented from different angles, but the end of all remarks must always and immutably be the slogan itself. . . .*
>
> *All advertising, whether in the field of business or politics,*

From *Mein Kampf* by Adolf Hitler, trans. by Ralph Manheim, copyright 1943. Reprinted by permission of Houghton Mifflin Company and Hutchinson Publishing Group Ltd.

*achieves success through the continuity and sustained uniformity
of its application.*

—Adolf Hitler, *Mein Kampf*

WAYS OF CIRCUMVENTING THOUGHT: "UP-LABELING" AND "DOWN-LABELING"

Up-labeling is the use of a symbol or sign to create in those who respond
to it a favorable attitude. Thus, words such as *good, bad,* and their
variants are often applied to objects and ideas in order to evoke positive
or negative reactions. One nation will extend such one-valued concepts
toward another: their own side is "good"; the other side is "bad." Or
consider the respective and hardly less subtle concepts engendered by
"defensive" and "offensive": U.S. missiles in Turkey are "defensive,"
while U.S.S.R. missiles in Cuba are "offensive." Russia considers the
involvement of the United States in Vietnam as "imperialist aggres-
sion," while its own suppression of the Hungarian Revolution is conceived of as the necessary rooting out of "traitorous revisionism." Most
of the Western world reported the movement of Russian troops across
the border of Czechoslovakia in August, 1968, as a "Soviet invasion,"
but the Russian press contended that its troops "came to the aid of" that
country "upon invitation." The United States refers to "Russia's satel-
lites," and Russia refers to the "colonist West." In the United States, the
U.S. is part of the "free world"; in Russia, Russian-bloc countries are
part of "the peace-loving nations."

Newspaper and magazine reporters, editors, and feature writers
may upgrade intentionally or unintentionally. To gain the advantageous
perspective and objectivity of history, let us examine the November 7,
1960, issue of *Time* in its coverage of Presidential candidates Richard
M. Nixon and John F. Kennedy. In "The Presidency" (p. 23), the *Time*
writer reports the entrance of the national hero and then-President
Eisenhower into the campaign; numerous laudatory terms are employed, some of them subtle verbs, adjectives, and morphological arrangements suggestive of propagandistic techniques rather than an
impartial conveyance of information (all italics added):

1. "Dwight Eisenhower *wheeled dramatically* onto the political
   firing line. . . ."
2. "Ike's best crack, by far, was *a stinging jab* at Kennedy's repeated references to a drop in U.S. prestige."
3. "Eisenhower *forcefully praised* the '*superlative team*' of *Nixon
   and Lodge.* . . ."
4. ". . . *he had not lost his old campaigner's touch* . . ." and "Ike
   had *carefully prepared* for its [his speech's] impact."

"*Wheeled dramatically*" is an up-labeling of "walked onto"; "*Ike's best
crack*" combines the *ad populum* technique of the illusory familiarity
of the nickname—nearly always a symbol of affection—with "best
crack" (a familiar, good-natured up-label). Similarly, the excessively

colorful *"forcefully praised"* replaces the less emotive *"complimented";* however, *"superlative team of Nixon and Lodge"* is allowed to stand in context as an original superlative, without interpretation (In the common law of England and America, silence implies consent or agreement). The affective *"he had not lost his old campaigner's touch"* is an approbative statement for the more substantive "effective campaigning methods"; and *"carefully prepared for its impact"* is an extolling of "studied his speech," and suggests that Eisenhower had the prescience to prepare for its reception and whatever followed. Perhaps the most subtle slanting of the political news is the juxtaposing and intermingling of the events surrounding ever-popular General Eisenhower with the actual Republican candidate of 1960, Mr. Nixon—an appeal *ad populum* through association.

The reportage on candidate Nixon himself (p. 25) also uses devices of up-labeling, even though the writer appears to have indicated several times that Mr. Nixon's receptions had been, generally, unsuccessful compared to those of Kennedy. Still, Mr. Nixon's advisers are termed *"top-level advisers";* his tiring campaign stops are *"grueling."* And when he speaks out, he *"lets go full jolt."* Sentimental stories of his youth are referred to, in one case, as a *"poor-boy anecdote,"* another *ad populum* device. Mr. Nixon, according to the *Time* writer, does not attack, but rather "strikes out" at Kennedy, a favorable verbal image connoting sudden motion and agility. Neither does he repeat energetically his views of the issues, but instead "pounds home" his arguments, a phrasing suggesting strength and determination. His "speech reserves" are upheld as his *"biggest guns"* (by implication, power and force), and when Mr. Nixon makes a promise, he does it *"in a manner reminiscent of Ike's 'I will go to Korea. . . .'"* The subtly intruded phrase serves as a panegyrical *ad vericundiam* of the presidential candidate.

The use of photographs is also illuminating: they are clearly forceful examples of up-labels. The one featured with the Eisenhower story depicts an ebullient and vigorous president caught in profile, replete with Homberg and neatly buttoned all-weather coat, engaging a grinning Senator Byrd (a Democrat) of Virginia in conversation. The photo is remarkable in its dexterity, for the Democrat in a closeup— with his hat doffed, his bright-eyed and broad-grinning expanse of face —radiates sheer admiration toward President Eisenhower, the symbol of Republicanism and, in this special instance, the symbol through association of Mr. Nixon. The caption reads, "President Eisenhower & Senator Byrd in Virginia/ *Not so strange bedfellows."* The caption fairly leaps at not-so-subtle implications: "Why *not* vote for the man whom the President supports so enthusiastically? Even in traditionally Democratic Virginia, its political leader is an intimate and admiring friend of the President. . . ."

Another high-speed snapshot emphasizes a white-toothed smile of a confident Mr. Nixon. The context is that of a parade. His camel-color coat is bunched ever so slightly, exaggerating the breadth of his shoulders, giving him a husky appearance; and his right arm is lost in a maze of grasping human hands, while in the wake of his open car an attractive young woman grins her elation. The caption reads: "Nixon in Cincinnati/ *Building up margins.*"

Down-labeling appears to be employed in the same issue of *Time*. Pejorative labels are repeated to describe John F. Kennedy's campaign, in contrast to the laudatory labels applied to Mr. Nixon's. The title of the report is "Democrats/ *Candidate in Orbit*," and it begins with two depreciative anecdotes which, in effect, link Kennedy to (1) a boss politician who warns the boys "not to miss the boat," and (2) "a cheap trick to dredge California for last-minute votes" (p. 26). Kennedy appears as *"grey with fatigue,"* rather than tired. The governor of Pennsylvania (a Democrat) is referred to as *"mutter[ing] old Governor Dave Lawrence,"* in preference to the more objective Governor David Lawrence. In effect, Kennedy is down-labeled through *ad hominem* and associative devices. Even the crowds the candidate addresses are denigrated, for Kennedy speaks to "a wall-to-wall *carpet of humanity* spread out for 12 blocks around him" in Manhattan. Hence, although the presence of large crowds is reported, the effect is subtly diluted by associating those who heard Kennedy with a carpet, that is, something most people walk on. In the observation, "What Kennedy said made no difference; he could have recited the *Boy Scout oath* and brought forth ovations," the candidate's youth is emphasized over any substance of what he may have said. Indeed, the substance is altogether ignored as being of no difference. The implication is again denunciatory, implying that those to whom the inexperienced, youthful candidate appeals are vacuous and emotional, rather than solid in their judgment. In more subtle ways, Jack Kennedy is castigated (pp. 26–27, italics added):

1. He is surrounded by *"the flinty eyes of unforgiving political bosses."*
2. Kennedy possesses a *"cool calculation"* and has *"met head-on the political problem of his Roman Catholic faith, may even have turned it into a sizable political asset."*
3. "He *campaigns with Depression fervor for welfare-state reform* ('I am not satisfied that 17 million Americans go to bed hungry every night. . . .')."
4. "There was, in fact, *very little in the Kennedy message to make the crowds bust the barricades, to explain the ecstasy of teenagers or the wild urge of the throngs* to touch him."
5. ". . . speaking in *short, terse sentences in a chowderish New England accent* that he *somehow makes attractive* (even when he pronounces Cincinnati as 'Since-in-notty'). . . ."
6. "In *the salad days of the New Deal,* Jack grew up, *absorbing his father's ambiguous politics. . . . Unlike . . . (. . . Richard Nixon, for example), he was untouched by the Depression and unaware, except* through reading and conversations, of the traumatic effect it had on the U.S."

7. "By the time he decided to enter public life, *Kennedy was a cool and detached young man* and *a political mugwump.*
   [Intervening head reads: *"Mixed Package"*] His decision was *almost capricious.* . . . He meticulously *served the parochial interests of his district—Boston's poorest.* . . . Much of his *time was spent in pursuit of pretty girls* and *higher elective office,* and *his absenteeism was notorious.* . . ."

These down-labels clearly dominate the factual coverage of the campaign and are so obvious that they require little comment; read as a news story, however, the italicized statements, taken in such repetitive profusion, are not only disparaging, but also censorious, caviling, and snidely insinuating. The effect is closer to propaganda than to candid news coverage. In the midst of such slanted reportage are two sudden, contrasting insertions of laudatory up-labels: (1) President Eisenhower under whom the "country . . . *has marched down the middle of the road behind Dwight Eisenhower to the highest level of shared prosperity of any nation in history;* and (2) "To a nation winding up *eight comfortable years under the leadership of one of the most popular Presidents* in U.S. history, *he* [Kennedy] *brings a message of anxiety and discontent.*"

At least on the surface, the photographs and captions related to Kennedy are severe: the first depicts the candidate seated on the track of a railroad next to a workman's firmly planted boot; Kennedy appears to be looking up and talking with begrimed and helmeted miners. The caption reads: "With West Virginia Miners / *An ear for distress.*" The second shows Kennedy in a somewhat wooden attitude, his coat tightly buttoned and wrinkled about the hips, behind and to the side of a Negro speaker, whose face bears the suggestion of a snarl; a nondescript woman in the background looks curiously, if not askance, at Kennedy. The caption states, "With Harlem Leader*/ *An eye for blocs,*" and the asterisk identifies "Congressman Adam Clayton Powell." The third picture reveals Kennedy bending over what appears to be the paneled railing of a dais, shaking hands, as the caption designates them, "With Houston Ministers / *A voice for reason.*" Each photograph, at least superficially, links the candidate respectively to laboring people close to the dirt; a minority group involved in a controversial quest for civil rights and led by a leader whose ethics had frequently been questioned; and querying Protestant ministers, who had been raising the "Roman Catholic problem." Intentionally or unintentionally, the down-labels of candidate John F. Kennedy in this issue of the magazine tend to appeal to the emotions rather than to thought; they indicate a desire to persuade subtly rather than to report objectively. And the calm integrity of facts and events frequently gives way to a penchant for the startling word, the loaded anecdote, and the clever phrase.

THE ABUSE OF LANGUAGE: A SUMMARY

Up-labeling and down-labeling are abuses of the legitimate use of language. Such devices tell more about how certain people feel, and how they want others to feel, than they do about subverbal reality. They are a kind of verbal legerdemain or word magic, presenting an illusion. Without the interjection of thought, one can see only what the word manipulators want him to see, especially if they skillfully circumvent his mind and appeal directly to his emotions and feelings. Is it any wonder that Talleyrand cynically observed, "Speech was given to man to disguise his thoughts," or that Bertrand Russell, endeavoring to alert us to the abuses of language, amended the statement, ". . . to prevent thought"? If the thought process can indeed be cut off, or patterned to a direct, emotive response, then word magic prevails, the spell is woven, and the slight-of-hand illusionist has his victims at his mercy, no matter how pathogenic his ends may be.

QUESTIONS ON READINGS

SCIENCE AND THE HUMANITIES IN CONFLICT

After reviewing *"Good and poor analogies"* in Chapter 6, and noting the four major qualities of a *good analogy,* apply this information to the thorough analogy extracted from Sir Charles Sherrington's "The Brain and Its Work" (p. 171). Is his basic analogy a good one? If so, why? Discuss.

LANGUAGE AND REALITY

As illustrations of confusions of words with objects or ideas, consider the following expressions and their possible meanings:
  1. "The many-splendored thing" (p. 185).
  2. "The robbed that smiles, steals something from the thief" (p. 182).
  3. "Walk with the Gods" (p. 183).
  4. "The Way of all flesh . . ." (p. 184).

After discussing these, examine the original contexts indicated by page references. Are the original accurate contexts of the statements different from the meanings you considered? Discuss. How would you relate the results of your discussion to other kinds of *verbal confusions*? Discuss.

WAR AND DEHUMANIZATION

Review the sections in Chapter 6 on *"The language of literature"* and *"The language of propaganda,"* and then read the excerpts from Thomas Paine's "The American Crisis" (p. 233) and Anton Chekhov's short story "The Lament" (p. 249). To which work does the *language of literature* more accurately apply? Why? Do both works contain aspects of the language of literature and propaganda? Discuss, giving specific reasons from your text.

THE CAMPUS TODAY: REBELLION AND CONFORMITY

Look over *"The use and abuse of language: Word magic"* in Chapter 6, and especially note the four listed uses of language—*general communication, specific information, hortative use,* and *persuasion.* Now read Mario Savio's "An End to History" (p. 262), applying these various uses to selected portions of his essay. Especially, consider the following:

1. The paragraph beginning, "In our free speech fight at the University of California, we have come up against what may emerge as the greatest problem of our nation—depersonalized, unresponsive bureaucracy" (p. 262).
2. The third paragraph, commencing, "As bureaucrat, an administrator believes that nothing new happens. He occupies an ahistorical point of view" (p. 262).
3. Then Savio's conclusion *in re* "bureaucracies" in the fourth paragraph (p. 262).

In addition, how does the author use language when he states, "The most crucial problems facing the United States today are the problem of automation and the problem of racial injustice," and in the related sentences which follow (p. 263)? When he writes of due process of law, contending that although such phrases "are all pretty old . . . they are not being taken seriously in America today, nor are they being taken seriously on the Berkeley campus" (p. 263)? Also examine closely the following: the paragraph commencing, "The university is the place where people begin . . ." (p. 263); the one which starts, "Many students here at the University . . ." (p. 264); and the final paragraph of the essay. In your discussion of the various uses of language, does Savio also employ the *language of literature*? Of *propaganda*? Do you detect any *verbal confusions*? Good and poor *analogies*? Ways of circumventing thought, especially *up-labeling* and *down-labeling*? *Logical fallacies*? Discuss.

THE SEARCH FOR IDENTITY

Examine Ernest Hemingway's "Une Génération Perdue" ("the lost generation") from *A Moveable Feast* (p. 292). First, treat the short passage as the *language of literature,* and notice how this use of language "communicates," "informs," employs "sensuous devices" (especially the auditory sense, evident in frequent passages of dialogue), "emotional," and "imaginative" dimensions, which characterize the *language called literature*. Discuss. Does Hemingway make you feel as if Gertrude Stein truly lived in Paris and talked with him? Does she emerge with distinct personality traits—both strengths and weaknesses which humanize? Why? Notice Hemingway's use of *analogy* when he writes of Sherwood Anderson, James Joyce, and other artists in relation to Gertrude Stein and refers to them as generals (p. 293). What does Hemingway reveal through this *analogy,* and is it effective? Discuss. Does Hemingway also employ *up-labels* and *down-labels*? Why? Discuss.

LOVE, SEX, AND CENSORSHIP

Read Lord Byron's letter to Countess Guiccioli, "Amor Mio" (p. 308). It is a love letter, of course. In April, 1819, in Venice Byron met the Countess Teresa Guiccioli, a beautiful girl fresh out of a convent, who, at sixteen, had wed a man in his sixties. She and Byron fell passionately in love, and this letter was composed only a few months later. Byron was thirty-one years old. Discuss the letter as *information*, as *persuasion;* finally, discuss the letter as *literature.*

INDIVIDUAL RESPONSIBILITY

Read the excerpt in your text from Adolf Hitler's *Mein Kampf* (p. 111). Working close to the text, distinguish the various *uses of language:* general communication, specific information, hortative use, and persuasion. Also discuss the piece as *literature;* as *propaganda.* In connection with your analysis of the excerpt as *propaganda,* compare and contrast it with any other examples of propaganda which you can think of. Discuss.

GOD, MAN, AND MORAL CONSCIOUSNESS

Read "Tom Dooley Writes to a Young Doctor" (p. 363). This fourteen-paragraph letter to "Bart," a young doctor who has just graduated and is about to do his internship, is an excellent example of the various uses of language. Examine the letter closely by paragraphs to determine how Dr. Dooley used language:

1. *General communication*—paragraphs 4, 5, 12, especially.
2. *Specific information*—paragraphs 3, 4, especially.
3. *Hortatory use*—paragraphs 8, 9, 10, 14, especially.
4. *Persuasion*—paragraphs 3, 6, 7, 12, especially.

What was Dooley's opinion of America, expressed in paragraph 5 (p. 363)? Discuss his concept of its strengths and weaknesses. Did Dooley have any ideas about modern concepts of medical practice, particularly about "specialists" and "general practitioners" (p. 363)? Discuss. Give several examples of Dooley's sense of humor (paragraphs 7, 12, especially). How does he bring the idea of man's responsibility to his fellow man alive, especially in paragraph 5? Discuss. Notice how Dooley also employs the *literary use* of language, most obviously in paragraphs 1, 5, 11, and 12. Discuss. Finally, notice the well-balanced logic of paragraph 6. Does it strengthen his *persuasive* and *hortatory* uses of language? How? Discuss.

LITERATURE AND GOOD WRITING

W. Somerset Maugham in the excerpt "Lucidity, Simplicity, and Euphony in Writing Well," from his autobiography, *The Summing Up,* relates some valuable concepts in avoiding verbal confusions and using language effectively. He begins by pointing out his own limitations as a writer (p. 388). Discuss his weaknesses; his strengths. "On taking thought," he writes, "it seemed to me that I must aim at lucidity, simplicity, and euphony," and he places "these three qualities in the order of importance . . ." (p. 388).

He proceeds to take up the three aspects of good writing, one by one, beginning with *lucidity* (p. 388). Discuss his statement that one "cause of obscurity is that the writer is himself not sure of his meaning," that "He has a vague impression of what he wants to say," but fails to do so either from "lack of mental power" or "from laziness" (p. 388). Unfortunately, "many writers think, not before, but as they write" (p. 388). Discuss his concept of the danger of "a sort of magic in the written word" (p. 388). In emphasizing the lack of clear thinking in writing, note how Maugham states a writer's rationalization concerning obscure writing, "Some writers who do not think clearly are inclined to suppose that their thoughts have a significance greater than at first sight appears" (p. 388) and his expansion upon the idea. Is this so? Discuss. What is the author's view of what he terms "the faculty of precise reflection" (p. 388)? Relate it to his contrary view of murky writing: "Fools can always be found to discover a hidden sense in them" (p. 389); also note the phrase "aristocratic exclusiveness" (p. 389). What does he mean by it? Is Maugham himself lucid or clear? Does he use language in different ways? How? Does he employ *down-labels* in this section of his autobiography? Discuss.

In dealing with *simplicity* (p. 389) Maugham discusses John Ruskin, Sir Thomas Browne, Shakespeare, Sir Thomas More, the King James Bible and its influence, "plain, honest English speech" (p. 390), John Dryden, the writers of Queen Anne (who reigned 1702–1714; the period included Daniel Defoe, Jonathan Swift, Richard Steele, Joseph Addison, and Alexander Pope), and Charles Lamb "at his best"; then Thomas De Quincey, Thomas Carlyle, George Meredith, Walter Pater; and, finally, Matthew Arnold. What is his opinion of these writers? Have you read any of them? Discuss. What does Maugham mean when he states, "But words are tyrannical things, they exist for their meanings, and if you will not pay attention to these, you cannot pay attention at all. Your mind wanders" (p. 389)? According to Maugham, is *simplicity* in writing easy to attain? Does it come to one by nature? What does the author think of "the purple patch" in English writing? Discuss the section dealing with *simplicity* in writing, beginning, "It has been said that good prose should resemble the conversation of a well-bred man . . ." and continuing through ". . . must be neither flippant nor solemn, but always apt" (p. 390). Discuss this portion of the work carefully. What do you think of Maugham's analogy of good prose, conversation, and what we may term "personhood" to clothes (p. 390)? Discuss. What is Maugham's opinion of Voltaire?

Euphony, briefly, may be looked upon as a pleasing style, which depends upon the selection and arrangement of words which do not detract from the sense, but rather add to it, and in doing so fall pleasantly upon the ear; thus, the best writers as a rule avoid *cacophony* (the combination of harsh, clashing sounds), unintentional rhyming, awkward or exalted repetitions of sounds—especially *alliteration* (the repetition of initial consonantal sounds, as in "To sit in solemn silence") in prose. What does Maugham say about these points and others? Does he think that a writer should "make . . . concession to pleasant sound" (p. 392)? Yet, Maugham states, "Anything is better than not to write clearly"; "against simplicity" the only argument is "the possibility of dryness" (p. 392); and "This is a risk that is well worth taking when you reflect how much better it is to be bald than to wear a curly wig" (p. 392). What does he mean in relation to *euphony,* and what are its dangers (p. 392)? In your discussion of this question, include Maugham's reference to George Moore, Matthew Arnold, and Colette.

This selected portion of Maugham's autobiography concludes with his opinion of Hazlitt and Cardinal Newman. Discuss his opinion of the two men; by blending their best talents with Matthew Arnold, how does he summarize his opinion of the best use of the language of literature?

AGE OF CONTROVERSY

Read James Wright's poem "Mutterings over the Crib of a Deaf Child" (p. 444). In the language of literature, how does the poet avoid verbal confusions, in spite of the depth and tragedy of his subject?

Similarly, read Jesse Stuart's short story "Corbie" (p. 446). Now read his introduction to "Corbie" (p. 445). Does Stuart himself suggest in his words the power of the use of literary language? Discuss. Have you ever known a "Corbie"? How did you feel about him? Does Stuart suggest that there are deeper hypocrisies in American society than surface ones involving daily social relationships; prejudices deeper than skin, race, religion, creed, and national origin—a kind of ingrained *propaganda* out of which we habitually think and are taught to think? Discuss.

7
CONTEXT AND MEANING

In the narrowest word sense, *context* indicates the parts of a sentence, paragraph, or larger statement which go before and follow a specified word or unit of language, the completeness of which must be kept intact in order to determine the specific meaning. When for whatever purpose people quote the extracted word or unit of language, they are said to be "quoting out of context."

For example, let us suppose that a Chicago drama critic, Justin O. Meanie, objects to Arthur Miller's *After the Fall* in this caustic review:

> The play is a perfect example of the perversion of Aristotelian tragedy. Instead of the spectators being purged of the emotions of pity and fear, they are instead subjected to the protracted nausea of a pitiful and frightened protagonist wallowing in the offal of his self-pity. Despite the author's protestations to the contrary, the horizontal Maggie-Quentin scenes of Part II seem to have come full-blown with shockingly frank emotion, as well as sartorial dishabille, from the bedroom of Marilyn Monroe. They are crudely unimaginative; moreover, they are cruel to that gossamer illusion of her poor and only legacy of carnal beauty. Now that's dead, too —like kicking a dead horse, beating a dead bitch, or pummeling Lazarus come back to tell us—nothing. Doubtless, sadomasochists will get terrific aesthetic kicks from seeing an aberrant patient regurgitate his unrestrained maunderings, amid all too rare ejaculations of insight, on a psychiatrist's couch, but the experience is hardly prime fillet from the Blackhawk or juicy *escargot* from Jacques. For the ticket or the meal, though, the price you'll pay is about the same. The only other stupendous aspects of this abortion in experimental theatre are the conceit of the author and the endurance of the audience.

Quoted out of context by the advertising agents of the Lost Cause Theatre, however, Justin O. Meanie, to his angry astonishment, may later read his own words arranged above his name and that of his newspaper as follows:

". . . A PERFECT EXAMPLE OF . . . ARISTOTELIAN TRAGEDY. . . . SPECTATORS PURGED OF THE EMOTIONS OF PITY AND FEAR. . . . HORIZONTAL MAGGIE-QUENTIN SCENES . . . FULL-BLOWN WITH SHOCKINGLY FRANK EMOTION . . . DISHABILLE FROM THE BEDROOM OF MARILYN MONROE . . . GOSSAMER ILLUSION OF . . . CARNAL BEAUTY. . . . TERRIFIC AESTHETIC KICKS . . . EJACULATIONS OF IN-SIGHT . . . PRIME FILLET FROM THE BLACKHAWK . . . JUICY ESCARGOT FROM JACQUES . . . STUPENDOUS!"

Why is he angry and astonished? They *are* his own words quoted in sequential order, true—but not *all* of his own words. The words that make the meaning clear are left out, as indicated by the ellipses.

Portions of a critical review may be, and often are, extracted for advertising purposes; but if the excerpts are ethical and valid, they must represent the intent of the author as fully as possible, as necessary parts make a meaningful whole. Certainly the parts extracted should not misrepresent his views. Here, Justin O. Meanie is not only quoted unfairly out of context, but the context is purposely distorted.

In the broadest sense, language and its context are inseparable. The words we use are not isolated chatter, independent of other aspects of civilization—its history, traditions, and culture. Words cannot be detached from the circumstances in which they are spoken or from which they are written without distorting the particular thought process, feeling, or attitude they were meant to represent. Every statement derives from a context—the collective conditions, the whole background and situation relevant to the statement. Thus, for words to be comprehended as fully as possible, the whole context of situation is important.

Once we understand that language can never be isolated as an entity unto itself, then we see that words in themselves have only a potential meaning, just as tools in themselves cannot do work out of the context of human intelligence, plans, or guiding purposes, and the application of a preferably creative force—actuating manpower itself.

Meaning, one perceives, depends upon surrounding events and stimuli. These may involve complex attitudes, the desire for food and survival, a variety of psychological situations, purposes, and motivations. Words may *mean* in the ramified context of emotions, economic considerations, social settings, the desire for friendship, sexual attitudes, and intellectual curiosity. Contexts may vary as widely as man's interests, involving his physical senses, his needs beyond the scope of sensory experience, his particular desires for entertainment, imitation, or search for meaning. Indeed, he may be motivated by such widely diverging extremes as power or peace, self-destruction or love.

The environment in which we use language, then, is always relevant to the fullness of communication. The way people live—ways

different from our own life—may require us to know about as many of
the circumstances as possible (unfortunately, we can never know all)
in order to understand and to be understood.

MEANING AND THE NATURE OF CONTEXT

When we use language (symbols) in conversation, our words become
meaningful through the thinking processes of those involved. As we
have seen, the word is not the thing, but merely stands for the thing.
Between the words we use (symbols) and the things to which we refer
(referents), there is no *direct* relationship, for *meaning takes place
through human minds* (thoughts or references). But people do not
think in a vacuum, either. As we converse with others, or read a book,
our thoughts are constantly qualified, altered, and reshaped by contexts
which affect the meaning of what we say, hear, read, perceive. In much
the same way, others with whom we talk and correspond experience a
similar process of mental responses (references), but never precisely
the same way in which we do. Even though a person as he speaks may
tend to behave as if his views are *the* truth, *the* reality, we know that
there may be many truths, many realities. As we have seen in Chapter
5, the awareness of *multiordinality* vastly widens the range of human
perceptions. Just as many approaches may exist in relation to music in
a discussion among five college students (Remember the conversation
in Chapter 5?), similarly, many contexts may cut through and tend to
shape in various ways the thought processes (references) of two people
as they converse.

Among the contexts which may influence words and conceptualizing are the following:

1. Culture (nationality, religion, socioeconomic relationships,
   related environmental matters).
2. Language and the nature of communication (same or different languages; aspects of conversation, its closeness, distract-
   ing obstacles, distance; influence of mechanical devices such
   as telephones, with which one hears but cannot see; gestures
   [kinesics] which qualify the meaning of verbal symbols; writing and reading, in which thought takes place through non-
   verbal symbols; and the various levels of meaning treated in
   Chapter 2).
3. Age and time (similarities and differences of experience, language, habits, interests).
4. Knowledge (what is mutually known, degrees of potential understanding).
5. Physical-mental-nervous similarities and differences (circumstances of attention, work, and preoccupations of the moment,
   mutual abilities to respond to physical stimuli, to cerebrate, to
   react to the five senses).
6. Social relationships (mutually shared).
7. Intellectual affinity (not the same as knowledge, but rather

the ability to think in mutually enlightening ways and to transmute these thoughts into shared understanding).

8. Psychological factors (mental attitudes; for example, adult-child, father-son, adult-adult relationships; other similarities or differences such as fear, extrovertism, introvertism, reticence, caution, boldness, friendliness, hostility).
9. Political persuasions (similarities and differences).
10. Purposes for symbolizing (information, entertainment, warning, desire to give or to get something, etc.).

Let us consider a simple dialogue in which these contexts operate as influences on the meaning of language:

Son (bounding into the living room): "Dad, need to scoop tonight. Stone fox—really together, I mean. A pot grabber named Mary Jane. What about your wheels?"

Father (looking up from newspaper): "Sorry, it's too dangerous."

Although the son walks away mumbling and the father goes back to his newspaper with a shouted afterthought, "You'd better watch out, son!" thought processes have taken place. And most of the contexts listed above have influenced meaning. Ideally, the references (thought processes) of two people who talk with each other should coincide (as nearly as possible) through the language symbols used. But the truth of the matter is that the references never coincide, although in some fortunate instances they may overlap to a highly meaningful extent. In this case, however, little communication has taken place. The entire process may be illustrated with three circles: Circle "A" represents the acts of reference (thought processes) of the son; circle "B" the referents (words spoken by son and father); and circle "C" the acts of reference of the father. Cutting through all three circles are strata of contexts which influence meaning on the part of both son and father, explained by the legend at the bottom of the diagram and its analysis.

ANALYSIS

By reviewing the conversation of the son and father, along with the contexts which influenced their words and thought processes, one can graphically see how various contexts have detracted from what could otherwise have been a different kind of understanding between the two. Among the strongest contexts for communication is that of *culture*. Father and son, of course, are members of the same family; they share a similar environment and general cultural background. Another strong context is knowledge, for both father and son have been together for nearly twenty years. Therefore, each knows much about the other, including such intimate matters as personal habits and what may be termed the stronger bridges of understanding, established through repeated experiences in talking with each other. Similarly, the *purposes for symbolizing* (conversation) are not subject to the same kinds of economic and self-serving motivations one may encounter outside the family circle. Thus, a general awareness of purposes already exists.

Diagram of Contexts, Words, References

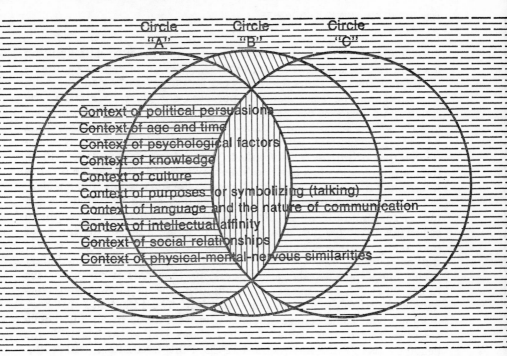

Circle "A"   Circle "B"   Circle "C"

Context of political persuasions
Context of age and time
Context of psychological factors
Context of knowledge
Context of culture
Context of purposes for symbolizing (talking)
Context of language and the nature of communication
Context of intellectual affinity
Context of social relationships
Context of physical-mental-nervous similarities

Other contexts outside the present experience of both individuals concerned, potentially available but as yet unrealized, attainable but unattained by either at the present time.

Contexts operative within the two individuals' conceptualizing processes but outside the symbolical language used; further communication between the two would diminish these areas and simultaneously enlarge the contexts of mutual understanding.

Contexts of potential mutual understanding inherent in the symbols (language) used, but for various reasons not shared by the two conversers; further conceptualizing on the bases of the symbols alone would diminish these areas while enlarging the contexts of mutual understanding.

Contexts of a complete lack of communication, potentially within the symbols (language) used but simultaneously outside the present experience of both speakers, at least for the present, potentially available but as yet unrealized because of limited linguistic achievements.

Contexts of mutual understanding and communication within the potential of the symbols (language) used; could be enlarged as the two thought processes converge; ideally a full circle with convergence of thought processes with symbols shared.

Specifically, the son wants most to impress an attractive date by using his father's car, while the father realizes, in an ill-defined way unfortunately, that his son wants the family car for purposes of a date.

Although the son's detailed purposes are clear to himself, the father's knowledge is comparatively vague; for the context of *language and the nature of communication*—potentially strong—is in fact weak here. Another context, *psychological factors,* has been nearly as operative as that of *intellectual affinity* in disrupting communication. First, the communication has been considerably reduced because the son has interrupted his father's reading. Moreover, the son's words, though clear to him, are not comprehended as fully as they could be. What the son means to communicate to his father is that he has a date with an especially attractive girl, and he wants to impress her by driving a car that really moves—accelerates quickly—especially through freeway traffic. However, "need," "scoop," "stone fox," "pot grabber named Mary Jane," and "your wheels" are expressions that do not *mean* for the father what the son intended. In addition, the psychological factors have widened the gap of misunderstanding. The father has just been reading about some college students who were killed in an automobile accident, and on the same page has glanced at an article with the heading "INSURANCE RATES UPPED FOR UNDER-25 DRIVERS," scanning such adjectives as "young," "immature," "hopped-up drivers," and the phrase "errors in judgment." In the context of his reading, his son's effusiveness bespeaks these very negative concepts. As the father emerges from his verbal fog, he perceives the words of his son, but the words are not as clear as they might be. The *argot* is not new to him, but in his present mood he associates some of the words with erroneous referents. To him "scoop" does not mean merely "to drive fast," or what the son has intended it to mean in this instance—"accelerate quickly" (the son's car has clutch trouble), that is, "more quickly than my own car," but, since the father has heard "scoop" and "scooping" used by television commentators of stock-car races, it is to him a descriptive term for excessive speed. Moreover, he is concerned about his son's date (whose real name happens to be Mary Jane Hopkins). By "pot grabber," the son has meant to say that her major is archeology, and he represents his admiration of her beauty, modish garments, and feminine appeal by "stone fox"—a rare compliment among his peers. But the father has read about college students who smoke marijuana, and he knows the term "Mary Jane" may refer to the drug. "Stone fox" means little to him except for the vaguest kinds of connotations (perhaps a somewhat hard-hearted, clever vixen?), but the term "pot grabber" settles the whole confusing matter in his mind, for he equates "pot" with marijuana.

In lesser ways the contexts of *social relationships, political persuasions,* and *physical-mental-nervous similarities* are involved in the acts of reference the two men make. The context of *age and time,* however, most clearly evinced in language rather than dissimilarities of experience and interests, has interfered with the breadth of mutual understanding and communication which could be enlarged.

Circle "A" (son's thought processes, references) and Circle "C" (father's thought processes, references) have converged—as the diagram illustrates—just enough to permit the two to share the "edges of their thought processes," so to speak. Within the symbols (words) used (Circle "B"), indicated by diagonal lines, are small areas of potential communication, available but as yet outside the present experience of both speakers. The contexts of some psychological factors, age and time, political persuasions, intellectual affinity, social relationships, and physical-mental-nervous similarities are potentially inherent in the use of words, but not in the references of the two. For example, the son tends to use *argot* when asking his father for a favor—here the loan of his car—possibly in order to affirm his own independence, or to assert his own identity, so to speak, but he would not know how to put this psychological tendency into words. The father, in turn, tends to be paternal and, hence, protective in dealing with his son. As a result, a kind of unconscious hostility, evinced in an inability to communicate, or to communicate indirectly, builds up between the two. Doubtless, psychologists would have more profound observations to make about the relationship, but these observations will serve to illustrate how attitudes may often inhere in family conversations without conscious thought processes accompanying the language used.

The greater pity of this specific kind of conversation between father and son is indicated in the diagram by solid horizontal lines— huge areas within Circles "A" and "C"—contexts of potential mutual understanding inherent in the words used, but for various reasons previously explained, simply not shared by the two conversers. If the father could put aside his newspaper and consider his son's words carefully, and the son could drop his bouncy posing and *argot* long enough to approach his father more thoughtfully, the two could then enter into a more meaningful dialogue.

HUMOR THROUGH CHANGE OF CONTEXT

Humor is often the result of a sudden change in what may be termed "a preconditioned direction of meaning." Consider, for example, the statement: "If everything else fails, follow directions." The context of "If everything else fails . . ." suggests the precondition of a series of efforts, each resulting in vain attempts. The context connotes a lack of success, disappointment, perhaps frustration—even hopelessness and despair. Thus, the reader is prepared contextually for a possible solution; the short form of the statement suggests an epigram, and perhaps the reader may expect some kind of enlightening advice in the face of dejection resulting from repeated failure. Then, when he continues to read, ". . . *follow directions*," the earnest entreaty which he has been led by context to expect simply changes context, as it were. His shifting of mental gears is rapid, unexpected, and peculiar—the contexts and causal relationships between words (symbols) and thoughts (references) are turned awry, and momentarily the expectation of context breaks down. The only sense that connects the two (symbols-references) is so far out of the range of expectation that one laughs at the disparity.

A similar change of context may be found in the advice from W. C. Fields: "If at first you don't succeed, try, try again. Then give up. There's no use being a damn fool about it." Here, the shift of context is made more universal in its appeal because Fields' adjuration is out of context with the old classic adage.

Change of context, of course, is not always humorous; it may be poetic or serious, as, for example, in Alexander Pope's

> The hungry judges soon the sentence sign,
> And wretches hang that jury-men may dine.

Here the shift of context comes so quickly and with such contrastive force, one clause balancing the other like counterweights on a scale, that the word unit becomes a distinctive figure of speech known as *antithesis*. A philosophical statement such as, "The more a man learns, the more aware he becomes of his ignorance," while apparently contradictory, upon closer examination may be true. The sudden shift in context from learning to ignorance produces an emphatic rhetorical effect known as *paradox*.

Humor through change of context should not be confused with a pun. The pun, though it may involve a shift in context like humor through change of context, is a figurative expression which depends upon a play on words similar in sound but different in meaning. One of the most famous examples of the pun is Thomas Hood's "They went and told the sexton and the sexton tolled the bell." Or consider "psyche-Cola, for those who think Jung." The actor Peter Ustinov, who wears a beard, maintains that people can hear him better when "I speak above a whisker." Joyce Megginson wrote in *The Wall Street Journal:* "Though companies . . . convene with good intention, one wonders if necessity is the mother of convention." A congressman was queried, "How many members compromise the House of Representatives?" Although the context shifts in all these examples, the primary humorous emphasis depends upon the similarities of the sounds of words. For the pun the sound is essential, the shift of context secondary.

Following are several examples of humor through change of context. In considering them, trace the direction of context, and then determine just how the context shifts and thereby creates humor:

1. I remember the name, but I forget your face.
2. Flattery will get you everywhere.
3. "Ladies and gentlemen, I wish to present to you a man whose great learning and veneration for truth are only exceeded by his high moral character and majestic presence."
   —Mark Twain, introducing himself to an audience.
4. Avoid tight shoes, and keep your feet off your mind.
5. George Bernard Shaw's definition of *heartbreak:* "The end of happiness and the beginning of peace."

6. The only thing he ever took out in the moonlight was his false teeth.
7. Jonathan Swift's definition of *inconstancy:* "The only thing in the world that is constant."
8. It's as simple as the look on your face.
9. Ambrose Bierce's definition of *jealous:* "Unduly concerned about the preservation of that which can be lost only if not worth having."
10. Husband to wife on a shopping spree during a sale: "You're going to save us into bankruptcy!"
11. Senior to freshman: "I'd like to lend you the money, but all my assets are tied up in cash."
12. There goes a sheep in sheep's clothing.
13. Definition of a cowardly skindiver: Chicken of the Sea.
14. Thou shalt not spit thy pits.
15. You know, an empty car pulled up in front of Number 10 Downing Street, and Mr. Clement Atlee got out.
        —attributed to Winston Churchill
16. The four seasons: salt, pepper, vinegar, and sugar.
17. Happiness is an empty bladder.
18. Headline in the *Los Angeles Times:* "Typewriter Heiress XXX's out Husband."
19. Did Will Rogers say, "We're all ignorant, just in different ways"?
20. Early to bed, early to rise means you're going out on the paper route, the milk route, or the graveyard shift.
21. An apple for the computer.
22. "While returnin' from Idynoplus t'day a sudden lurch o' the train caused Lafe Budd t' be vi'lently thrown t' the ground, but fortunately only one bottle was broke."
        —Kin Hubbard
23. "I'll take an excessively gentle horse, a crippled one if you have him."
        —Mark Twain
24. Hippie slogan: "Nextness is Godlier than cleanliness."
25. Definition of an *optimist:* A fat man who shaves before he gets on the bathroom scales to weigh.

QUESTIONS ON READINGS

SCIENCE AND THE HUMANITIES IN CONFLICT

Note Henry James' epigraph—a definition of art in relationship to the *context* of science: "Art is nothing more than the shadow of humanity" (p. 156). It is important to relate this statement to the context of science and the humanities in conflict, in order for it to be as meaningful as possible. Otherwise, its meaning would be out of context. Discuss the meaning of the statement within the context indicated. Specifically, how can "art" be the "shadow of humanity"? Or "nothing more than the shadow of humanity"? In this sense, may art embody science? Discuss.

Taking James' statement further, examine Dante's comment, the epigraph, "Nature is the art of God" (p. 156). Consider the intended context in your analysis of Dante's statement.

Look over the excerpts from Charles Dickens' *Hard Times* (p. 166) and examine them in relation to aspects of *context and meaning*. What is the *importance of context* here? In determining *meaning and the nature of context*, analyze the various contexts of the following: the names and characters of Thomas Gradgrind, student number twenty (Cecilia "Sissy" Jupe), the student Bitzer (he has no number), the educational Commissioner, and Mr. M'Choakumchild. What is the possible contextual significance of the following incidents:

1. The description of the "plain, bare, monotonous vault of a schoolroom" (p. 167)?
2. Thomas Gradgrind's emphasis on the "facts," or as he puts it, "In this life, we want nothing but Facts, sir; nothing but Facts" (p. 167)! and later the detailed treatment of "Fact, fact, fact" (p. 170)! during which Gradgrind asserts, "We hope to have, before long, a board of fact, composed of commissioners of fact, who will force the people to be a people of fact, and of nothing but fact. You must discard the word Fancy altogether" (p. 170)?
3. The repeated analogy of the students to "the inclined plane of little vessels then and there arranged in order, ready to have imperial gallons of facts poured into them until they were full to the brim" (p. 167)?
4. The student Bitzer's ready factual answer, giving the definition of a quadruped (p. 168)?
5. The questions and ideas of Thomas Gradgrind regarding the definition of a horse (p. 168)? The educational Commissioner's dealing with papering a room with representations of horses (p. 169) and specifically, "Do you ever see horses walking up and down the sides of rooms in reality—in fact"

(p. 169)? His statement that "What is called Taste, is only another name for fact" (p. 169)? His question "Would you use a carpet having a representation of flowers upon it" (p. 170)? The questions implied in Thomas Gradgrind's summary, including, "You don't find that foreign birds and butterflies come and perch upon your crockery? You never meet with quadrupeds going up and down walls; you must not have quadrupeds represented upon walls" (p. 170). Gradgrind's assertion that "for all these purposes, combinations and modifications (in primary colours) of mathematical figures which are susceptible of proof and demonstration" must be used for all these purposes?

6. The comparison and contrast of the two students' appearances —Bitzer's and Sissy Jupe's (p. 168)? The fact that Bitzer is called by his name and Sissy Jupe by a number?

7. Mr. M'Choakumchild's name, educational background and training, the emphasis on his specialty of "All the Water Sheds of all the world (whatever they are) . . ." (p. 171)?

8. The author's editorializing in regard to M'Choakumchild, "If he had only learnt a little less, how infinitely better he might have taught much more" (p. 171)?

9. The *rhetorical question* and *paradox* of M'Choakumchild's trying to "fill each jar brim full," but still having to face the challenge of "Fancy lurking within" (p. 171)?

10. Thomas Gradgrind's self-satisfaction at the conclusion of the passage?

LANGUAGE AND REALITY

Read the excerpts from Walt Whitman's "Preface to the 1855 Edition of *Leaves of Grass*" (p. 186). From the section of your text subtitled "Analysis" in Chapter 7 and the previous "Diagram of Contexts, Words, References" (p. 127), develop various *contexts* of understanding of the following points Whitman makes, and in doing so be as complete as possible:

1. The paragraph beginning, "The Americans of all nations at any time upon the earth have probably the fullest poetical nature" (p. 186), and such *paradoxes* as "the President's taking off his hat to them not they to him."

2. The significance of the many geographical references following, "America is the race of races. Of them a bard is to be commensurate with a people . . ." (p. 187).

3. The various comments about poets and their natures, beginning with "He is the arbiter of the diverse and he is the key. He is the equalizer of his age and land"; the poet's liberality, continuing, "He judges not as the judge judges but as the sun falling around a helpless thing. As he sees the farthest he has the most faith. His thoughts are the hymns of the praise of

things. Also, the poet and faith, beginning, "He sees eternity less like a play with a prologue and denouement . . . he sees eternity in men and women. . . . he does not see men and women as dreams or dots. Faith is the antiseptic of the soul . . . it pervades the common people and preserves them" (p. 187). Similarly, the poet's largeness of soul, commencing, "The greatest poet hardly knows pettiness or triviality" (p. 187); the "greatest poet" as the "one complete lover" of the universe (p. 189). And the affirmation of life in the face of earthly sorrow, consistent with the poet's vision, "Nothing can jar him. . . . suffering and darkness cannot—death and fear cannot. To him complaint and jealousy and envy are corpses buried and rotten in the earth. . . . he saw them buried" (p. 189).

4. The importance of the freedom of poetry, "the poetic quality" of which "is not marshalled in rhyme or uniformity or abstract addresses to things . . ." (p. 188).
5. The statement, "The art of art, the glory of expression, and the sunshine of the light of letters is simplicity" (p. 190).
6. Whitman's attitude toward political liberty, starting, "In the make of the great masters the idea of political liberty is indispensable" (p. 192).
7. In relation to freedom [remember, the time is 1855], his statements about the institution of slavery.
8. The most difficult challenges to the poet of "today"—his "direct trial" and the greatness of poets and poems, the "final test of poems or any character or work" (p. 194).
9. Whitman's comments on "A great poem. . . . for all ages and ages in common . . ." (p. 195).
10. His concluding observations on the English language (p. 195).

WAR AND DEHUMANIZATION

One of the most difficult contexts of human experience is war and the dehumanization which accompanies it. Notice how E. E. Cummings distinguishes between *poetry* and *propaganda* (two different uses of language) in "Is Something Wrong" (p. 225)? Then examine the two poems, Randall Jarrell's "Death of the Ball-Turret Gunner" and Dylan Thomas' "A Refusal to Mourn the Death, by Fire, of a Child in London" (p. 223). Do these poets succeed in creating a vivid context of war? How do they do so? In your discussion, include as many contexts as possible to promote an understanding of the poets' works and allude to those contexts especially, which are treated in the "Diagram of Contexts, Words, References" (p. 127). What are some problems in communication which may be analyzed contextually? Explain. Strengths of communication? Discuss.

THE CAMPUS TODAY: REBELLION AND CONFORMITY

After having examined closely Mario Savio's essay, "An End to History," from *Revolution at Berkeley* in Question 4 following the previous chapter of this text, now examine the editorial, "Who Is to Run the University?" reprinted from the *Chicago Tribune*. Review the list of ten contexts which may influence words and conceptualizing from Chapter 7 in your text (p. 125). Applying these contexts, and any others which may come to mind, discuss the *contextual significance* of the editorial. In your discussion, consider from the editorial the following references:

1. To hippies and agitators.
2. Free speech, tenure or reappointment of professors, traveling college and university presidents.
3. Indifference toward students from professors, from administrators, from deans and other educational officials.
4. More student voice in management of the university.
5. Ultimate responsibility for governing the university.
6. Presidential reports to students.
7. The need for "channels," organization, etc.
8. Weakness and "permissive" dealing with student agitation (In this connection, compare Berkeley today with the Berkeley of 1966.).
9. "Thousands of deserving high school graduates . . . being turned away from universities all thru the land," and the "malcontents who hold the places to which they aspire."
10. Preconditions for admission of students to colleges and universities as "simple corrective measures."

THE SEARCH FOR IDENTITY

The *contexts* of the search for identity vary widely. Consider, for example, how Ernest Hemingway exposes the fallacious context of the famous (and often misunderstood) statement, the *"génération perdue"* (the "lost generation") in his conversation as a young writer in France with Gertrude Stein (p. 292). What is the objective context of the original statement? Stein's application of it? Hemingway's response to it? What does Hemingway mean by placing the phrase "lost generation" within the context of "all the dirty, easy labels" (p. 295)?

Similarly, what is the *context* of Eliot's statement from *The Elder Statesman* (p. 295)? Do people in a sense wear masks by making up their faces before they can look into the mirror in the morning? Is the context of the statement figurative for men and literal for women; or does it apply to both in a figurative sense? Discuss the various contexts of meaning including (1) failure in life; (2) self-delusion; (3) pretense and artificiality; (4) honesty toward self; (5) honesty toward others; and (6) illusion and honesty as they relate to individual integrity.

Individual needs. Individual survival. Can everyone live all the time without illusions? Discuss, clarifying specific contexts to support your views.

Now reread the excerpt from Emerson's "The American Scholar" (p. 298). Emerson treats books and reading from several *contexts*. As Emerson views each, how do books and reading relate to the various contexts of

1. Books in relation to the age in which they are written?
2. Books in relation to subsequent and preceding generations?
3. Books well used? Abused?
4. Books for the purpose of inspiration?
5. Reading for "creative actions"?
6. Books as a source of receiving truth from other minds?
7. Books used for "the scholar's idle times"? For pleasure? For "intervals of darkness"?
8. Books as they evince convictions of authors and readers?
9. Books as they may be identified across the reaches of time with one's own unwritten thoughts—mind identifying with mind across the span of centuries?
10. Books as sources for invention, creative reading, and creative writing?
11. Books as a source for basic, necessary information?
12. Books as a source of, and stimulation to, wit?

How do you see each one of these contexts in relation to your own time, concepts, duties, attitudes? May one's opinions concerning such matters as books and reading vary within the context being considered? Discuss, giving examples or anecdotes to support your views. May the accuracy of thinking, discussion, and writing depend upon the *context of meaning*? Again, declare your answers as substantively as possible.

Review your answer to Question No. 5 under "the search for identity," Chapter 5, in Part I (p. 92). How may the term "identity crisis" be related to various *contexts*? Being as broad as definiteness will permit in your reasoning, consider some of the following contexts:

1. Crisis of infancy.
2. Crisis of childhood when one's individuality begins to develop. When one's will begins to develop.
3. Crisis within the family, especially during early adolescence.
4. Sexual identity. In relation to parents. Confusions of identity in sexuality. Normal patterns and perversion.
5. Social identity, especially with groups as the individual desires to work with others. Advantages. Disadvantages. Finding and losing identity through group associations.
6. Identity of self with what may be termed moral standards. Conflict between the ideal and the real. Disillusionment as it affects individuation. Is it possible to retain one's ideals and yet live in a real world? Discuss. How may one alter his ideals,

bringing them within the realm of reality (possibility of accomplishment), yet retain the best of them? Put another way, how does one adjust his ideals practicably within the context of reality, without losing his sense of integrity and developing a destructive inner conflict leading to demoralization? Discuss as concretely as possible.

7. The crises of adulthood, middle age, occupational selection, and fulfillment. Need one's identity be fixed? May one find identity through mobility? May one's identity be, in a sense, dynamic (changing) within still workable limits? Discuss in relation to geographic, social, economic, and spiritual mobility.

8. The crisis of old age and death. How may one give his life meaning, even through death? Can you give specific examples of people who have done so? Discuss.

Finally, examine closely Clark Kerr's statement from *Industrialism and Industrial Man* in the epigraph of Part II, Chapter 12 (p. 261). Assuming some truth in Kerr's contentions, how may problems of personal identity be related to extremist behavior on the part of college and university students? Be as precise as possible in your comments. For example, may some students tend to respond in an extremist manner (from chauvinistic displays of patriotism to anarchistic riots) because of an anxiety impressed upon them through a lack of "belonging," feelings of alienation from society, a sense of failure, a response to being an "outsider"? Discuss concretely. Do all people, at times, feel like striking back? Becoming a "disaffiliate" from one's peers and dominant culture? Do all feel "fed up"? When do these moments occur? In your own experience? In those of others about whom you have heard or read? Discuss. Conversely, how may acquiring mooring cables of identity, so to speak, tend to decrease extremist responses to reality? Can you give examples with your answers?

LOVE, SEX, AND CENSORSHIP

Relate the contexts of young love, lost love, nostalgic love, physical love, and spiritual love to the following works:

1. William Shakespeare, excerpt from *Romeo and Juliet* (p. 304).
2. John Donne, "A Valediction: Forbidding Mourning" (p. 307).
3. Ernest Dowson, "Non Sum Qualis Eram Bonae Sub Regno Cynarae" (p. 309).
4. Rupert Brooke, "The Hill" (p. 310).
5. Edwin Arlington Robinson, "Another Dark Lady" (p. 311).
6. William Butler Yeats, "A Deep-Sworn Vow" (p. 311).
7. Theodore Roethke, "I Knew a Woman" (p. 312).

In what other contexts do you find any one or more of these works especially meaningful? Through consideration of various contexts, endeavor to build as many bridges of communication as possible with the poet or maker of the poems. Discuss as concretely as possible, within clear reference points of defined *contexts*.

INDIVIDUAL RESPONSIBILITY

Compare and contrast the two works "Dover Beach" (p. 440), by Matthew Arnold, and "The Myth of Sisyphus" (p. 441), by Albert Camus. Read the introduction to Arnold's poem, first published in 1867, and relating the work to the age out of which it originated, discuss the various *contexts* of "faith," "doubt," "self-examination," "historical past," "meaning in life," "wars," "love," and other dimensions of significant meaning.

Similarly, examine the following *contexts* and *meanings*, comparing them with Arnold's where appropriate:
1. Sisyphus as myth(s).
2. Sisyphus as a "futile and hopeless" laborer.
3. Sisyphus as a god who has "put Death in chains."
4. Sisyphus as a lover of life, punished for his passions.
5. Sisyphus as an "absurd hero," whose "whole being is exerted toward accomplishing nothing.
6. Sisyphus as a symbol of man, the "wholly human security of two earth-clotted hands."
7. Sisyphus' face which "toils so close to stones" that it is "already stone itself!" and the following four sentences, concluding, "He is stronger than his rock."
8. Sisyphus as a tragic hero because he is "conscious"
9. The context of *paradox* in the statement, "The lucidity that was to constitute his torture at the same time crowns his victory," or ". . . crushing truths perish from being acknowledged."
10. The comparison to Sophocles' tragic hero (Œdipus).
11. "Happiness and the absurd are two sons of the same earth."
12. "Sisyphus' silent joy" in making of fate "a human matter, which must be settled among men," and the pithy, "His rock is his thing."
13. The contexts of life and death in the statement, "There is no sun without shadow, and it is essential to know the night."
14. Contrast especially Camus's statement, "This universe henceforth without a master seems to him neither sterile nor futile," with Arnold's ". . . the world, which seems/ To lie before us like a land of dreams . . . Hath really neither joy, nor peace, nor help for pain. . . ."
15. "One must imagine Sisyphus happy," for "The struggle itself toward the heights is enough to fill a man's heart."

GOD, MAN, AND MORAL CONSCIOUSNESS

What are the various contexts of Gerard Manley Hopkins' famous poem, "God's Grandeur"? Of Robert Frost's "Stopping by Woods on a Snowy Evening" (p. 362)? In which poem can you develop a wider range of meaningful contexts? Discuss.

LITERATURE AND GOOD WRITING

After reading the first chapter of this text, the question on Literature and Good Writing dealt with Walt Whitman's "O Captain! My Captain!" a well-known elegy to Abraham Lincoln. Now read what is, perhaps, the greatest tribute ever written on Abraham Lincoln, Walt Whitman's "When Lilacs Last in the Dooryard Bloom'd" (p. 396), certainly one of Whitman's greatest poems. Read the fifteen sections of the poem carefully, and in so doing, note the many *contexts* with which the poet communicates his ideas in the language of poetry, among them the following:

1. The life and death of Lincoln.
2. Beauty of nature, especially spring.
3. The symbolism of the "powerful western fallen star!"
4. The "lilac bush tall-growing with heart-shaped leaves of rich green," as well as the emblematical meaning of "A sprig with its flower I break."
5. The ultimate meaning of the hermit thrush. Why does the bird sing a "Song of the bleeding throat"?
6. The solemn journey of the train across the country westward to Illinois, the description along the way.
7. The universal meaning of death within the particularity of the tragic death of the American President.
8. The growing strength of the thrush's song, and its relationship to the poet's song.
9. The meaning of death itself; its relationship to the song of the hermit thrush.
10. The choric praise to death, the nature of suffering in war (examine as *paradox* in Section 14), and the strikingly evocative power of unity of the final fifteenth section, in which the poet weaves the three symbols ("Lilac and star and bird") together with his soul in the midst of life and nature.

AGE OF CONTROVERSY

In what *contexts* is Faulkner's "The Tribute to the Mule" from *Sartoris* (p. 452) an affirmation of life? Is it a *paradoxical* affirmation? Discuss. Similarly, within the dominant *context* of the affirmation of life, apply as many specific *contexts* of meaning as possible to selected works from the following:

1. Edgar Lee Masters, "Lucinda Matlock" (p. 453).
2. Henry David Thoreau, excerpts from *Walden* (p. 454).
3. Henry James, excerpt from *The Ambassadors* (p. 459).
4. Leo Tolstoy, "To Love Life Is to Love God," excerpt from *War and Peace* (p. 461).

8
CHAPTER THE LAST

Mastering the basic elements of composition is important. Such fundamental skills as the development of "sentence sense," consistently accurate punctuation, spelling, capitalization, grammatical construction, and a knowledge of paragraph and theme organization are essential skills and can and should be reviewed in a good handbook of English. (The "Composition Symbol Chart" in this text has been designed to help in such reviews.) But we have also seen that the elementary tools of composition, though they require repeated study and practice, represent only minimal knowledge. The bedrock of good writing is *natural fluency,* which springs from original thinking transmuted into lucid verbal expression—which *means* that we must think as accurately as possible. Such writing never emerges from careless thinking, or the use of trite expressions, vague generalizations, or clichés. Neither does a good writer use the easy phrase, time-worn expression, or abstractions, polysyllabic words intended to impress rather than to convey meaning, purple passages, or a cheap sloganizing to persuade. Good writing is not made up of parroting habits or preconceived thought and word patterns. Rather, as simple as it sounds, the student who writes well will first think clearly. His mind will govern the words (symbols) he chooses to communicate his thoughts. Nor will he give in to the tendency to let habitual word and sentence patterns control his thinking. When he writes he will be primarily concerned with saying what he means to say. If what he has written does not reflect his thought, he will rethink his ideas. By concentrated effort he will pull the stuff of original thinking from his mind and shape it into word and sentence patterns that satisfy his sense of what might be termed writing honesty. He will, in short, match the thought to the word as precisely as he can, knowing as he does so that he must break through old shells of preconceived expressions—indeed, ignore them even as their barriers tend to channel his thinking into the old grooves and to weaken the force of his ideas.

Aware of the changing nature of language, the student who wants to think and to write well sees a basic contradiction between clear thought and language usage: many people conceive of language as permanent, never-changing, static. Because they do not move from thoughts to words, or because their thoughts do not activate their word choices, they often allow their thought processes to be imprisoned by a kind of "verbal environment." Much as people develop other kinds of personal habits, they tend also to develop verbal habits. Habits tend to become automatic; hence, the thoughts and words of many people often seem to be unreflective, rigid, static, cut off from further development. Such people tend to be nearsighted about the reality around them. They falsely assume things have always been more or less as they perceive them. They tend to think of language as meaning precisely what *they* "mean," what *they* "think," and they attach an illusory permanence to the language they use.

We do not know precisely how language developed, although there are various theories of its origin. Most linguists believe that thought had to precede or develop along with the evolution of language. And just as language has evolved over a long period of time, it is still evolving. A tracing of the origins of our own English language demonstrates the point. Emerging out of the West German division of the Germanic or Teutonic branch of the Indo-European group, Old English may seem as foreign to us today as another language. The changes which occurred by the Middle English period (1066–1500) were profound in all aspects, including vocabulary, grammar, spelling, and pronunciation, and even early modern English (that in Shakespeare's plays, for example), when judged by college students of the 1970's, may at times be difficult to understand because of continuing shifts in meaning and usage.

Change of meaning is natural, since the circumstances with which man deals in everyday reality situations change about him. Language, we remember, reflects thinking; it is a way of expressing ideas. The meaning of a word, therefore, may be restricted or narrowed (for example, *deer*); its meaning can be transferred or changed until original concepts may be altogether lost (for example, *gossip*); or its meaning may be extended, and the word may gain a variety of newer meanings (for example, *board*). Transfers of meaning continue also in the form of metaphors, as when we say, "I'm blue," "She's with it," or "Joe's uptight." Likewise, extensions of meaning are evident in the slang of today which may become the accepted language of tomorrow (although most slang expressions are short-lived). Even though we may tend to think and behave otherwise, there is little that is permanent or sacred about words. Indeed, language is so changeable that over periods of time words may come to mean the opposite of what they once meant (for example, *calm*).

Words are symbols, not things. The perceptive student knows this, for he is aware that any word or group of words merely *represents* a thought about something. And he does not mistake the thought for the thing. Even so, he may at times unthinkingly confuse what he says or writes with reality itself. But if he realizes that words *cannot be* things, then he will tend to avoid the confusions which arise from this verbal illusion. In doing so, he will become more aware of the world as it is, he will be better able to cope with changes, and he will recognize words as tools with which to find better communication between people rather than to protect any personal distortions of reality.

Language is flexible when properly understood. There are many meanings of a word, and people use words to mean different things. If people fail to perceive the flexibility of language, they may sometimes lead themselves into foolish behavior, sometimes with tragic consequences. Some people have such a strange understanding of reality that they conceive of words as being things, and hence of people as being objects. Such people tend to "use" other human beings for their own selfish purposes; that is, they look upon people as mere names, as so many "its" to be manipulated. They tend to confuse *their own way* of thinking with *the way* people should think. Thus, when thwarted, their responses to life are childishly concerned with self rather than with others. In moments of crisis, they tend to become personally involved in a highly emotional sense. They may be angry and throw fits and tantrums. Of course, we are aware that children often confuse one thing with another, or the name with the thing, and we laugh at their mistakes, but what of the adults who confuse a man with a particular name for an abstract cause, and then, in slaying the man, think they have slain the cause? Or, on another level, what of those women who pathogenically confuse a product with a particularly emotive name with such realities as beauty, romance, sex appeal, cleanliness, slimness, youth, vivacity, and charm? Although such an adult may be laughed at, he seldom sees his own confusion of words (symbols) with the things (referents) for which they stand.

Various levels of language include the meaning without the word, the dictionary meaning of the word (denotation), the associated meanings of the word (connotations), and the private meaning of the word (concepts remote from reality). The student who thinks and writes clearly will be aware that the reality which a word represents is always subverbal and exists without the word. All words, therefore, mean different (sometimes slightly, sometimes widely different) things each time they are used. The perceptive student will try to think matters out clearly with all his senses before attaching words to his thoughts and then writing them; such a student is like the chemist who discovers "new" things before he names them, or the poet who looks at life and expresses what he senses in new and excitingly different ways. In short, the perceptive student tries to understand life about him *subverbally*. Similarly, in his thinking, speaking, and writing, such a student endeavors to stay as close to subverbal reality as possible by using denotations of words, and by rendering his ideas through direct or explicit words which first report the basics of his insights. The student who thinks and writes clearly tries to choose his words and arrange them in ways which force us to feel and to understand him in ways as close to his original intentions as possible. In attempting to communicate concretely, he may use metaphors, comparisons, contrasts, and richly connotative words that suggest other associations which he desires us to make. Such a creative student wants us to think of and to sense the color of life itself, much as he does.

The most treacherous level of language is the private one, which is remote from reality. It is at least three levels removed from reality and may be even farther away than that. Often the private meaning is cut off, separate from reality. To the extent that a person's response to reality involves a pattern of remoteness, he may tend to be unsane in his thinking, although we should remember that all people at times react "privately," hence irrationally, and their language upon such occasions reflects it.

Awareness of subverbal reality and the ability to recognize generalizations are closely related. Generalizations are vague words which often omit important details and concrete terms, often broadly emphasizing more than what is meant and employing abstract terms to hazy ends. Properly oriented students of language tend to strike through generalizations and become aware of the meaning without the word. Hence, their views of reality are often much better balanced than those of students whose thought processes are usually lost in a maze of abstract words.

Clear thinking is the major prerequisite of good writing. Language itself, however, tends to move toward abstraction, away from rather than closer to reality. Hence, the natural tendency in thinking and writing is to let our thoughts fall back on familiar and comfortable generalizations. It is easy to be unoriginal. Originality, on the other hand, demands a subverbal habit—clear thinking controlled and kept close to the reality about which we are cogitating, speaking, or writing.

Words and human behavior are closely related. Although, in the broadest sense, signs may be said to include symbols, for purposes of this text a distinction is made: *signs point directly* to the existence, either past, present, or future, of something else, while *symbols* are made by man to *stand for, to represent,* something. Symbols must be accompanied by an active thought process. Man is the only symbol-making creature, and only he can hold onto his symbols and write them down. He is the only "time-binding" creature.

Man, along with other animals, uses signs, and he may use them incorrectly. For example, upon emerging from the theater he may mistake freshly washed streets for rain. He does not "think" in such cases. There is a tendency for man to create signs and then to use them in place of thought. Propaganda slogans are one example; advertising slogans are another. Some politicians try to keep their constituents from thinking by using signs to appeal to their emotions rather than symbols to appeal to their reason. Signs differ among different peoples of the world.

A knowledgeable student of language is aware of Aristotelian ways of thinking which have, through the ages, virtually become laws: the law of identity, the law of the excluded middle, and the law of contradiction. Generalizations based on Aristotle's logic may seem to be only common sense, but they do not work in all situations. Often, they are misapplied, as when a convict is "overidentified" as a convict even after he is no longer in prison and has become in reality a reformed man. "Two-valued thinkers" tend to rely heavily on the law of the excluded middle; thus, they may think of ideas in extremes of good-bad, possible-impossible, new-old, true-false. They may look upon their fellow human beings as strong-weak, beautiful-ugly, smart-dumb, sociable or antisocial, hardworking or lazy. Similarly, the law of contradiction sanctions two-valued approaches, denying simultaneous possibilities.

Modern concepts of language and reality are less rigid. By 1660 John Locke observed that people supposed their words to stand for the reality of things, but pointed out the fallacy of the assumption, especially Aristotle's law of identity. Foremost among a group of modern thinkers who attempted to study language and to make it more consistent with the constructive behavior of mankind was Alfred Korzybski. His premises of nonidentity, non-allness, and self-reflexiveness, when placed alongside Aristotle's three laws, appeared at first to be virtual obverse reflections of them, but actually they were simply a more accurate filling out of what Aristotle had begun. Before Korzybski, people had known that words were not the things, but only represented the things. They knew, too, that no word or group of words could represent all the reality for which they were fallaciously presumed to stand. And certainly most people realized that the more people treated an idea in language, the further they tended to stray from the essentials and the more tangential their discussion became. But these modern premises of language had never been systemized before; they had never been closely examined as more accurate approaches than those of Aristotle. Students of language and logic began to see and to communicate to their students the many implications of these premises. For example, two-valued approaches were immediately exposed as fallacious, and the misapplications and inaccuracies of Aristotle's law of the excluded middle were repeatedly demonstrated. Similarly, the premise of non-allness demonstrated the higher logic of multiordinal or infinite-valued responses to situations encountered in reality. The ultimate effect has been, in part at least, to give perceptive students of language much more accurate concepts of subverbal reality than they had previously experienced—concepts which, in turn, promote original thinking and better writing. In order to achieve these results, however, it is necessary *to implement* these modern concepts of language, not only in what we read, say, and write, but also in the everyday reality situations we encounter. That is, modern concepts of language should emerge in habits of thought and action.

To deal effectively with generalizations, the student must first recognize them. Generalizations give us the main or overall features of something; they are not specific and detailed, but instead are vague and lacking in precision. Some generalizations are necessary in family situations and everyday greetings—in telling people how we feel rather than how we think about matters of information. But in order to get closer to meanings which lie under the level of language itself (subverbal realities), it is first necessary to *recognize* generalizations. If one wishes to think close to reality, he must *index* misleading generalizations; for example, he can avoid erroneous descriptions of groups by pointing out the ways individuals within the group differ from each other.

Even though the world is in flux and all things in process of change, the behavior responses of most people are, comparatively, fixed. We tend to be imprisoned by the language we use; even professionals are often limited by their jargon. If one expects to think close to reality, he must *date* a fact or event in order to place it in time, relative to change, to place, and to circumstances. Indexing and dating must be implemented frequently in order for these very processes to become part of our thinking habits. In so doing, we can deal with generalizations more successfully—think and express ourselves more accurately and meaningfully.

Cliché was originally a French term meaning a "stereotype plate," although it was applied in French to mean a "stereotyped phrase." A cliché means, then, an expression that has become trite. There are so many clichés in the language that a particularly energetic and sensitive composition student finds that he must run them like an obstacle course when he tries to write something well. Like the generalization, a cliché handicaps thinking. In a sense, clichés may be looked upon as extreme, compressed forms of generalizations. But we can avoid them in the same way we avoid generalizations. We first recognize the expression as a cliché; then we index it and date it. We may use an anecdote or a comparison to make what is vague more concrete. We try to particularize the general by thinking clearly and by placing our thoughts into new shapes of words, as it were.

Generalizations imply that one can treat different things in the same way. If a person does not limit his generalizations to such understandable uses as, let us say, greeting friends and socializing, but instead allows generalizations to replace thinking, then he is in danger of oversimplifying the complex realities of life. No matter what the individual's generation—whether he is old or young—he tends to develop generalized ways of looking at things. Gradually one's vision of reality in a given instance is symbolized by a word or phrase: "the age of reason," "the mauve decade," "the lost generation," "the roaring twenties," "the big apple generation," "the beat generation," "the hippie generation." Group labels are seldom accurate; the thinking person is always suspicious of them, for they are generalizations, too frequently evasions of thought. If one insists on using generalizations, fails to recognize them, to correct them by indexing and dating—in brief, fails to say and write what he really means—then he becomes lost in a kind of verbal crazy-house of mirrors constructed by his own distorted imaginings and, hence, remote from subverbal reality.

The basic problems in the abstraction of language stem from the self-reflexive nature of word usage. Usually, the more we talk about something, the farther away we tend to move from it. Misunderstandings occur. Communication breaks down. We fail to learn. One way of checking the tendency to stray far afield is to refer to the subverbal level of reality as closely as possible. In addition, we should be aware of concrete as opposed to abstract terms as we use them.

The relativity of concreteness and abstractness is another more complex consideration. As we saw illustrated in the "Cycle of Relativity," there may be many legitimately "real" views of even a simple concept, each more concrete than any other in relation to a particular person who considers certain characteristics of a thing more important than all others. As helpful as the terms *concrete* and *abstract* may be, then, they are not always enough; for the context of meaning often governs significance and accuracy. The ability to examine a time-space event (pig, human being, object, etc.) with a multiplicity of views is important in keeping ourselves closely oriented to subverbal levels of reality. In doing so we can better see relationships between ideas, cross over the boundaries of narrow concepts, encompass new ideas, and consider many approaches to whatever we may confront in life about us. Multiordinal concepts, however, must be implemented in order to be useful. They must be consciously employed each day, for theory without practice is a dream without fulfillment.

Among the various problems in logic are some common fallacies which are obstacles to communication; if permitted to go unchallenged, they contribute to false and mistaken ideas, opinions, and illogical modes of argument. These abuses of logic include the broad generalization; the generalized prediction; the argument against the man; the cause-effect fallacy; the false analogy; the appeal to authority; the appeal to the public; a begging of the question or arguing in a circle; overidentity or the fallacy of false identity; and the excluded-middle fallacy.

Verbal confusions largely derive from certain basic problems which may be summarized as follows: excessive application of what may be termed "overidentity"; the remote, "private meaning" of or "response" to language; the use of unrecognized generalizations; the tendency to use words about words (self-reflexiveness); and the failure to be aware of and to use as many approaches to a given circumstance as possible (multiordinality).

Similarly, various kinds of ambiguities add to verbal confusions: the *double entendre*, vague pronoun references, unclear or misplaced modifiers, overcompression, faulty inversions, "overwriting," and incomplete comparisons. Often ambiguities represent thinking gone awry in such a way that the resulting lack of clarity produces comical responses—sadly, when the speaker or writer may want to be deadly serious, as, for example, the welfare recipient who dutifully reported to the proper authorities: "I have just given birth to twins, as you can see, enclosed in the envelope."

An analogy is a kind of extended comparison in which one concept is explained in terms of another. Misconceptions are sometimes derived from poor analogies, just as good analogies may produce a clearer understanding of ideas. The quality of an analogy depends upon the similarities of the unlike items compared, the scarcity of the dissimilarities, and—the most important point—the relevance of the analogy in explaining the purpose of the speaker or writer. The perceptive student of language should be able to recognize strong analogies so as to effectuate clear thinking and good writing, and he should be able to expose false analogies, which muddle thinking and weaken expression.

Language may be used for many purposes; it may even, unfortunately, be used to disguise or to prevent thought. Among its more obvious uses are those of imparting general or specific communication, the hortative use (inciting by words), and persuasion. Of course, language is used in other ways, too. The language of literature communicates on the level of information, but it also appeals to the reader's senses. The sensuous level of language gives rise to a more or less emotional response, and all three levels working together produce the "imaginative dimension" of the language of literature, one of the highest uses of language. But language may be used for base, selfish purposes, to serve profit motives, to convince people to think in a certain way which benefits those aims. Such uses of language usually operate from the thesis that people are things rather than human beings, objects rather than fellowmen capable of independent thought, and therefore are subject to manipulation, channeling into grooves. People are to be herded as so many cattle for nonhuman purposes. The worst of these self-serving uses of language is *propaganda,* and all these uses, to varying degrees, are pathogenic—hence, intended to deceive man in his thinking, or even to "help" him to avoid thinking altogether.

Thought also may be circumvented in various other ways, among them *up-labeling* and *down-labeling.* No matter how subtle efforts may be to tempt people to avoid thinking for themselves, to lead their thinking into certain planned "molds," or to supplant their thinking completely—they are all abuses of language.

Context indicates the parts of a statement which go before and follow a specified word or unit of language, all parts of which are necessary for the determination of specific meaning. If any part of a statement is taken out and quoted, the quotation is said to be taken "out of context." In a broader sense, however, language itself has a context involving the collective conditions, background, and situation relevant to the statement—all of which are important. Language can never be isolated as an entity unto itself. Meaning is dependent upon surrounding events and stimuli. Words mean in many contexts, among them emotions, economic considerations, social settings, the desire for friendship, sexual attitudes, and intellectual curiosity.

Meaning is closely related to the nature of context, for our words mean through the thinking processes of those involved; that is, meaning takes place through human minds. Since people do not think in a vacuum, their thoughts are constantly qualified, altered, and reshaped by what may be said, heard, read, and perceived through other media. Among the contexts which may influence words and conceptualizing are these: culture, language and the nature of communication, age and time, knowledge, physical-mental-nervous similarities and differences, social relationships, intellectual affinity, psychological factors, political persuasions, and purposes for symbolizing. To the extent that people ignore these contexts in their efforts to communicate with each other, even members of the same family may find mutual understanding is diminished, as illustrated in the "Diagram of Contexts, Words, and References" (Chapter 7). However, if efforts are made to deal with various contexts—to be aware of them, to approach communication thoughtfully before speaking, to follow through simply, clearly, and directly, and to listen to and to understand the other person as well— then what we speak and write will be far more effective, for meaning and contexts will tend to coincide.

Humor through change of context is often the result of a sudden change in a preconditioned direction of meaning. There are many examples of such humor. If the shift of context consists of one clause balancing another, and the contrast is direct and strong, then the distinctive form is known as *antithesis;* other forms of change of context may involve *paradox,* in which an apparent contradiction, upon closer examination, proves to be true. Another example, "He is so fat that when he takes a shower his feet don't get wet," involves a change of context (shower-dryness) which may be termed *hyperbole.* Humor through change of context should not be confused with a *pun,* however; for a pun involves primarily a play on words and word sounds. Countless illustrations of the pun exist. For example, there was the girl who went to college to learn art but instead eloped her freshman year: She put her heart before the course.

THE LANGUAGE CLINIC

Many problems in thinking and writing can be readily identified and dealt with. Elementary difficulties in basic English, for example, may be met through a conscientious use of the "Composition Symbol Chart" and the repeated practice its use entails. A person who is unaware of the changing nature of language may insist on spelling words in ways that no longer reflect usage. To illustrate, forty years ago *today* was spelled *to-day;* thirty years ago *judgment* was spelled *judgement;* more recently *catalogue* has given way to *catalog;* and soon *cigarette* may be largely supplanted by *cigaret.*

Similarly, a person who confuses words with things may repeatedly be at odds with reality situations; if his meanings are *private,* he may be constantly thwarted and frustrated. We all have known people who have made grotesques of their lives by confusing one exalted idea with a totalistic concept of reality. Thus, if the spiritual dimension of life becomes "the all" of existence for a person, he may become what we call a "religious fanatic"; the student who virtually lives in a library, reading, becomes a "bookworm"; the one who frantically seeks a round of parties is known as a "playboy" or "playgirl"; and the ever gung-ho athlete may become a narcissistic "physical culturist." All such people, failing to conceive of the various levels of language, and lapsing into the most dangerous *private level,* may live their lives remote from reality in a constant illusion of the imposed "rightness" of their eccentric selfhoods.

In the same way, one who fails to be aware of modern concepts of language may tend to *overidentify* people, ideas, and institutions. Such a person tends to confuse the individual with a class, or the class with an individual, as if both were one and the same. Common illustrations of *overidentity* involve sweeping *generalizations* about national and racial groups; about political, social, and philosophical ideas and parties or groups identified with them; and about religions. Such people may become *two-valued* in their views of the truly *infinite-valued* aspects of human existence. Or as they examine and discuss events and ideas, they may let the *symbol* supplant original thought and fall into the habit of using words about words, hence moving farther away from, rather than closer to reality.

The *generalization* is, perhaps, the major obstacle of the would-be thinker and writer. Often he is not even aware of the generalizations he uses. Once he is made sensitive to them (as to clichés), he can *index* and *date* them, and then, perhaps, can begin to reshape them, giving them new and fresh word patterns.

In striving for new shapes of language, he can supplant the *abstract* with the *concrete*, but always within the context of a proper *relativity*, being aware of the *infinite number* of approaches to a given animal, object, or concept, thus qualifying his expressed and particularized idea even while acknowledging the wide range of other possibilities. In this instance, *multiordinality* would replace *overidentity* and the general would become more specific.

Common fallacies, too, can be readily identified and treated as can other more general kinds of verbal confusions, including *ambiguities* and *false analogies.* The abuses of language such as *up-labeling, down-labeling, propaganda,* and other *pathogenic misapplications* can be exposed for what they are. *Contexts* of language and meaning can be explored in an effort to establish new bridges of communication, and even humor may be more richly understood and readily created by a knowledge of the celerity with which contexts may shift, turn awry into new and antic currents.

Most problems in thinking and writing fall into one, or perhaps a few more of these innumerable categories. If a person is aware of such errors, and has developed the habit of implementing corrective measures and proceeds to do so, he can quickly improve his understanding, speaking, and writing.

But there are more complex situations, more profound problems which involve not merely one or a few corrective implementations, but rather a whole range of approaches. Here, the problem may not be solved with mere *analysis* and the application of a few corrective measures. Rather, the problem invites a pulling together of *multiordinal* approaches, what might be termed a *synthesis* of nearly all the student has learned in his study of language and its modern concepts. Not only the basic knowledge itself will be involved, but also the *how* of using it. In addition, the perceptive student will not only exhaust numerous possible approaches, but will bring repeatedly fresh thought processes and original ideas to the inquiry. He will scrutinize, rethink, attack the problem repeatedly, regroup his approaches, question, puzzle, and keep trying until he makes some kind of order out of a seeming chaos.

If a problem is one of this kind—too complex to be treated by the substance of one of the previous chapters—then it may be placed into the *language clinic*, where all of the resources of this text as well as the student's ingenuity may be brought to bear upon the search for solution. Following are some sample topics which fall into this category:

1. What do most students in American colleges and universities want today? What explains their unrest, and what common meanings may be found in their restlessness?

2. When is war justified? When is the killing of one human being by another human being justified?

3. Under what circumstances would nuclear war be logical? What is the major reason for nuclear stockpiling? Is it rational?

4. Why do major nations in the world today place budgetary emphasis on their military-industrial complexes (for example, about sixty percent of the national budget of the United States is absorbed by defense)? If the rationale for sophisticated weapons systems is that by having one we can keep any other nation from using its own against us, can you think of other answers with better rationales?

5. It has been said that a knowledge of science is more practicable (workable) today than a knowledge of the humanities. Comment.

6. Is man evil and suicidal by nature? Why does he desire power over others? Why does he behave violently, hurt other people, and destroy himself and others in violence?

7. Is man innately a good and loving creature who desires to survive and to procreate his kind above all else? Why does he affirm life frequently, even in the midst of tragedy?

8. Some people have stated that man is a "group animal." Assuming that the statement is generally accurate, why do men then divide the world into subgroups, creeds, and nations; and then contend with each other, often fighting and killing each other? What are such "group animals" trying to prove?

9. Are men (*homo sapiens*) one species in one world? If so, in what ways should man try to overcome his group distinctions and, perhaps, transcend them? Discuss consequences and rationales.

10. The population of the United States reached 100 million in 1917, rose to 200 million by 1967, and, at the present rate of growth, it will reach nearly 308 million by the year 2000. The population of the underdeveloped nations of the world will double in about half the time ours has taken. Most biologists and ecologists who have studied population trends and its dangers believe that if we do not take effective measures to

limit overpopulation our civilization cannot endure. Discuss possible solutions. Implications of urgency?

11. In the context of man in 1350, 1850, and the present, respectively, discuss the meaning of the following terms: *success, nature, competition, peace, love, progress, good, evil, beauty, wisdom, compassion, sacrifice, pride, victory, defeat, sanity, insanity (unsanity), endurance, industry, temperance (moderation), humility, tragedy,* and *humor.*

PART 2

PART 2

9
SCIENCE AND THE HUMANITIES IN CONFLICT

"Science is a first-rate piece of furniture for a man's upper-chamber, if he has common-sense on the ground floor."

—Oliver Wendell Holmes,
The Poet at the Breakfast Table, Ch. 5

SOME DEFINITIONS OF "SCIENCE" AND THE "HUMANITIES"

1. William H. Smyth, a definition of "technocracy" from *Concerning Irascible Strong* (1926), used by Smyth first in *Industrial Management*, March 1919: "Scientific reorganization of national energy and resources, coordinating industrial democracy to effect the will of the people."
2. Miguel de Unamuno, a definition from *The Tragic Sense of Life*, p. 93: "True science teaches, above all, to doubt and to be ignorant."
3. Henry James, a definition of art, an aspect of the humanities: "Art is nothing more than the shadow of humanity," from *Lectures: University in Arts.*
4. Dante, an inclusive definition from *De Monarchia*, Pt. I, 1. 3: "Nature is the art of God."

C. P. Snow

THE TWO CULTURES

"It's rather odd," said G. H. Hardy, one afternoon in the early Thirties, "but when we hear about 'intellectuals' nowadays, it doesn't include people like me and J. J. Thomson and Rutherford." Hardy was the first mathematician of his generation, J. J. Thomson the first physicist of his; as for Rutherford, he was one of the greatest scientists who has ever lived. Some bright young literary person (I forget the exact context) putting them outside the enclosure reserved for intellectuals seemed to Hardy the best joke for some time. It does not seem quite such a good joke now. The separation between the two cultures has been getting deeper under our eyes; there is now precious little communication between them, little but different kinds of incomprehension and dislike.

The traditional culture, which is, of course, mainly literary, is behaving like a state whose power is rapidly declining—standing on its precarious dignity, spending far too much energy on Alexandrian intricacies, occasionally letting fly in fits of aggressive pique quite beyond its means, too much on the defensive to show any generous imagination to the forces which must inevitably reshape it. Whereas the scientific culture is expansive, not restrictive, confident at the roots, the more confident after its bout of Oppenheimerian self-criticism, certain that history is on its side, impatient, intolerant, creative rather than critical, good-natured and brash. Neither culture knows the virtues of the other; often it seems they deliberately do not want to know. The resentment which the traditional culture feels for the scientific is shaded with fear;

Reprinted from *New Statesman and Nation*, LII, October 6, 1956, pp. 413–414, by permission.

from the other side, the resentment is not shaded so much as brimming with irritation. When scientists are faced with an expression of the traditional culture, it tends (to borrow Mr. William Cooper's eloquent phrase) to make their feet ache.

It does not need saying that generalizations of this kind are bound to look silly at the edges. There are a good many scientists indistinguishable from literary persons, and vice versa. Even the stereotype generalizations about scientists are misleading without some sort of detail—e.g., the generalization that scientists as a group stand on the political Left. This is only partly true. A very high proportion of engineers is almost as conservative as doctors; of pure scientists, the same would apply to chemists. It is only among physicists and biologists that one finds the Left in strength. If one compared the whole body of scientists with their opposite numbers of the traditional culture (writers, academics, and so on), the total result might be a few percent more towards the Left wing, but not more than that. Nevertheless, as a first approximation, the scientific culture is real enough, and so is its difference from the traditional. For anyone like myself, by education a scientist, by calling a writer, at one time moving between groups of scientists and writers in the same evening, the difference has seemed dramatic.

The first thing, impossible to miss, is that scientists are on the up and up; they have the strength of a social force behind them. If they are English, they share the experience common to us all—of being in a country sliding economically downhill—but in addition (and to many of them it seems psychologically more important) they belong to something more than a profession, to something more like a directing class of a new society. In a sense oddly divorced from politics, they are the new men. Even the staidest and most politically conservative of scientific veterans, lurking in dignity in their colleges, have some kind of link with the world to come. They do not hate it as their colleagues do; part of their mind is open to it; almost against their will, there is a residual glimmer of kinship there. The young English scientists may and do curse their luck; increasingly they fret about the rigidities of their universities, about the ossification of the traditional culture which, to the scientists, makes the universities cold and dead; they violently envy their Russian counterparts who have money and equipment without discernible limit, who have the whole field wide open. But still they stay pretty resilient: they are swept on by the same social force. Harwell and Winscale have just as much spirit as Los Alamos and Chalk River: the neat petty bourgeois houses, the tough and clever young, the crowds of children: they are symbols, frontier towns.

There is a touch of the frontier qualities, in fact, about the whole scientific culture. Its tone is, for example, steadily heterosexual. The difference in social manners between Harwell and Hampstead, or as far as that goes between Los Alamos and Greenwich Village, would make an anthropologist blink. About the whole scientific culture, there is an absence—surprising to outsiders—of the feline and oblique. Sometimes it seems that scientists relish speaking the truth, especially when it is unpleasant. The climate of personal relations is singularly bracing, not to say harsh: it strikes bleakly on those unused to it, who suddenly find that the scientists' way of deciding on action is by a full-dress argument, with no regard for sensibilities and no holds barred. No body of people ever believed more in dialectic as the primary method of attaining sense; and if you want a picture of scientists in their off-moments it could be just one of a knock-about argument. Under the argument there glitter egotisms as rapacious as any of ours: but, unlike ours, the egotisms are driven by a common purpose.

How much of the traditional culture gets through to them? The answer is not simple. A good many scientists, including some of the most gifted, have the tastes of literary persons, read the same things, and read as much. Broadly, though, the infiltration is much less. History gets across to a certain extent, in particular social history: the sheer mechanics of living, how men ate, built, travelled, worked, touches a good many scientific imaginations, and so they have fastened on such works as Trevelyan's *Social History,* and Professor Gordon Childe's books. Philosophy, the scientific culture views with indifference, especially metaphysics. As Rutherford said cheerfully to Samuel Alexander: "When you think of all the years you've been talking about those things, Alexander, and what does it all add up to? *Hot air,* nothing but *hot air."* A bit less exuberantly, that is what contemporary scientists would say. They regard it as a major intellectual virtue, to know what not to think about. They might touch their hats to linguistic analysis, as a relatively honourable way of wasting time; not so to existentialism.

The arts? The only one which is cultivated among scientists is music. It goes both wide and deep; there may possibly be a greater density of musical appreciation than in the traditional culture. In comparison, the graphic arts (except architecture) score little, and poetry not at all. Some novels work their way through, but not as a rule the novels which literary persons set most value on. The two cultures have so few points of contact that the diffusion of novels shows the same sort of delay, and exhibits the same oddities, as though they were getting into translation in a foreign country. It is only fairly recently, for instance, that Graham Greene and Evelyn Waugh have become more than names. And, just as it is rather startling to find that in Italy Bruce Marshall is by a long shot the best-known British novelist, so it jolts one to hear scientists talking with attention of the works of Nevil Shute. In fact, there is a good reason for that: Mr. Shute was himself a high-class engineer, and a book like *No Highway* is packed with technical stuff that is not only accurate but often original. Incidentally, there are benefits to be gained from listening to intelligent men, utterly removed from the literary scene and unconcerned as to who's in and who's out. One can pick up such a comment as a scientist once made, that it looked to him as though the current preoccupations of the New Criticism, the extreme concentration on a tiny passage, had made us curiously insensitive to the total flavour of a work, to its cumulative effects, to the epic qualities in literature. But, on the other side of the coin, one is just as likely to listen to three of the most massive intellects in Europe happily discussing the merits of *The Wallet of Kai-Lung.*

When you meet the younger rank-and-file of scientists, it often seems that they do not read at all. The prestige of the traditional culture is high enough for some of them to make a gallant shot at it. Oddly enough, the novelist whose name to them has become a token of esoteric literary excellence is that difficult highbrow Dickens. They approach him in a grim and dutiful spirit as though tackling *Finnegan's Wake,* and feel a sense of achievement if they manage to read a book through. But most young technicians do not fly so high. When you ask them what they read—"As a married man," one says, "I prefer the garden." Another says: "I always like just to use my books as tools." (Difficult to resist speculating what kind of tool a book would make. A sort of hammer? A crude digging instrument?)

That, or something like it, is a measure of the incommunicability of the two cultures. On their side the scientists are losing a great deal. Some of that loss is inevitable: it must and would happen in any society at our technical level. But in this country we make it quite unnecessarily worse by our educational patterns. On the other side, how much does the traditional culture lose by the separation?

I am inclined to think, even more. Not only practically—we are familiar with those arguments by now—but also intellectually and morally. The intellectual loss is a little difficult to appraise. Most scientists would claim that you cannot comprehend the world unless you know the structure of science, in particular of physical science. In a sense, and a perfectly genuine sense, that is true. Not to have read *War and Peace* and *La Cousine Bette* and *La Chartreuse de Parme* is not to be educated; but so is not to have a glimmer of the Second Law of Thermodynamics. Yet that case ought not to be pressed too far. It is more justifiable to say that those without any scientific understanding miss a whole body of experience: they are rather like the tone deaf, from whom all musical experience is cut off and who have to get on without it. The intellectual invasions of science are, however, penetrating deeper. Psycho-analysis once looked like a deep invasion, but that was a false alarm; cybernetics may turn out to be the real thing, driving down into the problems of will and cause and motive. If so, those who do not understand the method will not understand the depths of their own cultures.

But the greatest enrichment the scientific culture could give us is —though it does not originate like that—a moral one. Among scientists, deep-natured men know, as starkly as any men have known, that the individual human condition is tragic; for all its triumphs and joys, the essence of it is loneliness and the end death. But what they will not admit is that, because the individual condition is tragic, therefore the social condition must be tragic, too. Because a man must die, that is no excuse for his dying before his time and after a servile life. The impulse behind the scientists drives them to limit the area of tragedy, to take nothing as tragic that can conceivably lie within men's will. They have nothing but contempt for those representatives of the traditional cul-

ture who use a deep insight into man's fate to obscure the social truth
—or to do something pettier than obscure the truth, just to hang on to
a few perks. Dostoevski sucking up to the Chancellor Pobedonostsev,
who thought the only thing wrong with slavery was that there was not
enough of it; the political decadence of the *avant garde* of 1914, with
Ezra Pound finishing up broadcasting for the Fascists; Claudel agreeing
sanctimoniously with the Marshal about the virtue in others' suffering;
Faulkner giving sentimental reasons for treating Negroes as a different species. They are all symptoms of the deepest temptation of the
clerks—which is to say: "Because man's condition is tragic, everyone
ought to stay in their place, with mine as it happens somewhere near
the top." From that particular temptation, made up of defeat, self-
indulgence, and moral vanity, the scientific culture is almost totally
immune. It is that kind of moral health of the scientists which, in the
last few years, the rest of us have needed most; and of which, because
the two cultures scarcely touch, we have been most deprived.

National Review

OPERATION SNOW REMOVAL

As literary vendettists, the British are superb; with a flick of the wrist
and a delicate slash they can disembowel an opponent as neatly as they
trim a cucumber sandwich for a Buckingham Palace tea party. So it was
good news last week when one of the top duelists, the distinguished
literary critic F. H. Leavis, a Reader in English at Cambridge, took out
after Sir Charles Percy Snow, a scientist turned novelist who has
promoted himself as one of Britain's reigning literary greats through a
series of ponderous, middlebrow, pseudo-philosophic novels.

In a farewell lecture at Downing College, Cambridge (to a small,
but select audience, which was part of his ploymanship), Mr. Leavis
disposed of C. P. Snow's literary pretensions by announcing that, "as a
novelist, C. P. Snow doesn't begin to exist." "Snow's books," he went on,
"must be composed for him by an electronic brain called Charlie, into
which the instructions are fed in the form of chapter headings." And
the critical fallout was, as you would guess, tremendous.

But far more important was Mr. Leavis' thoughtful criticism of the
"two cultures" thesis which Sir Charles outlined in his now-celebrated
Rede Lectures in 1959. In them, Snow maintained that society is
dividing into two cultures, one scientific and one literary. He suggested
that, given advancing technologies and the increasing complexities of
modern life, science would and should become the predominant culture; the scientists, the new ruling elite. It was a major boost for the
thesis the atomic physicists have been pushing ever since Hiroshima:

Reprinted from *National Review*, XII (March 27, 1962) by permission of National Review,
150 East 35 Street, New York, N.Y. 10016.

that the scientists should not only build bombs but decide what to do with them; that the scientists should, in short, rule the world. Sir Charles' inflated reputation gave this position a seeming imprimatur.

Mr. Leavis deplored the intellectual climate that had allowed Sir Charles to assume a role of "master mind and sage." He contended that the advance of science means a future change so momentous that it is more than ever essential that mankind be in possession not of mere technical competence but of a "full humanity" to cope with it. The Rede Lectures, Mr. Leavis concluded, exhibited "an utter lack of intellectual distinction and embarrassing vulgarity of style."

Sir Charles was so astounded by this *lèse majesté* that he has so far only spluttered in reply.

Jonathan Swift

GULLIVER'S TRAVELS

The humours and dispositions of the Laputians *described. An account of their learning. Of the King and his Court. The Author's reception there. The inhabitants subject to fear and disquietudes. An account of the women.*

At my alighting I was surrounded by a crowd of people, but those who stood nearest seemed to be of better quality. They beheld me with all the marks and circumstances of wonder; neither, indeed, was I much in their debt, having never till then seen a race of mortals so singular in their shapes, habits, and countenances. Their heads were all reclined either to the right or the left; one of their eyes turned inward, and the other directly up to the zenith. Their outward garments were adorned with the figures of suns, moons, and stars, interwoven with those of fiddles, flutes, harps, trumpets, guitars, harpsichords, and many other instruments of music, unknown to us in Europe. I observed here and there many in the habit of servants, with a blown bladder fastened like a flail to the end of a short stick, which they carried in their hands. In each bladder was a small quantity of dried pease, or little pebbles (as I was afterwards informed). With these bladders they now and then flapped the mouths and ears of those who stood near them, of which practice I could not then conceive the meaning; it seems, the minds of these people are so taken up with intense speculations, that they neither can speak, nor attend to the discourses of others, without being roused by some external taction upon the organs of speech and hearing; for which reason, those persons who are able to afford it always keep a flapper (the original is *climenole*) in their family, as one of their domestics, nor ever walk abroad or make visits without him. And the business of this officer is, when two or more persons are in company, gently to strike with his bladder the mouth of him who is to speak, and the right ear of him or them to whom the speaker addresseth himself. This flapper is likewise employed diligently to attend his master in his walks, and upon occasion to give him a soft flap on his eyes, because he is always so wrapped up in cogitation, that he is in manifest danger of falling down every precipice, and bouncing his head against every post, and in the streets, of justling others, or being justled himself into the kennel.

It was necessary to give the reader this information, without which he would be at the same loss with me, to understand the proceedings of these people, as they conducted me up the stairs, to the top of the island, and from thence to the royal palace. While we were ascending, they forgot several times what they were about, and left me to myself, till their memories were again roused by their flappers; for they appeared altogether unmoved by the sight of my foreign habit and countenance, and by the shouts of the vulgar, whose thoughts and minds were more disengaged.

At last we entered the palace, and proceeded into the chamber of presence, where I saw the King seated on his throne, attended on each side by persons of prime quality. Before the throne, was a large table filled with globes and spheres, and mathematical instruments of all kinds. His Majesty took not the least notice of us, although our entrance was not without sufficient noise, by the concourse of all persons belonging to the court. But he was then deep in a problem, and we attended at least an hour, before he could solve it. There stood by him on each side, a young page, with flaps in their hands, and when they saw he was at leisure, one of them gently struck his mouth, and the other his right ear; at which he started like one awaked on the sudden, and looking towards me, and the company I was in, recollected the occasion of our coming, whereof he had been informed before. He spoke some words, whereupon immediately a young man with a flap came up to my side, and flapped me gently on the right ear; but I made signs, as well as I could, that I had no occasion for such an instrument; which, as I afterwards found, gave his Majesty and the whole court a very mean opinion of my understanding. The King, as far as I could conjecture, asked me several questions, and I addressed myself to him in all the languages I had. When it was found, that I could neither understand nor be understood, I was conducted by his order to an apartment in his palace (this prince being distinguished above all his predecessors for his hospitality to strangers), where two servants were appointed to attend me. My dinner was brought, and four persons of quality, whom I remembered to have seen very near the King's person, did me the honour to dine with me. We had two courses, of three dishes each. In the first course, there was a shoulder of mutton, cut into an equilateral triangle, a piece of beef into a rhomboides, and a pudding into a cycloid. The second course was two ducks, trussed up into the form of fiddles; sausages and puddings resembling flutes and haut-boys, and a breast of veal in the shape of a harp. The servants cut our bread into cones, cylinders, parallelograms, and several other mathematical figures.

While we were at dinner, I made bold to ask the names of several things in their language; and those noble persons, by the assistance of their flappers, delighted to give me answers, hoping to raise my admiration of their great abilities, if I could be brought to converse with them. I was soon able to call for bread and drink, or whatever else I wanted.

After dinner my company withdrew, and a person was sent to me by the King's order, attended by a flapper. He brought with him pen, ink, and paper, and three or four books, giving me to understand by signs, that he was sent to teach me the language. We sat together four hours, in which time I wrote down a great number of words in columns, with the translations over against them. I likewise made a shift to learn several short sentences. For my tutor would order one of my servants to fetch something, to turn about, to make a bow, to sit, or stand, or walk, and the like. Then I took down the sentence in writing. He showed me also in one of his books, the figures of the sun, moon, and stars, the zodiac, the tropics, and polar circles, together with the denominations of many planes and solids. He gave me the names and descriptions of all the musical instruments, and the general terms of art in playing on each of them. After he had left me, I placed all my words with their interpretations in alphabetical order. And thus in a few days, by the help of a very faithful memory, I got some insight into their language.

The word, which I interpret the *Flying* or *Floating Island,* is in the original *Laputa,* whereof I could never learn the true etymology. *Lap* in the old obsolete language signifieth *high,* and *untuh,* a *governor,* from which they say, by corruption, was derived *Laputa,* from *Lapuntuh.* But I do not approve of this derivation, which seems to be a little strained. I ventured to offer to the learned among them a conjecture of my own, that *Laputa* was *quasi lap outed; lap* signifying properly the dancing of the sunbeams in the sea, and *outed,* a wing, which however I shall not obtrude, but submit to the judicious reader.

Those to whom the King had entrusted me, observing how ill I was clad, ordered a tailor to come next morning, and take my measure for a suit of clothes. This operator did his office after a different manner from those of his trade in Europe. He first took my altitude by a quadrant, and then with a rule and compasses, described the dimensions and outlines of my whole body, all which he entered upon paper, and in six days brought my clothes very ill made, and quite out of shape, by happening to mistake a figure in the calculation. But my comfort was, that I observed such accidents very frequent, and little regarded.

During my confinement for want of clothes, and by an indisposition that held me some days longer, I much enlarged my dictionary; and when I went next to court, was able to understand many things the King spoke, and to return him some kind of answers. His Majesty had given orders that the island should move north-east and by east, to the vertical point over Lagado, the metropolis of the whole kingdom below upon the firm earth. It was about ninety leagues distant, and our voyage lasted four days and an half. I was not in the least sensible of the progressive motion made in the air by the island. On the second morning about eleven o'clock, the King himself in person, attended by his nobility, courtiers, and officers, having prepared all their musical instruments, played on them for three hours without intermission, so that I was quite stunned with the noise; neither could I possibly guess the meaning, till my tutor informed me. He said that the people of their island had their ears adapted to hear the music of the spheres, which always played at certain periods, and the court was now prepared to bear their part in whatever instrument they most excelled.

In our journey towards Lagado, the capital city, his Majesty ordered that the island should stop over certain towns and villages, from whence he might receive the petitions of his subjects. And to this purpose several packthreads were let down with small weights at the bottom. On these packthreads the people strung their petitions, which mounted up directly like scraps of paper fastened by school-boys at the end of the string that holds their kite. Sometimes we received wine and victuals from below, which were drawn up by pulleys.

The knowledge I had in mathematics gave me great assistance in acquiring their phraseology, which depended much upon that science and music; and in the latter I was not unskilled. Their ideas are perpetually conversant in lines and figures. If they would, for example, praise the beauty of a woman, or any other animal, they describe it by rhombs, circles, parallelograms, ellipses, and other geometrical terms, or by words of art drawn from music, needless here to repeat. I observed in the King's kitchen all sorts of mathematical and musical instruments, after the figures of which they cut up the joints that were served to his Majesty's table.

Their houses are very ill built, the walls bevil, without one right angle in any apartment, and this defect ariseth from the contempt they bear to practical geometry, which they despise as vulgar and mechanic, those instructions they give being too refined for the intellectuals of their work-men, which occasions perpetual mistakes. And although they are dexterous enough upon a piece of paper in the management of the rule, the pencil, and the divider, yet in the common actions and behaviour of life, I have not seen a more clumsy, awkward, and unhandy people, nor so slow and perplexed in their conceptions upon all other subjects, except those of mathematics and music. They are very bad reasoners, and vehemently given to opposition, unless when they happen to be of the right opinion, which is seldom their case. Imagination, fancy, and invention, they are wholly strangers to, nor have any words in their language by which those ideas can be expressed; the whole compass of their thoughts and mind being shut up within the two forementioned sciences.

Most of them, and especially those who deal in the astronomical part, have great faith in judicial astrology, although they are ashamed to own it publicly. But what I chiefly admired, and thought altogether unaccountable, was the strong disposition I observed in them towards news and politics, perpetually enquiring into public affairs, giving their judgments in matters of state, and passionately disputing every inch of a party opinion. I have indeed observed the same disposition among most of the mathematicians I have known in Europe, although I could never discover the least analogy between the two sciences; unless those people suppose, that because the smallest circle hath as many degrees as the largest, therefore the regulation and management of the world require no more abilities than the handling and turning of a globe. But I rather take this quality to spring from a very common infirmity of human nature, inclining us to be more curious and conceited in matters where we have least concern, and for which we are least adapted either by study or nature.

These people are under continual disquietudes, never enjoying a minute's peace of mind; and their disturbances proceed from causes which very little affect the rest of mortals. Their apprehensions arise from several changes they dread in the celestial bodies. For instance; that the earth, by the continual approaches of the sun towards it, must in course of time be absorbed, or swallowed up. That the face of the sun will by degrees be encrusted with its own effluvia, and give no more light to the world. That the earth very narrowly escaped a brush from the tail of the last comet, which would have infallibly reduced it to ashes; and that the next, which they have calculated for one and thirty years hence, will probably destroy us. For, if in its perihelion it should approach within a certain degree of the sun (as by their calculations they have reason to dread), it will receive a degree of heat ten thousand times more intense than that of red-hot glowing iron; and in its absence from the sun, carry a blazing tail ten hundred thousand and fourteen miles long; through which if the earth should pass at the distance of one hundred thousand miles from the nucleus or main body of the comet, it must in its passage be set on fire, and reduced to ashes. That the sun daily spending its rays without any nutriment to supply them, will at last be wholly consumed and annihilated; which must be attended with the destruction of this earth, and of all the planets that receive their light from it.

They are so perpetually alarmed with the apprehensions of these and the like impending dangers, that they can neither sleep quietly in their beds, nor have any relish for the common pleasures or amusements of life. When they meet an acquaintance in the morning, the first question is about the sun's health, how he looked at his setting and rising, and what hopes they have to avoid the stroke of the approaching comet. This conversation they are apt to run into with the same temper that boys discover, in delighting to hear terrible stories of spirits and hobgoblins, which they greedily listen to, and dare not go to bed for fear.

The women of the island have abundance of vivacity: they contemn their husbands, and are exceedingly fond of strangers, whereof there is always a considerable number from the continent below, attending at court, either upon affairs of the several towns and corporations of their own particular occasions, but are much despised, because they want the same endowments. Among these the ladies choose their gallants: but the vexation is, that they act with too much ease and security, for the husband is always so rapt in speculation, that the mistress and lover may proceed to the greatest familiarities before his face, if he be but provided with paper and implements, and without his flapper at his side.

The wives and daughters lament their confinement to the island, although I think it the most delicious spot of ground in the world; and although they live in the greatest plenty and magnificence, and are allowed to do whatever they please, they long to see the world, and take the diversions of the metropolis, which they are not allowed to do without a particular licence from the King; and this is not easy to be obtained, because the people of quality have found, by frequent experience, how hard it is to persuade their women to return from below. I was told that a great court lady, who had several children, is married to the prime minister, the richest subject in the kingdom, a very graceful person, extremely fond of her, and lives in the finest palace of the island, went down to Lagado, on the pretence of health, there hid herself for several months, till the King sent a warrant to search for her, and she was found in an obscure eating-house all in rags, having pawned her clothes to maintain an old deformed footman, who beat her every day, and in whose company she was taken much against her will. And although her husband received her with all possible kindness, and without the least reproach, she soon after contrived to steal down again with all her jewels, to the same gallant, and hath not been heard of since.

This may perhaps pass with the reader rather for an European or English story, than for one of a country so remote. But he may please to consider, that the caprices of womankind are not limited by any climate or nation, and that they are much more uniform than can be easily imagined.

In about a month's time I had made a tolerable proficiency in their language, and was able to answer most of the King's questions, when I had the honour to attend him. His Majesty discovered not the least curiosity to enquire into the laws, government, history, religion, or manners of the countries where I had been, but confined his questions to the state of mathematics, and received the account I gave him with great contempt and indifference, though often roused by his flapper on each side.

Charles Dickens

HARD TIMES

THE ONE THING NEEDFUL

"Now, what I want is, Facts. Teach these boys and girls nothing but Facts. Facts alone are wanted in life. Plant nothing else, and root out everything else. You can only form the minds of reasoning animals upon Facts: nothing else will ever be of any service to them. This is the principle on which I bring up my own children, and this is the principle on which I bring up these children. Stick to Facts, sir!"

The scene was a plain, bare, monotonous vault of a schoolroom, and the speaker's square forefinger emphasised his observations by underscoring every sentence with a line on the schoolmaster's sleeve. The emphasis was helped by the speaker's square wall of a forehead, which had his eyebrows for its base, while his eyes found commodious cellarage in two dark caves, overshadowed by the wall. The emphasis was helped by the speaker's mouth, which was wide, thin, and hard set. The emphasis was helped by the speaker's voice, which was inflexible, dry, and dictatorial. The emphasis was helped by the speaker's hair, which bristled on the skirts of his bald head, a plantation of firs to keep the wind from its shining surface, all covered with knobs, like the crust of a plum pie, as if the head had scarcely warehouse-room for the hard facts stored inside. The speaker's obstinate carriage, square coat, square legs, square shoulders,—nay, his very neckcloth, trained to take him by the throat with an unaccommodating grasp, like a stubborn fact, as it was,—all helped the emphasis.

"In this life, we want nothing but Facts, sir; nothing but Facts!"

The speaker, and the schoolmaster, and the third grown person present, all backed a little, and swept with their eyes the inclined plane of little vessels then and there arranged in order, ready to have imperial gallons of facts poured into them until they were full to the brim.

MURDERING THE INNOCENTS

Thomas Gradgrind, sir. A man of realities. A man of facts and calculations. A man who proceeds upon the principle that two and two are four, and nothing over, and who is not to be talked into allowing for anything over. Thomas Gradgrind, sir—peremptorily Thomas—Thomas Gradgrind. With a rule and a pair of scales, and the multiplication table always in his pocket, sir, ready to weigh and measure any parcel of human nature, and tell you exactly what it comes to. It is a mere question of figures, a case of simple arithmetic. You might hope to get some other nonsensical belief into the head of George Gradgrind, or Augustus Gradgrind, or John Gradgrind, or Joseph Gradgrind (all suppositious, nonexistent persons), but into the head of Thomas Gradgrind—no, sir!

In such terms Mr. Gradgrind always mentally introduced himself, whether to his private circle of acquaintance, or to the public in general. In such terms, no doubt, substituting the words "boys and girls," for "sir," Thomas Gradgrind now presented Thomas Gradgrind to the little pitchers before him, who were to be filled so full of facts.

Indeed, as he eagerly sparkled at them from the cellarage before mentioned, he seemed a kind of cannon loaded to the muzzle with facts, and prepared to blow them clean out of the regions of childhood at one discharge. He seemed a galvanizing apparatus, too, charged with a grim mechanical substitute for the tender young imaginations that were to be stormed away.

"Girl number twenty," said Mr. Gradgrind, squarely pointing with his square forefinger, "I don't know that girl. Who is that girl?"

"Sissy Jupe, sir," explained number twenty, blushing, standing up, and curtseying.

"Sissy is not a name," said Mr. Gradgrind. "Don't call yourself Sissy. Call yourself Cecilia."

"It's father as calls me Sissy, sir," returned the young girl in a trembling voice, and with another curtsey.

"Then he has no business to do it," said Mr. Gradgrind. "Tell him he mustn't. Cecilia Jupe. Let me see. What is your father?"

"He belongs to the horse-riding, if you please, sir."

Mr. Gradgrind frowned, and waved off the objectionable calling with his hand.

"We don't want to know anything about that, here. You mustn't tell us about that, here. Your father breaks horses, don't he?"

"If you please, sir, when they can get any to break, they do break horses in the ring, sir."

"You mustn't tell us about the ring, here. Very well, then. Describe your father as a horsebreaker. He doctors sick horses, I dare say?"

"Oh yes, sir."

"Very well, then. He is a veterinary surgeon, a farrier, and horse-breaker. Give me your definition of a horse."

(Sissy Jupe thrown into the greatest alarm by this demand.)

"Girl number twenty unable to define a horse!" said Mr. Gradgrind, for the general behoof of all the little pitchers. "Girl number twenty possessed of no facts, in reference to one of the commonest of animals! Some boy's definition of a horse. Bitzer, yours."

The square finger, moving here and there, lighted suddenly on Bitzer, perhaps because he chanced to sit in the same ray of sunlight which, darting in at one of the bare windows of the intensely white-washed room, irradiated Sissy. For, the boys and girls sat on the face of the inclined plane in two compact bodies, divided up the centre by a narrow interval; and Sissy, being at the corner of a row on the sunny side, came in for the beginning of a sunbeam, of which Bitzer, being at the corner of a row on the other side, a few rows in advance, caught the end. But, whereas the girl was so dark-eyed and dark-haired, that she seemed to receive a deeper and more lustrous colour from the sun, when it shone upon her, the boy was so light-eyed and light-haired that the self-same rays appeared to draw out of him what little colour he ever possessed. His cold eyes would hardly have been eyes, but for the short ends of lashes which, by bringing them into immediate contrast with something paler than themselves, expressed their form. His short-cropped hair might have been a mere continuation of the sandy freckles on his forehead and face. His skin was so unwholesomely deficient in the natural tinge, that he looked as though, if he were cut, he would bleed white.

"Bitzer," said Thomas Gradgrind. "Your definition of a horse."

"Quadruped. Graminivorous. Forty teeth, namely twenty-four grinders, four eye-teeth, and twelve incisive. Sheds coat in the spring; in marshy countries, sheds hoofs, too. Hoofs hard, but requiring to be shod with iron. Age known by marks in mouth." Thus (and much more) Bitzer.

"Now girl number twenty," said Mr. Gradgrind. "You know what a horse is."

She curtseyed again, and would have blushed deeper, if she could have blushed deeper than she had blushed all this time. Bitzer, after rapidly blinking at Thomas Gradgrind with both eyes at once, and so catching the light upon his quivering ends of lashes that they looked like the antennae of busy insects, put his knuckles to his freckled forehead, and sat down again.

The third gentleman now stepped forth. A mighty man at cutting and drying, he was; a government officer; in his way (and in most other people's too), a professed pugilist; always in training, always with a system to force down the general throat like a bolus, always to be heard of at the bar of his little Public-office, ready to fight all England. To continue in fistic phraseology, he had a genius for coming up to the scratch, wherever and whatever it was, and proving himself an ugly customer. He would go in and damage any subject whatever with his right, follow up with his left, stop, exchange, counter, bore his opponent (he always fought All England) to the ropes, and fall upon him neatly. He was certain to knock the wind out of common sense, and render that unlucky adversary deaf to the call of time. And he had it in charge from high authority to bring about the great public-office Millennium, when Commissioners should reign upon earth.

"Very well," said this gentleman, briskly smiling, and folding his arms. "That's a horse. Now, let me ask you girls and boys, Would you paper a room with representations of horses?"

After a pause, one half of the children cried in chorus, "Yes, sir!" Upon which the other half, seeing in the gentleman's face that Yes was wrong, cried out in chorus, "No, sir!"—as the custom is, in these examinations.

"Of course, No. Why wouldn't you?"

A pause. One corpulent slow boy, with a wheezy manner of breathing, ventured the answer, Because he wouldn't paper a room at all, but would paint it.

"You *must* paper it," said the gentleman, rather warmly.

"You must paper it," said Thomas Gradgrind, "whether you like it or not. Don't tell *us* you wouldn't paper it. What do you mean, boy?"

"I'll explain to you, then," said the gentleman, after another and a dismal pause, "why you wouldn't paper a room with representations of horses. Do you ever see horses walking up and down the sides of rooms in reality—in fact? Do you?"

"Yes, sir!" from one half. "No, sir!" from the other.

"Of course, No," said the gentleman, with an indignant look at the wrong half. "Why, then, you are not to see anywhere, what you don't see in fact; you are not to have anywhere, what you don't have in fact. What is called Taste, is only another name for Fact."

Thomas Gradgrind nodded his approbation.

"This is a new principle, a discovery, a great discovery," said the gentleman. "Now, I'll try you again. Suppose you were going to carpet a room. Would you use a carpet having a representation of flowers upon it?"

There being a general conviction by this time that "No, sir!" was always the right answer to this gentleman, the chorus of No was very strong. Only a few feeble stragglers said Yes: among them Sissy Jupe.

"Girl number twenty," said the gentleman, smiling in the calm strength of knowledge.

Sissy blushed, and stood up.

"So you would carpet your room—or your husband's room, if you were a grown woman, and had a husband—with representations of flowers, would you?" said the gentleman. "Why would you?"

"If you please, sir, I am very fond of flowers," returned the girl.

"And is that why you would put tables and chairs upon them, and have people walking over them with heavy boots?"

"It wouldn't hurt them, sir. They wouldn't crush and wither, if you please, sir. They would be the pictures of what was very pretty and pleasant, and I would fancy—"

"Ay, ay, ay! But you mustn't fancy," cried the gentleman, quite elated by coming so happily to his point. "That's it! You are never to fancy."

"You are not, Cecilia Jupe," Thomas Gradgrind solemnly repeated, "to do anything of that kind."

"Fact, fact, fact!" said the gentleman. And, "Fact, fact, fact!" repeated Thomas Gradgrind.

"You are to be in all things regulated and governed," said the gentleman, "by fact. We hope to have, before long, a board of fact, composed of commissioners of fact, who will force the people to be a people of fact, and of nothing but fact. You must discard the word Fancy altogether. You have nothing to do with it. You are not to have, in any object of use or ornament, what would be a contradiction in fact. You don't walk upon flowers in fact; you cannot be allowed to walk upon flowers in carpets. You don't find that foreign birds and butterflies come and perch upon your crockery; you cannot be permitted to paint foreign birds and butterflies upon your crockery. You never meet with quadrupeds going up and down walls; you must not have quadrupeds represented upon walls. You must use," said the gentleman, "for all these purposes, combinations and modifications (in primary colours) of mathematical figures which are susceptible of proof and demonstration. This is the new discovery. This is fact. This is taste."

The girl curtseyed, and sat down. She was very young, and she looked as if she were frightened by the matter of fact prospect the world afforded.

"Now, if Mr. M'Choakumchild," said the gentleman, "will proceed to give his first lesson here, Mr. Gradgrind, I shall be happy, at your request, to observe his mode of procedure."

Mr. Gradgrind was much obliged. "Mr. M'Choakumchild, we only wait for you."

So, Mr. M'Choakumchild began in his best manner. He and some one hundred and forty other schoolmasters, had been lately turned at the same time, in the same factory, on the same principles, like so many pianoforte legs. He had been put through an immense variety of paces, and had answered volumes of head-breaking questions. Orthography, etymology, syntax, and prosody, biography, astronomy, geography, and general cosmography, the sciences of compound proportion, algebra, land-surveying and levelling, vocal music, and drawing from models, were all at the ends of his ten chilled fingers. He had worked his stony way into Her Majesty's most Honourable Privy Council's Schedule B, and had taken the bloom off the higher branches of mathematics and physical science, French, German, Latin, and Greek. He knew all about all the Water Sheds of all the world (whatever they are), and all the histories of all the peoples, and all the names of all the rivers and mountains, and all the productions, manners, and customs of all the countries, and all their boundaries and bearings on the two and thirty points of the compass. Ah, rather overdone, M'Choakumchild. If he had only learnt a little less, how infinitely better he might have taught much more!

He went to work in this preparatory lesson, not unlike Morgiana in the Forty Thieves: looking into all the vessels ranged before him, one after another, to see what they contained. Say, good M'Choakumchild. When from thy boiling store, thou shalt fill each jar brim full by-and-by, dost thou think that thou wilt always kill outright the robber Fancy lurking within—or sometimes only maim him and distort him . . . !

Mr. Gradgrind walked homeward from the school, in a state of considerable satisfaction. It was his school, and he intended it to be a model. He intended every child in it to be a model—just as the young Gradgrinds were all models.

Sir Charles Sherrington

THE BRAIN AND ITS WORK

Not so long since science inclined to look upon all nature somewhat as a feat of engineering. That phase passed with the coming of present-day mathematical outlook.

A scheme of lines and nodal points, gathered together at one end into a great ravelled knot, the brain, and at the other trailing off to a sort of stalk, the spinal cord. Imagine activity in this shown by little points of light. Of these some stationary flash rhythmically, faster or slower. Others are travelling points, streaming in serial trains at various speeds. The rhythmic stationary lights lie at the nodes. The nodes are both goals whither converge, and junctions whence diverge, the lines of

From *Man on His Nature,* copyright 1951 by permission of Cambridge University Press.

travelling lights. The lines and nodes where the lights are, do not remain, taken together, the same even a single moment. There are at any time nodes and lines where lights are not.

Suppose we choose the hour of deep sleep. Then only in some sparse and out of the way places are nodes flashing and trains of light-points running. Such places indicate local activity still in progress. At one such place we can watch the behaviour of a group of lights perhaps a myriad strong. They are pursuing a mystic and recurrent manœuvre as if of some incantational dance. They are superintending the beating of the heart and the state of the arteries so that while we sleep the circulation of the blood is what it should be. The great knotted headpiece of the whole sleeping system lies for the most part dark, and quite especially so the roof-brain. Occasionally at places in it lighted points flash or move but soon subside. Such lighted points and moving trains of lights are mainly far in the outskirts, and wink slowly and travel slowly. At intervals even a gush of sparks wells up and sends a train down the spinal cord, only to fail to arouse it. Where however the stalk joins the headpiece, there goes forward in a limited field a remarkable display. A dense constellation of some thousands of nodal points bursts out every few seconds into a short phase of rhythmical flashing. At first a few lights, then more, increasing in rate and number with a deliberate crescendo to a climax, then to decline and die away. After due pause the efflorescence is repeated. With each such rhythmic outburst goes a discharge of trains of travelling lights along the stalk and out of it altogether into a number of nerve-branches. What is this doing? It manages the taking of our breath the while we sleep.

Should we continue to watch the scheme we should observe after a time an impressive change which suddenly accrues. In the great head-end which has been mostly darkness spring up myriads of twinkling stationary lights and myriads of trains of moving lights of many different directions. It is as though activity from one of those local places which continued restless in the darkened main-mass suddenly spread far and wide and invaded all. The great topmost sheet of the mass, that where hardly a light had twinkled or moved, becomes now a sparkling field of rhythmic flashing points with trains of travelling sparks hurrying hither and thither. The brain is waking and with it the mind is returning. It is as if the Milky Way entered upon some cosmic dance. Swiftly the head-mass becomes an enchanted loom where millions of flashing shuttles weave a dissolving pattern, always a meaningful pattern though never an abiding one; a shifting harmony of subpatterns. Now as the waking body rouses, subpatterns of this great harmony of activity stretch down into the unlit tracks of the stalk-piece of the scheme. Strings of flashing and travelling sparks engage the lengths of it. This means that the body is up and rises to meet its waking day.

Albert Einstein

ON EDUCATION

A day of celebration generally is in the first place dedicated to retro-spect, especially to the memory of personages who have gained special distinction for the development of the cultural life. This friendly service for our predecessors must indeed not be neglected, particularly as such a memory of the best of the past is proper to stimulate the well-disposed of today to a courageous effort. But this should be done by someone who, from his youth, has been connected with this State and is familiar with its past, not by one who like a gypsy has wandered about and gathered his experiences in all kinds of countries.

Thus, there is nothing else left for me but to speak about such questions as, independently of space and time, always have been and will be connected with educational matters. In this attempt I cannot lay any claim to being an authority, especially as intelligent and well-mean-ing men of all times have dealt with educational problems and have certainly repeatedly expressed their views clearly about these matters. From what source shall I, as a partial layman in the realm of pedagogy, derive courage to expound opinions with no foundations except per-sonal experience and personal conviction? If it were really a scientific matter, one would probably be tempted to silence by such considera-tions.

However, with the affairs of active human beings it is different. Here knowledge of truth alone does not suffice; on the contrary this knowledge must continually be renewed by ceaseless effort, if it is not to be lost. It resembles a statue of marble which stands in the desert and is continuously threatened with burial by the shifting sand. The hands of service must ever be at work, in order that the marble continue lastingly to shine in the sun. To these serving hands mine also shall belong.

The school has always been the most important means of transfer-ring the wealth of tradition from one generation to the next. This applies today in an even higher degree than in former times, for through modern development of the economic life, the family as bearer of tradition and education has been weakened. The continuance and health of human society is therefore in a still higher degree dependent on the school than formerly.

Sometimes one sees in the school simply the instrument for trans-ferring a certain maximum quantity of knowledge to the growing generation. But that is not right. Knowledge is dead; the school, how-ever, serves the living. It should develop in the young individuals those qualities and capabilities which are of value for the welfare of the commonwealth. But that does not mean that individuality should be destroyed and the individual become a mere tool of the community, like

From Albert Einstein's *Out of My Later Years,* New York, 1950, by permission of the Estate of Albert Einstein.

a bee or an ant. For a community of standardized individuals without personal originality and personal aims would be a poor community without possibilities for development. On the contrary, the aim must be the training of independently acting and thinking individuals, who, however, see in the service of the community their highest life problem. So far as I can judge, the English school system comes nearest to the realization of this ideal.

But how shall one try to attain this ideal? Should one perhaps try to realize this aim by moralizing? Not at all. Words are and remain an empty sound, and the road to perdition has ever been accompanied by lip service to an ideal. But personalities are not formed by what is heard and said, but by labor and activity.

The most important method of education accordingly always has consisted of that in which the pupil was urged to actual performance. This applies as well to the first attempts at writing of the primary boy as to the doctor's thesis on graduation from the university, or as to the mere memorizing of a poem, the writing of a composition, the interpretation and translation of a text, the solving of a mathematical problem or the practice of physical sport.

But behind every achievement exists the motivation which is at the foundation of it and which in turn is strengthened and nourished by the accomplishment of the undertaking. Here there are the greatest differences and they are of greatest importance to the educational value of the school. The same work may owe its origin to fear and compulsion, ambitious desire for authority and distinction, or loving interest in the object and a desire for truth and understanding, and thus to that divine curiosity which every healthy child possesses, but which so often is weakened early. The educational influence which is exercised upon the pupil by the accomplishment of one and the same work may be widely different, depending upon whether fear of hurt, egoistic passion, or desire for pleasure and satisfaction is at the bottom of this work. And nobody will maintain that the administration of the school and the attitude of the teachers do not have an influence upon the molding of the psychological foundation for pupils.

To me the worst thing seems to be for a school principally to work with methods of fear, force, and artificial authority. Such treatment destroys the sound sentiments, the sincerity, and the self-confidence of the pupil. It produces the submissive subject. It is no wonder that such schools are the rule in Germany and Russia. I know that the schools in this country are free from this worst evil; this also is so in Switzerland and probably in all democratically governed countries. It is comparatively simple to keep the school free from this worst of all evils. Give into the power of the teacher the fewest possible coercive measures, so that the only source of the pupil's respect for the teacher is the human and intellectual qualities of the latter.

The second-named motive, ambition or, in milder terms, the aiming at recognition and consideration, lies firmly fixed in human nature. With absence of mental stimulus of this kind, human cooperation would be entirely impossible; the desire for the approval of one's fellow-man certainly is one of the most important binding powers of society. In this complex of feelings, constructive and destructive forces lie closely together. Desire for approval and recognition is a healthy motive; but the desire to be acknowledged as better, stronger, or more intelligent than a fellow being or fellow scholar easily leads to an excessively egoistic psychological adjustment, which may become injurious for the individual and for the community. Therefore the school and the teacher must guard against employing the easy method of creating individual ambition, in order to induce the pupils to diligent work.

Darwin's theory of the struggle for existence and the selectivity connected with it has by many people been cited as authorization of the encouragement of the spirit of competition. Some people also in such a way have tried to prove pseudo-scientifically the necessity of the destructive economic struggle of competition between individuals. But this is wrong, because man owes his strength in the struggle for existence to the fact that he is a socially living animal. As little as a battle between single ants of an ant hill is essential for survival, just so little is this the case with the individual members of a human community.

Therefore one should guard against preaching to the young man success in the customary sense as the aim of life. For a successful man is he who receives a great deal from his fellowmen, usually incomparably more than corresponds to his service to them. The value of a man, however, should be seen in what he gives and not in what he is able to receive.

The most important motive for work in the school and in life is the pleasure in work, pleasure in its result, and the knowledge of the value of the result to the community. In the awakening and strengthening of these psychological forces in the young man, I see the most important task given by the school. Such a psychological foundation alone leads to a joyous desire for the highest possessions of men, knowledge and artist-like workmanship.

The awakening of these productive psychological powers is certainly less easy than the practice of force or the awakening of individual ambition but is the more valuable for it. The point is to develop the childlike inclination for play and the childlike desire for recognition and to guide the child over to important fields for society; it is that education which in the main is founded upon the desire for successful activity and acknowledgment. If the school succeeds in working successfully from such points of view, it will be highly honored by the rising generation and the tasks given by the school will be submitted to as a sort of gift. I have known children who preferred schooltime to vacation.

Such a school demands from the teacher that he be a kind of artist in his province. What can be done that this spirit be gained in the school? For this there is just as little a universal remedy as there is for an individual to remain well. But there are certain necessary conditions which can be met. First, teachers should grow up in such schools. Second, the teacher should be given extensive liberty in the selection of the material to be taught and the methods of teaching employed by him. For it is true also of him that pleasure in the shaping of his work is killed by force and exterior pressure.

If you have followed attentively my meditations up to this point, you will probably wonder about one thing. I have spoken fully about in what spirit, according to my opinion, youth should be instructed. But I have said nothing yet about the choice of subjects for instruction, nor about the method of teaching. Should language predominate or technical education in science?

To this I answer: in my opinion all this is of secondary importance. If a young man has trained his muscles and physical endurance by gymnastics and walking, he will later be fitted for every physical work. This is also analogous to the training of the mind and the exercising of the mental and manual skill. Thus the wit was not wrong who defined education in this way: "Education is that which remains, if one has forgotten everything he learned in school." For this reason I am not at all anxious to take sides in the struggle between the followers of the classical philologic-historical education and the education more devoted to natural science.

On the other hand, I want to oppose the idea that the school has to teach directly that special knowledge and those accomplishments which one has to use later directly in life. The demands of life are much too manifold to let such a specialized training in school appear possible. Apart from that, it seems to me, moreover, objectionable to treat the individual like a dead tool. The school should always have as its aim that the young man leave it as a harmonious personality, not as a specialist. This in my opinion is true in a certain sense even for technical schools, whose students will devote themselves to a quite definite profession. The development of general ability for independent thinking and judgment should always be placed foremost, not the acquisition of special knowledge. If a person masters the fundamentals of his subject and has learned to think and work independently, he will surely find his way and besides will better be able to adapt himself to progress and changes than the person whose training principally consists in the acquiring of detailed knowledge.

Finally, I wish to emphasize once more that what has been said here in a somewhat categorical form does not claim to mean more than the personal opinion of a man, which is founded upon *nothing but* his own personal experience, which he has gathered as a student and as a teacher.

10
LANGUAGE AND REALITY

"Whatever we conceive well we express clearly."
—Nicolas Boileau, *L'Art Poétique*

Helene and Charlton Laird

HOW DID LANGUAGE BEGIN?

Let's keep on supposing you are living in a world where no one can talk. You live in a cave with your mother and father and brothers and sisters. Your bed of skins is at the side of the cave, where the roof curves down to meet the floor. The roof, then, is close above you, and at night you crawl into your bed, keeping low so as not to strike your head. In the morning you wake early, full of energy, and sit up—with a bang! For you have forgotten how low the roof is and have hit your head on it hard. A second before you hit, but too late, your father made a sharp sound of warning—let us say it was "dop." The next morning, just as you wake and before you can move, your father says, "Dop!" again. You remember the day before, you remember hitting your head, you feel the bump with your fingers, and then you crawl out to where the roof of the cave is higher before you sit up. After that you always remember about the low roof, and your father does not need to say "Dop!" to you any more for that.

But perhaps in a day or two you are walking with your father. He is ahead of you and suddenly he makes the same sound, "Dop!", but this time in a low voice. The sound isn't exactly a word yet, but it does have some meaning to you. You remember the other times your father said it —those times it meant, "Don't keep on moving the way you are moving or you will get hurt." When he gave the warning in the family cave there was no one but the family to hear. Since he did not have to be careful, your father spoke in rather a loud voice. But this time his voice is soft—that could mean he doesn't want anyone but you to hear him. You do not think all this in words, because so far you have no real words, but you feel it. Anyway, you stop and hold still. And then you see some distance away a huge, hairy rhinoceros with a dangerous looking tusk. The wind is blowing toward you, and you hope the rhinoceros will not be able to smell you. He doesn't. He grubs around, finds a few roots, eats them, and goes slowly on. All the time you stand there behind your father, perfectly still, almost holding your breath. Finally your father thinks the rhinoceros has gone far enough away so that he can't hear you any more, and you move.

Now your father has come to realize that his warning exclamation can be very useful. If you and the whole family will always stop moving when he says "dop," he can often keep you out of trouble or danger, and there is lots of trouble and danger in your primitive world. When he first said it, "dop" was a cry, and perhaps it was an accident that he said it twice. But now he has said it three times, and in two different situations. It is a word, and he resolves to teach it to all the family.

That may have been the way the first word was invented. Then, when other words had been invented and proved to be useful too, people may have gone on rather rapidly to invent more and more. We can guess that necessary words came first—warnings, commands, names of things and actions—and later on abstract words—names for ideas and emotions.

It may have been that language was invented because it was needed. But it is also possible that it was invented for fun. Imagine again that you are living in the time before anyone could talk. There are all sorts of sounds in the world around you, but no words. The wind in the trees goes "whoosh." The thunder goes "boom." The rain on the tight skin of a tent goes "pitter-patter." The wild geese say "honk." The half-wild dogs that live with your tribe make an abrupt, harsh noise which sounds to you like "bowwow." For fun you begin to imitate these noises. You run as fast as you can with your arms outspread, pretending you are the wind, and say softly, "Whoosh, whoo-oosh." Then, in your pretending, a storm comes up. The lightning flashes, and you yell, "Boom, boom!" as loud as you can, because now you're thunder. After the thunder and lightning the rain comes, and you almost whisper, "Pitter-patter, pitter-patter." The rain stops. You pretend that geese are flying over, and say, "Honk, honk." This is a loud, funny noise so you say it again. Your brother hears you, and he says, "Honk, honk," too, because he recognizes it as the sound the geese make and is amused that you are imitating them. You and your brother make so much noise that the dogs get excited and bark, and you both bark right back. The game of imitating natural sounds is fun, and you play it often enough so that after a while you've invented some words. *Whoosh, boom, pitter-patter, honk, bowwow* are no longer just amusing, imitative sounds to you; they are *words* which represent the sounds and similar sounds under all circumstances. *Boom* isn't just the noise of the thunder, it is also the sound of a falling tree or rock, the sound of the ocean waves breaking on the shore in a storm.

The words we've been talking about are all real words, they are in the dictionary, and they must have been invented in some such way as we've described. They, and hundreds of others, such as *squeak, clatter, bang,* are called echoic words—that is, they echo or imitate sounds. The idea that speech came to be invented by someone imitating natural sounds is called the bowwow theory. It is a fairly recent theory, yet people who study language no longer believe in it. Although scholars don't accept this particular theory as the origin of language itself, but rather as the origin of many individual words, they would almost certainly be willing to say that it is just as probable that language was invented for fun as for necessity.

All this is guessing, and people have been trying to guess for centuries how speech began. Plato, a Greek philosopher who lived some four hundred years before Christ, thought that everything in the world had a natural name—a name which suited that thing and no other—and that it was the job of human beings to discover these natural names. It would seem that Plato thought there was a perfect language given to man by the creator of the universe.

The ancient Hebrews had somewhat the same idea. In the Bible, after God created the heaven and the earth, He said, "Let there be light," and there was light. Next He arranged the earth just the way He wanted it, making oceans and rivers, forests and gardens, fish and birds and animals. At last He made Adam. Then He brought all the animals to Adam to be named. "And Adam gave names to all cattle, and to the fowl of the air, and to every beast of the field."

The ancient Hebrews thought the language that God and Adam spoke was Hebrew, and for centuries many people believed this to be true. Sir Thomas Browne, an English doctor and writer who was born in 1605, had a theory that any child brought up away from human beings and never hearing anyone speak would speak Hebrew naturally. But from time to time children have been discovered—one was found in India just recently—who had lived with animals apparently since before they learned to talk. The sounds they made were animal sounds, and only after they had lived with people did they learn to speak as people.

It seems clear that man invented speech, just as he invented the wheel and the steam engine and the jet plane. When and how he invented it we may never find out. Somewhere, long ago, someone said the first word, but we don't know what the word was, or who the someone was, or where he lived. It was so long before history—history means "recorded events," and events cannot be recorded without words —that we can only say, as in a fairy tale, "Once upon a time man learned to talk."

Editor's note: The following eleven selections are designed to show the derivation of certain common expressions.

Robert Browning

THE BEST IS YET TO BE

Context: The old rabbi refutes the idea that youth is the only good time of life. God planned man's life as a continuous growth which reaches its greatest development just before death. In youth, men gain experience which ripens into wisdom in later life, and it is this wisdom that God values in His creatures. God is compared to a potter making a cup, the cup representing a man's life: the base of the cup is his early years; only when the cup is completed—when his life is ending—does it begin to have use to God. Thus, men should not become saddened as the years

The following ten selections are from *Magill's Quotations in Context* edited by Frank N. Magill. Copyright © 1965 by Frank N. Magill. Reprinted by permission of Harper & Row, Publishers, Inc.

of their lives slip away, but should anticipate greater development and greater value in the sight of God.

> Grow old along with me!
> The best is yet to be,
> The last of life, for which the first was made:
> Our times are in His hand
> Who saith, "A whole I planned,
> Youth shows but half; trust God: see all, nor be afraid!"

Elbert Green Hubbard

CARRY A MESSAGE TO GARCIA

Context: Elbert Hubbard's essay *A Message to Garcia* was written shortly after the Spanish-American war. Hubbard very briefly relates several details of the beginning of the conflict. The President of the United States needed the co-operation of Garcia, leader of the Cuban insurgents. Someone suggested that a man by the name of Rowan could get a message through to the insurgent leader, who was somewhere in the mountains of Cuba. President McKinley handed his letter over to Rowan. Without asking questions, Rowan put the letter in a pouch, strapped it to his body, went in a boat to the coast of Cuba, made his way through the island jungles, and eventually delivered the message to Garcia. Hubbard says that that is the kind of model young men should follow:

> *By the Eternal! there is a man whose form should be cast in death-less bronze and the statue placed in every college of the land. It is not book-learning young men need, nor instruction about this and that, but a stiffening of the vertebrae which will cause them to be loyal to a trust, to act promptly, concentrate their energies: do the thing—"Carry a message to Garcia."*

William Wordsworth

THE CHILD IS FATHER OF THE MAN

Context: This phrase, which Wordsworth later used as an epigraph for his "Ode on the Intimations of Immortality," is central to his thinking about childhood. It is the child who, in his innocence and freshness, is more open to the beauty of nature, more susceptible to its influence. So it was in his own youth, and, happily, so it has continued to be as he has grown older. What the child is, the man will become—in this case, a lover of nature, able to be moved by its beauty. In the last line of the short poem, Wordsworth uses the word "piety" in its sense of "reverence." The poem follows:

> My heart leaps up when I behold
>   A rainbow in the sky:
> So was it when my life began;
> So is it now I am a man;
> So be it when I shall grow old,
>   Or let me die!
> The Child is father of the Man;
> And I could wish my days to be
> Bound each to each by natural piety.

John Heywood

A NEW BROOM SWEEPS CLEAN

Context: The author is advising a young man about whether he should marry a young maid for love or an old widow for money. In advising, he is including all the old proverbs he can think of. He has finished a story about a young couple who married for love and foundered on the rocks of poverty. Now he has turned to the story of a young man who married for money. This rich old widow, whose "age and appetite fell at a strong strife," was "made like a beer port, or a barrel," and was "as coy as a croker's mare." In talking about her, her neighbors finally decided she would do for the young fool, for "every man as he loveth/ Quoth the good man when that he kissed his cow." The author further tells his story:

> It would have made a horse break his halter sure
> All the first fortnight their ticking might have taught
> Any young couple their love ticks to have wrought.
> Some laughed, and said: all thing is gay that is green.
> Some thereto said: the green new broom sweepeth clean.
> But since all thing is the worse for the wearing,
> Decay of clean sweeping folk had in fearing.

William Shakespeare

THE ROBBED THAT SMILES, STEALS SOMETHING FROM THE THIEF

Context: Othello, a Moor and a military commander in the service of Venice, elopes with Desdemona, daughter of a Venetian senator, Brabantio. Brought before the duke by the irate father, and accused of using witchcraft to win the girl, Othello denies the charge, sends for his bride, and relates how he courted Desdemona. She comes to the duke's council chamber. Brabantio immediately puts her to a test of affection —she must choose between her husband and him. She chooses Othello. To comfort the grieving father, the duke offers sage advice.

> *When remedies are past, the griefs are ended*
> *By seeing the worst, which late on hopes depended.*
> *To mourn a mischief that is past and gone*
> *Is the next way to draw new mischief on.*
> *What cannot be preserved when fortune takes,*
> *Patience her injury a mockery makes.*
> *The robbed that smiles, steals something from the thief;*
> *He robs himself, that spends a bootless grief.*

Publius Syrus

A ROLLING STONE GATHERS NO MOSS

Context: The disputed authorship of many of these copybook sentences, perhaps used as models for the education of the young, gives rise to many theories concerning these familiar quotations. They were first attributed to Seneca, but Pliny and others give evidence of a slave from Syrus who was a mime in the first century B.C., having arrived in Rome with the astronomer Manilius and the grammarian Staberius. His plays seem to have been admired during the Augustan age and survived, according to Petronius, to the time of Nero, and the writer himself may have lived into the Christian era. In the Middle Ages the texts were bowdlerized and misplaced, and it is certain that the accretion of maxims under this name is not definitely Publius', as he is popularly called. The proverb is current today, having come to us from many sources, among which are John Heywood's *"The rolling stone never gathereth mosse"* (1546) and Tusser's *"The stone that is rolling can gather no moss."* (1557) The meaning remains constant: it is not a good thing to be always on the move, for stability gives repose and wealth. The popular version of the saying is:

> *A rolling stone gathers no moss.*

Marcus Aurelius Antoninus

WALK WITH THE GODS

Context: Marcus Aurelius, the Roman emperor who wrote his meditations in Greek, was a Stoic philosopher. He believed that man should rely on the divine reason within himself and that external pleasures and sufferings should be matters of indifference. In order to walk or live with the gods, man should use their gift of reason.

> *Walk with the Gods! And he does walk with the Gods, who lets them see his soul invariably satisfied with its lot and carrying out the will of that "genius," a particle of himself, which Zeus has given to every man as his Captain and guide—and this is none other than each man's intelligence and reason.*

William Tecumseh Sherman

WAR IS HELL

Context: William Tecumseh Sherman, general in the Union army and participant in most of the major battles of the Civil War, is noted chiefly for his devastating march from Atlanta to Savannah. Before his death, the saying "War is hell" came to be ascribed to him, but a search of newspapers and speeches produces no such memorable remark. Attributed to speeches at various occasions, the exact remark may not have been uttered, but on August 11, 1880, at Columbus, Ohio, following a speech by President Hayes, Sherman spoke briefly to the Union veterans the words seemingly closest in meaning to his famous statement. The *Ohio State Journal* reported the words:

> *There is many a boy here today who looks on war as all glory, but, boys, it is all hell. You can bear this warning voice to generations yet to come. I look upon war with horror, but if it has to come I am here.*

John Webster with Thomas Dekker

THE WAY OF ALL FLESH

Context: In *Westward Ho!* the expression "going the way of all flesh" is a joke. Monopoly, a nephew of the Earl, asks Mistress Birdlime, a procuress, if she has seen his uncle. She says she just saw him going the way of all flesh—into the kitchen. Although the inference here is that flesh is cooked in the kitchen, the expression usually means to die, as all flesh is mortal; for instance, Thomas Heywood in *The Golden Age* (1611) says: "If I go by land, and miscarry, then I go the way of all flesh"; in other words, he will die. So it is in Thomas Heywood's *Second Part of the Fair Maid of the West* (1631): "She by this is gone the way of all flesh." In his *Sketches by Boz:* "Mr. Watkins Tottle" (1835), Charles Dickens brings out the meaning in: "He . . . allowed us something to live on till he went the way of all flesh." When Samuel Butler names his novel *The Way of All Flesh,* he is referring to the frailties of humanity caused by the desires of the flesh. The passage in *Westward Ho!* is:

Monopoly: Saw you my uncle?

Birdlime: I saw him even now going the way of all flesh, that's to say, toward the kitchen. . . .

Miguel de Cervantes Saavedra

WITH A GRAIN OF SALT

Context: The Romans spoke of taking an unbelievable story "cum grano salis," (with a grain of salt), to make it easier to swallow. The druggist mentioned by Sancho did not like "old waiting women," and required a grain of salt to make them more palatable. The arrival of the Disconsolate Matron is announced. She is coming to beg Don Quixote to redress her wrongs. Sancho, taking her Spanish title of Dueña to mean a waiting woman, is sure her coming will spoil his chances to receive preferment.

> *I remember I once knew a Toledo pothecary, that talked like a canary bird, and used to say, wherever come old waiting-women, good luck can happen there to no man. Body of me, he knew them too well and therefore valued them accordingly. He could have eaten them all with a grain of salt.*

Francis Thompson

THE MANY-SPLENDOURED THING

Context: In many of his poems the Catholic poet Francis Thompson treats profound religious themes. Much of the beauty of the poem entitled "The Kingdom of God" ("In No Strange Land") comes from the simplicity of the treatment of the subject. The theme is first developed through analogy. The poet asks: "Does the fish soar to find the ocean,/ The eagle plunge to end the air— . . . ?" Then discarding the ideas of the Kingdom of God lying "where the wheeling systems darken,/ And our benumbed conceiving soars!," the poet says the beating of the wings of angels is at "our own clay-shuttered doors," if we would only listen. Man has become estranged from Heaven; Heaven is in the same place it has always been. The poet gives the theme of his poem in the following lines:

From *Complete Poems of Francis Thompson*, Random House, Inc.

> The angels keep their ancient places;—
> Turn but a stone, and start a wing!
> 'Tis ye, 'tis your estrangèd faces,
> That miss the many-splendoured thing.

Walt Whitman

PREFACE TO THE 1855 EDITION OF
LEAVES OF GRASS

America does not repel the past, or what the past has produced under its forms, or amid other politics, or the idea of castes, or the old religions—accepts the lesson with calmness—is not impatient because the slough still sticks to opinions and manners in literature, while the life which served its requirements has passed into the new life of the new forms—perceives that the corpse is slowly borne from the eating and sleeping rooms of the house—perceives that it waits a little while in the door—that it was fittest for its days—that its action has descended to the stalwart and well-shaped heir who approaches—and that he shall be fittest for his days.

The Americans of all nations at any time upon the earth have probably the fullest poetical nature. The United States themselves are essentially the greatest poem. In the history of the earth hitherto, the largest and most stirring appear tame and orderly to their ampler largeness and stir. Here at last is something in the doings of man that corresponds with the broadcast doings of the day and night. Here is action untied from strings, necessarily blind to particulars and details, magnificently moving in masses. Here is the hospitality which forever indicates heroes. Here the performance, disdaining the trivial, unapproach'd in the tremendous audacity of its crowds and groupings, and the push of its perspective, spreads with crampless and flowing breadth, and showers its prolific and splendid extravagance. One sees it must indeed own the riches of the summer and winter, and need never be bankrupt while corn grows from the ground, or the orchards drop apples, or the bays contain fish, or men beget children upon women.

Other states indicate themselves in their deputies—but the genius of the United States is not best or most in its executives or legislatures, nor in its ambassadors or authors, or colleges or churches or parlors, nor even in its newspapers or inventors—but always most in the common people, South, North, West, East, in all its States, through all its mighty amplitude. The largeness of the nation, however, were monstrous without a corresponding largeness and generosity of the spirit of the citizen. Not swarming states, nor streets and steamships, nor prosperous business, nor farms, nor capital, nor learning, may suffice for the ideal of man—nor suffice the poet. No reminiscences may suffice either. A live nation can always cut a deep mark, and can have the best authority the cheapest—namely, from its own soul. This is the sum of the profitable uses of individuals or states, and of present action and grandeur, and of the subjects of poets. (As if it were necessary to trot back generation after generation to the Eastern records! As if the beauty and sacredness of the demonstrable must fall behind that of the mythical! As if men do not make their mark out of any times! As if the opening of the Western Continent by discovery, and what has transpired in North and South America, were less than the small theatre of the antique, or the aimless sleep-walking of the Middle Ages!) The pride of the United States leaves the wealth and finesse of the cities, and all returns of commerce and agriculture, and all the magnitude of geography or shows of exterior victory, to enjoy the sight and realization of full-sized men, or one full-sized man unconquerable and simple.

The American poets are to enclose old and new, for America is the race of races. The expression of the American poet is to be transcendent and new. It is to be indirect, and not direct or descriptive or epic. Its quality goes through these to much more. Let the age and wars of other nations be chanted, and their eras and characters be illustrated, and that finish the verse. Not so the great psalm of the republic. Here the theme is creative, and has vista. Whatever stagnates in the flat of custom or obedience or legislation, the great poet never stagnates. Obedience does not master him, he masters it. High up out of reach he stands, turning a concentrated light—he turns the pivot with his finger —he baffles the swiftest runners as he stands, and easily overtakes and envelopes them. The time straying toward infidelity and confections and persiflage he withholds by steady faith. Faith is the antiseptic of the soul—it pervades the common people and preserves them—they never give up believing and expecting and trusting. There is that indescribable freshness and unconsciousness about an illiterate person, that humbles and mocks the power of the noblest expressive genius. The poet sees for a certainty how one not a great artist may be just as sacred and perfect as the greatest artist.

The power to destroy or remould is freely used by the greatest poet, but seldom the power of attack. What is past is past. If he does not expose superior models, and prove himself by every step he takes, he is not what is wanted. The presence of the great poet conquers—not parleying, or struggling, or any prepared attempts. Now he has passed that way, see after him! There is not left any vestige of despair, or misanthropy, or cunning, or exclusiveness, or the ignominy of a nativity or color, or delusion of hell or the necessity of hell—and no man thenceforward shall be degraded for ignorance or weakness or sin. The greatest poet hardly knows pettiness or triviality. If he breathes into anything that was before thought small, it dilates with the grandeur and life of the universe. He is a seer—he is individual—he is complete in himself—the others are as good as he, only he sees it, and they do not. He is not one of the chorus—he does not stop for any regulation— he is the president of regulation. What the eyesight does to the rest, he does to the rest. Who knows the curious mystery of the eyesight? The other senses corroborate themselves, but this is removed from any proof but its own, and foreruns the identities of the spiritual world. A single

glance of it mocks all the investigations of man, and all the instruments
and books of the earth, and all reasoning. What is marvellous? what is
unlikely? what is impossible or baseless or vague—after you have once
just open'd the space of a peach-pit, and given audience to far and near,
and to the sunset, and had all things enter with electric swiftness, softly
and duly, without confusion or jostling or jam?

The land and sea, the animals, fishes and birds, the sky of heaven
and the orbs, the forests, mountains and rivers, are not small themes—
but folks expect of the poet to indicate more than the beauty and
dignity which always attach to dumb real objects—they expect him to
indicate the path between reality and their souls. Men and women
perceive the beauty well enough—probably as well as he. The passionate tenacity of hunters, woodmen, early risers, cultivators of gardens
and orchards and fields, the love of healthy women for the manly form,
sea-faring persons, drivers of horses, the passion for light and the open
air, all is an old varied sign of the unfailing perception of beauty, and of
a residence of the poetic in out-door people. They can never be assisted
by poets to perceive—some may, but they never can. The poetic quality
is not marshal'd in rhyme or uniformity, or abstract addresses to things,
nor in melancholy complaints or good precepts, but is the life of these
and much else, and is in the soul. The profit of rhyme is that it drops
seeds of a sweeter and more luxuriant rhyme, and of uniformity that it
conveys itself into its own roots in the ground out of sight. The rhyme
and uniformity of perfect poems show the free growth of metrical laws,
and bud from them as unerringly and loosely as lilacs and roses on a
bush, and take shapes as compact as the shapes of chestnuts and
oranges, and melons and pears, and shed the perfume impalpable to
form. The fluency and ornaments of the finest poems or music or
orations or recitations are not independent but dependent. All beauty
comes from beautiful blood and a beautiful brain. If the greatnesses are
in conjunction in a man or woman, it is enough—the fact will prevail
through the universe; but the gaggery and gilt of a million years will
not prevail. Who troubles himself about his ornaments or fluency is lost.
This is what you shall do: Love the earth and sun and the animals,
despise riches, give alms to every one that asks, stand up for the stupid
and crazy, devote your income and labor to others, hate tyrants, argue
not concerning God, have patience and indulgence toward the people,
take off your hat to nothing known or unknown, or to any man or
number of men—go freely with powerful uneducated persons, and with
the young, and with the mothers of families—re-examine all you have
been told in school or church or in any book, and dismiss whatever
insults your own soul; and your very flesh shall be a great poem, and
have the richest fluency, not only in its words, but in the silent lines of
its lips and face, and between the lashes of your eyes, and in every
motion and joint of your body. The poet shall not spend his time in
unneeded work. He shall know that the ground is already plough'd and
manured; others may not know it, but he shall. He shall go directly to
the creation. His trust shall master the trust of everything he touches—
and shall master all attachment.

The known universe has one complete lover, and that is the greatest poet. He consumes an eternal passion, and is indifferent which chance happens, and which possible contingency of fortune or misfortune, and persuades daily and hourly his delicious pay. What balks or breaks others is fuel for his burning progress to contact and amorous joy. Other proportions of the reception of pleasure dwindle to nothing to his proportions. All expected from heaven or from the highest, he is rapport with in the sight of the daybreak, or the scenes of the winter woods, or the presence of children playing, or with his arm round the neck of a man or woman. His love above all love has leisure and expanse—he leaves room ahead of himself. He is no irresolute or suspicious lover—he is sure—he scorns intervals. His experience and the showers and thrills are not for nothing. Nothing can jar him—suffering and darkness cannot—death and fear cannot. To him complaint and jealousy and envy are corpses buried and rotten in the earth—he saw them buried. The sea is not surer of the shore, or the shore of the sea, than he is the fruition of his love, and of all perfection and beauty.

The fruition of beauty is no chance of miss or hit—it is as inevitable as life—it is exact and plumb as gravitation. From the eyesight proceeds another eyesight, and from the hearing proceeds another hearing, and from the voice proceeds another voice, eternally curious of the harmony of things with man. These understand the law of perfection in masses and floods—that it is profuse and impartial—that there is not a minute of the light or dark, nor an acre of the earth and sea, without it—nor any direction of the sky, nor any trade or employment, nor any turn of events. This is the reason that about the proper expression of beauty there is a precision and balance. One part does not need to be thrust above another. The best singer is not the one who has the most lithe and powerful organ. The pleasure of poems is not in them that take the handsomest measure and sound.

Without effort, and without exposing in the least how it is done, the greatest poet brings the spirit of any or all events and passions and scenes and persons, some more and some less, to bear on your individual character as you hear or read. To do this well is to compete with the laws that pursue and follow Time. What is the purpose must surely be there, and the clue of it must be there—and the faintest indication is the indication of the best, and then becomes the clearest indication. Past and present and future are not disjoin'd but join'd. The greatest poet forms the consistence of what is to be, from what has been and is. He drags the dead out of their coffins and stands them again on their feet. He says to the past, Rise and walk before me that I may realize you. He learns the lesson—he places himself where the future becomes present. The greatest poet does not only dazzle his rays over character and scenes and passions—he finally ascends, and finishes all—he exhibits the pinnacles that no man can tell what they are for, or what is beyond—he glows a moment on the extremest verge. He is most wonderful in his last half-hidden smile or frown; by that flash of the moment of parting the one that sees it shall be encouraged or terrified afterward for many years. The greatest poet does not moralize or make applications of morals—he knows the soul. The soul has that measureless pride which consists in never acknowledging any lessons or deductions but its own. But it has sympathy as measureless as its pride, and the one balances the other, and neither can stretch too far while it stretches in company with the other. The inmost secrets of art sleep with the twain. The greatest poet has lain close betwixt both, and they are vital in his style and thoughts.

The art of art, the glory of expression and the sunshine of the light of letters, is simplicity. Nothing is better than simplicity—nothing can make up for excess, or for the lack of definiteness. To carry on the heave of impulse and pierce intellectual depths and give all subjects their articulations, are powers neither common nor very uncommon. But to speak in literature with the perfect rectitude and insouciance of the movements of animals, and the unimpeachableness of the sentiment of trees in the woods and grass by the roadside, is the flawless triumph of art. If you have look'd on him who has achiev'd it you have look'd on one of the masters of the artists of all nations and times. You shall not contemplate the flight of the gray gull over the bay, or the mettlesome action of the blood horse, or the tall leaning of sunflowers on their stalk, or the appearance of the sun journeying through heaven, or the appearance of the moon afterward, with any more satisfaction than you shall contemplate him. The great poet has less a mark'd style, and is more the channel of thoughts and things without increase or diminution, and is the free channel of himself. He swears to his art, I will not be meddlesome, I will not have in my writing any elegance, or effect, or originality, to hang in the way between me and the rest like curtains. I will have nothing hang in the way, not the richest curtains. What I tell I tell for precisely what it is. Let who may exalt or startle or fascinate or soothe, I will have purposes as health or heat or snow has, and be as regardless of observation. What I experience or portray shall go from my composition without a shred of my composition. You shall stand by my side and look in the mirror with me.

The old red blood and stainless gentility of great poets will be proved by their unconstraint. A heroic person walks at his ease through and out of that custom or precedent or authority that suits him not. Of the traits of the brotherhood of first-class writers, savans, musicians, inventors and artists, nothing is finer than silent defiance advancing from new free forms. In the need of poems, philosophy, politics, mechanism, science, behavior, the craft of art, an appropriate native grand opera, shipcraft, or any craft, he is greatest for ever and ever who contributes the greatest original practical example. The cleanest expression is that which finds no sphere worthy of itself, and makes one.

The messages of great poems to each man and woman are, Come to us on equal terms, only then can you understand us. We are no better than you, what we inclose you inclose, what we enjoy you may enjoy. Did you suppose there could be only one Supreme? We affirm there can be unnumber'd Supremes, and that one does not countervail another any more than one eyesight countervails another—and that men can be good or grand only of the consciousness of their supremacy within

them. What do you think is the grandeur of storms and dismember-
ments, and the deadliest battles and wrecks, and the wildest fury of the
elements, and the power of the sea, and the motion of Nature, and the
throes of human desires, and dignity and hate and love? It is that
something in the soul which says, Rage on, whirl on, I tread master
here and everywhere—Master of the spasms of the sky and of the
shatter of the sea, Master of nature and passion and death, and of all
terror and all pain.

The American bards shall be mark'd for generosity and affection,
and for encouraging competitors. They shall be kosmos, without monopoly or secrecy, glad to pass anything to any one—hungry for equals
night and day. They shall not be careful of riches and privilege—they
shall be riches and privilege—they shall perceive who the most affluent
man is. The most affluent man is he that confronts all the shows he sees
by equivalents out of the stronger wealth of himself. The American bard
shall delineate no class of persons, nor one or two out of the strata of
interests, nor love most nor truth most, nor the soul most, nor the body
most—and not be for the Eastern States more than the Western, or the
Northern States more than the Southern.

Exact science and its practical movements are no checks on the
greatest poet, but always his encouragement and support. The outset
and remembrance are there—there the arms that lifted him first, and
braced him best—there he returns after all his goings and comings. The
sailor and traveler—the anatomist, chemist, astronomer, geologist,
phrenologist, spiritualist, mathematician, historian, and lexicographer,
are not poets, but they are the lawgivers of poets, and their construction
underlies the structure of every perfect poem. No matter what rises or is
utter'd, they sent the seed of the conception of it—of them and by them
stand the visible proofs of souls. If there shall be love and content
between the father and the son, and if the greatness of the son is the
exuding of the greatness of the father, there shall be love between the
poet and the man of demonstrable science. In the beauty of poems are
henceforth the tuft and final applause of science.

Great is the faith of the flush of knowledge, and of the investigation of the depths of qualities and things. Cleaving and circling here
swells the soul of the poet, yet is president of itself always. The depths
are fathomless, and therefore calm. The innocence and nakedness are
resumed—they are neither modest nor immodest. The whole theory of
the supernatural, and all that was twined with it or educed out of it,
departs as a dream. What has ever happen'd—what happens, and
whatever may or shall happen, the vital laws inclose all. They are
sufficient for any case and for all cases—none to be hurried or retarded
—any special miracle of affairs or persons inadmissible in the vast clear
scheme where every motion and every spear of grass, and the frames
and spirits of men and women and all that concerns them, are unspeakably perfect miracles, all referring to all, and each distinct and in its
place. It is also not consistent with the reality of the soul to admit that
there is anything in the known universe more divine than men and
women.

Men and women, and the earth and all upon it, are to be taken as they are, and the investigation of their past and present and future shall be unintermitted, and shall be done with perfect candor. Upon this basis philosophy speculates, ever looking towards the poet, ever regarding the eternal tendencies of all toward happiness, never inconsistent with what is clear to the senses and to the soul. For the eternal tendencies of all toward happiness make the only point of sane philosophy. Whatever comprehends less than that—whatever is less than the laws of light and of astronomical motion—or less than the laws that follow the thief, the liar, the glutton and the drunkard, through this life and doubtless afterward,—or less than vast stretches of time, or the slow formation of density, or the patient upheaving of strata,—is of no account. Whatever would put God in a poem or system of philosophy as contending against some being or influence, is also of no account. Sanity and ensemble characterize the great master—spoilt in one principle, all is spoilt. The great master has nothing to do with miracles. He sees health for himself in being one of the mass—he sees the hiatus in singular eminence. To the perfect shape comes common ground. To be under the general law is great, for that is to correspond with it. The master knows that he is unspeakably great, and that all are unspeakably great—that nothing, for instance, is greater than to conceive children, and bring them up well—that to *be* is just as great as to perceive or tell.

In the make of the great masters the idea of political liberty is indispensable. Liberty takes the adherence of heroes wherever man and woman exist—but never takes any adherence or welcome from the rest more than from poets. They are the voice and exposition of liberty. They out of ages are worthy the grand idea—to them it is confided, and they must sustain it. Nothing has precedence of it, and nothing can warp or degrade it.

As the attributes of the poets of the kosmos concentre in the real body, and in the pleasure of things, they possess the superiority of genuineness over all fiction and romance. As they emit themselves, facts are shower'd over with light—the daylight is lit with more volatile light—the deep between the setting and rising sun goes deeper many fold. Each precise object or condition or combination or process exhibits a beauty—the multiplication table its—old age its—the carpenter's trade its—the grand opera its—the huge-hull'd clean-shap'd New York clipper at sea under steam or full sail gleams with unmatch'd beauty— the American circles and large harmonies of government gleam with theirs—and the commonest definite intentions and actions with theirs. The poets of the kosmos advance through all interpositions and coverings and turmoils and stratagems to first principles. They are of use— they dissolve poverty from its need, and riches from its conceit. You large proprietor, they say, shall not realize or perceive more than any one else. The owner of the library is not he who holds a legal title to it, having bought and paid for it. Any one and every one is owner of the library (indeed he or she alone is owner), who can read the same through all the varieties of tongues and subjects and styles, and in whom they enter with ease, and make supple and powerful and rich and large.

These American States, strong and healthy and accomplish'd, shall receive no pleasure from violations of natural models, and must not permit them. In paintings or mouldings or carvings in mineral or wood, or in the illustrations of books or newspapers, or in the patterns of woven stuffs, or anything to beautify rooms or furniture or costumes, or to put upon cornices or monuments, or on the prows or sterns of ships, or to put anywhere before the human eye indoors or out, that which distorts honest shapes, or which creates unearthly beings or places or contingencies, is a nuisance and revolt. Of the human form especially, it is so great it must never be made ridiculous. Of ornaments to a work nothing outré can be allow'd—but those ornaments can be allow'd that conform to the perfect facts of the open air, and that flow out of the nature of the work, and come irrepressibly from it, and are necessary to the completion of the work. Most works are most beautiful without ornament. Exaggerations will be revenged in human physiology. Clean and vigorous children are jetted and conceiv'd only in those communities where the models of natural forms are public every day. Great genius and the people of these States must never be demean'd to romances. As soon as histories are properly told, no more need of romances.

The great poets are to be known by the absence in them of tricks, and by the justification of perfect personal candor. All faults may be forgiven of him who has perfect candor. Henceforth let no man of us lie, for we have seen that openness wins the inner and outer world, and that there is no single exception, and that never since our earth gather'd itself in a mass have deceit or subterfuge or prevarication attracted its smallest particle or the faintest tinge of a shade—and that through the enveloping wealth and rank of a state, or the whole republic of States, a sneak or sly person shall be discover'd and despised—and that the soul has never once been fool'd and never can be fool'd—and thrift without the loving nod of the soul is only a fœtid puff—and there never grew up in any of the continents of the globe, nor upon any planet or satellite, nor in that condition which precedes the birth of babes, nor at any time during the changes of life, nor in any stretch of abeyance or action of vitality, nor in any process of formation or reformation anywhere, a being whose instinct hated the truth.

Extreme caution or prudence, the soundest organic health, large hope and comparison and fondness for women and children, large alimentiveness and destructiveness and causality, with a perfect sense of the oneness of nature, and the propriety of the same spirit applied to human affairs, are called up of the float of the brain of the world to be parts of the greatest poet from his birth out of his mother's womb, and from her birth out of her mother's. Caution seldom goes far enough. It has been thought that the prudent citizen was the citizen who applied himself to solid gains, and did well for himself and for his family, and completed a lawful life without debt or crime. The greatest poet sees and admits these economies as he sees the economies of food and sleep, but has higher notions of prudence than to think he gives much when he gives a few slight attentions at the latch of the gate. The premises of the prudence of life are not the hospitality of it, or the ripeness and harvest of it. Beyond the independence of a little sum laid aside for burial-money, and of a few clapboards around and shingles overhead on a lot of American soil own'd, and the easy dollars that supply the year's plain clothing and meals, the melancholy prudence of the abandonment of such a great being as a man is to the toss and pallor of years of money-making, with all their scorching days and icy nights, and all their stifling deceits and underhand dodgings, or infinitesimals of parlors, or shameless stuffing while others starve, and all the loss of the bloom and odor of the earth, and of the flowers and atmosphere, and of the sea, and of the true taste of the women and men you pass or have to do with in youth or middle age, and the issuing sickness and desperate revolt at the close of a life without elevation or naïveté, (even if you have achiev'd a secure 10,000 a year, or election to Congress or the Governorship,) and the ghastly chatter of a death without serenity or majesty, is the great fraud upon modern civilization and forethought, blotching the surface and system which civilization undeniably drafts, and moistening with tears the immense features it spreads and spreads with such velocity before the reach'd kisses of the soul.

Ever the right explanation remains to be made about prudence. The prudence of the mere wealth and respectability of the most esteem'd life appears too faint for the eye to observe at all, when little and large alike drop quietly aside at the thought of the prudence suitable for immortality. What is the wisdom that fills the thinness of a year, or seventy or eighty years—to the wisdom spaced out by ages, and coming back at a certain time with strong reinforcements and rich presents, and the clear faces of wedding-guests as far as you can look, in every direction, running gaily toward you? Only the soul is of itself—all else has reference to what ensues. All that a person does or thinks is of consequence. Nor can the push of charity or personal force ever be anything else than the profoundest reason, whether it brings argument to hand or no. No specification is necessary—to add or subtract or divide is in vain. Little or big, learn'd or unlearn'd, white or black, legal or illegal, sick or well, from the first inspiration down the windpipe to the last expiration out of it, all that a male or female does that is vigorous and benevolent and clean is so much sure profit to him or her in the unshakable order of the universe, and through the whole scope of it forever. The prudence of the greatest poet answers at last the craving and glut of the soul, puts off nothing, permits no let-up for its own case or any case, has no particular sabbath or judgment day, divides not the living from the dead, or the righteous from the unrighteous, is satisfied with the present, matches every thought or act by its correlative, and knows no possible forgiveness or deputed atonement.

The direct trial of him who would be the greatest poet is to-day. If he does not flood himself with the immediate age as with vast oceanic tides—if he be not himself the age transfigur'd, and if to him is not open'd the eternity which gives similitude to all periods and locations and processes, and animate and inanimate forms, and which is the bond of time, and rises up from its inconceivable vagueness and infiniteness in the swimming shapes of to-day, and is held by the ductile anchors of life, and makes the present spot the passage from what was to what shall be, and commits itself to the representation of this wave of an hour, and this one of the sixty beautiful children of the wave—let him merge in the general run, and wait his development.

Still the final test of poems, or any character or work, remains. The prescient poet projects himself centuries ahead, and judges performer or performance after the changes of time. Does it live through them? Does it still hold on untired? Will the same style, and the direction of genius to similar points, be satisfactory now? Have the marches of tens and hundreds and thousands of years made willing détours to the right hand and the left hand for his sake? Is he beloved long and long after he is buried? Does the young man think often of him? and the young woman think often of him? and do the middle-aged and the old think of him?

A great poem is for ages and ages in common, and for all degrees and complexions, and all departments and sects, and for a woman as much as a man, and a man as much as a woman. A great poem is no finish to a man or woman, but rather a beginning. Has any one fancied he could sit at last under some due authority, and rest satisfied with explanations, and realize, and be content and full? To no such terminus does the greatest poet bring—he brings neither cessation nor shelter'd fatness and ease. The touch of him, like Nature, tells in action. Whom he takes he takes with firm sure grasp into live regions previously unattain'd—thenceforward is no rest—they see the space and ineffable sheen that turn the old spots and lights into dead vacuums. Now there shall be a man cohered out of tumult and chaos—the elder encourages the younger and shows him how—they two shall launch off fearlessly together till the new world fits an orbit for itself, and looks unabash'd on the lesser orbits of the stars, and sweeps through the ceaseless rings, and shall never be quiet again.

There will soon be no more priests. Their work is done. A new order shall arise, and they shall be the priests of man, and every man shall be his own priest. They shall find their inspiration in real objects to-day, symptoms of the past and future. They shall not deign to defend immortality or God, or the perfection of things, or liberty, or the exquisite beauty and reality of the soul. They shall arise in America, and be responded to from the remainder of the earth.

The English language befriends the grand American expression—it is brawny enough, and limber and full enough. On the tough stock of a race who through all change of circumstance was never without the idea of political liberty, which is the animus of all liberty, it has attracted the terms of daintier and gayer and subtler and more elegant tongues. It is the powerful language of resistance—it is the dialect of common sense. It is the speech of the proud and melancholy races, and of all who aspire. It is the chosen tongue to express growth, faith, self-esteem, freedom, justice, equality, friendliness, amplitude, prudence, decision, and courage. It is the medium that shall wellnigh express the inexpressible.

No great literature, nor any like style of behavior or oratory, or social intercourse or household arrangements, or public institutions, or the treatment by bosses of employ'd people, nor executive detail, or detail of the army and navy, nor spirit of legislation or courts, or police or tuition or architecture, or songs or amusements, can long elude the jealous and passionate instinct of American standards. Whether or no the sign appears from the mouths of the people, it throbs a live interrogation in every freeman's and freewoman's heart, after that which passes by, or this built to remain. Is it uniform with my country? Are its disposals without ignominious distinctions? Is it for the ever-growing communes of brothers and lovers, large, well united, proud, beyond the old models, generous beyond all models? Is it something grown fresh out of the fields, or drawn from the sea for use to me to-day here? I know that what answers for me, an American, in Texas, Ohio, Canada, must answer for any individual or nation that serves for a part of my materials. Does this answer? Is it for the nursing of the young of the republic? Does it solve readily with the sweet milk of the nipples of the breasts of the Mother of Many Children?

America prepares with composure and good-will for the visitors that have sent word. It is not intellect that is to be their warrant and welcome. The talented, the artist, the ingenious, the editor, the statesman, the erudite, are not unappreciated—they fall in their place and do their work. The soul of the nation also does its work. It rejects none, it permits all. Only toward the like of itself will it advance half-way. An individual is as superb as a nation when he has the qualities which make a superb nation. The soul of the largest and wealthiest and proudest nation may well go half-way to meet that of its poets.

H. L. Mencken

AMERICAN SLANG

THE NATURE OF SLANG

Slang is defined by the Oxford Dictionary as "language of a highly colloquial type, considered as below the level of standard educated speech, and consisting either of new words or of current words employed in some special sense." The essence of slang is that it is of general dispersion, but still stands outside the accepted canon of the language. It is, says George H. McKnight,[1] "a form of colloquial speech

Condensed from H. L. Mencken's The American Language: Abridged, ed. by Raven I. McDavid and David W. Maurer. Copyright 1948, © 1963 by Alfred A. Knopf, Inc. Reprinted by permission of the publisher.

[1] English Words and Their Background; New York, 1923, p. 43.

created in a spirit of defiance and aiming at freshness and novelty. . . .
Its figures are consciously farfetched and are intentionally drawn from
the most ignoble of sources. Closely akin to profanity in its spirit, its
aim is to shock."

What chiefly lies behind it is simply a kind of linguistic exuber-
ance, an excess of word-making energy. But there is also something
else. The best slang is not only ingenious and amusing; it also embodies
a kind of social criticism. It not only provides new names for a series of
everyday concepts, some new and some old; it also says something
about them.[2] "Words which produce the slang effect," observes Frank K.
Sechrist,[3] "arouses associations which are incongruous or incompatible
with those of customary thinking." Everyone, including even the meta-
physician in his study and the eremite in his cell, has a large vocabulary
of slang, but the vocabulary of the vulgar is likely to be larger, in
proportion to the total vocabulary, than that of the cultured, and it is
harder-worked.

[Current investigation shows that even nuns in cloisters have
developed their own slang (amusing, but of course genteel) and that
Trappist monks, for whom silence is the rule, have introduced slang
among themselves. In a collection of some 1,000 entries of sign language (much of it undoubtedly very ancient) used by Trappists, there
are some which express attitudes and concepts which are more or less
taboo and are not used in the presence of the Bishop.]

Slang originates in the effort of ingenious individuals to make the
language more pungent and picturesque—to increase the store of terse
and striking words, to widen the boundaries of metaphor, and to provide a vocabulary for new shades of difference in meaning. As Jespersen has pointed out,[4] this is also the aim of poets (as, indeed, it is of
prose writers), but they are restrained by consideration of taste and
decorum, and also, not infrequently, by historical or logical considerations. The maker of slang is under no such limitations: he is free to
confect his neologism by any process that can be grasped by his customers, and out of any materials available, whether native or foreign.

The origin of the word *slang* is unknown. Ernest Weekley, in his
"Etymological Dictionary of Modern English" (1921), suggests that it
may have some relation to the verb *to sling,* and cites two Norwegian
dialect words, based upon the cognate verb *slenge* or *slengje,* that
appear to be its brothers: *slengjeord,* a neologism, and *slengjenamn,* a
nickname. But he is not sure, so he adds the note that "some regard it as
an argotic perversion of the French *langue,* language." A German
philologian, O. Ritter, believes that it may be derived, not from *langue,*
but from *language* itself, most probably by a combination of blending

---

[2] See American Slang, the London *Times* (editorial), May 11, 1931; and What Is Slang?
by H. F. Reeves, *AS,* Vol. I, Jan. 1926.

[3] The Psychology of Unconventional Language, *Pedagogical Seminary,* Dec. 1913, p. 443.

[4] Language: Its Nature, Development and Origin; London, 1922, p. 300.

and shortening, as in *thieve(s' lang)uage, beggar(s' lang)uage* and so on.[5]

When it first appeared in English, about the middle of the Eighteenth Century, it was employed as a synonym of *cant,* and so designated "the special vocabulary used by any set of persons of a low or disreputable character"; and half a century later it began to be used interchangeably with *argot,* which means the vocabulary special to any group, trade or profession. But during the past fifty years the three terms have tended to be more or less clearly distinguished.

The boundaries separating true slang from cant and argot are wavering and not easily defined, and there is a constant movement of words and phrases from one category to another. When, in 1785, Captain Francis Grose published the first edition of his "Classical Dictionary of the Vulgar Tongue," the word *slang* itself seems to have been confined mainly to the argot of criminals and vagabonds, but today it appears unchallenged in all dictionaries.

As everyone knows, most slang terms have relatively short lives, and nothing seems more stale than one that has passed out, *e.g., skiddoo, snake's hips, nerts, attaboy* and *I don't think,* but now and then one survives for years and even for centuries, without either going into eclipse on the one hand or being elevated to standard speech on the other. *To bamboozle* is still below the salt and would hardly be used by a bishop in warning against Satan, but it is more than two hundred years old and was listed as slang by Richard Steele in the *Tatler* in 1710. *Gas* (talk) has been traced to 1847, *kibosh* to 1836, *lip* (impudence) to 1821, *sap* to 1815, *cheese it* to 1811, *to chisel* to 1808, *racket* to 1785, *hush money* to 1709, *to knock off* (to quit) to 1662, *tick* (credit) to 1661, *grub* to 1659, *to cotton to* to 1605, *bat* (a loose woman) to 1612, *to plant* (to hide) to 1610, *brass* (impudence) to 1594, *duds* (clothes) to 1567 and *to blow* (to boast) to c. 1400: all remain in use today and all continue to be slang.[8] *Booze* has never got into Standard English, but it was used as slang as early as the Fourteenth Century.

It would be hard to figure out precisely what makes one slang term survive for years and another perish quickly and miserably, but some of the elements which may shape the process are discernible. One of them is the degree to which a neologism fills a genuine need. It may do so by providing a pungent name, nearly always metaphorical, for an object or concept that is new to the generality of people, *e.g., ghost writer* and *caterpillar* (running gear), or it may do so by supplying a more succinct or more picturesque designation for something already familiar in terms more commonplace, *e.g., bellhop, sorehead, rubberneck* and *killjoy.* Many of the best slang terms are simple compounds, as the exam-

---

[5] *Archiv für das Studium der neueren Sprachen,* Vol. CXVI, 1906. I am indebted for the reference to Concerning the Etymology of *Slang,* by Fr. Klaeber, *AS,* Vol. I, Apr. 1926. The process is not unfamiliar in English: *tawdry,* from *Saint Audrey,* offers an example.

[6] I take these from Modern Slang, by J. Louis Kuethe, *AS,* Vol. XI, Dec. 1936, pp. 293–7.

ples I have just given show; others are bold tropes, *e.g.*, *bull* (a police-man), *to squeal, masher, cold feet, yellow* (cowardly), *baloney, apple-sauce* and *chick* (from *chicken*, a girl); yet others are the products of a delirious delight in language making, *e.g.*, *fantods, heebie-jeebies, nifty, whoopee, hubba-hubba, to burp* and *oomph*. When a novelty is obvious it seldom lasts very long, *e.g.*, *shellacked* for drunk, *skirt* for woman, *peach* for a beautiful girl, and when its humor is strained it dies as quickly, like *movie cathedral, lounge lizard, third-termite* and the fre-quent inventions of the Broadway school. Moreover, its longevity seems to run in obverse proportion to its first success, so that overnight crazes like *yes, we have no bananas* and *goo-goo eyes* are soon done for, whereas novelties of slower growth, *e.g.*, *booze, to goose* and *gimcrack* last a long, long while. This auto-intoxication seems to cut short the silly phrases of negation that come and go, *e.g.*, *sez you, oh yeah, I don't think* and the numerous catch phrases that have little if any precise meaning but simply delight the moron by letting him show that he knows the latest.

Slang tends to multiply terms for the same concept: its chief aim seems to be to say something new, not necessarily something good. Thus there is a constant succession of novel synonyms for *girl, head, money, drunk, yes, good, bad* and other such words of everyday usage. Slang terms relating to the head always have a derogatory significance, and many of them hint at idiocy. In 1928 Mamie Meredith listed some of those then current, *e.g.*, *bean, coco* and *nut*, along with the fashion-able derivatives, *e.g.*, *bonehead, pinhead* and *mutt* (from *muttonhead*), but many of these are now obsolete. On the other hand, the French word *tête* has been a sound word for head for many centuries, but its origin was in *testa*, meaning a pot, exactly analogous to our *block, nut* and *bean*. The vast vogue of *sheik* (pronounced *sheek*, not *shike*) for a predatory male will be recalled by the middle-aged; it is now as extinct as *masher*.[7] The late George Ade, in 1935, attempted a list of substitutes for such words as *girl, married, idiot, begone* and *drunk*, arranging them in categories of "old," "later" and "latest." [8] Most of the terms he entered under the last heading are now almost forgotten, *e.g.*, *cutie, babe, eyeful, pip* and *wow* for a pretty girl. William Feather, searching "The American Thesaurus of Slang," by Lester V. Berrey and Melvin Van den Bark,[9] found that it listed 52 synonyms for *wife*, and that there was "not an affectionate reference in the lot." [10] Indeed, this attitude is characteristic of all slang, which commonly represents no more than the effort of some smartie to voice his derision, not infrequently for

---

[7] Sinclair Lewis, in Cass Timberlane, New York, 1945, pp. 323–4, listed some of the terms then in use for "the sort of male once described with relish as an agreeable scoun-drel," *e.g., lug, jerk, louse, stinker, twirp, rat, crumb, goon* and *wolf*. Most of them soon passed out.

[8] A Check-Up on Slang in America, Baltimore *Sun* (and other papers), Sept. 8, 1935.

[9] New York, 1942.

[10] *William Feather Magazine*, Oct. 1943, p. 19.

some person, object or idea obviously above his own lowly thought and station. The wit of Broadway, now the source of much American slang, is thus essentially opprobrious, and many of its brighter words and sayings may be readily reduced to "Oh, you son of a bitch."

[Today we know that much if not most slang is argot which emerges from or is discarded from the subcultures of the professional criminal on many levels and in many different specialties. The "wit of Broadway," while still the immediate source of much slang, always was —and still is—closely attuned to the underworld for new and salty terms. For example, Damon Runyon studied the fringes of criminal cultures closely, Wilson Mizner spent many years as a professional grifter before he became a writer and went right on writing just the way he talked, and S. J. Perelman has long been a discerning observer of the criminal world and its idiom. Nowadays there are many other channels which also pipe words from criminal subcultures into the speech and writing of the dominant culture—TV, movies, newspaper columnists, jazz musicians, teen-age pseudo-hoodlums, a few novelists and short-story writers and, certainly not to be overlooked, a growing body of trained sociologists and linguists who are bringing carefully documented, firsthand studies of underworld speech and behavior into professional literature. The contempt in which the criminal subcultures hold the dominant culture accounts for much of the element of derision mentioned above. Invention of slang words by the literati of the dominant culture appears to be meager; most of them, it seems, are borrowed from underworld sources. . . .]

CANT AND ARGOT

The cant of modern criminals, still somewhat international in nature, began to be formulated in western Europe in the early Fifteenth Century, when roving bands of a strange, dark race of petty thieves appeared from the mysterious East and were presently intermingled with the native tramps, beggars, parasite friars and other fly-by-night rogues. These newcomers, at the start, were assumed to be Egyptians, which explains our English name of *Gypsies* for them, but later studies of their history and language have demonstrated that they actually came from northwestern India. They were in Germany by 1414, in Italy by 1422, in France by 1427 and in England by the early 1500s. Two of the largest classes of indigenous vagabonds that they encountered were those of the begging friars and the displaced Jews. Both of these borrowed words and phrases from them and in turn reinforced their language with homemade inventions, and by the end of the Fifteenth Century there had developed in Germany a rogues' jargon that was based on German, but included many Hebrew and Gypsy terms. Some of these survive to the present day, even in the United States, *e.g., pal* from the Gypsy and *ganov* [*ganef*] from the Hebrew. . . .

The literature of criminals' cant since Grose [1785] has been voluminous, but on the whole it was of small value until recent years.

Godfrey Irwin's "American Tramp and Underworld Slang," brought out in 1931, was mainly devoted to the argot of tramps, but within its limits it was well done.[11] [Meanwhile there is the much more authentic "Dictionary of American Underworld Lingo," by Goldin, O'Leary and Lipsius,[12] and another dictionary, currently listing about 10,000 terms is being compiled by Frank Prewitt and Francis K. Schaeffer in a California prison.] At about the same time David W. Maurer, of the University of Louisville, began to interest himself in the subject, and has since become the chief American authority upon it. He has two important qualifications for his task: he is a man trained in scholarly and especially linguistic method, and he has an extraordinary capacity for gaining the confidence of criminals. He has published a book upon the techniques and speech of the confidence men who constitute the gentry of the underworld [13] and papers in the learned journals and elsewhere upon the argots of various lesser groups, ranging from forgers and safecrackers to drug peddlers and prostitutes. [His books "Whiz Mob" [14] and "Narcotics and Narcotic Addiction" [15] explore the relation of language to human behavior within the subcultures of the thief and the drug addict.] A century ago the cant of American criminals was still largely dependent upon that of their English colleagues, stretching back for centuries, but though it still shows marks of that influence [16] it is now predominantly on its own. Its chief characteristics, says Maurer, are "its machine-gun staccato, its hard timbre, its rather grim humor, its vivid imagery, and its remarkable compactness." [17] It differs considerably, of course, from specialty to specialty, but within a given specialty "it appears to be well standardized from coast to coast and from the Gulf into Canada." [Subsequently three geographical dialect areas have been tentatively identified—East Coast, Midwest and West Coast.] It shows the cosmopolitan quality of all American speech, and includes loans from Yiddish, Spanish, German, French, Chinese and even Hindustani. Like slang in general, it is the product, not of the common run of ordinary lawbreakers or amateur criminals, but of the well-established criminal subcultures; it tends to increase in picturesqueness as one goes up the scale of professional rank and dignity. Says Maurer:

[11] It is significant that Irwin had to go to England to find a publisher. There he got aid from Eric Partridge. His material was accumulated during "more than twenty years' experience as a tramp on the railroads and roads of the United States, Canada, Mexico and Central America, and on tramp steamers in Central American waters."

[12] [New York, 1950.]

[13] The Big Con; [3rd ed.; New York, 1963].

[14] [PADS, No. 24, 1955.]

[15] [2nd ed.; Springfield, Ill., 1962.]

[16] For example, in the survival of rhyming slang. An account of the argot of American criminals of the 1900 era is in The Lingo of the Good People, by David W. Maurer, AS, Vol. X, Feb. 1935, pp. 10–23. A great deal of it is now obsolete.

[17] The Argot of the Underworld, AS, Vol. VII, Dec. 1931, pp. 99–118.

*Why do criminals speak a lingo? There are several reasons, per-
haps the most widely accepted of which is that they must have
a secret language in order to conceal their plans from their victims
or from the police. In some instances it is undoubtedly used for
this purpose—for instance,* flat-jointers, three-card monte men,
and other short-con workers [18] *sometimes use it to confuse or
deceive their victims. But most professional criminals do not so use
it. They speak argot only among themselves, . . . for using it in
public would mark them as underworld characters whether or not
they were understood. . . . There is a very strong sense of camara-
derie among them, a highly developed group-solidarity. . . . A
common language helps to bind these groups together and gives
expression to the strong fraternal spirit. . . . Professional crime is
nothing more than a way of living and working within a great
variety of parasitic sub-cultures; hence it is only natural that many
of the same factors which operate in the dominant culture and
among legitimate craftsmen should affect criminal speech.* [19]

The vast upsurge of crime brought in by Prohibition made all
Americans familiar with a large number of criminal words and phrases,
and many of these, as I have noted, have entered into the everyday
speech of the country. How much of the argot of the Volsteadian
racketeers was the product of their own fancy and how much was
thrust upon them by outside admirers, *e.g.,* newspaper reporters and
movie writers, is not easily determined, but Maurer has cited some
examples from the latter, including even such apparently characteristic
terms as *big shot.* He says [20] that actual members of the *mob* called the
brass hats of the profession *wheels* (in the plural). But *trigger man,
torpedo, gorilla, pineapple* (bomb), *whiskers* (a federal agent: a reference to Uncle Sam), *hot* (a stolen object or a criminal pursued by the
law), *on the lam, to snatch* (to kidnap), *moll* and *racket,* whatever

---

[18] *Short-con workers* operate on a modest scale, and are usually content with whatever
money the victim has on him at the time he is rooked. They seldom employ the *send*—
that is, they seldom send him home for more. [*Short-con* argots have been studied by
Maurer in The Argot of the Three-Shell Game, *AS,* Vol. XXII, Oct. 1947, and The Argot of
the Faro Bank, *AS,* Vol. XVIII, Feb. 1943. Many additional examples of it occur in his The
Argot of the Dice Gambler, included in Scarne on Dice, by Clayton Rawson and John
Scarne, Harrisburg, Pa., 1945; in his The Argot of the Racetrack, *PADS,* No. 16, 1951; and
in his The Argot of the Professional Dice Gambler, *The Annals of the American Academy
of Political and Social Science,* Vol. 269, May 1950. Most *short-con* games are connected
with professional gambling, which has argots so voluminous that they cannot be treated
in this work, and which have, in turn, vastly enriched American slang. An excellent survey
of gambling, with much argot included, is John Scarne's classic book, Scarne's Complete
Guide to Gambling; New York, 1961.]

[19] The Big Con, before cited, pp. 270–1.

[20] Private communication, Apr. 7, 1940. The anonymous author of The Capone I Knew,
True Detective, June 1947, p. 80, says that *syndicate,* used by Al to describe his mob, was
"picked up from the newspaper stories about him."

their provenance, were indigenous to the subcultures using them. The gentlemen of the *big con, i.e.,* swindlers who specialize in rooking persons of means, constitute the aristocracy of the underworld, and hold aloof from all lesser criminals. They are, taking one with another, of superior intelligence, and not many of them ever land in prison. Their lingo thus shows a considerable elegance and also some humor, *e.g., apple, savage* or *Mr. Bates* for a victim; *big store,* the bogus gambling house or brokerage office to which *apples* are lured; *coarse ones,* large bills; *earwigger,* one who tries to eavesdrop; *excess baggage,* a member of a mob who fails to pull his weight in the boat; *to fit the mitt,* to bribe an official; *Joe Hep,* a victim who tumbles (or thinks he does) to what is happening; *larceny,* the itch for illicit money that lures a victim on: "He has *larceny* in his heart"; *to light a rag,* to run away; *to play the C,* to operate a confidence game; *to sting,* to swindle; *sucker word,* a term not used by professionals,[21] and *yellow,* a telegram. The craft is now called the *grift,* not the *graft;* [22] and is characterized by its lack of violence. . . .

The line separating the criminal argots from ordinary slang is hard to draw, and in certain areas the two are mixed. Consider, for example, the language of showfolks. At the top it is highly respectable, and some of it is of considerable antiquity, but on the lower levels, as with traveling carnivals, it coalesces with that of hoboes, Gypsies and thieves. Similarly, the transient slang of jitterbugs and other incandescent youngsters is connected through that of jazz musicians with that of drug addicts. All showfolks who work under canvas say that they are *on the show* or *with it,* not *in it,* just as pickpockets say they are *on the cannon* and yeggs that they are *on the heavy,* and there are many circus and carnival terms that are identical with criminal terms, *e.g., grift,* an illicit or half-illicit means of getting money; *benny,* an overcoat; *shill,* one hired to entice customers; *cheaters,* spectacles; *mouthpiece,* a lawyer; *to lam,* to depart hastily; *hoosier,* a yokel; *home guard,* those who do not travel; *leather,* a pocketbook; *moniker,* a person's name or nickname; *office,* a signal; and the various names for money, ranging from *ace* for a $1 bill to *grand* for $1,000. This lingo has been studied by David W. Maurer,[23] George Milburn,[24] Percy W. White,[25] E. P. Conkle,[26]

---

[21] I take all these from Maurer.

[22] The glossary in The Big Con is also in The Argot of Confidence Men, *AS,* Vol. XV, Apr. 1940, pp. 113–23, and Confidence Games, by Carlton Brown, *Life,* Aug. 12, 1946, pp. 45–52.

[23] Carnival Cant; a Glossary of Circus and Carnival Slang, *AS,* Vol. VI, June 1931, pp. 327–37.

[24] Circus Words, *American Mercury,* Nov. 1931, pp. 351–4.

[25] A Circus List, *AS,* Vol. I, Feb. 1926, pp. 282–3; More About the Language of the Lot, *AS,* Vol. III, June 1928, pp. 413–15.

[26] Carnival Slang, *AS,* Vol. III, Feb. 1928, pp. 253–4.

A. J. Liebling,[27] Marcus H. Boulware,[28] Joe Laurie, Jr.,[29] and Charles Wolverton.[30]

[Carnival workers, and especially *strong-joint* or *flat-joint* operators, have a more or less secret argot called *ceazarney* or *alfalfa*, which is based on phonetic distortion and cannot be reproduced in print without resort to a complex phonemic rendering. It is one of the few argots which are spoken with a deliberate attempt to deceive or to conceal meaning. . . .]

Many terms associated with the movies are the product of press agents,[31] *e.g.*, *wampas*, a female aspirant to stardom; *cobra*, a girl powerfully aphrodisiacal; *starlet*, *sex appeal*, *oomph*, *glamour girl* and the magnificent *super-colossal*. Some of the other terms emanating from Hollywood wits have their points, *e.g.*, *to go Hollywood*, meaning, when applied to an actor, to succumb to a suffocating sense of his own importance, and when applied to a movie writer or other intellectual, to abandon the habits and ideas of civilization and embrace the levantine life of the richer movie folks; *casting couch* for the divan in a casting director's office; *tear bucket* for an elderly actress playing heart-broken mothers; *finger wringer* for a star given to emoting; *baddie* for an actor playing villains; *cliff-hanger* for a serial melodrama; *sobbie* or *weepie* for a picture running to sadness; and *bump man* for a performer who undertakes dangerous stunts. *Variety* uses *flesh* to designate live players who appear in moviehouses.

The queer jargon called *jive*, which emerged in the early 1940s, was an amalgam of Negro slang from Harlem and the argots of drug addicts and the pettier sort of criminals, with occasional additions from the Broadway gossip columns and the high-school campus. It seems to have been current at the start among jazz musicians, many of them Negroes and perhaps more of them addicts, and its chief users were always youthful devotees of the more delirious type of dancing, *i.e.*, the so-called *jitterbugs*. It actually arose in the honky-tonks and tingle-tangles of the pre-jazz era, and many of its current names for musical instruments go back to that era or even beyond, *e.g.*, *bull fiddle* or *doghouse* for a double bass; *groan box* or *box of teeth* for an accordion; *slip horn, slush pump, gas pipe, syringe* or *push pipe* for a trombone; *thermometer* for an oboe; *iron horn, plumbing, squeeze horn* or *piston* for a trumpet; *pretzel* or *peck horn* for a French horn; *licorice stick, wop stick, gob stick, blackstick* or *agony pipe* for a clarinet; *foghorn, fishhorn* or *gobble pipe* for a saxophone; *box, moth box* or *88* for a

---

[27] Masters of the Midway, *The New Yorker*, Aug. 12, 1939, pp. 21–5.

[28] Circus Slang, Pittsburgh *Courier*, Mar. 20 and 27, 1943.

[29] Lefty's Notebook, *Variety*, Apr. 7, 1943.

[30] Mysteries of the Carnival Language, *American Mercury*, June 1936, pp. 227–31.

[31] *Variety* calls press agents *flacks*, a World War II term for antiaircraft fire. It was borrowed from the German *flak*, an abbreviation of *Fliegerabwehrkanone*, an antiaircraft cannon. Agents of extraordinary virulence are *blast artists*. They call themselves *publicists, public relations counsel* or *publicity engineers*. See Ch. VI, Sec. 7.

piano; *scratch box* for a violin; *chin bass* for a viola; *gitter, gitbox* or *belly fiddle* for a guitar; *grunt iron* for a tuba; *god box* for an organ; *woodpile* for a xylophone; and *skin* or *suitcase* for a drum. [Currently any instrument is an *ax*.] So with the names for performers, *e.g., skin tickler, skin beater, hide beater* or *brave boy* for a drummer; *squeaker* for a violinist; *sliver sucker* for a clarinetist; *whanger, plunker boy* or *plink-plonker* for a guitarist; *monkey hurdler* for an organist; *gabriel* for a trumpeter; and *brass officer* for a cornetist. Any performer on a brass wind instrument is a *lip splitter.*

The jazz band is a variable quantity, and may run from four or five men to what almost amounts to a symphony orchestra. Jazz itself is divided into two halves, the *sweet* kind and the *hot* kind or *jive* and *swing,* of which *boogie-woogie* is a subspecies. [*Sweet* jazz is usually played *straight* or according to the score, while *hot* jazz is played with plenty of leeway for improvisation.] [32] A performer who sticks to the printed notes is a *paperman,* and if he ever undertakes conventional music is a *commercial, salon man, long underwear* or *longhair.* An adept at *hot jazz* is a *cat,* and if he excels at arousing the libido of the fans (who are also, by courtesy, *cats*) he is said to *send* or *give* or *ride* or *go to town* or to be *in the groove,* and becomes a *solid sender* or *gate.* The test of his skill is his proficiency at adorning the music with *ad lib,* ornaments called *licks, riffs, get-offs* or *takeoffs.* The wilder they are the better. When swing performers meet to *lick* and *riff* for their own entertainment, they are said to hold a *jam session, clambake* or *barrel-house.* Music that is banal or stale is *corny. Boogie-woogie* accentuates a monotonous bass, usually of eight notes to a measure.[33] A woman singer is a *canary* or *chirp.* Any wind performer is a *Joe blow.* Tuning up is *licking the chops.* High trumpet notes are *Armstrongs.*[34] Notes are *spots.* Rests are *layouts.* To emphasize the rhythm is to *beat it out.* To be out of a job is to be *cooling.* Jazz in Negroid style is *gut-bucket.* To keep good time is to *ride.* The jazz bands have changed much of the conventional Italian terminology of music. Music played *dolce* is said to be *schmalz* (German for lard), *scherzo* is *medium bounce,* a grace note is a *rip,* the final chord is a *button,* a drop in pitch on a sustained note is a *bend* and a *glissando* is a *smear* or *slurp.*

[32] The structure of jazz is discussed learnedly in So This Is Jazz, by Henry Osborne Osgood, New York, 1926, and by the same author in The Anatomy of Jazz, *American Mercury,* Apr. 1926, pp. 385–95. Its history is recounted in Reflections on the History of Jazz, by S. I. Hayakawa, a lecture delivered before the Arts Club of Chicago, Mar. 17, 1945, and later printed as a pamphlet by the author. See also Is Jazz Music?, by Winthrop Parkhurst, *American Mercury,* Oct. 1943, pp. 403–9.

[33] It is discussed learnedly, and with approbation in *Étude,* the trade journal of American music teachers, Dec. 1943, p. 757, and by Nicholas Slonimsky in Jazz, Swing and Boogie-Woogie, *Christian Science Monitor,* May 20, 1944. Slonimsky says that it was launched by Meade Lewis and Albert Ammons, Negro pianists, at Carnegie Hall, New York, Dec. 23, 1938.

[34] From Louis *Armstrong,* alias Satchelmouth, alias Satchmo, a famous colored trumpet player. For his triumphs see Hot Jazz Jargon, by E. J. Nicholas and W. L. Werner, *Vanity Fair,* Nov. 1935, p. 38, and *Jazz,* by Robert Coffin; New York, 1946.

The vocabulary of the jazz addict is largely identical with that of the jazz performer. He himself is a *hepcat, alligator* or *rugcutter.* To him those who dislike swing music are *tin ears,* and are said to be *icky.* A dance is a *rat race* or *cement mixer;* anything excellent is *killer-diller, murder* or *Dracula;* a girl is a *chick, witch, drape, mouse, spook* or *bree;* face powder is *dazzle dust;* a shot of Coca-Cola is a *fizz;* a blind date is a *grab bag;* a hamburger is *ground horse;* a kiss is a *honey cooler;* money is *moola;* a sandwich is a *slab;* to sit down is to *swoon;* to dance wildly is to get *whacky;* an aggressive girl is a *vulture* or *wolverine;* a fat girl is a *five-by-five;* and a person disliked is a *specimen, herkle, prune, corpse, droop, fumb, gleep, cold cut, apple* or *sloop.*[35] When he encounters swing that really lifts him he says that he has been *sent down to the very bricks,* an experience comparable to suffering demoniacal possession or dying in the electric chair. This slang of the adolescent burgeons quickly, and just as quickly becomes as passé as a yearling egg. [Much of this jive lingo, modernized and intermingled with pseudo-intellectualisms, appears today in the patois of the beatnik.]

[*Beatnik* is said to have been coined by Herb Caen, a San Francisco newspaperman, in 1958, but one suspects antecedents in, and perhaps indebtedness to, Al Capp. *Beat,* in the sense of frustrated, has long been in the language, but the Beat Generation probably acquired it from the Negro *hipster* along with many other attitudes and cultural accouterments. However, the *beats,* both Negro and white, have given the *hipster* borrowings a mystic depth which is supposed to make up in inner intensity for any lack of communication, for to the *beat* any attempt at coherence is a sure indication of emotional death. Syntax is the sign of the *square,* whose world they have repudiated. *Beats* extend their introvert horizons largely by *digging,* by which they mean picking over their own psychic junkpiles in order to salvage some bits of emotional experience unattainable by *squares,* and one becomes truly *hip* only by *digging.* Once *digging* (and other mystic experiences) has produced, one is ready to *go,* that is, to *flip,* which may be either *up* or *down* on either side of the manic-depressive cycle, and most *cats* consider it necessary to probe the mystic depths with the assistance of wine, a *joint of pot* or perchance a *roach* or two salvaged in a *tea pad,* heroin via the *main line* by means of the needle, *peyote* buttons and large infusions of invigorating jazz music—most of which are indulged in as continuously as money provided by the *chick* permits, but in any event indulged in with friends as part of the *Saturday night kicks.* The *beat makes it* in friendship or in love largely by *swinging,* a subtle exchange of the very rhythms of internal being. A *cool cat*—and all aspire to this temperature—is one who knows he has stumbled on the

---

[35] I take most of these from Jabberwocky and Jive, by Nancy Pepper; New York, 1943. See also The New Cab Calloway's Hepster's Dictionary, New York, 1938; new editions, 1939 and 1944 (said by *Variety,* June 22, 1938, to have been written by Ned Williams, a press agent); Hepcats' Jive Dictionary, by Lou Shelly, Derby, Conn., 1945, and Really the Blues, by Milton "Mezz" Mezzrow and Bernard Wolfe, New York, 1946, pp. 371–80. The last is extremely interesting and also authoritative, for Mezzrow has functioned successfully as both jazz musician and marijuana peddler.

basic truths and eternal verities and is always well organized within, cautious but not fearful, reserved, inarticulate, and much of the time *stoned* on wine, *pot* (marijuana, from the Mexican Spanish *potiguaya*), heroin or an overdose of Zen Buddhism. Allen Ginsberg calls the beats "angel-headed *hipsters* burning for the ancient heavenly connection," but that *connection* is all too often a *cat* in *shades* who has a few *decks* or *caps* of *horse* stashed in the fly of his pants. This synthetic subculture has produced some literature (Ginsberg, Kerouac, Brossard and others) and their behavior has been analyzed by John Ciardi, Norman Mailer, John Cellon Holmes, David McReynolds and Ned Polsky, to mention a few. Most likely vocabulary survivals are *man, hip* (not new but durable; I published it in 1940 and ran it back as far as the 1890s), the widely applicable suffix -'*sville* as in *Square'sville, cool, flip, swing* or *swing with it* and *pad*. . . .]

The English apparently preferred the *European War* as a designation for the conflict of 1914–18, but in the United States it came to be known as the *World War*, and when another round began in 1939 it naturally became *World War II*. But there were poets who groped for something less prosaic, and one of them was President Franklin D. Roosevelt. So late as the spring of 1942 he was calling for suggestions, and many flowed in. The Hon. Thomas E. Dewey proposed the *War for Survival*, Mrs. Anne M. Rosenberg *Freedom's War*, Dr. William Lyon Phelps the *War of Liberty*, the Hon. Henry H. Curran the *Necessary War* and Jack Dempsey the *Fight to Live*. The Hon. Emil Schram, president of the New York Stock Exchange, put his hopes into the *Last World War*, and other less eminent persons contributed the *War to Save Humanity*, the *Fight for Right*, the *War to Save Civilization*, the *War of the Ages*, the *People's War*, the *Survival War*, the *War of World Freedom*, the *War Against Tyrants*, the *Hitler War* and the *World Order War*. There were even cynics who proposed the *Crazy War*, the *War of Illusions*, the *Meddler's War*, the *Roosevelt War*, the *Devil's War* and *Hell*. How and by whom the votes were counted I do not know, but when the uproar was over it was announced that *World War II* had won by a large plurality. Soon after Pearl Harbor, in fact, the Army and Navy had adopted *World War II*, and by the middle of 1942 it was appearing in the *Congressional Record*. By the end of that year it had obliterated all the other proposed names, and prophets were already beginning to talk hopefully of *World War III*.

Ernest K. Lindley and Forrest Davis say in "How War Came" [36] that *United Nations* was coined by President Roosevelt. This was during Winston Churchill's visit to Washington at the end of December 1941. He was a guest at the White House, and he and Roosevelt discussed the choice of a name for the new alliance. One morning, lying in bed, Roosevelt thought of *United Nations*, and at once sought Churchill, who was in his bath. "How about *United Nations*?" he called through the door. "That," replied Churchill, "should do it." And so it was.

[36] New York, 1942.

John Kenneth Galbraith

THE AGE OF THE WORDFACT

After the loss of New York and Long Island to Howe in 1776, General Washington made no effort to picture this misfortune as an important gain for the Continental army. Lincoln was similarly remiss after the debacle at First Manassas. In 1919 Wilson succeeded in persuading a clear majority of the Senate to vote in favor of the Covenant of the League of Nations, although not the necessary two thirds majority. Nothing whatever was made of this moral victory.

Things are different today. In June of 1960 President Eisenhower returned from a trip to the Pacific which would seem, superficially, to have been an unparalleled disaster of its kind. Japan, which was the principal object of his tour, had been beset by violent riots over the visit, and in the end it had been forced to urge him not to come. With the aid of his press secretary, however, the President was able to report on his return that the trip had been a success. A small number of Communists, acting under outside orders, had made things a trifle sour in Japan. But that was because they knew how powerful was the impression Mr. Eisenhower made on his trips to other lands, and they determined, as a result, that no such impression would be made on Japan. This was not the first time this kind of thing had happened. Two years earlier, Communists in South America had been forced to take similar preventive action because of the overwhelming appeal of Mr. Nixon to the Latin populace.

Some will perhaps conclude from this comparison that Mr. Eisenhower (and also Mr. Nixon and Mr. Hagerty) has a deeper and more perceptive insight into the ultimate meaning of events than did Washington, Lincoln, or Wilson. After all, the battles of Long Island, of Bull Run, and over the League all occurred in wars that were eventually won. Such a conclusion would be wrong. The earlier Presidents operated, in fact, without the help and support of one of the most important modern instruments of public administration. Just possibly they would not have used it, but the issue is academic, for it had not been invented. I refer to the institution of the "wordfact."

The wordfact makes words a precise substitute for reality. This is an enormous convenience. It means that to say that something exists is a substitute for its existence. And to say that something will happen is as good as having it happen. The saving in energy is nearly total.

There is a distinct possibility that the inventor of the wordfact was an editor or a newspaperman. But whatever its origins, it has come to have present-day importance less in journalism than in government. A press that fully accepts the institution is essential to its employment, but one of the principal functions of the modern public leader is to find

Published in *The Atlantic Monthly,* September 1960, pp. 87–89. Reprinted by permission of the author.

the language which adequately improves the reality. Where once it was said of a statesman that he suited action to the words, now he suits the words to the action. If past action (or inaction) has failed to produce the desired result, then, by resort to wordfact, he quickly establishes that the undesired result was more desirable than the desired result.

Lest any of this seem farfetched or complicated, let us remind ourselves of some of the achievements of wordfact in these last years. We agree, of course, that any manifestation of anti-American sentiment abroad is the work of a misguided minority. And until last summer there was no misunderstanding that could not be cured, no resentment that could not be alleviated, no fear that could not be dissipated by a smiling visit of two days to the capital of the country. It would then be stated with appropriate solemnity that the visit was a success; the papers would report that it was a great success; the problems then were presumably gone. Perhaps never before in history had diplomacy become so simple.

But not even traveling has always been necessary. By a bold use of wordfact, we were long able to convert South American dictators into bulwarks of the free world, although on occasion it was thought necessary to drive home the point by decorating them. The recent rise of military regimes in Asia is not a setback for democracy. Rather, it reflects the natural and inevitable difficulty in these countries of basing government on the consent of the governed.

Here at home it is no longer easy to think of unemployment as a misfortune. It reflects the introduction of needed and desirable slack in the system. No properly run economy can be without it. The drastic decline in farm income in recent years has become a manifestation of the vitality of the market system. Though farmers have been leaving their farms at an unprecedented rate, the forces making for this migration have been favorably described by the Secretary of Agriculture in a book with the agreeable title *Freedom to Farm*. Bad television programs were strongly defended early this year by the Federal Communications Commission as a precious manifestation of the freedom of speech. The networks found this a more than satisfactory substitute for any improvement in their programs. They are said, as a result, to be coming up with autumn offerings of unparalleled banality and horror. One hopes that some Sunday afternoon they will have a statesmanlike salute to the principal modern architects of the wordfact.

However, as an indication of what can be done by skillful deployment of the wordfact, with the aid of an acquiescent press, it is unlikely that any recent event matches that of the ill-fated U-2. Until Francis Powers made his unpremeditated landing, the sending of military or paramilitary aircraft by one country over another without the permission of the latter would have been considered a somewhat provocative act. (Even now the appearance of such planes over the United States would not be regarded with any real warmth and enthusiasm.) To have an aircraft shot down in the course of such an excursion into another country would have been regarded as a serious misfortune from which little comfort or reward of any kind could possibly be gleaned.

Yet in the days immediately following the last flight of the U-2, by the massive use of wordfact all of the relevant circumstances were changed. Flying planes over other countries became a kind of fifth freedom, to be justified, not without sanctimony, by the secrecy of the other country. The information gained justified the danger incurred and the mistrust aroused among our friends. Indeed, the flights would have to continue. The loss of the plane had proved, as nothing else, the weakness of the opposing defenses. The flights were then suspended, and this became an act of wise restraint. At this stage, the information being gathered ceased to be important as compared with the danger involved and the discomfort and mistrust created among our allies.

Such is the service of wordfact in transforming misfortune into fortune. But it has at least an equal value in transforming inaction into action. Thus, for a year and half now, a cabinet committee headed by Vice President Nixon has been dealing with the problem of inflation. This it has done all but exclusively by denouncing it, and so great has been the fury of its denunciation that it has not deemed it necessary to propose any concrete remedies of importance. In recent years, medical care for the aged has become a major political issue. As this is written, both parties in Congress are endeavoring to make a record on the issue. Records are made not by enacting legislation but by indicating an all but uncontrollable desire to enact legislation. Yet there is a difference, which is recognizable to those who are old and ill and faced with a terrible medical bill. Strong statements in favor of school integration and voting rights for Negroes are a widely accepted substitute for progress, and much less complicated in practice. To most congressional and campaign strategists, it would be considered little short of eccentric to inquire what might be accomplished. The important thing is to find the form of words that will satisfy, and if possible inspire, the Negro voters. One imagines, incidentally, that the invasion of the lunch counters by Negro students is related to the discovery that much of the civil rights discussion is purely inspirational.

On occasion, as when Republicans opposed slavery and Democrats favored alcohol, political platforms in the past have been a guide to ensuing action. But these, too, have been taken over by wordfact. In those hammered out this summer at Los Angeles and Chicago, little thought was given to whether the good things mentioned in them could or would be done. It would have been a jarring note had anyone on either platform committee asked: "Are we sure we can keep this promise?" (It *was* a jarring note at Los Angeles when Paul Ziffren, the California Democratic national committeeman, said that it was less important to write platforms than to get them enacted.) In the case of the platforms, the people appear to be fully aware of the use of wordfact. As a result, they pay them only the most perfunctory attention. It is unfortunate, but words have value only if they have some nexus, however tenuous, with action.

This truth is well illustrated on a global and tragic basis by the discussion of disarmament. Here it is all but taken for granted that no one means what he says, that proposals are made for their effect on public opinion and not on the arms race. And, as a result, people have ceased to pay any attention to the proposals. Civilized survival may in this instance depend on our ability to redeem this problem from the practitioners of wordfact.

But the redemption had better be general. To some extent, of course, it is automatic. It cannot be supposed that the vast verbal fallout of recent years is intrinsically attractive. It is certain to breed a reaction. Convention viewers doubtless saw the beginning of such a reaction this year in the massive inattention that was accorded these wordy proceedings. One sees it also in the tendency to assume, when the government explains that all is well, that something must be wrong.

In part, the control of wordfact requires only that our leaders be slightly more sensible in their approach to the American people. It would be to their own interest. When President Eisenhower described his trip to the vicinity of Japan as a success, he was fooling no one capable of consecutive thought. He did risk giving the impression that he was susceptible to such nonsensical conclusions. And certainly he revealed an unflattering attitude toward the gullibility of the American people.

This, to some extent, was their—or our—fault. We have come to suffer nonsense gladly, and pompous nonsense far too gladly. Elaborate rationalizations of failure should not be met by bored silence or even by a fishy stare. They should be greeted by loud and vulgar laughter, followed immediately by equally uncouth speeches and letters and, if nothing else is possible, by scribbling on walls. All who proclaim good intentions should be immediately asked for their program as to performance. Speeches of candidates for public office this autumn should be scrupulously clipped and saved—and sent to them at intervals over the next couple of years with a request for a progress report. Four years from now, when the parties meet to write their programs, a large number of articulate citizens must be on hand to inquire what in hell happened to the pious promises of 1960. They should have this year's copies in hand.

Perhaps, having organizations for almost everything else, we should have an organization for enforcing election promises and for fingering the man who imagines that he can make his record with words. At a minimum, however, we must reconstruct our hierarchy of political delinquency. The most serious delinquent, the man now to be marked for extinction even before the Florida free-loader, is the man of any political faith or persuasion whose talk shows any sign of being unmatched by intention. The windy liberal should go, along with the windy conservative, and, as a liberal, I devoutly hope that he will go first. And while dealing kindly with all who confess honest error, we should make a special bipartisan onslaught on any man who defends his mistakes by saying that the unintended was better than the intended and that it was really planned all along.

Susanne K. Langer

LANGUAGE

The fact is that our primary world of reality *is* a verbal one. Without words our imagination cannot retain distinct objects and their relations, but out of sight is out of mind. Perhaps that is why Köhler's apes could use a stick to reach a banana outside the cage so long as the banana and the stick could be seen in one glance, but not if they had to turn their eyes away from the banana to see the stick. Apparently they could not look at the one and *think of* the other.[1] A child who had as much practical initiative as the apes, turning away from the coveted object, yet still murmuring "banana," would have seen the stick in its instrumental capacity at once.

The transformation of experience into concepts, not the elaboration of signals and symptoms, is the motive of language. Speech is through and through symbolic; and only sometimes signific. Any attempt to trace it back entirely to the need of communication, neglecting the formulative, abstractive experience at the root of it, must land us in the sort of enigma that the problem of linguistic origins has long presented. I have tried, instead, to trace it to the characteristic human activity, symbolic transformation and abstraction, of which pre-human beginnings may perhaps be attributed to the highest apes. Yet we have not found the commencement of language anywhere between their state and ours. Even in man, who has all its prerequisites, it depends on education not only for its full development, but for its very inception. How, then, did it ever arise? And why do all men possess it?

It could only have arisen in a race in which the lower forms of symbolistic thinking—dream, ritual, superstitious fancy—were already highly developed, i.e. where the process of symbolization, though primitive, was very active. Communal life in such a group would be characterized by vigorous indulgence in purely expressive acts, in ritual gestures, dances, etc., and probably by a strong tendency to fantastic terrors and joys. The liberation from practical interests that is already marked in the apes would make rapid progress in a species with a definitely symbolistic turn of mind; conventional meanings would gradually imbue every originally random act, so that the group-life as a whole would have an exciting, vaguely transcendental tinge, without any definable or communicable body of ideas to cling to. A wealth of dance-forms and antics, poses and manoeuvres might flourish in a society that was somewhat above the apes' in non-practical interests, and rested on a slightly higher development of the symbolific brain-functions. There are quite articulated play-forms, verging on dance-

[1] Köhler, *The Mentality of Apes*, p. 37.

forms, in the natural repertoire of the chimpanzees; [2] with but a little further elaboration, these would become most obvious material for symbolic expression. It is not at all impossible that *ritual,* solemn and significant, antedates the evolution of language.

In a vocalizing animal, such actions would undoubtedly be accompanied by purely fanciful sounds—wavering tones, strings of syllables, echoing shouts. Voice-play, which as an instinct is lost after infancy, would be perpetuated in a group by the constant stimulation of response, as it is with us when we learn to speak. It is easy enough to imagine that young human beings would excite each other to shout, as two apes excite one another to jump, rotate, and strike poses; and the shouting would soon be formalized into song. Once the vocal habits are utilized, as in speech or song, we know that they do not become lost, but are fixed as a life-long activity. In a social group, the infantile lalling-instinct would be constantly reinforced, and instead of being outgrown, would become conventionalized in social play-forms. "Never a nomadic horde in the wilderness, but must already have had its songs," says Wilhelm von Humboldt, "for man as a species is a singing creature. . . ." [3] Song, the formalization of voice-play, probably preceded speech.

Jespersen, who is certainly one of our great authorities on language, suggests that speech and song may well have sprung from the same source (as Herder and Rousseau, without really scientific foundation, imagined long ago). "Word-tones were originally frequent, but meaningless," he observes; "afterwards they were dropped in some languages, while in others they were utilized for sense-distinguishing purposes." [4] Furthermore, he points out that in passionate speech the voice still tends to fluctuate, that civilization only reduces this effect by reducing passionate utterance, and that savages still use a sing-song

---

[2] Even at the risk of letting Köhler's apes steal the show in this chapter, I must quote his account of these plays. Tschego and Grande developed a game of spinning round and round like dervishes, which found favor with all the others. "Any game of two together," says Köhler, "was apt to turn into this 'spinning-top' play, which appeared to express a climax of friendly and amicable *joie de vivre.* The resemblance to a human dance became truly striking when the rotations were rapid, or when Tschego, for instance, stretched her arms out horizontally as she spun round. Tschego and Chica—whose favorite fashion during 1916 was this 'spinning'—sometimes combined a forward movement with the rotations, and so they revolved slowly round their own axes and along the playground.

"The whole *group* of chimpanzees sometimes combined in more elaborate *motion-patterns.* For instance, two would wrestle and tumble near a post; soon their movements would become more regular and tend to describe a circle round the post as a center. One after another, the rest of the group approach, join the two, and finally march in an orderly fashion round and round the post. The character of their movements changes; they no longer walk, they trot, and as a rule with special emphasis on one foot, while the other steps lightly; thus a rough approximate rhythm develops, and they tend to 'keep time' with one another. . . .

"It seems to me extraordinary that there should arise quite spontaneously, among chimpanzees, anything that so strongly suggests the dancing of some primitive tribes." (*The Mentality of Apes,* pp. 326–327.)

[3] *Die sprachphilosophischen Werke Wilhelm von Humboldts* (ed. Steinthal, 1884), p. 289.

[4] *Language,* p. 418, n.

manner of speaking; and in fine, he declares, "These facts and considerations all point to the conclusion that there was once a time when all
speech was song, or rather when these two actions were not yet
differentiated. . . ." [5]

Yet it is hard to believe that song was ever an essential form of
communication. How, then, was language derived from it? He does not
tell us; but the difficulty of tracing an instrument like language to a free
exercise like song is minimized in his sagacious reflection: "Although
we now regard the communication of thought as the main object of
speaking, there is no reason for thinking that this has always been the
case." [6]

Ralph Waldo Emerson

LANGUAGE

Words are signs of natural facts. The use of natural history is to give us
aid in supernatural history; the use of the outer creation, to give us
language for the beings and changes of the inward creation. Every word
which is used to express a moral or intellectual fact, if traced to its root,
is found to be borrowed from some material appearance. *Right* means
straight; wrong means *twisted. Spirit* primarily means *wind; transgres-
sion,* the crossing of a *line; supercilious,* the *raising of the eyebrow.* We
say the *heart* to express emotion, the *head* to denote thought; and
thought and *emotion* are words borrowed from sensible things, and now
appropriated to spiritual nature. Most of the process by which the
transformation is made, is hidden from us in the remote time when
language was framed; but the same tendency may be daily observed in
children. Children and savages use only nouns or names of things,
which they convert into verbs, and apply to analogous mental acts.

But this origin of all words that convey a spiritual import,—so
conspicuous a fact in the history of language,—is our least debt to
nature. It is not words only that are emblematic; it is things which are
emblematic. Every natural fact is a symbol of some spiritual fact. Every
appearance in nature corresponds to some state of the mind, and that
state of the mind can only be described by presenting that natural
appearance as its picture. An enraged man is a lion, a cunning man is a
fox, a firm man is a rock, a learned man is a torch. A lamb is innocence;
a snake is subtle spite; flowers express to us the delicate affections.
Light and darkness are our familiar expression for knowledge and
ignorance; and heat for love. Visible distance behind and before us, is
respectively our image of memory and hope.

Who looks upon a river in a meditative hour and is not reminded

[5] Ibid., p. 420.

[6] Ibid., p. 437.

of the flux of all things? Throw a stone into the stream, and the circles that propagate themselves are the beautiful type of all influence. Man is conscious of a universal soul within or behind his individual life, wherein, as in a firmament, the natures of Justice, Truth, Love, Freedom, arise and shine. This universal soul he calls Reason: it is not mine, or thine, or his, but we are its; we are its property and men. And the blue sky in which the private earth is buried, the sky with its eternal calm, and full of everlasting orbs, is the type of Reason. That which intellectually considered we call Reason, considered in relation to nature, we call Spirit. Spirit is the Creator. Spirit hath life in itself. And man in all ages and countries embodies it in his language as the FATHER. . . .

Because of this radical correspondence between visible things and human thoughts, savages, who have only what is necessary, converse in figures. As we go back in history, language becomes more picturesque, until its infancy, when it is all poetry; or all spiritual facts are represented by natural symbols. The same symbols are found to make the original elements of all languages. It has moreover been observed, that the idioms of all languages approach each other in passages of the greatest eloquence and power. And as this is the first language, so is it the last. This immediate dependence of language upon nature, this conversion of an outward phenomenon into a type of somewhat in human life, never loses its power to affect us. It is this which gives that piquancy to the conversation of a strong-natured farmer or backwoodsman, which all men relish.

A man's power to connect his thought with its proper symbol, and so to utter it, depends on the simplicity of his character, that is, upon his love of truth and his desire to communicate it without loss. The corruption of man is followed by the corruption of language. When simplicity of character and the sovereignty of ideas is broken up by the prevalence of secondary desires, the desire of riches, of pleasure, of power, and of praise,—and duplicity and falsehood take place of simplicity and truth, the power over nature as an interpreter of the will is in a degree lost; new imagery ceases to be created, and old words are perverted to stand for things which are not; a paper currency is employed, when there is no bullion in the vaults. In due time the fraud is manifest, and words lose all power to stimulate the understanding or the affections. Hundreds of writers may be found in every long-civilized nation who for a short time believe and make others believe that they see and utter truths, who do not of themselves clothe one thought in its natural garment, but who feed unconsciously on the language created by the primary writers of the country, those, namely, who hold primarily on nature.

But wise men pierce this rotten diction and fasten words again to visible things; so that picturesque language is at once a commanding certificate that he who employs it is a man in alliance with truth and God. The moment our discourse rises above the ground line of familiar facts and is inflamed with passion or exalted by thought, it clothes itself in images. A man conversing in earnest, if he watch his intellectual processes, will find that a material image more or less luminous arises in his mind, contemporaneous with every thought, which furnishes the vestment of the thought. Hence, good writing and brilliant discourse are perpetual allegories. This imagery is spontaneous. It is the blending of experience with the present action of the mind. It is proper creation. . . .

Edward L. Thorndike

THE PSYCHOLOGY OF SEMANTICS

THE MEANINGS OF WORDS TO HEARERS AND READERS

Meanings are in persons' minds, not in words, and when we say that a word has or possesses such and such meanings, we are really saying that it has evoked, or caused, those meanings. Until it gets into a mind, a word is only puffs of air or streaks of ink. What a word, sentence, or other expression means to hearer or reader is mainly what it makes him think or feel or do as a fairly direct consequence of hearing or seeing it, and, more narrowly, what it makes him think or think of as the direct and almost immediate consequence of hearing or seeing it. Consideration of the rarer operations in which a hearer asks the speaker for explanations, or a reader consults dictionaries, would add little of value. Consideration of the still rarer cases in which all or part of a meaning bursts upon the mind after an appreciable interval, perhaps of hours, would add little of value.[1]

At least ninety-nine percentage of meanings depend upon the part experience and present attitude or 'set' of the hearer (or reader). But it is desirable to clear the way for the facts about them by considering certain cases where single sounds or serial combinations of sounds have inherent meanings or influences on meaning apart from what they have been associated with in a hearer's experience.

Reprinted from *American Journal of Psychology*, LIX, October 1946 by permission.

[1] Certain philosophers have found it possible to treat declarative sentences apart from speakers, hearers, and the speaker-hearer relation, as a part of what they call pure semantics, which, however, they would not regard as a part of linguistic science. R. Carnap's *Introduction to Semantics*, 1942, 1–263, is an authoritative presentation of their extremely abstract and subtle doctrines.

Eleazer Lecky

WORDS AND THINGS

Proverbs, as universal declarations, can hardly avoid contradicting one another because there are so many of them. It is wise to look before you leap, but what if the sign you see reads, "He who hesitates is lost?" There will not be time to count ten.

Some proverbs, however, do get along well together even though they seem not to. Adages about language, for instance, often conflict superficially. One may say, "A blow with a word strikes deeper than a blow with a sword," and be contradicted by another which says, "A word does not make a hole in the head." But the two sayings are, in fact, compatible. Read as a description, the first makes figurative sense and the second literal. Both agree that words may induce psychic damage. But the second, despite its appearance, is less descriptive than prescriptive. It, too, has a figurative sense. It means: "Don't react to mere words as if they were actions—or tangible things. Don't be a fool."

In these anonymous views we meet, by implication, one of the central problems of language theory—the interrelationship between words and things. That words are not things is no modern discovery. Even "primitive" people, who attribute magical powers to some words, deny them to others. Yet the theoretical distinction between words and things has, throughout the history of western man, been irregularly maintained, and by varying arguments.

The records from "civilized" Greece and Rome are inconsistent. For Plato, words are but images of things and both are inferior to ideas (which, to Plato's critics, are no more than words). For Aristotle and Cicero and Quintilian, words are not the same as ideas or things. Yet from Sumerian times (3000 B.C. or earlier) men had sought to explain the orderly processes of the universe as manifestations of a spirit, or mind. The Greeks called this mind the "Logos," but they called the expression of mind "Logos" too. Thus the ambivalence of "the Word" in Christian theology.

From *Beowulf* to Chaucer to Shakespeare extends a consciousness of the difference between words and things. Then, remarkably, in the seventeenth century this consciousness becomes acute. The world, it seems, is turning with new speed. The philosophers—Bacon, Hobbes, Locke—and the men of letters—Davenant, Cowley, Dryden—write of it. Cowley, in fact, addresses an ode to the Royal Society praising Bacon because,

> *From Words, which are but pictures of the Thought*
> *(Though we our Thoughts from them perversely drew)*
> *To Things, the Mind's right Object, he it brought.*[1]

Reprinted by permission from *ETC; A Review of General Semantics,* Vol. XIII, No. 1; copyright 1955, by the International Society for General Semantics.

[1] *The English Writings of Abraham Cowley* (Cambridge, 1905), p. 449 f.

In the eighteenth century Cowley's argument, though frequently enough restated, sounds like settled doctrine. Addison could recommend Locke to those readers of *The Spectator* who hoped to "get a reputation by critical writings," for, "an author who has not learned the art of distinguishing words and things and of ranging his thoughts and setting them in proper lights, whatever notions he may have, will lose himself in confusion and obscurity." [2]

But the eighteenth century was also a time of change. Meyer Abrams, in his *The Mirror and the Lamp*, has described an important shift. By the end of the century the mind of the poet was said not to copy, but to make its world. What, then, is the role of language? Again we find opinion at the crossroads. Wordsworth in 1805 could say:

> *There are also various other reasons why repetition and apparent tautology are frequently beauties of the highest kind. Among the chief of these reasons is the interest which the mind attaches to words, not only as symbols of the passion, but as things, active and efficient, which are of themselves part of the passion.*[3]

At almost the same time Wordsworth could also sound like Addison:

> *Minute criticism is in its nature irksome, and as commonly practised in books and conversation, is both irksome and injurious. Yet every mind must occasionaly be exercised in this discipline, else it cannot learn the art of bringing words rigorously to the test of thoughts; and these again to a comparison with things, their archetypes, contemplated first in themselves, and secondly in relation to each other; in all which processes the mind must be skilful, otherwise it will be perpetually imposed upon.*[4]

Coleridge, too, expressed diverse opinions about language. He acknowledged the difference between words and things. In *Biographia Literaria*, as much as he disliked Hobbes' materialism, he quoted his warning against verbal traps. And yet Coleridge, who knew the Logos doctrine, wanted to merge words and things. In a letter to William Godwin in 1800, he had asked:

> *Are not words, etc. parts in germinations of the plant? And what is the law of their growth? In something of this sort I would endeavor to destroy the old antithesis between Words and Things; elevating, as it were, Words into Things, and living Things, too.*[5]

---

[2] (New York, 1924), II, 152.

[3] *The Poetical Works of William Wordsworth* (London, 1916), p. 899 f.

[4] *The Prose Works of William Wordsworth* (London, 1876), II, 57.

[5] *Unpublished Letters of Samuel Taylor Coleridge* (New Haven, 1933), I, 156.

I will not attempt, for the present, to balance these accounts, but will add one more opinion about words, this from a recent book, *Symbolism and American Literature,* by Charles Feidelson:

> *To consider the literary work as a piece of language is to regard it as a symbol, autonomous in the sense that it is distinct both from the personality of its author and from any world of pure objects, and creative in the sense that it brings into existence its own meaning.*[6]

Feidelson believes that the concern of other modern critics with form and structure indicates that they too regard, or should regard, words as autonomous.

In Coleridge's sense, are words things? In Feidelson's, are words autonomous? To reach an answer, one must, I am afraid, go "sounding on / through words and things, a dim and perilous way. . . ."

Man, it has been said, is *the* symbol-maker. Other living creatures may use symbols to a small degree, but none rivals man, and none shows the capacity to borrow from him. Man can turn any sign into a symbol. He can make it stand for something else—a shell for money. He can make a picture of the shell. He can coin silver. He can print paper dollars. He can name all these objects. Names are the commonest and most useful tokens for labeling whatever we want to classify. Though individuals differ, we do most of our thinking with symbols, usually with words.

Words are systematized human sounds. To the ear, as sounds, they are signs, but they are also symbols. They occur and have their meaning within a physical, psychological, and social setting. When represented graphically (in writing, printing, etc.) they are both visual and phonetic signs. The graphic devices may properly be considered symbols of sounds, which in turn are symbolic.

Words have only potential meaning until they are put to use. Then their actual meaning is determined by their context. Words work together. It is artificial to take any unit of meaning, regardless of size, out of context, but a tentative study may be made of words as symbols.

[6] (Chicago, 1953), p. 49.

11
WAR AND DEHUMANIZATION

"Dulce et decorum est pro patria mori." (*It is sweet and fitting to die for one's country.*)

—Horace

POETS ON WAR: POETRY

Wilfred Owen

DULCE ET DECORUM EST

Bent double, like old beggars under sacks,
Knock-kneed, coughing like hags, we cursed through sludge,
Till on the haunting flares we turned our backs,
And towards our distant rest began to trudge.
Men marched asleep. Many had lost their boots,
But limped on, blood-shod. All went lame, all blind;
Drunk with fatigue; deaf even to the hoots
Of gas-shells dropping softly behind.

Gas! Gas! Quick, boys!—An ecstasy of fumbling,
Fitting the clumsy helmets just in time,
But someone still was yelling out and stumbling
And floundering like a man in fire or lime.—
Dim through the misty panes and thick green light,
As under a green sea, I saw him drowning.

In all my dreams before my helpless sight
He plunges at me, guttering, choking, drowning.

If in some smothering dreams, you too could pace
Behind the wagon that we flung him in,
And watch the white eyes writhing in his face,
His hanging face, like a devil's sick of sin;
If you could hear, at every jolt, the blood
Come gargling from the froth-corrupted lungs,
Bitter as the cud
Of vile, incurable sores on innocent tongues,—
My friend, you would not tell with such high zest
To children ardent for some desperate glory,
The old Lie: Dulce et decorum est
Pro patria mori.

Randall Jarrell

THE DEATH OF THE BALL TURRET GUNNER

> From my mother's sleep I fell into the State
> And I hunched in its belly till my wet fur froze.
> Six miles from earth, loosed from its dream of life,
> I woke to black flak and the nightmare fighters.
> When I died they washed me out of the turret with a hose.

Dylan Thomas

A REFUSAL TO MOURN THE DEATH,
BY FIRE, OF A CHILD IN LONDON

> Never until the mankind making
> Bird beast and flower
> Fathering and all humbling darkness
> Tells with silence the last light breaking
> And the still hour
> Is come of the sea tumbling in harness
>
> And I must enter again the round
> Zion of the water bead
> And the synagogue of the ear of corn
> Shall I let pray the shadow of a sound
> Or sow my salt seed
> In the least valley of sackcloth to mourn
>
> The majesty and burning of the child's death.
> I shall not murder
> The mankind of her going with a grave truth
> Nor blaspheme down the stations of the breath
> With any further
> Elegy of innocence and youth.
>
> Deep with the first dead lies London's daughter,
> Robed in the long friends,
> The grains beyond age, the dark veins of her mother
> Secret by the unmourning water
> Of the riding Thames.
> After the first death, there is no other.

POETS ON WAR: STATEMENTS

John Manifold

WAR, POETRY, THE INDIVIDUAL

You can only do three things about a war—fight in it, protest against it, or ignore it. I'm not capable of ignoring it, as Yeats ignored the 1914–18 war. *Pour moi, le monde extérieur existe*. And, idiotic as it is, I don't protest against it, or rather not basically. Opposition is probably a better attitude for preserving one's "poetic integrity" in, but while people are being shot at I'd sooner be in the danger area. The process of fighting a war isn't very different from living in an alleged state of peace. Not from the way I am living, anyhow. I'm still nomadic, exposed to rather more boredom and rather more danger, surrounded by fewer friends of fewer different nationalities, subject to the same alternative of inactivity and furious concentration. The war has confirmed more of my beliefs than it has destroyed. I still think that the human race is on the average rather likable, that nationality is no more important than class or occupation in making people likable or not, that authority is bad for the soul and responsibility good for it, and that once a thing becomes official it's dead and damned. The war has given me a lot of experience that I share with other people, which is one of the real bases of poetry, and has considerably influenced my style and vocabulary, which is another. I like using precise words and phrases which have not had the meaning dulled out of them, and military vocabulary provides plenty of them—"resertion," "defilade," "échelon," "revetment," for example, all good lively words fit for metaphors and exact images. But on the average I think I should still be writing as I do even if the war we spent our lives waiting for had not actually been declared.

Dylan Thomas

WAR CAN'T PRODUCE POETRY

War can't produce poetry, only poets can, and war can't produce poets either because they bring themselves up in such a war that this outward *bang bang* of men against men is something they have passed a long time ago on their poems' way towards peace. A poet writing a poem is at peace with everything except words, which are eternal actions; only in the lulls between the warring work on words can he be at war with men. Poets can stop bullets, but bullets can't stop poets. What is a poet anyway? He is a man who has written or is writing what he, in his utmost human fallible integrity, necessarily communal, believes to be good poetry. As he writes good poetry very rarely, he is most often at peace with the eternal actions of words and is therefore very likely to be caught up in any *bang bang* that is going. When he is fighting, he is not a poet. Nor is a craftsman a craftsman. I think capital-lettered War can only in subject matter affect poetry. Violence and suffering are all the time, and it does not matter how you are brought up against them.

e. e. cummings

IS SOMETHING WRONG?

"Is something wrong with America's socalled creative artists? Why don't our poets and painters and composers and so forth glorify the war effort? Are they Good Americans or are they not?"

First: are they Good Americans. . . .

when I was a boy, Good Americans were—believe it or don't—adoring the Japanese and loathing the Russians; now, Good Americans are adoring the Russians and loathing the Japanese. Furthermore (in case you were born yesterday) yesterday Good Americans were adoring the Finns; today Good Americans are either loathing the Finns or completely forgetting that Finland exists. Not even the fact that twice during my lifetime Good Americans have succeeded in disliking the Germans can convince me that any human being (such as an artist) is a Good American.

Second: why don't they glorify . . .

when you confuse art with propaganda, you confuse an act of God with something which can be turned on and off like the hot water faucet. If "God" means nothing to you (or less than nothing) I'll cheerfully substitute one of your own favorite words, "freedom." You confuse freedom—the only freedom—with absolute tyranny. Let me, incidentally, opine that absolute tyranny is what most of you are really after; that your socalled ideal isn't America at all and never was America at all: that you'll never be satisfied until what Father Abraham called "a new nation, conceived in liberty" becomes just another subhuman superstate (like the "great freedom-loving democracy" of Comrade Stalin) where an artist—or any other human being—either does as he's told or turns into fertilizer.

Third: is something wrong. . . .

all over a socalled world, hundreds of millions of servile and insolent inhuman unbeings are busily rolling and unrolling in the enlightenment of propaganda. So what? There are still a few erect human beings in the socalled world. Proudly and humbly, I say to these human beings:

"O my fellow citizens, many an honest man believes a lie. Though you are as honest as the day, fear and hate the liar. Fear and hate him when he should be feared and hated: now. Fear and hate him where he should be feared and hated: in yourselves.

"Do not hate and fear the artist in yourselves, my fellow citizens. Honour him and love him. Love him truly—do not try to possess him. Trust him as nobly as you trust tomorrow.

"Only the artist in yourselves is more truthful than the night."

Karl Marx and Friedrich Engels
THE COMMUNIST MANIFESTO

A spectre is haunting Europe—the spectre of Communism. All the Powers of old Europe have entered into a holy alliance to exorcise this spectre; Pope and Czar, Metternich and Guizot, French Radicals and German police-spies.

Where is the party in opposition that has not been decried as communistic by its opponents in power? Where the Opposition that has not hurled back the branding reproach of Communism against the more advanced opposition parties, as well as against its reactionary adversaries?

Two things result from this fact.

I. Communism is already acknowledged by all European Powers to be itself a Power.

II. It is high time that Communists should openly, in the face of the whole world, publish their views, their aims, their tendencies, and meet this nursery tale of the spectre of Communism with a Manifesto of the party itself.

To this end, Communists of various nationalities have assembled in London and sketched the following Manifesto, to be published in the English, French, German, Italian, Flemish and Danish languages.

BOURGEOIS AND PROLETARIANS [1]

The history of all hitherto existing society [2] is the history of class struggles.

Freeman and slave, patrician and plebeian, lord and serf, guild-

[1] By bourgeoisie is meant the class of modern Capitalists, owners of the means of social production and employers of wage-labor. By proletariat, the class of modern wage laborers who, having no means of production of their own, are reduced to selling their labor-power in order to live.

[2] That is, all written history. In 1847, the pre-history of society, the social organization existing previous to recorded history, was all but unknown. Since then Haxthausen dis-

master[3] and journeyman, in a word, oppressor and oppressed, stood in constant opposition to one another, carried on uninterrupted, now hidden, now open fight, a fight that each time ended, either in a revolutionary re-constitution of society at large, or in the common ruin of the contending classes.

In the earlier epochs of history we find almost everywhere a complicated arrangement of society into various orders, a manifold gradation of social rank. In ancient Rome we have patricians, knights, plebeians, slaves; in the middle ages, feudal lords, vassals, guild-masters, journeymen, apprentices, serfs; in almost all of these classes, again, subordinate gradations.

The modern bourgeois society that has sprouted from the ruins of feudal society, has not done away with class antagonisms. It has but established new classes, new conditions of oppression, new forms of struggle in place of the old ones.

Our epoch, the epoch of the bourgeoisie, possesses, however, this distinctive feature; it has simplified the class antagonisms. Society as a whole is more and more splitting up into two great hostile camps, into two great classes directly facing each other: Bourgeoisie and Proletariat. . . .

The bourgeoisie, historically, has played a most revolutionary part.

The bourgeoisie, wherever it has got the upper hand, has put an end to all feudal, patriarchal, idyllic relations. It has pitilessly torn asunder the motley feudal ties that bound man to his "natural superiors," and has left no other nexus between man and man than naked self-interest, than callous "cash payment." It has drowned the most heavenly ecstasies of religious fervor, of chivalrous enthusiasm, of Philistine sentimentalism, in the icy water of egotistical calculation. It has resolved personal worth into exchange value, and in place of the numberless indefeasible chartered freedoms, has set up that single, unconscionable freedom—Free Trade. In one word, for exploitation, veiled by religious and political illusions, it has substituted naked, shameless, direct, brutal exploitation.

The bourgeoisie has stripped of its halo every occupation hitherto honored and looked up to with reverent awe. It has converted the physician, the lawyer, the priest, the poet, the man of science, into its paid wage laborers.

The bourgeoisie has torn away from the family its sentimental veil, and has reduced the family relation to a mere money relation.

---

covered common ownership of land in Russia, Maurer proved it to be the social foundation from which all Teutonic races started in history, and bye and bye village communities were found to be, or to have been, the primitive form of society everywhere from India to Ireland. The inner organization of this primitive Communistic society was laid bare, in its typical form, by Morgan's crowning discovery of the true nature of the gens and its relation to the tribe. With the dissolution of these primeval communities society begins to be differentiated into separate and finally antagonistic classes. I have attempted to retrace this process of dissolution in: "Der Ursprung der Familie, des Privateigenthums und des Staats," 2nd edit., Stuttgart, 1886.

[3] Guild-master, that is, a full member of a guild, a master within, not a head.

The bourgeoisie has disclosed how it came to pass that the brutal display of vigor in the Middle Ages, which reactionists so much admire, found its fitting complement in the most slothful indolence. It has been the first to show what man's activity can bring about. It has accomplished wonders far surpassing Egyptian pyramids, Roman aqueducts and Gothic cathedrals; it has conducted expeditions that put in the shade all former Exoduses of nations and crusades.

The bourgeoisie cannot exist without constantly revolutionizing the instruments of production, and thereby the relations of production, and with them the whole relations of society. Conservation of the old modes of production in unaltered form was, on the contrary, the first condition of existence for all earlier industrial classes. Constant revolutionizing of production, uninterrupted disturbance of all social conditions, everlasting uncertainty and agitation distinguish the bourgeois epoch from all earlier ones. All fixed, fast frozen relations, with their train of ancient and venerable prejudices and opinions, are swept away, all new formed ones become antiquated before they can ossify. All that is solid melts into the air, all that is holy is profaned, and man is at last compelled to face with sober senses, his real conditions of life, and his relations with his kind.

The need of a constantly expanding market for its products chases the bourgeoisie over the whole surface of the globe. It must nestle everywhere, settle everywhere, establish connections everywhere. . . . Modern bourgeois society with its relations of production, of exchange and of property, a society that has conjured up such gigantic means of production and of exchange, is like the sorcerer, who is no longer able to control the powers of the nether world whom he has called up by his spells. For many a decade past, the history of industry and commerce is but the history of the revolt of modern productive forces against modern conditions of production, against the property relations that are the conditions for the existence of the bourgeoisie and of its rule. It is enough to mention the commercial crises that by their periodical return put on its trial, each time more threateningly, the existence of the entire bourgeois society. In these crises a great part not only of the existing products, but also of the previously created productive forces, are periodically destroyed. In these crises there breaks out an epidemic that, in all earlier epochs, would have seemed an absurdity—the epidemic of overproduction. Society suddenly finds itself put back into a state of momentary barbarism; it appears as if a famine, a universal war of devastation, had cut off the supply of every means of subsistence; industry and commerce seem to be destroyed; and why? Because there is too much civilization, too much means of subsistence, too much industry, too much commerce. The productive forces at the disposal of society no longer tend to further the development of the conditions of the bourgeois property; on the contrary, they have become too powerful for these conditions by which they are fettered, and as soon as they overcome these fetters they bring disorder into the whole of bourgeois society, endanger the existence of bourgeois property. The conditions of bourgeois society are too narrow to comprise the wealth created by them. And how does the bourgeoisie get over these crises? On the one hand by enforced destruction of a mass of productive forces; on the other, by the conquest of new markets, and by the more thorough exploitation of the old ones. That is to say, by paving the way for more extensive and more destructive crises, and by diminishing the means whereby crises are prevented.

The weapons with which the bourgeoisie felled feudalism to the ground are now turned against the bourgeoisie itself.

But not only has the bourgeoisie forged the weapons that bring death to itself; it has also called into existence the men who are to wield those weapons—the modern working-class—the proletarians. . . .

The proletariat goes through various stages of development. With its birth begins its struggle with the bourgeoisie. At first the contest is carried on by individual laborers, then by the workpeople of a factory, then by the operatives of one trade, in one locality, against the individual bourgeois who directly exploits them. They direct their attacks not against the bourgeois conditions of production, but against the instruments of production themselves; they destroy imported wares that compete with their labor, they smash to pieces machinery, they set factories ablaze, they seek to restore by force the vanished status of the workman of the Middle Ages.

At this stage the laborers still form an incoherent mass scattered over the whole country, and broken up by their mutual competition. If anywhere they unite to form more compact bodies, this is not yet the consequence of their own active union, but of the union of the bourgeoisie, which class, in order to attain its own political ends, is compelled to set the whole proletariat in motion, and is moreover yet, for a time, able to do so. At this stage, therefore, the proletarians do not fight their enemies, but the enemies of their enemies, the remnants of absolute monarchy, the landowners, the non-industrial bourgeois, the petty bourgeoisie. Thus the whole historical movement is concentrated in the hands of the bourgeoisie, every victory so obtained is a victory for the bourgeoisie. . . .

Now and then the workers are victorious, but only for a time. The real fruit of their battle lies not in the immediate result but in the ever-expanding union of workers. This union is helped on by the improved means of communication that are created by modern industry, and that places the workers of different localities in contact with one another. It was just this contact that was needed to centralize the numerous local struggles, all of the same character, into one national struggle between classes. But every class struggle is a political struggle. And that union, to attain which the burghers of the Middle Ages with their miserable highways, required centuries, the modern proletarians, thanks to railways, achieve in a few years. . . .

Of all the classes that stand face to face with the bourgeoisie to-day the proletariat alone is a really revolutionary class. The other classes decay and finally disappear in the face of modern industry; the proletariat is its special and essential product.

The lower middle class, the small manufacturer, the shopkeeper, the artisan, the peasant, all these fight against the bourgeoisie, to save from extinction their existence as fractions of the middle class. They are therefore not revolutionary, but conservative. Nay, more; they are reactionary, for they try to roll back the wheel of history. If by chance they are revolutionary, they are so only in view of their impending transfer into the proletariat; they thus defend not their present, but their future interests; they desert their own standpoint to place themselves at that of the proletariat.

The "dangerous class," the social scum, that passively rotting mass thrown off by the lowest layers of old society, may, here and there, be swept into the movement by a proletarian revolution; its conditions of life, however, prepare it far more for the part of a bribed tool of reactionary intrigue.

In the conditions of the proletariat, those of the old society at large are already virtually swamped. The proletarian is without property; his relation to his wife and children has no longer anything in common with the bourgeois family relations; modern industrial labor, modern subjection to capital, the same in England as in France, in America as in Germany, has stripped him of every trace of national character. Law, morality, religion, are to him so many bourgeois prejudices, behind which lurk in ambush just as many bourgeois interests.

All the preceding classes that got the upper hand sought to fortify their already acquired status by subjecting society at large to their conditions of appropriation. The proletarians cannot become masters of the productive forces of society, except by abolishing their own previous mode of appropriation, and thereby also every other previous mode of appropriation. They have nothing of their own to secure and to fortify; their mission is to destroy all previous securities for and insurances of individual property.

All previous historical movements were movements of minorities, or in the interest of minorities. The proletarian movement is the self-conscious, independent movement of the immense majority. The proletariat, the lowest stratum of our present society, cannot stir, cannot raise itself up without the whole superincumbent strata of official society being sprung into the air.

Though not in substance, yet in form, the struggle of the proletariat with the bourgeoisie is at first a national struggle. The proletariat of each country must, of course, first of all settle matters with its own bourgeoisie.

In depicting the most general phases of the development of the proletariat, we traced the more or less veiled civil war, raging within existing society, up to the point where that war breaks out into open revolution, and where the violent overthrow of the bourgeoisie, lays the foundations for the sway of the proletariat.

Hitherto every form of society has been based, as we have already seen, on the antagonism of oppressing and oppressed classes. But in order to oppress a class, certain conditions must be assured to it under which it can, at least, continue its slavish existence. The serf, in the period of serfdom, raised himself to membership in the commune, just as the petty bourgeois, under the yoke of feudal absolutism managed to develop into a bourgeois. The modern laborer, on the contrary, instead of rising with the progress of industry, sinks deeper and deeper below the conditions of existence of his own class. He becomes a pauper, and pauperism develops more rapidly than population and wealth. And here it becomes evident that the bourgeoisie is unfit any longer to be the ruling class in society, and to impose its conditions of existence upon society as an over-riding law. It is unfit to rule, because it is incompetent to assure an existence to its slave within his slavery, because it cannot help letting him sink into such a state that it has to feed him, instead of being fed by him. Society can no longer live under this bourgeoisie; in other words, its existence is no longer compatible with society.

The essential condition for the existence, and for the sway of the bourgeois class, is the formation and augmentation of capital; the condition for capital is wage labor. Wage labor rests exclusively on competition between the laborers. The advance of industry, whose involuntary promoter is the bourgeoisie, replaces the isolation of the laborers, due to competition, by their involuntary combination, due to association. The development of Modern Industry, therefore, cuts from under its feet the very foundation on which the bourgeoisie produces and appropriates products. What the bourgeoisie therefore produces, above all, are its own grave diggers. Its fall and the victory of the proletariat are equally inevitable.

Mao Tse-Tung

SELECTED WORKS

Political power comes out of the barrel of a gun (1938).
Historical experience is written in blood and iron (1937).

THE WAR OBJECTIVE

Here we are not referring to the political objective of the war, because we have already defined the political objective of the Anti-Japanese War as "the ousting of Japanese imperialism and the building up of a new China of freedom and equality." We are here referring to the fundamental objective of war as man's politics of bloodshed, as the mutual slaughter of opposing armies. The objective of war is nothing but "to preserve oneself and to annihilate the enemy." (To annihilate the enemy means to disarm him or "to deprive him of his power of resistance," and not to annihilate him completely in a physical sense.) The spear and the shield were used in ancient warfare: the spear was used

From *Selected Works* by Mao Tse-Tung, reprinted by permission of International Publishers Co., Inc. Copyright © 1937–1938.

to attack and annihilate the enemy while the shield was used to defend and preserve oneself. The weapons of today are but a continuation of these two. The bomber, the machine gun, the long-range gun and poison gas develop from the spear, while the air-raid shelter, the steel helmet, concrete defence works and the gas mask, form the shield. The tank is a new weapon combining the functions of the spear and the shield. Attack is the chief means to annihilate the enemy but defence cannot be dispensed with. To attack is directly to annihilate the enemy but at the same time also to preserve oneself, for, if the enemy is not annihilated, one will be annihilated by him. To defend is directly to preserve oneself but at the same time it is also a means to supplement attack or to prepare to turn to attack. Retreat belongs to the category of defence and is a continuation of defence, while pursuit is a continuation of attack. It should be pointed out that the annihilation of the enemy is the main objective of war, while the preservation of oneself is the secondary one, because it is only by annihilating the enemy in large numbers that one can effectively preserve oneself. Therefore attack as the chief means to annihilate the enemy is primary, while defence, as an auxiliary means to annihilate the enemy or as a means to preserve oneself, is secondary. Although in actual warfare the chief role is sometimes played by defence and at other times by attack, yet if the war is viewed as a whole, attack remains primary.

How do we explain our advocacy of heroic sacrifice in war? Does it not contradict "self-preservation"? No, it is not contradictory; sacrifice and self-preservation are opposed to each other and yet complement each other. War is the politics of bloodshed, which exacts a price, sometimes an extremely high price. Partial and temporary sacrifice (non-preservation) is made for the sake of general and permanent preservation. This is precisely the reason why we say that attack, which is basically a means to annihilate the enemy, functions at the same time as a means of self-preservation. This is also the reason why defence must be accompanied by attack and ought not to be pure defence.

The objective of war, *i.e.*, the preservation of oneself and the annihilation of the enemy, is the essence of war and the basis of all war activities, and all war activities from technical to strategic are filled with this essence. The objective of war is the basic principle of war and all theories and principles relating to technology, tactics, campaign or strategy, cannot in the least be separated from it. What is meant by the principle of marksmanship, "taking cover and exploiting firing power"? The former is for self-preservation while the latter is for the annihilation of the enemy. From the former arise various methods like utilising the terrain and objects on the ground, making a hopping advance, and spreading out the troops. From the latter arise various methods like clearing the firing range and organising firing networks. As to the storm troops, the containing force and the reserve force in tactical operations, the first is for the annihilation of the enemy, the second for the preservation of oneself, and the third kept in reserve to be used according to circumstances for either of the two purposes—either to reinforce the storm troops or to serve as a pursuit force, both for annihilating the enemy, or to reinforce the containing force or to serve as a covering force, both for preserving oneself. Thus all principles relating to technology, tactics, campaign and strategy as well as all such operations cannot in the least be separated from the war objective which applies to every part of the war from beginning to end.

. . . The unfolding of these factors in war activities becomes a struggle on each side to preserve itself and to annihilate the other. Our war consists in our striving in every engagement to score victory, big or small, to disarm a section of the enemy, and to inflict losses on a part of the enemy's men and *matériel*. We have to accumulate the results of these partial annihilations into major strategic victories in order to achieve the political objective of ultimately ousting the enemy, defending our motherland and building up a new China.

Thomas Paine

THE AMERICAN CRISIS

These are the times that try men's souls: The summer soldier and the sunshine patriot will in this crisis, shrink from the service of his country; but he that stands it Now, deserves the love and thanks of man and woman. Tyranny, like hell, is not easily conquered; yet we have this consolation with us, that the harder the conflict, the more glorious the triumph. What we obtain too cheap, we esteem to[o] lightly:—'Tis dearness only that gives everything its value. Heaven knows how to put a proper price upon its goods; and it would be strange indeed, if so celestial an article as FREEDOM should not be highly rated. Britain, with an army to enforce her tyranny, has declared that she has a right (not only to) TAX but "to BIND *us in* ALL CASES WHATSOEVER," and if being *bound in that manner,* is not slavery, then is there not such a thing as slavery upon earth. Even the expression is impious for so unlimited a power can belong only to God.

Whether the Independence of the Continent was declared too soon, or delayed too long, I will not now enter into as an argument; my own simple opinion is, that had it been eight months earlier, it would have been much better. We did not make a proper use of last winter, neither could we, while we were in a dependent state. However, the fault, if it were one, was all our own; we have none to blame but ourselves. But no great deal is lost yet; all that Howe [1] has been doing for this month past, is rather a ravage than a conquest, which the spirit of the Jersies [2] a

---

All footnotes in this selection are by the editor of this text.

[1] The commander of British troops in the Colonies, 1775.

[2] *I.e.,* East Jersey and West Jersey, now New Jersey.

year ago would have quickly repulsed, and which time and a little resolution will soon recover.

I have as little superstition in me as any man living, but my secret opinion has ever been, and still is, that God Almighty will not give up a people to military destruction, or leave them unsupportedly to perish, who have so earnestly and so repeatedly sought to avoid the calamities of war, by every decent method which wisdom could invent. Neither have I so much of the infidel in me, as to suppose that he has relinquished the government of the world, and given us up to the care of devils; and as I do not, I cannot see on what grounds the king of Britain can look up to heaven for help against us: a common murderer, a highwayman, or a house-breaker, has as good a pretence as he.

'Tis surprising to see how rapidly a panic will sometimes run through a country. All nations and ages have been subject to them: Britain has trembled like an ague at the report of a French fleet of flat-bottomed boats; and in the fourteenth century the whole English army, after ravaging the kingdom of France, was driven back like men petrified with fear; and this brave exploit was performed by a few broken forces collected and headed by a woman, Joan of Arc. Would that heaven might inspire some Jersey maid to spirit up her countrymen, and save her fair fellow sufferers from ravage and ravishment! Yet panics, in some cases, have their uses; they produce as much good as hurt. Their duration is always short; the mind soon grows through them, and acquires a firmer habit than before. But their peculiar advantage is, that they are the touchstones of sincerity and hypocrisy, and bring things and men to light, which might otherwise have lain forever undiscovered. In fact, they have the same effect on secret traitors which an imaginary apparition would have upon a private murderer. They sift out the hidden thoughts of man, and hold them up in public to the world. Many a disguised tory has lately shown his head, that shall penitentially solemnize with curses the day on which Howe arrived upon the Delaware. . . .

I shall not now attempt to give all the particulars of our retreat to the Delaware; suffice it for the present to say, that both officers and men, though greatly harassed and fatigued, frequently without rest, covering, or provision, the inevitable consequences of a long retreat, bore it with a manly and martial spirit. All their wishes centered in one, which was, that the country would turn out and help them to drive the enemy back. *Voltaire* [3] has remarked that King William never appeared to full advantage but in difficulties and in action; the same remark may be made on General Washington, for the character fits him. There is a natural firmness in some minds which cannot be unlocked by trifles,

[3] Here the French author (1694–1778) is quoted concerning his remark about the English King William III. Termed "the supreme incarnation of the Enlightenment," he was a rabid critic of the established order. He believed reason and human experience to be the basic guides for mankind, and he unleashed his contempt upon the then popular idea that this is the "best of all possible worlds," which he satirized in his most famous work, *Candide, or Optimism* (*Candide, ou l'Optimisme*, 1752). He spent much of his later life in exile.

but which, when unlocked, discovers a cabinet of fortitude; and I reckon it among those kind of public blessings, which we do not immediately see, that God hath blessed him with uninterrupted health, and given him a mind that can even flourish upon care.

I shall conclude this paper with some miscellaneous remarks on the state of our affairs; and shall begin with asking the following question, Why is it that the enemy have left the New-England provinces, and made these middle ones the seat of war? The answer is easy: New England is not infested with tories, and we are. I have been tender in raising the cry against these men, and used numberless arguments to show them their danger, but it will not do to sacrifice a world either to their folly or their baseness. The period is now arrived, in which either they or we must change our sentiments, or one or both must fall. And what is a tory? Good God! what is he? I should not be afraid to go with a hundred Whigs against a thousand tories, were they to attempt to get into arms. Every tory is a coward; for servile, slavish, self-interested fear is the foundation of toryism; and a man under such influence, though he may be cruel, never can be brave.

But, before the line of irrecoverable separation be drawn between us, let us reason the matter together: Your conduct is an invitation to the enemy, yet not one in a thousand of you has heart enough to join him. Howe is as much deceived by you as the American cause is injured by you. He expects you will all take up arms, and flock to his standard, with muskets on your shoulders. Your opinions are of no use to him, unless you support him personally, for 'tis soldiers, and not tories, that he wants.

I once felt all that kind of anger, which a man ought to feel, against the mean principles that are held by the tories: A noted one, who kept a tavern at Amboy, was standing at his door, with as pretty a child in his hand, about eight or nine years old, as I ever saw, and after speaking his mind as freely as he thought was prudent, finished with this unfatherly expression, *"Well! give me peace in my day."* Not a man lives on the continent but fully believes that a separation must some time or other finally take place, and a generous parent should have said, *"If there must be trouble, let it be in my day, that my child may have peace;"* and this single reflection, well applied, is sufficient to awaken every man to duty. Not a place upon earth might be so happy as America. Her situation is remote from all the wrangling world, and she has nothing to do but to trade with them. A man can distinguish himself between temper and principle, and I am as confident, as I am that God governs the world, that America will never be happy till she gets clear of foreign dominion. Wars, without ceasing, will break out till that period arrives, and the continent must in the end be conqueror; for though the flame of liberty may sometimes cease to shine, the coal can never expire.

America did not, nor does not want force; but she wanted a proper application of that force. Wisdom is not the purchase of a day, and it is no wonder that we should err at the first setting off. From an excess of tenderness, we were unwilling to raise an army, and trusted our cause to the temporary defence of a well-meaning militia. A summer's experience has now taught us better; yet with those troops, while they were collected, we were able to set bounds to the progress of the enemy, and, thank God! they are again assembling. I always considered militia as the best troops in the world for a sudden exertion, but they will not do for a long campaign. Howe, it is probable, will make an attempt on this city; [4] should he fail on this side the Delaware, he is ruined. If he succeeds, our cause is not ruined. He stakes all on his side against a part on ours; admitting he succeeds, the consequence will be, that armies from both ends of the continent will march to assist their suffering friends in the middle states; for he cannot go everywhere, it is impossible. I consider Howe as the greatest enemy the tories have; he is bringing a war into their country, which, had it not been for him and partly for themselves, they had been clear of. Should he now be expelled, I wish with all the devotion of a Christian, that the names of whig and tory may never more be mentioned; but should the tories give him encouragement to come, or assistance if he come, I as sincerely wish that our next year's arms may expel them from the continent, and the Congress appropriate their possessions to the relief of those who have suffered in well-doing. A single successful battle next year will settle the whole. America could carry on a two years' war by the confiscation of the property of disaffected persons, and be made happy by their expulsion. Say not that this is revenge, call it rather the soft resentment of a suffering people, who, having no object in view but the GOOD of ALL, have staked their OWN ALL upon a seemingly doubtful event. Yet it is folly to argue against determined hardness; eloquence may strike the ear, and the language of sorrow draw forth the tear of compassion, but nothing can reach the heart that is steeled with prejudice.

Quitting this class of men, I turn with the warm ardor of a friend to those who have nobly stood, and are yet determined to stand the matter out: I call not upon a few, but upon all: not on THIS state or THAT state, but on EVERY state: up and help us; lay your shoulders to the wheel; better have too much force than too little, when so great an object is at stake. Let it be told to the future world, that in the depth of winter, when nothing but hope and virtue could survive, that the city and the country, alarmed at one common danger, came forth to meet and to repulse it. Say not that thousands are gone, turn out your tens of thousands; [5] throw not the burden of the day upon Providence, but *"show your faith by your works,"* [6] that God may bless you. It matters not where you live, or what rank of life you hold, the evil or the blessing will reach you all. The far and the near, the home counties and the back, the rich and the poor, will suffer or rejoice alike. The heart that

---

[4] Philadelphia, taken by the British September 26, 1777, seven months later.

[5] See the source, I Samuel, 8:7.

[6] See the source, James 2:18.

feels not now is dead; the blood of his children will curse his cowardice, who shrinks back at a time when a little might have saved the whole, and made *them* happy. I love the man that can smile in trouble, that can gather strength from distress, and grow brave by reflection. 'Tis the business of little minds to shrink; but he whose heart is firm, and whose conscience approves his conduct, will pursue his principles unto death. My own line of reasoning is to myself as straight and clear as a ray of light. Not all the treasures of the world, so far as I believe, could have induced me to support an offensive war, for I think it murder; but if a thief breaks into my house, burns and destroys my property, and kills or threatens to kill me, or those that are in it, and to *"bind me in all cases whatsoever"* to his absolute will, am I to suffer it? What signifies it to me, whether he who does it is a king or a common man; my country-man or not my countryman; whether it be done by an individual villain, or an army of them? If we reason to the root of things we shall find no difference; neither can any just cause be assigned why we should punish in the one case and pardon in the other. Let them call me rebel, and welcome, I feel no concern from it; but I should suffer the misery of devils, were I to make a whore of my soul by swearing allegiance to one whose character is that of a sottish, stupid, stubborn, worthless, brutish man. I conceive likewise a horrid idea in receiving mercy from a being, who at the last day shall be shrieking to the rocks and mountains to cover him, and fleeing with terror from the orphan, the widow, and the slain of America.

There are cases which cannot be overdone by language, and this is one. There are persons, too, who see not the full extent of the evil which threatens them; they solace themselves with hopes that the enemy, if he succeed, will be merciful. It is the madness of folly, to expect mercy from those who have refused to do justice; and even mercy, where conquest is the object, is only a trick of war; The cunning of the fox is as murderous as the violence of the wolf, and we ought to guard equally against both. Howe's first object is, partly by threats and partly by promises, to terrify or seduce the people to deliver up their arms and receive mercy. A peace which would be the immediate forerunner of a worse ruin than any we have yet thought of. Ye men of Pennsylvania, do reason upon these things! Were the back counties to give up their arms, they would fall an easy prey to the Indians, who are all armed: this perhaps is what some tories would not be sorry for. Were the home counties to deliver up their arms, they would be exposed to the resent-ment of the back counties, who would then have it in their power to chastise their defection at pleasure. And were any one state to give up its arms, THAT state must be garrisoned by all Howe's army of Britons and Hessians [7] to preserve it from the anger of the rest. Mutual fear is the principal link in the chain of mutual love, and woe be to that state that breaks the compact. Howe is mercifully inviting you to barbarous destruction, and men must be either rogues or fools that will not see it. I

---

[7] The hated troops from Hesse were German mercenaries, employed by the British.

dwell not upon the vapors of imagination; I bring reason to your ears, and, in language as plain as A, B, C, hold up truth to your eyes.

I thank *God* that I fear not. I see no real cause for fear. I know our situation well, and can see the way out of it. While our army was collected, Howe dared not risk a battle; and it is no credit to him that he decamped from the White Plains,[8] and waited a mean opportunity to ravage the defenceless Jerseys; but it is great credit to us, that, with a handful of men, we sustained an orderly retreat for near an hundred miles, brought off our ammunition, all our fieldpieces, the greatest part of our stores, and had four rivers to pass. None can say that our retreat was precipitate, for we were near three weeks in performing it, that the country [the local militia] might have time to come in. Twice we marched back to meet the enemy, and remained out till dark. The sign of fear was not seen in our camp, and had not some of the cowardly and disaffected inhabitants spread false alarms through the country, the Jersies had never been ravaged. Once more we are again collected and collecting, our new army at both ends of the continent is recruiting fast, and we shall be able to open the next campaign with sixty thousand men, well-armed and clothed. This is our situation, and who will may know it. By perseverance and fortitude we have the prospect of a glorious issue; by cowardice and submission, the sad choice of a variety of evils—a ravaged country—a depopulated city—habitations without safety, and slavery without hope—our homes turned into barracks and bawdy-houses for Hessians, and a future race to provide for, whose fathers we shall doubt of. Look on this picture and weep over it! and if there yet remains one thoughtless wretch who believes it not, let him suffer it unlamented.

---

[8] In New York, Howe failed to destroy the Continental Army of Washington after forcing his retreat.

DEHUMANIZATION

Harry M. Caudill

A LAND DIVIDED

In the early months after Fort Sumter, the conviction crystallized in the mountaineer's mind that he must fight for his slaves or lose them. As a highland slaveholder recruiting troops for the Confederacy once told a group of his fellow mountaineers: "We've got to jine and fight, 'cause if they can take our niggers away from us they can take our cows and hosses, and everything else we've got!" Though the slaveowners did not make up a large portion of the population, each of them could count a few kinsmen or friends who resented the idea that property earned by hard toil—even when that property consisted of fellow human beings —should be wrested from the owner. Many of these sympathizers were willing to support the Confederate cause and even to join its army with the sons of their wealthier neighbors.

But the great majority of the highlanders were, from the outset, sympathetic with the Union. Their reasons were not so simple or so easily defined as were those of their Rebel fellows. The inevitable and very human element of envy and resentment against their more successful neighbors was important and, in many instances, the real cause for their enmity to slavery. Nevertheless there is no doubt that Chad, the hero of John Fox's *Little Shepherd of Kingdom Come*, was not the only mountaineer to risk or endure death on the battlefields because of a sincere desire to see the shackles stricken from millions of men and women.

Perhaps the most important factor causing the mountaineer to enter the army, regardless of the side to which he gave his fealty, was boredom with his monotonous and innately melancholy existence. He and his forefathers had dwelt amid the primeval quiet of a great forest for generations. Life had flowed on in the same primitive routine for so long that a subconscious and deeply felt yearning for a break with his environment had come to beset him. As rumors began to filter in about the great events transpiring in the "outside world," they brought a craving to burst through the forest walls and to escape into the adventure and color of a realm which most of them had never seen and had sensed only from an almost impassable distance.

Too, these were not men who, in the modern sense, had to be trained and inured to the privations and bloodletting of warfare. They had known the discomforts of cold and heat, and sometimes of hunger and thirst, since boyhood. They could walk tirelessly for many miles and the use of the rifle came almost by instinct to their hands and eyes.

No great bridge between their life and the hardship of camp and battlefield had to be crossed, and it was with ever-quickening excitement that they heard tales of "the War."

For whatever reason individuals chose to enter military service, there was a great outpouring of men and boys into the recruitments of the two contending armies. The world may not see again the match for these men as soldiers. Indefatigable afoot or in the saddle, they fought on practically every battleground, ignoring the legislature of their state —which solemnly declared Kentucky to be neutral in the great struggle. The fierce cry that became famous as the bloodcurdling "Rebel Yell" had been learned by their forefathers from Indian warriors, and was now carried North and South by soldiers from the Southern mountains. But to their soldierly virtues was added a grave defect—an unrelenting hatred of discipline and order. The highland soldier wore the collar of military discipline with poor grace, frequently deserting when an officer "got too big for his britches." The Confederates generally elected their officers—a democratic but perilous practice—and at least one soldier refused to vote at all, explaining his stand with, "God damn it, I'm ag'in *all* officers."

From every valley went forth Confederate and Union men. Cousins took opposite sides, and sometimes brothers and even fathers and sons split on the issue. Such partings in the early stages of the war were relatively friendly, but it could not remain so for long. As the months passed wounded and crippled men began to return, and they brought reports of the deaths of others. When the occupants of a mountain cabin learned that a son, brother or father had died at the hands of Union or Rebel troops on some distant battlefield, they fixed their resentment, not against the far-off armies but against the known and near neighbors, relatives or former friends who had put on the uniform of the army at whose hands the loved one had perished. These were simple people lacking complexity in emotional or mental makeup. They were quick to anger and quick to carry that anger into effective action against the offender. And within a short time there grew up within the confines of these valleys a war in miniature, fought by the people back home, neighbor against neighbor, kinsman against kinsman. By the end of 1863 practically every household was involved in the struggle, at home or on the great battlefields of Virginia.

At first the two camps simply drew sullenly apart from each other; but, in an atmosphere charged with the electricity of ever-deepening hatred, outbreaks of violence were inevitable. They were not long in coming.

Sometimes the immediate cause was some trifling local incident. A man might find one of his hogs dead and jump to the conclusion that his neighbor of the opposite camp had killed it. Or a mountaineer might conclude that his former friend across the ridge had shot his missing hound. Such trifling sparks set fire to emotional powder kegs, and the battlefield in the mountains came to be almost as tragic as the ones developing before Vicksburg and Gettysburg. Men were killed from ambush when they left their cabins in the early dawn. They were ambushed on the trails and shot from the sheltering forests. Sometimes a cabin was attacked under cover of darkness and set afire, and the family shot as they fled the flames. Still children of the frontier, with traditions of warfare acquired in the cruel border struggles, they fought each other now with the same brutality and disregard of chivalrous restraints with which their grandsires had fought the hated Cherokee, Shawnee and Choctaw.

When men were killed in this harsh land women were left to till the land and raise children. They must plow and plant and harvest without help except for the small hands of those whom they toiled to feed. And all too frequently, when a crop had been raised and when a widow had butchered and salted her hogs with her own hands, partisans of the hated enemy swooped down and carried away her treasures. Sometimes the longest-lasting hatreds were planted in the bosoms of these bereaved women and of the children whom they sought to rear. Thus the land was sowed with bitterness, from which crops of bloodshed were to be harvested for generations to come.

As a child I heard my paternal grandmother tell countless tales of her wartime childhood. She was eleven when the conflict began, and when her Confederate father rode away to join General Lee in "Old Virginny." In 1864 he came home on a "crop leave"—to plant corn and vegetables for his family. One day while he was at work in his field a half-dozen pro-Union guerrillas swept down on him. Seeing that escape was impossible and resistance futile, he attempted to surrender. But the guerrillas were implacable and riddled him with bullets. His teen-age daughter held his shattered head while his brains ran out onto her aproned lap. To the day of her death she was an unreconstructed Rebel, and her eyes glinted and her lips tightened into a thin line at the merest mention of even the grandchildren of her father's killers.

The "war tales" still remembered and retold by the old bring into focus a vivid tableau from this most bitter of battlefields. In generations of retelling they have lost little of the hatred and vengefulness which flamed so intensely a century ago.

In 1941 a ninety-year-old mountaineer led me and my father to a "sinkhole" on a hillside near his family cemetery and pointed to the spot where, nearly eighty years before, he and his fifteen-year-old brother had buried the body of a Yankee cavalryman. It was a still, droning day in July, and in the rich bottom beyond his house his grandchildren were dutifully "hoeing out grandpap's corn patch." We sat on a fallen log while he recollected the details.

Pap warn't no nigger lover and on t'other hand he didn't hate 'em. But he thought hit was right to own 'em because they are skasely human accordin' to th' Bible. So when the war started pap got ready and went off to fight fer the South.

Me and my brother was left at home to take keer of things. He was five years older than me and he sort of run things about the place. Ma and the girls worked, too, and we got along all right till the damned Yankees started stealin' everything a body could raise.

Well, about two years after the war started, about this time of year, a gang of Union soldiers come through this here country. They was camped at the Cumberland Gap and had to just take things to eat away from folks. They went through the country robbin' widders and orphans, and payin' 'em with greenbacks if they was on the Union side and nothin' atall if they was Democrats. They was about fifty in this gang and they was ridin' horses. They had a herd of cattle they had stole and was drivin' 'em to the Cumberland Gap. They called their robb'ry "foragin'."

They camped right thar in that bottom and cooked supper. They eat up all our ham meat and about ten fat hens. The next morning they left afore daylight and took all our cattle and work stock with 'em. Their captain said he didn't have to pay us a cent fer nothin' because pap was a traitor.

Well, ma cried and begged him to leave us a mule to plow with but the captain said, "No, let yore old man quit fightin' his country and come home and work fer ye." So just afore they rode off one of them sons-of-bitches went to the creek and got water and poured it in our bee gums and drownded our bees. All them other rascals just stood around and laughed.

As soon as they got gone brother Oliver grabbed pap's old hog-rifle and went to the mountain, and me right after him. He took a nigh cut and got ahead of them Yankees, so we could see 'em come in sight. Oliver put in a good smooth ball and a heavy charge of powder and waited. Pretty soon we seed 'em a-comin' and just waited real still till they was all out of sight except the last one. Then Oliver took good aim and shot him right betwixt his galluses. He yelled and fell out of his saddle and me and Oliver took off back to the house. We stopped just long enough to clean the gun, then hung it up over the fireboard and started hoein' corn just like nothin' had happened.

In about twenty minutes here come them Yankees with their dead buddy. They was awful mad and threatened to kill us fer shore. But the captain said we hadn't done hit and made his men leave us alone. He went up to the graveyard and had his men dig a grave and bury the dead Yankee. Then he come down to the house and all the men got a drink from our well afore they left. The old captain sort of softened up and give us back a plow mule and warned me and Oliver to stay out of trouble. He said he had two young-'uns about like us back home.

When they got plumb gone ma tol' me and Ol to go dig up that Yankee and git him outen our graveyard. So we uncovered him and pulled him up the hill and buried him in a sinkhole where a big tree had turned up by the roots. We didn't git him very deep though, 'cause a hog rooted him up and carried off his head. Ma said that proved that hogs and other Yankees was the only things that could stomach a Yankee, dead or alive!

Before the war ended conditions in the mountains defied description. Death, robbery, rapine and starvation were rampant and both civil and military authorities were helpless to restore order. At last the

"Federals" established camps on the fringes of the mountains and urged victims of the war within a war to find refuge in them. One such camp was established at Stevenson, Alabama, and sheltered refugees from many parts of the Southern highlands. A young private in the Union Army, Frank Wilkeson, a New Yorker, has left us a vivid description of these unfortunate mountaineers. His book, *The Recollections of a Private Soldier*,[1] is one of the finest commentaries on the War Between the States. He wrote:

At Stevenson there was a large refugee camp, where many women and children and a few crippled or age-enfeebled men had sought refuge from attacks by murderous bands of guerrillas. . . . These pretended soldiers, it mattered not which uniform they disgraced by wearing, were, almost without exception, robbers and murderers, who sought to enrich themselves by plundering their defenceless neighbors. They rode through the Southern highlands, killing men, burning houses, stealing cattle and horses. To-day a band of guerrillas, alleged Unionists, ravaged a mountain district. They killed their personal enemies, whom they said were Confederate sympathizers, and destroyed their property. Tomorrow other guerillas burned Union men's houses, and shot so-called Union men to death. This relentless, mountain warfare was exceedingly hard on women and children. Agriculture was suspended in the highlands. No man dared to till his lean fields for fear that some hidden enemy might kill him. No stack of unthrashed grain or garner of corn was safe from the torch. The defenseless women and children were starved out of their homes, and they sought safety and food within the Union lines. Our government established extensive camps for these war-stricken Southerners.

Curious to see these people I spent a day in camp at Stevenson. I saw hundreds of tall, gaunt, frouzy-headed, snuff-dipping, pipe-smoking, unclean women. Some were clad in homespun stuffs, others in calico, others in bagging. Many of them were unshod. There were hundreds and hundreds of vermin-infested and supremely dirty children in the camp. Some families lived in tents, some in flimsy barracks. All lived in discomfort. All drew rations from the government. All were utterly poor. It seemed that they were too poor to ever again get a start in life. Haggard, wind- and sun- and storm-burnt women, their gaunt forms showing plainly through their rags, sat, or lolled, or stood in groups, talking drawlingly. Their features were as expressionless as wood, their eyes lustreless. I talked to many of these women. All told stories of murder, of arson, of blood-curdling scenes. One, gray-eyed, bony, square-jawed, barefooted, forty years old, clad in a dirty, ragged, homespun dress, sat on a log outside of a tent sucking a corncob pipe. Her tow-headed children played around her. She told me that before the war she and her husband owned a mountain farm, where they lived in comfort; that they owned horses, cattle, and pigs, and raised plenty of

[1] G. P. Putnam's Sons, 1886.

corn and tobacco. One day her husband, who was a Union man, was shot dead as he stood by her side in the door of their house. She buried him in a grave she dug herself. She and her children tended the crops. These were burned shortly after they gathered them. Then her swine were stolen, and her cows and horse driven off. Finally her oldest son, a boy of fourteen, was shot dead at the spring, and her house and barn were burned in broad daylight, and she and her children were left homeless and without food on a desolate mountain side. Many of her neighbors had been burned out the same day. They joined forces and wandered down the mountain, hungry, cold, with little children tugging at women's dresses, to a Union camp. From there they had been sent to Stevenson. Long before this woman had finished her story she rose to her feet, her face was white with intense passion, her eyes blazed with fire, and her gaunt form quivered with excitement as she gesticulated savagely. She said that if she lived, and her boys lived, she would have vengeance on the men who had murdered her husband and son, and destroyed her home. As she talked so talked all. These women were saturating their children's minds with the stories of the wrongs they had endured. I heard them repeat over and over to their children the names of men which they were never to forget, and whom they were to kill when they had sufficient strength to hold a rifle. The stolid manners, the wooden faces, the lustreless eyes, the drawling speech of these people, concealed the volcanoes of fire and wrath which burned within their breasts. . . . It was easy to foresee the years of bloodshed, of assassination, of family feuds, that would spring from the recollections of the war, handed from widowed mothers to savage-tempered sons, in the mountain recesses of Georgia, Tennessee, Alabama, and Kentucky. And long after the war closed rifles continued to crack in remote mountain glens, as the open accounts between families were settled.

Here the mountains were like the walls of a great jail which shut in the combatants. After Appomattox it was as though mortal enemies had been locked in the same prison without taking away the deadly weapons they knew so well how to use.

Perhaps in no other region of the United States except the Southern mountains were the lives and property of a great number of pro-Union civilians lost in the war. In Pennsylvania, Kansas and a few other border areas the people were subjected to occasional Confederate forays, but those areas were comparatively rich and the losses were soon restored. But in the highlands much of the modest and slowly-built-up accumulations of three generations were destroyed, impoverishing virtually the entire population.

Thus the curtain rose upon one of the most fantastic dramas in American History—the ferocious Kentucky mountain feuds. Their story has gone largely unchronicled, but in savagery and stark horror they dwarf the cattle wars of the Great Plains and, by contrast, make the vendettas of Sicily look like children's parlor games.

The Kentucky mountain feuds commenced a few years after the

Civil War and continued with unchecked ferocity until about 1915, an interval of nearly half a century. These dreadful interfamily wars constitute a truly astounding chapter in American history. A few statistics from the region will reveal the stark outline of their horror. During the half-century mentioned, the nineteen counties of the plateau achieved a maximum average population of about fifteen thousand people. Careful research in the files of the Circuit Court Clerk's office in one of the counties disclosed that between 1865 and 1915 nearly one thousand murder indictments were returned by the local grand juries. Thus we know that twenty homicides per year occurred, and inevitably many killings must have taken place in which for one reason or another no indictments were made.

Some of the feuds involved whole armies. A wandering Presbyterian preacher arrived in Hazard, the county seat of Perry County, to find the town in the midst of a roaring battle. This feud, then called the "French-Eversole War," eventually caused an almost complete suspension of the law courts within the county. The preacher arrived at a time when the two factions were locked in mortal combat for the courthouse and its records. The Eversole clan had holed up in the structure, while the more numerous French faction fired at them from doors and windows of neighboring buildings. This siege lasted until the approach of a company of militiamen forced the besiegers to flee.

Probably the most famous of the feuds was the "Hatfield-McCoy War." This great struggle eventually involved, directly or indirectly, practically every inhabitant of Pike County, Kentucky and Logan County, West Virginia—and resulted in at least sixty-five deaths. This epic clan war was fought out to its grim conclusion with all the characteristic savagery and tenacity the borderers had displayed a century before in struggles with the Indians. The vendetta brought the governments of the two states to the brink of war, and the correspondence between the governors on the matter reveals a situation so fantastic as to defy belief.

During the war, according to a letter from West Virginia's governor, E. W. Wilson, the families fought on different sides and relations between them became unfriendly. In those days before voter-registration, the Hatfields habitually crossed the border to vote in Kentucky elections. This unlawful franchise was resented by the McCoys and one of them, Tolbert by name, stabbed "Big Ellison" Hatfield to death at a voting precinct in 1882. Tolbert McCoy and his brothers Hurmer and Randolf were arrested for the slaying, and law officers undertook to deliver them to the jailer at Pikeville. A dozen or more mounted men armed with Winchester rifles and Colt revolvers crossed the Tug river and, at gunpoint, took the prisoners from the custody of the officers. They were taken out into the mountains, tied to paw-paw bushes and shot. Their killers were led by Anderson Hatfield, a brother of "Big Ellison."

The McCoys retaliated with murderous raids into West Virginia after the killers of their kinsmen. Jim Vance and William Dempsey,

Hatfield warriors, were killed on one of these raids and six captured Hatfields were carried back to Pikeville under guard. Eyewitnesses reported that two of the surviving McCoy brothers shook hands in self-congratulation over the dead bodies of their enemies, and "crowed like roosters," while their father, Randall McCoy, vowed he would not rest until he had slain Anderson Hatfield with his own hands and had "cut a slice of meat from his body and broiled it and eat it."

In due course, the Hatfields returned the raid. They surrounded Randall McCoy's cabin at night and set it afire. Another son, Calvin, was slain in the gunfire that followed. The vengeance seekers this time turned their guns on women and children when they fled the cabin. But old Randall escaped to continue the feud. Four of his sons died in the long vicious struggle. Both counties were occupied by militiamen time after time, and civil authorities were helpless and hopeless. Legend has it, however, that the feud at last ended happily in the marriage of two of the few survivors—a Hatfield youth to a McCoy girl.

Knott County was riven by the terrible "Knott County War," which raged for many years between the followers of "Cap" Hays and Clabe Jones. Hays had been a cavalry captain in the Confederate army and Jones a pro-Union, guerrilla leader. When these two strong-willed men resumed the war in Knott County most of the population enlisted in one faction or the other and in a pitched battle at McPherson Post Office (which later became Hindman, the county seat) a half-dozen men were shot to death. Old Clabe Jones was renowned in song as a "booger," little less evil than the devil himself. When he was not feuding with the followers of "Cap" Hays he warred with "Bad John" Wright, his neighbor in Letcher County. This mountain baron was an ex-Confederate who was captured during the war and imprisoned in Ohio. He escaped and thereafter acquired a small fortune by repeatedly enlisting in the Union Army for the bounties which were paid. With his roll of "Yankee greenbacks" he returned to his Rebel unit, where he remained until the war ended. He and Hays were eventually able to decimate the Jones crowd and bring this war, at least, to a close.

One dreadful feud began when a family which had given its support to the Union buried the body of a little girl on land which a family of ex-Confederates claimed as its own. The latter unhesitatingly dug into the grave and pitched the coffined body across the fence onto land recognized as belonging to the offenders. This hideous act elicited murderous retaliation and plunged the county into a war that lasted more than two decades and cost unnumbered lives.

In 1888 conditions became so tumultuous in feud-riven Rowan County that a special committee of the Legislature was appointed to investigate the situation. It recommended that the act establishing the county be repealed, and that the territory be thenceforth governed by martial law. The committee found no disposition on the part of the officials to enforce the law or on the part of the populace to obey it. Twenty "open murders and secret assassinations" had been committed in the county without a single conviction having been secured in the courts. In addition, sixteen other persons had been wounded in shooting affrays. And this in a county shown by the census of 1890 to have a population of 6129!

But hardly a county was without its "war," and some had a whole series. The "troubles" in Breathitt won for that county the somber sobriquet of "Bloody Breathitt" and gained for its populace the shocked attention of the world. An eighty-year-old lawyer once related to me the unique manner in which court adjournments were occasionally obtained in its Circuit Court. A murder case was docketed for trial and numerous friends of the defendant appeared at the courthouse heavily armed and in a belligerent mood. When the judge called the case for trial, the defendant's father, a man of about fifty with huge handle-bar whiskers and two immense pistols, rose and walked to the judicial bench. Wringing the gavel from the fingers of the startled judge, the feudist rapped the bench and announced, "Court's over and ever'body can go. We ain't agoin' to have any court here this term, folks." The red-faced judge hastily acquiesced in this extraordinary order and promptly left town. When court convened at the next term the court and sheriff were bolstered by sixty militiamen, but by then the defendant was not available for trial. He had been slain from ambush.

Nor was this incident the only one of its kind. Sometimes, though, the feudists were not satisfied with seeing a trial delayed or a judge run out of town. At least four men have been shot to death on the lawn or within the walls of the crumbling, ancient Breathitt County Courthouse at Jackson. And at Hillsville, Virginia, not far from the state line, feudists in the "Allen-Edwards Wars," enraged by the outcome of a trial, entered the circuit courtroom and shot to death the circuit judge, commonwealth attorney, sheriff and three of the jurors.

Clay County was the scene of the "White-Baker War," that terrible and prolonged war of attrition in which countless participants died in grim gun battles, some of them on the streets of Manchester, the dusty little county seat.

Immediately after the Civil War, a struggle for political power was waged within each county. Union and Rebel forces fought for ascendancy by seeking to capture local offices. In no more than four counties were the discredited ex-Confederates able to succeed. Elsewhere the "good old Union boys" elected their former comrades to fill the log courthouses and to run the counties. These backwoods politicians promptly set out to harass their old foes with indictments for wartime crimes. Long dockets accumulated in the Circuit Courts as Republican grand jurors charged defeated rebels with every imaginable crime— murder, arson, rape, grand and petty larceny, treason against the Commonwealth, unlawful assembly, conspiracy to commit unlawful acts and "obtaining property by false tokens." This last offense referred to purchases made with Confederate currency. So formidable were the assaults made on them through the courts that the unregenerate Confederates were in grave peril.

Their reaction was deadly. Jurors learned quickly that to convict a man was to risk prompt and certain death. Not all rebels could be imprisoned, and once court was over and the juror was at home his back became a target for rifles hidden on the hillsides that overlooked his cabin. Even rabid, vengeance-thirsty "Yankees" became slow to convict.

The courtroom perpetuation of war and feud, though it imprisoned few people, added fuel to the fires of hatred and kindled new violence on every hand. Nor did conviction by a court and jury mean the sentences would be carried out. When officers attempted to convey prisoners to the state penitentiary at Frankfort they had to traverse the baronies of many heavily armed feudal lords. Often, indeed, these mountain chiefs "took pity" on the prisoners and, supported by small armies of retainers, demanded that the officers surrender their charges. Knott County's Clabe Jones acted as a one-man appellate court and freed many malefactors whose crimes were no greater than his own. He stirred up no little trouble by entering the bailiwicks of other war lords and rescuing men whose sad plight touched his tender heart. During the feuds such a friend was infinitely more valuable to a defendant than any number of skilled lawyers.

In at least one county, officials resorted to a unique device in an effort to preserve the life of the trial judge: sheets of steel were bolted together around the judicial bench to form a protective box or canopy. By this means it was sought to lessen the danger of having the judge shot by an irate spectator or, perhaps, with a high-powered rifle from a wooded hillside. Mountain judges during these years risked their lives daily, and some died in an effort to bring respect for law to a grim and savage people.

So diabolical did the feuds become and so long did they persist that they sparked a considerable exodus from the region. Thoughtful men who had no interest in the wars which so engrossed the energies of their kinsmen began "moving west." The disorders in Kansas, Texas and New Mexico were as teapot tempests compared to those raging in their own mountains. Today countless mountaineers have distant relatives residing half a continent westward.

A terrible quality of these monstrous adventures in homicide was that they were virtually self-perpetuating. Without distractions from the larger "outside world" to attract the highlanders' attention and hold their interests, each personal affront or injury was remembered and recounted. The ties of blood kinship were exceedingly important and an injury, real or imagined, even to a "third or fourth cousin" was likely to instill indignant umbrage. Their thoughts tended to dwell on the accumulating grievances of the decades and frequently hatreds came to center on an entire family because of some act of one of its long-dead ancestors. Sometimes such hatreds persisted even after the name of the original offender was only dimly remembered and the offensive act itself was forgotten. Thus the mountaineer came to inherit the hatreds of his father along with his name. Corn liquor copiously consumed to induce relief from boredom often fired vengeful excursions against the foe. The mountaineers' hatreds became so many-layered, so deeply ingrained and so tenaciously remembered that they were subconscious, and as such they have, to a remarkable degree, been transmitted to his present-day descendants. This accounts largely for the remarkably personal turn which politics always takes in the highlands even now—a fact which will be discussed at length in later chapters. Even today a mountain officeseeker is likely to find it impossible to win by taking a stand on public issues. His electorate is far more likely to vote for or against him because of something his uncle or grandfather did, perhaps before the candidate's birth, than because he proposes to improve schools or construct new roads. . . .

Anton Chekhov

THE LAMENT

It is twilight. A thick wet snow is twirling around the newly lighted street lamps, and lying in soft thin layers on roofs, on horses' backs, on people's shoulders and hats. The cabdriver Iona Potapov is quite white, and looks like a phantom; he is bent double as far as a human body can bend double; he is seated on his box; he never makes a move. If a whole snowdrift fell on him, it seems as if he would not find it necessary to shake it off. His little horse is also quite white, and remains motionless; its immobility, its angularity, and its straight wooden-looking legs, even close by, give it the appearance of a ginger-bread horse worth a *kopek*. It is, no doubt, plunged in deep thought. If you were snatched from the plow, from your usual gray surroundings, and were thrown into this slough full of monstrous lights, unceasing noise, and hurrying people, you too would find it difficult not to think.

Iona and his little horse have not moved from their place for a long while. They left their yard before dinner, and up to now, not a fare. The evening mist is descending over the town, the white lights of the lamps replacing brighter rays, and the hubbub of the street getting louder. "Cabby for Viborg way!" suddenly hears Iona. "Cabby!"

Iona jumps, and through his snow-covered eyelashes sees an officer in a greatcoat, with his hood over his head.

"Viborg way!" the officer repeats. "Are you asleep, eh? Viborg way!"

With a nod of assent Iona picks up the reins, in consequence of which layers of snow slip off the horse's back and neck. The officer seats himself in the sleigh, the cabdriver smacks his lips to encourage his horse, stretches out his neck like a swan, sits up, and, more from habit than necessity, brandishes his whip. The little horse also stretches its neck, bends its wooden-looking legs, and makes a move undecidedly.

"What are you doing, werewolf!" is the exclamation Iona hears from the dark mass moving to and fro, as soon as they have started.

"Where the devil are you going? To the r-r-right!"

"You do not know how to drive. Keep to the right!" calls the officer angrily.

A coachman from a private carriage swears at him; a passerby, who has run across the road and rubbed his shoulder against the horse's nose, looks at him furiously as he sweeps the snow from his sleeve. Iona shifts about on his seat as if he were on needles, moves his elbows as if he were trying to keep his equilibrium, and gapes about like someone suffocating, who does not understand why and wherefore he is there.

"What scoundrels they all are!" jokes the officer; "one would think they had all entered into an agreement to jostle you or fall under your horse."

Iona looks round at the officer, and moves his lips. He evidently wants to say something, but the only sound that issues is a snuffle.

"What?" asks the officer.

Iona twists his mouth into a smile, and with an effort says hoarsely:

"My son, *barin*, died this week."

"Hm! What did he die of?"

Iona turns with his whole body toward his fare, and says:

"And who knows! They say high fever. He was three days in the hospital, and then died. . . . God's will be done."

"Turn round! The devil!" sounds from the darkness. "Have you popped off, old doggie, eh? Use your eyes!"

"Go on, go on," says the officer, "otherwise we shall not get there by tomorrow. Hurry up a bit!"

The cabdriver again stretches his neck, sits up, and, with a bad grace, brandishes his whip. Several times again he turns to look at his fare, but the latter has closed his eyes, and apparently is not disposed to listen. Having deposited the officer in the Viborg, he stops by the tavern, doubles himself up on his seat, and again remains motionless, while the snow once more begins to cover him and his horse. An hour, and another. . . . Then, along the footpath, with a squeak of galoshes, and quarreling, come three young men, two of them tall and lanky, the third one short and humpbacked.

"Cabby, to the Police Bridge!" in a cracked voice calls the humpback. "The three of us for two *griveniks!*"

Iona picks up his reins, and smacks his lips. Two *griveniks* is not a fair price, but he does not mind whether it is a *rouble* or five *kopeks*—to him it is all the same now, so long as they are fares. The young men, jostling each other and using bad language, approach the sleigh, and all three at once try to get onto the seat; then begins a discussion as to which two shall sit and who shall be the one to stand. After wrangling, abusing each other, and much petulance, it is at last decided that the humpback shall stand, as he is the smallest.

"Now then, hurry up!" says the humpback in a twanging voice, as he takes his place and breathes in Iona's neck. "Old furry! Here, mate, what a cap you have! There is not a worse one to be found in all Petersburg! . . ."

"He-he!—he-he!" giggles Iona. "Such a . . ."

"Now you, 'such a,' hurry up, are you going the whole way at this pace? Are you? . . . Do you want it in the neck?"

"My head feels like bursting," says one of the lanky ones. "Last night at the Donkmasovs, Vaska and I drank the whole of four bottles of cognac."

"I don't understand what you lie for," says the other lanky one angrily; "you lie like a brute."

"God strike me, it's the truth!"

"It's as much the truth as that a louse coughs!"

"He, he," grins Iona, "what gay young gentlemen!"

"Pshaw, go to the devil!" says the humpback indignantly.

"Are you going to get on or not, you old pest? Is that the way to drive? Use the whip a bit! Go on, devil, go on, give it to him well!"

Iona feels at his back the little man wriggling, and the tremble in his voice. He listens to the insults hurled at him, sees the people, and little by little the feeling of loneliness leaves him. The humpback goes on swearing until he gets mixed up in some elaborate six-foot oath, or chokes with coughing. The lankies begin to talk about a certain Nadejda Petrovna. Iona looks round at them several times; he waits for a temporary silence, then, turning round again, he murmurs:

"My son . . . died this week."

"We must all die," sighs the humpback, wiping his lips after an attack of coughing. "Now, hurry up, hurry up! Gentlemen, I really cannot go any farther like this! When will he get us there?"

"Well, just you stimulate him a little in the neck!"

"You old pest, do you hear, I'll bone your neck for you! If one treated the like of you with ceremony one would have to go on foot! Do you hear, old serpent Gorinytch! Or do you not care a spit?"

Iona hears rather than feels the blows they deal him.

"He, he," he laughs. "They are gay young gentlemen, God bless 'em!"

"Cabby, are you married?" asks a lanky one.

"I? He, he, gay young gentlemen! Now I have only a wife and the moist ground. . . . He, ho, ho . . . that is to say, the grave. My son has died, and I am alive. . . . A wonderful thing, death mistook the door . . . instead of coming to me, it went to my son. . . ."

Iona turns round to tell them how his son died, but at this moment, the humpback, giving a little sigh, announces, "Thank God, we have at last reached our destination," and Iona watches them disappear through the dark entrance. Once more he is alone, and again surrounded by silence. . . . His grief, which has abated for a short while, returns and rends his heart with greater force. With an anxious and hurried look, he searches among the crowds passing on either side of the street to find whether there may be just one person who will listen to him. But the crowds hurry by without noticing him or his trouble. Yet it is such an immense, illimitable grief. Should his heart break and the grief pour out, it would flow over the whole earth, so it seems, and yet no one sees it. It has managed to conceal itself in such an insignificant shell that no one can see it even by day and with a light.

Iona sees a hall porter with some sacking, and decides to talk to him.

"Friend, what sort of time is it?" he asks.

"Past nine. What are you standing here for? Move on."

Iona moves on a few steps, doubles himself up, and abandons himself to his grief. He sees it is useless to turn to people for help. In less than five minutes he straightens himself, holds up his head as if he felt some sharp pain, and gives a tug at the reins; he can bear it no longer. "The stables," he thinks, and the little horse, as if it understood, starts off at a trot.

About an hour and a half later Iona is seated by a large dirty stove. Around the stove, on the floor, on the benches, people are snoring; the air is thick and suffocatingly hot. Iona looks at the sleepers, scratches himself, and regrets having returned so early.

"I have not even earned my fodder," he thinks. "That's what's my trouble. A man who knows his job, who has had enough to eat, and his horse too, can always sleep peacefully."

A young cabdriver in one of the corners half gets up, grunts sleepily, and stretches towards a bucket of water.

"Do you want a drink?" Iona asks him.

"Don't I want a drink!"

"That's so? Your good health! But listen, mate—you know, my son is dead. . . . Did you hear? This week, in the hospital. . . . It's a long story."

Iona looks to see what effect his words have, but sees none—the young man has hidden his face and is fast asleep again. The old man sighs, and scratches his head. Just as much as the young one wants to drink, the old man wants to talk. It will soon be a week since his son died, and he has not been able to speak about it properly to anyone. One must tell it slowly and carefully; how his son fell ill, how he suffered, what he said before he died, how he died. One must describe every detail of the funeral, and the journey to the hospital to fetch the dead son's clothes. His daughter Anissia has remained in the village—one must talk about her too. Is it nothing he has to tell? Surely the listener would gasp and sigh, and sympathize with him? It is better, too, to talk to women; although they are stupid, two words are enough to make them sob.

"I'll go and look after my horse," thinks Iona; "there's always time to sleep. No fear of that!"

He puts on his coat, and goes to the stables to his horse; he thinks of the corn, the hay, the weather. When he is alone, he dares not think of his son; he can speak about him to anyone, but to think of him, and picture him to himself, is unbearably painful.

"Are you tucking in?" Iona asks his horse, looking at its bright eyes; "go on, tuck in, though we've not earned our corn, we can eat hay. Yes! I am too old to drive—my son could have, not I. He was a first-rate cabdriver. If only he had lived!"

Iona is silent for a moment, then continues:

"That's how it is, my old horse. There's no more Kuzma Ionitch. He has left us to live, and he went off pop. Now let's say, you had a foal, you were the foal's mother, and suddenly, let's say, that foal went and left you to live after him. It would be sad, wouldn't it?"

The little horse munches, listens, and breathes over its master's hand. . . .

Iona's feelings are too much for him, and he tells the little horse the whole story.

Joseph Wood Krutch

MAN'S ANCIENT POWERFUL LINK TO NATURE: A SOURCE OF FEAR AND JOY

What is "Nature"? One standard reference devotes five columns to 15 different and legitimate definitions of the word. But for the purposes of this article the meaning is simple. Nature is that part of the world which man did not make and which has not been fundamentally changed by him. It is the mountains, the woods, the rivers, the trees, the plants and the animals which have continued to be very much what they would have been had he never existed.

In another sense man is, of course, himself a part of Nature. But he is also in so many ways so unique that it is convenient to speak of man *and* Nature, especially of man's relation to the rest of this Nature of which he is also a part.

The relationship is something which he can never forget; but he responds to it in the most diverse ways. He regards Nature sometimes as a friend and sometimes as an enemy. He loves it and he fears it. He uses it and destroys it. Nature is what he tries to get away from and then something he wishes to keep. He replaces it with his homes and factories, then wishes to return to it. He tries to impose on it human order and civilization, and then suddenly finds himself dreaming of a golden age when man and Nature were one.

This paradox is as old as civilization itself. Though it is true that man never admired the more savage aspects of Nature until life had become comparatively safe, it is equally true that he had scarcely built the first cities before he began to try to get away from them. In ancient Greece poets idealized the shepherd's life, and in imperial Rome the literary cult of the simple life had already reached the point where satirists ridiculed it. In our modern world the engineer, the industrialist and the builder of skyscrapers moves his family to a country house in the suburbs. He plants trees and cultivates a garden. He acquires animals as pets, and perhaps he takes up bird watching—all of which reveals his unwillingness to let go of what, in theory at least, he has not valued.

Ancient as these paradoxes and conflicts are, there is today one supremely important respect in which they pose a problem that never existed in so acute a form before: now for the first time man can effectively act out his impulses and his decisions. He can, if he so desires, all but banish Nature and the natural from the earth he has come to rule.

Until a few centuries ago man was not even a very numerous species. It has been an even shorter time since his technology became sufficiently advanced to the point where he could upset seriously the ancient balances of the natural world. Formerly he might love Nature or hate her, might attempt to preserve her or destroy her; but she was more powerful than he. Except over relatively small areas she remained in control. Now the balance has shifted. Man controls forces which at least rival and seem on the point of surpassing hers. He can decide as never before what part, if any, of the natural world will be permitted to exist. Thus the question "What is man's place in Nature and what ought to be his relation to her?" is fateful as it never was before.

In its most abstract form this fundamental question was asked and opposing answers were given by the ancient religions. In the Hebraic tradition man was the child of God, and God was separate from, rather than a part of, Nature. Greek paganism, on the other hand, worshiped gods who were themselves aspects of Nature and it taught man to think of himself also as part of her. These gods were more at home in the woods and streams and mountains than in the temples built for them. Nature was the source of health, beauty and joy, and to live in accord with Nature's laws was wisdom. The Great God Pan, or Nature god, was one of the most ancient and powerful of deities, so much so indeed that an early Christian tradition made the exclamation "Great Pan is dead" a cry of victory announcing the triumph for the new faith; and many centuries later, the neopagan poet Swinburne could turn it into a lament to Christ Himself: "Thou hast conquered, O pale Galilean; the world has grown grey from thy breath."

To Noah, unloading his animals after the flood, Jehovah said, "And the fear of you and the dread of you shall be upon every beast of the earth, and upon every fowl of the air, upon all that moveth upon the earth, and upon all the fishes of the sea; into your hand are they delivered." Throughout the Greek and Roman ascendencies and all through the Middle Ages the most admired aspects of Nature were those which man had tamed, at least to a degree. It has often been said that the 14th Century Italian scholar Petrarch was the first man who ever confessed to climbing a mountain just for the sake of the view, and it is not so often added that, at the end of his description, he apologized for this eccentricity.

The conflicting attitudes which even today sometimes relate "the natural" to "the divine" began to emerge some three centuries ago. The first great English biologist, the pious John Ray, in his enormously popular *The Wisdom of God Manifested in the Works of the Creation* (1691), maintained that God did not create the living world exclusively for man's use but that, on the contrary, He "takes pleasure that all His creatures enjoy themselves." And Ray urged that men should study Nature as well as books because it was by such study that the greatness and goodness of God was most clearly revealed.

A bare generation later Alexander Pope, the most read English poet except Shakespeare, could put the same thing in epigrammatic couplets:

> Has God, thou fool! work'd solely for thy good,
> Thy joy, thy pastime, thy attire, thy food? . . .
> Is it for thee the lark ascends and sings?
> Joy tunes his voice, joy elevates his wings.
> Is it for thee the linnet pours his throat?
> Loves of his own and raptures swell the note. . . .
> Know Nature's children all divide her care;
> The fur that warms a monarch warm'd a bear.

Already we were halfway to Wordsworth's "the meanest flower that blows can give / Thoughts that do often lie too deep for tears" or Blake's "Kill not the Moth nor butterfly / For the Last Judgment draweth nigh."

Out of such attitudes emerged the whole romantic glorification of Nature which blossomed in the 18th Century and continued almost unchecked to the middle of the 19th, when scientific objectivity began to struggle against it. By that time life had become comparatively secure and men increasingly were finding the somewhat terrifying spectacle of Nature's savage grandeur thrillingly beautiful. Mountains, as modern scholarship has pointed out, were almost always called "sublime." The philosopher-statesman Edmund Burke devoted one of his earliest writings to distinguishing between "The Beautiful" (that which is soothing and reassuring) and "The Sublime" (that which strikes us with awe and with something almost like terror). Everywhere men were beginning to exclaim over thunderstorms, lashing seas and icy peaks—over whatever suggested something grander and less comfortable than their own cities or, even, their own lawns and gardens.

In this period also the cult of Nature as "the kind mother" or, in the words of Goethe, as "the living garment of God" grew. This wildly unrealistic view attributed to Nature below the human level a consistent kindliness and benevolence which man himself to this day has by no means achieved. Nature is not always a kind mother; she is as often a stern, and sometimes a brutal, one. Yet Burns spoke of "Man's inhumanity to man" and contrasted it with "Nature's social union" which, he said, man had so cruelly disturbed. Wordsworth's God had his dwelling in "the light of setting suns," and "Nature," he proclaimed, "never did betray the heart that loved her."

It was against such romantic idealism that the 19th Century gradually rebelled until, just after the mid-century, Charles Darwin took a position at the opposite extreme and drew his picture of a natural world which assumed its form through the operation of mechanical processes, and which was devoid of anything which could be called moral values.

If few today doubt that Darwin's theory of "natural selection through the struggle for survival" explains much, there are many who insist that it does not explain everything. Some of the most primitive organisms have survived for many millions of years—far longer than other more advanced organisms and possibly longer than man himself will prevail. If only "the fittest survive," then the sea squirt is fitter than any mammal—including, perhaps, man. And "natural selection" cannot account for the intensification of man's consciousness or the value which he puts upon such ideals as justice, fair play and benevolence. It cannot account for them inasmuch as creatures in which these traits are not conspicuous are at least as successful in the "struggle for survival" as he is.

If Nature herself has exhibited a tendency, if she seems to "want" anything, it is not merely to survive. She has tended to realize more and more completely the potentialities of protoplasm and these include much that has no demonstrable "survival value." Evolution itself has spread before us the story of a striving toward "the higher," not merely toward that which enables an organism to survive.

If the romantic view of Nature was mere wishful thinking, merely the projection upon Nature of our own fully developed desires and ideals, then Darwinism generated a romanticism in reverse in which all is conflict, violence and blood. But the fact is that animals do not spend all their time fighting for survival, though for the sake of excitement antiromantic popular books and films do strive to give that impression. Animals also give tender love to their offspring as well as, sometimes, to their mates and the fellow members of their group. Those theories of human society which propose ruthless, devil-take-the-hindermost political and social systems sometimes claim that they are in accord with the laws of Nature, but they are not.

There was a time not too long ago when orthodox science talked only of instincts, behavior patterns, chemical drives and the like, while any tendency to see in the animal even faint analogies to the conscious processes, the intelligence or the emotions of man was ridiculed as sentimental and "anthropomorphic"—*i.e.*, stated in terms appropriate to man only. But the tide has turned. So notable a student of animal behavior as Konrad Lorenz has protested against what he named "mechanomorphism"—the interpretation of animal behavior exclusively in terms of the mechanical—which he calls an error no less grave than anthropomorphism. Animals are not men, but neither are they machines. If they cannot think as man does in terms of abstract concepts, neither are they controlled entirely by push-button reflexes. To some extent they exhibit the beginnings of "the human." They can sometimes take in a situation and modify their behavior in the light of circumstances. They have individuality also; one does not behave exactly like another. Even insects, once thought to be the most automatic and invariable of creatures, seem to be able sometimes to change purposely the pattern of their conduct.

As a matter of fact, the life of the senses in some of the higher animals is possibly more vivid than ours, and in some of them the emotions may be more powerful also. As Sir Julian Huxley, one of the greatest living authorities on evolution, has said of the birds he has observed with scientific exactitude: "Their lives are often emotional, and their emotions are richly and finely expressed. . . . In birds the advance on the intellectual side has been less, on the emotional side greater: so that we can study in them a part of the single stream of life where emotion, untrammeled by much reason, has the upper hand."

Thus all the strange powers and potentialities of the living thing are diffused throughout animate Nature—which remains mysterious, and our relation to it no less so. The universe is not the mere machine which early Darwinians tended to make it; the man who thinks of his dog as another human being is wrong, but no more so perhaps than his opposite who refuses to acknowledge any kinship. Yet an appreciation of this truth still leaves unanswered the question of man's own position. To what extent is he unique; to what extent is he not only "higher" than any other animal, but also radically different from, and discontinuous with, that great chain which connects by close links the humblest one-celled animal with the most intelligent of the apes?

The traditional answer, given by some philosophers and theologians, is that man is an animal to which something (a soul, if you like) has been added and that this something distinguishes him absolutely from all other living creatures. This answer is at least logically tenable, whether you accept it or not. If, on the other hand, you say, as some old-fashioned biologists did, that though man has "evolved" by purely natural process, he is nevertheless endowed with capacities of which not a trace is to be found in any other animal, that is not logically tenable. "Evolution" implies the growing complexity of things previously existing in simpler form. Hence man's consciousness, thought and sense of purpose must either have been added to his natural endowment by something outside Nature, or they must have truly evolved from something in the "lower" forms of life.

William Morton Wheeler, the late great student of the social insects, once wrote that we can only guess why animals are as they are and can never know except very imperfectly how they came to be what they are. Nevertheless, he added, "[the fact] that organisms are as they are, that apart from members of our own species they are our only companions in an infinite and unsympathetic waste of electrons, planets, nebulae and stars, is a perennial joy and consolation." It is upon this "perennial joy and consolation" that the deepest and most rewarding "love of Nature" must rest.

Even to say that we can and should know this joy and consolation is not to answer all the questions. How far should we not only enjoy Nature but also follow her; to what extent should we take our cue, as it were, from the natural world? We are something more than merely part of it. However we came to be where we are, our position is, as an 18th Century poet put it, "on the isthmus of a middle state." We face back towards our primitive ancestors, perhaps even to the ape; but we also look forward to we know not what.

To what extent then should man, to what extent dare he renounce

Nature; take over the management of the earth he lives on; and use it exclusively for what he sometimes regards as his higher purposes?

Extremists give and have always given extreme answers. Let us, say some, "return to Nature," lead the simple life, try to become again that figment of the romantic imagination, "the noble savage." Henry David Thoreau, the greatest of American "Nature lovers," is sometimes accused of having advocated just that. But he did not do so; he advocated only that we should live more simply and more aware of the earth which, he said with characteristic exaggeration, "is more wonderful than it is convenient; more beautiful than it is useful; it is more to be admired and enjoyed than used."

Others suggest a different extreme. They talk about "the biosphere" (loosely, that which has been here defined as the natural world) as contrasted with "the noosphere" (translate as that portion of the earth upon which man has imposed his own will so successfully that whatever conditions prevail there do so because of his will). It appears that civilization, according to this notion, is to be completed only when the noosphere is the whole earth and the biosphere is completely subordinated to the human will.

Within the last one hundred years we have approached faster and closer to that condition than in all the preceding centuries of civilization. But would man, whose roots go so deep into Nature, be happy should he achieve such a situation? Certainly he would become a creature very different from what he is, and the experience of living would be equally different from what it has always been. He would, indeed, have justified his boast that he can "conquer Nature" but he would also have destroyed it. He would have used every spot of earth for homes, factories and farms, or perhaps got rid of farms entirely, because by then he could synthesize food in the laboratory. But he would have no different companions in the adventures of living. The emotions which have inspired much of all poetry, music and art would no longer be comprehensible. He would have all his dealings with things he alone has made. Would we then be, as some would imagine, men like gods? Or would we be only men like ants?

That we would not be satisfied with such a world is sufficiently evidenced by the fact that, to date at least, few do not want their country house, their country vacation, their camping or their fishing trip—even their seat in the park and their visit to the zoo. We need some contact with the thing we sprang from. We need Nature at least as a part of the context of our lives. Though we are not satisfied with Nature, neither are we happy without her. Without cities we cannot be civilized. Without Nature, without wilderness even, we are compelled to renounce an important part of our heritage.

The late Aldo Leopold, who spent his life in forestry and conservation, once wrote, "For us of the minority, the opportunity to see geese is more important than television, and the chance to find a pasque-flower is a right as inalienable as free speech."

Many of us who share this conviction came to it only gradually. On some summer vacation or some country weekend we realize that what we are experiencing is more than merely a relief from the pressures of city life; that we have not merely escaped *from* something but also *into* something; that we have joined the greatest of all communities, which is not that of men alone but of everything which shares with us the great adventure of being alive.

This sense, mystical though it may seem, is no delusion. Throughout history some have felt it and many have found an explanation of it in their conviction that it arises out of the fact that all things owe their gift of life to God. But there is no reason why the most rationalistic of evolutionists should not find it equally inevitable. If man is only the most recent and the most complex of Nature's children, then he must feel his kinship with them. If even his highest powers of consciousness, intellect and conscience were evolved from simpler forms of the same realities, then his kinship with those who took the earlier steps is real and compelling. If Nature produced him, and if she may some day produce something far less imperfect, then he may well hesitate to declare that she has done all she can for him and that henceforth he will renounce her to direct his own destiny.

In some ways man may seem wiser than she is, but it is not certain that he is wiser in all ways. He dare not trust her blindly, but neither does he dare turn his back upon her. He is in danger of relying too exclusively upon his own thoughts, to the entire neglect of her instincts; upon the dead machine he creates, while disregarding the living things of whose adventure he is a part.

We have heard much about "our natural resources" and of the necessity for conserving them, but these "resources" are not merely materially useful. They are also a great reservoir of the life from which we evolved, and they have both consolation to offer and lessons to teach which are not alone those the biologist strives to learn. In their presence many of us experience a lifting of the heart for which mere fresh air and sunshine is not sufficient to account. We feel surging up in us the exuberant, vital urge which has kept evolution going but which tends to falter amid the complexities of a too civilized life. In our rise to the human state we have lost something, despite all we have gained.

Is it merely a sentimental delusion, a "pathetic fallacy," to think that one sees in the animal a capacity for joy which man himself is tending to lose? We have invented exercise, recreation, pleasure, amusement and the rest. To "have fun" is a desire often expressed by those who live in this age of anxiety and most of us have at times actually "had fun." But recreation, pleasure, amusement, fun and all the rest are poor substitutes for joy; and joy, I am convinced, has its roots in something from which civilization tends to cut us off.

Are at least some animals capable of teaching us this lesson of joy? Some biologists—but by no means all and by no means the best—deny categorically that animals feel it. The gift for real happiness and joy is not always proportionate to intelligence, as we understand it, even among the animals. As Professor N. J. Berrill has put it, "To be a bird is to be alive more intensively than any other living creature. . . . [Birds] live in a world that is always in the present, mostly full of joy."

Similarly Sir Julian Huxley, no mere sentimental Nature lover, wrote after watching the love play of herons: "I can only say that it seemed to bring such a pitch of emotion that I could have wished to be a Heron that I might experience it."

This does not mean that Sir Julian would desire, any more than you or I, to be permanently a bird. Perhaps some capacity for joy has been, must be, and should be sacrificed to other capacities. But some awareness of the world outside of man must exist if one is to experience the happiness and solace which some of us find in an awareness of Nature and in our love for her manifestations.

Those who have never found either joy or solace in Nature might begin by looking not for the *joy they can get*, but for the *joy that is there* amid those portions of the earth man has not yet entirely preempted for his own use. And perhaps when they have become aware of joy in other creatures they will achieve joy themselves, by sharing it.

QUOTATION:

"The problem today is to save the individual from anonymity before it is too late and humanity has vanished from the animal called man."

—William Faulkner, *Faulkner in the University* (pp. 244–245)

12
THE CAMPUS TODAY: REBELLION AND CONFORMITY

(Rebellion) *"The intellectuals (including the university students) are a particularly volatile element . . . capable of extreme reactions to objective situations —more extreme than any group in society. They are by nature irresponsible, in the sense that they have no continuing commitment to any single institution or philosophical outlook and they are not fully answerable for consequences. They are, as a result, never fully trusted by anybody, including themselves."*

—Clark Kerr, describing the coming New Order in *Industrialism and Industrial Man*

(Conformity) *"If you will give me six lines written by the hand of the most honest of men, I will find something in them which will hang him."*

—Cardinal Richelieu, *Mirame*

Mario Savio

AN END TO HISTORY

Last summer I went to Mississippi to join the struggle there for civil rights. This fall I am engaged in another phase of the same struggle, this time in Berkeley. The two battlefields may seem quite different to some observers, but this is not the case. The same rights are at stake in both places—the right to participate as citizens in democratic society and the right to due process of law. Further, it is a struggle against the same enemy. In Mississippi an autocratic and powerful minority rules, through organized violence, to suppress the vast, virtually powerless, majority. In California, the privileged minority manipulates the University bureaucracy to suppress the students' political expression. That "respectable" bureaucracy masks the financial plutocrats; that impersonal bureaucracy is the efficient enemy in a "Brave New World."

In our free speech fight at the University of California, we have come up against what may emerge as the greatest problem of our nation —depersonalized, unresponsive bureaucracy. We have encountered the organized status quo in Mississippi, but it is the same in Berkeley. Here we find it impossible usually to meet with anyone but secretaries. Beyond that, we find functionaries who cannot make policy but can only hide behind the rules. We have discovered total lack of response on the part of the policy makers. To grasp a situation which is truly Kafkesque, it is necessary to understand the bureaucratic mentality. And we have learned quite a bit about it this fall, more outside the classroom than in.

As bureaucrat, an administrator believes that nothing new happens. He occupies an ahistorical point of view. In September, to get the attention of his bureaucracy which had issued arbitrary edicts suppressing student political expression and refused to discuss its action, we held a sit-in on the campus. We sat around a police car and kept it immobilized for over thirty-two hours. At last, the administrative bureaucracy agreed to negotiate. But instead, on the following Monday, we discovered that a committee had been appointed, in accordance with usual regulations, to resolve the dispute. Our attempt to convince any of the administrators that an event had occurred, that something new had happened, failed. They saw this simply as something to be handled by normal University procedures.

The same is true of all bureaucracies. They begin as tools, means to certain legitimate goals, and they end up feeding their own existence. The conception that bureaucrats have is that history has in fact come to an end. No events can occur now that the Second World War is over which can change American society substantially. We proceed by standard procedures as we are.

Reprinted from *Humanity*, December, 1964 by permission.

The most crucial problems facing the United States today are the problem of automation and the problem of racial injustice. Most people who will be put out of jobs by machines will not accept an end to events, this historical plateau, as the point beyond which no change occurs. Negroes will not accept an end to history here. All of us must refuse to accept history's final judgment that in America there is no place in society for people whose skins are dark. On campus students are not about to accept it as fact that the university has ceased evolving and is in its final state of perfection, that students and faculty are respectively raw material and employees, or that the university is to be autocratically run by unresponsive bureaucrats.

Here is the real contradiction: the bureaucrats hold history as ended. As a result significant parts of the population both on campus and off are dispossessed, and these dispossessed are not about to accept this ahistorical point of view. It is out of this that the conflict has occurred with the university bureaucracy and will continue to occur until that bureaucracy becomes responsive or until it is clear the university can not function.

The things we are asking for in our civil rights protests have a deceptively quaint ring. We are asking for the due process of law. We are asking for our actions to be judged by committees of our peers. We are asking that regulations ought to be considered as arrived at legitimately only from the consensus of the governed. These phrases are all pretty old, but they are not being taken seriously in America today, nor are they being taken seriously on the Berkeley campus.

I have just come from a meeting with the dean of students. She notified us that she was aware of certain violations of University regulations by certain organizations. University friends of SNCC, which I represent, was one of these. We tried to draw from her some statement on these great principles, consent of the governed, jury of one's peers, due process. The best she could do was to evade or to present the administration party line. It is very hard to make any contact with the human being who is behind these organizations.

The university is the place where people begin seriously to question the conditions of their existence and raise the issue of whether they can be committed to the society they have been born into. After a long period of apathy during the fifties, students have begun not only to question but, having arrived at answers, to act on those answers. This is part of a growing understanding among many people in America that history has not ended, that a better society is possible, and that it is worth dying for.

This free speech fight points up a fascinating aspect of contemporary campus life. Students are permitted to talk all they want so long as their speech has no consequences.

One conception of the university, suggested by a classical Christian formulation, is that it be in the world but not of the world. The conception of Clark Kerr, by contrast, is that the university is part and parcel of this particular stage in the history of American society; it stands to serve the need of American industry; it is a factory that turns out a certain product needed by industry or government. Because speech does often have consequences which might alter this perversion of higher education, the university must put itself in a position of censorship. It can permit two kinds of speech, speech which encourages continuation of the status quo, and speech which advocates changes in it so radical as to be irrelevant in the foreseeable future. Someone may advocate radical change in all aspects of American society, and this I am sure he can do with impunity. But if someone advocates sit-ins to bring about changes in discriminatory hiring practices, this cannot be permitted because it goes against the status quo of which the university is a part. And that is how the fight began here.

The administration of the Berkeley campus has admitted that external, extra-legal groups have pressured the University not to permit students on campus to organize picket lines, not to permit on campus any speech with consequences. And the bureaucracy went along. Speech with consequences, speech in the area of civil rights, speech which some might regard as illegal, must stop.

Many students here at the University, many people in society, are wandering aimlessly about. Strangers in their own lives, there is no place for them. They are people who have not learned to compromise, who for example have come to the University to learn to question, to grow, to learn—all the standard things that sound like clichés because no one takes them seriously. And they find at one point or other that for them to become part of society, to become lawyers, ministers, business-men, people in government, that very often they must compromise those principles which were most dear to them. They must suppress the most creative impulses that they have; this is a prior condition for being part of the system. The University is well structured, well tooled, to turn out people with all the sharp edges worn off, the well-rounded person. The University is well equipped to produce that sort of person, and this means that the best among the people who enter must for four years wander aimlessly much of the time questioning why they are on cam-pus at all, doubting whether there is any point in what they are doing, and looking toward a very bleak existence afterward in a game in which all of the rules have been made up, which one cannot really amend.

It is a bleak scene, but it is all a lot of us have to look forward to. Society provides no challenge. American society in the standard concep-tion it has of itself is simply no longer exciting. The most exciting things going on in America today are movements to change America. America is becoming ever more the Utopia of sterilized, automated contentment. The "futures" and "careers" for which American students now prepare are for the most part intellectual and moral wastelands. This chrome-plated consumers' paradise would have us grow up to be well-behaved children. But an important minority of men and women coming to the front today have shown that they will die rather than be standardized, replaceable and irrelevant.

Lee Pennington

INTRODUCTION TO *TOMORROW'S PEOPLE*

The poet walks in the sun and the rain, the snow and the wind, and there is in his hands a soul pleading to know the earth.

His hands are anxious, come spring, to touch the early dogwood blooms, to know a death on death when winter falters, and to know a life reaching toward the sky and roots reaching earthward.

The poet walks in moonlight where shadows speak out like all those yesterdays of the forgotten earth.

His ears hear the songs of roaring mountains and dying rivers and lonely men crying in the streets and children screaming in the night and dogs howling on rat-infested trash heaps and a baby's sigh.

The poet walks in darkness with laughter on his face and tears in his eyes.

His eyes search the black world like a blind man picking roses, like a thin ray of light peeking through a crack in the attic and gathering all the dust particles only the sun can know.

The poet walks in time with the constant clicking of clocks, of beating hearts, of swirling planets, of calender pages being ripped off and fed to the wind.

He can smell spring coming and winter going and the restless summer days of sweaty July leaves begging dew and the yellow pollen assuring life to the weeds.

The poet walks in life but knows the tombstones on the briar loved hills.

He knows the hungry children crying and the old women laughing, the noisy guns singing in the dark woods and the warm silence of longing eyes, the falling rains and the hot suns, the flowers blooming in the kingdom of the dead, the brown weeping goldenrod stems in the December fields. He knows some young boy sitting alone in the alley and the crowded streets and the dirty rivers washing their way back to clean rain.

The poet walks in youth and sings to the earth, the wind and the rain.

INTRODUCTION by Lee Pennington from *Tomorrow's People*, April 1967, reprinted by permission.

He sings to the high mountains where the wounds now stand out in pain. He sings to the hissing grass and the lonely streets in the moonlight. He sings to the windows with broken glass and to the rusty rails and rotting crossties.

The poet walks in Harlan County like the last hope whispering to the darkness, like the last love wishing the sun.

Tomorrow's People is a record of his walking.

K. D. Petrey

OF THIS TOWN

Ripped like paper by railroad cars.
Half of the lights make it glow like death—
while unwed mothers are its pride.

Water is staggered by chemicals and waste.
Church members support the whiskey stores—
while garbage men knife the dogs.

Moonshine rolls from the blood-stained hills.
Drunken officers delight in finding parked kids—
while the county sheriff has a son by a local woman.

Mayor's son works on the poverty program;
Children starve with rocks between their teeth—
while beggars eat dust from the rooftops.

Parents fight for their sons' victory, but only in a dream.
Rich men walk on the hands of children—
while the swimming pool is filled with mating frogs.

Side walks are kept clean by local drunks.
Jail is broken by a ten-year-old kid—
while people cheat the shoeshine boy.

"Of This Town" by H. D. Petrey
"Omnipotent Boob" by Angie M. Skidmore
"Fool's Intersanctum" by Angie M. Skidmore
"Back To Earth Today" by Carson Hansel
"By Love Possessed" and *"Dreamer"* by James D. Asher
"Hay Barn," "Owned Desire," "To a Poet With a Crooked Stem Pipe" all by James Goode
The above nine poems are from *Tomorrow's People,* April 1967, reprinted by permission.

Prices are high; the food is cheap,
Money in the pockets of few—
while men are left dead on garbage piles.

Dog flesh is used in hamburger meat.
People steal the paper from the press—
while a woman tells their future.

Of This Town:
               Bones and dust will be the victors.

Angie Skidmore

OMNIPOTENT BOOB

God, if you're there
   You're a fool,
God, if you've been there
   Shouldn't you be senile by now?
God, if you're omnipotent
   Why don't you help?
God, if you're omniscient
   Why don't you know?
God.............Damn it!

FOOL'S INTERSANCTUM

Cracked pulpits, bleeding fists, and
   Crumbling plaster,
Ecstatic shouts of fantasy that fall on
   Already numbed ears,
Obese Deacons with sticky fingers
   Greedily grasping wooden plates,
Silent meditation that evokes knowing
   Whispers of night's experiences,
Promises made to the apathetic followers
   Of the non-existent,
The exodus bells that release the long
   Suppressed yawns!

Carson Hansel

BACK TO EARTH TODAY

Jesus came back to earth today
to destroy it and all of its corruption.
Jesus came back to earth today
to become king of man.
He started his slaughter
but met one he could not kill.
He fell in love with Brigitte Bardot.
God came back to earth today
to talk to his son.

James D. Asher

BY LOVE POSSESSED

No one worth possessing
Can ever be possessed.
Lay that on your heart
My young angry dear
This truth,
     This hard and precious stone.
Lay this on your hot cheek
Let it hide your tears.
Hold it like a crystal
When you are alone, and
Gaze into the depths of this icy stone
Lona,
     Look long, and you will be blessed.
No one worth possessing
Can ever be possessed.

DREAMER

Dreams are fragile lovely things—
Mental butterflies:
Wear no mourning, shield of tears
When a dream child dies.
It was not reality;
Dreams do not abide.
They are daisy chains of thought
To wear—and toss aside.

Never let them rule your heart
Nor leave it to vain sorrow;
Throw a kiss to parting dreams
And dream again tomorrow.

James Goode

HAY BARN

The secrets lost in Grandpa's barn
I always wanted to find;
they ran and hid behind shadows
and laughed from high above.

Cows, restless in their stalls,
heard our running feet
on boards of floor above,
our screams of glee slipped through.

Mice lived in our corn,
always lost their home
when we picked up cobs
to throw at coming foe.

Beneath the smell of hay,
a castle all my own,
to rule the grass stems,
until darkness called me home.

OWNED DESIRE

Flesh, hot white flesh of desire
seizes my wanting body,
and bends my aching limbs,
then disappears in air
of density from my sweat.

Heart beats like hammer on steel,
never ending rings of metallic sound
are caught by walls and pitched about.
I listen as I hear them travel,
the hall and down the stairs.

Senses tell me that I can,
but reason tells me I must not,

because society knows what's right.
I am their doll to be played with,
hair to be pulled and combed.

TO A POET WITH A CROOKED STEM PIPE

Hands push words across
the lines and off the page
that has no room for
all he puts there.

Understanding drips from eyes
upon my head to puddle
in a book he writes,
a book with arms and legs of him.

Words about the earth,
all that's on the living stage
sleeps on paper watched
by all eyes of window light.

His page I read tonight,
a panorama from a star,
where secrets unfold
and shine down from the moon.

The Mountain Eagle

POEMS STIR DISPUTE

A University of Kentucky teacher at Southeast Community College is in hot water because of a book of poems.

Lee Pennington, 28, who has been teaching at Cumberland for two years, considers the crisis serious enough to have thought about moving out of Harlan County until tempers cool.

Pennington teaches creative writing at Cumberland. This year, thirteen of his students published a book of poems, titled *Tomorrow's People* and dedicated to Harlan County. The book was published April 17. Since then, Pennington and his poets have been in deep trouble with the people to whom they dedicated the book.

From *The Mountain Eagle*, May 4, 1967, Vol. 59, no. 51.

Three poems have especially come in for attack. One, by sopho-more K. D. Petrey, refers to a sheriff of an unnamed county. A poem by sophomore Angie Skidmore calls God an "omnipotent boob." Another by freshman Carson Hansel contains a line about Christ returning to earth only to fall in love with Brigitte Bardot.

A number of Harlan County residents have risen up in anger against the poems.

Some ministers have preached sermons against Pennington's stu-dents, one of whom claims that his minister told him to go find another church. The Harlan County Sheriff, Jason Howard, telephoned Pen-nington demanding an explanation of Petrey's poem. Pennington ex-plained that the poem was literary and not political, but he feels that the Sheriff was unsatisfied by the explanation. According to Penning-ton, Howard told him, "You either clear this up or I'll be to see you."

In the past few days, Pennington's students have told him of overhearing a number of people talking about doing violence to him. Several students have reported receiving threatening phone calls. Pen-nington is convinced that his phone is being tapped and that his home is being watched. He has begun to think seriously about whether he and his wife should move away until the political climate of Harlan County quiets down.

The problem has become complicated by Pennington's belief that Cumberland director James Falkenstine wants him to resign. According to Pennington, Falkenstine told him early this week, "We have a real problem here, and I think it would be best for you to leave."

Falkenstine would not comment on the problem to *The Mountain Eagle*. He did admit that "there's certainly pressure on the college from the community when a book like that comes out with the college's name on it." He demanded to know how the newspaper had learned of the furor created by the poems and said the paper had no right to ask questions concerning the matter or to print anything concerning it.

Falkenstine would not identify the source of the pressure of which he spoke.

In Lexington, Dr. Ellis Hartford, dean of the UK Community Colleges, did discuss the situation and commented that "the matter of teacher tenure is not something for the general public to decide upon."

"As far as I am personally concerned," Hartford said, "it's not for any outside group to tell us how to deal with our faculty. And I don't feel that anyone should question whether students have a right to raise questions about the world they live in. They have a sacred privilege, a right, and a responsibility to raise questions."

Despite pressure from parents and friends, most of Pennington's students are sticking by him. "He's a fine teacher," said one sophomore —who asked not to be identified. "He doesn't push us into attitudes. But he opens our eyes. He encourages freedom."

Carson Hansel, whose poem about Christ and Brigitte Bardot has been offensive to many Harlan Countians, says of the whole crisis: "I enjoy it. I hope it will wake Harlan County up a little bit."

But Pennington feels that the controversy will make it difficult for him to continue teaching at Cumberland.

"I think the academic climate here has been very difficult," he says, "because people are too ready to yell 'trash' without judging things on their merits."

He is pessimistic about his future at the college. "I think some people will always feel that I have motives other than the teaching of creative writing. If I feel I can't operate here to the best of my ability—I might not be able to stay on."

Cumberland's school year ends this week, so for the immediate future Pennington only has to worry about getting through the next few days. After that, he will have the summer to contemplate the political and literary climate at Cumberland. At the very least, he has a local best seller on his hands; *Tomorrow's People* sold out of its first edition—500 copies—in five days.

Kyle Vance

STUDENTS' POEMS WHIP UP FUROR AT CUMBERLAND

A book of freewheeling poems by a college poetry writing class has stirred tumult, anger and even terror in the coal mining communities of Harlan County.

An instructor and two of his student poets, reportedly frightened by implied threats from outraged citizens, have moved to other regions.

Administrators of Southeast Community College, a branch of the University of Kentucky, are trying to pacify seething clergymen and parents and prevent a mass withdrawal of students.

The book, called *Tomorrow's People* and published from the writings of a poetry class at the college, deals freely with ignorance, poverty, decay, pollution, sickness and scum in coal camps and towns.

Sin, sex, love, blood and death inspire descriptives in the poems, written mostly in non-rhyming, free verse.

Taking a critical look at their own environs, the young poets also swipe poetically at cripples, half-breeds, unwed mothers, beggars, drunkards and harlots.

Other targets are rotting tipples, strip-mined mountains and the war in Vietnam.

The furor came soon after the book was published and circulated in mid-April. Lee Pennington, professor of English and conductor of the poetry-writing class, said the first in a series of telephone calls at his

Reprinted from *Courier-Journal*, May 13, 1967, by permission.

home came from a man who identified himself as Harlan County Sheriff Jason Howard.

Pennington said the caller was angered by K. D. Petrey's poem, "Of This Town," especially one verse reading:

"Moonshine rolls from the bloodstained hills; Drunken officers delight in finding parked kids; while the county sheriff has a son by a local woman."

Pennington said he tried to reason with his caller that the poem was fiction, dealing with no specific sheriff or town. The man nevertheless admonished him, he said, to "clear it up or I'll be out to see you."

Sheriff Howard has denied talking with Pennington. He said it was true, however, that he was disturbed by the poem's implications. "So are some former sheriffs and their families," he said.

A series of calls followed the one from the man who identified himself as the sheriff, Pennington said.

"There was no voice when we answered these calls, just hard breathing on the other end of the line," he said.

Pennington said he and his wife returned from the college one day and discovered a man running from their lawn with a roll of insulated wire. He said he searched for dynamite before entering the home.

On another occasion, he continued, a visitor in his home spotted from a window two men on the lawn pointing at the house. He and Mrs. Pennington were at school, he said, but the visitor "went out with a shotgun and the men got away from there as fast as they could."

Pennington said he decided to leave Cumberland after a student told him a man—"he identified the man"—was going to kill him. He said shortly afterward, a driver tried to force young Petrey off the highway when Petrey was driving from Cumberland to Harlan.

Now driving from place to place visiting friends, Pennington was reached in Bowling Green. He said Petrey and another student, Carson Hansel, left when he did. Petrey is from Cumberland and Hansel from nearby Lynch.

Petrey, now in Lexington, agreed with Pennington's story. He said a man who identified himself as the sheriff first called him, talking "menacingly" and enquiring about Pennington. He said Hansel and others were present when Pennington received his call from the man who said he was Howard.

At the college, Dr. J. C. Falkenstein, the director, said that however distasteful the book might be, it was published in the spirit of university policy giving complete freedom of expression to students and faculty.

He said that while such academic freedom is a privilege, his own feeling is that it shouldn't be abused. Also, he said, the school feels it should not be judged too severely for the work of 14 students out of a total of 400.

The Rev. Edward E. Gorsuch, pastor of Cumberland Baptist Church, said the publication created a regrettable situation which is being smoothed over. He commented that notwithstanding the poor taste of some of the material, "It was mild by comparison with some I have seen at larger universities."

Ministers and religion were targets for ridicule in some of the poems, as, for example: "He stood behind the wooden box; Hatred flowing from his dry tongue. . . ."

One poem imagined a love affair between Jesus and Brigitte Bardot. Another, taking God to task, is entitled "Omnipotent Boob."

Student reaction to the book was mixed. The students, including some of the contributing poets, said some of the poems should have been rejected before publication.

Linda Vicini, assistant editor of the book, said she regretted that her poems were published under the same cover as some of the others. At the same time, she said, Pennington is bearing too much of the blame.

"I believe he (Pennington) was disturbed about the book, too," she said. "He just didn't try to tell them (students) what to say. He read his own poetry in class and nothing sacrilegious was ever in any of them."

Mrs. Lillian Simpson, a student and member of the editorial board, described Pennington as "a gentleman through and through."

"I have never heard him mention God, pro or con," she said. "I have never heard him say anything bad about anybody. Still, while I do not hold Mr. Pennington responsible for the type of poetry the students wrote, I do hold him responsible for what went into the book."

Jesse Stuart, prize-winning poet and author from Pennington's hometown of Greenup, said he has reviewed *Tomorrow's People* and found it to be "maybe not good poetry, but mighty powerful writing."

Pennington defends the works of his students with zeal.

"This is creative work, done by kids given complete freedom of expression for the first time," he said.

"It is based on real, raw experience. These kids have already lived through what most of us only read about.

"There is a great potential for writing in Appalachia, especially in Harlan County. All these kids need is the opportunity to express themselves. Appalachia will never get off of its back-end until the youth brings in new ideas.

"I hate to see the program fall down."

H. Lynn Sheller

WHAT THE STUDENTS ARE SAYING TO US

During the last several years we have been reading of student demonstrations on college and university campuses throughout the United States. The public has been alarmed by these demonstrations; college faculties have been disturbed; and students have been avidly interested

Address to the faculty of the North Orange County Junior College District, Fullerton, California, on September 8, 1966.

if not militantly responsive. The sympathetic student response to these demonstrations indicates that the demonstrators are expressing feelings that are common among college students everywhere. In these demonstrations the students have been, and are, saying things to their institutions and to us as faculty members. What are they saying?

As I tell you what the students are saying to us, please remember that I do not pretend that I am speaking for *all* students; that I do not mean to suggest that they are speaking to *all* of us; and that I do not mean to say that *all* they say is right. However, I do mean to say that a significant number are speaking; that those who are speaking are strongly supported by a much larger group who are not speaking; that the articulate ones are speaking to a significant number of teachers and administrators; and that there is enough truth and sincerity in what they say to warrant serious consideration.

Before telling you what the students are saying, I ought to tell you something about the students themselves, that is, about the militant leaders. If the facts concerning the students who participated in the demonstrations at the University of California at Berkeley in 1964 and 1965 are applicable elsewhere in the United States—and I think they are—we may say that the militants constitute at most about four percent of any student body. I arrived at this estimate from the fact that about 1,000 of Berkeley's 26,000 students participated in the 1964 sit-in at Sproul Hall. Though this percentage may seem small, we should note that, according to a survey of Berkeley students in April, 1965, over four-fifths of the students agreed with the goals of the Free Speech Movement and that three-fourths of them believed the leaders of the movement to be idealistic and motivated by moral values. We should note further that the University of California purports to draw its students from the upper eighth of California's high school graduates and that nearly half of the students included in the four percent that I mentioned had grade-point averages of 3.0 or better, while only 21 percent of the total student body had averages that high.

Some of the ideas and attitudes commonly found among the leaders of these students should be mentioned briefly. First they reject much of contemporary America. In general they reject big business, which they call "economic imperialism." They reject our increasingly bureaucratic, machine-like society, which they think is resulting from technology and cybernation and which they think is leading to technological slavery for all of us. They reject the Christian church and other institutions of our society, including institutions of higher education. They reject the colleges and universities as part of "the system," and one of their spokesmen has designated the big universities as a public utility, run by big business to produce workers for big business. They are contemptuous of patriotism; they denounce the bomb, and they denounce the use of force in settling international disputes. Generally they reject conventional values and have a tolerant attitude toward obscenity in speech, books, or films; toward free sex relations, and toward the use of alcohol, narcotics, and the hallucinatory drugs. They reject work and thrift as virtues. One student said, "Abstract values are entirely dead for my generation, though they had a meaning for my father and grandfather." They object to conformity and "role playing." They are impatient and suspicious of the older generation, expressing these feelings in the often-heard statement, Trust no one over thirty.

They feel that those over thirty are too willing to tolerate the evils of our society and the world. The militant student leaders tend to be contemptuous of gradualism and of compromise in negotiations. They are strongly for social and economic justice and for individual freedom, but they are skeptical of the belief that wrongs can eventually be adjusted within the democratic process. Often they seem to be nihilistic and anarchistic. They are generally cynical and existentialist in their outlook, considering life to be empty and devoid of meaning. Some of their favorite words and phrases are hypocrisy; middle class (a term of disdain); style; bureaucracy; the system, the establishment, or the power structure (referring to society, government, and institutions in general); exploitation; confrontation; eyeball-to-eyeball confrontation; dialogue; activist; and existential. One writer on "The New Radical Spirit" said this: "Most Free Speech Movement leaders make no attempt to disguise their deep alienation from American society, but they regard allegiance to any specific alternative as utopian, divisive, immobilizing, and—perhaps most significant—not their 'style.'" [1]

May I here reemphasize that I do not apply the description that I have just given you to all the militant students of revolt. I do not believe in such blanket inclusions. I only say that the ideas and attitudes that I have given you are commonly found among these leaders and that they are the ideas and attitudes of "the new radical spirit."

Now, what are these students saying to us—these students whose goals at Berkeley were supported by four-fifths of the student body, these students who find a large measure of support on our own campus, if I read rightly the thirty pages of single-spaced, open-ended comments copied verbatim from the 450 follow-up questionnaires returned by our own graduates of 1965?

The students are saying this: We want the same rights of free press, free speech, and free action on campus as other citizens have off campus. We want the right to publish what we please in the college newspaper or literary magazine without hindrance or the possibility of veto by a faculty adviser. We want the right of unrestricted free speech, not only for ourselves but for any off-campus persons whom we may choose to invite to the campus or who may come without invitation. This includes freedom not only to question, explain, argue, defend, advocate, and persuade, but also to recruit members for the Communist Party, the Birch Society, the Ku Klux Klan, or the American Nazi Party. We want the right to participate in political activities at the national, state, or local levels; to solicit funds for political or social purposes; and to organize marches, strikes, sit-ins, sit-downs, campaigns, or demon-

---

[1] Miller, Michael V., and Gilmore, Susan (eds.), *Revolution at Berkeley* (The Dial Press, N. Y., 1965), p. 274.

strations, legal or illegal, the legality to be judged not by college officials, but by the courts at law. The only restriction that students would recognize would be that their campus activities not interfere with the normal activities of the institution.

The students are saying this: We want an end to *in loco parentis; i.e.,* to our supervision by the college or university in the place of a parent. Our activities outside the classroom are our own business. If we are attending a residential college or university, we, as men and women, want freedom to visit each other as we please in our dormitory rooms. We want no restrictions on hours. We want no prohibitions on alcohol, narcotics, or hallucinatory drugs. We want no college or university discipline for what we may do off campus. We want to be the same free agents as students as are persons over twenty-one who have left home and are wholly on their own. Our lives are our own, and we want no parental supervision or regulation by the college.

The students are saying this: We want genuine student government without restrictions, not "sand box" student government. We want to operate our own bookstore and cafeteria, and we want to control our own funds without the aid or interference of faculty advisers or administrators.

They are saying this: We want the elimination of bureaucracy—bureaucracy with all its red tape, canned greetings, depersonalization, unresponsiveness to individual needs, and lack of imagination. We despise the bureaucratic functionaries who don't know, who don't care, who send us from place to place, who operate by, and hide behind rules. We want to deal with clerks who are human, who are efficient, who are genuinely interested in serving us, who have some resourcefulness in helping us solve our problems, and who are willing and able to make or obtain exceptions where exceptions are warranted.

The students are saying this: We want administrators in the college who are "interested in what people are complaining about," not just interested in "how to keep them from complaining." We want administrators who are willing to listen to us and talk honestly with us and who will do what they can to correct faults. We don't want foot-dragging. We don't want double talk. We don't want one set of answers today and another tomorrow or one set of answers for us and another for the newspapers. We don't want broken promises. We want to be dealt with openly, frankly, and fairly as equal human beings.

The students are saying this: We want teachers, librarians, and counselors who are interested in us as individuals and who do not regard the college as a "knowledge factory" that exists so that they may have jobs. We want counselors who know their business, who are available to us, and who are concerned. We want librarians who are approachable, interested in us, and glad to help. We want teachers to regard us, to listen to us, to talk with us, to teach us as persons of equal worth and dignity with themselves. We want teachers who understand our loneliness, our conflicts, frustrations, defeats, rejections, doubts, questioning, fears, hopes, and yearnings; teachers who can help us to experience a sense of personal worth and who can help us to find purpose and meaning in life. We want teachers who know their fields and are prepared when they come to class, teachers who will challenge us in our studies, not by making them more difficult, but by making them more relevant and meaningful. We want teachers who are reasonably demanding but who at the same time are understanding and sympathetic without being condescending. We want teachers who invite us with genuine sincerity to confer with them and who even seek us out when we need assistance but are too timid to ask for it.

Finally the students are saying this to us: We want a voice in curriculum and instruction. We want a voice in determining course offerings, course content, course standards, and course requirements for majors. We feel that many courses are trivial, outmoded, or irrelevant; that certain important fields are not included in the curriculum; and that standards are often unrealistic. Moreover we feel that we should have a voice in evaluating the quality of instruction in our classes. We would, bluntly, like to evaluate our teachers.

These are the things that students all over the United States are saying with varying degrees of insistence to the faculties and classified personnel of their institutions, and they are the things that some of our students are saying in this College.

What is to be our response as teachers and administrators to these insistent demands of our students?

First, we need to be up-to-date, well prepared, relevant, and strong in our teaching. We need to be teaching the facts, theories, and skills of our various courses with economy, clarity, and humanity.

Second, we must continue to resist the depersonalization that results from numbers. We need to treat our students, the public, and each other with genuine respect for ideas and personality. We need to be warm, approachable, interested, genuinely concerned, human, and honest in all our interpersonal relations.

Third, we need to break down, or keep down, the barriers that inhibit communication between students and teachers. Communication can be encouraged on our part by familiarizing ourselves with the ideas and problems of youth in revolt so that we can understand our students and talk with them helpfully. It can be encouraged further by an attitude of openness and receptivity to ideas different from our own. We must be willing to consider student suggestions honestly and to adopt them if they seem better than our own. I do not mean that we should allow ourselves to be pushed into accepting ideas or policies that do not merit acceptance. Beyond a willingness to accept innovations we should be minded to innovate on our own initiative, thinking ahead of the students, noting the needs of the times, and proposing measures to meet those needs before they ever become serious issues in the minds of the students. Inclusion of students on curriculum, instruction, and student personnel committees, on administrative initiative, is one of several important steps that can be made in this direction.

Finally we need to encourage college-wide forums on all the issues of the day that students wish to discuss. These open, inter-divisional discussions should be planned jointly by students and faculty. Two years ago I proposed a series of such forums and the results were gratifying. Large groups of interested students turned out to discuss Red China, Vietnam, moral values, Is God Dead? and other subjects. They want to know what you and I think as well as to express their own thoughts. We are not doing our full job as a college if we do not discuss with our students the great questions that concern them.

These responses on the part of teachers and administrators will go far toward establishing understanding, trust, and cooperation between students and faculty and thus toward establishing a climate favorable to the intellectual development of students.

CONFORMITY

Wilbert James McKeachie and Charlotte Lackner Doyle

WHAT FACTORS CONTRIBUTE TO COMPLIANCE?

CONFORMITY: COMPLIANCE TO A MAJORITY

When a person changes his behavior in order to comply with the norms of a group, we say he is *conforming* to the group. Since Asch's pioneering study, a number of experiments have been carried out which permit us to see which variables influence conformity. We can classify the variables into four groups: (1) the nature of the group; (2) the nature of the stimuli presented; (3) the consequences of conformity; and (4) individual differences in the crucial subject.

THE NATURE OF THE GROUP

As you might expect, the size and the unanimity of the prearranged "peer" group affect the amount of conformity. In a two-person group, the subject's opinion may have little effect; a group of three produces more conformity, and groups of four and five produce as much conformity as groups that are considerably larger.

In the original experiment, the crucial subject was faced with unanimous consensus. What would happen if the majority of group members made incorrect judgments but if one person other than the crucial subject gave the correct answer? Asch (1951) tried such a condition and found that the amount of conformity dropped sharply. Now only 5.5 percent of the subject's opinions were incorrect. With one other person to support his judgments, the critical subject was able to oppose the opinions expressed by the majority of the group.

THE NATURE OF THE STIMULI

Using an experimental situation similar to Asch's, Crutchfield (1955) found that group unanimity produced conformity to a number of different kinds of items: perceptual judgments, agreement with factual statements, attitudes on issues, and personal evaluations of self. This last type of item is particularly interesting since presumably each group member is evaluating only himself. When subjects were asked individu-

Reprinted by permission from W. J. McKeachie and C. L. Doyle, *Psychology*, 1966, Addison-Wesley, Reading, Mass.

Tables from Milgram, S. "Behavioral study of obedience," *Journal of Abnormal and Social Psychology*, 67, 4, 371–378 (1963). Reprinted by permission of the author and the American Psychological Association.

ally to agree or disagree with the statement "I doubt whether I would make a good leader," not one subject agreed. In the experimental group situation in which a prearranged number of the group agreed with the statement, so also did 37 percent of the subjects.

In our analysis of perception, we saw that the degree to which factors other than stimulus factors determine perception depends in part on the ambiguity of the stimuli. Thus we might expect that ambiguous stimuli would result in more conformity than unambiguous ones. Crutchfield (1955) found that there was considerable conformity with both kinds of material, but that ambiguous stimuli accentuated the conformity effect.

THE CONSEQUENCES OF CONFORMITY

We can look at conformity as a learned general habit in which a person learns to model his behavior on that of other group members. This implies that a person learns to conform or not to conform in a situation depending on the rewards and punishment in the situation. In most of the conformity studies, the subject hears the opinions of his peers and states his own opinion, but there is no further feedback. It has been suggested that an implicit motive in such a situation is desire for group approval, which tends to produce conformity. This interpretation is supported by a study reported by Walker and Heyns (1962). In this study, conformity increased when the subjects were told that people tend to like one another more when they are in agreement about common problems.

There is evidence that informational as well as affective feedback influences conformity behavior.

Crutchfield (1955) investigated the effects of this variable. He used two conditions: one in which on each trial the experimenter confirmed the judgments of the group, and one in which the experimenter confirmed the judgments of the individual. Confirmation of the group opinion increased the percentage of conforming judgments by the subjects from 45 percent to 70 percent. Confirmation of the individual subject's lone opinion greatly increased resistance to conformity.

If conformity varies as a function of the amount of reinforcement for such behavior, we might expect to find cross-cultural differences. Milgram (1961) found that Norwegians showed significantly more conformity than Frenchmen in the Asch-type of experiment. These results, Milgram felt, seemed to be in accordance with the cultural tradition of the two countries: The people of Norway are highly cohesive, with a strong sense of social responsibility and a heritage of political stability. The people of France on the other hand have a tradition of dissent. It may be that these traditions are continued in each culture through a pattern of reinforcements for conformity and/or dissent.

INDIVIDUAL DIFFERENCES

The habit of conformity is not all-pervasive in the sense that one person conforms either in every situation or in no situation. The behavior depends, as we have seen, on a number of conditions. Nevertheless, we can look at the differences, in a given situation, between those who conform and those who do not, and ask the question "Is the tendency toward greater conformity coupled with other tendencies which form more general traits?" Personality inventories suggest that subjects who tend to conform are less intelligent, more anxious, more prone to feelings of inferiority, less realistic in self-perception and more dependent than independent subjects. Furthermore, the high conformity subjects also tend to be high in authoritarianism. (The correlation between conformity score and *F*-scale score is 0.48.) If skilled observers are asked to rate subjects on various personality traits, they tend to rate the independent subjects as more original, more self-reliant, more emotionally expressive, and insightful. (Crutchfield, 1955)

OBEDIENCE: COMPLIANCE TO LEGITIMATE AUTHORITY

In the conformity experiments, an individual is faced with the presence of a number of people who disagree with his private judgments. In our society, there are many situations in which we feel social pressure, even though it is transmitted to us by a single person. For example, the laws enacted by our representatives may be enforced by a single police officer. As part of the process of socialization, we learn to obey our parents, our teachers, our judges, our policemen, and other agents of society who appear to have legitimate authority.

To what extent will people obey the commands of a person in authority when the behavior demanded is contrary to the beliefs, motives, and habits of the individual? Milgram (1963) sought an answer to this very serious question with the following study:

As each subject came into the experiment, an experimenter asked him to serve as a "teacher" for a study on the effects of punishment on learning. The job of this "teacher"-subject was to give electrical shocks to another subject in another room, increasing the shock level with each error. The victim was in reality a collaborator of the experimenter, and no shocks were actually administered. The shock apparatus looked authentic however; voltage levels were clearly marked and verbal descriptions ranging from "Slight Shock," to "Danger: Severe Shock," to "XXX," appeared below the numerical designations. As the number of "errors" made by the person in the next room increased, the subject serving as "teacher" increased the shock level. If he hesitated in administering the required shock, the experimenter who was sitting behind the "teacher" asked him to go on. As the shock level got higher and higher the "teacher"-subject began to hear more and more protest from the "victim" in the adjoining room. But still the order to give more shock was repeated. What did the "teacher"-subject do? How high a shock level would he be willing to administer on the orders of an authority?

The results appear in Fig. 1. As you can see, 26 our of 40 subjects were totally obedient; that is, they administered every shock they were ordered to administer. Only 14 of the subjects were defiant at some point in the experiment and refused to give further shocks. But you should not conclude from this experiment that the obedient subjects were aggressive, sadistic people. They showed great hesitancy in administering the high shock levels. As the shock got stronger and stronger, they showed signs of extreme tension and emotional strain: sweating, trembling, groaning, lip-biting, stuttering. Many subjects had fits of nervous smiling and bizarre laughter. One observer gave this report of a subject's behavior:

> *"I observed a mature and initially poised businessman enter the laboratory, smiling and confident. Within 20 minutes he was reduced to a twitching, stuttering wreck, who was rapidly approaching a point of nervous collapse. He constantly pulled on his ear lobe, and twisted his hands. At one point, he pushed his fist into his forehead and muttered: 'Oh, God, let's stop it.' And yet he continued to respond to every word of the experimenter and obeyed to the end."* [1]

In a control study, subjects were permitted to select whatever shock levels they desired to "punish" the errors. In this case almost all subjects selected shock levels in the mild ranges. Thus motives for aggressive behavior cannot account for the results. In another study, the orders for shock levels were delivered by telephone. Under these conditions subjects agreed to follow the orders, but did not actually deliver shocks as intense as the orders demanded. In still another variation, the subjects believed that the man giving the orders was not a scientist, but another subject who happened to "take over" when the experimenter was called away. In this case most of the subjects were defiant. In fact, when the "subject" giving the orders responded to the defiance by saying he would deliver the shock himself, the subjects sometimes physically prevented him from doing so. A subject who happens to give orders is not a sufficient authority.

All these results suggest that the obedient subjects were faced with extreme conflict. Their behavior was contrary to what they would ordinarily do. But the habits and motives for obedience to legitimate authority were so strong that they overrode other attitudes.

Experiments in the proximity of the victim illustrated the extremes to which a few subjects would go to obey orders. Milgram hypothesized that the more the subject was aware of the presence of his victim, the less willing he would be to administer severe shocks. Therefore Milgram

---

[1] From Milgram, S., "Behavioral study of obedience," *J. abnorm. soc. Psychol.*, 67, 4, 371–378 (1963). Reprinted by permission.

DISTRIBUTION OF BREAKOFF POINT

NUMBER OF SUBJECTS FOR WHOM THIS WAS MAXIMUM SHOCK	VERBAL DESIGNATION AND VOLTAGE INDICATION
Slight shock	
15	0
30	0
45	0
60	0
Moderate shock	
75	0
90	0
105	0
120	0
Strong shock	
135	0
150	0
165	0
180	0
Very strong shock	
195	0
210	0
225	0
240	0
Intense shock	
255	0
270	0
285	0
300	5
Extreme intensity shock	
315	4
330	2
345	1
360	1
Danger: Severe shock	
375	1
390	0
405	0
420	0
XXX	
435	0
450	26

FIG. 1. The numbers of people who refused to continue after each shock level in Milgram's study. Twenty-six subjects were obedient throughout the experiment. (From Milgram, 1963)

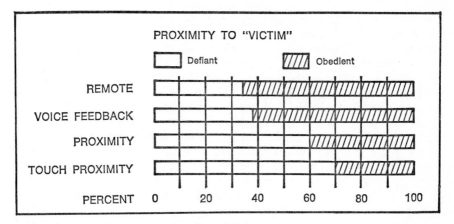

FIG. 2. The effect of proximity on the percentage of subjects who were defiant at any point in the experiment. (After Milgram, 1965)

used four conditions: (1) remote feedback in which the subject heard his victim pounding on the wall at some shock levels up to 300 volts and thereafter heard nothing; (2) voice feedback in which the subject heard protests, moaning, and finally cries that the victim could not stand the pain; (3) proximity, in which the victim was seated a foot-and-a-half from the subject and reacted in the same way as in the voice feedback condition; and (4) touch-proximity, which involved the same conditions as proximity except that the victim received the shock only if he touched a shockplate. At the 150-volt level, the victim refused to put his hand on the plate and the experimenter commanded the subject to physically hold the victim's hand on the shockplate. (Insulation was provided so that the subject would not feel the shock.) The results supported Milgram's prediction. The more aware the subject was of his victim's presence, the lower the mean maximum shock level, and the more subjects defied the experimenter (see Fig. 2). But even with the subjects only a foot-and-a-half from the victim, hearing him cry out that he could not stand the pain, 30 percent of the subjects held their victim's hand on the shockplate to receive a shock level marked "Danger: Severe Shock"!

A FINAL COMMENT

We have seen that the social environment has tremendous effects on the thinking and behavior of individuals. This is not surprising when we realize how strongly and consistently habits such as conformity and obedience are rewarded. As we have grown up, we have learned to depend on the people around us to confirm our judgments, to suggest opinions, to provide models for our actions. If a person did not learn this, he would be unable to become a civilized member of society.

Compliance and attitude change are, on many occasions, necessary and appropriate. If individuals did not comply with traffic laws, the results would be chaotic and dangerous. If people did not change their attitudes when confronted with new information, then their rigidity could preclude the possibility of progress.

We saw earlier that habits that are strongly rewarded may themselves become motives. The research on obedience and conformity suggests that these habits become powerful motives indeed. But both habits and motives are aroused by situations. In the studies we described, some people discriminated one situation from another, obeying, complying, and agreeing in some cases and not doing so in others. But many people generalized obedience and conformity to such an extent that they failed to act on their own thinking. Herein lies a very serious problem: To distinguish between situations in which compliance is appropriate and those in which it is not.

Recent history has a striking example to remind us of the importance of the resolution of this problem. In Germany from 1933 to 1945, millions of people died partly because of blind obedience to Nazi authority. Milgram's studies were originally undertaken in an attempt to understand the behavior of the German people before and during World War II. Milgram's research suggests that the German people were not unique in their willingness to harm others on command.

Is it inevitable, then, that people become creatures determined by their social environments? The answer to this question has to be "No!" In the experiments in obedience and conformity, some individuals remained independent. However, this independence was possible only if the individual trusted his own ability to perceive, to interpret, and to evaluate independently of his peers and his superiors.

In discussing the person in society, we should never lose sight of the fact that society is not an impersonal abstraction, but a living, changing entity, itself made up of individuals. In a democratic society, each individual must share in deciding the direction in which the society shall move. It is extremely important that each person add his independent evaluation of issues and actions, if the society is to be truly democratic. He must decide when to conform and when to defy, when to agree and when to dissent, when to trust and when to be skeptical. In order to make appropriate decisions, he needs access to objective, accurate information.

We hope that an understanding of psychological processes can make a contribution.

William Cowper

VARIETY'S THE VERY SPICE OF LIFE

> Variety's the very spice of life,
> That gives it all its flavour. We have run
> Through ev'ry change, that Fancy at the loom

Exhausted, has had genius to supply;
And studious of mutation still, discard
A real elegance, a little us'd,
For monstrous novelty and strange disguise
We sacrifice to dress, till household joys
And comforts cease.

John Dos Passos

PROTEUS

Steinmetz was a hunchback,
son of a hunchback lithographer.

He was born in Breslau in eighteen sixtyfive, graduated with highest honors at seventeen from the Breslau Gymnasium,[1] went to the University of Breslau to study mathematics;

mathematics to Steinmetz was muscular strength and long walks over the hills and the kiss of a girl in love and big evenings spent swilling beer with your friends;

on his broken back he felt the topheavy weight of society the way workingmen felt it on their straight backs, the way poor students felt it, was a member of a socialist club, editor of a paper called *The People's Voice.*

Bismarck[2] was sitting in Berlin like a big paperweight to keep the new Germany feudal, to hold down the empire for his bosses the Hohenzollerns.

Steinmetz had to run off to Zurich for fear of going to jail; at Zurich his mathematics woke up all the professors at the Polytechnic;

but Europe in the eighties was no place for a penniless German student with a broken back and a big head filled with symbolic calculus and wonder about electricity that is mathematics made power

and a socialist at that.

With a Danish friend he sailed for America steerage on an old French line boat *La Champagne,*

lived in Brooklyn at first and commuted to Yonkers where he

Reprinted from *The 42nd Parallel* by John Dos Passos, copyright by John Dos Passos 1930 and 1948, published by the Houghton Mifflin Company. All footnotes in this selection are by the editor of this text.

[1] German college preparatory institute.

[2] Prince Otto Eduard Leopold von Bismarck-Schönhausen (1815–1898), German statesman called "the Iron Chancellor"; he was anti-socialist in his views, and did much to promote the unification of Germany as an empire.

had a twelvedollar a week job with Rudolph Eichemeyer[3] who was a German exile from fortyeight an inventor and electrician and owner of a factory where he made hatmaking machinery and electrical generators.

In Yonkers he [i.e., Steinmetz] worked out the theory of the Third Harmonics

and the law of hysteresis which states in a formula the hundredfold relations between the metallic heat, density, frequency when the poles change places in the core of a magnet under an alternating current.

It is Steinmetz's law of hysteresis that makes possible all the transformers that crouch in little boxes and gableroofed houses in all the hightension lines all over everywhere. The mathematical symbols of Steinmetz's law are the patterns of all transformers everywhere.

In eighteen ninetytwo when Eichemeyer sold out to the corporation that was to form General Electric, Steinmetz was entered in the contract along with other valuable apparatus. All his life Steinmetz was a piece of apparatus belonging to General Electric.

First his laboratory was at Lynn, then it was moved and the little hunchback with it to Schenectady, the electric city.

General Electric humored him, let him be a socialist, let him keep a greenhouseful of cactuses lit up by mercury lights, let him have alligators, talking crows and a gila monster for pets and the publicity department talked up the wizard, the medicine man who knew the symbols that opened up the doors of Ali Baba's cave.[4]

Steinmetz jotted a formula on his cuff and next morning a thousand new powerplants had sprung up and the dynamos sang dollars and the silence of the transformers was all dollars,

and the publicity department poured oily stories into the ears of the American public every Sunday and Steinmetz became the little parlor magician,

who made a toy thunderstorm in his laboratory and made all the toy trains run on time and the meat stay cold in the icebox and the lamp in the parlor and the great lighthouses and the searchlights and the revolving beams of light that guide airplanes at night towards Chicago, New York, St. Louis, Los Angeles,

and they let him be a socialist and believe that human society could be improved the way you can improve a dynamo and

[3] Bavarian inventor, who immigrated to the United States in 1850.

[4] The hero of the tale *Ali Baba and the Forty Thieves,* who learned the passwords to the treasure cave, "Open, Sesame," and, thereby, enriched himself.

they let him be pro-German and write a letter offering his services to Lenin because mathematicians are so impractical who
make up formulas by which you can build powerplants, factories, subway systems, light, heat, air, sunshine but not human
relations that affect the stockholders' money and the directors'
salaries.

    Steinmetz was a famous magician and he talked to Edison
tapping with the Morse code on Edison's knee
    because Edison was so very deaf
    and he went out West
    to make speeches that nobody understood
    and he talked to Bryan about God on a railroad train
    and all the reporters stood round while he and Einstein
    met face to face,
    but they couldn't catch what they said
    and Steinmetz was the most valuable piece of apparatus
General Electric had
    until he wore out and died.

Chicago Tribune

WHO IS TO RUN THE UNIVERSITY?

'I, Said the Student'

The academic year is approaching its end, and as one contemplates the
year's developments on American campuses the view is disquieting. It
has been a year of ferment at many universities. The anarchic tactics of
the civil rights demonstrators have come to the quadrangles. There have
been demonstrations, picketing, sit-ins, protests, rebellions, and riots by
students from Berkeley to Brooklyn and New Haven.

    Beatniks and agitators, often abetted by radicals from outside the
student body, have had a field day. The demands and complaints cut a
wide swath. Here it is charged that "free speech" is infringed. There
that popular professor has been denied tenure or reappointment. Or the
protest is that the university has grown so large that the student is an
undifferentiated entity, unknown to his professors, out of touch with
the administration.

    But all of these allegations and activities are directed to one end.
That is to give the student a greater voice in the management of the
university. Some would say that the students want more than to be
recognized, heeded, or consulted. They want to govern. They would
have the president, the chancellor, the provost, even the trustees or

Reprinted, courtesy of the *Chicago Tribune*, May 11, 1966.

regents, take a back seat while they make the decisions and lay down the rules.

The latest of these petitions of "grievance" to come to hand asserts that the president is away too much on fund-raising trips, that some of the better professors are leaving, that the faculty and administration are out of touch with the student body. Therefore the "remedy" should be for students to sit in at faculty meetings and offer their suggestions on how the curriculum should be shaped and taught, and that the president should submit himself once a month to the student body, to be cross-examined, in effect.

It seems to us that these are hardly modest petitions. If the president is working in the best interests of the university, it is his business how he schedules his time. As for communication, there are established channels available to the student. He can go first to his professor. He will find the student counselor and the dean ready to listen to him. If he is still frustrated, he may ask the chancellor or the president for an interview.

But we feel that he is out of bounds when he bypasses all these avenues and addresses petitions directly to the trustees.

On the record of this academic year, presidents and university administrations as a whole have been weak and "permissive" in dealing with student agitation. The faculty, conspicuously at the University of California, lined up with the students and supported their remonstrances. Disciplinary action, when taken, was belated and indecisive. These are all elements in a prescription, not to keep the university system strong, but to see it fall apart.

Thousands of deserving high school graduates this year are being turned away from universities all thru the land. The malcontents hold the places to which they aspire. Why do not the universities, before accepting any entering student, tell him the conditions under which he will be registered? That would be to hold off the trouble before it develops.

"We will accept you," they need only say, "if you abide by our rules, our codes of student conduct, the terms of our charter, and accept the authority of the university and agree to conduct yourself with decorum and responsibility. Otherwise, we shall dismiss you and we shall give your place to another student willing to live up to the contract."

These simple corrective measures, we are confident, would bring order where now there is none.

13
THE SEARCH FOR IDENTITY

"The unexamined life is not worth living."

—Socrates

"Ich bin's nit! Ich bin's nit!"
(rendered, "It isn't me! It isn't me!")

—Martin Luther,
as he collapsed on a monastery floor

Ernest Hemingway

UNE GÉNÉRATION PERDUE

It was easy to get into the habit of stopping in at 27 rue de Fleurus late
in the afternoon for the warmth and the great pictures and the conversation. Often Miss Stein would have no guests and she was always very
friendly and for a long time she was affectionate. When I had come
back from trips that I had made to the different political conferences or
to the Near East or Germany for the Canadian paper and the news
services that I worked for she wanted me to tell her about all the
amusing details. There were funny parts always and she liked them and
also what the Germans call gallows-humor stories. She wanted to know
the gay part of how the world was going; never the real, never the bad.

I was young and not gloomy and there were always strange and
comic things that happened in the worst time and Miss Stein liked to
hear these. The other things I did not talk of and wrote by myself.

When I had not come back from any trips and would stop in at the
rue de Fleurus after working I would try sometimes to get Miss Stein to
talk about books. When I was writing, it was necessary for me to read
after I had written. If you kept thinking about it, you would lose the
thing that you were writing before you could go on with it the next day.
It was necessary to get exercise, to be tired in the body, and it was very
good to make love with whom you loved. That was better than anything.
But afterwards, when you were empty, it was necessary to read in order
not to think or worry about your work until you could do it again. I had
learned already never to empty the well of my writing, but always to
stop when there was still something there in the deep part of the well,
and let it refill at night from the springs that fed it.

To keep my mind off writing sometimes after I had worked I would
read writers who were writing then, such as Aldous Huxley, D. H.
Lawrence or any who had books published that I could get from Sylvia
Beach's library or find along the quais.

"Huxley is a dead man," Miss Stein said. "Why do you want to read
a dead man? Can't you see he is dead?"

I could not see, then, that he was a dead man and I said that his
books amused me and kept me from thinking.

"You should only read what is truly good or what is frankly bad."

"I've been reading truly good books all winter and all last winter
and I'll read them next winter, and I don't like frankly bad books."

"Why do you read this trash? It is inflated trash, Hemingway. By a
dead man."

"I like to see what they are writing," I said. "And it keeps my mind
off me doing it."

"Who else do you read now?"

"D. H. Lawrence," I said. "He wrote some very good short stories, one called 'The Prussian Officer.' "

"I tried to read his novels. He's impossible. He's pathetic and preposterous. He writes like a sick man."

"I liked *Sons and Lovers* and *The White Peacock*," I said. "Maybe that not so well. I couldn't read *Women in Love*."

"If you don't want to read what is bad, and want to read something that will hold your interest and is marvelous in its own way, you should read Marie Belloc Lowndes."

I had never heard of her, and Miss Stein loaned me *The Lodger*, that marvelous story of Jack the Ripper and another book about murder at a place outside Paris that could only be Enghien les Bains. They were both splendid after-work books, the people credible and the action and the terror never false. They were perfect for reading after you had worked and I read all the Mrs. Belloc Lowndes that there was. But there was only so much and none as good as the first two and I never found anything as good for that empty time of day or night until the first fine Simenon books came out.

I think Miss Stein would have liked the good Simenons—the first one I read was either *L'Ecluse Numéro 1,* or *La Maison du Canal*—but I am not sure because when I knew Miss Stein she did not like to read French although she loved to speak it. Janet Flanner gave me the first two Simenons I ever read. She loved to read French and she had read Simenon when he was a crime reporter.

In the three or four years that we were good friends I cannot remember Gertrude Stein ever speaking well of any writer who had not written favorably about her work or done something to advance her career except for Ronald Firbank and, later, Scott Fitzgerald. When I first met her she did not speak of Sherwood Anderson as a writer but spoke glowingly of him as a man and of his great, beautiful, warm Italian eyes and of his kindness and his charm. I did not care about his great beautiful warm Italian eyes but I liked some of his short stories very much. They were simply written and sometimes beautifully written and he knew the people he was writing about and cared deeply for them. Miss Stein did not want to talk about his stories but always about him as a person.

"What about his novels?" I asked her. She did not want to talk about Anderson's works any more than she would talk about Joyce. If you brought up Joyce twice, you would not be invited back. It was like mentioning one general favorably to another general. You learned not to do it the first time you made the mistake. You could always mention a general, though, that the general you were talking to had beaten. The general you were talking to would praise the beaten general greatly and go happily into detail on how he had beaten him.

Anderson's stories were too good to make happy conversation. I was prepared to tell Miss Stein how strangely poor his novels were, but this would have been bad too because it was criticizing one of her most loyal supporters. When he wrote a novel finally called *Dark Laughter*, so terribly bad, silly and affected that I could not keep from criticizing it in a parody,* Miss Stein was very angry. I had attacked someone that was a part of her apparatus. But for a long time before that she was not angry. She, herself, began to praise Sherwood lavishly after he had cracked up as a writer.

She was angry at Ezra Pound because he had sat down too quickly on a small, fragile and, doubtless, uncomfortable chair, that it is quite possible he had been given on purpose, and had either cracked or broken it. That he was a great poet and a gentle and generous man and could have accommodated himself in a normal-size chair was not considered. The reasons for her dislike of Ezra, skillfully and maliciously put, were invented years later.

It was when we had come back from Canada and were living in the rue Notre-Dame-des-Champs and Miss Stein and I were still good friends that Miss Stein made the remark about the lost generation. She had some ignition trouble with the old Model T Ford she then drove and the young man who worked in the garage and had served in the last year of the war had not been adept, or perhaps had not broken the priority of other vehicles, in repairing Miss Stein's Ford. Anyway he had not been *sérieux* and had been corrected severely by the *patron* of the garage after Miss Stein's protest. The *patron* had said to him, "You are all a *génération perdue.*"

"That's what you are. That's what you all are," Miss Stein said. "All of you young people who served in the war. You are a lost generation."

"Really?" I said.

"You are," she insisted. "You have no respect for anything. You drink yourselves to death. . . ."

"Was the young mechanic drunk?" I asked.

"Of course not."

"Have you ever seen me drunk?"

"No. But your friends are drunk."

"I've been drunk," I said. "But I don't come here drunk."

"Of course not. I didn't say that."

"The boy's *patron* was probably drunk by eleven o'clock in the morning," I said. "That's why he makes such lovely phrases."

"Don't argue with me, Hemingway," Miss Stein said. "It does no good at all. You're all a lost generation, exactly as the garage keeper said."

Later when I wrote my first novel I tried to balance Miss Stein's quotation from the garage keeper with one from Ecclesiastes. But that night walking home I thought about the boy in the garage and if he had ever been hauled in one of those vehicles when they were converted to ambulances. I remembered how they used to burn out their brakes going down the mountain roads with a full load of wounded and braking in low and finally using the reverse, and how the last ones were driven over the mountainside empty, so they could be replaced by big Fiats with a good H-shift and metal-to-metal brakes. I thought of Miss

* *The Torrents of Spring.*

Stein and Sherwood Anderson and egotism and mental laziness versus discipline and I thought who is calling who a lost generation? Then as I was getting up to the Closerie des Lilas with the light on my old friend, the statue of Marshal Ney with his sword out and the shadows of the trees on the bronze, and he alone there and nobody behind him and what a fiasco he'd made of Waterloo, I thought that all generations were lost by something and always had been and always would be and I stopped at the Lilas to keep the statue company and drank a cold beer before going home to the flat over the sawmill. But sitting there with the beer, watching the statue and remembering how many days Ney had fought, personally, with the rear-guard on the retreat from Moscow that Napoleon had ridden away from in the coach with Caulaincourt, I thought of what a warm and affectionate friend Miss Stein had been and how beautifully she had spoken of Apollinaire and of his death on the day of the Armistice in 1918 with the crowd shouting "*à bas Guillaume*" and Apollinaire, in his delirium, thinking they were crying against him, and I thought, I will do my best to serve her and see she gets justice for the good work she had done as long as I can, so help me God and Mike Ney. But the hell with her lost-generation talk and all the dirty, easy labels. When I got home and into the courtyard and upstairs and saw my wife and my son and his cat, F. Puss, all of them happy and a fire in the fireplace, I said to my wife, "You know, Gertrude *is* nice, anyway."

"Of course, Tatie."

"But she does talk a lot of rot sometimes."

"I never hear her," my wife said. "I'm a wife. It's her friend that talks to me."

T. S. Eliot

THE ELDER STATESMAN (QUOTATION)

"*What do you call a failure? The worst kind of failure, in my opinion, is the man who has to keep on pretending to himself that he's a success—the man who in the morning has to make up his face before he looks in the mirror.*"

Sherwood Anderson

THE BOOK OF THE GROTESQUE

The writer, an old man with a white mustache, had some difficulty in getting into bed. The windows of the house in which he lived were high and he wanted to look at the trees when he awoke in the morning. A carpenter came to fix the bed so that it would be on a level with the window.

Quite a fuss was made about the matter. The carpenter, who had been a soldier in the Civil War, came into the writer's room and sat down to talk of building a platform for the purpose of raising the bed. The writer had cigars lying about and the carpenter smoked.

For a time the two men talked of the raising of the bed and then they talked of other things. The soldier got on the subject of the war. The writer, in fact, led him to that subject. The carpenter had once been a prisoner in Andersonville prison and had lost a brother. The brother had died of starvation, and whenever the carpenter got upon that subject he cried. He, like the old writer, had a white mustache, and when he cried he puckered up his lips and the mustache bobbed up and down. The weeping old man with the cigar in his mouth was ludicrous. The plan the writer had for the raising of his bed was forgotten and later the carpenter did it in his own way and the writer, who was past sixty, had to help himself with a chair when he went to bed at night.

In his bed the writer rolled over on his side and lay quite still. For years he had been beset with notions concerning his heart. He was a hard smoker and his heart fluttered. The idea had got into his mind that he would some time die unexpectedly and always when he got into bed he thought of that. It did not alarm him. The effect in fact was quite a special thing and not easily explained. It made him more alive, there in bed, than at any other time. Perfectly still he lay and his body was old and not of much use any more, but something inside him was altogether young. He was like a pregnant woman, only that the thing inside him was not a baby but a youth. No, it wasn't a youth, it was a woman, young, and wearing a coat of mail like a knight. It is absurd, you see, to try to tell what was inside the old writer as he lay on his high bed and listened to the fluttering of his heart. The thing to get at is what the writer, or the young thing within the writer, was thinking about.

The old writer, like all of the people in the world, had got, during his long life, a great many notions in his head. He had once been quite handsome and a number of women had been in love with him. And then, of course, he had known people, many people, known them in a peculiarly intimate way that was different from the way in which you and I know people. At least that is what the writer thought and the thought pleased him. Why quarrel with an old man concerning his thoughts?

In the bed the writer had a dream that was not a dream. As he grew somewhat sleepy but was still conscious, figures began to appear before his eyes. He imagined the young indescribable thing within himself was driving a long procession of figures before his eyes.

You see the interest in all this lies in the figures that went before the eyes of the writer. They were all grotesques. All of the men and women the writer had ever known had become grotesques.

The grotesques were not all horrible. Some were amusing, some almost beautiful, and one, a woman all drawn out of shape, hurt the old man by her grotesqueness. When she passed he made a noise like a small dog whimpering. Had you come into the room you might have supposed the old man had unpleasant dreams or perhaps indigestion.

For an hour the procession of grotesques passed before the eyes of the old man, and then, although it was a painful thing to do, he crept out of bed and began to write. Some one of the grotesques had made a deep impression on his mind and he wanted to describe it.

At his desk the writer worked for an hour. In the end he wrote a book which he called "The Book of the Grotesque." It was never published, but I saw it once and it made an indelible impression on my mind. The book had one central thought that is very strange and has always remained with me. By remembering it I have been able to understand many people and things that I was never able to understand before. The thought was involved but a simple statement of it would be something like this:

That in the beginning when the world was young there were a great many thoughts but no such thing as a truth. Man made the truths himself and each truth was a composite of a great many vague thoughts. All about in the world were the truths and they were all beautiful.

The old man had listed hundreds of the truths in his book. I will not try to tell you of all of them. There was the truth of virginity and the truth of passion, the truth of wealth and of poverty, of thrift and of profligacy, of carelessness and abandon. Hundreds and hundreds were the truths and they were all beautiful.

And then the people came along. Each as he appeared snatched up one of the truths and some who were quite strong snatched up a dozen of them.

It was the truths that made the people grotesques. The old man had quite an elaborate theory concerning the matter. It was his notion that the moment one of the people took one of the truths to himself, called it his truth, and tried to live his life by it, he became a grotesque and the truth he embraced became a falsehood.

You can see for yourself how the old man, who had spent all of his life writing and was filled with words, would write hundreds of pages concerning this matter. The subject would become so big in his mind that he himself would be in danger of becoming a grotesque. He didn't, I suppose, for the same reason that he never published the book. It was the young thing inside him that saved the old man.

Concerning the old carpenter who fixed the bed for the writer, I only mentioned him because he, like many of what are called very common people, became the nearest thing to what is understandable and lovable of all the grotesques in the writer's book.

Ralph Waldo Emerson

THE AMERICAN SCHOLAR

Each age, it is found, must write its own books; or rather, each generation for the next succeeding. The books of an older period will not fit this.

Yet hence arises a grave mischief. The sacredness which attaches to the act of creation, the act of thought, is transferred to the record. The poet chanting was felt to be a divine man: henceforth the chant is divine also. The writer was a just and wise spirit: henceforward it is settled the book is perfect; as love of the hero corrupts into worship of his statue. Instantly the book becomes noxious: the guide is a tyrant. The sluggish and perverted mind of the multitude, slow to open to the incursions of Reason, having once so opened, having once received this book, stands upon it, and makes an outcry if it is disparaged. Colleges are built on it. Books are written on it by thinkers, not by Man Thinking; by men of talent, that is, who start wrong, who set out from accepted dogmas, not from their own sight of principles. Meek young men grow up in libraries, believing it their duty to accept the views which Cicero, which Locke, which Bacon, have given; forgetful that Cicero, Locke, and Bacon were only young men in libraries when they wrote these books.

Hence, instead of Man Thinking, we have the bookworm. Hence the book-learned class, who value books, as such; not as related to nature and the human constitution, but as making a sort of Third Estate with the world and the soul. Hence the restorers of readings, the emendators, the bibliomaniacs of all degrees.

Books are the best of things, well used; abused, among the worst. What is the right use? What is the one end which all means go to effect? They are for nothing but to inspire. I had better never see a book than to be warped by its attraction clean out of my own orbit, and made a satellite instead of a system. The one thing in the world, of value, is the active soul. This every man is entitled to; this every man contains within him, although in almost all men obstructed, and as yet unborn. The soul active sees absolute truth and utters truth, or creates. In this action it is genius; not the privilege of here and there a favorite, but the sound estate of every man. In its essence it is progressive. The book, the college, the school of art, the institution of any kind, stop with some past utterance of genius. This is good, say they,—let us hold by this. They pin me down. They look backward and not forward. But genius looks forward: the eyes of man are set in his forehead, not in his hindhead: man hopes: genius creates. Whatever talents may be, if the man create not, the pure efflux of the Deity is not his;—cinders and smoke there may be, but not yet flame. There are creative manners, there are creative actions, and creative words; manners, actions, words, that is, indicative of no custom or authority, but springing spontaneous from the mind's own sense of good and fair.

On the other part, instead of being its own seer, let it receive from another mind its truth, though it were in torrents of light, without periods of solitude, inquest, and self-recovery, and a fatal disservice is done. Genius is always sufficiently the enemy of genius by over-influence. The literature of every nation bears me witness. The English dramatic poets have Shakspearized now for two hundred years.

Undoubtedly there is a right way of reading, so it be sternly subordinated. Man Thinking must not be subdued by his instruments. Books are for the scholar's idle times. When he can read God directly, the hour is too precious to be wasted in other men's transcripts of their readings. But when the intervals of darkness come, as come they must, —when the sun is hid and the stars withdraw their shining,—we repair to the lamps which were kindled by their ray, to guide our steps to the East again, where the dawn is. We hear, that we may speak. The Arabian proverb says, "A fig tree, looking on a fig tree, becometh fruitful."

It is remarkable, the character of the pleasure we derive from the best books. They impress us with the conviction that one nature wrote and the same reads. We read the verses of one of the great English poets, of Chaucer, of Marvell, of Dryden, with the most modern joy,— with a pleasure, I mean, which is in great part caused by the abstraction of all *time* from their verses. There is some awe mixed with the joy of our surprise, when this poet, who lived in some past world, two or three hundred years ago, says that which lies close to my own soul, that which I also had well-nigh thought and said. But for the evidence thence afforded to the philosophical doctrine of the identity of all minds, we should suppose some preëstablished harmony, some foresight of souls that were to be, and some preparation of stores for their future wants, like the fact observed in insects, who lay up food before death for the young grub they shall never see.

I would not be hurried by any love of system, by any exaggeration of instincts, to underrate the Book. We all know, that as the human body can be nourished on any food, though it were boiled grass and the broth of shoes, so the human mind can be fed by any knowledge. And great and heroic men have existed who had almost no other information than by the printed page. I only would say that it needs a strong head to bear that diet. One must be an inventor to read well. As the proverb says, "He that would bring home the wealth of the Indies, must carry out the wealth of the Indies." There is then creative reading as well as creative writing. When the mind is braced by labor and invention, the page of whatever book we read becomes luminous with manifold allusion. Every sentence is doubly significant, and the sense of our author is as broad as the world. We then see, what is always true, that as the seer's hour of vision is short and rare among heavy days and months, so is its record, perchance, the least part of his volume. The discerning will read in his Plato or Shakspeare, only that least part,— only the authentic utterances of the oracle;—all the rest he rejects, were it never so many times Plato's and Shakspeare's.

Of course there is a portion of reading quite indispensable to a wise man. History and exact science he must learn by laborious reading. Colleges, in like manner, have their indispensable office,—to teach elements. But they can only highly serve us when they aim not to drill, but to create; when they gather from far every ray of various genius to their hospitable halls, and by the concentrated fires, set the hearts of their youth on flame. Thought and knowledge are natures in which apparatus and pretension avail nothing. Gowns and pecuniary foundations, though of towns of gold, can never countervail the least sentence or syllable of wit. Forget this, and our American colleges will recede in their public importance, whilst they grow richer every year. . . .

Russell Baker

IDENTITY CRISIS (THING THAT COUNTS: KNOWING WHO YOU AREN'T)

The psychiatric fad these days is "identity." Walk into any room full of strangers, lift a glass and two swallows later some sadist whose pleasure derives from splashing other persons' egos will be telling you, "The trouble with you is that you don't know who you really are."

Knowing "who you really are" is supposed, for reasons that no one can persuasively explain, to be essential to putting one's life on order. Those who do not know are said to be caught in the dreadful "identity crisis." Judging from the voluminous literature on the subject, American campuses today are swarming with victims of the "identity crisis" whose chances of salvation hinge upon discovering "who they really are."

It is hard to conceive of a more fallacious doctrine. For most people, nothing but the most abject depression can result from the sudden discovery of who they really are. Most of us have known at one time or another some perfectly happy soul who has breezed through 20 or 30 years of mature life under the happy impression that he was Napoleon, only to learn at last, to his utter dismay, that he was actually J. Kendall Throstlewaith, overaged accountant, father of seven and prize bore of the PTA.

Reprinted from *The New York Times*, © 1968 (Jan. 4) by the New York Times Company, by permission.

The true formula for happiness is knowing who you aren't. This is something that must be learned gradually, a step at a time. Let us consider, by way of example, a man who in 1932 was seven years old. At that age, it would have been natural for him to have spent long hours under the impression that he was Tom Mix. Just as naturally, he would probably have developed the illusion that he was a person capable of actually becoming Tom Mix some day.

The only important thing for that man today is that he be under absolutely no illusions that he has actually become Tom Mix.

There may be an outside chance that a man of 43 can find happiness while clattering around a split-level in spurs and ten-gallon hat whistling for Tony, but it is not a good bet. In fact, despite the millions who in 1932 thought they might become Tom Mix, probably only a handful remain who are still convinced that they are.

Happy progress through life requires a gradual shucking off of such identity illusions. By the age of 13 our hypothetical case probably admitted quietly to himself that he was no Tom Mix, nor was meant to be. What made the admission tolerable was the suspicion that he might be Johnny Weissmuller.

By 17, a few drubbings in the schoolyard would have relieved him of the illusion that he had the vigor and bicep to be Weissmuller. But that, too, was tolerable, for he had begun greasing his hair, and practicing a devilish wink and—who could tell?—maybe he was Clark Gable.

Within a few years a series of disastrous outings with hostesses at the USO would have persuaded him of the sad reality, but by this time practice at accepting the disappointment of discovering who he wasn't would have softened the readjustment.

And, after all, wasn't he young and immortal? Might he not become the next Lincoln? The next Hemingway? The next Einstein?

In a graduated program of happy adjustment, he would have put these illusions aside very slowly and with great care. Six or seven years is not too long to spend on admitting to yourself that you are not the next Lincoln, or even the next Eisenhower, and one surely wouldn't want to face it at the same time he was discovering that he was no longer young and terribly mortal.

The whole process might take 14 or 15 years and carry a man comfortably into his middle thirties. Fourteen or 15 years of suspecting that you may be not only immortal, but also the next Lincoln, Hemingway or Einstein is, after all, a large bloc of time traversed in considerable splendor.

It would have been foolish cruelty to have forced this man at the very outset to find out who he actually was, for he would almost surely have discovered that he was not much of anybody, and what's more, a not-much-of-anybody who was going to get old and mortal like everyone else. Why anyone should believe that this sort of self-knowledge is the key to happiness is a baffling question.

As he is, the fellow discovering in his mid-thirties that he is not going to be Lincoln and stay young forever is proceeding satisfactorily through life by gradually putting aside his more absurd delusions as absurdity ceases to befit his age, and adjusting happily to fresh scaled-down illusions which will get him through to the next depot.

It is enough for him to discover, in the nick of time, who he isn't. His answer to any tormentor who threatens to tell him who he actually is should be, "If you do so, I shall never be able to forgive you."

LOVE, SEX, AND CENSORSHIP

"A writer owned an asterisk,
And kept it in his Den,
Where he wrote tales (which had large sales)
Of frail and erring men;

And always, when he reached the point
Where carping Censors lurk,
He called upon the Asterisk
To do his dirty work.

—Stoddard King, *"The Writer and the Asterisk"*

"There is no such thing as a dirty theme.
There are only dirty writers."

—George Jean Nathan, *Testament of a Critic*

POETS ON LOVE

William Shakespeare

ROMEO AND JULIET

> *Juliet.*
> Spread thy close curtain, love-performing night,
> That runaways' eyes [1] may wink, and Romeo
> Leap to these arms, untalk'd of and unseen.
> Lovers can see to do their amorous rites
> By their own beauties; or, if love be blind,
> It best agrees with night. Come, civil [2] night,
> Thou sober-suited matron, all in black,
> And learn me how to lose a winning match,
> Play'd for a pair of stainless maidenhoods:
> Hood my unmann'd blood, bating [3] in my cheeks,
> With thy black mantle; till strange love, grown bold,
> Think true love acted simple modesty.
> Come, night; come, Romeo; come, thou day in night;
> For thou wilt lie upon the wings of night
> Whiter than new snow on a raven's back.
> Come, gentle night, come, loving, black-brow'd night,
> Give me my Romeo; and, when he shall die,
> Take him and cut him out in little stars,
> And he will make the face of heaven so fine
> That all the world will be in love with night
> And pay no worship to the garish sun.

SONNET 116

> 116
>
> Let me not to the marriage of true minds
> Admit impediments. Love is not love
> Which alters when it alteration finds,

All footnotes in this selection are by the editor of this text.

[1] Here Juliet may be referring either to the sunny day (Phoebus), or to the night (also, perhaps, a runaway); the point is open for discussion.

[2] acceptable, respectable.

[3] "Unmanned," in the Elizabethan sense of the word, meant "inexperienced" or "untrained"; thus, a lack of control or a "wildness" is suggested. "Bating" means "fluttering." The whole reference, including "Hood," relates to the Elizabethan sport of falconry.

Or bends with the remover to remove.[1]
O, no! it is an ever-fixéd mark
That looks on tempests and is never shaken;
It is the star to every wand'ring bark,
Whose worth's unknown, although his height be taken.
Love's not Time's fool,[2] though rosy lips and cheeks
Within his bending sickle's compass come;
Love alters not with his brief hours and weeks,
But bears it out even to the edge of doom.[3]
   If this be error and upon me proved,
   I never writ, nor no man ever loved.

Andrew Marvell

TO HIS COY MISTRESS

Had we but world enough, and time,
This coyness, Lady, were no crime;
We would sit down and think which way
To walk and pass our long love's day.
Thou by the Indian Ganges' side
Shouldst rubies find; I by the tide
Of Humber would complain. I would
Love you ten years before the Flood,
And you should, if you please, refuse
Till the conversion of the Jews.
My vegetable love should grow
Vaster than empires, and more slow;
An hundred years should go to praise
Thine eyes and on thy forehead gaze;
Two hundred to adore each breast,
But thirty thousand to the rest;
An age at least to every part,
And the last age should show your heart.
For, Lady, you deserve this state,
Nor would I love at lower rate.
   But at my back I always hear
Time's wingéd chariot hurrying near;
And yonder all before us lie

All footnotes in this selection are by the editor of this text.

[1] "Or bends with the remover to remove" may be paraphrased, "Or lends help in any way to any force which may adversely affect the love—even inconstancy."

[2] i.e., the fool ("jester") of Time; subject to be mocked by Time.

[3] Doomsday or the Day of Last Judgment.

Deserts of vast eternity.
Thy beauty shall no more be found,
Nor, in thy marble vault, shall sound
My echoing song; then worms shall try
That long preserved virginity,
And your quaint honor turn to dust,
And into ashes all my lust:
The grave's a fine and private place,
But none, I think, do there embrace.
   Now therefore, while the youthful hue
Sits on thy skin like morning dew,
And while thy willing soul transpires
At every pore with instant fires,
Now let us sport us while we may,
And now, like amorous birds of prey,
Rather at once our time devour
Than languish in his slow-chapt [1] power.
Let us roll all our strength and all
Our sweetness up into one ball,
And tear our pleasures with rough strife
Thorough the iron gates of life:
Thus, though we cannot make our sun
Stand still, yet we will make him run.

Robert Herrick

UPON JULIA'S CLOTHES

Whenas in silks my Julia goes,
Then, then (methinks) how sweetly flows
That liquefaction of her clothes.

Next, when I cast mine eyes and see
That brave vibration each way free;
O how that glittering taketh me!

Percy Bysshe Shelley

LOVE'S PHILOSOPHY

I
  The Fountains mingle with the River
    And the Rivers with the Ocean,

All footnotes in this selection are by the editor of this text.

[1] A "chap" meant "jaw"; therefore, Time is depicted as "devouring" human lives.

The winds of Heaven mix for ever
   With a sweet emotion;
Nothing in the world is single;
   All things by a law divine
In one spirit meet and mingle.
   Why not I with thine?—

II
See the mountains kiss high Heaven
   And the waves clasp one another;
No sister-flower would be forgiven
   If it disdained its brother,
And the sunlight clasps the earth
   And the moonbeams kiss the sea:
What is all this sweet work worth
   If thou kiss not me?

John Donne

A VALEDICTION: FORBIDDING MOURNING

As virtuous men pass mildly away,
   And whisper to their souls to go,
While some of their sad friends do say,
   The breath goes now, and some say, no:

So let us melt, and make no noise,
   No tear-floods, nor sigh-tempests move,
'Twere profanation of our joys
   To tell the laity our love.

Moving of th' earth brings harms and fears,
   Men reckon what it did and meant,
But trepidation of the spheres,
   Though greater far, is innocent.

Dull sublunary lovers' love
   (Whose soul is sense) cannot admit
Absence, because it doth remove
   Those things which elemented it.

But we by a love so much refined
   That ourselves know not what it is,
Inter-assurèd of the mind,
   Care less, eyes, lips, and hands to miss.

Our two souls therefore, which are one,
  Though I must go, endure not yet
A breach, but an expansion,
  Like gold to airy thinness beat.

If they be two, they are two so
  As stiff thin compasses are two,
Thy soul the fixed foot, makes no show
  To move, but doth, if th' other do.

And though it in the center sit,
  Yet when the other far doth roam,
It leans, and hearkens after it,
  And grows erect, as that comes home.

Such wilt thou be to me, who must
  Like th' other foot, obliquely run;
Thy firmness makes my circle just,
  And makes me end, where I begun.

George Gordon, Lord Byron

AMOR MIO

To the Countess Guiccioli

Bologna, August 25, 1819

My dearest Teresa,—

I have read this book in your garden;—my love, you were absent, or else I could not have read it. It is a favorite book of yours, and the writer was a friend of mine. You will not understand these English words, and *others* will not understand them,—which is the reason I have not scrawled them in Italian. But you will recognize the handwriting of him who passionately loved you, and you will divine that, over a book which was yours, he could only think of love. In that word, beautiful in all languages, but most so in yours—*Amor mio*—is comprised my existence here and hereafter. I feel I exist here, and I fear that I shall exist hereafter,—as to *what* purpose you will decide; my destiny rests with you, and you are a woman, seventeen years of age, and two out of a convent. I wish that you had staid there, with all my heart,—or, at least, that I had never met you in your married state.

But all this is too late. I love you, and you love me,—at least, you *say so*, and *act* as if you *did* so, which last is a great consolation in all events. But I more than love you, and cannot cease to love you.

Think of me, sometimes, when the Alps and the ocean divide us,—but they never will, unless you *wish* it.

Robert Browning

MEETING AT NIGHT

The gray sea and the long black land;
And the yellow half-moon large and low;
And the startled little waves that leap
In fiery ringlets from their sleep,
As I gain the cove with pushing prow,
And quench its speed i' the slushy sand.

Then a mile of warm sea-scented beach;
Three fields to cross till a farm appears;
A tap at the pane, the quick sharp scratch
And blue spurt of a lighted match,
And a voice less loud, through its joys and fears,
Than the two hearts beating each to each!

PARTING AT MORNING

Round the cape of a sudden came the sea,
And the sun looked over the mountain's rim:
And straight was a path of gold for him,
And the need of a world of men for me.

Ernest Dowson

NON SUM QUALIS ERAM BONAE SUB REGNO CYNARAE [1]

Last night, ah, yesternight, betwixt her lips and mine
There fell thy shadow, Cynara! thy breath was shed
Upon my soul between the kisses and the wine;
And I was desolate and sick of an old passion,
  Yea, I was desolate and bowed my head—
I have been faithful to thee, Cynara! in my fashion.

All night upon mine heart I felt her warm heart beat,
Night-long within mine arms in love and sleep she lay;

All footnotes in this selection are by the editor of this text.

[1] The Latin sentence may be translated, "I am not that which I was under the bewitchment of Cynara." Also see as influence Horace's ODES, IV, I, ll. 3–4. The name of the heroine is taken from Horace, but the subject is treated originally. It is likely that he had Adelaide Foltinowicz, the daughter of an émigré restauranteur, in mind as his "Cynara." She married a waiter in her father's café.

Surely the kisses of her bought red mouth were sweet;
But I was desolate and sick of an old passion,
When I awoke and found the dawn was gray—
I have been faithful to thee, Cynara! in my fashion.

I have forgot much, Cynara! gone with the wind,[2]
Flung roses, roses riotously with the throng,
Dancing, to put thy pale, lost lilies out of mind;
But I was desolate and sick of an old passion,
Yea, all the time, because the dance was long—
I have been faithful to thee, Cynara! in my fashion.

I cried for madder music and for stronger wine,
But when the feast is finished and the lamps expire,
Then falls thy shadow, Cynara! the night is thine;
And I am desolate and sick of an old passion,
Yea, hungry for the lips of my desire—
I have been faithful to thee, Cynara! in my fashion.

Rupert Brooke

THE HILL

Breathless, we flung us on the windy hill,
Laughed in the sun, and kissed the lovely grass.
You said, "Through glory and ecstasy we pass;
Wind, sun, and earth remain, the birds sing still,
When we are old, are old. . . ." "And when we die
All's over that is ours; and life burns on
Through other lovers, other lips," said I,
—"Heart of my heart, our heaven is now, is won!"

"We are Earth's best, that learnt her lesson here.
Life is our cry. We have kept the faith!" we said;
"We shall go down with unreluctant tread
Rose-crowned into the darkness!" . . . Proud we were,
And laughed, that had such brave true things to say.
—And then you suddenly cried, and turned away.

[2] Source for Margaret Mitchell's *Gone with the Wind*

Edwin Arlington Robinson

ANOTHER DARK LADY

Think not, because I wonder where you fled,
That I would lift a pin to see you there;
You may, for me, be prowling anywhere,
So long as you show not your little head:
No dark and evil story of the dead
Would leave you less pernicious or less fair—
Not even Lilith, with her famous hair;
And Lilith was the devil, I have read.

I cannot hate you, for I loved you then.
The woods were golden then. There was a road
Through beeches; and I said their smooth feet showed
Like yours. Truth must have heard me from afar,
For I shall never have to learn again
That yours are cloven as no beech's are.

William Butler Yeats

A DEEP-SWORN VOW

Others because you did not keep
That deep-sworn vow have been friends of mine;
Yet always when I look death in the face,
When I clamber to the heights of sleep,
Or when I grow excited with wine,
Suddenly I meet your face.

Theodore Roethke

I KNEW A WOMAN

I knew a woman, lovely in her bones,
When small birds sighed, she would sigh back at them;
Ah, when she moved, she moved more ways than one:
The shapes a bright container can contain!
Of her choice virtues only gods should speak,
Or English poets who grew up on Greek
(I'd have them sing in chorus, cheek to cheek).

How well her wishes went! She stroked my chin,
She taught me Turn, and Counter-turn, and Stand;
She taught me Touch, that undulant white skin;
I nibbled meekly from her proffered hand;
She was the sickle; I, poor I, the rake,
Coming behind her for her pretty sake
(But what prodigious mowing we did make).

Love likes a gander, and adores a goose:
Her full lips pursed, the errant note to seize;
She played it quick, she played it light and loose;
My eyes, they dazzled at her flowing knees;
Her several parts could keep a pure repose,
Or one hip quiver with a mobile nose
(She moved in circles, and those circles moved).

Let seed be grass, and grass turn into hay:
I'm martyr to a motion not my own;
What's freedom for? To know eternity.
I swear she cast a shadow white as stone.
But who would count eternity in days?
These old bones live to learn her wanton ways:
(I measure time by how a body sways).

SEX AND CENSORSHIP

Artemus Ward

ARTEMUS WARD: AMONG THE FREE LOVERS [1]

Some years ago I pitched my tent and onfurled my banner to the breeze, in Berlin Hites, Ohio. I had hearn that Berlin Hites was ockepied by a extensive seck called Free Lovers, who beleeved in affinertys and sich, goin back on their domestic ties without no hesitation whatsomever. They was likewise spirit rappers and high presher reformers on ginral principles. If I can improve these 'ere misgided peple by showin them my onparalleld show at the usual low price of admitants, methunk, I shall not hav lived in vane. But bitterly did I cuss the day I ever sot foot in the retchid place. I sot up my tent in a field near the Love Cure, as they called it, and bimeby the free lovers begun for to congregate around the door. A ornreer set I have never sawn. The men's faces was all covered with hare and they lookt half-starved to deth. They didn't wear no weskuts for the purpose (as they sed) of allowin the free air of hevun to blow onto their boozums. Their pockets was filled with tracks and pamplits and they was barefooted. They sed the Postles didn't wear boots, & why should they? That was their stile of argument. The wimin was wuss than the men. They wore trowsis, short gownds, straw hats with green ribbins, and all carried bloo cotton umbrellers.

Presently a perfeckly orful lookin female presented herself at the door. Her gownd was skanderlusly short and her trowsis was shameful to behold.

She eyed me over very sharp, and then startin back she sed, in a wild voice:

"Ah, can it be?"

"Which?" sed I.

"Yes, 'tis troo, O 'tis troo!"

"15 cents, marm," I anserd.

She bust out a cryin & sed:

"An so I hav found you at larst—at larst, O at larst!"

"Yes," I anserd, "you have found me at larst, and you would hav found me at fust, if you had cum sooner."

She grabd me vilently by the coat collar, and brandishin her umbreller wildly round, exclaimed:

"Air you a man?"

Sez I, "I think I air, but if you doubt it, you can address Mrs. A. Ward, Baldinsville, Injianny, postage pade, & she will probly giv you the desired informashun."

"Then thou ist what the cold world calls marrid?"

All footnotes in this selection are by the editor of this text.

[1] A "love cult" which established itself for a short time in Ohio and other places.

"Madam, I istest!"

The exsentric female then clutched me franticly by the arm and hollered:

"You air mine, O you air mine!"

"Scacely," I sed, endeverin to git loose from her. But she clung to me and sed:

"You air my Affinerty!"

"What upon arth is that?" I shouted.

"Dost thou not know?"

"No, I dostent!"

"Listen man, & I'll tell ye!" sed the strange female; "for years I hav yearned for thee. I knowd thou wast in the world, sumwhares, tho I didn't know whare. My hart sed he would cum and I took courage. He *has* cum—He's here—you air him—you air my Affinerty! O 'tis too mutch! too mutch!" and she sobbed agin.

"Yes," I anserd, "I think it is a darn site too mutch!"

"Hast thou not yearned for me?" she yelled, ringin her hands like a female play acter.

"Not a yearn!" I bellerd at the top of my voice, throwin her away from me.

The free lovers who was standin round obsarvin the scene commenst for to holler "shame!" "beast," etsettery, etsettery.

I was very mutch riled, and fortifyin myself with a spare tent stake, I addrest them as follers: "You pussylanermus critters, go away from me and take this retchid woman with you. I'm a law-abidin man, and beleeve in good, old-fashioned institutions. I am marrid & my orfsprings resemble me, if I am a showman! I think your Affinity bizniss is cussed noncents, besides bein outrajusly wicked. Why don't you behave desunt like other folks? Go to work and earn a honist livin and not stay round here in this lazy shiftless way, pizening the moral atmosphere with your pestifrous idees! You wimin folks go back to your lawful husbands if you've got any, and take orf them skanderlous gownds and trowsis, and dress respectful like other wimin. You men folks, cut orf them pirattercal whiskers, burn up them infurnel pamplits, put sum weskuts on, go to work choppin wood, splittin fence rales, or tillin the sile." I pored 4th my indignashun in this way till I got out of breth, when I stopt. I shant go to Berlin Hites agin, not if I live to be as old as Methooseler.

Stephen Crane

MAGGIE: A GIRL OF THE STREETS

Pete did not consider that he had ruined Maggie. If he had thought that her soul could never smile again, he would have believed the mother and brother, who were pyrotechnic over the affair, to be responsible for it. Besides, in his world, souls did not insist upon being able to smile. "What d' hell?"

He felt a trifle entangled. It distressed him. Revelations and scenes might bring upon him the wrath of the owner of the saloon, who insisted upon respectability of an advanced type. "What do dey wanna raise such a smoke about it fer?" demanded he of himself, disgusted with the attitude of the family. He saw no necessity that people should lose their equilibrium merely because their sister or their daughter had stayed away from home. Searching about in his mind for possible reasons for their conduct, he came upon the conclusion that Maggie's motives were correct, but that the two others wished to snare him. He felt pursued.

The woman whom he had met in the hilarious hall showed a disposition to ridicule him. "A little pale thing with no spirit," she said. "Did you note the expression of her eyes? There was something in them about pumpkin pie and virtue. That is a peculiar way the left corner of her mouth has of twitching, isn' it? Dear, dear, Pete, what are you coming to?"

Pete asserted at once that he never was very much interested in the girl. The woman interrupted him, laughing. "Oh, it's not of the slightest consequence to me, my dear young man. You needn't draw maps for my benefit. Why should I be concerned about it?" But Pete continued with his explanations. If he was laughed at for his tastes in women, he felt obliged to say that they were only temporary or indifferent ones.

The morning after Maggie had departed from home Pete stood behind the bar. He was immaculate in white jacket and apron, and his hair was plastered over his brow with infinite correctness. No customers were in the place. Pete was twisting his napkined fist slowly in a beer-glass, softly whistling to himself, and occasionally holding the object of his attention between his eyes and a few weak beams of sunlight that found their way over the thick screens and into the shaded rooms.

With lingering thoughts of the woman of brilliance and audacity, the bartender raised his head and stared through the varying cracks between the swaying bamboo doors. Suddenly the whistling pucker faded from his lips. He saw Maggie walking slowly past. He gave a great start, fearing for the previously mentioned eminent respectability of the place.

He threw a swift, nervous glance about him, all at once feeling guilty. No one was in the room. He went hastily over to the side door. Opening it and looking out, he perceived Maggie standing, as if undecided, at the corner. She was searching the place with her eyes. As she turned her face toward him, Pete beckoned to her hurriedly, intent upon returning with speed to a position behind the bar, and to the atmosphere of respectability upon which the proprietor insisted.

Maggie came to him, the anxious look disappearing from her face and a smile wreathing her lips. "Oh, Pete—" she began brightly.

The bartender made a violent gesture of impatience. "Oh, say," cried he vehemently. "What d' yeh wanna hang aroun' here fer? Do yer wanna git me inteh trouble?" he demanded with an air of injury.

Astonishment swept over the girl's features. "Why, Pete! yehs tol' me—"

Pete's glance expressed profound irritation. His countenance reddened with the anger of a man whose respectability is being threatened. "Say, yehs makes me tired! See! What'd yeh wanna tag aroun' atter me fer? Yeh'll do me dirt wid' d' ol' man an' dey'll be trouble! If he sees a woman roun' here he'll go crazy an' I'll lose me job! See? Ain' yehs got no sense? Don' be allus bodderin' me. See? Yer brudder came in here an' made trouble an' d' ol' man hadda put up fer it! An' now I'm done! See? I'm done."

The girl's eyes stared into his face. "Pete, don' yeh remem—"

"Oh, go ahn!" interrupted Pete, anticipating.

The girl seemed to have a struggle with herself. She was apparently bewildered and could not find speech. Finally she asked in a low voice, "But where kin I go?"

The question exasperated Pete beyond the powers of endurance. It was a direct attempt to give him some responsibility in a matter that did not concern him. In his indignation he volunteered information. "Oh, go to hell!" cried he. He slammed the door furiously and returned, with an air of relief, to his respectability.

Maggie went away. She wandered aimlessly for several blocks. She stopped once and asked aloud a question of herself: "Who?" A man who was passing near her shoulder humorously took the questioning word as intended for him. "Eh! What? Who? Nobody! I didn't say anything," he laughingly said, and continued his way.

Soon the girl discovered that if she walked with such apparent aimlessness, some men looked at her with calculating eyes. She quickened her step, frightened. As a protection, she adopted a demeanour of intentness as if going somewhere.

After a time she left rattling avenues and passed between rows of houses with sternness and stolidity stamped upon their features. She hung her head, for she felt their eyes grimly upon her.

Suddenly she came upon a stout gentleman in a silk hat and a chaste black coat, whose decorous row of buttons reached from his chin to his knees. The girl had heard of the grace of God and she decided to approach this man. His beaming, chubby face was a picture of benevolence and kind-heartedness. His eyes shone good will.

But as the girl timidly accosted him he made a convulsive movement and saved his respectability by a vigorous side-step. He did not risk it to save a soul. For how was he to know that there was a soul before him that needed saving?

Upon a wet evening, several months later, two interminable rows of cars, pulled by slipping horses, jangled along a prominent side street. A dozen cabs, with coat-enshrouded drivers, clattered to and fro. Electric lights, whirring softly, shed a blurred radiance. A flower-dealer, his feet tapping impatiently, his nose and his wares glistening with raindrops, stood behind an array of roses and chrysanthemums. Two or three theatres emptied a crowd upon the stormswept sidewalks. Men pulled their hats over their eyebrows and raised their collars to their ears. Women shrugged impatient shoulders in their warm cloaks and stopped to arrange their skirts for a walk through the storm. People who had been constrained to comparative silence for two hours burst into a roar of conversation, their hearts still kindling from the glowings of the stage.

The sidewalks became tossing seas of umbrellas. Men stepped forth to hail cabs or cars, raising their fingers in varied forms of polite request or imperative demand. An endless procession wended toward elevated stations. An atmosphere of pleasure and prosperity seemed to hang over the throng, born, perhaps, of good clothes and of two hours in a place of forgetfulness.

In the mingled light and gloom of an adjacent park, a handful of wet wanderers, in attitudes of chronic dejection, were scattered among the benches.

A girl of the painted cohorts of the city went along the street. She threw changing glances at men who passed her, giving smiling invitations to those of rural or untaught pattern and usually seeming sedately unconscious of the men with a metropolitan seal upon their faces. Crossing glittering avenues, she went into the throng emerging from the places of forgetfulness. She hurried forward through the crowd as if intent upon reaching a distant home, bending forward in her handsome cloak, daintily lifting her skirts, and picking for her well-shod feet the dryer spots upon the sidewalks.

The restless doors of saloons, clashing to and fro, disclosed animated rows of men before bars and hurrying barkeepers. A concert-hall gave to the street faint sounds of swift, machine-like music, as if a group of phantom musicians were hastening.

A tall young man, smoking a cigarette with a sublime air, strolled near the girl. He had on evening dress, a moustache, a chrysanthemum, and a look of *ennui,* all of which he kept carefully under his eye. Seeing the girl walk on as if such a young man as he was not in existence, he looked back transfixed with interest. He stared glassily for a moment, but gave a slight convulsive start when he discerned that she was neither new, Parisian, nor theatrical. He wheeled about hastily and turned his stare into the air, like a sailor with a searchlight.

A stout gentleman, with pompous and philanthropic whiskers, went stolidly by, the broad of his back sneering at the girl. A belated man in business clothes, and in haste to catch a car, bounced against her shoulder. "Hi, there, Mary, I beg your pardon! Brace up, old girl." He grasped her arm to steady her, and then was away running down the middle of the street.

The girl walked on out of the realm of restaurants and saloons. She passed more glittering avenues and went into darker blocks than those where the crowd travelled.

A young man in light overcoat and Derby hat received a glance shot keenly from the eyes of the girl. He stopped and looked at her, thrusting his hands into his pockets and making a mocking smile curl his lips. "Come, now, old lady," he said, "you don't mean to tell me that you sized me up for a farmer?"

A labouring man marched along with bundles under his arms. To her remarks he replied, "It's a fine evenin', ain't it?"

She smiled squarely into the face of a boy who was hurrying by with his hands buried in his overcoat pockets, his blond locks bobbing on his youthful temples, and a cheery smile of unconcern upon his lips. He turned his head and smiled back at her, waving his hands. "Not this eve—some other eve."

A drunken man, reeling in her pathway, began to roar at her. "I ain' go' no money!" he shouted, in a dismal voice. He lurched on up the street, wailing to himself: "I ain' go' no money. Ba' luck. Ain' go' no more money."

The girl went into gloomy districts near the river, where the tall black factories shut in the street and only occasional broad beams of light fell across the sidewalks from saloons. In front of one of these places, whence came the sound of a violin vigorously scraped, the patter of feet on boards, and the ring of loud laughter, there stood a man with blotched features.

Farther on in the darkness she met a ragged being with shifting, bloodshot eyes and grimy hands.

She went into the blackness of the final block. The shutters of the tall buildings were closed like grim lips. The structures seemed to have eyes that looked over them, beyond them, at other things. Afar off the lights of the avenues glittered as if from an impossible distance. Streetcar bells jingled with a sound of merriment.

At the feet of the tall buildings appeared the deathly black hue of the river. Some hidden factory sent up a yellow glare, that lit for a moment the waters lapping oilily against timbers. The varied sounds of life, made joyous by distance and seeming unapproachableness, came faintly and died away to a silence.

Plato

THE REPUBLIC

And shall we just carelessly allow children to hear any casual tales which may be devised by casual persons, and to receive into their minds ideas for the most part the very opposite of those which we shall wish them to have when they are grown up?

We cannot.

Then the first thing will be to establish a censorship of the writers of fiction, and let the censors receive any tale of fiction which is good,

From "The Republic" trans. by Benjamin Jowett from *The Dialogues of Plato*, 4th edition, 1953, Volume 2. Reprinted by permission of The Clarendon Press, Oxford.

and reject the bad; and we will persuade mothers and nurses to tell their children the authorized ones only. Let them fashion the mind with such tales, even more fondly than they mould the body with their hands; but most of those which are now in use must be discarded. . . .

But shall our superintendence go no further, and are the poets only to be required by us to express the image of the good in their works, on pain, if they do anything else, of expulsion from our State? Or is the same control to be extended to other artists, and are they also to be prohibited from exhibiting the opposite forms of vice and intemperance and meanness and deformity in sculpture and building and the other creative arts; and is he who cannot conform to this rule of ours to be prevented from practising his art in our State, lest the taste of our citizens be corrupted by him? We would not have our guardians grow up amid images of moral deformity, as in some noxious pasture, and there browse and feed upon many a baneful herb and flower day by day, little by little, until they silently gather a festering mass of corruption in their own soul. Let us rather search for artists who are gifted to discern the true nature of the beautiful and graceful; then will our youth dwell in a land of health, amid fair sights and sounds, and receive the good in everything; and beauty, the effluence of fair works, shall flow into the eye and ear, like a health-giving breeze from a purer region, and insensibly draw the soul from earliest years into likeness and sympathy with the beauty of reason.

There can be no nobler training than that, he replied.

Henry James

THE ART OF FICTION

[Fiction] must take itself seriously for the public to take it so. The old superstition about fiction being "wicked" has doubtless died out in England; but the spirit of it lingers in a certain oblique regard directed toward any story which does not more or less admit that it is only a joke. Even the most jocular novel feels in some degree the weight of the proscription that was formerly directed against literary levity; the jocularity does not always succeed in passing for gravity. It is still expected, though perhaps people are ashamed to say it, that a production which is after all only a "make believe" (for what else is a "story?") shall be in some degree apologetic—shall renounce the pretension of attempting really to compete with life. This, of course, any sensible wide-awake story declines to do; for it quickly perceives that the tolerance granted to it on such a condition is only an attempt to stifle it, disguised in the form of generosity. The old Evangelical hostility to the novel, which was as explicit as it was narrow, and which regarded it as little less favor-

All footnotes in this selection are by the editor of this text.

able to our immortal part than a stage-play, was in reality far less insulting. The only reason for the existence of a novel is that it *does* compete with life. When it ceases to compete as the canvas of the painter competes, it will have arrived at a very strange pass. It is not expected of the picture that it will make itself humble in order to be forgiven; and the analogy between the art of the painter and the art of the novelist is, so far as I am able to see, complete. Their inspiration is the same, their process (allowing for the different quality of the vehicle) is the same, their success is the same. They may learn from each other, they may explain and sustain each other. Their cause is the same, and the honor of one is the honor of another. . . . The Mahometans think a picture an unholy thing, but it is a long time since any Christian did, and it is therefore the more odd that in the Christian mind the traces (dissimulated though they may be) of a suspicion of the sister art should linger to this day. The only effectual way to lay it to rest is to emphasize the analogy to which I just alluded —to insist on the fact that, as the picture is reality, so the novel is history. That is the only general description (which does it justice) that we may give of the novel. But history also is allowed to compete with life, as I say; it is not, any more than painting, expected to apologize. The subject-matter of fiction is stored up likewise in documents and records, and if it will not give itself away, as they say in California, it must speak with assurance, with the tone of the historian. Certain accomplished novelists have a habit of giving themselves away which must often bring tears to the eyes of people who take their fiction seriously. I was lately struck, in reading over many pages of Anthony Trollope,[1] with his want of discretion in this particular. In a digression, a parenthesis or an aside, he concedes to the reader that he and this trusting friend are only "making believe." He admits that the events he narrates have not really happened, and that he can give his narrative any turn the reader may like best. Such a betrayal of a sacred office seems to me, I confess, a terrible crime; it is what I mean by the attitude of apology, and it shocks me every whit as much in Trollope as it would have shocked me in Gibbon or Macaulay.[2] It implies that the novelist is less occupied in looking for the truth than the historian, and in doing so it deprives him at a stroke of all his standing-room. To represent and illustrate the past, the actions of men, is the task of either writer, and the only difference that I can see is, in proportion as he succeeds, to the honor of the novelist, consisting as it does in his having more difficulty in collecting his evidence, which is so far from being purely literary. It seems to me to give him a great character, the fact that he has at once so much in common with the philosopher and the painter; this double analogy is a magnificent heritage. . . .

---

[1] Prolific English novelist (1815–1882), best known for his Barchester novels, including *Barchester Towers* (1857).

[2] Edward Gibbon was a widely known English historian (1737–1794), whose massive study *Decline and Fall* (8 vols., 1828) ensured his fame; Thomas Babington Macaulay was also a noted English historian (1800–1859).

"Art," in our Protestant communities, where so many things have got so strangely twisted about, is supposed, in certain circles, to have some vaguely injurious effect upon those who make it an important consideration, who let it weigh in the balance. It is assumed to be opposed in some mysterious manner to morality, to amusement, to instruction. When it is embodied in the work of the painter (the sculptor is another affair!) you know what it is; it stands there before you, in the honesty of pink and green and a gilt frame; you can see the worst of it at a glance, and you can be on your guard. But when it is introduced into literature it becomes more insidious—there is danger of its hurting you before you know it. Literature should be either instructive or amusing, and there is in many minds an impression that these artistic pre-occupations, the search for form, contribute to neither end, interfere, indeed, with both. They are too frivolous to be edifying, and too serious to be diverting; and they are, moreover, priggish and paradoxical and superfluous. That, I think, represents the manner in which the latent thought of many people who read novels as an exercise in skipping would explain itself if it were to become articulate. They would argue, of course, that a novel ought to be "good," but they would interpret this term in a fashion of their own, which, indeed, would vary considerably from one critic to another. One would say that being good means representing virtuous and aspiring characters, placed in prominent positions; another would say that it depends for a "happy ending" on a distribution at the last of prizes, pensions, husbands, wives, babies, millions, appended paragraphs, and cheerful remarks. Another still would say that it means being full of incident and movement, so that we shall wish to jump ahead, to see who was the mysterious stranger, and if the stolen will was ever found, and shall not be distracted from this pleasure by any tiresome analysis or "description." But they would all agree that the "artistic" idea would spoil some of their fun. One would hold it accountable for all the description, another would see it revealed in the absence of sympathy. Its hostility to a happy ending would be evident, and it might even, in some cases, render any ending at all impossible. The "ending" of a novel is, for many persons, like that of a good dinner, a course of dessert and ices, and the artist in fiction is regarded as a sort of meddlesome doctor who forbids agreeable aftertastes. It is therefore true that this conception of Mr. Besant's,[3] of the novel as a superior form, encounters not only a negative but a positive indifference. It matters little that, as a work of art, it should really be as little or as much concerned to supply happy endings, sympathetic characters, and an objective tone, as if it were a work of mechanics; the association of ideas, however incongruous, might easily be too much for

---

[3] Sir Walter Besant (1836–1901), an antiquarian who set scenes of his novels in eighteenth-century London and used his fiction to advocate social reforms, presented a lecture at the Royal Institution on April 25, 1884, treating fiction as "one of the Fine Arts." Besant endeavored to define laws for the writing of fiction, to which Henry James took exception. Besant's views seemed rigid, didactic, and restrictive. James took Besant to task in his "The Art of Fiction," and in so doing enunciated one of the great critical commentaries on fiction as art.

it if an eloquent voice were not sometimes raised to call attention to the fact that it is at once as free and as serious a branch of literature as any other.

Certainly, this might sometimes be doubted in presence of the enormous number of works of fiction that appeal to the credulity of our generation, for it might easily seem that there could be no great substance in a commodity so quickly and easily produced. It must be admitted that good novels are somewhat compromised by bad ones, and that the field at large suffers discredit from overcrowding. I think, however, that this injury is only superficial, and that the superabundance of written fiction proves nothing against the principle itself. It has been vulgarized, like all other kinds of literature, like everything else to-day, and it has proved more than some kinds accessible to vulgarization. But there is as much difference as there ever was between a good novel and a bad one; the bad is swept, with all the daubed canvases and spoiled marble, into some unvisited limbo or infinite rubbish-yard, beneath the back-windows of the world, and the good subsists and emits its light and stimulates our desire for perfection. . . . A novel is in its broadest definition a personal impression of life; that, to begin with, constitutes its value, which is greater or less according to the intensity of the impression. But there will be no intensity at all, and therefore no value, unless there is freedom to feel and say. The tracing of a line to be followed, of a tone to be taken, of a form to be filled out, is a limitation of that freedom and a suppression of the very thing that we are most curious about. The form, it seems to me, is to be appreciated after the fact; then the author's choice has been made, his standard has been indicated; then we can follow lines and directions and compare tones. Then, in a word, we can enjoy one of the most charming of pleasures, we can estimate quality, we can apply the test of execution. The execution belongs to the author alone; it is what is most personal to him, and we measure him by that. The advantage, the luxury, as well as the torment and responsibility, of the novelist, is that there is no limit to what he may attempt as an executant—no limit to his possible experiments, efforts, discoveries, successes. Here it is especially that he works, step by step, like his brother of the brush, of whom we may always say that he has painted his picture in a manner best known to himself. . . .

It goes without saying that you will not write a good novel unless you possess the sense of reality; but it will be difficult to give you a recipe for calling that sense into being. Humanity is immense, and reality has a myriad forms; the most one can affirm is that some of the flowers of fiction have the odor of it, and others have not; as for telling you in advance how your nosegay [4] should be composed, that is another affair. It is equally excellent and inconclusive to say that one must write from experience; to our supposititious aspirant such a declaration might savor of mockery. What kind of experience is intended, and where does it begin and end? Experience is never limited, and it is never

---

[4] A small bouquet of flowers.

complete; it is an immense sensibility, a kind of huge spider-web, of the finest silken threads, suspended in the chamber of consciousness and catching every air-borne particle in its tissue. It is the very atmosphere of the mind; and when the mind is imaginative—much more when it happens to be that of a man of genius—it takes to itself the faintest hints of life, it converts the very pulses of the air into revelations. . . .

We must grant the artist his subject, his idea, what the French call his *donnée;*[5] our criticism is applied only to what he makes of it. Naturally I do not mean that we are bound to like it or find it interesting; in case we do not, our course is perfectly simple, to let it alone. We may believe that of a certain idea even the most sincere novelist can make nothing at all, and the event may perfectly justify our belief; but the failure will have been a failure to execute, and it is in the execution that the fatal weakness is recorded. If we pretend to respect the artist at all we must allow him his freedom of choice, in the face, in particular cases, of innumerable presumptions that the choice will not fructify. Art derives a considerable part of its beneficial exercise from flying in the face of presumptions, and some of the most interesting experiments of which it is capable are hidden in the bosom of common things. Gustave Flaubert has written a story about the devotion of a servant-girl to a parrot, and the production, highly finished as it is, cannot on the whole be called a success.[6] We are perfectly free to find it flat, but I think it might have been interesting; and I, for my part, am extremely glad he should have written it. It is a contribution to our knowledge of what can be done—or what cannot. Ivan Turgénieff has written a tale about a deaf and dumb serf and a lap-dog, and the thing is touching, loving, a little masterpiece.[7] He struck the note of life where Gustave Flaubert missed it; he flew in the face of a presumption and achieved a victory.

Nothing, of course, will ever take the place of the good old fashion of "liking" a work of art or not liking it; the more improved criticism will not abolish that primitive, that ultimate, test. I mention this to guard myself from the accusation of intimating that the idea, the subject, of a novel or a picture does not matter. It matters, to my sense, in the highest degree, and if I might put up a prayer it would be that artists should select none but the richest. Some, as I have already hastened to admit, are much more substantial than others, and it would be a happily arranged world in which persons intending to treat them should be exempt from confusions and mistakes. This fortunate condition will arrive only, I fear, on the same day that critics become purged from error. Meanwhile, I repeat, we do not judge the artist with fairness unless we say to him: "Oh, I grant you your starting-point, because if I did not I should seem to prescribe to you, and heaven forbid I should take that responsibility. If I pretend to tell you what you must not take,

---

[5] That is, the writer's starting point; in a larger sense, his approach and subject.

[6] The story is, very likely, "A Simple Heart."

[7] "Mumu."

you will call upon me to tell you then what you must take; in which case I shall be nicely caught! Moreover, it isn't till I have accepted your data that I can begin to measure you.[8] I have the standard; I judge you by what you propose, and you must look out for me there. Of course I may not care for your idea at all; I may think it silly, or stale, or unclean; in which case I wash my hands of you altogether. I may content myself with believing that you will not have succeeded in being interesting, but I shall, of course, not attempt to demonstrate it, and you will be as indifferent to me as I am to you. I needn't remind you that there are all sorts of tastes; who can know it better? Some people, for excellent reasons, don't like to read about carpenters; others, for reasons even better, don't like to read about courtesans. Many object to Americans. Others (I believe they are mainly editors and publishers) won't look at Italians. Some readers don't like quiet subjects; others don't like bustling ones. Some enjoy a complete illusion; others revel in a complete deception. They choose their novels accordingly, and if they don't care about your idea they won't, *a fortiori*,[9] care about your treatment."

So that it comes back very quickly, as I have said, to the liking; in spite of M. Zola,[10] who reasons less powerfully than he represents, and who will not reconcile himself to this absoluteness of taste, thinking that there are certain things that people ought to like, and that they can be made to like. I am quite at a loss to imagine anything (at any rate in this matter of fiction) that people *ought* to like or to dislike. Selection will be sure to take care of itself, for it has a constant motive behind it. That motive is simply experience. As people feel life, so they will feel the art that is most closely related to it. This closeness of relation is what we should never forget in talking of the effort of the novel. Many people speak of it as a factitious, artificial form, a product of ingenuity, the business of which is to alter and arrange the things that surround us, to translate them into conventional, traditional moulds. This, however, is a view of the matter which carries us but a very short way, condemns the art to an eternal repetition of a few familiar *clichés*, cuts short its development, and leads us straight up to a dead wall. Catching the very note and trick, the strange irregular rhythm of life, that is the attempt whose strenuous force keeps Fiction upon her feet. In proportion as in what she offers us we see life *without* rearrangement, do we feel that we are touching the truth; in proportion as we see it *with* rearrangement do we feel that we are being put off with a substitute, a compromise and convention. . . . Art is essentially selection, but it is a selection whose main care is to be typical, to be inclusive. For many people art means

---

[8] In later editions, James inserted the line here, "I have the standard, the pitch; I have no right to tamper with your flute and then criticize your music."

[9] All the more.

[10] Emile Zola (1840–1902), a famous innovative French novelist and early prose naturalist; he experimented with "slice-of-life" fiction. His "empirical" ideals are stated in *Le roman expérimental,* in which he theorizes that humanity is controlled by natural forces and man's individual strength is limited.

rose-colored windows, and selection means picking a bouquet for Mrs. Grundy.[11] They will tell you glibly that artistic considerations have nothing to do with the disagreeable, with the ugly; they will rattle off shallow commonplaces about the province of art and the limits of art, till you are moved to some wonder in return as to the province and the limits of ignorance. It appears to me that no one can ever have made a seriously artistic attempt without becoming conscious of an immense increase—a kind of revelation—of freedom. One perceives, in that case —by the light of a heavenly ray—that the province of art is all life, all feeling, all observation, all vision. . . . it is all experience. That is a sufficient answer to those who maintain that it must not touch the painful, who stick into its divine unconscious bosom little prohibitory inscriptions on the end of sticks, such as we see in public gardens—"It is forbidden to walk on the grass; it is forbidden to touch the flowers; it is not allowed to introduce dogs, or to remain after dark; it is requested to keep to the right." The young aspirant in the line of fiction, whom we continue to imagine, will do nothing without taste, for in that case his freedom would be of little use to him; but the first advantage of his taste will be to reveal to him the absurdity of the little sticks and tickets. If he have taste, I must add, of course he will have ingenuity, and my disrespectful reference to that quality just now was not meant to imply that it is useless in fiction. But it is only a secondary aid; the first is a vivid sense of reality. . . .

I have just been reading, at the same time, the delightful story of "Treasure Island," by Mr. Robert Louis Stevenson, and the last tale from M. Edmond de Goncourt, which is entitled "Chérie." One of these works treats of murders, mysteries, islands of dreadful renown, hairbreadth escapes, miraculous coincidences and buried doubloons. The other treats of a little French girl who lived in a fine house in Paris and died of wounded sensibility because no one would marry her. I call "Treasure Island" delightful, because it appears to me to have succeeded wonderfully in what it attempts; and I venture to bestow no epithet upon "Chérie," which strikes me as having failed in what it attempts—that is, in tracing the development of the moral consciousness of a child. But one of these productions strikes me as exactly as much of a novel as the other, and as having a "story" quite as much. The moral consciousness of a child is as much a part of life as the islands of the Spanish Main, and the one sort of geography seems to me to have . . . "surprises" . . . quite as much as the other. . . .

The most interesting part of Mr. Besant's lecture is unfortunately the briefest passage—his very cursory allusion to the "conscious moral purpose" of the novel. Here again it is not very clear whether he is recording a fact or laying down a principle; it is a great pity that in the latter case he should not have developed his idea. This branch of the subject is of immense importance, and Mr. Besant's few words point to considerations of the widest reach, not to be lightly disposed of. He will

[11] Mrs. Grundy was a character known for her excessive prudery in Thomas Morton's *Speed the Plough* (1798), a comedy.

have treated the art of fiction but superficially who is not prepared to go
every inch of the way that these considerations will carry him. It is for
this reason that at the beginning of these remarks I was careful to
notify the reader that my reflections on so large a theme have no
pretension to be exhaustive. . . . I have left the question of the morality
of the novel till the last, and at the last I find I have used up my space.
It is a question surrounded with difficulties, as witness the very first
that meets us, in the form of a definite question, on the threshold.
Vagueness, in such a discussion, is fatal, and what is the meaning of
your morality and your conscious moral purpose? Will you not define
your terms and explain how (a novel being a picture) a picture can be
either moral or immoral? You wish to paint a moral picture or carve a
moral statue; will you not tell us how you would set about it? We are
discussing the Art of Fiction; questions of art are questions (in the
widest sense) of execution; questions of morality are quite another
affair, and will you not let us see how it is that you find it so easy to mix
them up . . . ? [Many] people . . . have been positively struck . . .
with the moral timidity of the usual English novelist; with his (or with
her) aversion to face the difficulties with which, on every side, the treatment of reality bristles. He is apt to be extremely shy . . . and the sign
of his work, for the most part, is a cautious silence on certain subjects.
In the English novel (by which I mean the American as well), more than
in any other, there is a traditional difference between that which people
know and that which they agree to admit that they know, that which
they see and that which they speak of, that which they feel to be a part
of life and that which they allow to enter into literature. There is the
great difference, in short, between what they talk of in conversation,
and what they talk of in print. The essence of moral energy is to survey
the whole field, and I . . . say, not that the English novel has a purpose,
but that it has a diffidence. To what degree a purpose in a work of art is
a source of corruption I shall not attempt to inquire; the one that seems
to me least dangerous is the purpose of making a perfect work. As for
our novel, I may say, lastly, on this score, that, as we find it in England
to-day, it strikes me as addressed in a large degree to "young people,"
and that this in itself constitutes a presumption that it will be rather
shy. There are certain things which it is generally agreed not to discuss,
not even to mention, before young people. That is very well, but the
absence of discussion is not a symptom of the moral passion. . . .

There is one point at which the moral sense and the artistic sense
lie very near together; that is, in the light of the very obvious truth that
the deepest quality of a work of art will always be the quality of the mind
of the producer. In proportion as that mind is rich and noble, will the
novel, the picture, the statue, partake of the substance of beauty and
truth. To be constituted of such elements is, to my vision, to have
purpose enough. No good novel will ever proceed from a superficial
mind; that seems to me an axiom which, for the artist in fiction, will
cover all needful moral ground; if the youthful aspirant take it to heart,
it will illuminate for him many of the mysteries of "purpose." There are
many other useful things that might be said to him, but I have come to

the end of my article, and can only touch them as I pass. The critic in the *Pall Mall Gazette*, whom I have already quoted, draws attention to the danger, in speaking of the art of fiction, of generalizing. The danger that he has in mind is rather, I imagine, that of particularizing; for there are some comprehensive remarks which . . . might, without fear of misleading . . . be addressed to the ingenuous student. I should remind him first of the magnificence of the form that is open to him, which offers to sight so few restrictions and such innumerable opportunities. The other arts, in comparison, appear confined and hampered; the various conditions under which they are exercised are so rigid and definite. But the only condition that I can think of attaching to the composition of the novel is, as I have already said, that it be interesting.[12] This freedom is a splendid privilege, and the first lesson of the young novelist is to learn to be worthy of it. "Enjoy it as it deserves," I should say to him; "take possession of it, explore it to its utmost extent, reveal it, rejoice in it. All life belongs to you, and don't listen either to those who would shut you up into corners of it and tell you that it is only here and there that art inhabits, or to those who would persuade you that this heavenly messenger wings her way outside of life altogether, breathing a superfine air and turning away her head from the truth of things. There is no impression of life, no manner of seeing it and feeling it, to which the plan of the novelist may not offer a place; you have only to remember that talents so dissimilar as those of Alexandre Dumas and Jane Austen, Charles Dickens and Gustave Flaubert, have worked in this field with equal glory. Don't think too much about optimism and pessimism; try and catch the color of life itself. In France to-day we see a prodigious effort (that of Emile Zola, to whose solid and serious work no explorer of the capacity of the novel can allude without respect), we see an extraordinary effort, vitiated by a spirit of pessimism on a narrow basis. M. Zola is magnificent, but he strikes an English reader as ignorant; he has an air of working in the dark; if he had as much light as energy, his results would be of highest value. As for the aberrations of a shallow optimism, the ground (of English fiction especially) is strewn with their brittle particles as with broken glass. If you must indulge in conclusions, let them have the taste of a wide knowledge. Remember that your first duty is to be as complete as possible—to make as perfect a work. Be generous and delicate, and then, in the vulgar phrase, go in!" [13]

---

[12] The word *Interesting* becomes *sincere* in subsequent publications.

[13] In later publications of the essay, the final sentence reads, "Be generous and delicate and pursue the prize."

Vance Packard

THE BUILT-IN SEXUAL OVERTONE

The potency of sex as a sales promoter was not, of course, an original discovery of the depth merchandisers. Sex images have long been cherished by ad men purely as eye stoppers. But with the depth approach, sex began taking on some interesting twists, ramifications, and subtleties. Penetration to deeper levels of consciousness was sought. Simple cheesecake and get-your-man themes of old, while used for routine selling, were regarded as limited-penetration weapons.

One shortcoming of get-your-man themes was that they frequently left the buyer disappointed and resentful. Perfume makers, in straining to outpromise each other in the early fifties with sex-drenched titles and themes, had trouble getting women to buy a second bottle when the first bottle, rich in sexual promise, had failed to deliver a satisfactory man into their arms. The Institute for Motivational Research, after exploring this problem, reported finding many women's dressers cluttered with "dead enthusiasm"—stale jars, unopened bottles, half-used boxes of cosmetics. It found that there is a dismally low rate of brand loyalty among users and that the industry has had to combat disappointment and raise new hopes by constantly bringing out new products, an expensive and discouraging process. (Ad men at conventions tell the story of the wistful girl who surveyed all the passionate labels on a perfume counter and asked bashfully if the store perhaps had something for beginners.) In 1955 more than 250 new trade-marks were issued in the toilet preparation field. Another difficulty harassing the cosmetics people was that modern women were no longer bewitched by a mere get-your-man or sexual enchantment promise. They wanted something more: to be accepted and respected by men as *partners,* and that of course was something a little more difficult for a mere perfume merchant to promise. It would take thought. In the words of the institute the situation called for "more subtle and more passive sex symbols than was the case a generation ago" with careful emphasis on such ingredients as poetry, fantasy, whimsey, and a distinct soft-pedaling of pure sex.

While sex was soft-pedaled for marketing in depth, its use as a simple eye stopper took more daring forms. The public had become jaded and permissive. The brassière and girdle appeals, for example, became bolder, with overtones of masochism, body exhibitionism, and so on. One ad widely exhibited showed a lovely girl with blond tresses, dressed only in her bra and girdle, being dragged by the hair across the floor by a modern caveman. The gay title was "Come out of the bone age, darling!" Another girdle ad showed a girl and her boyfriend at a Coney Island type of wind tunnel with the wind blowing her skirt above her head and exposing her entire midsection, which, of course, was encased in the girdle being offered for sale. She was giggling modestly.

The most controversial of the eye stoppers of this sort was the "I Dreamed I Stopped Traffic in My Maidenform Bra" campaign. The situations varied but always the girl involved, dressed fully except that she wore only a bra above the waist, was wandering about among normally dressed people. The theory was that since she was dreaming, her undressed state was permissible. The ad men themselves argued about the wisdom of this ad and the deep-down effect it had on women seeing it. Some were convinced, after talking with their psychological consultants, that the scene depicted would simply produce an anxiety state in women since it represented a common oneiric, or dream, expression of the neurotic anxieties experienced by many women. Others in the trade, however, became convinced after checking their psychologists that the ad was sound because the wish to appear naked or scantily clad in a crowd is "present in most of us" and "represents a beautiful example of wish fulfillment." This view evidently prevailed because the campaign was intensified and Maidenform began offering the public prizes up to $10,000 for ideas on dream situations that could be depicted.

The twists given sex in the hands of the depth merchandisers took some odd forms. A study was made for a major fountain-pen company in the Midwest on the sensuality and sexual connotations of pens. R. R. McMurry, psychological consultant of Chicago, made the study into the motivation for buying fountain pens and concluded that the pen is experienced as a body image by men—which is why they will pay up to fifteen dollars for a pen with an image particularly satisfying to them even though a cheaper one might write just as well.

An evidence of the extent to which sexual appeals have been carried is available in the so-called sport of wrestling. The discovery was made that the grunt-and-groan spectacles of professional wrestling, supposedly a sweaty he-man sport, survive only because of the feminine fans. A Nielsen check of TV fans watching wrestling matches revealed that ladies outnumbered men two to one. The promoters of the matches, shrewdly calculating the triggers that produced the most squeals from feminine fans, stepped up the sadism (men writhing in torture), the all-powerful male symbolism (chest beating and muscle flexing), and fashion interest (more and more elegant costumes for the performers).

A classic example of the way motivation analysts found merchandising possibilities in our deeper sexual yearnings was a study Dr. Dichter made for Chrysler Corporation in the early days of M.R. His study is now known as "Mistress versus Wife."

Dr. Dichter was called upon to explain a fact puzzling marketers of the auto. While most men bought sedans and rarely bought convertibles they evidently were more attracted to convertibles. Dealers had found that they could draw more males into their showrooms by putting convertibles in the window. After exploring the situation Dr. Dichter concluded that men saw the convertible as a possible symbolic mistress. It set them daydreaming of youth, romance, adventure just as they may dream of a mistress. The man knows he is not going to gratify his wish for a mistress, but it is pleasant to daydream. This daydreaming drew the man into the auto salesroom. Once there, he finally chose a four-door sedan just as he once married a plain girl who, he knew, would make a fine wife and mother. "Symbolically, he marries the sedan," a spokesman for Dr. Dichter explained. The sedan is useful, practical, down to earth, and safe. Dr. Dichter felt that the company would be putting its best foot backward if it puts its main emphasis on sedans simply because that was the car most men ended up buying. Instead, he urged the company to put the hope of mistress-adventure a little closer to males by giving most prominent display to the convertibles. The spokesman went on to explain Dr. Dichter's line of thinking: "If we get a union between the wife and mistress—all we sought in a wife plus the romance, youth, and adventure we want in a mistress—we would have . . . lo and behold, the hardtop!" The hardtop was soon to become the most successful new auto style introduced in the American market for several years, and Dr. Dichter's organization takes full credit for inspiring it by its "Mistress versus Wife" study.

The motivational analysts began finding that a major sexual need of both men and women in America at mid-century was sexual reassurance. Women by the millions were yearning for evidence that they were still basically feminine; and men by the millions were yearning for evidence they were still indisputably and virulently masculine. Merchandisers were quick to see the possibilities of offering both products that would serve as reassurance symbols.

Women were in need of evidences of reassurance because during the first half of the century their role in life had been undergoing radical changes: they had lost many of their old functions, had taken over many male functions, and in business had often fought to be accepted on the same basis as men. . . .

The beer brewers, too, had been caught napping. In 1955 the United States Brewers' Foundation exhorted members to stop assuming the average beer buyer was an older man. The average beer buyer, it said after researching the subject, was a woman between twenty-five and thirty-six who buys beer out of her weekly food budget and is particularly prone to female-oriented ads, nice packaging, and display.

The beer packagers began tampering with their can's sex appeal in ways that must have made some he-man customers uneasy. Pabst began stressing fashion as a selling lure by using the selling line "The finest is always in fashion," and its ads began showing stylish young people of both sexes partaking of beer. Budweiser, meanwhile, came out with a slim new beer can aimed at the woman buyer. The merchandising director explained that the can was being made "high style" to "appeal to the woman buyer. . . . We believe that the innate preference of women for grace, beauty, and style carries over to the purchase of beer."

A spectacular transvestism in the opposite direction was carried out in 1956 by Marlboro cigarettes, which used to be lipstick red and ivory tipped, designed primarily for women. Marlboro felt a little unhappy about its sexual designation because men smokers still outnumbered women two to one. When the cancer scare drove millions of men to show interest in filter tips, the Marlboro people decided to do a sexual flip-flop and go after the men, while holding onto as many women as they could. Their first move was to have Louis Cheskin, of the Color Research Institute, design a more masculine package. He did, in bold red and white. But that was only one of several significant changes. The Marlboro ads began featuring rugged, virile-looking men deep in work. To get the virile look desired the company used many nonprofessional models for the pictures (sailors, cowboys, and, reportedly, some men who worked at the company's ad agency). And the headlines of the ads began talking of Marlboro's "man-sized flavor."

Perhaps the most fascinating innovation was that all the rugged men shown in the long series—whether they were cowpokes, fishermen, skiers or writers—had one mark in common: they wore man-made stigmata. By an amazing coincidence they all had "tattoos," and still more amazing all the tattoos just happened to be on the back of the men's hands so that they showed in close-up photos. This tattoo motif puzzled some people since the tattoo is a common phenomenon among delinquents in reformatories. Marlboro, however, decided the tattoo was just what was needed to give its men a virile and "interesting past" look. The Marlboro people in fact became so pleased with this symbol of virility that they began distributing millions of transfer pictures of tattoos that men could stamp on their wrists just as children have long done.

Interestingly, first reports showed that Marlboro was, with this campaign, holding onto many women, while recruiting males. Many women seemed to enjoy gazing at the dashing-looking men in the ads. And Marlboro was still careful to call itself "A man's cigarette that women like too."

Motivational expert Pierre Martineau hailed the Marlboro campaign as investing its brand with a "terrifically exciting personality." He felt the highly masculine figures and the tattoo symbols set the cigarette "right in the heart of some core meanings of smoking: masculinity, adulthood, vigor, and potency. Quite obviously these meanings cannot be expressed openly. The consumer would reject them quite violently. The difference between a top-flight creative man and the hack is this ability to express powerful meanings indirectly. . . ."

15
INDIVIDUAL RESPONSIBILITY

*"If a man does not keep pace with his companions,
perhaps it is because he hears a different drummer.
Let him step to the music which he hears, however
measured or far away."*

—Henry David Thoreau, *Walden*

John Donne

MEDITATION 16

There is a story of a *Bell* in a *Monastery* [1] which, when any of the house was sicke to death, rung alwaies *voluntarily*, and they knew the inevitablenesse of the danger by that. It rung once, when no man was sick; but the next day one of the house, fell from the *steeple*, and died, and the *Bell* held the reputation of a *Prophet* still. If these *Bells* that warne to a *Funerall* now, were appropriated to none, may not I, by the houre of the *funerall*, supply? How many men that stand at an *execution*, if they would aske, for what dies that man, should heare their owne faults condemned, and see themselves executed, by *Atturney*? [2] We scarce heare of any man *preferred*, but wee thinke of our selves, that wee might very well have beene that *Man;* Why might not I have beene that *Man*, that is carried to his *grave* now? Could I fit my selfe, to *stand*, or *sit* in any Mans *place*, and not to lie in any mans *grave?* I may lacke much of the *good parts* of the meanest, but I lacke nothing of the *mortality* of the weakest; They may have acquired better *abilities* than I, but I was borne to as many *infirmities* as they. To be an *incumbent* [3] by lying down in a *grave*, to be a *Doctor* by teaching *Mortification* by *Example*, by *dying*, though I may have *seniors*, others may be *elder* than I, yet I have proceeded apace in a good *University*, and gone a great way in a little time, by the furtherance of a vehement *fever;* and whomsoever these *Bells* bring to the ground to day, if hee and I had beene compared yesterday, perchance I should have been thought likelier to come to this preferment, then, than he. *God* hath kept the power of *death* in his owne hands, lest any Man should *bribe death*. If man knew the *gaine of death*, the *ease of death*, he would solicite, he would provoke death to assist him, by any hand, which he might use. But as when men see many of their owne professions preferd, it ministers a hope that that may light upon them; so when these hourely *Bells* tell me of so many *funerals* of men like me, it presents, if not a *desire* that it may, yet a *comfort* whensoever mine shall come.

Reprinted with permission of The Macmillan Company from *Seventeenth-Century Verse and Prose*, Vol. 1 by H. C. White, R. C. Wallerstein & R. Quintana. Copyright 1951, by The Macmillan Company.

[1] "Roccha" (Donne's note), Angiolo Rocca, *De Campanis*, 1612

[2] deputy

[3] pun on two meanings, lying down and person in present possession of a benefice or office

MEDITATION 17

Nunc lento sonitu dicunt, Morieris. Now, this Bell tolling softly for another, sales to me, Thou must die.

Perchance [4] hee for whom this *Bell* tolls, may bee so ill, as that he knowes not it tolls for him; And perchance I may thinke my selfe so much better than I am, as that they who are about mee, and see my state, may have caused it to toll for mee, and I know not that. The *Church* is *Catholike, universall,* so are all her Actions; *All* that she does, belongs to *all.* When she *baptizes a child,* that action concernes mee; for that child is thereby connected to that *Head* which is my *Head* too, and engraffed into that *body,* whereof I am a *member.* And when she *buries a Man,* that action concernes me: All *mankinde* is of one *Author,* and is one *volume;* when one Man dies, one *Chapter* is not *torne* out of the *booke,* but *translated* into a better *language;* and every *Chapter* must be so translated; *God* emploies several *translators;* some peeces are translated by *Age,* some by *sicknesse,* some by *warre,* some by *justice;* but *Gods* hand is in every *translation;* and his hand shall binde up all our scattered leaves againe, for that *Librarie* where every *booke* shall lie open to one another: As therefore the *Bell* that rings to a *Sermon,* calls not upon the *Preacher* onely, but upon the *Congregation* to come; so this *Bell* calls us all: but how much more *mee,* who am brought so neere the *doore* by this *sicknesse.* There was a *contention* as farre as a *suite,* (in which both *pietie* and *dignitie, religion,* and *estimation,*[5] were mingled) which of the religious *Orders* should ring to *praiers* first in the *Morning;* and it was *determined,* that *they should ring first that rose earliest.* If we understand aright the *dignitie* of this *Bell,* that tolls for our *evening prayer,* wee would bee glad to make it ours, by rising early, in that *application,* that it might bee ours, as wel as his, whose indeed it is. The *Bell* doth toll for him that *thinkes* it doth; and though it *intermit* againe, yet from that *minute,* that that occasion wrought upon him, hee is united to *God.* Who casts not up his *Eye* to the *Sunne* when it rises? but who takes off his *Eie* from a *Comet* when that breakes out? who bends not his *eare* to any *bell,* which upon any occasion rings? but who can remove it from that *bell,* which is passing a *peece of himselfe* out of this *world?* No man is an *Iland,* intire of it selfe; every man is a peece of the *Continent,* a part of the *maine;* [6] if a *Clod* bee washed away by the *Sea, Europe* is the lesse, as well as if a *Promontorie* were, as well as if a *Mannor* of thy *friends* or of *thine owne* were; Any mans *death* diminishes *me,* because I am involved in *Mankinde;* And therefore never send to know for whom the *bell* tolls; It tolls for *thee.*

[4] perhaps

[5] prestige

[6] mainland

James Fenimore Cooper
THE AMERICAN DEMOCRAT

We live in an age when the words aristocrat and democrat are much used, without regard to the real significations. An aristocrat is one of a few who possess the political power of a country; a democrat, one of the many. The words are also properly applied to those who entertain notions favorable to aristocratical or democratical forms of government. Such persons are not necessarily either aristocrats or democrats in fact, but merely so in opinion. Thus a member of a democratical government may have an aristocratical bias, and vice versa.

To call a man who has the habits and opinions of a gentleman, an aristocrat from that fact alone, is an abuse of terms and betrays ignorance of the true principles of government, as well as of the world. It must be an equivocal freedom under which every one is not the master of his own innocent acts and associations; and he is a sneaking democrat indeed who will submit to be dictated to, in those habits over which neither law nor morality assumes a right of control.

Some men fancy that a democrat can only be one who seeks the level, social, mental and moral, of the majority, a rule that would at once exclude all men of refinement, education, and taste from the class. These persons are enemies of democracy, as they at once render it impracticable. They are usually great sticklers for their own associations and habits, too, though unable to comprehend any of a nature that are superior. They are, in truth, aristocrats in principle, though assuming a contrary pretension, the groundwork of all their feelings and arguments being self. Such is not the intention of liberty, whose aim is to leave every man to be the master of his own acts; denying hereditary honors, it is true, as unjust and unnecessary, but not denying the inevitable consequences of civilization.

The law of God is the only rule of conduct in this, as in other matters. Each man should do as he would be done by. Were the question put to the greatest advocate of indiscriminate association, whether he would submit to have his company and habits dictated to him, he would be one of the first to resist the tyranny; for they who are the most rigid in maintaining their own claims in such matters, are usually the loudest in decrying those whom they fancy to be better off than themselves. Indeed, it may be taken as a rule in social intercourse, that he who is the most apt to question the pretensions of others is the most conscious of the doubtful position he himself occupies; thus establishing the very claims he affects to deny, by letting his jealousy of it be seen. Manners, education, and refinement, are positive things, and they bring with them innocent tastes which are productive of high enjoyments; and it is as unjust to deny their possessors their indulgence as it would be to insist on the less fortunate's passing the time they would rather devote to athletic amusements, in listening to operas for which they have no relish, sung in a language they do not understand.

All that democracy means, is as equal a participation in rights as is practicable; and to pretend that social equality is a condition of popular institutions is to assume that the latter are destructive of civilization, for, as nothing is more self-evident than the impossibility of raising all men to the highest standard of tastes and refinement, the alternative would be to reduce the entire community to the lowest. The whole embarrassment on this point exists in the difficulty of making men comprehend qualities they do not themselves possess. We can all perceive the difference between ourselves and our inferiors, but when it comes to a question of the difference between us and our superiors, we fail to appreciate merits of which we have no proper conceptions. In face of this obvious difficulty, there is the safe and just governing rule, already mentioned, or that of permitting every one to be the undisturbed judge of his own habits and associations, so long as they are innocent and do not impair the rights of others to be equally judges for themselves. It follows, that social intercourse must regulate itself, independently of institutions, with the exception that the latter, while they withhold no natural, bestow no factitious advantages beyond those which are inseparable from the rights of property, and general civilization.

In a democracy, men are just as free to aim at the highest attainable places in society, as to attain the largest fortunes; and it would be clearly unworthy of all noble sentiment to say that the grovelling competition for money shall alone be free, while that which enlists all the liberal acquirements and elevated sentiments of the race, is denied the democrat. Such an avowal would be at once a declaration of the inferiority of the system, since nothing but ignorance and vulgarity could be its fruits.

The democratic gentleman must differ in many essential particulars from the aristocratical gentleman, though in their ordinary habits and tastes they are virtually identical. Their principles vary; and, to a slight degree, their deportment accordingly. The democrat, recognizing the right of all to participate in power, will be more liberal in his general sentiments, a quality of superiority in itself; but in conceding this much to his fellow man, he will proudly maintain his own independence of vulgar domination as indispensable to his personal habits. The same principles and manliness that would induce him to depose a royal despot would induce him to resist a vulgar tyrant.

There is no more capital, though more common error, than to suppose him an aristocrat who maintains his independence of habits; for democracy asserts the control of the majority, only in matters of law, and not in matters of custom. The very object of the institution is the utmost practicable personal liberty, and to affirm the contrary would be sacrificing the end to the means.

An aristocrat, therefore, is merely one who fortifies his exclusive privileges by positive institutions, and a democrat, one who is willing to admit of a free competition in all things. To say, however, that the last supposes this competition will lead to nothing is an assumption that means are employed without any reference to an end. He is the purest democrat who best maintains his rights, and no rights can be dearer to a man of cultivation than exemptions from unseasonable invasions on his time by the coarse minded and ignorant.

Henry David Thoreau

CIVIL DISOBEDIENCE

I heartily accept the motto,—"That government is best which governs least;" and I should like to see it acted up to more rapidly and systematically. Carried out, it finally amounts to this, which also I believe,— "That government is best which governs not at all;" the militia, jailers, constables, *posse comitatus*, etc. In most cases there is no free exercise whatever of the judgment or of the moral sense; but they put themselves on a level with wood and earth and stones; and wooden men can perhaps be manufactured that will serve the purpose as well. Such command no more respect than men of straw or a lump of dirt. They have the same sort of worth only as horses and dogs. Yet such as these even are commonly esteemed good citizens. Others—as most legislators, politicians, lawyers, ministers, and office-holders—serve the state chiefly with their heads; and, as they rarely make any moral distinctions, they are as likely to serve the devil, without *intending* it, as God. A very few, —as heroes, patriots, martyrs, reformers in the great sense, and *men*— serve the state with their consciences also, and so necessarily resist it for the most part; and they are commonly treated as enemies by it. A wise man will only be useful as a man, and will not submit to be "clay," and "stop a hole to keep the wind away," [1] but leave that office to his dust at least: —

> "I am too high-born to be propertied,
> To be a secondary at control,
> Or useful serving-man and instrument
> To any sovereign state throughout the world." [2]

He who gives himself entirely to his fellow-men appears to them useless and selfish; but he who gives himself partially to them is pronounced a benefactor and philanthropist.

How does it become a man to behave toward this American government to-day? I answer, that he cannot without disgrace be associated with it. I cannot for an instant recognize that political organization as *my* government which is the *slave's* government also.

All men recognize the right of revolution; that is, the right to

All footnotes in this selection are by the editor of this text.

[1] Allusion to Shakespeare's HAMLET, Act V, Sc. 1.

[2] See Shakespeare's KING JOHN, Act V, Sc. 2.

refuse allegiance to, and to resist, the government, when its tyranny or its inefficiency are great and unendurable. . . .[3]

All voting is a sort of gaming, like checkers or backgammon, with a slight moral tinge to it, a playing with right and wrong, with moral questions; and betting naturally accompanies it. The character of the voters is not staked. I cast my vote, perchance, as I think right; but I am not vitally concerned that that right should prevail. I am willing to leave it to the majority. Its obligation, therefore, never exceeds that of expediency. Even voting *for the right* is *doing* nothing for it. It is only expressing to men feebly your desire that it should prevail. A wise man will not leave the right to the mercy of chance, nor wish it to prevail through the power of the majority. There is but little virtue in the action of masses of men. When the majority shall at length vote for the abolition of slavery, it will be because they are indifferent to slavery, or because there is but little slavery left to be abolished by their vote. *They* will then be the only slaves. Only *his* vote can hasten the abolition of slavery who asserts his own freedom by his vote. . . .

It is not a man's duty, as a matter of course, to devote himself to the eradication of any, even the most enormous, wrong; he may still properly have other concerns to engage him; but it is his duty, at least, to wash his hands of it, and, if he gives it no thought longer, not to give it practically his support. If I devote myself to other pursuits and contemplations, I must first see, at least, that I do not pursue them sitting upon another man's shoulders. I must get off him first, that he may pursue his contemplations too. See what gross inconsistency is tolerated. I have heard some of my townsmen say, "I should like to have them order me out to help put down an insurrection of the slaves, or to march to Mexico;—see if I would go;" and yet these very men have each, directly by their allegiance, and so indirectly, at least, by their money, furnished a substitute. The soldier is applauded who refuses to serve in an unjust war by those who do not refuse to sustain the unjust government which makes the war; is applauded by those whose own act and authority he disregards and sets at naught; as if the state were penitent to that degree that it hired one to scourge it while it sinned, but not to that degree that it left off sinning for a moment. Thus, under the name of Order and Civil Government, we are all made at last to pay homage to and support our own meanness. After the first blush of sin comes its indifference; and from immoral it becomes, as it were, *un*moral, and not quite unnecessary to that life which we have made. . . .

How can a man be satisfied to entertain an opinion merely, and enjoy *it*? Is there any enjoyment in it, if his opinion is that he is aggrieved? If you are cheated out of a single dollar by your neighbor,

[3] The Jacksonian Democrat had narrowly defeated the Whig Henry Clay for the Presidency. Polk's administration [1845–1849] was condemned by both the Whigs and the Abolitionists; the latter were especially hostile to the fugitive-slave laws and the Mexican War, which, they believed, were merely disguises for the extension of the slaveocracy. Ironically, the most extreme of the Abolitionists had refused to support the more neutral Henry Clay in the presidential election, and by their very zealousness had let the election go to the Tennessean, who had solid Southern support.

you do not rest satisfied with knowing that you are cheated, or with saying that you are cheated, or even with petitioning him to pay you your due; but you take effectual steps at once to obtain the full amount, and see that you are never cheated again. Action from principle, the perception and the performance of right, changes things and relations; it is essentially revolutionary, and does not consist wholly with anything which was. It not only divides States and churches, it divides families; ay, it divides the *individual,* separating the diabolical in him from the divine.

Unjust laws exist: shall we be content to obey them, or shall we endeavor to amend them, and obey them until we have succeeded, or shall we transgress them at once? Men generally, under such a government as this, think that they ought to wait until they have persuaded the majority to alter them. They think that, if they should resist, the remedy would be worse than the evil. But it is the fault of the government itself that the remedy *is* worse than the evil. *It* makes it worse. Why is it not more apt to anticipate and provide for reform? Why does it not cherish its wise minority? Why does it cry and resist before it is hurt? Why does it not encourage its citizens to be on the alert to point out its faults, and *do* better than it would have them? Why does it always crucify Christ, and excommunicate Copernicus and Luther,[4] and pronounce Washington and Franklin rebels?

One would think, that a deliberate and practical denial of its authority was the only offense never contemplated by government; else, why has it not assigned its definite, its suitable and proportionate penalty? If a man who has no property refuses but once to earn nine shillings for the State, he is put in prison for a period unlimited by any law that I know, and determined only by the discretion of those who placed him there; but if he should steal ninety times nine shillings from the State, he is soon permitted to go at large again.

If the injustice is part of the necessary friction of the machine of government, let it go, let it go: perchance it will wear smooth,—certainly the machine will wear out. If the injustice has a spring, or a pulley, or a rope, or a crank, exclusively for itself, then perhaps you may consider whether the remedy will not be worse than the evil; but if it is of such a nature that it requires you to be the agent of injustice to another, then, I say, break the law. Let your life be a counter friction to stop the machine. What I have to do is to see, at any rate, that I do not lend myself to the wrong which I condemn.

As for adopting the ways which the State has provided for remedying the evil, I know not of such ways. They take too much time, and a man's life will be gone. I have other affairs to attend to. I came into this

---

[4] Nicolaus Copernicus (1473–1543) was the famous Polish astronomer who published his theory that the planets revolve around the sun and the earth turns on an axis, thus reversing man's previous idea that the earth was the center of the universe. His work, dedicated to Pope Paul III, first appeared in Nuremberg the year of Copernicus' death, and soon came under the censure of the Catholic Church.

Martin Luther founded the Protestant Reformation and was excommunicated in 1521 by Pope Leo X.

world, not chiefly to make this a good place to live in, but to live in it, be it good or bad. A man has not everything to do, but something; and because he cannot do *everything*, it is not necessary that he should do *something* wrong. It is not my business to be petitioning the Governor or the Legislature any more than it is theirs to petition me; and if they should not hear my petition, what should I do then? But in this case the State has provided no way: its very Constitution is the evil. This may seem to be harsh and stubborn and unconciliatory; but it is to treat with the utmost kindness and consideration the only spirit that can appreciate or deserves it. So is all change for the better, like birth and death, which convulse the body.

I do not hesitate to say, that those who call themselves Abolitionists should at once effectually withdraw their support, both in person and property, from the government of Massachusetts, and not wait till they constitute a majority of one, before they suffer the right to prevail through them. I think that it is enough if they have God on their side, without waiting for that other one.[5] Moreover, any man more right than his neighbors constitutes a majority of one already.

I meet this American government, or its representative, the State government, directly, and face to face, once a year—no more—in the person of its tax-gatherer; this is the only mode in which a man situated as I am necessarily meets it; and it then says distinctly, Recognize me; and the simplest, the most effectual, and, in the present posture of affairs, the indispensablest mode of treating with it on this head, of expressing your little satisfaction with and love for it, is to deny it then. My civil neighbor, the tax-gatherer, is the very man I have to deal with, —for it is, after all, with men and not with parchment that I quarrel,— and he has voluntarily chosen to be an agent of the government. How shall he ever know well what he is and does as an officer of the government, or as a man, until he is obliged to consider whether he shall treat me, his neighbor, for whom he has respect, as a neighbor and well-disposed man, or as a maniac and disturber of the peace, and see if he can get over this obstruction to his neighborliness without a ruder and more impetuous thought or speech corresponding with his action. I know this well, that if one thousand, if one hundred, if ten men whom I could name,—if ten *honest* men only,—ay, if *one* HONEST man, in this State of Massachusetts, *ceasing to hold slaves,* were actually to withdraw from this copartnership, and be locked up in the county jail therefor, it would be the abolition of slavery in America. For it matters not how small the beginning may seem to be: what is once well done is done forever. But we love better to talk about it: that we say is our mission. . . .

Under a government which imprisons any unjustly, the true place for a just man is also a prison. The proper place to-day, the only place which Massachusetts has provided for her freer and less desponding spirits, is in her prisons, to be put out and locked out of the State by her own act, as they have already put themselves out by their principles.

---

[5] "One on God's side is a majority," is a famous maxim.

It is there that the fugitive slave, and the Mexican prisoner on parole, and the Indian come to plead the wrongs of his race should find them; on that separate, but more free and honorable ground, where the State places those who are not *with* her, but *against* her,—the only house in a slave State in which a free man can abide with honor. If any think that their influence would be lost there, and their voices no longer afflict the ear of the State, that they would not be as an enemy within its walls, they do not know by how much truth is stronger than error, nor how much more eloquently and effectively he can combat injustice who has experienced a little in his own person. Cast your whole vote, not a strip of paper merely, but your whole influence. A minority is powerless while it conforms to the majority; it is not even a minority then; but it is irresistible when it clogs by its whole weight.[6] If the alternative is to keep all just men in prison, or give up war and slavery, the State will not hesitate which to choose. If a thousand men were not to pay their tax-bills this year, that would not be a violent and bloody measure, as it would be to pay them, and enable the State to commit violence and shed innocent blood. This is, in fact, the definition of a peaceable revolution, if any such is possible. If the tax-gatherer, or any other public officer, asks me, as one has done, "But what shall I do?" my answer is, "If you really wish to do anything, resign your office." When the subject has refused allegiance, and the officer has resigned his office, then the revolution is accomplished. But even suppose blood should flow. Is there not a sort of blood shed when the conscience is wounded? Through this wound a man's real manhood and immortality flow out, and he bleeds to an everlasting death. I see this blood flowing now. . . .

Some years ago, the State met me in behalf of the Church, and commanded me to pay a certain sum toward the support of a clergyman whose preaching my father attended, but never I myself. "Pay," it said, "or be locked up in the jail." I declined to pay. But, unfortunately, another man saw fit to pay it. I did not see why the schoolmaster should be taxed to support the priest, and not the priest the schoolmaster; for I was not the State's schoolmaster, but I supported myself by voluntary subscription. I did not see why the lyceum should not present its tax-bill, and have the State to back its demand, as well as the Church. However, at the request of the selection, I condescended to make some such statement as this in writing: —"Know all men by these presents, that I, Henry Thoreau, do not wish to be regarded as a member of any incorporated society which I have not joined." This I gave to the town clerk; and he has it. The State, having thus learned that I did not wish to be regarded as a member of that church, has never made a like demand on me since; though it said that it must adhere to its original presumption that time. If I had known how to name them, I should then have signed off in detail from all the societies which I never signed on to; but I did not know where to find a complete list.

I have paid no poll-tax for six years. I was put into a jail once on this account, for one night; [7] and, as I stood considering the walls of solid stone, two or three feet thick, the door of wood and iron, a foot thick, and the iron grating which strained the light, I could not help being struck with the foolishness of that institution which treated me as if I were mere flesh and blood and bones, to be locked up. I wondered that it should have concluded at length that this was the best use it could put me to, and had never thought to avail itself of my services in some way. I saw that, if there was a wall of stone between me and my townsmen, there was a still more difficult one to climb or break through before they could get to be as free as I was. I did not for a moment feel confined, and the walls seemed a great waste of stone and mortar. I felt as if I alone of all my townsmen had paid my tax. They plainly did not know how to treat me, but behaved like persons who are underbred. In every threat and in every compliment there was a blunder; for they thought that my chief desire was to stand the other side of that stone wall. I could not but smile to see how industriously they locked the door on my meditations, which followed them out again without let or hindrance, and *they* were really all that was dangerous. As they could not reach me, they had resolved to punish my body; just as boys, if they cannot come at some person against whom they have a spite, will abuse his dog. I saw that the State was half-witted, that it was timid as a lone woman with her silver spoons, and that it did not know its friends from its foes, and I lost all my remaining respect for it, and pitied it.

Thus the State never intentionally confronts a man's sense, intellectual or moral, but only his body, his senses. It is not armed with superior wit or honesty, but with superior physical strength. I was not born to be forced. I will breathe after my own fashion. Let us see who is the strongest. What force has a multitude? They only can force me who obey a higher law than I. They force me to become like themselves. I do not hear of *men* being *forced* to live this way or that by masses of men. What sort of life were that to live? When I meet a government which says to me, "Your money or your life," why should I be in haste to give it my money? It may be in a great strait, and not know what to do: I cannot help that. It must help itself; do as I do. It is not worth the while to snivel about it. I am not responsible for the successful working of the machinery of society. I am not the son of the engineer. I perceive that, when an acorn and a chestnut fall side by side, the one does not remain inert to make way for the other, but both obey their own laws, and spring and grow and flourish as best they can, till one, perchance, overshadows and destroys the other. If a plant cannot live according to its nature, it dies; and so a man.

The night in prison was novel and interesting enough. The prisoners in their shirt-sleeves were enjoying a chat and the evening air in the doorway, when I entered. But the jailer said, "Come, boys, it is time to lock up;" and so they dispersed, and I heard the sound of their steps re-

[7] Probably on July 23 or 24, 1846.

turning into the hollow apartments. My room-mate was introduced to me as "a first-rate fellow and a clever [good-natured] man." When the door was locked, he showed me where to hang my hat, and how he managed matters there. The rooms were whitewashed once a month; and this one, at least, was the whitest, most simply furnished, and probably the neatest apartment in the town. He naturally wanted to know where I came from, and what brought me there; and, when I had told him, I asked him in my turn how he came there, presuming him to be an honest man, of course; and, as the world goes, I believe he was. "Why," said he, "they accuse me of burning a barn; but I never did it." As near as I could discover, he had probably gone to bed in a barn when drunk, and smoked his pipe there; and so a barn was burnt. He had the reputation of being a clever man, had been there some three months waiting for his trial to come on, and would have to wait as much longer; but he was quite domesticated and contented, since he got his board for nothing, and thought that he was well treated.

He occupied one window, and I the other; and I saw that if one stayed there long, his principal business would be to look out the window. I had soon read all the tracts that were left there, and examined where former prisoners had broken out, and where a grate had been sawed off, and heard the history of the various occupants of that room; for I found that even here there was a history and a gossip which never circulated beyond the walls of the jail. Probably this is the only house in the town where verses are composed, which are afterward printed in circular form, but not published. I was shown quite a long list of verses which were composed by some young men who had been detected in an attempt to escape, who avenged themselves by singing them.

I pumped my fellow-prisoner as dry as I could, for fear I should never see him again; but at length he showed me which was my bed, and left me to blow out the lamp.

It was like traveling into a far country, such as I had never expected to behold, to lie there for one night. It seemed to me that I never had heard the town clock strike before, nor the evening sounds of the village; for we slept with the windows open, which were inside the grating. It was to see my native village in the light of the Middle Ages, and our Concord was turned into a Rhine stream, and visions of knights and castles passed before me. They were the voices of old burghers that I heard in the streets. I was an involuntary spectator and auditor of whatever was done and said in the kitchen of the adjacent village-inn,—a wholly new and rare experience to me. It was a closer view of my native town. I was fairly inside of it. I never had seen its institutions before. That is one of the peculiar institutions; for it is a shire town. I began to comprehend what its inhabitants were about.

In the morning, our breakfasts were put through the hole in the door, in small oblong-square tin pans, made to fit, and holding a pint of chocolate, with brown bread, and an iron spoon. When they called for the vessels again, I was green enough to return what bread I had left; but my comrade seized it, and said that I should lay that up for lunch or dinner. Soon after he was let out to work at haying in a neighboring field, whither he went every day, and would not be back till noon; so he bade me good-day, saying that he doubted if he should see me again.

When I came out of prison,—for some one interfered, and paid that tax,[8]—I did not perceive that great changes had taken place on the common, such as he observed who went in a youth and emerged a tottering and gray-headed man; and yet a change had to my eyes come over the scene,—the town, and State, and country,—greater than any that mere time could effect. I saw yet more distinctly the State in which I lived. I saw to what extent the people among whom I lived could be trusted as good neighbors and friends; that their friendship was for summer weather only; that they did not greatly propose to do right; that they were a distinct race from me by their prejudices and superstitions, as the Chinamen and Malays are; that in their sacrifices to humanity they ran no risks, not even to their property; that after all they were not so noble but they treated the thief as he had treated them, and hoped, by a certain outward observance and a few prayers, and by walking in a particular straight though useless path from time to time, to save their souls. This may be to judge my neighbors harshly; for I believe that many of them are not aware that they have such an institution as the jail in their village.

It was formerly the custom in our village, when a poor debtor came out of jail, for his acquaintances to salute him, looking through their fingers, which were crossed to represent the grating of a jail window, "How do ye do?" My neighbors did not thus salute me, but first looked at me, and then at one another, as if I had returned from a long journey. I was put into jail as I was going to the shoemaker's to get a shoe which was mended. When I was let out the next morning, I proceeded to finish my errand, and, having put on my mended shoe, joined a huckleberry party, who were impatient to put themselves under my conduct; and in half an hour,—for the horse was soon tackled,—was in the midst of a huckleberry field, on one of our highest hills, two miles off, and then the State was nowhere to be seen. . . .

No man with a genius for legislation has appeared in America. They are rare in the history of the world. There are orators, politicians, and eloquent men, by the thousand; but the speaker has not yet opened his mouth to speak who is capable of settling the much-vexed questions of the day. We love eloquence for its own sake, and not for any truth which it may utter, or any heroism it may inspire. Our legislators have not yet learned the comparative value of free trade and of freedom, of union, and of rectitude, to a nation. They have no genius or talent for comparatively humble questions of taxation and finance, commerce and manufactures and agriculture. If we were left solely to the wordy wit of legislators in Congress for our guidance, uncorrected by the seasonable experience and the effectual complaints of the people, America would not long retain her rank among the nations. For eighteen hundred years,

---

[8] The legend is that Ralph Waldo Emerson paid Thoreau's tax, but best evidence indicates that it was a member of Thoreau's family, possibly an aunt.

though perchance I have no right to say it, the New Testament has been written; yet where is the legislator who has wisdom and practical talent enough to avail himself of the light which it sheds on the science of legislation?

The authority of government, even such as I am willing to submit to,—for I will cheerfully obey those who know and can do better than I, and in many things even those who neither know nor can do so well,— is still an impure one; to be strictly just, it must have the sanction and consent of the governed. It can have no pure right over my person and property but what I concede to it. The progress from an absolute to a limited monarchy, from a limited monarchy to a democracy, is a progress toward a true respect for the individual. Even the Chinese philosopher was wise enough to regard the individual as the basis of the empire. Is a democracy, such as we know it, the last improvement possible in government? Is it not possible to take a step further towards recognizing and organizing the rights of man? There will never be a really free and enlightened State until the State comes to recognize the individual as a higher and independent power, from which all its own power and authority are derived, and treats him accordingly. I please myself with imagining a State at last which can afford to be just to all men, and to treat the individual with respect as a neighbor; which even would not think it inconsistent with its own repose if a few were to live aloof from it, not meddling with it, nor embraced by it, who fulfilled all the duties of neighbors and fellowmen. A State which bore this kind of fruit, and suffered it to drop off as fast as it ripened, would prepare the way for a still more perfect and glorious State, which also I have imagined, but not yet anywhere seen.

T. S. Eliot

THE LOVE SONG OF J. ALFRED PRUFROCK [1]

S'io credessi che mia risposta fosse
a persona che mai tornasse al mondo,
questa fiamma staria senza più scosse.

[1] Begun the year he received his M.A. at Harvard in 1910, when Eliot was twenty-one, the poem was first published in the Chicago magazine *Poetry* (June, 1915), after Ezra Pound's persistent badgering of editor Harriet Monroe; in book form first under the title *Prufrock and Other Observations* (June, 1917).

Concerning the title, although Eliot once remarked that the German surname was "quite unconscious," Hugh Kenner in *The Invisible Poet: T. S. Eliot* (New York: McDowell, Obolensky, 1959), p. 3, notes the advertisements of St. Louis furniture wholesalers Prufrock-Littau appeared while the poet was growing up there. "J. Alfred" and "Love Song" appear to create an ironic juxtaposition of opposites—a kind of fatuous priggishness set over against a persistently troubling rather than sentimental Romantic tradition, consistent with the *leitmotif* of clashing oppositions running throughout the poem.

Ma per clò che glammal dl questo fondo
non tornò vivo alcun, s'i'odo il vero,
senza tema d'Infamia ti rispondo.[2]

Let us go then, you and I,[3]
When the evening is spread out against the sky
Like a patient etherised upon a table;
Let us go, through certain half-deserted streets,
The muttering retreats
Of restless nights in one-night cheap hotels
And sawdust restaurants with oyster-shells:
Streets that follow like a tedious argument
Of insidious intent
To lead you to an overwhelming question. . .
Oh, do not ask, 'What is it?'
Let us go and make our visit.

In the room the women come and go
Talking of Michelangelo.[4]

The yellow fog that rubs its back upon the window-panes,
The yellow smoke that rubs its muzzle on the window-panes,
Licked its tongue into the corners of the evening,
Lingered upon the pools that stand in drains,
Let fall upon its back the soot that falls from chimneys,
Slipped by the terrace, made a sudden leap,
And seeing that it was a soft October night,
Curled once about the house, and fell asleep.[5]

[2] A damned soul in Dante's *Inferno* (canto xxvii, 11.61–66), Guido da Montefeltro, replies to a questioning of his name in these words: "If I thought my reply were being addressed to one who might return to the living earth, this flame would quiver no more [i.e., the spirit would not talk]. But since no one alive goes back from this depth, if what I hear be true, then without fear of infamy I answer you." This epigraph sets the tone for the opening of the poem and its continuing atmosphere and themes. For Eliot's interest in Dante, see his essay, "Dante," in *The Sacred Wood* (1922).

[3] Whether "you and I" be taken to refer to the generalized reader-poet, lady-lover, modern man-traditional man, twentieth-century man in dialogue with himself (i.e., the inner or subjective self with the outer or objective self)—or some other concept, such as man's real nature in contrast to the "mask" he presents to the external world—Eliot appears intentionally to have suggested more than he reveals, again within the context of clashing oppositions.

[4] The soothing sonority of the couplet is ironic and, once more, typical of Eliot's clashing oppositions. Following the first twelve lines, as they move out of the epigraphic Dantesque Hell and into the strange world of the Prufrockian hero, suggesting a half-alive, sick, and indecisive existence, the rhyming pair of lines serve as a kind of epiphany—a sudden and definite insight—of the modern world of artifice (bored women *talking* of art) contrasted with the energetic power and *creating* genius of the Renaissance artist, Michelangelo (1475–1564).

[5] The "yellow fog" passage represents the strong influence of Jules Laforgue and other French Symbolists upon Eliot's work; among their purposes in creating a new poetry were to "suggest" obliquely rather than to "state directly"; to make the abstract concrete (as fog here becomes a cat); and, conversely, to make the concrete abstract.

And indeed there will be time
For the yellow smoke that slides along the street
Rubbing its back upon the window-panes;
There will be time, there will be time
To prepare a face to meet the faces that you meet;
There will be time to murder and create,[6]
And time for all the works and days of hands[7]
That lift and drop a question on your plate;
Time for you and time for me,
And time yet for a hundred indecisions,
And for a hundred visions and revisions,
Before the taking of a toast and tea.

In the room the women come and go
Talking of Michelangelo.

And indeed there will be time
To wonder, 'Do I dare?' and, 'Do I dare?'
Time to turn back and descend the stair,
With a bald spot in the middle of my hair—
(They will say: 'How his hair is growing thin!')
My morning coat, my collar mounting firmly to the chin,
My necktie rich and modest, but asserted by a simple pin—
(They will say: 'But how his arms and legs are thin!')
Do I dare
Disturb the universe?[8]
In a minute there is time
For decisions and revisions which a minute will reverse.

For I have known them all already, known them all—[9]
Have known the evenings, mornings, afternoons,
I have measured out my life with coffee spoons;
I know the voices dying with a dying fall[10]

---

[6] Note again the clashing opposition. The tone is harshly cynical but also subtly didactic, even more subtly suggestive: is man essentially a destroyer or a creator? Is he evil or good? "Unnatural" or "natural"?

[7] Generally, perhaps, the weary round of life. More specifically, the Greek poet Hesiod (8th century B.C.) wrote *Works and Days,* a morally instructive piece in which he emphasized the advantages of his brother's working on his farm.

[8] Although Laforgue wrote, "Do I dare disturb the universe?" in an 1881 letter, thus presenting a possible source for Eliot, the latter here suggests much more than Laforgue: e.g., the over-intellectualized self juxtaposed with such ultimates as the meaning of life, awareness of self-discovery, of human responsibility, of death, and of eschatological mysteries.

[9] Laforgue anticipated these lines in his *Le Concile Féerique* (especially note II. 54, 62).

[10] In his opening speech of Shakespeare's *Twelfth Night*, Orsino, Duke of Illyria, declares, "If music be the food of love, play on; . . . . That strain again! it had **a dying fail**. . . ." Not unlike Prufrock, Orsino is "fancy-sick," capricious, outwardly false, inwardly unsound in his emotions, self-absorbed, and given to narcissistic exaggeration (like the fantastic Malvolio, to some extent). Given to talk rather than action, Orsino lacks the genuine thing.

Beneath the music from a farther room.
  So how should I presume?

And I have known the eyes already, known them all—
The eyes that fix you in a formulated phrase,
And when I am formulated, sprawling on a pin,
When I am pinned and wriggling on the wall,
Then how should I begin
To spit out all the butt-ends of my days and ways?
  And how should I presume?

And I have known the arms already, known them all—
Arms that are braceleted and white and bare
(But in the lamplight, downed with light brown hair!)
Is it perfume from a dress
That makes me so digress?
Arms that lie along a table, or wrap about a shawl.
  And should I then presume?
  And how should I begin?

                     .   .   .

Shall I say, I have gone at dusk through narrow streets
And watched the smoke that rises from the pipes
Of lonely men in shirt-sleeves, leaning out of windows? . . .

I should have been a pair of ragged claws
Scuttling across the floors of silent seas.[11]

                     .   .   .

And the afternoon, the evening, sleeps so peacefully!
Smoothed by long fingers,
Asleep . . . tired . . . or it malingers,
Stretched on the floor, here beside you and me.
Should I, after tea and cakes and ices,
Have the strength to force the moment to its crisis?
But though I have wept and fasted, wept and prayed,
Though I have seen my head (grown slightly bald) brought in
      upon a platter,
I am no prophet [12]—and here's no great matter;
I have seen the moment of my greatness flicker,
And I have seen the eternal Footman hold my coat, and snicker,
And in short, I was afraid.

---

[11] This image, the barest elemental form in the sea—not even a complete animal—is at least genuinely alive in its element, in opposition to Prufrock's unnatural functions in an unnatural world. Eliot once described the culture of his Boston world of 1912 as being "refined beyond the point of civilization."

[12] I.e., Prufrock is not a prophet like John the Baptist, who was decapitated at Herod's order, and whose head was presented to the spurned Herodias (Cf. Matthew, xiv:3–11; Oscar Wilde's play *Salomé*, 1894; and Richard Strauss' opera taken from it). No passionate dedication will dictate Prufrock's actions except, perhaps, in his daydreams where the external world "won't see."

And would it have been worth it, after all,
After the cups, the marmalade, the tea,
Among the porcelain, among some talk of you and me,
Would it have been worth while,
To have bitten off the matter with a smile,
To have squeezed the universe into a ball [13]
To roll it towards some overwhelming question,
To say: 'I am Lazarus, come from the dead,
Come back to tell you all,[14] I shall tell you all'—
If one, settling a pillow by her head,
  Should say: 'That is not what I meant at all.
  That is not it, at all.'

And would it have been worth it, after all,
Would it have been worth while,
After the sunsets and the dooryards and the sprinkled streets,
After the novels, after the teacups, after the skirts that trail
  along the floor—
And this, and so much more?—
It is impossible to say just what I mean!
But as if a magic lantern threw the nerves in patterns on a
  screen:
Would it have been worth while
If one, settling a pillow or throwing off a shawl,
And turning toward the window, should say:
  'That is not it at all,
  That is not what I meant, at all.'
                            .   .   .
No! I am not Prince Hamlet, nor was meant to be;
Am an attendant lord, one that will do
To swell a progress, start a scene or two,
Advise the prince; no doubt, an easy tool,
Deferential, glad to be of use,
Politic, cautious, and meticulous;
Full of high sentence, but a bit obtuse;
At times, indeed, almost ridiculous—
Almost, at times, the Fool.[15]

---

[13] Cf. and contrast the positive action of the lover in Andrew Marvell's poem "To His Coy Mistress" for whom time moves too fast: "Let us roll all our strength, and all/Our sweetness, up into one ball;/And tear our pleasures with rough strife,/Through the iron gates of life."

[14] Generally, the allusion to Lazarus (See John xi:1–44) is synthesized with the epigraph from Dante's Inferno, for both Dante and the persona of Eliot's poem "return" to the "world," but what kind of world is it? What kind of society is Prufrock's? Is Eliot suggesting a commentary upon 20th-century "civilized" man as well as the inner labyrinths of the Prufrockian narrator who symbolizes modern man's frustrations?

[15] Throughout the entire stanza Prufrock contends first that he is not young, heroic, and talented like Prince Hamlet, nor is he capable of taking action even after long indecision. Rather, he is comparable to sententious and ingratiating old Polonius or the deceptive and

I grow old . . . I grow old . . .
I shall wear the bottoms of my trousers rolled.

Shall I part my hair behind? Do I dare to eat a peach?
I shall wear white flannel trousers, and walk upon the beach.
I have heard the mermaids singing, each to each.

I do not think that they will sing to me.

I have seen them riding seaward on the waves
Combing the white hair of the waves blown back
When the wind blows the water white and black.

We have lingered in the chambers of the sea
By sea-girls wreathed with seaweed red and brown
Till human voices wake us, and we drown.[16]

Philip H. Phenix

REALMS OF MEANING

We now turn to a fourth realm, in which the selection and organization of experience is of a distinctively different logical kind from the three thus far considered. These meanings will be designated by the term "synnoetics." Briefly, this term refers to meanings in which a person has direct insight into other beings (or oneself) as concrete wholes existing in relation.

The general nature of synnoetics as a distinct realm of meaning may be made clear by indicating the main respects in which it differs from the other three realms thus far discussed. Knowledge in symbolics, empirics, and esthetics requires *detachment,* while synnoetic meaning requires *engagement.* In the first three realms the knower stands apart from what he knows. In the latter he effects a direct meeting.

---

fawning Rosencrantz or Guildenstern—even to the court jester or Fool. Chaucer in the Prologue to his *Canterbury Tales* describes his twelfth character, the "Clerk" of "Oxenford," as "ful of hy sentence" (l. 306). It is merely a pleasantry to note that Eliot himself was at Merton College, Oxford, in 1915, was a teacher at High Wycombe Grammar School outside London, and was also a clerk in Lloyd's Bank before *Prufrock* first appeared in book form.

[16] The mythic image suggests the encounter of the hero Ulysses with the sirens, irresistible creatures of magical beauty who enticed men and their ships to destruction upon their island. Prufrock may phantasize about walking upon the beaches and hearing the maidens' beautiful voices luring him seaward; but this seems to be as close to genuine passion as he will get. For he is a creature out of water—at least *natural* water—and will not drown in an epic adventure, but rather as he returns to his society, as he emerges to an uncertain self-awareness in the sea of humanity.

Knowledge in symbolics, empirics, and esthetics is *objective*, or better, it depends on a *subject-object relationship*. Synnoetic meanings relate *subjects* to *subjects*. Objectivity is eliminated and is replaced by *subjectivity*, or better, *intersubjectivity*. . . .

Synnoesis does not occur, of course, wholly without mediation. Subject relates to subject by a variety of means of communication, including ordinary language and perhaps even more often by the many sorts of nondiscursive symbolic forms. No realm of shared meaning can dispense with language of some kind. What is distinctive about synnoesis is that in this realm the function of the symbols used is to effect a relationship between the communicating beings themselves (or within themselves in the case of intrapersonal reflection) and not to establish a common orientation to some third objective entity. . . .

Meanings in this personal realm are *concrete* rather than *abstract*, as in language, science, and art. Language meanings are abstract in the sense that they are concerned with classes of sounds, semantic elements, and grammatical structures. Science meanings depend on concrete experience, through sense observation, but consist of the abstractions of classifications, generalizations, laws, and theories. Meanings in the arts are ideal abstractions presented in particular created works. In contrast with these, personal meanings are concrete in the sense that relational understanding is not a fragment, a perspective, or a transformation of some other more complete experience. Rather, it is itself the prototype of experience in its wholeness or concreteness.

In contrast to the realm of personal knowledge, symbolic, empirical, and esthetic meanings are impersonal. Language is for everybody's use, science is public knowledge, and art is presented for all to behold. Personal knowledge, on the other hand, is always on a one-to-one basis. It is not predicated upon the idea of "anyone" or "whosoever," but on confrontation with the singular being. Impersonal meanings presuppose the interchangeability of persons. Personal relations presuppose the uniqueness of the persons who enter into relation.

Language, science, and art are concerned with *essences,* while personal knowledge is *existential.* That is to say, the former fields deal with various kinds and qualities of being, while the latter has to do with *being itself*, that is, with concrete existence. To be is to be in relation. There is no such thing as absolutely solitary existence. The very concept of isolation has significance only against a background of others from whom one is separated. Separateness is relative nonbeing; all dividing of things depends upon their prior being in relation.

Having thus broadly characterized the synnoetic realm of personal knowledge, we proceed to a consideration of how these meanings are acquired and of some distinctive methods and concepts in this realm which may assist in teaching and learning such meanings.

For the most part, personal knowledge is not developed through formal instruction. It is a consequence of the basic fact of human association, beginning with the family and extending out in ever-widening circles to relationships in community, occupational life, and even with people in other nations and cultures. The quality of personal meanings therefore depends upon the nature of the common life, particularly upon the earliest and most intimate associations in the family, between parents and children.

Although personal knowledge is largely a product of ordinary social experience, it is not without benefit of theoretical study and concentrated consideration by specialized inquirers. However, those who are recognized as leaders in the practice and interpretation of meanings in this realm do not form as coherent and identifiable a company as do the linguists, scientists, and artists, respectively, in the first three realms of meaning. The subjectivity inherent in personal knowledge inhibits the formation of groups of persons who adhere to common objective criteria of meaning in this realm. Even more relevant is the fact that in personal understanding concern for critical theoretical judgments may militate against intersubjective awareness, somewhat as in the case of the arts, where overemphasis on critical evaluation may interfere with appreciative perception. Moreover, in personal insight the simplest and most untutored people can be as competent as, or even more competent than, people who devoted much time and thought to the perfecting of this aspect of life. The same cannot be said of linguists, scientists, or artists, all of whom become demonstrably expert through the deliberate cultivation of their specialized pursuits.

In spite of this somewhat embarrassing situation concerning practical expertise in the realm of personal knowledge, the insights of those who have considered the subject deeply may still be effective in making provision for the optimum development of these meanings. This assumption is necessary if the educator is not to abandon all hope and responsibility for improving the quality of human meanings at the deepest personal level.

Those who have been most concerned professionally with personal relations come mainly from four fields of endeavor, namely, religion, philosophy, psychology, and literature. As general disciplines the first two belong within the synoptic realm (see Chapters 19 and 20 below), the third within the empirical realm (see Chapter 10 above), and the last within the esthetic realm (see Chapter 15 above). Though workers from these fields provide most of the ideas for the understanding of personal awareness, the essential logic of meanings in this realm is neither that of the synoptic, the scientific, nor the esthetic disciplines, except insofar as the synoptic disciplines by their very nature integrate meanings from the other realms, including the synnoetic.

A classic discussion of the meaning of personal knowledge is found in the writings of Martin Buber.[1] According to Buber, fullness of being consists in *relation*. Relations are of two kinds: "I-Thou" and "I-It." I-Thou is a "primary word," not in the sense of a spoken utterance, but as a creative event. I-Thou arises out of the "reality of combination." I-It, on the contrary, arises out of separation. I-Thou, being primary, is not produced by the conjunction of a prior "I" with a prior "Thou." Rather,

[1] See especially his *I and Thou*, Charles Scribner's Sons, New York, 1958.

I-Thou is the primordial reality from which "I" and "Thou" are derived by abstraction. Thus, the infant's earliest life consists in relation, and only gradually are the self and the other discriminated as separable beings. On the other hand, I-It *is* derived from setting together "I" and "It." First comes the "I" (derived from I-Thou) as existing over against things (It), and from these two put in the relation of subject to object comes the I-It.

Buber adds that the "I" of I-Thou is not the same as the "I" of I-It. In being separated and then impersonally reconnected a fundamental alteration in the quality of being takes place. The "I" of I-Thou is a connected person with subjectivity; the "I" of I-It is a differentiated individual who is a subject over against a world of objects.

In the I-Thou relation the attitude of manipulation is absent. One does not try to *use* the other with whom he stands in relation, but rather affirms and respects the other's being. Others in relation are not objects to be comprehended, categorized, or abstracted. Relation is a state of being, not an emotional condition or an experience (both of which presuppose the isolation of the subject as over against objects). In the I-Thou relation others are set free to be themselves, not to be what I will them to be. At the same time, persons in relation are responsibly concerned for others, seeking their well-being, living to serve, to heal, to teach, and to strengthen them in every possible way that does not contradict their freedom.

Freedom is a central concept in the analysis of personal knowledge. Here freedom does not mean anarchy—the autonomy of isolation—nor does it mean release from responsibility by being submerged in social activities. It means the power to be and to become through relationships in which the integrity and worth of each person are responsibly affirmed by the others with whom he is associated.

Another fundamental concept in personal relations is *love*. Love is also an ambiguous term. In the present connection it does not refer to a subjective experience, state of feeling, or passion. It means simply the the reality of the active, caring, responsible relation of an "I" to a "Thou." The antithesis of love is not hate, which still manifests a kind of relation, but indifference, the cold exclusion of others by behaving as if they did not exist.

Although personal relations are usually thought of as occurring between human beings, in Buber's view they may also take place in our life with nature and in our spiritual life. One can regard the objects of nature as objects to be used and consumed (the I-It relation), or as beings in themselves, to be respected and loved (the I-Thou relation). This personalization of relationships with nature is the basis of animism and of the more sophisticated view (panpsychism) that everything existing has an inner consciousness. It also underlies the principle of noninjury of any living thing in Eastern religion—a principle that also governs Albert Schweitzer's basic ideal of "reverence for life." As for life in the spiritual sphere, Buber holds that every I-Thou relation is grounded in a relation to the eternal Thou and hence that all authentic personal relations are rooted in the life of the spirit. . . .

Loudon Wainwright

THE DYING GIRL THAT NO ONE HELPED

To judge from the recent, bitter example given us by the good folks of a respectable New York residential area, Samaritans are very scarce these days. In fact, if the reactions of the 38 heedless witnesses to the murder of Catherine Genovese provide any true reflection of a national attitude toward our neighbors, we are becoming a callous, chicken-hearted and immoral people. Psychiatrists, poking around in the ruins of character at the scene of the crime, have already come up with some generous, culture-blaming excuses for this grotesque piece of bad fellowship. But the matter calls for something more than sheer indignation. An examination of the pitiful facts of Miss Genovese's terminal experience makes very necessary the ugly personal question each of us must ask: What would *I* have done?

The story is simple and brutal. As she arrived home in the early morning darkness, Kitty Genovese, a decent, pretty young woman of 28, was stalked through the streets close to her Kew Gardens apartment and stabbed again and again by a man who had followed her home and who took almost a half hour to kill her. During that bloody little eternity, according to an extraordinary account published in the New York *Times,* Kitty screamed and cried repeatedly for help. Her entreaties were unequivocal. "Oh, my God!" she cried out at one point. "He stabbed me! Please help me! Someone help me!" Minutes later, before the murderer came back and attacked her for the final time, she screamed, "I'm dying! I'm dying!"

The reason the murderer's actions and his victim's calls are so well documented is that police were able to find 38 of Kitty's neighbors who admitted they witnessed the awful event. They heard the screams and most understood her cry for help. Peeking out their windows, many saw enough of the killer to provide a good description of his appearance and clothing. A few saw him strike Kitty, and more saw her staggering down the sidewalk after she had been stabbed twice and was looking for a place to hide. One especially sharp-eyed person was able to report that the murderer was sucking his finger as he left the scene; he had cut himself during the attack. Another witness has the awful distinction of being the only person Kitty Genovese recognized in the audience taking in her final moments. She looked at him and called to him by name. He did not reply.

No one really helped Kitty at all. Only one person shouted at the killer ("Let that girl alone!"), and the one phone call that was finally made to the police was placed after the murderer had got in his car and driven off. For the most part the witnesses, crouching in darkened windows like watchers of a Late Show, looked on until the play had passed beyond their view. Then they went back to bed.

Reprinted from *Life,* Vol. 56, April 10, 1964, p. 21, © Time Inc. 1964.

Not all of these people, it must be said, understood they were watching a murder. Some thought they were looking on at a lovers' quarrel; others saw or heard so very little that they could not have reached any conclusion about the disturbance. Even if one of her neighbors had called the police promptly, it cannot be definitely stated that Kitty would have survived. But that is quite beside the point. The fact is that no one, even those who were sure something was terribly wrong, felt moved enough to act. There is, of course, no law against not being helpful.

On the scene a few days after the killer had been caught and had confessed, Police Lieutenant Bernard Jacobs discussed the investigation. "The word we kept hearing from the witnesses later was 'involved,' " Jacobs said. A dark-haired, thoughtful man, he was standing on the sidewalk next to two fist-sized, dark-gray blotches on the cement. These were Kitty's bloodstains and it was there that the killer first stabbed her. "People told us they just didn't want to get involved," Jacobs said to me. "They don't want to be questioned or have to go to court." He pointed to an apartment house directly across the quiet street. "They looked down at this thing," he went on, "from four different floors of that building." Jacobs indicated the long, two-story building immediately next to him. A row of stores took up the ground floor; there were apartments on the upper floor. "Kitty lived in one of them," Jacobs said. "People up there were sitting right on top of the crime." He moved his arm in a gesture that included all the buildings. "It's a nice neighborhood, isn't it?" he went on. "Doesn't look like a jungle. Good, solid people. We don't expect anybody to come out into the street and fight this kind of bum. All we want is a phone call. We don't even need to know who's making it.

"You know what this man told us after we caught him?" Jacobs asked. "He said he figured nobody would do anything to help. He heard the windows go up and saw the lights go on. He just retreated for a while and when things quieted down, he came back to finish the job."

Later, in one of the apartment houses, a witness to part of Kitty Genovese's murder talked. His comments—agonized, contradictory, guilt-ridden, self-excusing—indicate the price in bad conscience he and his neighbors are now paying. "I feel terrible about it," he said. "The thing keeps coming back in my mind. You just don't want to get involved. They might have picked me up as a suspect if I'd bounced right out there. I was getting ready, but my wife stopped me. She didn't want to be a hero's widow. I woke up about the third scream. I pulled the blind so hard it came off the window. The girl was on her knees struggling to get up. I didn't know if she was drunk or what. I never saw the man. She staggered a little when she walked, like she had a few drinks in her. I forgot the screen was there and I almost put my head through it trying to get a better look. I could see people with their heads out and hear windows going up and down all along the street."

The man walked to the window and looked down at the sidewalk. He was plainly depressed and disappointed at his own failure. "Every time I look out here now," he said, "it's like looking out at a nightmare. How could so many of us have had the same idea that we didn't need to do anything? But that's not all that's wrong." Now he sounded betrayed and he told what was really eating him. Those 38 witnesses had, at least, talked to the police after the murder. The man pointed to a nearby building. "There are people over there who saw everything," he said. "And there hasn't been a peep out of them yet. Not one peep."

A VERY SPECIAL MURDERER

Once you accept the fact that he is what he is, the most shocking thing about Winston Moseley is the cool delicacy of his face. Framed by a perfectly symmetrical cap of black hair, it is all smooth olive and shadows, and the eyes look out from a distance somehow deeper than their sockets. When Moseley speaks, his mouth works with a dainty economy and his voice is even and well modulated. If Moseley is anything, he is convincing, especially when he is talking about the murders he has committed.

Winston Moseley is the very special murderer who was recently convicted of killing Kitty Genovese on a suburban New York street early one morning last March. Though 38 people watched or heard the murder, nobody helped Miss Genovese. Moseley, through his nightmare act, thus lacerated the consciences of people all over the United States. He did not just kill Kitty Genovese; he made a lot of people wonder about themselves, about their own courage and their attitudes toward their neighbors. More than the murder itself, the staggering reluctance to become involved caused a wave of reproach, often self-reproach, and the news around the country has been full of "apathy" stories about other people who refused to help those in trouble. Moseley's trial and conviction simply brought it all up again.

When I saw Winston Moseley last week, he was becoming involved with another man's problem: he was confessing a murder for which the other was being tried. The person on trial was Alvin Mitchell, a pale, weak-faced youth—"19 today," his stricken father announced from the witness stand, and the jury looked stunned as they grappled with visions of cake and ice cream and soundless echoes of "Happy Birthday, dear Alvin, Happy Birthday to you." Mitchell was on trial for the murder last summer of a 15-year-old friend of his named Barbara Kralik, whom he allegedly had stabbed to death with a pair of scissors as she lay in her bed. Mitchell confessed this crime to the police and the district attorney last August. But he has since recanted and now claims that the police extracted the confession from him through long hours of questioning and repeated beatings with rolled-up newspapers.

Now, here as a sworn witness was Winston Moseley, awaiting sure sentence of death for the Genovese murder, claiming one more awful credit. "I killed Barbara Kralik," he said with the patience of a man who is trying to clear up a minor misunderstanding. "I had a steak knife . . . I put my hand over her mouth . . . I stabbed her to death."

Reprinted from *Life*, Vol. 57, July 3, 1964, © Time Inc. 1964.

Moseley has developed a reputation for truthfulness in such matters. No one has had occasion to doubt one word of his detailed confession about killing Kitty Genovese. When at the same time he confessed the murder of a woman named Johnson, officials at first thought he was lying. He claimed to have shot Mrs. Johnson many times, while the official report said she died of stab wounds. But when the body was exhumed, it was discovered to be full of bullets fired from the gun Moseley declared he'd used to shoot Mrs. Johnson.

Moseley's statement in open court about the Kralik murder came as no real surprise. He has been saying right along that he did it. In an orange plaid shirt and black trousers, he described the way he had entered the house in the early hours of the morning, how he had crept past a sleeping child, up the stairs past the open door of a room where the girl's parents were sleeping, into the room where Barbara lay. He stabbed her, Moseley said, several times and then turned around and walked out of the house. J. Irwin Shapiro, the judge in the Mitchell trial, had also tried the Moseley case, and he asked Moseley for a clarification on the layout of the furniture in one room of the Kralik house. In answering, Moseley showed none of the tension one might look for in a man holding a conversation with the judge who would very soon pronounce his death sentence. Under cross-examination by a district attorney, Moseley admitted that he had read all about the killing in the papers and had indeed driven by the Kralik house months afterward. He was unsure of some details but he insisted throughout that this, too, was his murder.

If Moseley is telling the truth, is he doing it to satisfy the needs of his own sick conscience? Does he really want to save Alvin Mitchell? If Moseley is insane, which was the defense in his own trial, does he *imagine* that he killed Barbara Kralik? Does he *wish* that he had? If Moseley is lying, which the district attorney and the police are certain is the case, why? For publicity? For one false claim on a record that already contains two murders, about 40 burglaries and various assaults and rapes? Or is he playing some perverse private joke on the society which now seems determined to do away with him?

It is interesting to note that Moseley actually received his death sentence for Kitty Genovese's murder not from a judge, but from a jury. Under a recent change in the New York penal law, Moseley's trial took place in two sections. The first involved the trial proper, and the jury found him guilty. The second section involved a special hearing to help the jury arrive at a choice between life imprisonment and death. In such a hearing the ordinary rules of evidence do not apply.

Apparently nothing presented in the Moseley hearing for punishment inclined the jury toward mercy. Four women (who would not have been allowed to testify in the trial itself) came forth and told of Moseley's assaults upon them. The judge would not allow the defense lawyers to present evidence of medical insanity. He also advised the jury, as was entirely proper, that if they decided on a life sentence for Moseley, he might be released on parole in 26 years.

The jury's unanimous recommendation of death seemed fitting to many watchers in the courtroom. Like gleeful knitters at the guillotine, they burst into happy applause. The judge must have thought it was quite right, too, for in an extraordinary emotional comment from the bench he called Moseley a "monster" and said, "I wouldn't hesitate to pull the switch myself."

The whole thing sounds to me as if something more was going on in that courtroom than legal proceedings against a particularly vicious murderer. I wonder if the good citizens there weren't finding some hope of expiation in Winston Moseley's sentence. Moseley's death, if that indeed is his proper punishment, may pay for what he did to Kitty Genovese. But it will not mend the consciences of all those who did nothing for Kitty Genovese—or for that matter the consciences of countless others who were somewhere else that night.

16
GOD, MAN, AND MORAL CONSCIOUSNESS

"The most beautiful thing we can experience is the mysterious. To know that what is impenetrable to us really exists, manifesting itself as the highest wisdom and the most radiant beauty which our dull faculties can comprehend only in their most primitive forms—this knowledge, this feeling, is at the center of true religiousness."

—Albert Einstein, *I Believe*

Gerard Manley Hopkins

GOD'S GRANDEUR

The world Is charged with the grandeur of God.
It will flame out, like shining from shook foil;
It gathers to a greatness, like the ooze of oil
Crushed. Why do men then now not reck his rod?
Generations have trod, have trod, have trod;
And all is seared with trade; bleared, smeared with toil;
And wears man's smudge and shares man's smell—the soil
Is bare now, nor can foot feel, being shod.
And for all this, nature is never spent;
There lives the dearest freshness deep down things;
And though the last lights off the black West went
Oh, morning, at the brown brink eastward, springs—
Because the Holy Ghost over the bent
World broods with warm breast and with ah! bright wings.

Robert Frost

STOPPING BY WOODS ON A SNOWY EVENING

Whose woods these are I think I know.
His house is in the village though;
He will not see me stopping here
To watch his woods fill up with snow.

My little horse must think it queer
To stop without a farmhouse near
Between the woods and frozen lake
The darkest evening of the year.

He gives his harness bells a shake
To ask if there is some mistake.
The only other sound's the sweep
Of easy wind and downy flake.

The woods are lovely, dark and deep.
But I have promises to keep,
And miles to go before I sleep,
And miles to go before I sleep.

Thomas Anthony Dooley

PROMISES TO KEEP

Village of Muong Sing
Kingdom of Laos

Dear Bart:

It is far past midnight. I am sitting in my house at Muong Sing, high in the foothills of the Himalayas in northern Laos. The kerosene pressure lamps overhead are hissing at me, and the wind is lashing down my valley. It whips the palm and frangipani. All the earth on this sad cut of the world seems flooded in the monsoon rains. This is the season of the crashing violence of the tropical storm. The crickets, frogs and wilder jungle animals screech and scream. The high Lao night land is not calm.

But I feel calm in writing you. I feel as though I have just met you outside the medical-school auditorium. May I thrust my hand out and say, "Congratulations, Bart. Congratulations on your graduation from medical school. Congratulations on being a doctor." But along with my congratulations, I also want to offer you some thoughts to mull over during your coming year of internship.

As a doctor, you have glorious things ahead of you. I am going to presume that you will choose the life of a general practitioner. There is a place in the world for specialists, but this battered world of ours needs more country doctors. As a general practitioner, where will you practice? The world is lopsided in its distribution of doctors. Almost all corners of America have available doctors. With veterans' benefits, industrial group health plans, labor-union programs and all the others, there is hardly a citizen who cannot find medical attention if he is willing to make some effort.

This valley in Laos, prior to our Medico hospital, had nothing to offer the sick but black magic, necromancy, witchcraft, clay images, sorcery and betel juice. The villagers wallowed in monkeys' blood, cobwebs, tigers' teeth and incantations. You know the world's statistics. The Congo, 13 million people and not one native doctor. South Vietnam, 11 million people, about 180 doctors. Cambodia, five million people, seven doctors. Here in Laos, there are three million people and only one Lao doctor. Other nations' statistics are equally staggering.

Though this is sometimes called "the age of the shrug," I do not believe you would say, as some do, "So what, it's not my problem." You and I, Bart, are the heirs of all ages. We have been born and raised in freedom. We have justice, law and equality. But we have overlooked another side of our inheritance. We have also the legacy of hatred, bred by careless men before us. We have the legacy of abuse, degradation and the inhumanity of men blinded by prejudice and ignorance. To people like you and me, richer in educational opportunities than many, this is a challenge. To accept it is a privilege and a responsibility.

I believe that the unique aspect of this challenge to young doctors demands that we invest some of our lives in the practice of medicine in foreign fields. I say "some," not a lifetime. This is not expected of us. But we can give a year or two. It can be part of the maturation of a man, the metamorphosis of a doctor.

Your internship lies ahead, maybe residency, and then—come out to the developing nations of the world for a while, Bart. Bring your gadgets and the armamentarium of drugs, to be sure, but most of all bring your human spirit! Bring your youthful enthusiasm, your drive, your energy, your dedication to help the sick. Bring your belief in the good and the right. Bring along a sense of humor; you'll need it when the roof leaks, the patients eat all the pills the first dosage and the witch doctors put cow dung over your sterile compresses.

Bring also the spirit of adventure that our founding fathers possessed. Spend some time in valleys like Muong Sing. Splash some of your human warmth and goodness on people who heretofore have received few of these elements from Western man. You will find that just by being a doctor with qualities of the human heart you will help to unify men.

You are probably thinking, "But, Tom, what's in it for me? We are all a little selfish, you know." There is a great deal in it for you, Bart. By investing a portion of your life in work here, you will take back with you into private practice accomplishments beyond the narrow confines of continent and custom. Your accomplishments will be along the broad horizons of peace for the whole world.

Doctors know the alikeness of all human beings, and the world today demands a deeper emphasis on the brotherhood of man. This should be a force to unite men—as men. We young Americans must take the heritage of our freedoms, from disease as well as from tyranny, and project it into the future—for other men. We who have it must help those who do not have it.

The kerosene is running out, and the lamps are sputtering and flickering. I'll continue the letter tomorrow.

A day has passed since I began this letter. At clinic this morning we had 78 patients. Everything from a blazing malaria to a man who brought his donkey, requesting that we suture a laceration in its flank. Some children had diarrhea and eye inflammations, and one had head lice. My American corpsmen pulled some teeth. The kids howled, just like they do in America. The old gals complained about having to wait in line, just like they do in America. A few of the older gents wanted some "vigor pills," just like . . . well, anyway, there are no really deep differences between people. I have spent six years of my life among different men, and always I find that the similarities outweigh the differences. Each life is infinitely precious as a life. Everywhere.

To recapitulate, Bart, I believe that you should use your profession and your heart as a cable to bind men together. Kindness and gentleness, daily instruments of the doctor, can be potent weapons against the anger of the world. Bring your talents, and the spirituality of your heart, to distant valleys like mine. And take back with you a rich, rich reward.

So, along with my congratulations on your graduation, I send my wish that you will know the happiness that comes of serving others who have nothing.

Sincere best wishes always,
Tom

THE "GOD IS DEAD" CONTROVERSY

Stephen Crane

"GOD LAY DEAD IN HEAVEN"

God lay dead in heaven;
Angels sang the hymn of the end;
Purple winds went moaning,
Their wings drip-dripping
With blood
That fell upon the earth.
It, groaning thing,
Turned black and sank.
Then from the far caverns
Of dead sins
Came monsters, livid with desire.
They fought,
Wrangled over the world,
A morsel.
But of all sadness this was sad—
A woman's arms tried to shield
The head of a sleeping man
From the jaws of the final beast.

Thomas Hardy

GOD'S FUNERAL

I

I saw a slowly-stepping train—
Lined on the brows, scoop-eyed and bent and hoar—
Following in files across a twilit plain
A strange and mystic form the foremost bore.

II

And by contagious throbs of thought
Or latent knowledge that within me lay
And had already stirred me, I was wrought
To consciousness of sorrow even as they.

III

The fore-borne shape, to my blurred eyes,
At first seemed man-like, and anon to change
To an amorphous cloud of marvellous size,
At times endowed with wings of glorious range.

IV

And this phantasmal variousness
Ever possessed it as they drew along:
Yet throughout all it symboled none the less
Potency vast and loving-kindness strong.

V

Almost before I knew I bent
Towards the moving columns without a word;
They, growing in bulk and numbers as they went,
Struck out sick thoughts that could be overheard:—

VI

"O man-projected Figure, of late
Imaged as we, thy knell who shall survive?
Whence came it we were tempted to create
One whom we can no longer keep alive?

VII

"Framing him jealous, fierce, at first,
We gave him justice as the ages rolled,
Will to bless those by circumstance accurst,
And longsuffering, and mercies manifold.

VIII

"And, tricked by our own early dream
And need of solace, we grew self-deceived,
Our making soon our maker did we deem,
And what we had imagined we believed.

IX

"Till, in Time's stayless stealthy swing,
Uncompromising rude reality
Mangled the Monarch of our fashioning,
Who quavered, sank; and now has ceased to be.

X

"So, toward our myth's oblivion,
Darkling, and languid-lipped, we creep and grope
Sadlier than those who wept in Babylon,
Whose Zion was a still abiding hope.

XI

"How sweet it was in years far hied
To start the wheels of day with trustful prayer,
To lie down liegely at the eventide
And feel a blest assurance he was there!

XII

"And who or what shall fill his place?
Whither will wanderers turn distracted eyes
For some fixed star to stimulate their pace
Towards the goal of their enterprise?" . . .

XIII

Some in the background then I saw,
Sweet women, youths, men, all incredulous,
Who chimed: "This is a counterfeit of straw,
This requiem mockery! Still he lives to us!"

XIV

I could not buoy their faith: and yet
Many I had known: with all I sympathized;
And though struck speechless, I did not forget
That what was mourned for, I, too, long had prized.

XV

Still, how to bear such loss I deemed
The insistent question for each animate mind,
And gazing, to my growing sight there seemed
A pale yet positive gleam low down behind,

XVI

Whereof, to lift the general night,
A certain few who stood aloof had said,
"See you upon the horizon that small light—
Swelling somewhat?" Each mourner shook his head.

XVII

And they composed a crowd of whom
Some were right good, and many nigh the best. . . .
Thus dazed and puzzled 'twixt the gleam and gloom
Mechanically I followed with the rest.

Samuel L. Clemens

THE ADVENTURES OF HUCKLEBERRY FINN

So the king sneaked into the wigwam and took to his bottle for comfort and before long the duke tackled *his* bottle, and so in about a half an hour they was as thick as thieves again, and the tighter they got the lovinger they got, and went off a-snoring in each other's arms. They both got powerful mellow but I noticed the king didn't get mellow enough to forget to remember to not deny about hiding the money-bag again. That made me feel easy and satisfied. Of course when they got to snoring we had a long gabble and I told Jim everything.

We dasn't stop again at any town for days and days; kept right along down the river. We was down south in the warm weather now, and a mighty long ways from home. We begun to come to trees with Spanish moss on them, hanging down from the limbs like long, gray beards. It was the first I ever see it growing and it made the woods look solemn and dismal. So now the frauds reckoned they was out of danger, and they begun to work the villages again.

First they done a lecture on temperance, but they didn't make enough for them both to get drunk on. Then in another village they started a dancing-school, but they didn't know no more how to dance than a kangaroo does, so the first prance they made the general public jumped in and pranced them out of town. Another time they tried a go at yellocution, but they didn't yellocute long till the audience got up and give them a solid good cussing, and made them skip out. They tackled missionarying and mesmerizing and doctoring and telling fortunes, and a little of everything, but they couldn't seem to have no luck. So at last they got just about dead broke, and laid around the raft as she floated along, thinking and thinking, and never saying nothing, by the half a day at a time, and dreadful blue and desperate.

And at last they took a change and begun to lay their heads together in the wigwam and talk low and confidential two or three hours at a time. Jim and me got uneasy. We didn't like the look of it. We judged they was studying up some kind of worse deviltry than ever. We turned it over and over, and at last we made up our minds they was going to break into somebody's house or store, or was going into the counterfeit-money business, or something. So then we was pretty scared and made up an agreement that we wouldn't have nothing in the world to do with such actions, and if we ever got the least show we would give them the cold shake and clear out and leave them behind. Well, early one morning we hid the raft in a good, safe place about two mile below a little bit of a shabby village named Pikesville, and the king he went ashore and told us all to stay hid whilst he went up to town and smelt around to see if anybody had got any wind of the "Royal Nonesuch" there yet. ("House to rob, you *mean*," says I to myself; "and when you get through robbing it you'll come back here and wonder what has become of me and Jim and the raft—and you'll have to take it out in wondering.") And he said if he warn't back by midday the duke and me would know it was all right, and we was to come along.

So we stayed where we was. The duke he fretted and sweated around, and was in a mighty sour way. He scolded us for everything, and we couldn't seem to do nothing right; he found fault with every little thing. Something was a-brewing, sure. I was good and glad when midday come and no king; we could have a change, anyway—and maybe a chance for *the* change on top of it. So me and the duke went up to the village and hunted around there for the king, and by and by we found him in the back room of a little low doggery, very tight, and a lot of loafers bully-ragging him for sport, and he a-cussing and a-threatening with all his might, and so tight he couldn't walk and couldn't do nothing to them. The duke he begun to abuse him for an old fool, and the king begun to sass back, and the minute they was fairly at it I lit out and shook the reefs out of my hind legs, and spun down the river road like a deer, for I see our chance; and I made up my mind that it would be a long day before they ever see me and Jim again. I got down there all out of breath but loaded up with joy, and sung out:

"Set her loose, Jim; we're all right now!"

But there warn't no answer, and nobody come out of the wigwam. Jim was gone! I set up a shout—and then another—and then another one; and run this way and that in the woods, whooping and screeching; but it warn't no use—old Jim was gone. Then I set down and cried; I couldn't help it. But I couldn't set still long. Pretty soon I went out on the road, trying to think what I better do, and I run across a boy walking, and asked him if he'd seen a strange nigger dressed so and so, and he says:

"Yes."

"Whereabouts?" says I.

"Down to Silas Phelps's place, two mile below here. He's a runaway nigger and they've got him. Was you looking for him?"

"You bet I ain't! I run across him in the woods about an hour or two ago, and he said if I hollered he'd cut my livers out—and told me to lay down and stay where I was; and I done it. Been there ever since; afeard to come out."

"Well," he says, "you needn't be afeard no more, becuz they've got him. He run off f'm down South, som'ers."

"It's a good job they got him."

"Well I *reckon!* There's two hundred dollars' reward on him. It's like picking up money out'n the road."

"Yes, it is—and I could 'a' had it if I'd been big enough; I see him *first.* Who nailed him?"

"It was an old feller—a stranger—and he sold out his chance in him for forty dollars, becuz he's got to go up the river and can't wait. Think o' that, now! You bet I'd wait, if it was seven year."

"That's me, every time," says I. "But maybe his chance ain't worth no more than that, if he'll sell it so cheap. Maybe there's something ain't straight about it."

"But it *is,* though—straight as a string. I see the handbill myself.

It tells all about him, to a dot—paints him like a picture, and tells the plantation he's frum, below Newr*leans*. No-siree-*bob*, they ain't no trouble 'bout *that* speculation, you bet you. Say, gimme a chaw tobacker, won't ye?"

I didn't have none, so he left. I went to the raft, and set down in the wigwam to think. But I couldn't come to nothing. I thought till I wore my head sore, but I couldn't see no way out of the trouble. After all this long journey and after all we'd done for them scoundrels, here it was all come to nothing, everything all busted up and ruined, because they could have the heart to serve Jim such a trick as that and make him a slave again all his life, and amongst strangers, too, for forty dirty dollars.

Once I said to myself it would be a thousand times better for Jim to be a slave at home where his family was, as long as he'd *got* to be a slave, and so I'd better write a letter to Tom Sawyer and tell him to tell Miss Watson where he was. But I soon give up that notion for two things: she'd be mad and disgusted at his rascality and ungratefulness for leaving her, and so she'd sell him straight down the river again; and if she didn't, everybody naturally despises an ungrateful nigger and they'd make Jim feel it all the time, and so he'd feel ornery and disgraced. And then think of *me!* It would get all around that Huck Finn helped a nigger to get his freedom, and if I was to ever see anybody from that town again I'd be ready to get down and lick his boots for shame. That's just the way: a person does a low-down thing, and then he don't want to take no consequences of it. Thinks as long as he can hide it, it ain't no disgrace. That was my fix exackly. The more I studied about this the more my conscience went to grinding me, and the more wicked and low-down and ornery I got to feeling. And at last, when it hit me all of a sudden that here was the plain hand of Providence slapping me in the face and letting me know my wickedness was being watched all the time from up there in heaven, whilst I was stealing a poor old woman's nigger that hadn't ever done me no harm, and now was showing me there's One that's always on the lookout and ain't a-going to allow no such miserable doings to go only just so fur and no further, I most dropped in my tracks I was so scared. Well, I tried the best I could to kinder soften it up somehow for myself by saying I was brung up wicked and so I warn't so much to blame, but something inside of me kept saying, "There was the Sunday-school, you could 'a' gone to it; and if you'd 'a' done it they'd 'a' learnt you there that people that acts as I'd been acting about that nigger goes to everlasting fire."

It made me shiver. And I about made up my mind to pray and see if I couldn't try to quit being the kind of a boy I was and be better. So I kneeled down. But the words wouldn't come. Why wouldn't they? It warn't no use to try and hide it from Him. Nor from *me*, neither. I knowed very well why they wouldn't come. It was because my heart warn't right, it was because I warn't square, it was because I was playing double. I was letting *on* to give up sin but away inside of me I was holding on to the biggest one of all. I was trying to make my mouth *say* I would do the right thing and the clean thing, and go and write to that nigger's owner and tell where he was, but deep down in me I knowed it was a lie, and He knowed it. You can't pray a lie—I found that out.

So I was full of trouble, full as I could be; and didn't know what to do. At last I had an idea; and I says, I'll go and write the letter—and *then* see if I can pray. Why, it was astonishing, the way I felt as light as a feather right straight off and my troubles all gone. So I got a piece of paper and a pencil, all glad and excited, and set down and wrote:

Miss Watson, your runaway nigger Jim is down here two mile below Pikesville, and Mr. Phelps has got him and he will give him up for the reward if you send.

HUCK FINN.

I felt good and all washed clean of sin for the first time I had ever felt so in my life, and I knowed I could pray now. But I didn't do it straight off but laid the paper down and set there thinking—thinking how good it was all this happened so, and how near I come to being lost and going to hell. And went on thinking. And got to thinking over our trip down the river; and I see Jim before me all the time: in the day and in the nighttime, sometimes moonlight, sometimes storms, and we a-floating along, talking and singing and laughing. But somehow I couldn't seem to strike no places to harden me against him, but only the other kind. I'd see him standing my watch on top of his'n, 'stead of calling me, so I could go on sleeping; and see how glad he was when I come back out of the fog; and when I come to him again in the swamp, up there where the feud was; and such-like times; and would always call me honey and pet me and do everything he could think of for me, and how good he always was; and at last I struck the time I saved him by telling the men we had smallpox aboard, and he was so grateful, and said I was the best friend old Jim ever had in the world and the *only* one he's got now; and then I happened to look around and see that paper.

It was a close place. I took it up, and held it in my hand. I was a-trembling, because I'd got to decide, forever, betwixt two things, and I knowed it. I studied a minute, sort of holding my breath, and then says to myself:

"All right, then, I'll *go* to hell"—and tore it up.

It was awful thoughts and awful words but they was said. And I let them stay said; and never thought no more about reforming. I shoved the whole thing out of my head and said I would take up wickedness again, which was in my line, being brung up to it, and the other warn't. And for a starter I would go to work and steal Jim out of slavery again; and if I could think up anything worse, I would do that, too; because as long as I was in and in for good. I might as well go the whole hog.

Then I set to thinking over how to get at it and turned over considerable many ways in my mind, and at last fixed up a plan that suited me. So then I took the bearings of a woody island that was down the river a piece, and as soon as it was fairly dark I crept out with my raft and went for it and hid it there, and then turned in. I slept the night through and got up before it was light, and had my breakfast, and put on my store clothes and tied up some others and one thing or another in a bundle, and took the canoe and cleared for shore. I landed below where I judged was Phelps's place, and hid my bundle in the woods, and then filled up the canoe with water, and loaded rocks into her and sunk her where I could find her again when I wanted her, about a quarter of a mile below a little steam-sawmill that was on the bank.

Then I struck up the road, and when I passed the mill I see a sign on it, "Phelps's Sawmill," and when I come to the farm-houses, two or three hundred yards further along, I kept my eyes peeled but didn't see nobody around, though it was good daylight now. But I didn't mind because I didn't want to see nobody just yet—I only wanted to get the lay of the land. According to my plan, I was going to turn up there from the village, not from below. So I just took a look, and shoved along, straight for town. Well, the very first man I see when I got there was the duke. He was sticking up a bill for the "Royal Nonesuch"—three-night performance—like that other time. *They* had the cheek, them frauds! I was right on him before I could shirk. He looked astonished, and says:

"Hel-*lo!* Where'd *you* come from?" Then he says, kind of glad and eager, "Where's the raft?—got her in a good place?"

I says:

"Why, that's just what I was a-going to ask your grace."

Then he didn't look so joyful, and says:

"What was your idea for asking *me?*" he says.

"Well," I says, "when I see the king in that doggery yesterday I says to myself, we can't get him home for hours, till he's soberer; so I went a-loafing around town to put in the time and wait. A man up and offered me ten cents to help him pull a skiff over the river and back to fetch a sheep, and so I went along; but when we was dragging him to the boat, and the man left me a-holt of the rope and went behind him to shove him along, he was too strong for me and jerked loose and run, and we after him. We didn't have no dog and so we had to chase him all over the country till we tired him out. We never got him till dark; then we fetched him over and I started down for the raft. When I got there and see it was gone, I says to myself, "They've got into trouble and had to leave; and they've took my nigger, which is the only nigger I've got in the world, and now I'm in a strange country, and ain't got no property no more, nor nothing, and no way to make my living'; so I set down and cried. I slept in the woods all night. But what *did* become of the raft, then?—and Jim—poor Jim!"

"Blamed if *I* know—that is, what's become of the raft. That old fool had made a trade and got fourty dollars, and when we found him in the doggery the loafers had matched half-dollars with him and got every cent but what he'd spent for whisky; and when I got him home late last night and found the raft gone, we said, "That little rascal has stole our raft and shook us, and run off down the river.'"

"I wouldn't shake my *nigger,* would I?—the only nigger I had in the world, and the only property."

"We never thought of that. Fact is, I reckon we'd come to consider him *our* nigger; yes, we did consider him so—goodness knows we had trouble enough for him. So when we see the raft was gone and we flat broke, there warn't anything for it but to try the 'Royal Nonesuch' another shake. And I've pegged along ever since, dry as a powderhorn. Where's that ten cents? Give it here."

I had considerable money, so I give him ten cents, but begged him to spend it for something to eat and give me some, because it was all the money I had and I hadn't had nothing to eat since yesterday. He never said nothing. The next minute he whirls on me and says:

"Do you reckon that nigger would blow on us? We'd skin him if he done that!"

"How can he blow? Hain't he run off?"

"No! That old fool sold him, and never divided with me, and the money's gone."

"*Sold* him?" I says, and begun to cry; "why, he was *my* nigger, and that was my money. Where is he?—I want my nigger."

"Well, you can't *get* your nigger, that's all—so dry up your blubbering. Looky here—do you think *you'd* venture to blow on us? Blamed if I think I'd trust you. Why, if you *was* to blow on us—"

He stopped but I never see the duke look so ugly out of his eyes before. I went on a-whimpering, and says:

"I don't want to blow on nobody; and I ain't got no time to blow, nohow; I got to turn out and find my nigger."

He looked kinder bothered, and stood there with his bills fluttering on his arm, thinking, and wrinkling up his forehead. At last he says:

"I'll tell you something. We got to be here three days. If you'll promise you won't blow, and won't let the nigger blow, I'll tell you where to find him."

So I promised, and he says:

"A farmer by the name of Silas Ph—" and then he stopped. You see, he started to tell me the truth, but when he stopped that way and begun to study and think again, I reckoned he was changing his mind. And so he was. He wouldn't trust me; he wanted to make sure of having me out of the way the whole three days. So pretty soon he says:

"The man that bought him is named Abram Foster—Abram G. Foster—and he lives forty mile back here in the country, on the road to Lafayette."

"All right," I says, "I can walk it in three days. And I'll start this very afternoon."

"No you won't, you'll start *now;* and don't you lose no time about it, neither, nor do any gabbling by the way. Just keep a tight tongue in your head and move right along, and then you won't get into trouble with *us,* d'ye hear?"

That was the order I wanted, and that was the one I played for. I wanted to be left free to work my plans.

"So clear out," he says; "and you can tell Mr. Foster whatever you want to. Maybe you can get him to believe that Jim *is* your nigger— some idiots don't require documents—leastways I've heard there's such down South here. And when you tell him the handbill and the reward's bogus, maybe he'll believe you when you explain to him what the idea was for getting 'em out. Go 'long now, and tell him anything you want to; but mind you don't work your jaw any *between* here and there."

So I left, and struck for the back country. I didn't look around but I kinder felt like he was watching me. But I knowed I could tire him out at that. I went straight out in the country as much as a mile before I stopped; then I doubled back through the woods towards Phelps's. I reckoned I better start in on my plan straight off without fooling around, because I wanted to stop Jim's mouth till these fellows could get away. I didn't want no trouble with their kind. I'd seen all I wanted to of them and wanted to get entirely shut of them.

Nikos Kazantzakis

THE LAST TEMPTATION OF CHRIST

Jesus and the disciples sat warming themselves in front of the lighted fire while old Salome went in and out, overjoyed. All her illnesses had disappeared. She went in and out, setting the table, and her pride in her sons and in serving the holy man who would bring the kingdom of heaven was insatiable. John leaned over and whispered into his mother's ear. By glancing at the disciples he made her notice how they shivered, still dressed as they were in summer linens. The mother smiled, went inside, opened her trunks and took out woolen clothes. Then, quickly— before her husband's return—she divided them up among the companions. The thickest robe, one of brilliantly white wool, she threw tenderly over Jesus' shoulders.

He turned and smiled at her. "Bless you, Mother Salome," he said. "It is right and just that you should care for the body. The body is the camel on which the soul mounts in order to traverse the desert. Care for it, therefore, so that it will be able to endure."

Old Zebedee entered and looked at the unexpected visitors. He greeted them halfheartedly, then sat down in a corner. These robbers (that is what he called them) did not please him at all. Who invited them to come and take over his home? And his lavish wife had already laid them out a magnificent feast! Curse the day this new fanatic sprouted up. It wasn't bad enough that he had stolen both his sons! No, besides that there were the arguments all day long with his idiotic wife, who took the two boys' part. They had acted well, she said. This man was a true prophet: he would become king, throw out the Romans and sit on Israel's throne. Then John would be enthroned to his right, Jacob to his left—great lords, not fishermen in rowboats, but great important lords! Why, do you think they should rot away their entire lives here on the water? Day and night Zebedee was nagged with this— and more—by the old idiot, who would bang her foot on the floor and shout. Sometimes he cursed and smashed whatever happened to be in front of him; sometimes he gave up in despair and went off to roam the edge of the lake like a madman. In the end he had taken to drink. And now—what next!—all these lawbreakers had moved into his house: nine immense mouths; and they had with them that whore a thousand times kissed, that Magdalene. They sat themselves down in a circle around the table and did not even turn to look at him—him, the master of the house—nor even ask his permission. So that's what we've come to! Was it for these parasites that he and his ancestors had slaved for so many years? He flew into a rage and, jumping up, shouted, "Just a minute, my good men—whose house is this, yours or mine? Two and two make four. Will you tell me, please!"

"It's God's," answered Peter, who had downed quite a few drinks and was in a merry mood. "God's, Zebedee. Haven't you heard the news? Nothing any more is yours or mine; everything is God's."

"The law of Moses—" Zebedee began, but Peter interrupted him before he could work up steam.

"What do I hear—the law of Moses? That's done with, Zebedee, finished, gone for a nice long walk and never coming back. Now we have the Law of the Son of man. Understand? We're all brothers! Our hearts have broadened, and with our hearts the law has also broadened. It now embraces the whole of mankind. The entire world is the Promised Land. The frontiers are gone! I, the very man you see before you, Zebedee, shall go proclaim the word of God to the nations. I'll get clear to Rome—yes, don't laugh—and I'll grab the emperor by his Adam's apple, knock him down and sit myself on the throne. And why not! As the master said, we're no longer your kind of fishermen. We don't catch fish; we're fishers of men. And a word to the wise: flatter us, bring us plenty of wine and food, because one day—and quickly too—we'll be great lords. You give us one dry piece of bread, and we'll repay you with a whole ovenful in a few days. And what loaves! Immortal! You'll eat and eat, and they'll never be consumed."

"Poor fellow, I already see you crucified upside down," growled Zebedee, who had slunk away again to his corner. Listening to Peter's words, he had gradually begun to feel afraid. I'd better keep my mouth shut, he thought. You never know what will happen. The world is a sphere, and turns. It's just possible that one day these madmen . . . Let's play safe, then, whatever happens!

The disciples laughed in their beards. They knew perfectly well that Peter was in a merry mood and joking; but inside themselves—though they still were not drunk enough to speak out—they secretly spun the same thoughts. Impressiveness, rank, clothes of silk, golden rings, abundant food—and to feel the world under the Jewish heel: that was the kingdom of heaven.

Old Zebedee took another drink and mustered up courage. "And you, teacher," he said, "aren't you going to open your mouth? You started all this, and now you sit back as cool as a cucumber while we others sweat it out. . . . Look here, can you tell me in the name of your God why I should see my goods scattered and not scream about it?"

"Zebedee," Jesus answered, "there was once a very rich man who reaped, vintaged, gathered in the olives, stuffed his jugs, ate, filled himself and then lay down on his back in his yard. 'My soul,' he said, 'you have many belongings. Eat, drink and be merry!' But as he said this a voice was heard from the sky: 'Fool, fool—this night you shall surrender your soul to hell. What will you do with all the goods you have amassed?' Zebedee, you have ears, you hear what I say to you; you have a mind, you understand what I mean. May this voice of heaven be above you, Zebedee, night and day!"

The old proprietor lowered his head and did not speak again.

Just then the door opened and Philip appeared on the threshold. Behind him was an immense gawky bean stalk, Nathanael. His heart no longer chimed two bells at once: he had made his decision. He approached Jesus, stooped and kissed his feet.

"My master," he said, "I am with you to the death."

Jesus placed his hand on the curly buffalolike head. "Welcome, Nathanael. You make sandals for everyone else and go barefoot yourself. That pleases me very much. Come with me!" He seated him at his right and handed him a slice of bread and a cup of wine. "To become mine," he said, "eat this mouthful of bread and drink this cup of wine."

Nathanael ate the bread, drank the wine and all at once felt strength flow into his bones and soul. The wine rose like the sun and vermeiled his mind. Wine, bread and soul became one.

He was sitting on hot coals. He wanted to speak but was too bashful.

"Speak, Nathanael," the master said to him. "Open your heart and relieve yourself."

"Rabbi," he replied, "I want you to know that I've always been poor. I've lived and eaten from day to day and have never had time to study the Law. I'm blind, Rabbi. Forgive me. . . . That's what I want you to know. I've had my say and I feel better."

Jesus caressingly touched the newly enlightened man's broad shoulders. "Don't sigh, Nathanael," he said, laughing. "Two paths lead to God's bosom. One is the path of the mind, the other the path of the heart. Listen to the story I shall tell you:

"A poor man, a rich man and a rake died on the same day and appeared before God's tribunal at the same hour. None of them had ever studied the Law. God frowned and asked the poor man, 'Why didn't you study the Law while you were alive?'

"'Lord,' he answered, 'I was poor and hungry. I slaved day and night to feed my wife and children. I didn't have time.'

"'Were you poorer than my faithful servant Hillel?' God asked angrily. 'He had no money to pay to enter the synagogue and hear the Law being explained, so he climbed onto the roof, stretched himself out and listened through the skylight. But it snowed and he was so absorbed in what he heard that he did not realize it. In the morning when the rabbi entered the synagogue he saw that it was dark. Raising his eyes, he discovered a man's body over the skylight. He mounted to the roof, dug away the snow and exhumed Hillel. He took him in his arms, carried him down, lighted a fire and brought him back to life. Then he gave him permission to enter and listen after that without paying, and Hillel became the famous rabbi whom the whole world has heard of. . . . What do you have to say to that?'

" 'Nothing, Lord,' murmured the poor man, and he began to weep.

"God turned to the rich man. 'And you, why didn't you study the Law while you were alive?'

" 'I was too rich. I had many orchards, many slaves, many cares. How could I manage?'

" 'Were you richer,' God snapped, 'than Harsom's son Eleazar, who inherited a thousand villages and a thousand ships? But he abandoned them all when he learned the whereabouts of a sage who was explaining the Law. What do you have to say for yourself?'

" 'Nothing, Lord,' the rich man murmured in his turn, and he too began to weep.

"God then turned to the rake. 'And you, my beauty, why didn't you study the Law?'

" 'I was exceedingly handsome and many women threw themselves at me. With all the amusement I had, where could I find time to look at the Law?'

" 'Were you handsomer than Joseph, who was loved by the wife of Putiphar? He was so beautiful that he said to the sun, "Shine, sun, so that I may shine." When he unfolded the Law the letters opened up like doors and the meaning came out dressed in light and flames. What do you have to say?'

" 'Nothing, Lord,' murmured the rake, and he too began to weep.

"God clapped his hands and called Hillel, Eleazar and Joseph out from Paradise. When they had come, he said, 'Judge these men who because of poverty, wealth and beauty did not study the Law. Speak, Hillel. Judge the poor one!'

" 'Lord,' answered Hillel, 'how can I condemn him? I know what poverty means, I know what hunger means. He should be pardoned!'

" 'And you, Eleazar?' said God. 'There is the rich one. I hand him over to you!'

" 'Lord,' replied Eleazar, 'how can I condemn him? I know what it is to be rich—death! He should be pardoned!'

" 'And you, Joseph? It's your turn. There is the handsome one!'

" 'Lord, how can I condemn him? I know what a struggle it is, what a terrible martyrdom, to conquer the body's loveliness. He should be pardoned!' "

Jesus paused, smiled, and looked at Nathanael. But the cobbler felt uneasy.

"Well, what did God do next?" he asked.

"Just what you would have done," Jesus answered with a laugh.

The simple cobbler laughed too. "That means I'm saved!" He seized both of the master's hands and squeezed them hard. "Rabbi," he shouted, "I understand. You said there were two paths leading to God's bosom, the path of the mind and the path of the heart. I took the path of the heart and found you!"

Rising, Jesus went to the door. A strong wind had come up and the lake was billowing. The stars in the heavens were innumerable fine grains of sand. He recalled the desert, shuddered, and closed the door. "Night is a great gift from God," he said. "It is the mother of man and comes quietly and tenderly to cover him. It rests its cool hand on his forehead and effaces the day's cares from his body and soul. Brothers, it is time to surrender ourselves to night's embrace."

Old Salome heard him and rose. Magdalene also got up from the corner by the fire where, bowed over, she had been happily listening to the Beloved's voice. The two women laid out the mats and brought covers. Jacob went to the yard, carried in an armful of olive logs and heaped them on the fire. Jesus, standing erect in the middle of the house with his face turned toward Jerusalem, lifted his hands and in a deep voice pronounced the evening prayer: "Open your doors to us, O Lord. The day goes down; the sun falls, the sun disappears. Eternal, we come to your doors. We implore you: Pardon us. We implore you: Have mercy upon us. Save us!"

"And send us good dreams, Lord," Peter added. "In my sleep, Lord, let me see my aged green boat all new and with a red sail!" He had drunk much and was in a jolly mood.

Jesus lay down in the center, surrounded by the disciples. They occupied the entire length and breadth of the house. Zebedee and his wife, finding no room, went to an outbuilding; and with them went Magdalene. The old man grumbled. He was deprived of his comforts. Turning in a rage to his wife, he said in a loud voice, so that Magdalene would hear, "What next! Thrown out of my own house by a pack of foreigners. Look what we're reduced to!"

But the old lady turned to the wall and did not answer him.

This night Matthew again remained awake. He squatted under the lamp, removed the partly filled notebook from under his shirt and began to compose—how Jesus entered Capernaum, how Magdalene joined them, and the parable told by the master: There was once a very rich man. . . . When he finished writing he blew out the lamp and then he too went to bed, but a little to one side, because the disciples still had not become accustomed to his breath.

No sooner had Peter closed his eyes than he fell asleep. Straightway an angel came down from heaven, quietly opened his temples and entered him in the form of a dream. A great crowd seemed to be assembled on the shore of the lake. The teacher stood there too, admiring a brand-new boat, green with a red sail, which was drifting in the water. On the rear part of her prow gleamed a great painted fish, identical with the fish that was tattooed on Peter's chest. "Who does that beautiful boat belong to?" Jesus asked. "It's mine," Peter proudly replied. "Go, Peter, take the rest of the companions and sail out to the middle so that I can admire your courage!"

"With pleasure, Rabbi," said Peter. He detached the cable. The rest of the companions jumped in. A favorable wind blew over the stern, the sail swelled out and they reached the open sea singing.

But suddenly a whirlwind arose. The boat twirled around, her creaking hull ready to crack. She started to ship water and sink. The disciples, fallen face-down on the deck, raised a great lament. Peter seized hold of the mast and shouted, "Rabbi, Rabbi, help!" and lo! there in the thick darkness he perceived the white-clad rabbi walking toward them over the waters. The disciples lifted their heads and saw him. "A ghost! A ghost!" they cried out, trembling.

"Don't be afraid," Jesus said to them, "it's me!"

Peter answered him, "Lord, if it is really you, order me also to walk on the waves and to come and meet you."

"Come!" Jesus ordered him.

Peter jumped out of the boat, stepped on the waves, and began to walk. But when he saw the enraged sea he became paralyzed with fear. He started to sink. "Lord, save me," he screamed, "I'm drowning!"

Jesus put out his hand and pulled him up. "Man of little faith," he said, "why were you afraid? Have you no confidence in me? Look!" He raised his hand over the waves and said, "Be still!" and all at once the wind subsided, the waters became calm.

Peter burst into tears. His soul had been put to the test this time also, and once more it had emerged with disgrace.

Uttering a loud shout, he awoke. His beard was sprinkled with tears. He sat up on the mat, leaned his back against the wall and sighed.

Matthew, who was still awake, heard him. "Why did you sigh, Peter?" he asked.

For a second Peter resolved to play deaf and not answer him. To be sure, he did not relish conversations with publicans. But the dream was choking him and he felt he had to pull it out from within him in order to find relief. He therefore crawled near to Matthew and began to relate it to him, and the more he related, the more he embroidered. Matthew listened insatiably, recording it all in his mind. Tomorrow at daybreak, God willing, he would copy it into his book.

Peter finished, but within his breast his heart still pitched, just just like the boat in the dream. Suddenly he shook with fright. "Could the master really have come in the night and taken me with him to the open sea in order to test me? Never in my life have I seen a sea more alive, a boat more real or fear more palpable. Perhaps it wasn't a dream. . . . What do you think, Matthew?"

"It most certainly wasn't a dream. This miracle definitely took place," Matthew answered, and he began to turn over deeply in his mind how he could set it down the next day on paper. It would be extremely difficult because he was not entirely sure it was a dream, nor was he entirely sure it was the truth. It was both. The miracle happened, but not on this earth, not on this sea. Elsewhere—but where?

He closed his eyes to meditate and find the answer. But sleep came and took him along.

The next day there was a continuous downpour with strong winds, and the fishermen did not set sail. Shut up in their huts they mended their nets and talked about the odd visitor who was lodging at old Zebedee's. It seemed he was John the Baptist resuscitated. Immediately after the executioner's stroke the Baptist bent down, picked up his head, replaced it on his neck and was off in a flash. But to prevent Herod from catching him again and once more cutting off his head, he went and entered the son of the Carpenter of Nazareth and they became one. Seeing him, you went out of your mind. Was he one, or two? It was bewildering. If you looked him straight in the face, he was a simple man who smiled at you. If you moved a bit, one of his eyes was furious and wanted to eat you, the other encouraged you to come closer. You approached and grew dizzy. Without knowing what was happening to you, you abandoned your home and children and followed him!

An old fisherman heard all this and shook his head. "This is what happens to those who don't get married," he said. "All they want to do is save the world, by hook or by crook. The sperm rises to their heads and attacks their brains. For God's sake, all of you: get married, let your forces loose on women and have children in order to calm yourselves!"

Old Jonah had heard the news the previous evening and had waited and waited in his shack. This can't last, he thought. Surely my sons will come to see if I'm dead or alive. He waited the whole night, hoped and then lost hope, and in the morning put on the high captain's boots which were made when he got married and which he wore only on great occasions, encased himself in a torn oilcloth and went off in the rain toward the house of his friend Zebedee. Finding the door open, he entered.

The fire was lighted. Ten or so men and two women sat cross-legged in front of the fire. He recognized one of the women—it was old Salome. The other was young. He had seen her somewhere, but he could not remember where. The house was in half darkness. He recognized his two sons Peter and Andrew when they turned momentarily and their faces were illuminated by the fire glow. But no one heard him come in and no one turned to see him. All were listening with heads thrust forward and mouths agape to someone who faced directly toward him. What was he saying? Old Jonah, all ears, opened his mouth and listened. Now and then he caught a word: "justice," "God," "kingdom of heaven. . . ." The same and more of the same—year in, year out! He was sick of it. Instead of telling you how to catch a fish, mend a sail, caulk a boat, or how to avoid getting cold, wet or hungry, they sat there and spoke about heaven! Confound it, didn't they have anything to say about the earth and the sea? Old Jonah became angry. He coughed so that they would hear him and turn around. No one turned. He raised his huge leg and brought his captain's boot thundering down—but in vain. They were all hanging on the lips of the pale speaker.

Old Salome was the only one who turned. She looked at him but did not see him. Old Jonah went forward, therefore, and squatted in front of the fireplace, just behind his two sons. Putting out his huge hand, he touched Peter on the shoulder and shook him. Peter turned, saw his father, placed his finger to his lips in a signal for him not to speak, and once again turned his face toward the pale youth just as though this was not Jonah, his own father, just as though it was not months since he had seen him last. First Jonah felt aggrieved, then angry. He took off his boots (which had begun to pinch him) so that by throwing them in the teacher's face he could silence him at long last and be able to talk to his children. He had already lifted the boots and was swinging them to gather momentum when he felt a restraining hand behind him. Turning, he saw old Zebedee.

"Get up, Jonah," his friend whispered into his ear. "Let's go inside. Poor fellow, I've got something to tell you."

The old fisherman put his boots under his arm and followed Zebedee. They entered the inner part of the house and sat down side by side on Salome's trunk.

"Jonah," Zebedee began, stammering because he had drunk too much in an attempt to drown his rage, "Jonah, my much-buffeted friend, you had two sons—write them off. I too had a pair of sons, and I wrote them off. It seems their father is God, so why are we butting in? They look at us as if to ask, 'Who are you, graybeard?' . . . It's the end of the world, my poor Jonah!

"At first I got angry too. I felt like grabbing the harpoon and throwing them out. But afterward I saw there was no solution, so I crawled back into my shell and handed the keys over to them. My wife sees eye to eye with them, poor thing. She's getting a little senile, you know. So mum's the word, old Zebedee, and mum's the word, old Jonah —that's what I wanted to tell you. What's the use of lying to ourselves? Two and two make four: we're beaten!"

Once more old Jonah put on his boots and wrapped himself in his oilskin. Then he gazed at Zebedee to see if he had anything more to say. He had not, so Jonah opened the door, looked at the sky, looked at the earth: darkness like pitch; rain, cold. . . . His lips moved: "We're beaten," he grumbled, "we're beaten," and he splashed through the mud back toward his hut.

While Jonah went puffing along, the son of Mary held his palms out to the fire as if praying to the spirit of God which, hidden in the flames, gives warmth to men. His heart had opened up; he held out his palms and spoke.

"Think not that I have come to abolish the law and the prophets; I have come not to abolish the old commandments but to extend them. You have seen inscribed on the tables of Moses: You shall not kill! But I say to you that whoever is even angry with his brother and lifts his hand against him, or only speaks an unkind word to him, will be hurled down into the flames of hell. You have seen inscribed on the tables of Moses: You shall not commit adultery! But I say to you that whoever even looks at a woman lustfully has already committed adultery in his heart. The impure glance brings the lecher down to hell. . . .

"The old law instructs you to honor your father and your mother; but I say, Do not imprison your heart within your parents' home. Let it emerge and enter all homes, embrace the whole of Israel from Mount Hermon to the desert of Idumea and even beyond: east and west—the entire Universe. Our father is God, our mother is Earth. We are half soil and half sky. To honor your father and your mother means to honor Heaven and Earth."

Old Salome sighed. "Your words are hard, Rabbi, hard for a mother."

"The word of God is always hard," Jesus replied.

"Take my two sons," the old mother murmured, crossing her hands. "Take them; they are yours."

Jesus heard the orphaned mother and felt that all the sons and daughters of the world were suspended from his neck. He recalled the black he-goat he had seen in the desert with all the sins of the people enclosed in blue amulets and hanging from its neck. Without speaking, he leaned toward the old Salome, who had given him her two sons. He seemed to be saying to her, Look, here is my neck; hang your sons around it. . . .

He threw a handful of vine branches onto the fire. The flames swept over them. For a long time Jesus watched the fire hissingly consume the branches; then he turned again to the companions.

"He who loves father and mother more than me is not worthy to come with me; and he who loves son or daughter more than me is not worthy to come with me. The old commandments are no longer large enough to hold us; neither are the old loves."

He paused for a moment, then continued. "Man is a frontier, the place where earth stops and heaven begins. But this frontier never ceases to transport itself and advance toward heaven. With it the commandments of God also transport themselves and advance. I take God's commandments from the tables of Moses and extend them, make them advance."

"Does God's will change, then, Rabbi?" asked John, surprised.

"No, John, beloved. But man's heart widens and is able to contain more of God's will."

"Forward, then," shouted Peter, jumping up. "Why are we sitting? Let's go proclaim the new commandments to the world."

"Wait for the rain to stop so we don't get wet!" hissed Thomas mockingly.

Judas shook his head, infuriated. "First, we've got to chase out the Romans," he said. "We must liberate our bodies before we liberate our souls—each in its proper order. Let's not start building from the roof downward. First comes the foundation."

"The foundation is the soul, Judas."

"I say the foundation is the body!"

"If the soul within us does not change, Judas, the world outside us will never change. The enemy is within, the Romans are within, salvation starts from within!"

Judas jumped up, boiling. For a long time he had kept his heart from crying out. He had listened and listened, storing everything in his breast, but now he could bear it no longer.

"First throw out the Romans!" he shouted again, choking. "First the Romans!"

"But how can we throw them out?" asked Nathanael, who had begun to feel uneasy and to cast sidelong glances at the door. "Will you tell us how, Iscariot?"

"Revolution! Remember the Maccabees! They expelled the Greeks. It's our turn now; it's time for new Maccabees to expel the Romans. Afterward, when everything is in our own hands again, we can settle about rich and poor, injured and injurer."

No one spoke. The disciples were not sure which of the two roads to take. They gazed at the teacher and waited. He was looking thoughtfully at the flames. . . . When would men understand that only one thing exists in both the visible and invisible worlds—the soul!

Peter rose. "Excuse me," he said, "but these are complicated discussions and I don't understand them. Experience will teach us which is the foundation. Let's wait and see what happens. Master, give us the authority to go out by ourselves in order to bring the Good News to men. When we return we'll talk it all over again."

Jesus raised his head and swept his eyes over the disciples. He nodded to Peter, John and Jacob. They came forward and he placed his hands heavily on their heads.

"Go, with my blessing," he said. "Proclaim the Good News to men. Do not be afraid. God will hold you in his palm and keep you from perishing. Not a single sparrow falls from the sky without his will, and you are worth many sparrows. God be with you! Come back quickly, and may thousands of souls be suspended from your necks. You are my apostles."

The three apostles received the blessing. Opening the door, they went out into the tempest, and each took a different road.

The days went by. Zebedee's yard filled with people in the morning and emptied in the evening. The sick, the lame and those possessed with devils came from every direction. Some wept, others grew furious and shouted at the Son of man to perform a miracle and cure them. Wasn't this why God had sent him? Let him appear, then, in the courtyard! . . .

Hearing them day after day, Jesus became sad. He would go out to the yard and touch and bless each one saying, "There are two kinds of miracles, my brothers, those of the body and those of the soul. Have faith only in the miracles of the soul. Repent and cleanse your souls, and your flesh will be cleansed. The soul is the tree. Sickness, health, Paradise and the Inferno are its fruits."

Many believed and as soon as they believed felt their blood spurt up and fill their benumbed bodies. They threw away their crutches and danced. Others, as Jesus leaned his hand against their extinguished eyes, felt light flow out from the tips of his fingers. They raised their eyelids and shouted with joy, for now they saw the world!

Matthew kept his quill ready and his eyes and ears open. He did not allow even a single word to fall to the ground, but collected everything and placed it on paper. And thus little by little, day by day, the Gospel—the Good News—was composed. It took root, threw out branches and became a tree to bear fruit and nourish those born and yet to be born. Matthew knew the Scriptures by heart. He noticed how the teacher's sayings and deeds were exactly the same as the prophets, centuries earlier, had proclaimed; and if once in a while the prophecies and Jesus' life did not quite match, it was because the mind of man was not eager to understand the hidden meaning of the sacred text. The word of God had seven levels of meaning, and Matthew struggled to find at which level the incompatible elements could find their mates. Even if he occasionally matched things by force, God forgives! Not only would he forgive, he desired this. Every time Matthew took up his quill, did not an angel come and bend over his ear to intone what he was to write?

C. H. Dodd
THE AUTHORITY OF THE BIBLE

It is often claimed that the Bible must be an infallible external authority, because it is "the Word of God". God certainly is the Author of truth; if He has spoken, His Word must possess absolute authority. Let us hold to that maxim: authority belongs to God, and what He says, and that alone, infallibly compels assent. But in the expression "the Word of God" lurks an equivocation. A word is properly a means of communicating thought, through vibrations of the vocal cords, peculiar to the human species. The Eternal has neither breath nor vocal cords; how should He speak words? Clearly enough the term "Word of God" is a metaphorical expression. We mean by it, a means whereby the "thought" of God, which is the truth, is mediated to the human mind. That the Bible as a whole is such a means will be maintained throughout this book. But in the literal sense the Bible consists of the "words" of men— or rather of their visible symbols in writing. It is not the utterance of God *in the same sense* in which it is the utterance of men. Not God but Paul is the author of the Epistle to the Romans, though in a transferred sense we may describe the Epistle to the Romans as a "Word of God", meaning that in some way it mediates to the reader the truth which is the thought of God. God is the Author not of the Bible, but of the life in which the authors of the Bible partake, and of which they tell in such imperfect human words as they could command. The importance of this fairly obvious and elementary distinction is that it exposes the fallacy of arguing from an admission that the Bible is "the Word of

Reprinted from *The Authority of the Bible*, pp. 16–17, 2nd edition, copyright 1938, James Nisbet & Co. Ltd.

God" to the conclusion that it must possess God's own infallibility. The words of a man, assuming that they are the deliberate expression of his meaning, command just that measure of authority which we recognize in the man himself. Thus the words of the Epistle to the Romans carry just as much weight as we are prepared to allow to Paul as a religious teacher. But the question, how far and in what way God "speaks" through Paul, is quite another question, which is in no sense answered by asserting that the Epistle to the Romans is "the Word of God." The mystery of revelation is not to be so lightly disposed of. It is the mystery of the way in which God uses the imperfect thoughts and feelings, words and deeds, of fallible men, to convey eternal truth, both to the men themselves and through them to others.

I do not propose here to attempt to set forth a philosophy of revelation. In so far as this book is to make any contribution to such a philosophy, it must be by way of studying the character of the biblical writings themselves, without any prior assumption other than the manifest fact that readers of these writings have actually found themselves brought nearer to God. My present purpose is simply to clear out of the way of the argument the chimerical idea that we may seek in the Bible, or indeed anywhere else, an expression of the mind of God so direct and so independent of human mediation that it could claim infallible authority over against all other means of apprehending truth. . . .

News Tribune

HELP BUILD THE SPIRITUAL STRENGTH OF OUR NATION

HELP BUILD

THE SPIRITUAL STRENGTH OF OUR NATION

CONGRESSMAN James B.

UTT SAYS:

"For many years, and particularly during my eight years as a Representative in the United States Congress, I have been concerned with the decay of the moral fiber of our nation. I have felt that when this nation fails to realize its dependence upon God, that will be the time it will be destroyed.

"For this reason, I introduced a resolution in the Con-

From the *News Tribune*, November 23, 1960. Reprinted by permission of the Croddy Corporation.

gress, along with other Congressmen, to insert the words 'Under God' in our Pledge of Allegiance. This became law. For the same reason, I was one of a number of Congressmen who, several years ago, introduced a resolution seeking to affirm the basic belief in God and to have it become part of our Constitution.

"Wordage of the first section of this resolution has led to some honest misinterpretation, but it must be understood that during action upon it by the committees of Congress such wordage will be debated and worked out to satisfy all loyal American citizens, individually and as groups.

"At the same time, I want to call special attention to the second section of the resolution which SPECIFICALLY prohibits its being considered as establish-ing a national religion or ecclesiastical body. All of my life I have been a staunch supporter of the doctrine of separation of Church and State and I will work just as hard to keep this doctrine in effect as I am working for the strengthening of the spiritual base of our country.

"The third section of the resolution permits the establishment of a special oath for anyone whose religious scruples might prevent them from giving wholehearted allegiance to the Constitution because of any special wordage. In other words, every effort has been taken throughout this resolution to protect the right of every loyal citizen to his belief in the religion of his choice, to his Freedoms guaranteed to him under the First Amendment to our Constitution."

VOTE FOR and RE-ELECT UTT TO CONGRESS

17
LITERATURE AND GOOD WRITING

"Knowledge is the foundation and source of good writing."

—Horace, *Ars Poetica*

W. Somerset Maugham

THE SUMMING UP

Since then I have written many other books; and though ceasing my methodical study of the old masters (for though the spirit is willing, the flesh is weak), I have continued with increasing assiduity to try to write better. I discovered my limitations and it seemed to me that the only sensible thing was to aim at what excellence I could within them. I knew that I had no lyrical quality. I had a small vocabulary and no efforts that I could make to enlarge it much availed me. I had little gift of metaphor; the original and striking simile seldom occurred to me. Poetic flights and the great imaginative sweep were beyond my powers. I could admire them in others as I could admire their far-fetched tropes and the unusual but suggestive language in which they clothed their thoughts, but my own invention never presented me with such embellishments; and I was tired of trying to do what did not come easily to me. On the other hand, I had an acute power of observation and it seemed to me that I could see a great many things that other people missed. I could put down in clear terms what I saw. I had a logical sense, and if no great feeling for the richness and strangeness of words, at all events a lively appreciation of their sound. I knew that I should never write as well as I could wish, but I thought with pains I could arrive at writing as well as my natural defects allowed. On taking thought it seemed to me that I must aim at lucidity, simplicity and euphony. I have put these three qualities in the order of the importance I assigned to them. . . .

Another cause of obscurity is that the writer is himself not quite sure of his meaning. He has a vague impression of what he wants to say, but has not, either from lack of mental power or from laziness, exactly formulated it in his mind and it is natural enough that he should not find a precise expression for a confused idea. This is due largely to the fact that many writers think, not before, but as they write. The pen originates the thought. The disadvantage of this, and indeed it is a danger against which the author must be always on his guard, is that there is a sort of magic in the written word. The idea acquires substance by taking on a visible nature, and then stands in the way of its own clarification. But this sort of obscurity merges very easily into the wilful. Some writers who do not think clearly are inclined to suppose that their thoughts have a significance greater than at first sight appears. It is flattering to believe that they are too profound to be expressed so clearly that all who run may read, and very naturally it does not occur to such writers that the fault is with their own minds which have not the faculty of precise reflection. Here again the magic of the written word obtains. It is very easy to persuade oneself that a phrase that one does not quite understand may mean a great deal more than one realizes. From this there is only a little way to go to fall into the habit of setting down one's impressions in all their original vagueness. Fools can always be found to discover a hidden sense in them. There is another form of wilful obscurity that masquerades as aristocratic exclusiveness. The author wraps his meaning in mystery so that the vulgar shall not participate in it. His soul is a secret garden into which the elect may penetrate only after overcoming a number of perilous obstacles. But this kind of obscurity is not only pretentious; it is short-sighted. For time plays it an odd trick. If the sense is meagre time reduces it to a meaningless verbiage that no one thinks of reading. This is the fate that has befallen the lucubrations of those French writers who were seduced by the example of Guillaume Apollinaire. But occasionally it throws a sharp cold light on what had seemed profound and thus discloses the fact that these contortions of language disguised very commonplace notions. There are few of Mallarmé's poems now that are not clear; one cannot fail to notice that his thought singularly lacked originality. Some of his phrases were beautiful; the materials of his verse were the poetic platitudes of his day.

Simplicity is not such an obvious merit as lucidity. I have aimed at it because I have no gift for richness. Within limits I admire richness in others, though I find it difficult to digest in quantity. I can read one page of Ruskin with delight, but twenty only with weariness. The rolling period, the stately epithet, the noun rich in poetic associations, the subordinate clauses that give the sentence weight and magnificence, the grandeur like that of wave following wave in the open sea; there is no doubt that in all this there is something inspiring. Words thus strung together fall on the ear like music. The appeal is sensuous rather than intellectual, and the beauty of the sound leads you easily to conclude that you need not bother about the meaning. But words are tyrannical things, they exist for their meanings, and if you will not pay attention to these, you cannot pay attention at all. Your mind wanders. This kind of writing demands a subject that will suit it. It is surely out of place to write in the grand style of inconsiderable things. No one wrote in this manner with greater success than Sir Thomas Browne, but even he did not always escape this pitfall. In the last chapter of *Hydriotaphia* the matter, which is the destiny of man, wonderfully fits the baroque splendour of the language, and here the Norwich doctor produced a piece of prose that has never been surpassed in our literature; but when he describes the finding of his urns in the same splendid manner the effect (at least to my taste) is less happy. When a modern writer is grandiloquent to tell you whether or no a little trollop shall hop into bed with a commonplace young man you are right to be disgusted.

But if richness needs gifts with which everyone is not endowed, simplicity by no means comes by nature. To achieve it needs rigid discipline. So far as I know ours is the only language in which it has been found necessary to give a name to the piece of prose which is described as the purple patch; it would not have been necessary to do so unless it were characteristic. English prose is elaborate rather than simple. It was not always so. Nothing could be more racy, straightforward and alive than the prose of Shakespeare; but it must be remembered that this was dialogue written to be spoken. We do not know how he would have written if like Corneille he had composed prefaces to his plays. It may be that they would have been as euphuistic as the letters of Queen Elizabeth. But earlier prose, the prose of Sir Thomas More, for instance, is neither ponderous, flowery nor oratorical. It smacks of the English soil. To my mind King James's Bible has been a very harmful influence on English prose. I am not so stupid as to deny its great beauty. It is majestical. But the Bible is an oriental book. Its alien imagery has nothing to do with us. Those hyperboles, those luscious metaphors, are foreign to our genius. I cannot but think that not the least of the misfortunes that the Secession from Rome brought upon the spiritual life of our country is that this work for so long a period became the daily, and with many the only, reading of our people. Those rhythms, that powerful vocabulary, that grandiloquence, became part and parcel of the national sensibility. The plain, honest English speech was overwhelmed with ornament. Blunt Englishmen twisted their tongues to speak like Hebrew prophets. There was evidently something in the English temper to which this was congenial, perhaps a native lack of precision in thought, perhaps a naïve delight in fine words for their own sake, an innate eccentricity and love of embroidery, I do not know; but the fact remains that ever since, English prose has had to struggle against the tendency to luxuriance. When from time to time the spirit of the language has reasserted itself, as it did with Dryden and the writers of Queen Anne, it was only to be submerged once more by the pomposities of Gibbon and Dr. Johnson. When English prose recovered simplicity with Hazlitt, the Shelley of the letters and Charles Lamb at his best, it lost it again with De Quincey, Carlyle, Meredith and Walter Pater. It is obvious that the grand style is more striking than the plain. Indeed many people think that a style that does not attract notice is not style. They will admire Walter Pater's, but will read an essay by Matthew Arnold without giving a moment's attention to the elegance, distinction and sobriety with which he set down what he had to say. . . .

It has been said that good prose should resemble the conversation of a well-bred man. Conversation is only possible when men's minds are free from pressing anxieties. Their lives must be reasonably secure and they must have no grave concern about their souls. They must attach importance to the refinements of civilization. They must value courtesy, they must pay attention to their persons (and have we not also been told that good prose should be like the clothes of a well-dressed man, appropriate but unobtrusive?), they must fear to bore, they must be neither flippant nor solemn, but always apt; and they must look upon "enthusiasm" with a critical glance. This is a soil very suitable for prose. It is not to be wondered at that it gave a fitting opportunity for the appearance of the best writer of prose that our modern world has seen, Voltaire. The writers of English, perhaps owing to the poetic nature of the language, have seldom reached the excellence that seems to have come so naturally to him. It is in so far as they have approached the ease, sobriety and precision of the great French masters that they are admirable. . . .

Whether you ascribe importance to euphony, the last of the three characteristics that I mentioned, must depend on the sensitiveness of your ear. A great many readers, and many admirable writers, are devoid of this quality. Poets as we know have always made a great use of alliteration. They are persuaded that the repetition of a sound gives an effect of beauty. I do not think it does so in prose. It seems to me that in prose alliteration should be used only for a special reason; when used by accident it falls on the ear very disagreeably. But its accidental use is so common that one can only suppose that the sound of it is not universally offensive. Many writers without distress will put two rhyming words together, join a monstrous long adjective to a monstrous long noun, or between the end of one word and the beginning of another have a conjunction of consonants that almost breaks your jaw. These are trivial and obvious instances. I mention them only to prove that if careful writers can do such things it is only because they have no ear. Words have weight, sound and appearance; it is only by considering these that you can write a sentence that is good to look at and good to listen to.

I have read many books on English prose, but have found it hard to profit by them; for the most part they are vague, unduly theoretical, and often scolding. But you cannot say this of Fowler's *Dictionary of Modern English Usage*. It is a valuable work. I do not think anyone writes so well that he cannot learn much from it. It is lively reading. Fowler liked simplicity, straightforwardness and common sense. He had no patience with pretentiousness. He had a sound feeling that idiom was the backbone of a language and he was all for the racy phrase. He was no slavish admirer of logic and was willing enough to give usage right of way through the exact demesnes of grammar. English grammar is very difficult and few writers have avoided making mistakes in it. So heedful a writer as Henry James, for instance, on occasion wrote so ungrammatically that a schoolmaster, finding such errors in a schoolboy's essay, would be justly indignant. It is necessary to know grammar, and it is better to write grammatically than not, but it is well to remember that grammar is common speech formulated. Usage is the only test. I would prefer a phrase that was easy and unaffected to a phrase that was grammatical. One of the differences between French and English is that in French you can be grammatical with complete naturalness, but in English not invariably. It is a difficulty in writing English that the sound of the living voice dominates the look of the printed word. I have given the matter of style a great deal of thought and have taken great pains. I have written few pages that I feel I could not improve and far too many that I have left with dissatisfaction because, try as I would, I could do no better. I cannot say of myself what Johnson said of Pope: "He never passed a fault unamended by indifference, nor quitted it by despair." I do not write as I want to; I write as I can.

But Fowler had no ear. He did not see that simplicity may sometimes make concessions to euphony. I do not think a far-fetched, an archaic or even an affected word is one of place when it sounds better than the blunt, obvious one or when it gives a sentence a better balance. But, I hasten to add, though I think you may without misgiving make this concession to pleasant sound, I think you should make none to what may obscure your meaning. Anything is better than not to write clearly. There is nothing to be said against lucidity, and against simplicity only the possibility of dryness. This is a risk that is well worth taking when you reflect how much better it is to be bald than to wear a curly wig. But there is in euphony a danger that must be considered. It is very likely to be monotonous. When George Moore began to write, his style was poor; it gave you the impression that he wrote on wrapping paper with a blunt pencil. But he developed gradually a very musical English. He learnt to write sentences that fall away on the ear with a misty languor and it delighted him so much that he could never have enough of it. He did not escape monotony. It is like the sound of water lapping a shingly beach, so soothing that you presently cease to be sensible of it. It is so mellifluous that you hanker for some harshness, for an abrupt dissonance, that will interrupt the silky concord. I do not know how one can guard against this. I suppose the best chance is to have a more lively faculty of boredom than one's readers so that one is wearied before they are. One must always be on the watch for mannerisms and when certain cadences come too easily to the pen ask oneself whether they have not become mechanical. It is very hard to discover the exact point where the idiom one has formed to express oneself has lost its tang. As Dr. Johnson said: "He that has once studiously formed a style, rarely writes afterwards with complete ease." Admirably as I think Matthew Arnold's style was suited to his particular purposes, I must admit that his mannerisms are often irritating. His style was an instrument that he had forged once for all; it was not like the human hand capable of performing a variety of actions.

If you could write lucidly, simply, euphoniously and yet with liveliness you would write perfectly: you would write like Voltaire. And yet we know how fatal the pursuit of liveliness may be: it may result in the tiresome acrobatics of Meredith. Macaulay and Carlyle were in their different ways arresting; but at the heavy cost of naturalness. Their flashy effects distract the mind. They destroy their persuasiveness; you would not believe a man was very intent on ploughing a furrow if he carried a hoop with him and jumped through it at every other step. A good style should show no sign of effort. What is written should seem a happy accident. I think no one in France now writes more admirably than Colette, and such is the ease of her expression that you cannot bring yourself to believe that she takes any trouble over it. I am told that there are pianists who have a natural technique so that they can play in a manner that most executants can achieve only as the result of unremitting toil, and I am willing to believe that there are writers who are equally fortunate. Among them I was much inclined to place Colette. I asked her. I was exceedingly surprised to hear that she wrote everything over and over again. She told me that she would often spend a whole morning working upon a single page. But it does not matter how one gets the effect of ease. For my part, if I get it at all, it is only by strenuous effort. Nature seldom provides me with the word, the turn of phrase, that is appropriate without being far-fetched or commonplace. . . .

For my part the two writers I have found most useful to study for this purpose are Hazlitt and Cardinal Newman. I would try to imitate neither. Hazlitt can be unduly rhetorical; and sometimes his decoration is as fussy as Victorian Gothic. Newman can be a trifle flowery. But at their best both are admirable. Time has little touched their style; it is almost contemporary. Hazlitt is vivid, bracing and energetic; he has strength and liveliness. You feel the man in his phrases, not the mean, querulous, disagreeable man that he appeared to the world that knew him, but the man within of his own ideal vision. (And the man within us is as true in reality as the man, pitiful and halting, of our outward seeming.) Newman had an exquisite grace, music, playful sometimes and sometimes grave, a woodland beauty of phrase, dignity and mellowness. Both wrote with extreme lucidity. Neither is quite as simple as the purest taste demands. Here I think Matthew Arnold excels them. Both had a wonderful balance of phrase and both knew how to write sentences pleasing to the eye. Both had an ear of extreme sensitiveness.

If anyone could combine their merits in the manner of writing of the present day he would write as well as it is possible for anyone to write.

Henry David Thoreau

NATURE AND ANTIQUITY: THE POET OF GENIUS AND THE POET OF TASTE

Our own country furnishes antiquities as ancient and durable, and as useful, as any; rocks at least as well covered with moss, and a soil which if it is virgin, is but virgin mould, the very dust of nature. What if we cannot read Rome, or Greece, Etruria, or Carthage, or Egypt, or Babylon, on these; are our cliffs bare? The lichen on the rocks is a rude and simple shield which beginning and imperfect Nature suspended there. Still hangs her wrinkled trophy. And here too the poet's eye may still detect the brazen nails which fastened Time's inscriptions, and if he has the gift, decipher them by this clue. The walls that fence our fields, as well as modern Rome, and not less the Parthenon[1] itself, are all built of *ruins*. Here may be heard the din of rivers, and ancient winds which

---

All footnotes in this selection are by the editor of this text.

[1] Athens was the fountainhead of the culture of Western Civilization. The Parthenon, the temple of Athena (goddess of skills, wisdom, and warfare), was completed about 432 B.C. It stands today a model of classic purity: its columns are Doric; it is 228 feet long and 101 feet wide; and it contains friezes, statues, reliefs, and other decorations, some attributed to Phidias and of unsurpassed beauty.

have long since lost their names sough through our woods;—the first faint sounds of spring, older than the summer of Athenian glory, the titmouse lisping in the wood, the jay's scream, and blue-bird's warble, and the hum of

> "bees that fly
> About the laughing blossoms of sallowy." [2]

Here is the gray dawn for antiquity, and our to-morrow's future should be at least paulo-post[3] to theirs which we have put behind us. There are the red-maple and birchen leaves, old runes which are not yet deciphered; catkins,[4] pine-cones, vines, oak-leaves, and acorns; the very things themselves, and not their forms in stone,—so much the more ancient and venerable. And even to the current summer there has come down tradition of a hoary-headed master of all art, who once filled every field and grove with statues and god-like architecture, of every design which Greece has lately copied; whose ruins are now mingled with the dust, and not one-block remains upon another. The century sun and unwearied rain have wasted them, till not one fragment from that quarry now exists; and poets perchance will feign that gods sent down the material from heaven. . . .

Poetry is the mysticism of mankind.

The expressions of the poet cannot be analyzed; his sentence is one word, whose syllables are words. There are indeed no *words* quite worthy to be set to his music. But what matter if we do not hear the words always, if we hear the music?

Much verse fails of being poetry because it was not written exactly at the right crisis, though it may have been inconceivably near to it. It is only by a miracle that poetry is written at all. It is not recoverable thought, but a hue caught from a vaster receding thought.

A poem is one undivided, unimpeded expression fallen ripe into literature, and it is undividedly and unimpededly received by those for whom it was matured.

If you can speak what you will never hear,—if you can write what you will never read, you have done rare things.

There are two classes of men called poets. The one cultivates life, the other art,—one seeks food for nutriment, the other for flavor; one satisfies hunger, the other gratifies the palate. There are two kinds of writing, both great and rare; one that of genius, or the inspired, the other of intellect and taste, in the intervals of inspiration. The former is above criticism, always correct, giving the law to criticism. It vibrates and pulsates with life forever. It is sacred, and to be read with reverence, as the works of nature are studied. There are few instances of a sustained style of this kind; perhaps every man has spoken words, but the speaker

---

[2] "Sallowy" or "willows."

[3] Latin expression for "shortly afterward."

[4] "Catkins" or "cat's tails"; they are tassellike spikes of clustered flowers.

is then careless of the record. Such a style removes us out of personal relations with its author, we do not take his words on our lips, but his sense into our hearts. It is the stream of inspiration, which bubbles out, now here, now there, now in this man, now in that. It matters not through what ice-crystals it is seen, now a fountain, now the ocean stream running under ground. It is in Shakespeare, Alpheus, in Burns, Arethuse,[5] but ever the same.—The other is self-possessed and wise. It is reverent of genius, and greedy of inspiration. It is conscious in the highest and the least degree. It consists with the most perfect command of the faculties. It dwells in a repose as of the desert, and objects are as distinct in it as oases or palms in the horizon of sand. The train of thought moves with subdued and measured step, like a caravan. But the pen is only an instrument in its hand, and not instinct with life, like a longer arm. It leaves a thin varnish or glaze over all its work. The works of Goethe furnish remarkable instances of the latter.

There is no just and serene criticism as yet. Nothing is considered simply as it lies in the lap of eternal beauty, but our thoughts, as well as our bodies, must be dressed after the latest fashions. Our taste is too delicate and particular. It says nay to the poet's work, but never yea to his hope. It invites him to adorn his deformities, and not to cast them off by expansion, as the tree its bark. We are a people who live in a bright light, in houses of pearl and porcelain, and drink only light wines, whose teeth are easily set on edge by the least natural sour. If we had been consulted, the backbone of the earth would have been made, not of granite, but of Bristol spar.[6] A modern author would have died in infancy in a ruder age. But the poet is something more than a scald,[7] "a smoother and polisher of language"; he is a Cincinnatus[8] in literature, and occupies no west end of the world. Like the sun, he will indifferently select his rhymes, and with a liberal taste weave into his verse the planet and the stubble.

In these old books the stucco has long since crumbled away, and we read what was sculptured in the granite. They are rude and massive in their proportions, rather than smooth and delicate in their finish. The workers in stone polish only their chimney ornaments, but their pyra-

---

[5] Reference to the famous myth of Alpheus and Arethuse. Alpheus, the river god, was attracted to Arethuse, who bathed in his waters. Alarmed, she escaped through the intervention of the goddess Diana, who transported her to Sicily and turned her into a fountain. But Alpheus followed her through a subterranean route to Sicily, emerged in Arethuse's fountain, and was united with her there, where they mingled their waters. See Thoreau's previous sentence for the complete analogy of the myth: the inspiration of Alpheus is likened to the power of the writer of genius, who finds a way, as it were, bubbling up first here and then there, in order to reach into the hearts of Mankind.

[6] "Bristol spar" is a lustrous rock, but crumbles easily with time; however, "granite," though it possesses less sheer brilliance, endures and gleams subtly.

[7] The "scald" was a Norse poet, sometimes a court entertainer, who recited or "sang" conventional works.

[8] Lucius Quintus Cincinnatus, a symbol of Roman patriotism and humility, was born about 519 B.C. He twice defended his country in times of danger, but then returned to the simple life of his farm, a life which he preferred to the dictatorship to which he was appointed.

mids are roughly done. There is a soberness in a rough aspect, as of un-hewn granite, which addresses a depth in us, but a polished surface hits only the ball of the eye. The true finish is the work of time and the use to which a thing is put. The elements are still polishing the pyramids. Art may varnish and gild, but it can do no more. A work of genius is rough-hewn from the first, because it anticipates the lapse of time, and has an ingrained polish, which still appears when fragments are broken off, an essential quality of its substance. Its beauty is at the same time its strength, and it breaks with a lustre.

Walt Whitman

WHEN LILACS LAST IN THE DOORYARD BLOOM'D

1

When lilacs last in the dooryard bloom'd,
And the great star early droop'd in the western sky in the night,
I mourn'd, and yet shall mourn with ever-returning spring.

Ever-returning spring, trinity sure to me you bring,
Lilac blooming perennial and drooping star in the west,
And thought of him I love.

2

O powerful western fallen star!
O shades of night—O moody, tearful night!
O great star disappear'd—O the black murk that hides the star!
O cruel hands that hold me powerless—O helpless soul of me!
O harsh surrounding cloud that will not free my soul.

3

In the dooryard fronting an old farm-house near the white-
    wash'd palings,
Stands the lilac-bush tall-growing with heart-shaped leaves of
    rich green,
With many a pointed blossom rising delicate, with the perfume
    strong I love,
With every leaf a miracle—and from this bush in the dooryard,
With delicate-color'd blossoms and heart-shaped leaves of rich
    green,
A sprig with its flower I break.

4

In the swamp in secluded recesses,
A shy and hidden bird is warbling a song.

Solitary the thrush,
The hermit withdrawn to himself, avoiding the settlements,
Sings by himself a song.

Song of the bleeding throat,
Death's outlet song of life, (for well dear brother I know,
If thou wast not granted to sing thou would'st surely die.)

5

Over the breast of the spring, the land, amid cities,
Amid lanes and through old woods, where lately the violets
    peep'd from the ground, spotting the gray debris,
Amid the grass in the fields each side of the lanes, passing the
    endless grass,
Passing the yellow-spear'd wheat, every grain from its shroud
    in the dark-brown fields uprisen,
Passing the apple-tree blows of white and pink in the orchards,
Carrying a corpse to where it shall rest in the grave,
Night and day journeys a coffin.

6

Coffin that passes through lanes and streets,
Through day and night with the great cloud darkening the land,
With the pomp of the inloop'd flags with the cities draped in
    black,
With the show of the States themselves as of crape-veil'd
    women standing,
With processions long and winding and the flambeaus of the
    night,
With the countless torches lit, with the silent sea of faces and
    the unbared heads,
With the waiting depot, the arriving coffin, and the sombre
    faces,
With dirges through the night, with the thousand voices rising
    strong and solemn,
With all the mournful voices of the dirges pour'd around the
    coffin,
The dim-lit churches and the shuddering organs—where amid
    these you journey,
With the tolling tolling bells' perpetual clang,
Here, coffin that slowly passes,
I give you my sprig of lilac.

7

(Nor for you, for one alone,
Blossoms and branches green to coffins all I bring,
For fresh as the morning, thus would I chant a song for you
    O sane and sacred death.

All over bouquets of roses,
O death, I cover you over with roses and early lilies,
But mostly and now the lilac that blooms the first,
Copious I break, I break the sprigs from the bushes,
With loaded arms I come, pouring for you,
For you and the coffins all of you O death.)

8

O western orb sailing the heaven,
Now I know what you must have meant as a month since I
    walk'd,
As I walk'd in silence the transparent shadowy night,
As I saw you had something to tell as you bent to me night
    after night,
As you droop'd from the sky low down as if to my side, (while
    the other stars all look'd on,)
As we wander'd together the solemn night, (for something I
    know not what kept me from sleep,)
As the night advanced, and I saw on the rim of the west how
    full you were of woe,
As I stood on the rising ground in the breeze in the cool trans-
    parent night,
As I watch'd where you pass'd and was lost in the netherward
    black of the night,
As my soul in its trouble dissatisfied sank, as where you sad
    orb,
Concluded, dropt in the night, and was gone.

9

Sing on there in the swamp,
O singer bashful and tender, I hear your notes, I hear your call,
I hear, I come presently, I understand you,
But a moment I linger, for the lustrous star has detain'd me,
The star my departing comrade holds and detains me.

10

O how shall I warble myself for the dead one there I loved?
And how shall I deck my song for the large sweet soul that has
    gone?
And what shall my perfume be for the grave of him I love?

Sea-winds blown from east and west,
Blown from the Eastern sea and blown from the Western sea,
    till there on the prairies meeting,
These and with these and the breath of my chant,
I'll perfume the grave of him I love.

11

O what shall I hang on the chamber walls?
And what shall the pictures be that I hang on the walls,
To adorn the burial-house of him I love?

Pictures of growing spring and farms and homes,
With the Fourth-month eve at sundown, and the gray smoke
    lucid and bright,
With floods of the yellow gold of the gorgeous, indolent, sink-
    ing sun, burning, expanding the air,
With the fresh sweet herbage under foot, and the pale green
    leaves of the trees prolific,
In the distance the flowing glaze, the breast of the river, with a
    wind-dapple here and there,
With ranging hills on the banks, with many a line against the
    sky, and shadows,
And the city at hand with dwellings so dense, and stacks of
    chimneys,
And all the scenes of life and the workshops, and the workmen
    homeward returning.

12

Lo, body and soul—this land,
My own Manhattan with spires, and the sparkling and hurrying
    tides, and the ships,
The varied and ample land, the South and the North in the
    light, Ohio's shores and flashing Missouri,
And ever the far-spreading prairies cover'd with grass and corn.

Lo, the most excellent sun so calm and haughty,
The violet and purple morn with just-felt breezes,
The gentle soft-born measureless light,
The miracle spreading bathing all, the fulfill'd noon,
The coming eve delicious, the welcome night and the stars,
Over my cities shining all, enveloping man and land.

13

Sing on, sing on you gray-brown bird,
Sing from the swamps, the recesses, pour your chant from the
    bushes,
Limitless out of the dusk, out of the cedars and pines.

Sing on dearest brother, warble your reedy song,
Loud human song, with voice of uttermost woe.

O liquid and free and tender!
O wild and loose to my soul—O wondrous singer!

You only I hear—yet the star holds me, (but will soon depart,)
Yet the lilac with mastering odor holds me.

14

Now while I sat in the day and look'd forth,
In the close of the day with its light and the fields of spring,
    and the farmers preparing their crops,
In the large unconscious scenery of my land with its lakes and
    forests,
In the heavenly aerial beauty, (after the perturb'd winds and
    the storms,)
Under the arching heavens of the afternoon swift passing, and
    the voices of children and women,
The many-moving sea-tides, and I saw the ships how they
    sail'd,
And the summer approaching with richness, and the fields all
    busy with labor,
And the infinite separate houses, how they all went on, each
    with its meals and minutia of daily usages,
And the streets how their throbbings throbb'd, and the cities
    pent—lo, then and there,
Falling upon them all and among them all, enveloping me with
    the rest,
Appear'd the cloud, appear'd the long black trail,
And I knew death, its thought, and the sacred knowledge of
    death.

Then with the knowledge of death as walking one side of me,
And the thought of death close-walking the other side of me,
And I in the middle as with companions, and as holding the
    hands of companions,
I fled forth to the hiding receiving night that talks not,
Down to the shores of the water, the path by the swamp in the
    dimness,
To the solemn shadowy cedars and ghostly pines so still.

And the singer so shy to the rest receiv'd me,
The gray-brown bird I know receiv'd us comrades three,
And he sang the carol of death, and a verse for him I love.

From deep secluded recesses,
From the fragrant cedars and the ghostly pines so still,
Came the carol of the bird.

And the charm of the carol rapt me,
As I held as if by their hands my comrades in the night,
And the voice of my spirit tallied the song of the bird.

Come lovely and soothing death,
Undulate round the world, serenely arriving, arriving,

In the day, in the night, to all, to each,
Sooner or later delicate death.

Prais'd be the fathomless universe,
For life and joy, and for objects and knowledge curious,
And for love, sweet love—but praise! praise! praise!
For the sure-enwinding arms of cool enfolding death.

Dark mother always gliding near with soft feet,
Have none chanted for thee a chant of fullest welcome?
Then I chant it for thee, I glorify thee above all,
I bring thee a song that when thou must indeed come, come
*   unfalteringly.*
Approach strong deliveress,
When it is so, when thou hast taken them I joyously sing the
*   dead,*
Lost in the loving floating ocean of thee,
Laved in the flood of thy bliss O death.

From me to thee glad serenades,
Dances for thee I propose saluting thee, adornments and feast-
*   ings for thee,*
And the sights of the open landscape and the high-spread sky
*   are fitting,*
And life and the fields, and the huge and thoughtful night.

The night in silence under many a star,
The ocean shore and the husky whispering wave whose voice
*   I know,*
And the soul turning to thee O vast and well-veil'd death,
And the body gratefully nestling close to thee.

Over the tree-tops I float thee a song,
Over the rising and sinking waves, over the myriad fields and
*   the prairies wide,*
Over the dense-pack'd cities all and the teeming wharves and
*   ways,*
I float this carol with joy, with joy to thee O death.

15

To the tally of my soul,
Loud and strong kept up the gray-brown bird,
With pure deliberate notes spreading filling the night.

Loud in the pines and cedars dim,
Clear in the freshness moist and the swamp-perfume,
And I with my comrades there in the night.

While my sight that was bound in my eyes unclosed,
As to long panoramas of visions.

And I saw askant the armies,
I saw as in noiseless dreams hundreds of battle-flags,
Borne through the smoke of the battles and pierc'd with mis-
    siles I saw them,
And carried hither and yon through the smoke, and torn and
    bloody,
And at last a few shreds left on the staffs, (and all in silence,)
And the staffs all splinter'd and broken.

I saw battle-corpses, myriads of them,
And the white skeletons of young men, I saw them,
I saw the debris and debris of all the slain soldiers of the war,
But I saw they were not as was thought,
They themselves were fully at rest, they suffer'd not,
The living remain'd and suffer'd, the mother suffer'd,
And the wife and the child and the musing comrade suffer'd,
And the armies that remain'd suffer'd.

16

Passing the visions, passing the night,
Passing, unloosing the hold of my comrades' hands,
Passing the song of the hermit bird and the tallying song of my
    soul,
Victorious song, death's outlet song, yet varying ever-altering
    song,
As low and wailing, yet clear the notes, rising and falling, flood-
    ing the night,
Sadly sinking and fainting, as warning and warning, and yet
    again bursting with joy,
Covering the earth and filling the spread of the heaven,
As that powerful psalm in the night I heard from recesses,
Passing, I leave thee lilac with heart-shaped leaves,
I leave thee there in the dooryard, blooming, returning with
    spring.

I cease from my song for thee,
From my gaze on thee in the west, fronting the west, commun-
    ing with thee,
O comrade lustrous with silver face in the night.

Yet each to keep and all, retrievements out of the night,
The song, the wondrous chant of the gray-brown bird,
And the tallying chant, the echo arous'd in my soul,
With the lustrous and drooping star with the countenance full
    of woe,
With the holders holding my hand nearing the call of the bird,
Comrades mine and I in the midst, and their memory ever to
    keep, for the dead I loved so well,

For the sweetest, wisest soul of all my days and lands—and
this for his dear sake,
Lilac and star and bird twined with the chant of my soul,
There in the fragrant pines and the cedars dusk and dim.

O CAPTAIN! MY CAPTAIN!

O Captain! my Captain! our fearful trip is done,
The ship has weather'd every rack, the prize we sought is won,
The port is near, the bells I hear, the people all exulting,
While follow eyes the steady keel, the vessel grim and daring;
    But O heart! heart! heart!
     O the bleeding drops of red,
      Where on the deck my Captain lies,
      Fallen cold and dead.

O Captain! my Captain! rise up and hear the bells;
Rise up—for you the flag is flung—for you the bugle trills,
For you bouquets and ribbon'd wreaths—for you the shores
a-crowding,
For you they call, the swaying mass, their eager faces turning;
    Here Captain! dear father!
     This arm beneath your head!
      It is some dream that on the deck,
      You've fallen cold and dead.

My Captain does not answer, his lips are pale and still,
My father does not feel my arm, he has no pulse nor will,
The ship is anchor'd safe and sound, its voyage closed and
done,
From fearful trip the victor ship comes in with object won;
    Exult O shores, and ring O bells!
     But I with mournful tread,
      Walk the deck my Captain lies,
      Fallen cold and dead.

Kelly Thurman

TEACHING LITERATURE BY A SYNAPTIC METHOD

Nearly any teacher of literature begins his performance in the classroom with certain basic assumptions: that the nature of literature is to
delight and to instruct; that the study of literature involves an author-

Reprinted from *The Oklahoma Teacher,* March, 1966, pp. 10–11 by permission.

work-reader relationship; that the experience of a reader confronting a piece of literature has some relevancy to that reader's self-discovery, self-commitment and self-containment.

Transmitting these assumptions to a class is not an easy matter. What brings delight to one student may bore another; establishing relationships between an author and his work is often a limiting experience; and many students have difficulty visualizing how they can appropriate directly and immediately any segment of their reading experience. Finally, one should mention the recalcitrants who pretend they do not want instruction, who scoff at the appreciation of beauty, who fight self-discovery and self-improvement.

What the literature teacher needs is a method, and, fortunately, numerous methods for transmitting any literary assumption are available. Digests, analyses, films, slides, tapes, controlled research booklets —you name it—abound and may be profitably employed in making the reader's experience with a literary work more fruitful. Yet it is the raw experience of reader handling book which seems basic to the teacher of literature. Whatever method chosen by the instructor for imparting his material, the results of his efforts are more often *synoptic* than they are *synaptic,* thus in effect negating what ideally should be a rewarding and self-assuring experience.

Let me hasten to define my terms and to illustrate. By *synoptic* results, I mean that the student merely receives a grab bag of data; a general, useful digest; a Christmas package that needs not be unwrapped. This rich miscellany may include, if the piece of literature under study is a novel, a host of helpful biographical and historical anecdotes, meaningful intrinsic observations about structure, style, symbolism, genre; insightful statements about characters, theme, plot; but it is all canned, programmed, prescribed, and may be passed down from generation to generation. Think how many diluted "Kittredgeisms" and "Brooks-isms" are still circulated, though obviously shop worn; think how many "Frye-isms" remain to be served up in the next literary generation! Yet it is possible to pursue antiquarian delights as did Kittredge, and to find irony, paradox, and rich symbolism, as did Brooks, and to make meaningful comparisons through myth and genre, as does Frye, and do it freshly and imaginatively and creatively.

This can come by what I shall designate as the *synaptic* approach. Here I draw from physiology and biology: an impulse passes from one neuron to another; a conjugation and splitting of pairs of chromosomes occurs, resulting in a new nucleus. Something like this goes on in the learning process, especially when we rise above the elementary level of learning by rote. Synaptic learning then presupposes that a stimulus acting upon an object, i.e., a literary work eliciting from a reader, will effect a novel and original response. These are the responses which will endure: they are meaningful, leading to self-commitment and self-containment. I think they may be elicited from any reader, varying, of course, in number and degree and in intensity.

To illustrate the differences between the two approaches, let us use *Romeo and Juliet,* a play often read in Grades 9 or 10. However long the student is exposed to the play by the synoptic method, he is likely to be given packaged information about Shakespeare, about the Elizabethan theater, about Brooke's famous poem, "The Tragicall Historye of Romeus and Juliet," about pirated quartos, about myths and Queen Mab; about puns, conceits, sonnets, rimed couplets, and epithets in the play; about the violations of the unities in *Romeo and Juliet;* about the well-developed characters and the richness of language. The list could be expanded indefinitely, and few teachers would quarrel with the worth of such enterprises.

Neither do I, but I do question the methodology employed. Often I find myself engaged in lectures brimming with information similar to the above. Repeatedly, to my chagrin, I discover that the "inoculation" lasts only through the final examination. Once credit is earned in the course, such information is filed away into a compartment and forgotten.

But if a *synaptic* method can be found, the case is altered, and the student finds a relevancy between the literary work and his own experiences. He becomes involved and, like Adam naming the flora and fauna in Eden, starts creatively to name, assign, appropriate for himself. In the sense that all snowflakes differ, so do all naming and appropriating experiences differ. To every man falling in love is original, creative, committing, containing. Likewise are one's responses to works of art, making for differences in evaluative processes, in taste, in comprehensiveness.

Instead of being given information about a work of art, a student must "find" information about it by plumbing his own experiences. He must relate himself to it in order for an impulse to pass to another neuron, for a chromosome to conjugate and later to split, for a new nucleus to be born, for advanced learning to occur. The wise teacher employs such tactics or strategies as he possesses in order to precipitate the advanced learning state.

Again using *Romeo and Juliet* as a model, let us see how some form of cajolery, magic, or dramatization through discussion may lead a student to a position where he "possesses" the play himself. An intelligent examination of character and language may do the trick. If a student can identify himself with the realities of Tybalt's extremism, can see that a coarse-talking nurse has little effect upon Juliet's innocence and purity, that the broad-witted and high-spirited tongue of Mercutio cannot muster sufficient grace to avoid a clash, that Romeo's peace-making efforts lead to his own undoing, or that Friar Lawrence's gamble to subordinate his duties to his vows in order to patch up a quarrel between two feuding families succeeds—but at the sacrifice of the lives of the purest representatives of those families—he is beginning to see how literature poses (and answers) problems central to the most perplexing problems of human existence. Note that he reaches this discovery through playing as if he were one of the characters in the drama, an act which he repeats when he becomes one of the voices who speaks in any other literary genre. Character it must be remembered is as important in a lyric poem or a short story as it is in drama.

But a synaptic process can as easily be effected through questions relating to the functional aspects of the language used in *Romeo and*

Juliet, or in any other literary work, for that matter. Space will permit only one example. Consider Juliet's declaration that "when he (Romeo) shall die / Take him and cut him out in little stars / And he will make the heaven so fine / That all the world will be in love with night." Since the dullest clod in a classroom understands something of the beauty of twinkling stars, it should not be difficult to establish how that one passage tells something about the warmth, ardor, exhilaration, innocency of a young lover who can hardly await the next visit from her beloved. That an inscrutable Providence thwarts the lovers and chills the sensitivities of the reader, but, in doing so, registers a permanent impression. The chromosomes connected with an advanced learning process undergo a nuclear change; self-discovery ensues, a response that endures is elicited. The teacher no longer needs to inoculate; the student has passed the pre-packaging stage. What the student has received through a synaptic method is as meaningful to him as were Adam's initial impressions, for in truth the learner is a second Adam with new names to assign, new commitments to make, as he journeys on the road to fuller self-containment.

Jacques Barzun

HOW TO WRITE AND BE READ

Here and there a touch of good grammar for picturesqueness.—Mark Twain

Writing comes before reading, in logic and also in the public mind. No one cares whether you read fast or slow, well or ill, but as soon as you put pen to paper, somebody may be puzzled, angry, bored, or ecstatic; and if the occasion permits your reader is almost sure to exclaim about the schools not doing their duty. This is the oldest literary tradition, of which here is a modern instance:—

WHAT KIND OF TEACHING IN THE PRIMARY SCHOOLS?
By "Disgusted"   Recently a letter came into my office from a boy who described himself as a first-year high school student. He wanted *infirmation* about *Africia,* because for his project in the social studies class he had *chozen Africia.* If we could not help him, *were* could he write? In closing, he was ours *sinceerly.* His handwriting was comparable to that of my 6-year-old nephew.

Too bad, but I am not alarmed. This student of "Africia" may or may not learn to spell: it is not nearly so important as his diction and his sentence structure, which the plaintiff withheld, though they would have better enabled us to judge what the schools were really doing. What

I fear about this boy is that when grown-up and provided with a secretary who can spell, he will write something like this: —

DEAR SIR: —

As you know, security prices have been advancing rapidly in the recent past *in belated recognition of the favorable fundamentals that exist.* [Italics mine]

What is decadent about this I shall shortly explain. Meantime, the fact should be faced squarely that good writing is and has always been extremely rare. I do not mean fine writing, but the simple, clear kind that everyone always demands—from others. The truth is that Simple English is no one's mother tongue. It has to be worked for. As an historian, I have plowed through state papers, memoirs, diaries, and letters, and I know that the ability to write has only a remote connection with either intelligence, or greatness, or schooling. Lincoln had no schooling yet became one of the great prose writers of the world. Cromwell went to Cambridge and was hardly ever able to frame an intelligible sentence. Another man of thought and action, Admiral Lord Howe, generally refrained from writing out his plan of battle, so as to save his captains from inevitable misunderstanding. Yet Howe managed to win the famous First of June by tactics that revolutionized the art, and led directly to Nelson's Trafalgar plan—itself a rather muddled piece of prose. Let us then start with no illusion of an imaginary golden age of writing.

Which leaves the problem of doing the best with what nature gives us. And here I have some convictions born of long struggle, with myself and with others. First, I pass by all considerations of penmanship and elementary spelling to remark only that I think it a mistake to start children writing on typewriters, and worse yet to let them grow up unable to do anything but print capitals.

Above the beginner's level, the important fact is that writing cannot be taught exclusively in a course called English Composition. Writing can only be taught by the united efforts of the entire teaching staff. This holds good of any school, college, or university. Joint effort is needed, not merely to "enforce the rules"; it is needed to insure accuracy in every subject. How can an answer in physics or a translation from the French or an historical statement be called correct if the phrasing is loose or the key word wrong? Students argue that the reader of the paper knows perfectly well what is meant. Probably so, but a written exercise is designed to be read; it is not supposed to be a challenge to clairvoyance. My Italian-born tailor periodically sends me a postcard which runs: "Your clothes is ready and should come down for a fitting." I understand him, but the art I honor him for is cutting cloth, not precision of utterance. Now a student in college must be inspired to achieve in all subjects the utmost accuracy of perception combined with the utmost artistry of expression. The two merge and develop the sense of good workmanship, of preference for quality and truth, which is the chief mark of the genuinely educated man.

This is obviously a collective task, in which every department and every faculty has a common stake. But it is not enough to give notice that these are the faculty's sentiments. Even supposing that all teachers were willing and able to exert vigilance over written work, there would still be many practical problems of detail. And first, what motive for writing well can the student be made to feel? There is only one valid motive: the desire to be read. You will say that most students have no urge either to write or to be read. True, but (*a*) they know that they have to write and (*b*) most of them want to be well thought of. They should accordingly be made to see that reading the ordinary student paper can be a nuisance and a bore to the teacher, and that the proper aim of writing should be to make it a pleasure. This is another way of saying that most school writing is bad because student and teacher play at writing and reading instead of taking it seriously. The teacher expects second-rate hokum and the student supplies it. Let the teacher assert his rights just as the students do: in many college classes the men protest—quite rightly—when they are asked to read a dull or ill-organized book. Similarly, the instructor may warn the students that when they turn in filler and padding, jargon and lingo, stuff and nonsense, he will mark them down, not only in his grade book, but in his violated soul.

Naturally, this conscious brutality must go with a helping hand; in fact a revision of all usual practices is in order. The embargo on hokum will already work a healthy elimination of bad prose. Then the long Term Paper must be discarded and replaced with the short essay, not more than five typewritten pages in length. Students always ask how long a final paper should be and they are absolutely right in believing that most instructors are impressed by mere bulk. But when one knows how difficult it is to articulate even three measly thoughts around a single point, it is folly to ask eighteen-year-olds to produce thirty- or forty-page monographs that shall be readable. What they produce is an uncarded mattress of quotations, paraphrase, "however's," and "Thus we see's." Size being aimed at, there is no time for rewriting or reordering the material culled from half a dozen books, and the main effort goes into the irrelevant virtues of neat typing, plentiful footnotes, and the mannerisms of scholarship.

The short paper—and I speak from a large pile accumulated over twelve years—aims and arrives at different ends. It answers the reader's eternal question: Just what are you trying to tell me? It is in that spirit that student writing must be read, corrected, and if need be rewritten. When first presented, it must already be a second or third draft. The only reason I can think of for the somewhat higher average of good writing in France is that the *brouillon* is a national institution. The *brouillon* (literally: scrambled mess) is the first draft, and even the concierge writing to the police about anarchists on the third floor begins with a *brouillon*, later found by his heirs.

Of course it is no use telling an American boy or girl that the essay must be written, laid aside, and rewritten at least once before handing in: the innocents do not know what to do after their first painful delivery. So the simplest thing is to ask early in the term for a good five-page essay, which turns out to be pretty bad. This is fully annotated by the reader and turned back before the next one is called for. But the corrections on it are not merely the conventional *sp., ref., punc.,* and *awk.* which the writers have seen in their margins from the seventh grade on. The comments are intensely and painfully personal, being the responses that an alert reader would feel if he were encountering the essay in print. The result is that even the best students feel abashed, if not actually resentful. To which one can only say that they should resent the neglect in which all their previous teachers have left them.

This neglect has not damaged their grammar so much as their vocabulary. Since the last thing any writer learns is the uses of words, it is no wonder if untutored youths of ability write like the stockbroker whom I quoted about "favorable fundamentals that exist"—spineless, vague, and incoherent prose. Indeed, the exact parallel comes this moment under my hand, taken from a very able student's report on Newman's *University Sketches:* "A University that rests on a firm financial foundation has the greater ability to unleash the minds of its students." Despite the difference in names, the stockbroker is that boy's putative father. Their failure comes from a like inattention to meaning—their own and that of the words they use.

This means that words and tone are the main things to be taught. Spelling, grammar, and punctuation do not precede but follow in the order of importance. They follow also quite naturally in the order of facility. Accordingly, the teacher-critic must slowly and carefully explain to the student what each word conveys in its particular context. I find that in the essay just cited I have written such comments as: "I can't follow—This repeats in disguise—'avocational fruit' suggests alligator pears: why?—We now have about eight 'problems' on hand: Begin!—What! more issues and problems?—Commercial lingo—Who is 'we'?—Why 'cradle': the metaphor is lost—Who says this?—'Patina' is not 'clothing'—Don't scold and then trail off in this way—This is your point at last." In addition, images are changed, synonyms proposed, and bad sentences recast, sometimes in alternative ways, in order to show precisely how the original misleads and how clarity is to be reached.

Tone grows naturally out of diction, but the choice of words betrays feelings of which the young writer is usually unaware. "Are you pleading, denouncing, coaxing, or laughing? Do you back up this exaggeration? Why suddenly talk down, or turn pedant? If you want to change the mood inside the piece, you must modulate, otherwise your reader will stumble and you will lose him." The student who learns to quiz himself in this fashion over his first draft is learning not only something about English, about writing, and about thinking, but about the human heart as well.

At the risk of tediousness I repeat that what has to be done is to dramatize the relation between writer and reader. The blunt comments are just a device to break the spell of routine, and though they administer an unpleasant shock at first, they are also flattering. "Somebody cares about what I want to say." The teacher is no longer a paid detective hunting stray commas.

To point these lessons up in minute detail to a student of average powers is of course time-consuming—but what else is the teacher there for? Time spent on reading and writing, in any subject, is never a waste, and the reward almost always comes, often astonishingly great. The excitement aroused by the discovery that words live is like finding that you can balance on skates. A new world of motion and of feeling is opened out to the student, a source of some anguish balanced by lifelong delight. George Gissing writes somewhere that he saw an excursion steamer advertised as being "Replete with Ladies' Lavatories" and he comments on how many people could pass by the sign without a smile. My own favorite recollection is of a guarantee pasted on a modest shop window: "Hats fitted to the head exclusively"—fun in every ad and at the company's expense.

The pleasure to be taken in words is as innocent and satisfying as the moral effect is clear: unless words are used deftly to set the imagination on its travels, language, literature, conversation, and friendship are full of snares. Much of our modern anxiety about the tyranny of words and of our desire for foolproof Basic comes from the uneasy suspicion that we have lost the art of diction and with it the control over our own minds. This is more serious than it seems, for there is no doubt that the world outside the school largely checks what present instruction attempts, as we shall see. But having spoken of the imagination, let me first meet a likely objection to the advice here proposed. I can fancy some reader for whom school compositions were torture shaking a skeptical head and saying: "Most young children have very little to say and school assignments blot out even that little." I agree and the second great practical problem is, What to ask boys and girls to write about?

The don'ts are easy. Don't ask them for "A vacation experience," or "My most embarrassing moment," or "I am the Mississippi River." Such topics will only elicit the driest kind of hokum, though to be fair I must say that they are an improvement on the older practice of expecting infant moralizing and "What the flag means to me." Although as a child I enjoyed writing—history chiefly—I can remember the blankness of mind that overtook me when we had to do a *dissertation morale*. I still have a school text with some of those themes checked as having been done—for example: "*The Faithful Dog.*—A poor man has resolved to drown his dog. Thrown into the river, the dog tries to scramble up the bank, but his master lunges out to kill him with a stick. In so doing, he slips and falls. The dog saves him. Remorse of the owner."

I regret to say that French school life is stuffed with such thorns as these, but I am not sure that the opposite "progressive" extreme of turning children into researchers on their own is desirable either. The eleven-year-old son of a friend of mine once told me that he was writing a "project" on Papyrus. Why papyrus? Well, the class had been "doing" Egypt and each child was assigned one aspect of Egyptian civilization. Where was the information to come from? From encyclopedias, museums, friends, and paper manufacturers—hence such letters to strangers as the one about "Africia" quoted earlier. As I see it, two things are wrong with this scheme. One is that it gives a false freedom; the other is that it hardly trains in the art of composing. Did this boy care at all about

Egypt, let alone about the technicalities of papyrology? A child should select a topic that truly engages his interest. To eliminate pretense he must be helped to do this by means of questions and suggestions. At any age, it is very reassuring to be told that you don't really want to write about the Tariff. After two or three casts a real subject emerges, satisfactory to both parties.

Next should come into play the single good feature of the French dissertation, namely its furnishing a plan or program. Depending on the child's age a briefer or longer table of contents should be set out for each theme, either in logically organized form, or pell-mell for the student himself to disentangle. After all, what is wanted is prose, not a riot of fancy. In my experience, even examination questions are answered better when they consist of five or six sentences outlining a topic for discussion. This means further that brevity should never be accounted a fault in itself. After thirty, we can all spin tall tales, mostly secondhand,[1] but students, even of college age, have had very little conscious experience of life or books and it is no wonder their minds are bone dry. One should moreover keep in view the possibility that in some of them brevity may come from genius. American schoolmarms who relate the anecdote of Lincoln's "failure" with the Gettysburg Address are just as likely to say at one glance, "Jane, this is too short." How do they know? Perhaps they unwittingly agree with the Gettysburg crowd that Everett's speech, being longer, was better.

Some secondary schools, particularly the private ones, require the writing of verse as well as of prose. If the students are really shown how to go about versifying and are not expected to be "poetic," there is no harm in it. Verse writing is excellent practice for the prose writer and the striving for correct rhythm and rhyme gives the student of literature a feeling for words that may not otherwise be obtained. What can be done in this way before college by a gifted teacher has been shown by the experience of my friend, the poet Dudley Fitts, formerly at Choate and now at Andover. In collegiate circles, it is now well known that a freshman prepared under him is a literate, sometimes a polished writer, who can be safely allowed to skip into advanced work. No doubt Fitts has had his failures like all of us, but it is the successes we are looking for and that count in leavening the mass.

I am not so foolish as to think that carrying out my few suggestions would get rid of illiterate A.B.'s. I am too conscious of my initial point about "Education," which is that the school does not work in a vacuum but rather in a vortex of destructive forces. As regards writing, we in the twentieth century must offset not only the constant influence of careless speech and the indifference of parents, but the tremendous output of jargon issuing from the new mechanical means at man's disposal. Worst of all, circumstances have conspired to put the most corrupting force at the very heart of the school system. It is not newspapers, radio scripts,

---

[1] No course, therefore, should ever be called Creative Writing. Let us have at least a collective modesty and leave to charlatans the advertising of "How to Write Powerful Plays."

and movies that spoil our tongue so much as textbooks, official documents, commencement speeches, and learned works.[2]

The rise, at the turn of the century, of what James called "the softer pedagogy" is responsible for a debasement of language beyond all bounds of forgiveness. The desire to be kind, to sound new, to foster useful attitudes, to appear "scientific," and chiefly also the need to produce rapidly, account for this hitherto unheard-of deliquescence. In the victims, the softness goes to the very roots of the mind and turns it into mush. And among the "new" educators thus afflicted, the Progressive vanguard has naturally outstripped the rest. I shall not multiply examples from catalogues, reports, and speeches, though over the years I have gathered a blush-making collection. I want only to identify the evil because it spreads like the plague.

It consists mainly of what our forefathers called "cant phrases," strung together without continuity, like wash on a line. At a faculty meeting, a teacher asks the Director of Admissions why there seem to be more music students applying than before. The Director replies, "Well, I should say that the forces undergirding the process are societal." Or a committee chairman wants to know what we do next. "I think," says the secretary, "that we should go on to institute actual implementation."

Teachers steeped in this medium are bound to ooze it out themselves, particularly if weekly and daily they receive official instructions like these: "Specify the kinds of change or permanence the student seems to crave, reject, or fear; the reasons given for liking-disliking, giving up-persistence; complaining-boasting. . . . It cannot be too strongly emphasized that the observations of characteristics associated with age and background are not being made in the general area of adolescent behavior but under specific and limited conditions—those set by the aims, emphases, and assumptions of one particular faculty.[3] Moreover, the observations of what appear to be the interests of freshmen conceal a possible ambiguity. The term 'interests' may refer to fairly superficial interests in the sense of surprise, pleasure, enjoyment, which are comparatively temporary; or 'interests' may involve an awakening curiosity which leads to consistent inquiry along the lines of some project." The reader must imagine not merely a paragraph taken at random, but pages and pages of similar woolly abstractions, mimeographed at the rate of nine and one-half pounds per person per semester. If the words "specific" and "objective" were blotted out of the English language, Progressive Education would have to shut up . . . shop.

As for students in teachers' colleges, the long climb up the ladder of learning comes to mean the mastering of this ghoulish *Desperanto,* so

---

[2] See Mr. Maury Maverick's excellent denunciation of what he calls Gobbledygook in the *New York Times* for May 21, 1944. The rebuttals attempting to show that roundabout expressions spare shocks to the sick are hardly to the point. The healthy ought to be able to stand directness and even mention of "death and taxes." "Loss of life" and "fiscal levies" cost just as much in the end.

[3] I regret to say that "faculty" here means "faculty member"—a usage so far confined to the progressive schools.

that with the attainment of the M.A. degree, we get the following utterance: —

> In the proposed study I wish to describe and evaluate representative programs in these fields as a means of documenting what seems to me a trend of increasing concern with the role of higher education in the improvement of interpersonal and intergroup relations and of calling attention in this way to outstanding contributions in practice.

Some readers might think this quotation very learned and highbrow indeed. But in fact it says nothing definite. It only embodies the disinclination to think. This is a general truth, and nothing is more symptomatic of the whole jargon than the fantastic use and abuse it makes of the phrase "in terms of." The fact is worth a moment's attention. "In terms of" used to refer to things that had terms, like algebra. "Put the problem in terms of *a* and *b*." This makes sense. But in educational circles today "in terms of" means any connection between any two things. "We should grade students in terms of their effort"—that is, *for* or *according to* their effort. The *New York Public Library Bulletin* prints: "The first few months of employment would be easier . . . and more efficient in terms of service . . ."—that is, would yield more efficient service. But no one seems to care how or when or why his own two ideas are related. The gap in thought is plugged with "in terms of." I have been asked, "Will you have dinner with me, not tonight or tomorrow, but *in terms of* next week?" A modern Caesar would write: "All Gaul is to be considered in terms of three parts." [4]

From this Educator's patois, easily the worst English now spoken, we ought to pass to the idiom of textbooks, since they are written either by educators or by teachers. Happily, there is a standard set by other books—trade books—and it is not true that all textbooks are as badly written as those on education. On the contrary, it is very encouraging that the leading ones in every field are usually well planned *and* well written. The success of Morison and Commager's *Growth of the American Republic* is only the most recent case in point. Students, nevertheless, are asked to read many ill-written books. There is no excuse for this, though it is by no means the only source of error. We must remember that students do not read only books; they read what every man reads, and this would do no harm—it does no harm—when the mind is trained to resilience by the kind of writing practice I have advocated.

Unfortunately, with the vast increase in public schooling since 1870, an entirely new notion of what is good English has come to prevail. Awakened by free schooling, the people have shown worthy intentions. They want to be right and even elegant, and so become at once suspicious of plainness and pedantic. They purchase all sorts of handbooks that make a fetish of spelling, of avoiding split infinitives, of saying "it is I" (with the common result of "between you and I")—in short,

---

[4] The objectionable phrase is now to be found in newspapers, business reports, and private correspondence. It is a menace *in terms of* the whole nation.

dwell on trivialities or vulgarisms which do not affect style or thought in the slightest. But with this intolerance towards crude and plain error goes a remarkable insensitivity to inflated nonsense. Most bad journalism is only highbrow verbosity, yet the popular mind continues to believe that the pedantry which it likes is simple and the simplicity which it finds hard is complex. Here is the opening of a serial thriller in a Boston paper: —

Strange things happen in Chinatown. But even that exotic and perverse district seldom presented drama as fantastic as the secret that hid among the silk and jade and porcelain splendors of the famous House of the Mandarin on Mulberry Lane.

There is a certain art in this, and I take note of "porcelain splendors" as the *mot juste* for bathtubs on exhibit. But the passage as a whole contains nothing but arty and highfalutin words, joined by the good will of the reader rather than the mind of the writer. Still, every newspaper reader feels he understands it. Take now a well-known sentence composed of common words, all but two of them single syllables: "If there are more trees in the world than there are leaves on any one tree, then there must be at least two trees with the same number of leaves." Read this aloud and almost any listener will respond with "Huh? Say that again." For this sentence records a thought, and the Chinatown "drama" did not.

The close logic in the truly "simple" sentence makes the contrast sharper, but it would be just as sharp between a feeling clearly put and a feeble attempt to thrill. Thus there is a superstition that the novels of Henry James are written in a "difficult style." Yet if you examine them, you will find that the words and sentences—in *The Ambassadors*, for example—are in themselves quite usual. But the feelings they convey are unusual and subtle, and require attention. At the same time they also compel it, which is all that an artist takes pains for in writing.

Conversely, the only thing that can be asked of a writer is that he should know his own meaning and present it as forcibly as he can. The rule has not changed since Byron affirmed that "easy writing makes damned hard reading." Hence there is great value, as I think, in having college graduates recognize good prose when they see it, know that a tolerable paragraph must have gone through six or seven versions, and be ready to follow athletically on the trail of articulate thoughts, rather than look for the soapy incline to muddled meaning.

One does not have to go very far for the enjoyment of precise, sinewy writing. The same newspaper that furnishes tripe for the morning meal also brings such rarer tidbits as these: "They [the robot bombs] are of much the same shape and size as a small fighter plane, with stubby wings. They come over with tails aglow from the propelling rocket force, like little meteors moving at a nightmare pace by dark, and by day like little black planes with tails afire." This is perfection; and here is poetry: "Mr. McCaffrey, himself the father of two children, *and therefore schooled in apprehension,* ran across the street . . . shouting a warning."

When the daily reporter, harried by falling bombs or hustled by a city editor, can write like this, it is depressing to return to agencies closer to the school and find verbal laziness encouraged and imbecility taken for granted. One publisher of reference works sends out a circular stressing the fact that his books give the pronunciation of "all difficult— 'hard-to-say'—words." Is this where we are after fifty years of quasi-universal literacy? Is the word "difficult" so difficult that it has to be translated in its own sentence? The question is one for readers, and it is to the subject of reading that I now turn. . . .

18
AGE OF CONTROVERSY

"I am that gadfly which God has attached to the state, and all day long and in all places am always fastening upon you, arousing and persuading and reproaching you . . ."

—Plato
Socrates' *Apology*

RACIAL PREJUDICE

William Shakespeare
THE MERCHANT OF VENICE

Salarino. Why, I am sure, if he forfeit, thou wilt not take his flesh: what's that good for?

Shylock. To bait fish withal: if it will feed nothing else, it will feed my revenge. He hath disgraced me, and hinder'd me half a million; [1] laugh'd at my losses, mock'd at my gains, scorned my nation, thwarted my bargains, cooled my friends, heated mine enemies; and what's his reason? I am a Jew. Hath not a Jew eyes? hath not a Jew hands, organs, dimensions, senses, affections, passions? fed with the same food, hurt with the same weapons, subject to the same diseases, healed by the same means, warmed and cooled by the same Winter and Summer, as a Christian is? If you prick us, do we not bleed? if you tickle us, do we not laugh? if you poison us, do we not die? and if you wrong us, shall we not revenge? if we are like you in the rest, we will resemble you in that. If a Jew wrong a Christian, what is his humility? revenge: if a Christian wrong a Jew, what should his sufferance be by Christian example? why, revenge. The villainy you teach me, I will execute; and it shall go hard, but I will better the instruction.[2]

Barrows Dunham
MAN AGAINST MYTH

"Yes, they get in everywhere," said my next neighbor, lifting a forkful of meat to his mouth. We had arrived at the main course and the main topic of conversation, for in higher circles food and talk run parallel— or perhaps it would be truer to say that in higher parallels food and talk run in circles.

The dinner had begun with soup and with lively concern over the safety of Iran. The roast having appeared, a lady across the table, who bore some resemblance to the animal we were eating, began to comment upon the rarity of such meals and the sad emptiness of kitchens.

All footnotes in this selection are by the editor of this text.

[1] *I.e.,* half a million ducats. The famous ducat of Venice was struck about 1280; its value has varied from $2.32 to about 83¢.

[2] I shall commit the wrong which you have taught me, and do my best to surpass those who have taught me.

"They all want jobs in industry nowadays," she said reproachfully. "They don't know their place any more."

"Who?" I asked. But she looked at me pityingly and fell into talk with her hostess. It was then that my next neighbor leaned over, as one having wisdom to communicate.

"Yes, they get in everywhere," he said. "Why, only yesterday I had lunch at *Maxim's*. There was a whole tableful of them there."

"Who?" I asked.

"Why, Jews, of course. They get in everywhere."

"Is there any reason why they shouldn't get in?"

His mouth fell open so far that I could see a piece of the roast nestling against his lower teeth. Then he closed his mouth, and for the rest of dinner gave it over entirely to mastication. . . .

In January, 1946, the Senate of the United States prepared to debate the Fair Employment Practices Bill. A motion was offered to bring the bill before the Senate, and upon this motion there developed a filibuster. Now, filibustering is, of course, a parliamentary device for preventing the passage of a bill which, if put to a vote, would be carried. A minority in opposition can prevent the enactment of legislation, provided the members of the minority are willing to undergo the physical rigors of talking indefinitely. As a matter of fact, the talking is never interminable, for after a time senators show a willingness to let the measure drop and to proceed with other business.

The filibuster on the FEPC Bill was led by Senator Bilbo of Mississippi. In the course of it, he revealed a good many of the political principles actuating his conduct. Among the most interesting was this:

> Mr. Johnston of South Carolina. *I should like to ask the Senator from Mississippi a question. Does he not believe that if 60 or even 75 per cent of the laws which have been passed by the House and the Senate had been killed the nation would have been better off?*
> Mr. Bilbo. *I always thought there was more virtue in killing legislation than in passing it.*[1]

More relevant to our purpose, however, were the Senator's social views and the Senate's response to them. We shall meet some of them again, later on. Just now I want to present, exactly as it appears in the *Congressional Record*, the first paragraph of a letter which Mr. Bilbo announced he had sent to a certain Dr. James A. Dombrowski:

> *Dear Dombrowski:* [Laughter]
> I *have just received through a friend of mine in Jackson, Mississippi, two sheets that your un-American, Negro social equality, communistic, mongrel outfit is sending out throughout the country in your mad desire to build up a factual case against the right and*

---

[1] *Congressional Record*, Vol. 92, No. 14, p. 648.

prerogative of a United States Senator or Senators to filibuster any objectionable legislation that is proposed in this great body.[2]

The content of the paragraph is not so startling, in view of its source. What is startling is the introduction:

Dear Dombrowski: [Laughter]

In other words, at the mention of the name "Dombrowski" there was laughter in the Senate of the United States. . . .

Near Maidenek, in Poland, the Nazis erected a vast community of destruction.[3] Scores of buildings stood within a circumference of barbed wire, but of them all two have especial interest. In one of these was found the store of clothes accumulated from the victims—a pathetic heap, which contained everything from men's suits to babies' shoes.

The other building had three rooms. In the first of these the prisoners were made to remove their clothing; in the second they were passed under a series of shower baths; and in the third they were packed so tightly that no one could possibly fall. Three pipes led into this room from the outside, and there was a fourth aperture through which a guard might watch the happenings within.

When the room had been filled with perhaps two hundred persons, there suddenly came a shower of crystals through the pipes. On contact with the air, these crystals generated deadly gases. Then the guard, through his aperture, had the duty, pleasant doubtless to him, of deciding at what moment all two hundred persons might be considered dead.

For a time the corpses were buried, layer upon layer, in enormous trenches; but, as the tide of battle began to move westward, the Nazis sought to remove all traces of their crimes. For this purpose they built a crematory, a series of five ovens, each just large enough to hold a human body. The bodies were shoveled in on ladles of precisely the right shape and size. At first the cremations proceeded slowly, because the ovens were not hot enough. But then Nazi "science" worked the oven heat up to 1500 degrees Centigrade, and the furnaces began to consume as many as 2000 bodies a day. In this manner no less than 1,500,000 people perished at Maidenek.

One evening, when the furnaces were in full blast, a group of newly arrived prisoners came by. It was an error, for prisoners were not supposed to know of these events. By chance also the Nazi commandant was present at that moment. A woman among the prisoners, seeing thus suddenly the fate which awaited them all, shrieked aloud. The com-

---

[2] *Congressional Record*, Vol. 92, No. 13, p. 591.

[3] Sources for the information in this passage are AP and UP dispatches of September 1, 1944, and two bulletins of the Soviet Embassy in Washington (August 27 and September 1). The account in the two bulletins was written by the Russian dramatist, Konstantin Simonov.

mandant ordered her to be silent, but hysteria had overcome her. Then, at a further command, two guards seized her and threw her alive into one of the furnaces. There was a flash of light as the hair caught fire, a last horrible cry. Then silence, silence, the silence of fascist death. . . .

These episodes form a pattern, not of past history exactly, but of events as they may yet occur. There is a straight, direct line running from my friend at the dinner table . . . and the senatorial laughter, to the death factory at Maidenek. It is the path which Germany trod during the last twenty years. Other nations can tread it, too.

As journeys do not begin at their destinations, so not even the most wishful racist can build a death camp right away. He has to travel toward his goal, and he hopes, in the traveling, to take you with him. For, indeed, if you do not go with him, he will not get there at all.

Accordingly, he plays upon every sneer and whisper, upon idle talk and careless conversation, upon the newspaper practice of identifying Negroes while never identifying anybody else, upon the haunts of "restricted clientele," upon the quota systems of schools and colleges, upon the secret clauses in club and fraternity charters, upon the thousand spurious inequalities which feed his general campaign. He plays upon human vanity, upon the wish of abused and frustrated men to feel superior at least to something. And as if these things were not enough, our society implants the racial myths in children before they have any chance to be frustrated at all.

Thus the racists have set us a great and terrible problem. There is no other problem so large, except that of the entire reconstruction of society. We shall have to meet racism with every valid weapon: with the suffrage, to remove racists from public life; with legislation, to illegalize such practices; and with education, to protect all people against the corrupting myth. It is a matter of simple personal safety. For it always turns out that social inequality, from segregation to mass murder, consumes and devours everyone who is not willing to live and die a slave. . . .

What is it that racism asserts? It asserts that there exist groups of human beings, identifiable by certain physical traits, who, by reason of their birth, constitute some sort of menace to the rest of mankind, and whom mankind is therefore justified in ostracizing, punishing, or, indeed, destroying. In order to establish this contention, the racists would have to demonstrate the following propositions:

(1) That certain groups of men are so unlike in nature to the rest of mankind that their behavior differs radically also.

(2) That these traits of behavior are hereditary, so that no member of these groups can avoid having them or can succeed in ridding himself of them.

(3) That some at least of these traits are "bad" and that the "bad" traits are dominant.

(4) That other groups whose members possess "good" traits are

thereby entitled to domination over the groups whose members possess "bad" traits.

A little reflection will show that these are the propositions which the racist must hold. His wish to segregate minorities and to contrive various discriminations against them must be validated by some principle, and he therefore appeals to the moral superiority of his own group as against others. If he were to be granted this proposition, it might nevertheless be argued that the higher group ought to educate the lower group up to its level. But the racist does not want to educate; he wants to oppress. He therefore holds that the behavior traits of the lower group are ineradicable, because they are hereditary. Now, if they are hereditary, they must be bound up with the essential nature of that group; and that essential nature must be profoundly unlike the nature of other groups. This difference can be esteemed so highly that the members of "inferior" groups will appear to have the likeness, but not the reality, of men. A believing Nazi was fully persuaded that his victims were scarcely distinguishable from animals. The rest of the world came to have a comparable opinion of Nazis.

Such are the four postulates on which the racist view is erected. And, although they are men of turgid passion and dreary mind, the racists evince a dim awareness that this is what they mean. What they neither know nor want to know is that all four postulates, together with the conclusion, are false.

THE CRITIQUE OF RACISM

We have, thus, four statements whose truth is assumed, and a fifth statement which forms the basis of action. The relation between the four and the one is that of premises to conclusion. Ordinarily, if any premise in an argument is proved false, the conclusion becomes, not false, but merely doubtful. It might, that is to say, be true for other reasons. But in the argument before us there can be no other reasons. For, in discovering by analysis what the racist postulates are, we chose only the ones whose truth must be assumed if the conclusion is to be true. We were saying, "If E is to be considered true, then A and B and C and D must already be true." And from this we can infer that if A *or* B *or* C *or* D is false, then E is false. In other words, we need only show the falsity of *one* of these postulates in order to show the falsity of the conclusion. As a matter of fact, all four of the postulates are false. We have an embarrassment of riches.

I propose, then, that we take these postulates one by one in the order in which they are given, and subject them to analysis. The advantage of this procedure lies in the fact that it will fully reveal the inner absurdity of the racist view. For it does not suffice, I think, merely to assemble a quantity of facts on the opposing side. The argument becomes much more cogent when we show that racism is not only contrary to fact, but is by any rational criterion nonsense. Well, then, let us take the first postulate:

(1) That certain groups of men are so unlike in nature to the rest of mankind that their behavior differs radically also.

When any two groups differ radically from each other, they do so in respect of their appearance, their actions, and their relationships to the rest of the world. In such a circumstance the members of each class resemble one another far more than they resemble the members of other classes. Lions, for example, are unguiculates (clawed animals), and horses are ungulates (hoofed animals). Their appearance, their modes of life, and their relationships with the rest of the world differ accordingly. They cannot mate with each other; they cannot even associate, since the lion will regard the horse as a palatable meal, and the horse will regard the lion as a peril to be escaped. Evidently we have here two basically different animal types. If it could be shown (as it decidedly cannot) that racial differences are like those between the lion and the horse, racism could pretend to some scientific foundation.

Now suppose another example. If you were to compare a tiger with a leopard, you would immediately observe that the one has his stripes and the other his spots. You would notice, however, that the tiger and the leopard have very considerable resemblances. Both of them are unguiculates and both are felines. Moreover, they are the kind of felines that can roar, when others can only purr. If you weigh the importance of these various qualities, you will find that although the tiger's stripes and the leopard's spots provide a vivid means of distinguishing the two species, these qualities have rather less to do with their behavior. Their nature and their modes of life derive from the fact that they are feline. If it can be shown that racial differences are like those between the tiger and the leopard, then racism will be found to have no scientific basis at all.

In the opinion of the senatorial anthropologist, Mr. Bilbo, racial differences are like those of the horse and the lion:

> I said that segregation was a law of nature. Segregation is perfectly natural in nature. It is natural in the animal world. We do not see horses out in the meadow land lining up with the cows. No; the cows go by themselves this way, and the horses by themselves the other way. Hogs and sheep keep apart. Hogs go by themselves and sheep by themselves. That general law also applies to the human race. People of the Mongolian races associate together. They intermarry and want to live together and do business together. The same is true of the Indians. The Negro race is the only one I know of which is ashamed of its race and which tries to obtain for itself social equality with the white race. Most of its leaders preach that segregation and mongrelization and intermarriage between the whites and blacks is the only solution for the race question in this country.[5]

---

[5] *Congressional Record*, Vol. 92, No. 14, p. 649. The contradictory juxtaposition of "segregation," "mongrelization," and "intermarriage" is in the original text.

Senator O'Daniel agrees, except on the question of how Negroes feel about their own group:

> *Texas is a wonderful state. I make that statement so that any-thing I say against FEPC will not be construed as an infringement of the rights of the colored race. In the South we like the colored folk and they like us. Each of us keeps his place. I do not know what we would do without them or they without us. We get along well, but we do not live together. We do not marry each other. The colored people in Texas are proud of their race. They are just as proud of their race as the white people are proud of their race.*[6]

Senator Johnston passes through science into theology:

> *I notice, when I go to New York, that the colored people have congregated in Harlem. That is due to an inborn instinct. It will be found that the members of races congregate together; they want to be together. They do not want other races to interfere with them. That is nothing but human nature. It has always been true in the past. By this bill (FEPC) there is an attempt to change something that God made. We did not make it. God made my face white and made some other face yellow and some other face black. I did not do it. Congress cannot change that state of affairs.*[7]

Now, the qualities which scientists take as the basis of racial dif-ferences are primarily physical, and consist of height, head shape, color of skin, of eyes, and of hair, and the texture and quantity of hair. According to racism, which also makes some use of this basis, the most improved human being is perhaps six feet tall, long-headed, blond, and wavy-haired. Departures from this norm will, in their varying degrees, meet different intensities of disapproval.

Such are the assumed differences. From them the racists expect to be able to infer certain traits of behavior. They believe, for example, that a person who is curly of hair and negroid of skin will also be lazy; that a person whose hair is black, whose color is swarthy, and whose nose is aquiline will be usurious in his business dealings. They are full of examples, real and fancied, which are to be cited *ad infinitum* in substantiation of their beliefs. They employ, also, other examples, fewer and less spectacular, which are to be cited as "exceptions," so as to produce a gratifying display of fair-mindedness. But, scientifically, the effort is vain. No rule is proved by the first set of examples, and there-fore no rule exists to which the second set can be exceptions.

What connection can there possibly be between the way people "look" and the way they behave? What could one possibly predict about behavior, basing oneself on the mere evidence of skin color, hair tex-

---

[6] *Congressional Record,* Vol. 92, No. 14, p. 670.

[7] *Congressional Record,* Vol. 92, No. 13, p. 579.

ture, and height? It is quite obvious that one could predict nothing. If men who are tall and blond—"Nordics," as they used to be called; "Aryans," as they are called now—are by that fact virtuous and intelligent, then virtue in our day has become singularly easy. If men who are short and black are therefore vicious, then vice is for them unavoidable. They can incur no blame, as their self-styled betters can incur no praise.

Finding it difficult to establish a relation between skin color and character, some racists have put their faith in the shape and size of the head. A large skull will house a large brain, and a large brain, it might seem, would give one more to think with. But, alas for such hopes! The largest brain thus far found is that of an imbecile, whilst several men of great intelligence have had rather small brains. The size of the human brain and the shape of the human head have nothing whatever to do with intelligence.

Thus it is quite impossible to join the physical attributes which distinguish races with any behavior which could be called good or bad. Still more perplexing, however, is the fact that no groups can be found which exclusively possess even the designated physical attributes. Height varies *within* groups: The Shilluk Negroes, who live at the sources of the Nile, are six feet two, whereas the neighboring brown pigmies are only four feet eight. Tall and short people are found together all over the world.[8] Head shape varies *within* groups: both long heads and round heads will be found among the American Indians, for example, or the peoples of Asia Minor—even, indeed, among close relatives.

As for skin color, the facts are perhaps most remarkable of all. Speaking geographically, you can say that the darkest skins will be found in West Africa, the lightest in Northwest Europe, and the yellowest in Southeast Asia. But it turns out that these are extremes rather than norms, for most skins in the world are of intermediate shades. In all probability these intermediate shades represent the common original, and the extremes represent a later development. Any racial classification rigorously based on skin color would therefore have its evolutionary data exactly reversed.

It is now known, moreover, that skin color is determined by two chemicals, one of which (carotene) produces the yellow tint, and the other (melanin) the brown. It is known, also, that every one of us has these chemicals in his skin, though in varying proportions. These variations, together with the color provided by the blood vessels underneath the skin, will account for every difference observable.

I think it is very striking how the unity of mankind is proclaimed in the very attributes which are thought to divide us. We may be black or white or yellow, but we have all got melanin and carotene. We are brothers in the skin, as well as under it. And, without laboring too much

---

[8] These facts, and others in the present passage, are taken from *The Races of Mankind*, by Ruth Benedict and Gene Weltfish, Public Affairs Pamphlets, No. 85. This is the pamphlet which the House Military Affairs Committee refused to permit to be distributed throughout the Army in April, 1944. "This stone which the builders rejected. . . ."

the platitudes of old Kipling, now safely laid away with the lore of empire, we may add that East (which, as we know, is East) and West (which is West) now meet daily and forever upon the surface of the human body. . . .

In view of the vast community of human characteristics, it is wholly incredible that racial differences are in any way fundamental. If they were so, we should have to suppose that nature went to the trouble of producing the same anatomy, the same physiology, the same psychology over and over again in slightly different ways, starting anew after each effort. Obviously no such thing occurred. Obviously the various human groups have a common origin. Obviously the differences are not primordial, but are of rather recent development in evolutionary time. And as if this were not enough, nature has so mingled the various "stocks" by intermarriage over some fifty millennia that not a single representative of any imaginable pure race can possibly be found.

We therefore dismiss the first of the racists' assertions: that certain groups of men are so unlike in nature to the rest of mankind that their behavior differs radically also. In the largest sense, the nature and behavior of men are similar. And if, as racists sometimes say, it is proper for each to stick to his kind, it will follow that the supreme duty of men is to stick to one another. Logic vindicates, not fascism, but democracy. I suppose this is why fascists prefer to think with their blood.

THE MYTHOLOGY OF BLOOD

We take next the second of the racist postulates:

> (2) That these traits of behavior are hereditary, so that no member of these groups can avoid having them or can succeed in ridding himself of them.

Of all the mysticisms which have plagued mankind for innumerable years, the mysticism of blood is perhaps the most fanatical. Now, blood is a genial fluid, without which none of us can survive. It is therefore precious. Blood lies close to our physical existence and is therefore intimate. It runs beneath the skin and is therefore hidden. Something precious, something intimate, something hidden—this is all that any mysticism can require.

Blood, moreover, has had a long career as poetic metaphor, during which it has been made to symbolize both life and the sacrifice of life, both redemption and damnation, both the incidence of things new and the survival of things old. An image which thus suggests so many contraries will admirably suit the needs of men who desire it to mean anything they please. By concealing the difference between metaphor and fact, they can pass the concept off as a description of the real world. And they can find believers.

In feudal society, where nobles had the problem of keeping their estates in the family, it was useful to suppose that property could move from father to son along with "the blood." With colorful garments of this sort, apologists of the system were able to clothe the bare economic fact that each aristocratic family was the center of a large property holding. Under capitalism, where wealth derives from control of factory systems and from access to large markets, the concept (or image) of blood has necessarily been extended to include whole peoples. This extension was achieved in the nineteenth century by a union of the concepts "blood" and "nation." The Comte de Gobineau, more flatteringly known as a writer of detective stories, erected his theory of social superiority upon national divisions. It remained for the twentieth century to disclose the ingenuities of combining "blood" with "race."

The concept of racial blood ties has served two chief purposes: it has provided nations with an excuse for foreign conquest, and it has enabled them to divide their own populations at home. Since, for example, German nationals and their descendants are scattered all over the world, it has been very useful for Nazis to be able to say that Germany exists wherever there is German "blood." Each time the territory of the Reich expanded, the Germans thus newly brought back into the Fatherland could be said to have been "rescued" from the oppression of an alien and inferior people. The *Wehrmacht* undoubtedly hoped to move on until all persons of German stock had been thus rescued. From these saviors the world has had to save itself.

At the same time, the Nazis consolidated their rule at home by creating a spurious division within their own people. Availing themselves of a prejudice already widely and fanatically held, they caused the Jews to be deemed responsible for the evils they had themselves intensified or ordained. The brutalization of a whole people followed by swift, yet subtle, stages, until those of them who were not actual murderers were willing at least to adorn themselves with the clothes of the victims.

If a study of the social uses of blood-myths does not suffice to display their falsity, a few scientific facts ought to be conclusive. For one thing, blood is divisible into types, but these types bear no relation whatever to racial groupings. They will be found, in fact, among the members of every conceivable race. Men of democratic mind should derive some pleasure from knowing that they share the blood types of Australian bushmen and American aborigines. And to set a seal upon the unity of mankind, one may observe that the part of the blood most needed for transfusion is the plasma, which is altogether the same in everybody.

In the second place, blood is not the bearer of hereditary traits, which are in fact carried by biological units called "genes." The evidence of genetics appears, like all the other evidence, to point toward mankind as a community rather than a hierarchy of races. Since men presumably have a common origin, and since human groupings have intermarried throughout history, the possession of any particular gene for any particular physical characteristic will now be found in various peoples all over the world. If, therefore, you were to mark off a "race" on the basis of certain qualities, you would find that individuals who might be included because they have one of the qualities would have to be excluded for lacking the others.

In the third place, racism attempts to pass off, as hereditary, behavior traits which are not hereditary at all. Deaf-mutism and hemophilia are determined by genes, but there is no evidence to indicate that political and social behavior is so determined. If, for instance, we were to suppose the existence of a gene for profit-making in the capitalist sense, we should have to suppose that the feudal lords and the ancient slaveowners were motivated by yet other genes, which have ceased to be dominant. We should have to say that the genes for capitalist behavior were either recessive in feudal times or came into existence by mutation. Thus a frank historical account of social change would give way to an obscure and mythical application of genetics.

Within the extremely broad limits of an inherited anatomy and physiology, human behavior is determined by environmental influences. The greatest of these is society itself. Capitalists exist not because of any special hereditary equipment, but because of a particular social mode of producing and distributing goods. The same social mode determines the existence and the nature of industrial workers. There is no genetic reason why either group is what it is, or why any supposed racial group should be attached to one or the other. Even the reigning folklore admits this fact, when it advertises the possibility of ascent from the one class to the other.

Thus there is only a social, and never a biological, reason why Negroes are "last to be hired, first to be fired," why they have access mainly to menial jobs. There is only a social, and never a biological, reason why Jews are to be found chiefly in a few particular trades and professions. And the social reasons reflect little credit upon the rulers of society, for the Negroes owe their plight to their having been kept as a huge reservoir of the cheapest possible labor, and the Jews owe theirs to the desire of "Aryan" businessmen for the elimination of astute competitors.

Well, if the Nazis provided us with the myth that human behavior is predetermined by a "racial soul," it must be confessed that they also provided us with the completest refutation of that doctrine. For, when they came to the problem of consolidating their regime and of organizing the German people for conquests abroad, they trusted not at all to any sublime Teutonic personality nor to any primeval forest whispers. On the contrary, they seized the press, the radio, the schools, the universities, the various cultural media, and bent them to their purposes. They utilized, that is to say, every conceivable means of *conditioning* their people into the desired modes of behavior.

Whatever fascist theory may say, fascist practice clearly admits that social behavior is the result of conditioning. If it is so, then we may reasonably expect that conditioning will change it. Accordingly, if we find in some people behavior traits which we deem to be undesirable, our duty will lie not in segregating or exterminating the people, but in removing the environmental causes. If research should reveal an occasional lazy Negro, our duty would not lie in increasing his poverty and therefore his laziness. We have only to give him adequate food, and the laziness will disappear.

ARE THERE "BAD" RACES?

Let us take the last two postulates together, for both of them have to do with ethics:

(3) That some at least of these traits are "bad" and that the "bad" traits are dominant.

(4) That other groups whose members possess "good" traits are thereby entitled to domination over the groups whose members possess "bad" traits.

These blanket moralizings are extremely unpersuasive, for they conceal what we most need to know—the behavior of individual people. They show every sign of a wish to condemn in advance or to justify in advance, before actual behavior has been studied at all. Moreover, if it is impossible to generalize very accurately upon the physical characteristics of races, there is not likely to be any greater success in generalizing upon moral characteristics. We shall have trouble enough deciding what "good" means and what "bad" means, without applying the term to whole groups of people and disposing of their destinies in accordance with the application. We shall have trouble enough determining the content of moral principles, without imposing upon multitudes all the torments which bigotry can devise. It is not so much a common sinfulness as a lack of understanding which impedes the execution of moral judgments. It is one's *eye* that the beam is in, when one objects to the mote in another's.

But I think the question can be settled more simply and without recourse to metaphysical refinements. Suppose we compare the behavior of allegedly inferior races with that of the allegedly superior races. The results are as plain as they are devastating. It was not a Negro or a Jew who sat next me at that dinner. It was not a Negro or a Jew who franked the slanderous postcard, or invented the insidious slogan. It was not Negroes or Jews who built the death camp at Maidenek. No, all these people were (God save the mark) "Aryan." In the whole of history, no Negroes or Jews, no members indeed of any "inferior" races, have inflicted upon mankind sufferings which remotely compare with those inflicted by the self-styled "superior" races.

The moral balance is thus precisely the reverse of what racists affirm it to be. If to possess every conceivable vice is to be virtuous, then racists are virtuous. If to contrive every manner of injustice is to be just, then racists are just. If to bathe in abominable impurities is to be pure, then racists are pure. But to these "Aryans" and all their insufferable kin more rightfully belongs the famous judgment of Jonathan Swift: they are "the most pernicious race of little odious vermin, that Nature ever suffered to crawl upon the surface of the earth."

If groups of men are to submit to moral judgment, the savagery of recent years makes it very plain where the proper attributions lie.

But let us entertain one final supposition, the wildest of all. Let us suppose that these "Aryans," with all their equipment of whips, gas chambers, and portable gallows, with all their sneers, exclusions, and segregations, are nevertheless morally superior to other groups. Would this superiority entitle them to dominate the others, governing and oppressing at pleasure? How could so monstrous a thing be true? Oppression is a forcible and often violent exploitation by a small group of men. Superiority in power will achieve and sustain it; but no superiority, physical or moral, can justify it. A democratic ethics must abhor it and seek its universal destruction.

Thus, even if a racist could show (as he cannot) that human groups differ profoundly, even if he could show (as he cannot) that such differences are transmitted as hereditary traits of behavior, and even if he could show (as he cannot) that the traits of some groups are good and of others bad, he still could not show that the group with the good traits is justified in dominating the others. On his four statements he has a perfect score, which is zero. One shudders to think how close such men have come to achieving control over the entire world.

One shudders, but then one resolves to act. And act we must. By patient education and by effective political control we must bring it to pass that the public life of nations will exhibit no more Maideneks, no more Hitlers, no more Quislings, no more congressional racists, and no more anti-Semitic slogans. When this has happened, it may be possible to break one's bread in friendliness, and to eat it without a chattering accompaniment of hate.

There is no reason why we should not succeed. The Master Race produced its greater masters, and it found them in us, the democratic peoples of the world. We have the necessary knowledge; we have the necessary power; we have the necessary union of knowledge and power to effectuate the victory. The myths of race, however fortified with violence and hate, will not in the end prevail against us.

James Gould Cozzens

BY LOVE POSSESSED

"I'd be careful about that jury. I'd study the panel. In selecting jurors, I'd use my challenges with the general idea of keeping off, as far as I could, anyone with a foreign name and anyone I'd learned was a Roman Catholic. The precaution seems to you extreme?"

"Yes," Arthur Winner said. "I can't feel religion needs to be brought in. To suppose, because Jerry's a Catholic, Catholics would try to find for him, seems to me a view of prejudice."

"I merit the reproof, no doubt," Julius Penrose said. "I can't say instinct is silenced; but I, perhaps, ought to be! Perhaps I should not glance at Mr. Brophy's religion. First; prejudice is in itself held censurable; an evil thing. So I'm anti-Catholic, am I? Still, in passing, I'll confess I wonder, as one of them, why the only people who may be openly criticized, found fault with, and spoken ill of, are those of white, Protestant, and more or less Nordic extraction. I, it seems, am game and fair game for everybody—a kind of *caput lupinum*.[1] Nobody writes the papers threateningly when I'm decried or disparaged. I don't say this is unreasonable. I myself have no wish to abridge any man's right not to like me if he so chooses. Only, in my bewildered way, I keep thinking there ought to be a turnabout. There isn't! Not only may each bumptious Catholic freely rate and abuse me if I reflect in the least on his faith; but each self-pitying Jew, each sulking Negro, need only holler that he's caught me not loving him as much as he loves himself, and a rabble of professional friends of man, social-worker liberals, and practitioners of universal brotherhood—the whole national horde of nuts and queers —will come at a run to hang me by the neck until I learn to love."

---

[1] Literally, "a kind of chief of wolves," or "head of the pack."

TRADITIONAL FALLACIES

Ben Jonson

IT IS NOT GROWING LIKE A TREE

It is not growing like a tree
In bulk, doth make Man better be;
Or standing long an oak, three hundred year,
To fall a log at last, dry, bald, and sere:
     A lily of a day
     Is fairer far in May,
Although it fall and die that night;
It was the plant and flower of Light.
In small proportions we just beauties see;
And in short measures life may perfect be.

Remy de Gourmont

THE DISASSOCIATION OF IDEAS

There are two ways of thinking. One can either accept current ideas and associations of ideas, just as they are, or else undertake, on his own account, new associations or, what is rarer, original disassociations. The intelligence capable of such efforts is, more or less, according to the degree, or according to the abundance and variety of its other gifts, a creative intelligence. It is a question either of inventing new relations between old ideas, old images, or of separating old ideas, old images united by tradition, of considering them one by one, free to work them over and arrange an infinite number of new couples which a fresh operation will disunite once more, and so on till new ties, always fragile and doubtful, are formed.

There are associations of ideas so durable that they seem everlasting, so closely knit that they resemble those stars which the naked eye seeks in vain to separate. They are usually called "commonplaces." This expression, relic of an old rhetorical term, *loci communes sermonis*, has, especially since the development of individualism, assumed a slighting sense which it was far from possessing at the start, and even as late as the seventeenth century. The meaning of "commonplace" has also been narrowed, as well as debased, till it has come to be a variant of *cliché*, or hackneyed expression—that which has already been seen or heard; and, for the mass of men, who employ words without precision, com-

From *Decadence and Other Essays on the Culture of Ideas*, translated by William Aspenwall Bradley. Reprinted by permission of Harcourt Brace Jovanovich, Inc.

monplace is now one of the synonyms of *cliché*. But *cliché* refers to the words, commonplace to the ideas. *Cliché* defines the form or the letter, commonplace the substance or the sense. To confound them is to confound the thought with the expression of the thought. The *cliché* is immediately perceptible. The commonplace very often escapes notice if clothed in an original dress. There are not many examples, in any literature, of new ideas expressed in a new form. The most captious mind must commonly content itself with one or other of these pleasures, only too happy when not deprived of both at once, which is not very rarely the case.

The commonplace is both more and less than a hackneyed expression. It is hackneyed, but sometimes unavoidably so. It is hackneyed, but so universally accepted that it comes consequently to be called a truth. Most truths which travel the world (truths are great travellers) may be regarded as commonplaces, that is to say, associations of ideas common to a large number of men, none of whom would dare deliberately to disassociate them. Man, in spite of his lying tendency, has great respect for what he calls the truth. This is because truth is the staff with which he travels through life, because commonplaces are the bread in his wallet, the wine in his gourd. Deprived of the truth contained in commonplaces, men would be without defence, without support, and without nourishment. They have so great a need of truths that they adopt new ones without rejecting the old. Civilized man's brain is a museum of contradictory truths. This does not disturb him, because he is a "successive." He ruminates his truths one after the other. He thinks as he eats. We should vomit with horror if we had presented to us, in a large dish, the various aliments, from meat to fruit, mixed with soup, wine and coffee, destined to form our "successive" repast. Our horror would be as great were we shown the repellent amalgam of contradictory truths which find lodgment in our mind. Some few analytical intelligences have sought vainly to draw up in cold blood the inventory of their contradictions. To each objection offered by reason, sentiment opposes an immediately valid excuse; for . . . sentiments are what is strongest in us, representing the elements of permanence and continuity. . . .

Man associates ideas, not at all in accordance with verifiable exactitude, but with his pleasure and his interest. That is why most truths are merely prejudices. Those that are least open to question are also those that he has always sought to combat cunningly with the ruse of silence. The same inertia is opposed to the work of disassociation seen operating slowly on certain truths.

The state of disassociation reached by moral commonplaces seems to bear a rather close relation to the degree of intellectual civilization. Here, too, it is a question of a sort of struggle, carried on, not by individuals, but by peoples formed into nations, against palpable facts which, while augmenting the intensity of the individual life, diminish, for that very reason, as experience proves, the intensity of collective life and energy. There is no doubt that a man can derive from immorality itself—from his refusal to subscribe to the prejudices inscribed in a decalogue—a great personal benefit; but a collectivity of individuals too strong, too mutually independent, makes but a mediocre people. We have, in such cases, the spectacle of the social instinct entering the lists against the individual instinct, and of societies professing, as such, a morality that each of its intelligent members, followed by a very large part of the herd, deems vain, outworn or tyrannical.

A rather curious illustration of these principles will be found by examining the present state of sexual morality. This morality, peculiar to Christian peoples, is based upon the exceedingly close association of two ideas—that of carnal pleasure and that of generation. Any man or people that has not disassociated these two ideas, has not mentally liberated the elements of this truth, namely, that outside of the properly generative act, accomplished under the protection of the laws, whether religious or civil—the second being mere parodies of the first, in our essentially Christian civilizations—sexual acts are sins, errors, faults, weaknesses. Whoever consciously adopts this rule, sanctioned by the codes, belongs evidently to a still rudimentary civilization. The highest civilization being that in which the individual is freest, the most exempt from obligations, this proposition would be open to question only if taken as a provocation to libertinism, or as a depreciation of asceticism. It does not matter here whether it be moral or immoral. It ought, if exact, to be seen, at the first glance, in the facts. Nothing is easier. A statistical table of European natality will convince the stubbornest that there is a very close bond—a bond of cause and effect—between a people's intellectuality and its fecundity. The same is true for individuals as for social groups. It is as a result of intellectual weakness that working-men allow their homes to be flooded with offspring. The slums are full of unfortunate individuals who, having begotten a dozen children, are surprised to find life harsh. These poor creatures, who lack even the excuse of religious beliefs, have not yet learned to disassociate the idea of carnal pleasure and that of generation. In their case, the first determines the second, and their acts respond to a childish, almost animal cerebral process. The man who has reached a really human stage in the scale of intelligence, limits his offspring at will. It is one of his privileges, but it is among those that he attains only to die of them.

Fortunate for the individual whom it sets free, this particular disassociation is, in fact, far less fortunate for a people. However, it will favour the further development of civilization, by maintaining upon the earth the spaces required for human evolution.

It was not till fairly late that the Greeks succeeded in separating the idea of woman and that of generation; but they had already disassociated, at a very early date, the idea of generation and that of carnal pleasure. When they ceased to consider woman solely as an instrument of generation, the reign of the courtesans began. The Greeks seem, moreover, always to have had an extremely vague sexual morality, though this did not prevent them from cutting a certain figure in history.

Christianity could not, without forswearing its own principles, encourage the disassociation of the idea of carnal pleasure and that of generation; but it successfully promoted, on the other hand, the disassociation of the idea of love and that of carnal pleasure, and this was

one of the great conquests of humanity. The Egyptians were so far in-
capable of understanding such a disassociation, that the love of a brother
and sister would have seemed nothing to them if it had not led to sexual
intercourse. The lower classes of great cities are often enough quite
Egyptian in this regard. The different sorts of incest which occasionally
come to our notice, testify to the fact that an analogous state of mind
is not absolutely incompatible with a certain intellectual culture. The
peculiarly Christian form of chaste love, freed from all idea of physical
pleasure, is divine love, such as it is seen flowering in the mystical
exaltation of the contemplatives. This is the really pure love, since it
corresponds to nothing that can be defined. It is the intelligence adoring
itself in its own infinite self-made image. Whatever sensual element may
be involved has its source in the very constitution of the human body,
and in the law governing the interdependence of the organs. No account should, therefore, be taken of it in a non-physiological study.
What has been clumsily called Platonic love is thus a Christian creation.
It is in the last analysis a passionate friendship, as vital and jealous as
physical love, but freed from the idea of carnal pleasure, just as the
latter had already been freed from the idea of generation. This ideal
state of the human affections is the first stage on the road to asceticism,
and asceticism might be defined as the state of mind in which all ideas
are disassociated.

With the waning of the Christian influence, the first stage of asceticism has become a less and less frequent halting-place, and asceticism
itself, grown equally rare, is often reached by another route. In our day
the idea of love has once more been closely connected with the idea of
physical pleasure, and moralists are busy refashioning its primitive association with the idea of generation. It is a rather curious retrogres-
sion. . . .

What idea, at any given moment, did each class of society form
of the soldier? Would not the answer to this question contain a whole
course in history? Coming down to our own time, it might be asked at
what moment the idea of honour and the military idea became united in
the common mind. Is the union a survival of the aristocratic conception
of the army? Was the association formed as a result of the events of
thirty years ago, when the people decided to exalt the soldier for its own
encouragement? This idea of honour should be clearly understood. It
contains several other ideas—ideas of bravery, of disinterestedness, of
discipline, of sacrifice, of heroism, of probity, of loyalty, of frankness, of
good humour, of openness, of simplicity, etc. The word itself would, in
fine, be found to sum up the qualities of which the French race believes
itself to be the expression. To determine its origin would be, then, to determine automatically the period when the Frenchman began to believe
himself a compendium of all the manly virtues. The military man has
remained in France, in spite of recent objections, the very type of the
man of honour. The two ideas are united very energetically. They form
a truth which is scarcely disputed to-day, except by individuals of slight
authority or of doubtful sincerity. Its disassociation is, therefore, very
little advanced, as regards the nation as a whole. It was, however, for

a moment at least, completely effected in certain minds. This involved, from the strictly intellectual point of view, a considerable effort of abstraction which we cannot but admire when we regard dispassionately the cerebral machine in its functioning. Doubtless the result achieved was not the product of normal reasoning. The disassociation was accomplished in a fit of fever. It was unconscious, and it was momentary; but it *was*, and that is the important point for the observer. The idea of honour, with all it implies, became separated from the military idea, which, in this instance, is the factual idea, the female idea, ready to receive all the modifiers, and it was perceived that, if there was a certain logical relation between them, this relation was not necessary. There is the decisive point. A truth is dead when it has been shown that the relations between the elements are habitual, and not necessary; and, as the death of a truth is a great benefit for mankind, this disassociation would have been very important if it had been definitive, if it had remained stable. Unfortunately, after the effort to attain the pure idea, the old mental habits resumed their sway. The former modifying element was instantly replaced by an element by no means new, less logical than the other, and even less necessary. The operation seemed to have miscarried. Association of ideas occurred again in the very same form as before, though one of the elements had now been turned inside out, like an old glove. For honour had been substituted dishonour, with all the adventitious ideas belonging to the old element transformed into cowardice, deceitfulness, lack of discipline, falseness, duplicity, wickedness, etc. This new association of ideas may have a destructive value, but it offers no intellectual interest.

The moral of this anecdote is that the ideas which seem to us the clearest, the most evident,—the most palpable, as it were—are, even so, not strong enough to impose themselves in all their nakedness upon the average mind. In order to assimilate the idea of the army, a contemporary brain must swathe it with elements which have only a chance or current relation with the main idea. A humble politician cannot, doubtless, be expected to adopt Napoleon's simple idea of an army as a sword. Very simple ideas lie within the reach of very complicated minds only. It seems, however, that it should not be absurd to regard the army merely as the exteriorized force of a nation, and then to demand of this particular force only those very qualities which are demanded of force in general. But perhaps even this is too simple . . . ?

Ideas cannot be classed as true and false. The idea is necessarily true. An idea that can be disputed is an idea mingled with concrete notions, that is to say, a truth. The work of disassociation tends, precisely, to free the truth from all its fragile part, in order to obtain the pure, one, and consequently unassailable idea. But if words were never used save in their unique and absolute sense, connected discourse would be difficult. There must be left a little of that vagueness and flexibility which usage has given them; and, in particular, too much stress must not be laid upon the gap separating the abstract from the concrete. There is an intermediate state between ice and water—that in which the latter begins to congeal, when it still cracks and yields under the pressure of the hand plunged into it. Perhaps we should not even demand that the words contained in philosophic handbooks should abdicate all pretension to ambiguity. . . .

We might here examine this question: do abstract words really exist for the people, for the average man? Probably not. It would even seem as if the same word attained only graduated stages of abstraction, according to the degree of intellectual culture. The pure idea is more or less contaminated by concern for personal, caste or group interests, and the word justice, for example, thus clothes all sorts of particular and limited meanings under the weight of which its supreme sense disappears, overwhelmed. . . .

It is under one of these motleys that the idea of liberty is presented to us by the politicians. Hearing this word, we now perceive little other than the idea of political liberty, and it would seem as if all the liberties which man is capable of enjoying were summed up in this ambiguous expression. Moreover, it is the same with the pure idea of liberty, as with the pure idea of justice; it is of no use to us in the ordinary business of life. Neither man nor nature is free, any more than either is just. Reasoning has no hold upon such ideas. To express them is to assert them, but they would necessarily falsify every argument into which one might wish to introduce them. Reduced to its social significance, the idea of liberty is still incompletely disassociated. There is no general idea of liberty, and it is difficult to form one, since the liberty of an individual is exercised only at the expense of the liberty of others. Formerly liberty was called privilege. Taking everything into account, that is perhaps its true name. Even to-day one of our relative liberties—the liberty of the press—is an ensemble of privileges. Privileges also are the liberty of speech granted to lawyers, the liberty of trade unions, and, to-morrow, the liberty of association as it is now proposed to us. The idea of liberty is perhaps only an emphatic corruption of the idea of privilege. The Latins, who made great use of the word liberty, meant by it the privilege of the Roman citizen. . . .

I am ignorant of their origins, but they are later than the classic languages, which possess no fixed and precise words to express them, though the ancients were as well able as we to enjoy the reality they contain—better, even. They are intertangled. The idea of art is dependent upon the idea of beauty; but this latter idea is itself nothing but the idea of harmony, and the idea of harmony reduces itself to the idea of logic. The beautiful is that which is in its place. Thence arise the sentiments of pleasure given us by beauty. Or rather, beauty is a logic which is perceived as a pleasure. If this be admitted, it will at once be understood why the idea of beauty, in societies dominated by women, is almost always restricted to the idea of feminine beauty. Beauty is a woman. There is in this an interesting subject for analysis, but the question is somewhat complicated. It would be necessary to show, first, that woman is no more beautiful than man; that, situated on the same plane in nature, constructed on the same model, made of the same flesh, she would appear to a sensitive intelligence, exterior to humanity, exactly the female of man—exactly what, for man, a jenny is to a jack.

And, observing them more closely, the Martian, who wished to learn something concerning the aesthetics of terrestrial forms, would even note that, if there be a real difference in beauty between a man and a woman of the same race, of the same caste, and of the same age, this difference is almost always in favour of the man; and that, moreover, if neither the man nor the woman be entirely beautiful, the defects of the human race are more accentuated in the woman, where the twofold projection of the belly and the buttocks—sexual attractions, no doubt—breaks unpleasantly the double line of the silhouette. The curve of the breasts is almost inflected under the influence of the back, which has a hollow tendency. Cranach's nudes confess naïvely these eternal imperfections of woman. Another defect which artists, when they have taste, remedy instinctively, is the shortness of the legs, so marked in the photographs of nude women. This cold anatomy of feminine beauty has often been made. It is, then, useless to insist upon it—all the more because, unfortunately, its verification is only too easy. But if woman's beauty be so vulnerable to criticism, how does it happen that, in spite of all, it remains indisputable—that it has become for us the very basis and leaven of the idea of beauty? It is a sexual illusion. The idea of beauty is not a pure idea. It is intimately connected with the idea of carnal pleasure. Stendhal had an obscure perception of this line of reasoning when he defined beauty as "a promise of happiness." Beauty is a woman, even for women themselves, who have carried docility with regard to men to the point of adopting this aphorism which they are capable of understanding only under the form of extreme sensual perversion. We know, however, that women have a particular type of beauty, which men have naturally branded "doll-like." If women were sincere, they would long ago have stigmatized equally the type of feminine beauty by which man most readily lets himself be seduced.

This identification of woman and beauty goes so far to-day that we have had innocently proposed us the "apotheosis of woman," meaning the glorification of beauty, with all the promises contained in Stendhal's definition taken in its erotic sense. Beauty is a woman and woman is a beauty. The caricaturists accentuate the common sentiment by invariably coupling with a woman, whom they strive to render beautiful, a man whose ugliness they stress to the extreme of vulgarity; and this in spite of the fact that pretty women are so rare in life, that after thirty a woman is almost always inferior, age for age, in plastic beauty, to her husband or lover. It is true that this inferiority is no easier to demonstrate than it is to feel, and that reasoning remains ineffective, once the page is finished, for the reader as well as for the writer; and this is very fortunate.

The idea of beauty has never been disassociated save by aestheticians. The common run of men accept Stendhal's definition, which amounts to saying that this idea does not exist—that it has been absolutely devoured by the idea of happiness—of sexual happiness, happiness given by a woman. That is why the cult of beauty is suspect for moralists who have analyzed the value of certain abstract words. They translate this one by the cult of the flesh, and they would be right, if that last expression did not imply a somewhat silly attack upon one of man's most natural tendencies. The necessary result has been that, in opposing such excessive apotheosis of woman, they have infringed upon the rights of art. Art being the expression of beauty, and it being possible to understand beauty only under the material aspects of the true idea which it contains, art has become almost uniquely feminine. Beauty is woman; and art, also, is woman. But the latter is less absolute. The notion of art is even fairly clear for artists and for the élite. The idea of art has been extremely well liberated. There is a pure art which is concerned exclusively with self-realization. No definition of it even should be given; for such a definition could not be made without connecting the idea of art with ideas which are foreign to it, and which would tend to obscure and sully it. . . .

Certain associations, though very recent, have rapidly acquired a singular authority, like those of education and intelligence, of education and morality. But, at most, education may have something to say for one of the particular forms of memory, or for a literal knowledge of the commonplaces contained in the Decalogue. The absurdity of these forced relations appears very clearly in that which concerns woman. It seems clear that there is a certain sort of education—that which they receive to-day—which, far from stimulating their intelligence, tends rather to blunt it. Since they have been educated seriously, they no longer have the least influence either in politics or in literature. Compare, in this connection, our last thirty years with the last thirty years of the *ancien régime*. These two associations of ideas have, nevertheless, become veritable commonplaces—truths which it is as useless to expose as to combat. They take their place with all those which infest books and the degenerate lobes of man's brain—with old and venerable truths like: virtue-recompense, vice-punishment, God-goodness, crime-remorse, duty-happiness, authority-respect, unhappiness-punishment, future-progress, and thousands of others, some of which, though absurd, are useful to mankind.

It would be equally possible to make a long catalogue of the ideas which men refuse to associate, while delighting in the most disconcerting débauches. We have given above the explanation of this stubborn attitude, namely, that their principal occupation is the pursuit of happiness, and that they are much more concerned with reasoning in accordance with their interests than with the rules of logic.

Thence the universal aversion to connecting the idea of nothingness with the idea of death. Though the former is evidently contained in the latter, humanity insists upon considering them separately. It opposes their union with all its force, never tiring of driving between them a chimerical wedge upon which resound the hammer-blows of hope. This is the finest example of the illogical that we can offer ourselves for our diversion, and the best proof that, in the gravest matters, as in those of slightest concern, it is sentiment which always triumphs over reason.

Is it a great thing to have learned that? Perhaps.

The Venerable Bede

THE CONVERSION OF KING EDWIN

Another of the king's chief men, approving of his words and exhortations, presently added: "The present life of man, O king, seems to me, in comparison to that time which is unknown to us, like to the swift flight of a sparrow through the room wherein you sit at supper in winter, with your commanders and ministers, and a good fire in the midst, whilst the storms of rain and snow prevail abroad; the sparrow, flying in at one door, and immediately out at another, whilst he is within, is safe from the wintry storm; but after a short space of fair weather, he immediately vanishes out of your sight, into the dark winter from which he had emerged. So this life of man appears for a short space, but of what went before, or what is to follow, we are utterly ignorant. If, therefore, this new doctrine contains something more certain, it seems justly to deserve to be followed." The other elders and king's counselors, by Divine inspiration, spoke to the same effect.

Matthew Arnold

DOVER BEACH

The sea is calm to-night.
The tide is full, the moon lies fair
Upon the straits; on the French coast, the light
Gleams and is gone; the cliffs of England stand,
Glimmering and vast, out in the tranquil bay.
Come to the window, sweet is the night-air!
Only, from the long line of spray
Where the sea meets the moon-blanched land,
Listen! you hear the grating roar
Of pebbles which the waves draw back, and fling,
At their return, up the high strand,
Begin and cease, and then again begin,
With tremulous cadence slow, and bring
The eternal note of sadness in.

Sophocles long ago
Heard it on the Aegean, and it brought
Into his mind the turbid ebb and flow
Of human misery: we
Find also in the sound a thought,
Hearing it by this distant northern sea.

The sea of faith
Was once, too, at the full, and round earth's shore
Lay like the folds of a bright girdle furled.

But now I only hear
Its melancholy, long, withdrawing roar,
Retreating, to the breath
Of the night-wind, down the vast edges drear
And naked shingles of the world.

Ah, love, let us be true
To one another, for the world, which seems
To lie before us like a land of dreams,
So various, so beautiful, so new,
Hath really neither joy, nor love, nor light,
Nor certitude, nor peace, nor help for pain;
And we are here as on a darkling plain
Swept with confused alarms of struggle and flight,
Where ignorant armies clash by night.

Albert Camus

THE MYTH OF SISYPHUS

The gods had condemned Sisyphus to ceaselessly rolling a rock to the top of a mountain, whence the stone would fall back of its own weight. They had thought with some reason that there is no more dreadful punishment than futile and hopeless labor.

If one believes Homer, Sisyphus was the wisest and most prudent of mortals. According to another tradition, however, he was disposed to practice the profession of highwayman. I see no contradiction in this. Opinions differ as to the reasons why he became the futile laborer of the underworld. To begin with, he is accused of a certain levity in regard to the gods. He stole their secrets. Ægina, the daughter of Æsopus, was carried off by Jupiter. The father was shocked by that disappearance and complained to Sisyphus. He, who knew of the abduction, offered to tell about it on condition that Æsopus would give water to the citadel of Corinth. To the celestial thunderbolts he preferred the benediction of water. He was punished for this in the underworld. Homer tells us also that Sisyphus had put Death in chains. Pluto could not endure the sight of his deserted, silent empire. He dispatched the god of war, who liberated Death from the hands of her conqueror.

It is said also that Sisyphus, being near to death, rashly wanted to test his wife's love. He ordered her to cast his unburied body into the middle of the public square. Sisyphus woke up in the underworld. And there, annoyed by an obedience so contrary to human love, he obtained from Pluto permission to return to earth in order to chastise his wife.

But when he had seen again the face of this world, enjoyed water and sun, warm stones and the sea, he no longer wanted to go back to the infernal darkness. Recalls, signs of anger, warnings were of no avail. Many years more he lived facing the curve of the gulf, the sparkling sea, and the smiles of earth. A decree of the gods was necessary. Mercury came and seized the impudent man by the collar and, snatching him from his joys, led him forcibly back to the underworld, where his rock was ready for him.

You have already grasped that Sisyphus is the absurd hero. He *is*, as much through his passions as through his torture. His scorn of the gods, his hatred of death, and his passion for life won him that unspeakable penalty in which the whole being is exerted toward accomplishing nothing. This is the price that must be paid for the passions of this earth. Nothing is told us about Sisyphus in the underworld. Myths are made for the imagination to breathe life into them. As for this myth, one sees merely the whole effort of a body straining to raise the huge stone, to roll it and push it up a slope a hundred times over; one sees the face screwed up, the cheek tight against the stone, the shoulder bracing the clay-covered mass, the foot wedging it, the fresh start with arms outstretched, the wholly human security of two earth-clotted hands. At the very end of his long effort measured by skyless space and time without depth, the purpose is achieved. Then Sisyphus watches the stone rush down in a few moments toward that lower world whence he will have to push it up again toward the summit. He goes back down to the plain.

It is during that return, that pause, that Sisyphus interests me. A face that toils so close to stones is already stone itself! I see that man going back down with a heavy yet measured step toward the torment of which he will never know the end. That hour like a breathing-space which returns as surely as his suffering, that is the hour of consciousness. At each of those moments when he leaves the heights and gradually sinks toward the lairs of the gods, he is superior to his fate. He is stronger than his rock.

If this myth is tragic, that is because its hero is conscious. Where would his torture be, indeed, if at every step the hope of succeeding upheld him? The workman of today works every day in his life at the same tasks, and this fate is no less absurd. But it is tragic only at the rare moments when it becomes conscious. Sisyphus, proletarian of the gods, powerless and rebellious, knows the whole extent of his wretched condition: it is what he thinks of during his descent. The lucidity that was to constitute his torture at the same time crowns his victory. There is no fate that cannot be surmounted by scorn.

If the descent is thus sometimes performed in sorrow, it can also take place in joy. This word is not too much. Again I fancy Sisyphus returning toward his rock, and the sorrow was in the beginning. When the images of earth cling too tightly to memory, when the call of happiness becomes too insistent, it happens that melancholy rises in man's heart: this is the rock's victory, this is the rock itself. The boundless grief is too heavy to bear. These are our nights of Gethsemane. But crushing truths perish from being acknowledged. Thus, Œdipus at the outset obeys fate without knowing it. But from the moment he knows, his tragedy begins. Yet at the same moment, blind and desperate, he realizes that the only bond linking him to the world is the cool hand of a girl. Then a tremendous remark rings out: "Despite so many ordeals, my advanced age and the nobility of my soul make me conclude that all is well." Sophocles' Œdipus, like Dostoevsky's Kirilov, thus gives the recipe for the absurd victory. Ancient wisdom confirms modern heroism.

One does not discover the absurd without being tempted to write a manual of happiness. "What! by such narrow ways—?" There is but one world, however. Happiness and the absurd are two sons of the same earth. They are inseparable. It would be a mistake to say that happiness necessarily springs from the absurd discovery. It happens as well that the feeling of the absurd springs from happiness. "I conclude that all is well," says Œdipus, and that remark is sacred. It echoes in the wild and limited universe of man. It teaches that all is not, has not been, exhausted. It drives out of this world a god who had come into it with dissatisfaction and a preference for futile sufferings. It makes of fate a human matter, which must be settled among men.

All Sisyphus' silent joy is contained therein. His fate belongs to him. His rock is his thing. Likewise, the absurd man, when he contemplates his torment, silences all the idols. In the universe suddenly restored to its silence, the myriad wondering little voices of the earth rise up. Unconscious, secret calls, invitations from all the faces, they are the necessary reverse and price of victory. There is no sun without shadow, and it is essential to know the night. The absurd man says yes and his effort will henceforth be unceasing. If there is a personal fate, there is no higher destiny, or at least there is but one which he concludes is inevitable and despicable. For the rest, he knows himself to be the master of his days. At that subtle moment when man glances backward over his life, Sisyphus returning toward his rock, in that slight pivoting he contemplates that series of unrelated actions which becomes his fate, created by him, combined under his memory's eye and soon sealed by his death. Thus, convinced of the wholly human origin of all that is human, a blind man eager to see who knows that the night has no end, he is still on the go. The rock is still rolling.

I leave Sisyphus at the foot of the mountain! One always finds one's burden again. But Sisyphus teaches the higher fidelity that negates the gods and raises rocks. He too concludes that all is well. This universe henceforth without a master seems to him neither sterile nor futile. Each atom of that stone, each mineral flake of that night-filled mountain, in itself forms a world. The struggle itself toward the heights is enough to fill a man's heart. One must imagine Sisyphus happy.

THE SPECIAL CHILD

James Wright

MUTTERINGS OVER THE CRIB OF A DEAF CHILD

"How will he hear the bell at school
Arrange the broken afternoon
And know to run across the cool
Grasses where the starlings cry,
Or understand the day is gone?"

Well, someone lifting cautious brows
Will take the measure of the clock.
And he will see the birchen boughs
Outside sagging dark from the sky, and
The shade crawling upon the rock.

"And how will he know to rise at morning?
His mother has other sons to waken,
She has the stove she must build to burning
Before the coals of the night-time die,
And he never stirs when he is shaken."

I take it the air affects the skin,
And you remember, when you were young,
Sometimes you could feel the dawn begin,
And the fire would call you, by and by,
Out of the bed and bring you along.

"Well, good enough. To serve his needs
All kinds of arrangements can be made.
But what will you do if his finger bleeds?
Or a bobwhite whistles invisibly
And flutes like an angel off in the shade?"

He will learn pain. And, as for the bird,
It is always darkening when that comes out.
I will putter as though I had not heard,
And lift him into my arms and sing
Whether he hears my song or not.

Jesse Stuart

INTRODUCTION TO "CORBIE"

I couldn't find a magazine editor in America who would take *Corbie*. I had to send *Corbie* eight thousand miles away from the United States where he lived, grew to manhood, and died, to the Philippines, where Teodoro Locsin, Editor of *Free Press* accepted this story. The *Free Press* is to the Filipinos what a combination of *The Saturday Evening Post* and *Saturday Review* (if these could be combined) would be to the American people. Mr. Locsin not only accepted this story but he also printed a fine comment about it and he guessed my feelings for the people of whom I write who were part of my Appalachian-Kentucky background; and yet this editor had never experienced my background.

When he read this story he immediately sensed my feeling for a little boy, one of unsound mind, who was my classmate at a one-room school, Plum Grove, in the hills of Kentucky. All Corbie's classmates felt about him as I felt. We loved Corbie. And after leaving school I lost all trace of him, but he is one classmate I never forgot. Many, many years after he and I had gone to school together, I was reading the paper and in the obituaries I came across the account of Corbie's death. I threw the paper across the room. I went to my typewriter and wrote *Corbie*. I did very little revision. The story is almost repertorial of our early days at Plum Grove and the few other brief episodes in our lives when I watched him dancing on the Greenup streets.

Why wasn't *Corbie* an acceptable story in America? The fact is there are many taboos among editors regarding short stories and *Corbie* fell into one of these categories. I was writing of a little boy who had an unsound mind. No matter how well I wrote the story, how great my sympathies for my little friend had been, when I sent the story out it was returned from magazines. And I write for magazines. I love magazines. But the literary mediums in America in which an author can exercise his greatest freedom of thought and exercise it in subject matter that might be questionable for magazines, are the novel and the drama.

After *Corbie* was published in *Free Press*, Manila, Philippines, it was reprinted in *Sunday Magazine* of the *Herald Advertiser,* since this was my three hundredth published short story. . . . It was immediately reprinted in a magazine which specialized in stories and articles for and about the retarded and handicapped children. It was selected as the lead story for my last story collection, *My Land Has a Voice.* Here a collection of twenty stories was selected from more than one hundred magazine published stories . . . . I have received hundreds of letters on it. The story was singled out by reviewers as one of the best stories in *My Land Has a Voice.* . . .

When I wrote *Corbie* I thought that it was a story with some quality and that I should send it to magazine editors whom I knew, editors who had used my stories and who in my estimation worked for our finest quality magazines. I tried *Corbie* on five of these editors. And when the story was returned quickly by these editors, I thought I would try editors on other magazine levels. I tried it on eighteen more editors, thus making twenty-three rejections before I sent it to Teodoro Locsin, Editor of *Free Press*. There are no taboos on stories accepted by *Free Press*. The editorial staff seeks quality in stories and timely well-written articles on their country and the world and in their relations to each other. For each item used more than one hundred are rejected on quality, not because of taboos. This is true with many other publications in many other lands where I have been published, Denmark, West Pakistan, Taiwan and Korea. Each of these countries would have published a story like *Corbie*. . . .

In my lifetime I have tried to write of the whole, of people from all walks of life who make a world and, therefore, a Literature. To me, there are no taboos when a piece is well written and the character and characters are portrayed as they are in life, the story told by a writer-storyteller, put on the written page for the future and, perhaps, the best of the present to last as long as the language in which the story was written. This to me is literature and in real literature there are no taboos. . . .

Now, *Corbie*, has been read around the world, especially among Orientals where there is no taboo regarding little boys such as he. Perhaps we no longer look upon the child with the unsound mind as one to be shunted off and hidden, but as one being a part of the whole of mankind; and now that we are trying to do something to help the Corbies in America, this taboo must be changing. And, maybe, Corbie had something to do with helping change this taboo. I would like to think that he had. In my youth I never knew a nicer young boy than Corbie or one who asked for and expected so little from life as Corbie.

—Jesse Stuart
W-Hollow
Greenup, Kentucky

CORBIE

The first day I went to Plum Grove School, a little one-room school on a hilltop where one teacher taught all the first eight grades, I met Corbie. This was his first day of school, too. He and I were the same age. I went to school barefooted, since our school began in July. All the other boys and girls came barefooted, too. Corbie was the only one in school who came wearing shoes. Corbie's two brothers, Seymour and Kim, and his two sisters, Ellie Marie and Kate, came to school barefooted.

Corbie was the different pupil among us. He was the best-dressed pupil in Plum Grove School, and there were fifty of us. I wondered why he was so much better dressed than his sisters and brothers. And I wondered why somebody didn't call Corbie a "dood." Well, no one did. Just about everybody liked Corbie.

On our first day of school, I walked up to him and looked him over. He looked me over, I smiled at him, standing there in his corduroy suit, his white shirt and black bow tie, his black stockings and well-shined shoes. When I smiled at him he smiled back at me.

"You're all dressed up," I said. "Why do you wear shoes to school? We don't wear shoes here until frost comes in October and the weather gets cold."

"Yes, but you see, I dance," he said. "I can't dance very well bare-footed."

"Let me see you dance," I said. "I'll bet you're just telling me you can dance."

"No, I'm not just telling you this, either," he said. "I can dance and I play my own music when I dance. Have you got a penny?"

"Yes, I've got a penny."

"If you give me a penny, I'll dance. I don't work without pay."

"But dancing isn't work. It's fun."

"It is work for me, but I like to do it. And I don't like to dance unless I get paid. You give me the penny and I'll dance for you."

"Here in the schoolyard?"

"Yes, what's wrong with dancing here? I dance anywhere people want me to dance, if they will pay me a penny."

"I'll give you a penny to dance 'Turkey in the Straw.' "

"Pay me now," he said. "People say they'll give me a penny, and after I dance, I don't get paid. People won't always do what they say they will."

I gave Corbie a penny.

When he opened his little coin purse, I had never seen so many pennies. He didn't have any other kind of coins. Then he reach into his inside coat pocket and pulled out a harmonica.

"Now I got this French harp," he said. "And I got a jews-harp. I can play either one. Which would you rather hear?"

"I got another penny," I said. "Play the French harp when you dance 'Turkey in the Straw.' Now can you play and dance 'Corinna,' 'Stackoles,' or 'Sourwood Mountain'?"

"Yes, all of them," he said. "And I can dance a lot more, too."

Corbie took off his coat and laid it on the grass. The white sleeves of his shirt were held up by armbands. He was really a well-dressed dancer. Now he walked over to a place in the schoolyard where there wasn't any grass. It was a place where the ground had been trampled by many feet until it was too hard for the grass to grow. Here Corbie began to play his harmonica and dance. I don't know how much he weighed, but he seemed to float, and his body was as limp as wilted pods of oak leaves hanging in the July heat. He played "Turkey in the Straw" until I felt like dancing too. And when he played and danced all the Plum Grove pupils, plus our teacher, Mr. Clarke, came running. They formed a circle around Corbie where the dust rose up from his flying feet. It was a yellow dust, and it settled on our clothes and on Corbie's shoes. But Corbie danced on, and he gave us a penny's worth of music and dancing. I thought Corbie was great.

"Now, 'Sourwood Mountain' on the jews-harp," I said, and I gave Corbie another penny.

His breath was coming a little fast after dancing and playing that number. He took his time putting the penny away, he went over to his coat and put away the harmonica in a pocket, then took his jews-harp from another.

"It's harder to play the jews-harp and dance," he said. "I have to use both hands to play it. But I can do it."

When he had played the harmonica, he had to use only one hand to hold the harmonica to his mouth. His other arm was down by his side, and it had moved and swayed to the rhythm of his dance and song.

When Corbie put the jews-harp to his mouth, he held it tightly with one hand and with the index finger of the other hand began to play a tune that went like a buzzing bee. Again the yellow dust came up from the ground as we listened to "Sourwood Mountain." Then he went back to the jews-harp before he finished his dance. And when he finished, all of us clapped our hands. Little Corbie knew we liked to hear him play his music, sing his songs, and dance to the tunes.

We were still clapping our hands and telling him how well we liked to hear him play and watch him dance when he went over to get his coat. The morning sun was very warm now, and Corbie's face was damp with sweat. His damp shirt was sticking to his body. But Corbie put his coat on.

And Mr. Clarke went back in the schoolroom and got his bell. He came to the door and rang the bell. And we formed lines, boys on one side and girls on the other. The girls marched in first, and we followed. I was behind Corbie. Since his name was Corbett Sinnett and mine was Shan Stringer, we sat together. Mr. Clarke arranged the seating that way.

So Corbie and I sat in the back of the schoolroom by the window. He wanted the side next to the window, where he could hear the wind blow and could watch the birds. I let him have the side he wanted. I liked Corbie and he seemed to like me. But everybody liked Corbie. And everybody understood about Corbie. But they didn't understand why he came so well-dressed when his brothers and sisters didn't.

Corbie had brought a new book to school with him. I'd brought one too. We had brought our new primers. Each of us had brought a slate, a tablet, and a pencil. When the school day began, Corbie sat and looked at the picture in his primer. Then he looked out the window. Acorns were falling from the oaks and the bluejays flew down to the ground and picked them up in their short bills. They flew back up to the tops of the old trees and stored these acorns in the hollow branches for winter, when snow would lie on the ground and food would be scarce.

"Funny how birds will work like that," Corbie whispered to me. "But I like to watch how they fan their wings and work their feet when they fly."

I sat beside Corbie my first year at school. All Corbie ever did was watch the bluejays in summer, storing acorns in the hollow branches of the trees. And he looked at the Jim Young farm and the cattle in the pasture. When autumn came, he watched the crows flying over. From the window he watched the leaves come down from the trees. And in the wintertime he watched the snowflakes zigzag down to cover the Plum Grove hills.

Corbie never looked at his primer except, perhaps, once a month. Then he opened his primer and looked at the pictures. I learned my ABC's in a short time until I could say them from memory. I could recite them backwards and forwards and I could print them with chalk on the blackboard.

"Wish I could learn my ABC's like you," Corbie said to me once.

He looked at me and smiled.

"I wish I could dance and play like you, Corbie," I said.

Then I looked at him and smiled.

Before our six-month school term was over, I could read everything in my primer. I was ready for another book. But my seatmate, Corbie, couldn't say his ABC's, and Mr. Clarke never said anything to Corbie. He was very nice to Corbie. Often he looked at Corbie and smiled, and Corbie smiled back. And when Corbie danced, Mr. Clarke would come to the schoolyard and watch him. He didn't mind us giving Corbie a penny to dance.

The school year passed, and Corbie never learned his ABC's. He didn't get promoted from the Chart Class and the Primer. And until school began the next year, I never saw Corbie but once. I was in Blakesburg. Corbie was dancing and playing his harmonica in the street. A man had given him a penny to dance. Everybody liked Corbie. Some man stepped up and said, "How would you like to dance for this?" He held a quarter in his hand.

"It's too much," Corbie said. "I just want a penny."

Everybody laughed when Corbie wouldn't dance for a quarter, but he danced again and again for pennies.

In my second year in school at Plum Grove, I was the first pupil on the schoolground the day school began. Then Corbie came up the hill ahead of his brothers and sisters.

"I want to sit with you, Shan," he said.

"Then we'll sit together, Corbie," I said. "I want to sit with you too."

Corbie couldn't get a prize in spelling or in arithmetic, or in handwriting. Mr. Clarke gave us prizes for these things. But if there had been a prize for the best harmonica player, or the best jews-harp player, Corbie would have got it. And if there had been a prize for the best-dressed pupil in the Plum Grove School, Corbie surely would have taken it. And he might have won a prize for being the best-behaved boy in Plum Grove School, if such a prize had been given. He didn't get into any mischief. He never said a bad word, and when Mr. Clarke told Corbie to do something he always tried to do it. He didn't do anything wrong in school, just looked out the window at the hill slopes in their changing seasons and watched the animals and the birds.

"Another year has passed at Plum Grove," I told my father and mother. "And my seatmate, Corbie Sinnett, hasn't learned his ABC's.

He can't read in his primer. Honest, Mom, I don't believe Corbie can learn. Maybe he doesn't want to learn. I'll be in another grade next year. But I can't dance," I told them, "and I can't play music like Corbie."

My mother and father didn't say anything.

"And he comes to school better dressed than anybody," I said. "He wears shoes in the summertime when everybody else in school is going barefooted."

"Yes, I know," my mother said. "He wears shoes, a suit of clothes, white shirt, and a hat. He even wears armbands to hold up his shirt-sleeves. But Corbie isn't a dood. I think he wears shoes so he can dance. That's what he told me."

My parents didn't say anything when I told them we had to pay him a penny every time he danced.

"Does anybody ever tease Corbie at school?" my mother asked me.

"Oh no, everybody likes Corbie," I said.

In my third year at Plum Grove, when Corbie, who stood up front with the beginners, said all of his ABC's, there was great rejoicing among us at Plum Grove. When Mr. Clarke came to the letter "I" on the old chart that stood up against the wall, I saw him point to his own eye when Corbie was having trouble. Then, very suddenly, Corbie said "Eye." This got the attention of everybody in school. We put our books down. We stopped whatever we were doing. Mr. Clarke didn't say anything to us. He knew we wanted Corbie to go all the way through the alphabet. Mr. Clarke wanted him to go too, or he wouldn't have been helping him. And when he came to the letter "T," Corbie stumbled. Mr. Clarke picked up a cup, and Corbie started to say "coffee," but Mr. Clarke shook his head real quick and Corbie said "T." And when Corbie went all the way through, we all clapped our hands.

So Corbie was promoted to the first grade. Corbie would get to use a new book. He'd worn out two primers. He carried his primer in his pocket, and one just lasted him a year. His third primer was about worn out when he got promoted.

My father and mother didn't know that I was hearing them talk. They were in the little dining room and I'd just come in at the kitchen door. When my father said "Corbie," I stopped to listen.

"Yes, I picked up Felix Sinnett today," he said. "He rode out to the turnpike with me in my express wagon. And we got to talking about the Plum Grove School and he was telling me how well his boy Corbett likes our boy Shan. And he was braggin' on Mr. Clarke, the teacher. You know, Marth," he said to Mom, "this boy Corbie, he just can't get learning, his pappy Felix said. He don't have everything he should in his head. He said they bought the best of everything for Corbie. They wanted to do this while they lived to show their love for this child. I've been thinking about what old Felix said. He is a big coalminer with big fire-shovel hands and shoulders as broad as a corncrib door. How that big Felix can ever crawl back in one of those little joltwagon mines and lay on his side and dig coal from a twenty-four-inch vein, I don't know. But he does it, and he buys Corbie good clothes, fine shoes, harmonicas, and jews-harps."

Not all there in the head, I thought. Now I knew why Mr. Clarke, our teacher, was so nice to him. And I knew why his brothers and sisters never kicked about his going better dressed than they did. And I understood why all the older pupils at Plum Grove in the seventh and eighth grades were so nice to him.

I was ten years old and in the fifth grade when Corbie raised his price for dancing. Corbie was ten years old too. "Too many people ask me to dance," Corbie said. "A penny is not enough. I've got to raise my price to a nickel." And when he raised his price, fewer people asked him to dance. But he made more money dancing for a nickel than he did for a penny, and he didn't dance as much.

I was thirteen years old when I finished the eighth grade at Plum Grove. And I was still sitting with Corbie. But Corbie hadn't finished the first grade. He liked our old seat by the window, where he could look out at the landscape when it changed from summer to autumn and from autumn to winter. He liked to sit there where he could watch the birds and the animals and he could watch the autumn-colored leaves zigzag down from the trees after the first frost.

The next year I went to Blakesburg High School. I don't know how far Corbie got in school. Maybe he got to the second grade. I don't know. But I do know that if grades had been given for dancing, playing the harmonica and jews-harp and for going well-dressed, Corbie would have made the highest grades in school.

In my four years in Blakesburg High School during noon hours I often walked through the town with some of my classmates. Once we heard a fiddle in the courthouse square. And we heard the tapping of shoes on a concrete sidewalk. The dancer was keeping time to the music. And when we got there I saw Corbie. He didn't see me, for there was a crowd gathered around. Some man was playing a fiddle, and Corbie was dancing to its music.

"Here, I like the way you dance," a man said. "I want to give you this."

The man had a dollar bill.

"No, no," Corbie said. "That's too much. I used to dance for a penny. Then I danced for a nickel. Maybe sometime I'll charge more. Not now."

Then the man put the dollar in his pocket and gave Corbie a dime. The fiddler wasn't ready. But Corbie reached into his inside coat pocket. He pulled out his harmonica and began to play "Turkey in the Straw." And as he played, his feet tapped out the tune on the concrete. His hamonica playing was better than the fiddle. And everybody applauded Corbie.

This was the last time I ever saw Corbie. When I returned from college Felix Sinnett and his family had moved away from the Plum Grove hills.

And later I read a piece about him in the paper, where it said he had been preceded in death by a brother, a sister, his father and his mother. I threw the paper. For I wondered how Corbie had fared after his father Felix got too old to work in the mine and the family had moved to Auckland.

AFFIRMATION OF LIFE

William Faulkner
SARTORIS

The gin had been running steadily for a month, now, what with the Sartoris cotton and that of other planters further up the valley, and of smaller croppers with their tilted fields among the hills. The Sartoris place was farmed on shares. Most of the tenants had picked their cotton, and gathered the late corn; and of late afternoons, with Indian summer on the land and an ancient sadness sharp as wood-smoke on the windless air, Bayard and Narcissa would drive out where, beside a spring on the edge of the woods, the negroes brought their cane and made their communal winter sorghum molasses. One of the negroes, a sort of patriarch among the tenants, owned the mill and the mule that furnished the motive power. He did the grinding and superintended the cooking of the sap for a tithe, and when Bayard and Narcissa arrived the mule would be plodding in its monotonous and patient circle, its feet rustling in the dried cane-pith, while one of the patriarch's grandsons fed the cane into the crusher.

Round and round the mule went, setting its narrow, deerlike feet delicately down in the hissing cane-pith, its neck bobbing limber as a section of rubber hose in the collar, with its trace-galled flanks and flopping, lifeless ears and its half-closed eyes drowsing venomously behind pale lids, apparently asleep with the monotony of its own motion. Some Homer of the cotton fields should sing the saga of the mule and of his place in the South. He it was, more than any other one creature or thing, who, steadfast to the land when all else faltered before the hopeless juggernaut of circumstance, impervious to conditions that broke men's hearts because of his venomous and patient preoccupation with the immediate present, won the prone South from beneath the iron heel of Reconstruction and taught it pride again through humility, and courage through adversity overcome; who accomplished the well-nigh impossible despite hopeless odds, by sheer and vindictive patience. Father and mother he does not resemble, sons and daughters he will never have; vindictive and patient (it is a known fact that he will labor ten years willingly and patiently for you, for the privilege of kicking you once); solitary but without pride, self-sufficient but without vanity; his voice is his own derision. Outcast and pariah, he has neither friend, wife, mistress, nor sweetheart; celibate, he is unscarred, possesses neither pillar nor desert cave, he is not assaulted by temptations nor flagellated by dreams nor assuaged by vision; faith, hope and charity are not his. Misanthropic, he labors six days without reward for one creature whom he hates, bound with chains to another whom he despises, and spends the seventh day kicking or being kicked by his fellows. Misunderstood even by that creature, the nigger who drives him, whose impulses and mental processes most closely resemble his, he performs alien actions in alien surroundings; he finds bread not only for a race, but for an entire form of behavior; meek, his inheritance is cooked away from him along with his soul in a glue factory. Ugly, untiring and perverse, he can be moved neither by reason, flattery, nor promise of reward; he performs his humble monotonous duties without complaint, and his meed is blows. Alive, he is haled through the world, an object of general derision; unwept, unhonored and unsung, he bleaches his awkward accusing bones among rusting cans and broken crockery and worn-out automobile tires on lonely hillsides while his flesh soars unawares against the blue in the craws of buzzards.

As they approached, the groaning and creaking of the mill would be the first intimation, unless the wind happened to blow toward them; then it would be the sharp, subtly exciting odor of fermentation and of boiling molasses. Bayard liked the smell of it and they would drive up and stop for a time while the boy rolled his eyes covertly at them as he fed cane into the mill, while they watched the patient mule and the old man stooped over the simmering pot. Sometimes Bayard got out and went over and talked to him, leaving Narcissa in the car, lapped in the ripe odors of the failing year and all its rich, vague sadness, her gaze brooding on Bayard and the old negro—the one lean and tall and fatally young and the other stooped with time, and her spirit went out in serene and steady waves, surrounding him unawares.

Then he would return and get in beside her and she would touch his rough clothing, but so lightly that he was not conscious of it, and they would drive back along the faint, uneven road, beside the flaunting woods, and soon, above turning locusts and oaks, the white house simple and huge and steadfast, and the orange disk of the harvest moon getting above the ultimate hills, ripe as cheese.

Sometimes they went back after dark. The mill was still then, its long arm motionless across the firelit scene. The mule was munching in stable, or stamping and nuzzling its empty manger, or asleep standing, boding not of tomorrow; and against the firelight many shadows moved. . . .

Edgar Lee Masters

LUCINDA MATLOCK

I went to the dances at Chandlerville,
And played snap-out at Winchester.
One time we changed partners,

Driving home in the moonlight of middle June,
And then I found Davis.
We were married and lived together for seventy years,
Enjoying, working, raising the twelve children,
Eight of whom we lost
Ere I had reached the age of sixty.
I spun, I wove, I kept the house, I nursed the sick,
I made the garden, and for holiday
Rambled over the fields where sang the larks,
And by Spoon River gathering many a shell,
And many a flower and medicinal weed—
Shouting to the wooded hills, singing to the green valleys.
At ninety-six I had lived enough, that is all,
And passed to a sweet repose.
What is this I hear of sorrow and weariness,
Anger, discontent and drooping hopes?
Degenerate sons and daughters,
Life is too strong for you—
It takes life to love Life.

Henry David Thoreau

WALDEN

I went to the woods because I wished to live deliberately, to front only the essential facts of life, and see if I could not learn what it had to teach, and not, when I came to die, discover that I had not lived. I did not wish to live what was not life, living is so dear; nor did I wish to practise resignation, unless it was quite necessary. I wanted to live deep and suck out all the marrow of life, to live so sturdily and Spartan-like as to put to rout all that was not life, to cut a broad swath and shave close, to drive life into a corner, and reduce it to its lowest terms, and, if it proved to be mean, why then to get the whole and genuine meanness of it, and publish its meanness to the world; or if it were sublime, to know it by experience, and be able to give a true account of it in my next excursion. For most men, it appears to me, are in a strange uncertainty about it, whether it is of the devil or of God, and have *somewhat hastily* concluded that it is the chief end of man here to "glorify God and enjoy him forever."

Still we live meanly, like ants; though the fable tells us that we were long ago changed into men; like pygmies[1] we fight with cranes; it is error upon error, and clout upon clout, and our best virtue has for its occasion a superfluous and evitable wretchedness. Our life is frittered

All footnotes in this selection are by the editor of this text.

[1] In Homer's *Iliad*, the "pygmies" were small people, who were attacked by cranes.

away by detail. An honest man has hardly need to count more than his ten fingers, or in extreme cases he may add his ten toes, and lump the rest. Simplicity, simplicity, simplicity! I say, let your affairs be as two or three, and not a hundred or a thousand; instead of a million count half a dozen, and keep your accounts on your thumb-nail. In the midst of this chopping sea of civilized life, such are the clouds and storms and quicksands and thousand-and-one items to be allowed for, that a man has to live, if he would not founder and go to the bottom and not make his port at all, by dead reckoning,[2] and he must be a great calculator indeed who succeeds. Simplify, simplify. Instead of three meals a day, if it be necessary eat but one; instead of a hundred dishes, five; and reduce other things in proportion. Our life is like a German Confederacy,[3] made up of petty states, with its boundary forever fluctuating, so that even a German cannot tell you how it is bounded at any moment. The nation itself, with all its so-called internal improvements, which, by the way are all external and superficial, is just such an unwieldy and over-grown establishment, cluttered with furniture and tripped up by its own traps, ruined by luxury and heedless expense, by want of calculation and a worthy aim, as the million households in the land; and the only cure for it, as for them, is in a rigid economy, a stern and more than Spartan simplicity of life and elevation of purpose. It lives too fast. Men think that it is essential that the *Nation* have commerce, and export ice, and talk through a telegraph, and ride thirty miles an hour, without a doubt, whether *they* do or not; but whether we should live like baboons or like men, is a little uncertain. If we do not get out sleepers,[4] and forge rails, and devote days and nights to the work, but go to tinkering upon our *lives* to improve *them*, who will build railroads? And if railroads are not built, how shall we get to heaven in season? But if we stay at home and mind our business, who will want railroads? We do not ride on the railroad; it rides upon us. Did you ever think what those sleepers are that underlie the railroad? Each one is a man, an Irishman, or a Yankee man. The rails are laid on them, and they are covered with sand, and the cars run smoothly over them. They are sound sleepers, I assure you. And every few years a new lot is laid down and run over; so that, if some have the pleasure of riding on a rail, others have the misfortune to be ridden upon. And when they run over a man that is walking in his sleep, a supernumerary sleeper in the wrong position, and wake him up, they suddenly stop the cars, and make a hue and cry about it, as if this were an exception. I am glad to know that it takes a gang of men for every five miles to keep the sleepers down and level in their beds as it is, for this is a sign that they may sometime get up again.

[2] Calculation of a ship's direction or location by use of simple devices, such as a compass, the speed and distance of the vessel, as opposed to more sophisticated astronomical observations and instruments. "Dead reckoning" may be used in emergencies, such as fog.

[3] A loosely organized league or alliance; in Germany ca. 1815.

[4] Ties of a railroad, across which tracks are laid.

Why should we live with such hurry and waste of life? We are determined to be starved before we are hungry. Men say that a stitch in time saves nine, and so they take a thousand stitches to-day to save nine to-morrow. As for *work*, we haven't any of any consequence. We have the Saint Vitus' dance, and cannot possibly keep our heads still. If I should only give a few pulls at the parish bell-rope, as for a fire, that is, without setting the bell,[5] there is hardly a man on his farm in the outskirts of Concord, notwithstanding that press of engagements which was his excuse so many times this morning, nor a boy, nor a woman, I might almost say, but would forsake all and follow that sound, not mainly to save property from the flames, but, if we will confess the truth, much more to see it burn, since burn it must, and we, be it known, did not set it on fire,—or to see it put out, and have a hand in it, if that is done as handsomely; yes, even if it were the parish church itself. Hardly a man takes a half-hour's nap after dinner, but when he wakes he holds up his head and asks, "What's the news?" as if the rest of mankind had stood his sentinels. Some give directions to be waked every half-hour, doubtless for no other purpose; and then, to pay for it, they tell what they have dreamed. After a night's sleep the news is as indispensable as the breakfast. "Pray tell me anything new that has happend to a man anywhere on this globe,"—and he reads it over his coffee and rolls, that a man has had his eyes gouged out this morning on the Wachito River;[6] never dreaming the while that he lives in the dark unfathomed mammoth cave of this world,[7] and has but the rudiment of an eye himself.

For my part, I could easily do without the post-office. I think that there are very few important communications made through it. To speak critically, I never received more than one or two letters in my life—I wrote this some years ago—that were worth the postage. The penny-post is, commonly, an institution through which you seriously offer a man that penny for his thoughts which is so often safely offered in jest. And I am sure that I never read any memorable news in a newspaper. If we read of one man robbed, or murdered, or killed by accident, or one house burned, or one vessel wrecked, or one steamboat blown up, or one cow run over on the Western Railroad, or one mad dog killed, or one lot of grasshoppers in the winter,—we never need read of another. One is enough. If you are acquainted with the principle, what do you care for a myriad instances and applications? To a philosopher all *news*, as it is called, is gossip, and they who edit and read it are old women over their tea. Yet not a few are greedy after this gossip. There was such a rush, as I hear, the other day at one of the offices to learn the foreign news by the last arrival, that several large squares of plate glass belonging to the

---

[5] *I.e.*, without making it "rotate" instead of swing back and forth.

[6] "Wachito River": a river in Arkansas, sometimes spelled "Ouachita"; "gouging" also refers to a rough form of fighting on the frontier, sometimes resulting in mayhem.

[7] "Mammoth Cave" may be an allusion to the enormous caverns in Mammoth Cave National Park in southwestern Kentucky, which contains over 78 square miles, including underground rivers.

establishment were broken by the pressure,—news which I seriously think a ready wit might write a twelvemonth, or twelve years, beforehand with sufficient accuracy. . . .

Shams and delusions are esteemed for soundest truths, while reality is fabulous. If men would steadily observe realities only, and not allow themselves to be deluded, life, to compare it with such things as we know, would be like a fairy tale and the Arabian Nights' Entertainments. If we respected only what is inevitable and has a right to be, music and poetry would resound along the streets. When we are unhurried and wise, we perceive that only great and worthy things have any permanent and absolute existence, that petty fears and petty pleasures are but the shadow of the reality. This is always exhilarating and sublime. By closing the eyes and slumbering, and consenting to be deceived by shows, men establish and confirm their daily life of routine and habit everywhere, which still is built on purely illusory foundations. Children, who play life, discern its true law and relations more clearly than men, who fail to live it worthily, but who think that they are wiser by experience, that is, by failure. I have read in a Hindoo book, that "there was a king's son, who, being expelled in infancy from his native city, was brought up by a forester, and, growing up to maturity in that state, imagined himself to belong to the barbarous race with which he lived. One of his father's ministers having discovered him, revealed to him what he was, and the misconception of his character was removed, and he knew himself to be a prince. So soul," continues the Hindoo philosopher, "from the circumstances in which it is placed, mistakes its own character, until the truth is revealed to it by some holy teacher, and then it knows itself to be Brahme." [8] I perceive that we inhabitants of New England live this mean life that we do because our vision does not penetrate the surface of things. We think that that *is* which *appears* to be. If a man should walk through this town and see only the reality, where, think you, would the "Mill-dam" go to? [9] If he should give us an account of the realities he beheld there, we should not recognize the place in his description. Look at a meeting-house, or a court-house, or a jail, or a shop, or a dwelling-house, and say what that thing really is before a true gaze, and they would all go to pieces in your account of them. Men esteem truth remote, in the outskirts of the system, behind the farthest star, before Adam and after the last man. In eternity there is indeed something true and sublime. But all these times and places and occasions are now and here. God himself culminates in the present moment, and will never be more

---

[8] In Hindu religion, the reference is to God; to the "Transcendentalist" of Thoreau's time, the reference implied the fluid concept of a living Oversoul, which, they believed, existed coterminously with the great Creative Energy (or God) and the individual (man). Thus, Thoreau's profound respect for the individual takes on metaphysical dimensions; *i.e.*, each man had a "Divine spark" within him.

[9] *I.e.*, a common place in every village; like Plato, to some extent, the Transcendentalist thought that reality transcended the power of the five senses to comprehend. To them, reality lay behind objects subject to verification by the five senses. Intuition was a higher knowledge (see Immanuel Kant's *Critique of Pure Reason*, and his concept of a *priori* knowledge, that is "knowledge in man from the beginning," hence "intuitive" knowledge).

divine in the lapse of all the ages. And we are enabled to apprehend at all what is sublime and noble only by the perpetual instilling and drenching of the reality that surrounds us. The universe constantly and obediently answers to our conceptions; whether we travel fast or slow, the track is laid for us. Let us spend our lives in conceiving then. The poet or the artist never yet had so fair and noble a design but some of his posterity at least could accomplish it.

Let us spend one day as deliberately as Nature, and not be thrown off the track by every nutshell and mosquito's wing that falls on the rails. Let us rise early and fast, or break fast, gently and without perturbation; let company come and let company go, let the bells ring and the children cry,—determined to make a day of it. Why should we knock under and go with the stream? Let us not be upset and overwhelmed in that terrible rapid and whirlpool called a dinner, situated in the meridian shallows. Weather this danger and you are safe, for the rest of the way is down hill. With unrelaxed nerves, with morning vigor, sail by it, looking another way, tied to the mast like Ulysses.[10] If the engine whistles, let it whistle till it is hoarse for its pains. If the bell rings, why should we run? We will consider what kind of music they are like. Let us settle ourselves, and work and wedge our feet downward through the mud and slush of opinion, and prejudice, and tradition, and delusion, and appearance, that alluvion which covers the globe, through Paris and London, through New York and Boston and Concord, through Church and State, through poetry and philosophy and religion, till we come to a hard bottom and rocks in place, which we can call *reality*. . . .

If you stand right fronting and face to face to a fact, you will see the sun glimmer on both its surfaces, as if it were a scimitar, and feel its sweet edge dividing you through the heart and marrow, and so you will happily conclude your mortal career. Be it life or death, we crave only reality. If we are really dying, let us hear the rattle in our throats and feel cold in the extremities; if we are alive, let us go about our business. . . .

Why should we be in such desperate haste to succeed and in such desperate enterprises? If a man does not keep pace with his companions, perhaps it is because he hears a different drummer. Let him step to the music which he hears, however measured or far away. It is not important that he should mature as soon as an apple tree or an oak. Shall he turn his spring into summer? If the condition of things which we were made for is not yet, what were any reality which we can substitute? We will not be shipwrecked on a vain reality. Shall we with pains erect a heaven of blue glass over ourselves, though when it is done we shall be sure to gaze still at the true ethereal heaven far above, as if the former were not . . . ?

---

[10] In the *Odyssey*, Ulysses (Latin for the Greek Odysseus) required his men to bind him to the mast to avoid the spell of the Sirens, the songs of whom caused sailors to be lured to their destruction. The sirens were nymphs, and here the rocky coast refers to Scylla; Charybdis was a whirlpool off the coast of Sicily opposite Scylla; thus, Scylla and Charybdis refer to a choice of two extreme dangers.

Henry James

THE AMBASSADORS

He sank again upon his bench and, while his eyes followed the party, reflected, as he had done before, on Chad's strange communities. He sat there alone for five minutes, with plenty to think of; above all with his sense of having suddenly been dropped by a charming woman overlaid now by other impressions and in fact quite cleared and indifferent. He had not yet had so quiet a surrender; he didn't in the least care if nobody spoke to him more. He might have been, by his attitude, in for something of a march so broad that the want of ceremony with which he had just been used could fall into its place as but a minor incident of the procession. Besides, there would be incidents enough, as he felt when this term of contemplation was closed by the reappearance of little Bilham, who stood before him a moment with a suggestive "Well?" in which he saw himself reflected as disorganized, as possibly floored. He replied with a "Well!" intended to show that he was not floored in the least. No indeed; he gave it out, as the young man sat down beside him, that if, at the worst, he had been overturned at all, he had been overturned into the upper air, and sublimer element with which he had an affinity and in which he might be trusted a while to float. It was not a descent to earth to say, after an instant, in sustained response to the reference: "You're quite sure her husband's living?"

"Oh dear, yes."

"Ah then—!"

"Ah then what?"

Strether had, after all, to think. "Well, I'm sorry for them." But it didn't matter, for the moment, more than that. He assured his young friend he was quite content. They wouldn't stir; were all right as they were. He didn't want to be introduced; had been introduced already about as far as he could go. He had seen moreover an immensity; liked Gloriani, who, as Miss Barrace kept saying, was wonderful; had made out, he was sure, the half-dozen other men who were distinguished, the artists, the critics and, oh, the great dramatist—*him* it was easy to spot; but wanted—no, thanks, really—to talk with none of them; having nothing at all to say and finding it would do beautifully as it was; do beautifully because what it was—well, was just simply too late. And when, after this, little Bilham, submissive and responsive, but with an eye to the consolation nearest, easily threw off some "Better late than never!" all he got in return for it was a sharp "Better early than late!" This note, indeed, the next thing, overflowed, for Strether, into a quiet stream of demonstration that, as soon as he had let himself go, he felt as the real relief. It had consciously gathered to a head, but the reservoir had filled sooner than he knew, and his companion's touch was to make the waters spread. There were some things that had to come in time if they were to come at all. If they didn't come in time they were lost forever. It was the general sense of them that had overwhelmed him with its long, slow rush.

"It's not too late for *you,* on any side, and you don't strike me as in danger of missing the train; besides which people can be in general pretty well trusted, of course—with the clock of their freedom ticking as loud as it seems to do here—to keep an eye on the fleeting hour. All the same, don't forget that you're young—blessedly young; be glad of it, on the contrary, and live up to it. Live all you can; it's a mistake not to. It doesn't so much matter what you do in particular, so long as you have your life. If you haven't had that, what *have* you had? This place and these impressions—mild as you may find them to wind a man up so; all my impressions of Chad and of people I've seen at *his* place—well, have had their abundant message for me, have just dropped *that* into my mind. I see it now. I haven't done so enough before—and now I'm old; too old at any rate for what I see. Oh, I *do* see, at least; and more than you'd believe or I can express. It's too late. And it's as if the train had fairly waited at the station for me without my having had the gumption to know it was there. Now I hear its faint, receding whistle miles and miles down the line. What one loses one loses; make no mistake about that. The affair—I mean the affair of life—couldn't, no doubt, have been different for me; for it's, at the best, a tin mould, either fluted and embossed, with ornamental excrescences, or else smooth and dreadfully plain, into which, a helpless jelly, one's consciousness is poured—so that one 'takes' the form, as the great cook says, and is more or less compactly held by it: one lives, in fine, as one can. Still, one has the illusion of freedom; therefore don't be, like me, without the memory of that illusion. I was either, at the right time, too stupid or too intelligent to have it; I don't quite know which. Of course, at present, I'm a case of reaction against the mistake; and the voice of reaction should, no doubt, always be taken with an allowance. But that doesn't affect the point that the right time is now yours. The right time is *any* time that one is still so lucky as to have. You've plenty; that's the great thing; you're, as I say, damn you, so happily and hatefully young. Don't, at any rate, miss things out of stupidity. Of course I don't take you for a fool, or I shouldn't be addressing you thus awfully. Do what you like so long as you don't make *my* mistake. For it was a mistake. Live!" . . . . Slowly and sociably, with full pauses and straight dashes, Strether had so delivered himself; holding little Bilham, from step to step, deeply and gravely attentive. The end of all was that the young man had turned quite solemn, and that this was a contradiction of the innocent gayety the speaker had wished to promote. He watched for a moment the consequence of his words, and then, laying a hand on his listener's knee and as if to end, properly, with a joke: "And now for the eye I shall keep on you!"

"Oh, but I don't know that I want to be, at your age, too different from you!"

"Ah, prepare, while you're about it," Strether said, "to be more amusing."

Little Bilham continued to think; then at last he had a smile. "Well, you *are* amusing—to *me*. . . ."

Leo Tolstoy

WAR AND PEACE

After the execution, Pierre was parted from the others, and placed by himself in a small, dilapidated church which had been burned.

Just before the evening, a non-commissioned officer of the guard, accompanied by two soldiers, came into the church, and explained to Pierre that he was reprieved, and was to be put into the barracks of the prisoners of war.

Without comprehending what was said to him, Pierre got up and went with the soldiers.

He was conducted to some huts at the upper part of the field, constructed of burned planks, beams, and scantling, and introduced into one of them. Pierre found himself in the dark, surrounded by a score of various men. He looked at these men, without comprehending who they were, why they were there, or what they wanted of him. He heard the words that they spoke, but he saw no connection or coherence in them; he did not comprehend their meaning. He answered their questions, but he had no idea who listened to him, or how his answers were received. He looked at the faces and forms, and they all alike seemed to him meaningless.

From the moment that Pierre had looked on that horrid massacre perpetrated by men who did not wish to do it, the mainspring by which everything had been coördinated and kept alive in his mind seemed to have been torn away, and everything had crumbled into a heap of incoherent dust. Although he made no attempt to explain how it happened, his faith in the beneficent ordering of the universe, in the human soul, and in his own and in God, was destroyed.

Pierre had passed through such a mental crisis before, but never one of such violence as this. Before, when doubts of this kind had come on Pierre, they had their origin in his own wrong-doing. And then Pierre had felt in the depths of his heart that his salvation from such despair and doubt was in himself. But now he was conscious that it was not his own fault that the universe had collapsed before his eyes, leaving only incoherent ruins. He felt that it was not in his power to return to faith in life.

Around him in the darkness stood a number of men; apparently they found something in him to interest them. They told him things, they asked questions of him; then they led him somewhere, and at last he found himself in a corner of the hut, together with certain men who were talking and laughing together. "Here, now, my brothers, ... this very prince *who*. . . ." (special stress was laid on the word "who") some one was saying in the opposite corner of the balagan.

Pierre sat motionless and silent on the straw next the wall, now opening and now closing his eyes. But as soon as he closed his eyes he saw before him the factory workman's face, terrible, especially terrible, from its very simplicity, and the still more terrible faces of the reluctant executioners, with their anxious looks. And he would again open his eyes and stare inanely into the darkness around him.

Next him sat a little man all doubled up, whose presence Pierre was made aware of from the very first by the strong odor of sweat which emanated from him every time he moved. This man was engaged in do-ing something to his feet, and though it was so dark Pierre could not see his face, he felt conscious that this man kept looking at him. By strain-ing his eyes to suit the darkness, Pierre made out that this man was baring his feet. And Pierre began to grow interested in the way he did it.

Having unwound the long band which was twisted around one foot and leg, he carefully rolled it up, and then went to work on the other foot the same way, constantly glancing at Pierre. While one hand was hang-ing up the first leg-wrapper, the other had instantly begun to undo the one on the other leg. Having thus bared his feet with precise but flowing, well-directed motions whereby no time was lost, the man spread out his foot-gear on the pegs which were driven in just above his head, took out his pocket-knife, pared off something, shut up his knife, thrust it under his pillow, and, having settled himself more comfortably, he clasped his raised knees with both hands and stared straight at Pierre.

For Pierre there was something agreeable, soothing, and satisfying in these well-regulated motions, and in this man's making himself so at home in his corner,—even in the odor emanating from him; and Pierre, without dropping his eyes, returned his gaze.

"Well, have you seen pretty hard times, barin? hah?" suddenly asked the little man.

And there was such an expression of gentleness and simple-hearted goodness in the man's singsong voice that Pierre would have instantly replied, but his jaw trembled and the tears came into his eyes. The little man at the same second, not giving Pierre time to betray his confusion, went on in the same pleasant voice:—

"Ah, my dear friend,[1] don't repine," said he, in that gentle, singsong, affectionate tone with which old Russian peasant women talk, "don't repine, my friend. An hour to suffer, but an age to live! That's the way it is, my dear! But we live here, thank God, without offense. There's bad men and there's good men as well," said he, and, while still speaking, he got up on his knees with an agile motion, arose, and, coughing, went somewhere.

"Here, you little rascal,[2] you've come, have you!" Pierre heard the same caressing voice at the other end of the hut, saying, "You remem-bered me, did you? There, there! that'll do!"

---

[1] E sokolik (little hawk).

[2] Ish shelma.

And the soldier, pushing off a puppy that was jumping up on him, returned to his place and sat down. He carried in his hand something wrapped up in a rag.

"Here's something to eat, barin," said he, returning to his former respectful tone, and, unwrapping the bundle, he gave to Pierre several baked potatoes. "We had porridge for dinner. But potatoes are excellent."

Pierre had eaten nothing all day, and the smell of the potatoes seemed to him extraordinarily pleasant. He thanked the soldier and began to eat.

"Well, how is it?" asked the soldier, with a smile, and taking one of the potatoes,—"do you relish it?"—He again got out his jack-knife, laid the potato on his palm, and cut it into halves, sprinkled salt on from the rag, and offered it to Pierre. "Potatoes excellent," he reiterated. "Eat it that way!"

It seemed to Pierre that he had never eaten any viands that tasted more appetizing.

"No, it makes no difference to me, one way or the other," said Pierre. "But why did they shoot those poor wretches? . . . . The last one wasn't twenty."

"*Tts! tts!*" . . . . said the little man. "A sin!—a sin!" he quickly added; and as if words were always ready to his lips, and winged to fly away very unexpectedly from them, he added: —

"How was it, barin, that you stayed in Moscow?"

"I did not think they would come so soon. It was by accident I stayed," replied Pierre.

"And how came they to take you? Was it from your own house, my dear?" [3]

"No; I was going to the fire, and then they seized me, and tried me as an incendiary."

"Where the tribunal is, there is injustice," said the little man, sententiously.

"Have you been long here?" asked Pierre, as he munched the last potato.

"I? Since Sunday. I was taken from the hospital in Moscow."

"So you were a soldier, were you?"

"One of Apsheron's regiment. I was dying of fever. No one had ever told us anything about it. There were twenty of us lying there. We had no idea of such a thing . . . didn't dream of it!"

"Well, are you bored at being here?"

"How can I help being, my dear? [4] My name is Platon; surname, Karatayef," he added, evidently so as to make Pierre's intercourse with him less formal. "They always called me sokolik in the army. How can one help being bored, my dear? Moscow is the mother of our cities! How can one look on and see her destruction and not be blue? 'The worm

[3] Sokolik, darling (little hawk).

[4] Sokolik, darling (little hawk).

gnaws the cabbage, but perishes before it;' that's the old folks' saying," he added quickly.

"How, how did you say that?" asked Pierre.

"I?" asked Karatayef. "Oh, I say, 'Not by our wit, but as God sees fit,'"[5] said he, thinking he was repeating the former proverb. And immediately he went on: —

"And you have property, haven't you, barin? And have a house? Your cup must be full. And have a wife?[6] And old folks alive?" he asked.

And Pierre, though he could not see because it was so dark, still knew that the soldier's lips were curved in a respectful smile of friendliness as he asked these questions.

He was evidently grieved to learn that Pierre had no parents, especially no mother.

"A wife for advice, a wife's mother for a welcome, but nothing sweeter than one's own matushka!" said he. "But have you any children?" he proceeded to inquire. Pierre's negative reply again evidently grieved him, and he hastened to add: "Well, you are young yet; God may give them. Only you should live in good understanding. . . ."

"It's all the same to me now," said Pierre, involuntarily.

"Ekh! My dear man!" exclaimed Platon. "There's no getting rid of the beggar's sack nor of the prison cell!" He got into a more comfortable attitude, cleared his throat, and was evidently preparing to spin a long yarn. "This was the way, my dear friend,[7] I lived when I was at home," he began. "We had a rich estate . . . much land . . . peasants lived well, and we in the house too, glory to thee, O God! My own batyushka would go out and mow. Lived well, as *Christians* should! But it happened . . . ."

And Platon Karatayef related a long story about how he went into another man's grove after fire-wood, and the watchman had caught him; how he had been flogged, tried, and sent off as a soldier.

"Well, my dear friend,"[8] said he, his voice altered by his smile, "it seemed a misfortune; on the contrary, good thing! My brother would have had to go if it hadn't been for my sin. But my younger brother had five children, while, you see, I had only a wife to leave. I had a little girl once, but God took her back before I went soldiering. I went home on leave once. I will tell you about it. I see they live better than they did before. Yard full of live stock; women at home; two brothers off at work. Only Mikhaïlo, the youngest, at home. And my batyushka, he says, says he, 'All my children's alike to me; no matter which finger you pinch, it hurts just the same. And if they had not taken Platon, Mikhaïlo'd had to go.' He took us all in front of the 'images'—would you believe it?—and made us stand there. 'Mikhaïlo,' says he, 'come here. Bow down to the

---

[5] Nye nashim umom a Bozhyim sudom.

[6] Khozyaika, mistress of the house.

[7] Druk moi liubeznui.

[8] Sekolik.

ground before him; and you, woman, bow down; and you, little ones, bow down, all of you! Have you understood?' says he. And that's the way it is, my dear friend. 'No escaping Fate.' [9] And we are always declaring, 'This is not good, or this is all wrong.' But our happiness is like water in a net; put it in, and it's full; take it out, and it's empty! That's the way it is."

And Platon shifted his seat on his straw.

After a little space of silence, Platon arose: "Well, I suppose you'd like to go to sleep?" said he, and he began to cross himself, muttering, "Lord Jesus Christ! Saint Nikola! Frola and Lavra! Lord Jesus Christ, Saint Nikola! Frola and Lavra, Lord Jesus Christ—have mercy upon us and save us!" he said in conclusion, bowed down to the very ground, got up, drew a deep sigh, and lay down on his straw. "Now, O God! let me 'sleep like a stone and rise like a loaf,'" [10] he exclaimed, and lay down, covering himself with his soldier's coat.

"What was that prayer you were repeating?" asked Pierre.

"Heh?" said Platon. He was already dozing. "Repeated what? I was praying to God. Don't you say your prayers?"

"Certainly I say my prayers," replied Pierre. "But what was that about Frola and Lavra?" [11]

"Why," swiftly replied Platon, "that's the horses' saints. For we must have pity on the cattle," said Karatayef. "Oh, you rascal! you have come back, have you? You want to get warm, do you, you nice little bitch?" said he, fondling the puppy at his feet, and, turning over again, instantly fell asleep.

Outside in the distance were heard the sounds of wailing and yells, and through the cracks in the hut the glare of the fire could be seen, but within it was dark and still. It was long before Pierre could go to sleep; and he lay in his place in the darkness with wide-open eyes, listening to Platon's measured snoring, as he lay near him, and feeling that that formerly ruined world was now arising again in his soul, in new beauty and with new and steadfast foundations. . . .

The *balagan*, or hut, where Pierre was confined, and where he spent four weeks, contained twenty-three soldiers, three officers, and two chinovniks,—all prisoners.

Afterwards all of them seemed to be misty memories to Pierre; but Platon Karatayef forever remained in Pierre's mind as a most powerful and precious recollection, the very embodiment of all that was good and worthy and truly Russian.

When, on the following day, at dawn, Pierre saw his neighbor, the first impression of something rotund was fully confirmed; Platon's whole figure, in his French overcoat belted with a rope, in his forage-cap and bast shoes, was rotund. His head was perfectly round; his back, his chest,

---

[9] Literally, Fate, destiny, seeks heads. A variant of the proverb reads "If Fate does not find the man, the man goes to Fate."

[10] Kalachik (kalatch), a sort of pretzel, or light loaf.

[11] Frola and Lavra: Flora and Laura.

his shoulders, even his arms, which he always carried as if he were ready to throw them around something, were round; his pleasant smile and his large, thick brows and his gentle eyes were round.

Platon Karatayef must have been more than fifty, to judge by his stories of campaigns in which he had taken part as a soldier. He himself had no idea, and could never have told with any accuracy, how old he was. But his teeth, brilliantly white and strong, were always displayed in two unbroken rows whenever he laughed,—which he often did,—and not one was not good and sound. There was not a trace of gray in beard or hair, and his whole frame had the appearance of agility and especially of steadfastness and endurance.

His face, in spite of a multitude of delicate round wrinkles, gave the impression of innocence and youth; his voice was agreeable in its melodious singsong. But the chief peculiarity of his speech consisted in its spontaneity and shrewdness. He evidently never thought of what he said or what he was going to say. And from this arose the irresistible persuasiveness that was found in the rapidity and certainty of his intonations.

His physical powers and activity were so great during the early part of their term of captivity that it seemed as if he knew not what weariness or ill-health meant. Every morning and evening, as he lay on his couch of straw, he would say, "Lord let me sleep like a stone and rise like a loaf."

When he got up in the morning he always shrugged his shoulders in a certain way and said, "Turn over when you lie down, shake yourself when you get up."

And, in point of fact, all he had to do was to lie down, and instantly he would be asleep like a stone; and all he had to do was to shake himself, and without a second's delay he would be ready to take up anything, just as children, when they are once up, take to their toys.

He was a jack-at-all-trades, but neither very good nor very bad at any. He could bake, cook, sew, cut hair, cobble boots. He was always busy, and only when it came night did he allow himself to enjoy social converse, though he enjoyed it, and to sing. He sang his songs, not as singers usually sing, knowing that they will be heard; but he sang as the birds sing, evidently because it was just as much a necessity for him as it was for him to stretch himself or to walk. And these sounds were always gentle, soft, almost like a woman's, plaintive, and his face, while he was engaged in this, was very grave.

During his captivity he let his beard grow, and evidently discarded everything extraneous which was foreign or military, and involuntarily returned to his former condition of the peasant and man of the people.

" 'A soldier on leave is a shirt made out of drawers,' " he would quote. He was not fond of talking about his soldiering days, although he had no regret for them, and often declared that during all his term in the service he had not once been flogged. When he had stories to tell he much preferred to confine them to old and evidently precious recollections of the time when he was a serf—*Khristianin,* Christian, he called it, instead of *Krestyanin!*

The proverbs of which he made so much use were not that generally coarse and vulgar slang which soldiers are apt to employ, but were genuine popular "saws," which seem perfectly insignificant when taken out of connection, but which suddenly acquire a meaning of deep wisdom when applied appositely.

He often said things that were diametrically opposed to what he had said before, but yet each statement would be correct. He loved to talk, and talked well, embellishing his discourse with affectionate diminutives and proverbs, which, it seemed to Pierre, the man himself improvised; but the chief charm of his narrations arose from the fact that the simplest events, those which Pierre himself had seen without taking account of them, assumed a character of solemn beauty.

He liked to listen to the yarns—though they were all of a single stamp—which a certain soldier used to tell evenings, but above all he liked to listen to tales of actual life.

He smiled blithely while listening to such tales, suggesting words and asking questions conducive to bringing out all the beauty of what was related to him.

Special attachments, friendships, loves, as Pierre understood them, Karatayef had none; but he liked all men, and lived in a loving way with all with whom his life brought him into contact, and especially with men —not any particular men—but with such as were in his sight. He loved his dog; he loved his comrades, the French; he loved Pierre, who was his companion; but Pierre felt that Karatayef, in spite of all that affectionate spirit which he manifested toward him,—and which he could not help giving as a tribute to Pierre's spiritual life,—not for one moment would grieve over separation. And Pierre also began to have the same feeling toward Karatayef.

Platon Karatayef was, in the eyes of all the other prisoners, a most ordinary soldier. They called him *sokolik*, "little hawk," or *Platosha*, good-naturedly quizzed him, made him do odd jobs for them.

But for Pierre, he remained forever what he had seemed to him the first night,—the incomprehensible, "all round," and eternal personification of simplicity and truth. . . .

The provision train and the prisoners and the marshal's baggage wagons were halting at the village of Shamsheva. All gathered in groups around the bivouac fires. Pierre went to a camp-fire, and, after eating some roasted horse-flesh, lay down with his back to the fire and instantly fell asleep. He slept the same kind of sleep which he had slept at Mozhaïsk after Borodino.

Once more real events mingled with visions, and once more some one, either himself or some other person, uttered thoughts, even the same thoughts which had been spoken to him at Mozhaïsk.

"Life is everything. Life is God. Everything changes and is in a state of flux, and this movement is God. And as long as there is life, there is enjoyment of the self-consciousness of the Divinity. To love life is to love God. More difficult and more blessed than all else is it to love this life in its sufferings, in undeserved sufferings."

"Karatayef!" occurred to Pierre.

And suddenly there seemed to be standing before Pierre, as if alive, a dear little old man, long forgotten, who in Switzerland had taught Pierre geography.

"Wait," said the little man. And he showed Pierre a globe. This globe was a living, rolling ball, and had no natural divisions. The whole surface of the globe consisted of drops closely squeezed together. And these drops were all in motion, changing about, sometimes several coalescing into one, sometimes one breaking up into many. Each drop tried to expand, to occupy as much space as possible; but others, striving for the same end, crushed it, sometimes annihilated it, sometimes coalesced with it.

"Such is life," said the little old teacher.

"How simple and how clear," thought Pierre. "Why is it I never knew this before?"

"In the center is God, and each drop strives to spread out, to expand, so as to reflect Him in the largest possible proportions. And each expands, and coalesces, and is pressed down, and is to all outward appearance annihilated, and sinks into the depths and comes out again."

"That was the case with Karatayef; he overflowed and vanished."

"*Vous avez compris, mon enfant*—you understand now, my boy!" said the teacher.

"*Vous avez compris! Sacré nom!*—You understand? The devil take you!" cried a voice, and Pierre awoke.

He sat up. Squatting on his heels by the camp-fire sat a Frenchman who had just been pushing away a Russian soldier, and was now broiling a piece of meat stuck on a ramrod. His muscular, red hand, covered with hairs, with short fingers, was skilfully twirling the ramrod. His cinnamon-colored, scowling face and knitted brows could be clearly seen in the light of the coals.

"*Ça lui est bien égal*—It's all the same to him," he growled out, addressing the soldier standing near him. "*Brigand! Va!*"

And the soldier, twirling the ramrod, glared gloomily at Pierre. Pierre turned away and gazed into the darkness.

A Russian soldier, one of the prisoners, the very same whom the Frenchman had pushed away, was sitting by the fire and was patting something with his hand. Looking closer, Pierre recognized that it was the little bandy-legged, pink dog, which was wagging her tail as she crouched down next the soldier.

"Ah! She's come, has she?" said Pierre, "but Plat. . . ." he began, but did not finish the name.

Suddenly in his imagination, all blended together,—the recollection of the look which Platon had given him as he sat under the tree, the shot which he had heard at that same place, the howling of the dog, the guilty faces of the two Frenchmen who hastened past him, the empty, smoking musket, Karatayef left behind at that halting-place,—and this now made him realize that Platon was dead, but at the same instant, suggested by God knows what, there arose in his mind the recollection of an evening that he had spent in company with a Polish beauty one summer, on the balcony of his mansion at Kief. And, nevertheless, without making any effort to coördinate his recollections, and drawing no conclusions from them, Pierre closed his eyes, and the vision of the summer scene mingled with his recollections of bathing, of the fluid, rolling globe, and he seemed to be sinking in water, so that the water went over his head.

Before sunrise he was wakened by loud and frequent firing and shouts. The French were flying past him.

"*Les Cosaques!*" cried one of them, and in a moment Pierre was surrounded by a throng of Russians.

It was some time before Pierre could realize what had happened to him. On all sides he heard the joyful vociferations of his comrades. "Brothers! comrades! friends!" shouted old soldiers, and burst into tears as they embraced Cossocks and hussars. Cossacks and hussars surrounded the prisoners and made haste to offer them—one man, clothes; another, shoes; another, bread.

Pierre stood in the midst of them, sobbing, and could not speak a word. He threw his arms around the first soldier whom he met, and kissed him, weeping. . . .

INDEX

The items included in this Index relate to the substance of the chapters of Part I. Items in questions at the end of each chapter, as well as those in the readings of Part II, are not included.

1 2 3 4 5 6 7 8 9 10 11 12 13 14 15 16 17 18 19 20 21 22 23 24 25   78 77 76 75 74 73 72 71 70